"With this handbook, you will benefit fr⊔ __ ⊔ne who is at the same time a Roman historian, a Greek scholar, ⊔⊔ ⊔ pastor who regularly preaches the Word of God. The concise introductions, sentence-flow diagrams, insightful comments on the Greek text, and homiletical suggestions make this handbook an indispensible tool for working through the apostle Paul's rich and profound letter to the Philippians. Keep your eyes out for the illuminating gems from the Roman context of the letter that Hellerman weaves into his presentation—a feature that gives this book added value."

Clinton E. Arnold, *Talbot School of Theology*

"Hellerman has done the seemingly impossible—presented detailed exegetical and grammatical material in wonderfully readable prose. His concise and thorough explanation of the Greek text lays the ground for exploring Paul's theology and instruction to the church. Hellerman's well-informed understanding of the ancient world brings the Philippians' context to life. Students, pastors, and professors will want this volume close at hand when preparing a sermon or lecture."

Lynn H. Cohick, *Wheaton College*

"Thankfully, there is an explosion of interest today in doing Greek exegesis, but pastors and students need help, and there simply isn't time to cover all that is needed in the classroom. Hellerman's work on Philippians is a model for what is needed. He is conversant with the most recent work on Greek grammar; he demonstrates expertise in his exegesis of Philippians; his work is concise and accessible for the busy student and pastor. I recommend Hellerman's commentary enthusiastically."

Thomas R. Schreiner, *The Southern Baptist Theological Seminary*

"Clear, concise, accurate—these are the things I'm looking for in a commentary. Joe Hellerman's exegetical handbook on Philippians is a model for all three qualities. The Greek text is expertly handled, with various interpretive options set forth and judiciously examined. Every passage is presented in a Greek syntactical display. Additional bibliography on key issues is provided for those wanting to go deeper. Finally, various homiletical outlines are suggested. Students of the Greek New Testament interested first and foremost in exegeting and preaching the text will find everything they want here, with little padding or fluff."

Mark L. Strauss, *Bethel Seminary, San Diego*

EXEGETICAL
GUIDE TO THE
GREEK
NEW
TESTAMENT

PHILIPPIANS

The Exegetical Guide to the Greek New Testament

Volumes Available

Philippians	Joseph H. Hellerman
Colossians, Philemon	Murray J. Harris
James	Chris A. Vlachos
1 Peter	Greg W. Forbes

Forthcoming Volumes

Matthew	Charles L. Quarles
Mark	Joel F. Williams
Luke	Alan J. Thompson
John	Murray J. Harris
Acts	L. Scott Kellum
Romans	John D. Harvey
1 Corinthians	Jay E. Smith
2 Corinthians	Don B. Garlington
Galatians	David A. Croteau
Ephesians	Benjamin L. Merkle
1–2 Thessalonians	David W. Chapman
1–2 Timothy, Titus	Ray Van Neste
Hebrews	Dana M. Harris
2 Peter, Jude	Terry L. Wilder
1–3 John	Robert L. Plummer
Revelation	Bruce N. Fisk

Joseph H. Hellerman

EXEGETICAL
GUIDE TO THE **PHILIPPIANS**
GREEK
NEW
TESTAMENT

Andreas J. Köstenberger
Robert W. Yarbrough
GENERAL EDITORS

Nashville, Tennessee

Exegetical Guide to the Greek New Testament: Philippians

Copyright © 2015 Joseph H. Hellerman

Broadman & Holman Publishing Group
Nashville, Tennessee

ISBN: 978-1-4336-7686-4

Dewey Decimal Classification:
Subject Heading: BIBLE. N.T. Philippians—STUDY\BIBLE—CRITICISM

The Greek text of Philippians is from *The Greek New Testament*, Fifth Revised Edition, edited by Barbara Aland, Kurt Aland, Johannes Karavidopoulos, Carlo M. Martini, and Bruce M. Metzger in cooperation with the Institute for New Testament Textual Research, Münster/Westphalia, © 2014 Deutsche Bibelgesellschaft, Stuttgart. Used by permission.

Printed in the United States of America

1 2 3 4 5 6 7 8 9 10 • 20 19 18 17 16 15

BethP

*To all God's shepherds who learned Greek in seminary,
who made it a priority over the years to retain the language,
and who continue to draw upon the riches of the Greek New
Testament for ministry in the church today.*

Contents

PHILIPPIANS

Publisher's Preface

It is with great excitement that we publish this volume of the Exegetical Guide to the Greek New Testament series. When the founding editor, Dr. Murray J. Harris, came to us seeking a new publishing partner, we gratefully accepted the offer. With the help of the coeditor, Andreas J. Köstenberger, we spent several years working together to acquire all of the authors we needed to complete the series. By God's grace we succeeded and contracted the last author in 2011. Originally working with another publishing house, Murray's efforts spanned more than twenty years. As God would have it, shortly after the final author was contracted, Murray decided God wanted him to withdraw as coeditor of the series. God made clear to him that he must devote his full attention to taking care of his wife, who faces the daily challenges caused by multiple sclerosis.

Over the course of many years, God has used Murray to teach his students how to properly exegete the Scriptures. He is an exceptional scholar and professor. But even more importantly, Murray is a man dedicated to serving Christ. His greatest joy is to respond in faithful obedience when his master calls. "There can be no higher and more ennobling privilege than to have the Lord of the universe as one's Owner and Master and to be his accredited representative on earth."[1] Murray has once again heeded the call of his master.

It is our privilege to dedicate the Exegetical Guide to the Greek New Testament series to Dr. Murray J. Harris. We pray that our readers will continue the work he started.

B&H Academic

---

1. Murray J. Harris, *Slave of Christ: A New Testament Metaphor for Total Devotion to Christ* (Downers Grove: InterVarsity, 1999), 155.

General Introduction to the EGGNT Series

Studying the New Testament in the original Greek has become easier in recent years. Beginning students will work their way through an introductory grammar or other text, but then what? Grappling with difficult verb forms, rare vocabulary, and grammatical irregularities remains a formidable task for those who would advance beyond the initial stages of learning Greek to master the interpretive process. Intermediate grammars and grammatical analyses can help, but such tools, for all their value, still often operate at a distance from the Greek text itself, and analyses are often too brief to be genuinely helpful.

The Exegetical Guide to the Greek New Testament (EGGNT) aims to close the gap between the Greek text and the available tools. Each EGGNT volume aims to provide all the necessary information for understanding of the Greek text and, in addition, includes homiletical helps and suggestions for further study. The EGGNT is not a full-scale commentary. Nevertheless these guides will make interpreting a given New Testament book easier, in particular for those who are hard-pressed for time and yet want to preach or teach with accuracy and authority.

In terms of layout, each volume begins with a brief introduction to the particular book (including such matters as authorship, date, etc.), a basic outline, and a list of recommended commentaries. At the end of each volume, you will find a comprehensive exegetical outline of the book. The body of each volume is devoted to paragraph-by-paragraph exegesis of the text. The treatment of each paragraph includes:

1. The Greek text of the passage, phrase by phrase, from the fifth edition of the United Bible Societies' *Greek New Testament* (UBS[5]).
2. A structural analysis of the passage. Typically, verbal discussion of the structure of a given unit is followed by a diagram, whereby the verbal discussion serves to explain the diagram and the diagram serves to provide a visual aid illumining the structural discussion. While there is no one correct or standard way to diagram Greek sentences, the following format is typically followed in EGGNT volumes:
   a. The original Greek word order is maintained.
   b. When Greek words are omitted, this is indicated by an ellipsis (. . .).

   c. The diagramming method, moving from left to right, is predicated upon the following. In clauses with a finite verb, the default order is typically verb-subject-object. In verbless clauses or clauses with nonfinite verb forms, the default order is typically subject-(verb)-object. Departures from these default orders are understood to be pragmatically motivated (e.g., contrast, emphasis, etc.).

   d. Indents are used to indicate subordination (e.g., in the case of dependent clauses).

   e. Retaining original word order, modifiers are centered above or below the word they modify (e.g., a prepositional phrase in relation to the verb).

   f. Where a given sentence or clause spans multiple lines of text, drawn lines are used, such as where a relative pronoun introduces a relative clause (often shifting emphasis).

   g. Underline is used to indicate imperatives; dotted underline is used to indicate repetition (the same word or cognate used multiple times in a given unit); the symbol ⁝ may be used where an article is separated from a noun or participle by interjected material (such as a prepositional phrase).

   h. In shorter letters diagrams are normally provided for every unit; in longer letters and Revelation, ellipses may be used to show less detail in diagramming (keeping larger blocks together on the same line) in order to focus primarily on the larger structure of a given unit; in the Gospels and Acts, detailed diagrams will usually not be provided, though less detailed diagrams may be used to illustrate important or more complex structural aspects of a given passage.

3. A discussion of each phrase of the passage with discussion of relevant vocabulary, significant textual variants, and detailed grammatical analysis, including parsing. When more than one solution is given for a particular exegetical issue, the author's own preference, reflected in the translation and expanded paraphrase, is indicated by an asterisk (*). When no preference is expressed, the options are judged to be evenly balanced, or it is assumed that the text is intentionally ambiguous. When a particular verb form may be parsed in more than one way, only the parsing appropriate in the specific context is supplied; but where there is difference of opinion among grammarians or commentators, both possibilities are given and the matter is discussed.

4. Various translations of significant words or phrases.

5. A list of suggested topics for further study with bibliography for each topic. An asterisk (*) in one of the "For Further Study" bibliographies draws attention to a discussion of the particular topic that is recommended as a useful introduction to the issues involved.

6. Homiletical suggestions designed to help the preacher or teacher move from the Greek text to a sermon outline that reflects careful exegesis. The first suggestion for a particular paragraph of the text is always more exegetical than homiletical and consists of an outline of the entire paragraph. These

detailed outlines of each paragraph build on the general outline proposed for the whole book and, if placed side by side, form a comprehensive exegetical outline of the book. All outlines are intended to serve as a basis for sermon preparation and should be adapted to the needs of a particular audience.[2]

The EGGNT volumes will serve a variety of readers. Those reading the Greek text for the first time may be content with the assistance with vocabulary, parsing, and translation. Readers with some experience in Greek may want to skip or skim these sections and focus attention on the discussions of grammar. More advanced students may choose to pursue the topics and references to technical works under "For Further Study," while pastors may be more interested in the movement from grammatical analysis to sermon outline. Teachers may appreciate having a resource that frees them to focus on exegetical details and theological matters.

The editors are pleased to present you with the individual installments of the EGGNT. We are grateful for each of the contributors who has labored long and hard over each phrase in the Greek New Testament. Together we share the conviction that "all Scripture is inspired by God and is profitable for teaching, for rebuking, for correcting, for training in righteousness" (2 Tim 3:16 HCSB) and echo Paul's words to Timothy: "Be diligent to present yourself approved to God, a worker who doesn't need to be ashamed, correctly teaching the word of truth" (2 Tim 2:15 HCSB).

Thanks to David Croteau, who served as assistant editor for this volume.

Andreas J. Köstenberger
Robert W. Yarbrough

---

2. As a Bible publisher, B&H Publishing follows the "Colorado Springs Guidelines for Translation of Gender-Related Language in Scripture." As an academic book publisher, B&H Academic asks that authors conform their manuscripts (including EGGNT exegetical outlines in English) to the B&H Academic style guide, which affirms the use of singular "he/his/him" as generic examples encompassing both genders. However, in their discussion of the Greek text, EGGNT authors have the freedom to analyze the text and reach their own conclusions regarding whether specific Greek words are gender-specific or gender-inclusive.

Abbreviations

For abbreviations used in discussion of text critical matters, the reader should refer to the abbreviations listed in the Introduction to the United Bible Societies' *Greek New Testament*.

*	indicates the reading of the original hand of a manuscript as opposed to subsequent correctors of the manuscript, *or*
	indicates the writer's own preference when more than one solution is given for a particular exegetical problem, *or*
	in the "For Further Study" bibliographies, indicates a discussion of the particular topic that is recommended as a useful introduction to the issues involved
§, §§	section, sections

Books of the Old Testament

Gen	Genesis	Song	Song of Songs	(Canticles)
Exod	Exodus	Isa	Isaiah	
Lev	Leviticus	Jer	Jeremiah	
Num	Numbers	Lam	Lamentations	
Deut	Deuteronomy	Ezek	Ezekiel	
Josh	Joshua	Dan	Daniel	
Judg	Judges	Hos	Hosea	
Ruth	Ruth	Joel	Joel	
1–2 Sam	1–2 Samuel	Amos	Amos	
1–2 Kgs	1–2 Kings	Obad	Obadiah	
1–2 Chr	1–2 Chronicles	Jonah	Jonah	
Ezra	Ezra	Mic	Micah	
Neh	Nehemiah	Nah	Nahum	
Esth	Esther	Hab	Habakkuk	
Job	Job	Zeph	Zephaniah	
Ps(s)	Psalm(s)	Hag	Haggai	
Prov	Proverbs	Zech	Zechariah	
Eccl	Ecclesiastes	Mal	Malachi	

Books of the New Testament

Matt	Matthew	1–2 Thess	1–2 Thessalonians
Mark	Mark	1–2 Tim	1–2 Timothy
Luke	Luke	Titus	Titus
John	John	Phlm	Philemon
Acts	Acts	Heb	Hebrews
Rom	Romans	Jas	James
1–2 Cor	1–2 Corinthians	1–2 Pet	1–2 Peter
Gal	Galatians	1–3 John	1–3 John
Eph	Ephesians	Jude	Jude
Phil	Philippians	Rev	Revelation
Col	Colossians		

Dead Sea Scrolls

1QH	*Thanksgiving Hymn*
1QM	*War Scroll*
1QS	*Rule of the Community*
CD	*Damascus Document*

General Abbreviations

ABD	D. N. Freedman, ed., *The Anchor Bible Dictionary*, 6 vols. New York: Doubleday, 1992
abs.	absolute(ly)
ABRL	Anchor Bible Reference Library
acc.	accusative
act.	active (voice)
adj.	adjective, adjectival(ly)
adv.	adverbial(ly)
anar.	anarthrous
aor.	Aorist
apod.	apodosis
appos.	apposition, appositive, appositional
Aram.	Aramaic, Aramaism
art.	(definite) article, articular
attrib.	attributive
ANRW	H. Temporini and W. Haase, eds., *Aufstieg und Niedergang der römisch Welt: Geschichte und Kultur Roms im Spiegel der neueren Forschung.* Berlin and New York: de Gruyter, 1972–
AThR	*Anglican Theological Review*
aug.	augment
AUSS	*Andrews University Seminary Studies*

Barclay	W. Barclay, *New Testament Words*. Philadelphia: Westminster, 1974
BBR	*Bulletin for Biblical Research*
BDAG	F. W. Danker, ed., *A Greek-English Lexicon of the New Testament and Other Early Christian Literature*, rev. Chicago/London: University of Chicago, 2000. Based on W. Bauer's *Griechisch-deutsches Wörterbuch* (6th ed.) and on previous English ed. W. F. Arndt, F. W. Gingrich, and F. W. Danker
	References to BDAG are by page number and quadrant on the page, *a* indicating the upper half and *b* the lower half of the left-hand column, and *c* and *d* the upper and lower halves of the right-hand column.
BDF	F. Blass and A. Debrunner, *A Greek Grammar of the New Testament and Other Early Christian Literature*, ET and rev. by R. W. Funk. Chicago: University of Chicago, 1961
BGk.	Biblical Greek (i.e., LXX and NT Greek)
Bib	*Biblica*
Bockmuehl	M. Bockmuehl, *The Epistle to the Philippians*. Black's New Testament Commentary. Peabody, MA: Hendrikson, 1998
BSac	*Bibliotheca Sacra*
BT	*The Bible Translator*
BTB	Biblical Theology Bulletin
Burton	E. D. Burton, *Syntax of the Moods and Tenses in New Testament Greek*, 3rd ed. Edinburgh: Clark, 1898
c.	*circa* (Lat.), about
Campbell	C. Campbell, *Paul and Union with Christ: An Exegetical and Theological Study*. Grand Rapids: Zondervan, 2012
Campbell, *Indicative Mood*	C. R. Campbell, *Verbal Aspect, the Indicative Mood, and Narrative: Soundings in the Greek of the New Testament*. New York: Peter Lang, 2007
Campbell, *Non-Indicative Verbs*	C. R. Campbell, *Verbal Aspect in the Greek of the New Testament: Non-Indicative Verbs in Narrative*. New York: Peter Lang, 2008
CBQ	*Catholic Biblical Quarterly*
Cassirer	H.W. Cassirer, *God's New Covenant: A New Testament Translation*. Grand Rapids: Eerdmans, 1989
CE	Common Era
CEV	Contemporary English Version (1995)
cf.	*confer* (Lat.), compare
CGk.	Classical Greek
Colloq	*Colloquium*
comp.	comparative, comparison

cond.	condition(al)
conj.	conjunctive, conjunction
consec.	consecutive
cstr.	construction, construe(d)
CTR	*Criswell Theological Review*
dat.	dative
DBI	L. Ryken, J. Wilhoit, and Tremper Longman III, eds., *Dictionary of Biblical Imagery*. Downers Grove: InterVarsity, 1998
decl.	declension, decline
Deissmann	G. A. Deissmann, *Bible Studies*. Translated by A. Grieve. Edinburgh: Clark, 1901; reprint, Peabody, MA: Hendrickson, 1988
def.	definite
dep.	deponent
DLNT	R. P. Martin and P. H. Davids, eds., *Dictionary of the Later New Testament and Its Developments*. Leicester / Downers Grove: InterVarsity, 1997
DNTB	C. A. Evans and S. E. Porter, eds., *Dictionary of New Testament Background*. Leicester / Downers Grove: InterVarsity, 2000
DOTWPW	T. Longman III and P. Enns, eds., *Dictionary of the Old Testament: Wisdom, Poetry, and Writings*. Downers Grove: InterVarsity, 2008
DPL	G. F. Hawthorne, R. P. Martin, and D. G. Reid, eds., *Dictionary of Paul and His Letters*. Leicester/Downers Grove: IVP, 1993.
DTIB	K. J. Vanhoozer et al., eds., *Dictionary for Theological Interpretation of the Bible*. Grand Rapids, Baker, 2005
dir.	direct
DSS	Dead Sea Scrolls
ed(s).	edited by, edition(s), editor(s)
EDNT	H. Balz and G. Schneider, eds., *Exegetical Dictionary of the New Testament*, 3 vols. Grand Rapids: Eerdmans, 1990–1993
EDT	W. A. Elwell, ed., *Evangelical Dictionary of Theology*. Grand Rapids: Baker, 1984
e.g.	*exempli gratia* (Lat.), for example
EGT	W. R. Nicholl, ed., *The Expositor's Greek Testament*, 5 vols. Grand Rapids: Eerdmans, 1970 reprint of 1897–1910 ed.
Eng.	English
epex.	epexegetic
esp.	especially
ESV	English Standard Version (2001)
ET	English translation

et al.	*et alii* (Lat.), and others
etym.	etymology, etymologically
EvQ	*Evangelical Quarterly*
EVV	English versions of the Bible
Exp	*Expositor*
ExpTim	*Expository Times*
f(f).	and the following (verse[s] or page[s])
Fanning	B. Fanning, *Verbal Aspect in New Testament Greek.* Oxford: Oxford University Press, 1991
Fee	G. D. Fee, *Paul's Letter to the Philippians.* New International Commentary on the New Testament. Grand Rapids: Eerdmans, 1995
fem.	feminine
fig.	figurative(ly)
fut.	future
gen.	genitive
Gk.	Greek
GNB	Good News Bible (1976)
GTJ	*Grace Theological Journal*
Hansen	G. W. Hansen, *The Letter to the Philippians.* Pillar New Testament Commentary. Grand Rapids: Eerdmans, 2009.
Harris	M. J. Harris, "Prepositions and Theology in the Greek New Testament," *NIDNTT* 3.1,171–215.
HBT	*Horizons in Biblical Theology*
HCSB	Holman Christian Standard Bible (2009)
HE	*Historia Ecclesiastica* (History of the Church)
Heb.	Hebrew, Hebraism
Hellerman	J. H. Hellerman, *Reconstructing Honor in Roman Philippi: Carmen Christi as Cursus Pudorum.* SNTSMS 136. Cambridge: Cambridge University Press, 2005
HGk.	Hellenistic Greek
H-M	R. P. Martin and Gerald F. Hawthorne, *Philippians, Revised Edition.* Word Biblical Commentary 43. Nashville: Thomas Nelson, 2004.
HTR	*Harvard Theological Review*
HTS	*Harvard Theological Studies*
ibid.	*ibidem* (Lat.), in the same place
IBS	*Irish Biblical Studies*
IDB	G. A. Buttrick, ed., *Interpreters Dictionary of the Bible*, 4 vols. plus supp. Nashville / New York: Abingdon, 1962–76
i.e.	*id est* (Lat.), that is
impers.	impersonal
impf.	imperfect (tense)

impv.	imperative (mood), imperatival(ly)
incl.	including, inclusive
indecl.	indeclinable
indef.	indefinite
indic.	indicative (mood)
indir.	indirect
inf.	infinitive
instr.	instrument, instrumental(ly)
Int	*Interpretation*
interr.	interrogative
intrans.	intransitive
iter.	iterative
JB	Jerusalem Bible (1976)
JBL	*Journal of Biblical Literature*
JETS	*Journal of the Evangelical Theological Society*
JOTT	*Journal of Translation and Textlinguistics*
JR	*Journal of Religion*
JSNT	*Journal for the Study of the New Testament*
JSOT	*Journal for the Study of the Old Testament*
JTS	*Journal of Theological Studies*
JTSA	*Journal of Theology for Southern Africa*
KJV	King James Version (= "Authorized Version") (1611)
κτλ.	Καὶ τὰ λοιπά (and the rest).
LB	*Linguistica Biblica*
Lendon	J. E. Lendon, *Empire of Honour: The Art of Government in the Roman World*. Oxford: Oxford University Press, 1997
lit.	literal(ly)
LN	J. P. Louw and E. A. Nida, eds., *Greek-English Lexicon of the New Testament Based on Semantic Domains, Vol. I: Introduction and Domains*. New York: United Bible Societies, 1988
locat.	locative, locatival(ly)
LS	*Louvain Studies*
LSJ	H. G. Liddell and R. Scott, *A Greek-English Lexicon*, rev. and augmented H. S. Jones et al., 9th ed. Oxford: Clarendon, 1940; *Supplement*, ed. E. A. Barber et al. (1968)
LTJ	*Lutheran Theological Journal*
LXX	Septuagint (= Greek Old Testament)
Macc	Maccabees
masc.	masculine
McKay	K. L. McKay, *A New Syntax of the Verb in New Testament Greek: An Aspectual Approach*. New York: Peter Lang, 1994

Metzger	B. M. Metzger, *A Textual Commentary on the Greek New Testament*. Stuttgart: Deutsche Bibelgesellschaft / New York: United Bible Societies, 1994; original ed. of 1971 based on UBS³
mg.	margin
MH	J. H. Moulton and W. F. Howard, *Accidence and Word-Formation*, vol. 2 of *A Grammar of New Testament Greek*, ed. J. H. Moulton. Edinburgh: T&T Clark, 1939
mid.	middle
MM	J. H. Moulton and G. Milligan, *The Vocabulary of the Greek Testament Illustrated from the Papyri and Other Non-Literary Sources*. Grand Rapids: Eerdmans, 1972; repr. of 1930 ed.
Moule	C. F. D. Moule, *An Idiom Book of New Testament Greek*, 2nd ed. Cambridge: Cambridge University Press, 1960
Moulton	J. H. Moulton, *A Grammar of New Testament Greek, Vol. I: Prolegomena*, 3rd ed. Edinburgh: Clark, 1908
mng.	meaning
ms(s).	manuscript(s)
MT	Masoretic Text
n.	note
NA/NA²⁸	B. Aland, K. Aland, J. Karavidopoulos, C. M. Martini, and B. M. Metzger, eds., *Novum Testamentum Graece,* 28th rev. ed. Stuttgart: Deutsche Bibelgesellschaft, 2012
NABRE	New American Bible Revised Edition (2011)
NASB	New American Standard Bible (1995)
NCV	New Century Version
NDBT	T. D. Alexander and B. S. Rosner, eds., *New Dictionary of Biblical Theology*. Downers Grove: InterVarsity, 2000
NEB	New English Bible (1970)
neg.	negative, negation
Neot	*Neotestamentica*
NET	New English Translation Bible (2005)
neut.	neuter
NewDocs	G. H. R. Horsley and S. Llewelyn, eds., *New Documents Illustrating Early Christianity*. North Ryde, N.S.W., Australia: Macquarie University, 1981– . These will be cited by volume.
NIDNTT	C. Brown, ed., *The New International Dictionary of New Testament Theology*, 4 vols. Grand Rapids: Zondervan, 1975–78
NIDOTTE	W. A. VanGemeren, ed., *The New International Dictionary of Old Testament Theology and Exegesis*, 5 vols. Grand Rapids: Zondervan, 1997
NIV	New International Version (2011)
NJB	New Jerusalem Bible (1985)

NKJV	New King James Version
NLT	New Living Translation of the Bible (1996)
nom.	nominative
NovT	*Novum Testamentum*
NRSV	New Revised Standard Version (1990)
NT	New Testament
NTS	*New Testament Studies*
Oakes	P. Oakes, *Philippians: From People to Letter.* SNTSMS 110. Cambridge: Cambridge University Press, 2001
O'Brien	P. T. O'Brien, *The Epistle to the Philippians.* New International Greek Testament Commentary. Grand Rapids: Eerdmans, 1991
obj.	object(ive)
Omanson	*A Textual Guide to the Greek New Testament.* Stuttgart: Deutsche Bibelgesellshaft, 2006
orig.	origin, original(ly)
Osiek	C. Osiek, *Philippians and Philemon.* Abingdon New Testament Commentaries. Nashville: Abingdon, 2000
OT	Old Testament
p(p).	page(s)
pace	(from Lat. *pax*, peace) (in stating a contrary opinion) with all due respect to (the person named)
par.	parallel
Park	M. S. Park, *Submission Within the Godhead and the Church in the Epistle to the Philippians.* Library of New Testament Studies 361. Edited by Mark Goodacre, London: T&T Clark, 2007
pass.	passive
periph.	periphrastic
pers.	person(al)
pf.	perfect
pl.	plural
Porter	S. E. Porter, *Idioms of the Greek New Testament.* Sheffield: JSOT, 1992
poss.	possessive, possession
pred.	predicate, predicative
pref.	prefix
prep.	preposition(al)
Presb	*Presbyterion*
pres.	present
PTR	*Princeton Theological Review*
pron.	pronoun, pronominal
prot.	protasis
ptc.	participle, participial(ly)

R   A. T. Robertson, *A Grammar of the Greek New Testament in the Light of Historical Research*, 4th ed. Nashville: Broadman, 1934
rdg(s).   (textual) reading(s)
REB   Revised English Bible (1990)
Reed   J. T. Reed, *A Discourse Analysis of Philippians: Method and Rhetoric in the Debate over Literary Integrity*. JSNTSup 136. Sheffield: Sheffield Academic Press, 1997
ref.   reference
refl.   reflexive
rel.   relative
Reumann   J. Reumann, *Philippians*. The Anchor Yale Bible Commentary. New Haven, CT: Yale University Press, 2008
rev.   revised, reviser, revision
RevExp   *Review and Expositor*
ResQ   *Restoration Quarterly*
Robertson, *Pictures* A. T. Robertson, *Word Pictures in the New Testament*, 6 vols. Nashville: Broadman, 1930–33
RSV   Revised Standard Version (1952)
Runge   S. E. Runge, *Discourse Grammar of the Greek New Testament: A Practical Introduction for Teaching and Exegesis*. Peabody, MA: Hendrickson, 2010
SBJT   *Southern Baptist Journal of Theology*
SBLSP   *Society of Biblical Literature Seminar Papers*
Scr   *Scripture*
SE   *Studia Evangelica*
Sem.   Semitic, Semitism
sg.   singular
Silva   M. Silva, *Philippians*. Baker Exegetical Commentary on the New Testament. Grand Rapids: Baker Academic, 2005
sim.   similar(ly)
Sir   Sirach/Ecclesiasticus
SJT   *Scottish Journal of Theology*
Spicq   C. Spicq, *Theological Lexicon of the New Testament*, 3 vols., ET and ed. by J. D. Ernest. Peabody, MA: Hendrickson, 1994
STJ   *Stulos Theological Journal*
subj.   subject(ive)
subjunc.   subjunctive
subord.   subordinate, subordination
subst.   substantive
suf.   suffix
Sumney   J. L. Sumney, *Philippians: A Greek Student's Intermediate Reader*. Peabody, MA: Hendrickson, 2007
superl.   superlative

SwJT	*Southwestern Journal of Theology*
T	N. Turner, *A Grammar of New Testament Greek*. Edited by J. H. Moulton, vol. III: *Syntax*. Edinburgh: Clark, 1963
TBT	*The Bible Today*
TDNT	G. Kittel and G. Friedrich, eds., *Theological Dictionary of the New Testament*, 9 vols. Translated by G. W. Bromiley. Grand Rapids: Eerdmans, 1964–74
temp.	temporal(ly)
Them	*Themelios*
TJ	*Trinity Journal*
TNIV	Today's New International Version (2001)
tr.	translate(d), translator, translation(s)
trans.	transitive
Trench	R. C. Trench, *Synonyms of the Greek New Testament*. London: Macmillan, 1876; repr., Grand Rapids: Eerdmans, 1975
TTE	*The Theological Educator*
Turner, *Insights*	N. Turner, *Grammatical Insights into the New Testament*. Edinburgh: Clark, 1965
Turner, *Style*	N. Turner, *Style*, vol. 4 of *A Grammar of New Testament Greek*. Edited by J. H. Moulton. Edinburgh: T&T Clark, 1976
Turner, *Words*	N. Turner, *Christian Words*. Edinburgh: Clark, 1980
TynBul	*Tyndale Bulletin*
v(v).	verse(s)
var.	variant (form or reading)
vb.	verb
VE	*Vox evangelica*
viz.	*videlicet* (Lat.), namely
voc.	vocative
vol(s).	volume(s)
VT	*Vetus Testamentum*
Wallace	D. B. Wallace, *Greek Grammar Beyond the Basics: An Exegetical Syntax of the New Testament*. Grand Rapids: Zondervan, 1996
Winer	G. B. Winer, *A Grammar of the Idiom of the New Testament: Prepared as a Solid Basis for the Interpretation of the New Testament*. Edited by Gottlieb Lünemann, 7th ed. Andover: Draper, 1872
Wis	Wisdom of Solomon
Witherington	B. Witherington, III, *Friendship and Finances in Philippi: The Letter of Paul to the Philippians*. New Testament In Context. Edinburgh: T&T Clark, 1994
Wright	N. T. Wright, *Paul and the Faithfulness of God*. Minneapolis: Fortress, 2013.
WTJ	*Westminster Theological Journal*

WW	*Word and World*
Z	M. Zerwick, *Biblical Greek Illustrated by Examples*. Translated by J. Smith. Rome: Pontifical Biblical Institute, 1963
ZG	M. Zerwick and M. Grosvenor, *A Grammatical Analysis of the Greek New Testament*, 5th rev. ed. Rome: Pontifical Biblical Institute, 1996
ZNW	*Zeitschrift für die neutestamentliche Wissenschaft und die Kunde der älteren Kirche*

PHILIPPIANS

Introduction

AUTHORSHIP AND LITERARY INTEGRITY

Nearly all scholars think Paul wrote Philippians (the so-called "Christ hymn," 2:6–11, is the exception, for which see discussion of 2:5–11). More contentious is the issue of the letter's integrity. Reumann is representative of many who find in Philippians several earlier documents, due to problematic transitions at several points in the text (Reumann 8–13). There is no evidence for multiple epistles in the textual tradition, however, nor are there known analogies from ancient letters. The argument from "the apparently unmanageable 'seams'" in the letter, moreover, cuts both ways, since a partition theory must now explain why a scribal redactor would retain the troublesome transitions (Fee 22). Why rearrange several letters into a single epistle without, for example, removing Τὸ λοιπόν, ἀδελφοί μου, χαίρετε ἐν κυρίῳ in 3:1? (Silva 143). For a helpful overview of the discussion, see D. E. Garland, "The Composition and Literary Unity of Philippians: Some Neglected Factors," *NovT* 27 (1985) 141–73; see also A. Köstenberger, L. S. Kellum, and C. L. Quarles, *The Cradle, the Cross, and the Crown* (Nashville: B&H Publishing, 2009), 561–63.

DATE AND PROVENANCE

Tradition places the writing of Philippians during Paul's Roman imprisonment (ca. AD 60–62), a view still defended by numbers of scholars across the theological spectrum (Bockmuehl 25–32; Fee 34–37; Fitzgerald, *ABD* 5:323; Köstenberger, et al., *The Cradle, the Cross, and the Crown*, 563–66; O'Brien 19–26; Silva 5–7). A Roman provenance is not without problems, however, and a strong case has been made in recent years for Ephesus in the mid-50s (Hansen 19–25; Reumann 14; F. Thielman, "Ephesus and the Literary Setting of Philippians," in *New Testament Greek and Exegesis: Essays in Honor of Gerald Hawthorne*, ed. Amy M. Donaldson and Timothy B. Sailors [Grand Rapids: Eerdmans, 2003], 205–23), and, to a lesser degree, for Caesarea ca. AD 59–60 (Hawthorne, *DPL* 711; H-M xxxix–l). The main objections to Rome are twofold. First, the distance between Rome and Philippi becomes problematic in light of the number of journeys between the cities that Philippians appears to assume. Second, the style and contents of the epistle seem to have more in common with Galatians and

3

1 Corinthians than with Ephesians and Colossians, letters written during the Roman imprisonment.

The decision is a difficult one. The data relating to the distance and journeys can reasonably be interpreted to support any of the three views (see on 2:25–30). The argument from Paul's concerns in the letter carries a bit more weight but not enough to overturn evidence to the contrary for Rome as the origin of Philippians: (1) the reference to ὅλῳ τῷ πραιτωρίῳ ("the whole praetorian guard" [1:13]); and (2) the greeting from οἱ ἐκ τῆς Καίσαρος οἰκίας ("those of Caesar's household" [4:22]). Although both praetorians and Caesar's civil servants were found elsewhere in the empire, 1:13 and 4:22 are more naturally taken to indicate a Roman provenance for Philippians. I assume that Paul wrote Philippians in Rome for the purposes of the volume.

OCCASION

The immediate occasion for Philippians was a gift Paul received from the church through their emissary Epaphroditus. Paul took the opportunity afforded by the gift (a) to express his gratitude (1:3; 4:10–20), (b) to challenge the Philippians to remain faithful to the gospel in the face of local opposition (1:27–30), and (c) to address issues of disunity (2:1–4; 4:2–3) and false teaching (3:2, 18–19) that Paul perceived as threats to the community.

Particularly illuminating for the interpretation of the letter is the location of the church in a highly Romanized sociopolitical environment. Philippi was an imperial colony, founded by Octavian and Antony in 42 BC, in the wake of the battle of Philippi, and, again, by Augustus, post-Actium, ca. 30 BC. Archaeological finds from the site reveal a socially stratified population obsessed with status markers such as Roman citizenship, public office, and prestigious titles (Hellerman, *Reconstructing Honor*, 64–109). Persons of every class competed with their peers for these coveted titles and offices, which the victors then displayed in "résumé form" on inscriptions erected throughout the colony (see on 2:5–11 and 3:1–11).

Paul strongly resisted the "race of honors" (Lat. *cursus honorum*) that marked social life in Philippi. The apostle recognized that a stridently Roman honor culture had the potential to seriously undermine the radically different relational *ethos* that Jesus intended for his community of followers. And so Paul confronts Roman social priorities throughout the letter, preeminently in the epistle's magnificent centerpiece, Philippians 2:5–11. In his portrayal of the humiliation and exaltation of Christ, Paul turns Rome's race of honors on its head, forcefully challenging anyone—then or now—who would utilize his power, authority, or social capital in the service of his own personal agenda.

LINGUISTIC AND RHETORICAL CONSIDERATIONS

The Greek Verb. Verb tense has become a central topic of discussion and discovery among specialists in Greek grammar in recent decades. Perhaps most contentious is the debate about whether tense grammaticalizes time in the indicative. Fortunately, this is a moot point in Philippians since every imperfect and aorist indicative in the epistle pragmatically marks past time from the author's perspective (the epistolary aorists in 2:25 [ἡγησάμην] and 2:28 [ἔπεμψα] mark past time from the perspective of readers). More pertinent in the present connection is the increased sensitivity among grammarians to the distinction between Aspect (tense ontology/semantics) and *Aktionsart* (tense phenomenology/pragmatics). Aspect is the unaffected significance of the tense. *Aktionsart* may be loosely defined as aspect constrained by lexical, grammatical, or other contextual features. An exegetical guidebook is concerned, of course, with the latter, i.e., the significance of a verb in a given context, in reference to which I will use the word *"Aktionsart"* in the pages that follow. The distinction between semantics and pragmatics is crucial. Earlier generations of scholars confused the two and argued, among other things, for the now much-maligned "once-and-for-all" aorist. Unfortunately, the categorical mistake of elevating phenomenology (*Aktionsart*) to ontology (Aspect) continues today in the treatment of the present tense. Virtually every present-tense verbal form in Philippians is viewed by at least one commentator as denoting "continual" or "ongoing" action. Reumann alone finds the notion in the majority of presents in the epistle. This, again, is erroneously to confuse a potential *Aktionsart* of the present with the Aspect of the tense itself. It may, indeed, be the case that more instances of the present signify "continual" action than, for example, an "instantaneous" *Aktionsart*, a "futuristic" *Aktionsart*, or any other of a number of possible contextual usages of the present (I continue to find these traditional categories useful as descriptive labels for talking about phenomena in the text). But the argument must be made on a case-by-case basis. Accordingly, I will claim that a present-tense verbal form signifies "ongoing" or "continual" action only when lexical, grammatical, or other contextual intrusions support such a notion—only, that is, in the case of "a legitimate phenomenological usage" (Wallace 716).

Rhetorical Analysis. In recent decades the analysis of Paul's letters via ancient rhetorical categories (e.g., *exordium, narratio, propositio,* etc.) has become something of a cottage industry in New Testament scholarship (e.g., the commentaries of Ben Witherington III). The methodology has not gone unchallenged (see esp. Stanley E. Porter and Bryan R. Dyer, "Oral Texts? A Reassessment of the Oral and Rhetorical Nature of Paul's Letters in Light of Recent Studies," *JETS* 55 [2012]: 323–41; Fee 14–17; Hansen 13–14; Reumann 188; Reed, *Discourse Analysis,* 156–68). Few would doubt that Paul employs rhetorical devices at the level of clause, sentence, and paragraph (e.g., alliteration, chiasm). Paul's epistles share certain structural features with other letters from the ancient world, as well. I have yet to be convinced, however, of the exegetical value of oral rhetorical practices for outlining the arguments of Paul's letters. For Philippians, in particular, contradictory analyses raise serious questions about the value of the methodology, as Hansen (14) has made readily apparent in a revealing side-by-side comparison of three recent breakdowns of the letter using the categories of ancient rhetoric (D. Watson, "Rhetorical Analysis of Philippians and Its Implications for the Unity Question," *NovT* 30 [1988]: 57–88; L. G. Bloomquist, *The Function of Suffering in Philippians* [Sheffield: Sheffield Academic Press, 1993]; B. Witherington, *Friendship and Finances in Philippi: The Letter of Paul to the*

Philippians [Edinburgh: T&T Clark, 1994], 13). Reed compares seven rhetorical analyses of Philippians and finds them "widely divergent," as well (*Discourse Analysis*, 165, cf. 442–54). Consequently, I do not employ ancient rhetorical categories in the analysis of Philippians in this volume.

OUTLINE

   I. Introduction (1:1–11)
      A. Greeting (1:1–2)
      B. Thanksgiving and Prayer for Participation in the Gospel (1:3–11)
   II. Paul's Circumstances and the Gospel (1:12–26)
      A. The Gospel Continues to Advance (1:12–18c)
      B. Paul's Future Expectations (1:18d–26)
  III. Body of the Letter (1:27–4:9)
      A. Summary Exhortation to Unity and Steadfastness (1:27–30)
      B. Unity Among Believers (2:1–30)
         1. Plea for Unity Through Humility (2:1–4)
         2. Christ Our Example (2:5–11)
         3. Humility Lived Out in Community with Others (2:12–18)
         4. Paul Commends Timothy as an Example of Humility (2:19–24)
         5. Paul Commends Epaphroditus as an Example of Humility (2:25–30)
      C. Steadfastness Toward Opponents (3:1–4:1)
         1. Resisting the Opponents' Fleshly Confidence (3:1–16)
           a. Paul's Relationship with Judaism (3:1–11)
           b. Pressing Toward the Goal (3:12–16)
         2. Resisting the Opponents' Fleshly Behavior (3:17–4:1)
      D. Final Words of Exhortation (4:2–9)
         1. Restoring a Broken Relationship (4:2–3)
         2. The Joy and Peace of Knowing Christ (4:4–7)
         3. The Common Good and the Apostle's Example (4:8–9)
  IV. Paul's Circumstances and the Philippians' Gift (4:10–20)
   V. Closing Greeting and Benediction (4:21–23)

RECOMMENDED COMMENTARIES

Six commentaries on Philippians served as the primary resources for this volume of *EGGNT*. They are cited throughout by the author's last name, except where noted:

Fee, Gordon D. *Paul's Letter to the Philippians*. New International Commentary on the New Testament. Grand Rapids: Eerdmans, 1995.

Hansen, G. Walter. *The Letter to the Philippians*. Pillar New Testament Commentary. Grand Rapids: Eerdmans, 2009.

Martin, Ralph P., and Gerald F. Hawthorne. *Philippians*. Revised ed. Word Biblical Commentary. Nashville: Thomas Nelson, 2004. [cited as H-M]

O'Brien, Peter T. *The Epistle to the Philippians*. New International Greek Testament Commentary. Grand Rapids: Eerdmans, 1991.

Reumann, John. *Philippians*. Anchor Bible. New Haven, CT: Yale University Press, 2008.
Silva, Moisés. *Philippians*. 2nd ed. Baker Exegetical Commentary on the New Testament.
Grand Rapids: Baker, 2005.

Fee and Hansen treat the English text of Philippians, often discussing issues related
to Greek syntax and lexicography in some detail in their footnotes. Martin and
Hawthorne, Silva, and O'Brien are the standard commentaries in English on the Greek
text of the letter. All are excellent works. Martin and Hawthorne are creative at times,
Silva more theological (e.g., on 2:12–13; 3:9–11). O'Brien is the most thorough of the
three. Reumann's work is a dense and exhaustive compendium of just about everything that had been said to date (2008) on Philippians, accompanied by the author's
own interpretation of the text. The commentary (a) is lengthy, (b) is not user-friendly,
and (c) assumes a three-document partition theory for Philippians that sometimes
influences the exegesis. For these reasons Reumann will serve the scholar more readily than the pastor.

The following works are occasionally referenced in the discussion of significant
issues of interpretation:

Commentaries

Bockmuehl, Markus. *The Epistle to the Philippians*. Black's New Testament Commentary.
  Peabody, MA: Hendrickson, 1998.
Hendrickson, William. *Philippians*. 2nd ed. New Testament Commentary. Grand Rapids:
  Baker, 1979.
Lightfoot, J. B. *St. Paul's Epistle to the Philippians*. London: Macmillan, 1913; reprint,
  Grand Rapids: Zondervan, 1978.
Osiek, Carolyn. *Philippians and Philemon*. Abingdon New Testament Commentaries.
  Nashville: Abingdon, 2000.
Witherington, Ben, III. *Friendship and Finances in Philippi: The Letter of Paul to the
  Philippians*. New Testament in Context. Edinburgh: T&T Clark, 1994.

Other Works Cited

Campbell, Constantine. *Paul and Union with Christ: An Exegetical and Theological Study*.
  Grand Rapids: Zondervan, 2012.
Guthrie, George H. "Cohesion Shifts and Stitches in Philippians." In *Discourse Analysis
  and Other Topics in Biblical Greek*. Edited by Stanley E. Porter and D. A. Carson. JSNT
  Supplement Series 113. Sheffield: Sheffield Academic Press, 1995.
Hellerman, Joseph H. *Reconstructing Honor in Roman Philippi:* Carmen Christi *as* Cursus
  Pudorum. SNTSMS 136. Cambridge: Cambridge University Press, 2005.
Lendon, Jon E. *Empire of Honour: The Art of Government in the Roman World*. Oxford:
  Oxford University Press, 1997.
Oakes, Peter. *Philippians: From People to Letter*. SNTSMS 110. Cambridge: Cambridge
  University Press, 2001.
Park, M. Sydney. *Submission Within the Godhead and the Church in the Epistle to the
  Philippians*. Library of New Testament Studies 361. Edited by Mark Goodacre. London:
  T&T Clark, 2007.

Peterlin, Davorlin. *Paul's Letter to the Philippians in the Light of Disunity in the Church.* NovTSupp 79. Leiden: Brill, 1995.

Porter, Stanley E. *Idioms of the Greek New Testament.* 2nd ed. Sheffield: JSOT Press, 1994.

Reed, Jeffrey T. *A Discourse Analysis of Philippians: Method and Rhetoric in the Debate over Literary Integrity.* JSNTSup 136. Sheffield: Sheffield Academic Press, 1997.

Runge, Steven E. *Discourse Grammar of the Greek New Testament.* Peabody, MA: Hendrickson, 2010.

Sumney, Jerry L. *Philippians: A Greek Student's Intermediate Reader.* Peabody, MA: Hendrickson, 2007.

Winter, Bruce W. *Seek the Welfare of the City: Christians as Benefactors and Citizens.* First-Century Christians in the Graeco-Roman World 1. Grand Rapids: Eerdmans, 1994.

Wright, N. T. *Paul and the Faithfulness of God.* Minneapolis: Fortress, 2013.

I. Introduction (1:1–11)

A. GREETING (1:1–2)

1 Παῦλος καὶ Τιμόθεος
δοῦλοι Χριστοῦ Ἰησοῦ

πᾶσιν τοῖς ἁγίοις ἐν Χριστῷ Ἰησοῦ
τοῖς οὖσιν ἐν Φιλίπποις
σὺν ἐπισκόποις καὶ διακόνοις,

2 χάρις ὑμῖν καὶ εἰρήνη
ἀπὸ θεοῦ πατρὸς ἡμῶν
καὶ κυρίου Ἰησοῦ Χριστοῦ.

VERSE 1

Παῦλος καὶ Τιμόθεος δοῦλοι Χριστοῦ Ἰησοῦ

Παῦλος begins all Paul's letters. Proper names are generally anar. in salutations (R 759). Σαῦλος is Paul's "synagogue name" from birth, Παῦλος, his name in the Greco-Roman world. Jews in the Gk. world adopted names that sounded similar to their Heb. names (O'Brien 44; "Paul[l]us" was a common Lat. cognomen [BDAG 789b]; H. Balz, *EDNT* 3.59d).

Τιμόθεος (etym. "[one who] honors God"; common Gk. name) was a convert (μου τέκνον [1 Cor 4:17; cf. Acts 16:1–3]) who became Paul's "co-worker" (ὁ συνεργός μου [Rom 16:21]) (BDAG 1006b; MM 635). Timothy is elsewhere included among the "apostles of Christ" (Χριστοῦ ἀπόστολοι [1 Thess 2:7]), a group of commissioned missionary-preachers who were not, however, apostles like Paul and the twelve (cf. Epaphroditus [2:26]). Timothy is neither (1) "co-writer" (*pace* BDAG 1006b; cf. εὐχαριστῶ [1:3]; 1 sg. "pervades Philippians" [H-M 4]), nor (2) Paul's secretary or amanuensis (*pace* Fee 61; Hansen 38). Timothy is included, rather, as (3) a co-sender (Reumann 53), because of his key role as a coworker (cf. 2:19–24), and because he was among those who first brought the gospel to Philippi (not mentioned in Acts 16:11–40, but cf. 16:3 and 1 Thess 1:1; 2:2).

Δοῦλοι (nom. pl. masc.; appos. to Παῦλος καὶ Τιμόθεος [Porter 85 n. 1]) is intended

9

*1. negatively, of the servility and obedience associated with ancient slavery ("slaves" [NLT, HCSB] is better than "servants" [NRSV, NIV, NJB]) (H-M 6; O'Brien 45; Silva 40), rather than

2. positively, via the LXX, where it was an honor to be designated a "servant (δοῦλος) of the Lord" (Moses [LXX Neh 10:30]; Joshua [LXX Jos 23:30]; David [LXX Ps 88:21]; cf. also the Greco-Roman world, where a "slave of [a high-status person]" gains status by association) (BDAG 260c; A. Weiser, *EDNT* 1.352c; Reumann 82–83).

Reasons: (a) the exclusively negative connotation of δοῦλος in its only other occurrence in the letter (2:7); (b) the intent of the anomalous greeting (see below). It is not likely that Paul intended both meanings (*pace* Fee 63; Hansen 38–39).

Χριστός, from χρίω, "anoint" (BDAG 1091d), is used in LXX of anointed kings and high priests, occasionally prophets. Paul was certainly familiar with this OT background (cf. 2 Cor 1:21–22), but his Gentile audience would have needed instruction about the titular meaning of Χριστός as "Messiah." Here Χριστός means not "Messiah" but functions, rather, as "the personal name ascribed to Jesus" (BDAG 1091b).

The etym. of Ἰησοῦς ("Yahweh saves" [cf. OT "Joshua"]), though familiar in Jewish-Christian circles (cf. Matt 1:21), would also have escaped Paul's Gentile readers. Χριστός Ἰησοῦς became a two-part name, on the analogy of Caesar Augustus (Reumann 57). The gen. Χριστοῦ Ἰησοῦ can be taken as poss. or obj. (Reumann 54).

1:1 is unique among Paul's salutations in two striking ways: (a) Elsewhere when Paul introduces himself as δοῦλος, he adds ἀπόστολος (Rom 1:1; Titus 1:1; often only ἀπόστολος [1–2 Cor; Gal; Eph; Col; 1–2 Tim]). (b) In no other greeting does Paul single out church leaders by the title (ἐπισκόποις καὶ διακόνοις). Commentators address the two anomalies separately. The absence of ἀπόστολος is explained by the "special bonds of affection" Paul shared with the Philippians (O'Brien 45; Silva 39; appropriate for the friendship genre [Fee 62]), or by a desire on Paul's part not to draw any distinction between himself and Timothy in the greeting (K. Rengstorf, *TDNT* 2.277 n. 111).

The inclusion of ἐπισκόποις καὶ διακόνοις is interpreted as an attempt on Paul's part

1. to buttress the leaders' authority in the face of grumbling among the Philippians (2:14–15);

2. to show his regard for them while at the same time preparing to challenge them to tackle the difficult issues the letter raises (O'Brien 49–50; Silva 41); or

3. to single out the leaders because they oversaw Epaphroditus's gift-bearing mission to Paul (Hansen 42; Chrysostom, *Homily on Philippians*, 2.1.1–2).

*4. But recent research points to another option. The two anomalies in the salutation should, instead, be taken together since they interpret one another when read against the social background of Roman Philippi. By (1) deemphasizing his own status (δοῦλος *sans* ἀπόστολος) and (2) honoring the congregation's leaders with their titles (ἐπισκόποις καὶ διακόνοις), Paul intentionally subverts the honor culture of Philippi, where rank and titles were viewed as prizes to be competitively sought and publicly proclaimed, in order to enhance the holder's social status. Paul thus begins, at the outset of the letter, to model a relational *ethos* he will later (1) commend to the Philippians (2:5) and (2) vividly portray in his remarkable narrative of the humiliation of Christ (2:6–8) (Hellerman 117–21).

πᾶσιν τοῖς ἁγίοις ἐν Χριστῷ Ἰησοῦ τοῖς οὖσιν ἐν Φιλίπποις

A verbless epistolary greeting with the recipients in the dat. (indir. obj. or dat. of "recipient" [Wallace 148]) is common ("not difficult to supply λέγει" [R 394]).

Though not a rarity in Paul's greetings (cf. 1–2 Cor; Gal), the adj. πᾶς (here dat. pl. masc.) is employed of the Philippians eight times in the letter (1:1, 3, 7 [2x], 8, 25; 2:17, 26; "startling frequency" [H-M 6]), likely to remind the readers of the need for unity in the congregation (Fee 66; Hansen 40; Reumann 57).

Ἁγίοις is dat. pl. masc., from the adj. ἅγιος, -α, -ον, "dedicated or consecrated to the service of God" (BDAG 10d; used w/art. as subst.; pass. sense explicit in 1 Cor 1:2: ἡγιασμένοις ἐν Χριστῷ Ἰησοῦ, κλητοῖς ἁγίοις [Reumann 83]). Paul variously uses ἅγιοι (Rom; Eph; Phil; Col), ἐκκλησία/ἐκκλησίαι (Gal; 1–2 Thess), or sometimes both (1–2 Cor) to identify the recipients of his letters. Ἅγιοι in the greetings denotes not primarily ethical character but a "special relationship to God" (H-M 6; H. Balz, *EDNT* 1.20c; "pre-ethical," but still "demands behaviour which rightly corresponds to the Holy Spirit" [C. Brown, *NIDNTT* 2.229–30]). In CGk. ἅγιος (etym. cf. ἅζομαι, "stand in awe") referred to "the deity whose manifestations are accompanied by marvelous signs and call forth fear and awe," i.e., "venerable, awe-inspiring" (H. Balz, *EDNT* 1.18a). The LXX background, where the term was used to describe a people that was "holy," and therefore "set apart" (e.g., λαὸς ἅγιος w/dat. κυρίῳ τῷ θεῷ [Deut 7:6; 14:2, 21; 26:19]), is decisive for its meaning in the NT. A communal emphasis is thus present in ἁγίοις, i.e., a dedicated people (O'Brien 46; Reumann 58, 84). Because "saints" (NASB, HCSB, ESV) is used in some traditions to denote a special class of believers, the tr. "God's holy people" (NJB, NLT) is best (Fee 65).

Scholars have commented extensively on the meaning of Paul's familiar expression ἐν Χριστῷ (Ἰησοῦ) ("in Christ Jesus" [most EVV]; Reumann discusses ten options [58–61]; M. Harris surveys seven [*NIDNTT* 3.1192]). Each instance must be evaluated in its own context (Campbell is now the standard treatment; cf., also, Matthew V. Novenson, *Christ Among the Messiahs* [Oxford: Oxford University Press, 2012], 119–26). The options are:

1. incorporation ("in union with Christ Jesus" [GNB]; Hansen 40; O'Brien 46);
2. instr. or causal dat., telling "how those in Philippi came to be 'saints,' namely, 'by (the work of) Jesus Christ'" (Reumann 84; O. Procksch, *TDNT* 1.107);
3. a locat. sense; ἐν Χριστῷ Ἰησοῦ "tells us where the Christian community lives, just as the phrase *in Philippi* tells us where the church resides" (Hansen 40); or

*4. ἐν Χριστῷ Ἰησοῦ simply identifies the recipients as Christian (Campbell 124; "those who belong to Christ Jesus" [CEV, NLT, NIV; Fee 65]).

The first view is theologically attractive, but the last alternative most naturally fits the context of a straightforward greeting. Τοῖς οὖσιν ἐν Φιλίπποις marks "the locale that distinguishes them from others as 'Christ's saints'" (Reumann 84). Τοῖς οὖσιν is an art. subst. ptc. (dat. pl. masc. of the pres. act. ptc. of εἰμί, "live," "reside") in simple appos. to ἁγίοις. Φιλίπποις, with ἐν, is dat. of place ("at/in Philippi" [EVV]; pl. place-name, like Ἀθῆναι [Acts 17:15–16]). On Philippi as a Roman colony, see Introduction and Hellerman 64–87.

σὺν ἐπισκόποις καὶ διακόνοις

The prep. σύν means (1) "including" (NLT), identifying the church leaders as part of τοῖς ἁγίοις . . . ἐν Φιλίπποις, not (2) "and" (cf. "Peter with John" [Acts 3:4]), distinguishing them from the rest of the community (O'Brien 48; "besides" [R 628]). Although its leaders, they serve "(together) with" the church (most EVV; W. Grundmann, TDNT 7,782; Hansen 42; Reed 190–91). Καί could mark a hendiadys (BDF §442[16]; "episkopoi who serve" [H-M 11]), but this is not likely given the distinction between "overseers" and "deacons" in 1 Timothy 3 (Fee 66 n. 43; H. Beyer, TDNT 2.616 n. 28).

Ἐπισκόποις is dat. pl. masc. from ἐπίσκοπος, "one who has a definite function or a fixed office of guardianship within a group" (BDAG 379d). Paul's audience would have been immediately familiar with the "ubiquitous" use of ἐπίσκοπος for overseers or supervisors in government, and in voluntary associations and cult groups in the Greco-Roman world (Reumann 63; H. Beyer, TDNT 2.619). Best to tr. "overseers" (NIV, HCSB, ESV; "church leaders/officials" [GNB/CEV]) to avoid the anachronistic "bishops" (NRSV), a term "loaded with late historical baggage" (BDAG 379d; "elders" [NJB, NLT] confuses ἐπίσκοπος with πρεσβύτερος). Though care must be taken given the variety of labels for church leaders in the NT (cf. 1 Cor 12:28; Eph 4:11; Heb 13:17), πρεσβύτερος ("elder"), ἐπίσκοπος ("overseer"), and ποιμήν ("pastor") appear to be used in the NT interchangeably for the same office (cf. Acts 20:17, 28; 1 Pet 5:1–3). Such leaders are always in the pl. when associated with a single locale (Acts 14:23; 20:17; Phil 1:1; Titus 1:5; Jas 5:14 [cf. 1:1]; 1 Pet 5:1 [cf. 1:1]). The function of these leaders must be derived from elsewhere in Scripture ("oversight, supervision, or protective care" [O'Brien 47; J. Rohde, EDNT 2.36a]; "administration, hospitality, and pastoral care" [Fee 69]).

Διάκονοις is dat. pl. masc. from διάκονος, which originally denoted a lowly servant, such as someone waiting on tables (Matt 22:13; John 2:5). Paul regularly uses the term functionally, for Christian ministry (2 Cor 3:6; 6:4; 11:23; Eph 3:7; Col 4:7; 1 Tim 4:6), so some reject the idea that διάκονος in 1:1 is an official title. The tr. "deacon" (most EVV) is "inadequate for rendering NT usage" (BDAG 230d–231a). A διάκονος is simply "one who gets someth[ing] done, at the behest of a superior," and should be tr. "assistant" (BDAG 231a; "helpers" [GNB]). To single out some of the Philippians who simply function as servants (διάκονοι) would make little sense, however, in the present context (A. Weiser, EDNT 1.303c; Fee 66–69; O'Brien 48). And just a few years later Paul will use διάκονος unambiguously as an official title (1 Tim 3:8, 12). The preoccupation in the colony of Philippi with honorific office further supports the view that ἐπισκόποις and διακόνοις are titles in 1:1, and we should continue to interpret the twofold expression as "two co-ordinated offices" (H. Beyer, *TDNT* 2.89, cf. 616; "officers" [CEV]; Silva 40–41). Note, finally, how such titles are first applied to Christ (L. Coenen, *NIDNTT* 1. 191; ἐπίσκοπος [1 Pet 2:25], διάκονος [Rom 15:8; cf. Mark 10:45]).

VERSE 2

χάρις ὑμῖν καὶ εἰρήνη

Paul's characteristic greetings in all his letters (χάρις and εἰρήνη are nom. abs. [Porter 85; Wallace 51]). Some think a traditional Jewish greeting, "mercy and peace" (2 Bar 78:2; cf., in reverse order, εἰρήνη ἐπ' αὐτοὺς καὶ ἔλεος [Gal 6:16]), became "grace and peace" (EVV) in Christian circles (V. Hasler, *EDNT* 1.396d). More likely Paul worked from a Gk. archetype. Nonliterary papyri letters usually began: "A (sender) to B (recipient), greetings (χαίρειν)" (Reumann 74). Paul (a) substitutes χάρις for the typical initial χαίρειν ("greetings" [BDAG 1075b]; Acts 15:23; 23:26; Jas 1:1), and (b) adds the traditional Jewish greeting εἰρήνη (Judg 6:23; 19:20; 2 Kgs 5:22; cf. Dan 4:1 for "peace" in Babylonian letters) (BDAG 288a; H. Conzelmann, *TDNT* 9.394; Fee 70; Hansen 43; H-M 12–13; Reed 192–97). The Gk. word order may be significant ("grace to you and peace" [NRSV, HCSB, ESV], not "grace and peace to you" [NIV, NJB]). God's gives grace; peace is the result of that gift (Fee 70).

Χάρις ("a beneficent disposition toward someone" [BDAG 1079b]) would have made sense to new converts since it was used in the context of Greco-Roman benefaction for favors bestowed by the gods and by Roman emperors (Spicq 3.500; Reumann 65). For Paul, of course, the favor bestowed by God is his great eschatological act of putting forth Christ as the propitiation for our sin (Rom 3:24–25; 5:15–16, cf. v. 2). Paul's gospel was τὸ εὐαγγέλιον τῆς χάριτος τοῦ θεοῦ (Acts 20:24).

Like Eng. "peace" (EVV), εἰρήνη can denote either (a) "a state of concord" between parties or (b) "a state of well-being," individually or collectively (BDAG 287b–288a). The meanings broadly correspond to the Gk. and Heb. backgrounds, respectively. Εἰρήνη in Gk. writings referred not to "peace within" but, rather, to relations between persons, or the state of society: "quiet or rest, law and order, not strife or disturbance" (Reumann 66; Spicq 1.424–25; cf. 1 Cor 14:33 for εἰρήνη versus ἀκαταστασία). The pacification of the known world by Roman arms was called the *pax Romana/Augusta*. The ideology of universal peace and prosperity under Rome and her emperor was disseminated throughout the empire by coins bearing the terms *Securitas*, *Salus*, *Concordia*, and *Libertas* ("security," "safety," "concord," and "freedom") (Reumann 67). Peace had a somewhat different connotation in the OT, where *shalom* refers preeminently to a state of well-being that often involves health and material prosperity (Judg 19:20; 2 Sam 18:28–29; but cf. Deut 20:20). For εἰρήνη in 1:2, the Heb. background is likely dominant (the use in greetings likely informed Paul's understanding

[Gen 29:6; 2 Sam 20:9–10]): not peace "with God" (cf. πρὸς τὸν θεόν [Rom 5:1]) but peace "from God" (ἀπὸ θεοῦ), though the distinction must be qualified, since one cannot experience the latter apart from the former. God's peace, moreover, is associated by Paul with relational concord among God's people so that the Gk. sense of εἰρήνη remains on the horizon, as well (cf. Eph 2:14–18; Col 3:13b; Fee 71 n. 62).

ἀπὸ θεοῦ πατρὸς ἡμῶν καὶ κυρίου Ἰησοῦ Χριστοῦ

We would expect θεοῦ πατρός to have an art. since it is modified by the pers. pron. ἡμῶν; the stylized formula (ἀπὸ θεοῦ πατρὸς ἡμῶν) of Paul's salutations, however, accounts for the anar. cstr. here (BDF §268[2]; T 206).

Chiasm places θεοῦ in a position parallel to Ἰησοῦ Χριστοῦ, each with a respective title: πατρός to show which god and κυρίου to emphasize Christ's authority. The parallel bears witness to "the exalted place Christ occupied in Paul's thought" (O'Brien 52; Paul normally uses ἀπό ["from" = source] with God; διά ["through" = mediator] with Jesus [Reumann 68]). Ἡμῶν modifies both θεοῦ and κυρίου; it is not repeated with κυρίου in order to maintain structural balance. Take κυρίου with ἀπό, not as poss. gen. with πατρός: "father of us," not "father of us and of the Lord Jesus Christ" (H-M 13–14; Reumann 68). Paul's central affirmation as a Jew had been the Shema: "Hear, O Israel, the Lord our God, the Lord is one." Retaining "Lord" and "God," Paul now includes Jesus: "The Lord (Jesus Christ) (and) God (our Father), the Lord is one" (Hansen 43; W. Grundmann, TDNT 9.554; more clearly, 1 Cor 8:6).

Gentiles would have heard θεός (here gen. sg. masc.) against the background of polytheism and the ruler cult. For Paul, the content of θεός is rooted in the OT understanding of God as the holy and righteous One who creates, elects, enters into a covenant with, and delivers his people—the "living and true God" (1 Thess 1:9) before whom all are ultimately accountable (Rom 2:2; 3:19; 14:10) (Reumann 68). Paul's Jewish monotheism had to do with loyalty to the one true God, who alone is Creator and Redeemer, not philosophical speculation about the inner workings of divine ontology (Wright 619–33).

God as Father was a common idea in the Greco-Roman world due to the patriarchal orientation of family and society. Zeus "is the Father who cares for all" (Epictetus, 3.24.16). OT references are relatively rare, almost never to God as Father of individual Israelites (perhaps Ps 68:5) but, rather, as Father of the people (Isa 63:16; 64:8) or the king (2 Sam 7:14). "Father" is never used in the OT of God's relationship with all of humankind (Reumann 70). Jesus' use of Father, addressing God with the intimate, filial term Abba, was likely a significant factor for early Christian use (cf. Rom 8:15; Gal 4:6).

Κύριος can mean "owner," "by virtue of possession" (Matt 20:8; Gal 4:1; Rom 14:8, 12) or (here) "one who is in a position of authority," "lord, master" (BDAG 577a–b; W. Foerster, TDNT 3.1,041–42). The word was associated with gods and rulers in the ancient world, especially the Roman emperors (e.g., "To Caesar, ruler of the sea and holding sway over boundless lands, Zeus, from Father Zeus, . . . [who] arose (as) great Savior Zeus" [CIG 4923, cited by W. Foerster, TDNT 3.1056; cf. an inscription honoring Nero: ὁ τοῦ παντὸς κόσμου κύριος Νέρων [ibid.]). Domitian would later begin official letters with *dominus et deus* ("lord and god") (Suet. *Dom.* 13.2). "Jesus is Lord" (cf. Phil 2:11) became for the Christians "the basic theological assertion" (Reumann 71). In the OT, κύριος often tr. the tetragrammaton YHWH.

FOR FURTHER STUDY

1. Slave (1:1)

*Bartchy, S. S. *ABD* 6.65–73.
Bradley, K. R. *Slaves and Masters in the Roman Empire: A Study in Social Control.* Oxford: Oxford University Press, 1987.
Glancey, Jennifer A. *Slavery in Early Christianity.* Minneapolis: Fortress, 2006.
Harrill, J. Albert. *Slaves in the New Testament: Literary, Social, and Moral Dimensions.* Minneapolis: Fortress, 2005.
Joshel, Sandra R. *Slavery in the Roman World. Cambridge Introduction to Roman Civilization.* Cambridge: Cambridge University Press, 2010.
Rengstorf, K. *TDNT* 2.261–80.
Repprecht, A. A. *DPL* 881–83.
Tuente, R., and H. G. Link. *NIDNTT* 3.592–98.
Weiser, A. E. *EDNT* 1.349–52.

2. The "In Christ" Formula (1:1)

Best, Ernest. *One Body in Christ.* London: SPCK, 1955. See pages 1–33.
*Campbell.
Dunn, James D. G. *The Theology of Paul the Apostle.* Grand Rapids: Eerdmans, 1998. See pages 390–401.
Longenecker, Richard N. *Paul, Apostle of Liberty.* New York: Harper, 1964. See pages 160–70.
Moule, C. F. D. *The Origin of Christology.* New York: Cambridge University, 1977. See pages 47–96.
Oepke, A. *TDNT* 2.541–42.
Seifrid, M. A. *DPL* 433–36.
Wedderburn, A. J. M. "Some Observations on Paul's Use of the Phrases 'in Christ' and 'with Christ.'" *JSNT* 25 (1985): 83–87.

3. Overseers (1:1)

Banks, Robert J. *DPL* 131–37.
Best, Ernest. "Bishops and Deacons: Philippians 1,1." *Studia Evangelica* 4 (1968): 371–76.
Beyer, H. *TDNT* 2.599–622.
Burtchaell, James T. *From Synagogue to Church: Public Services and Offices in the Earliest Christian Communities.* New York: Cambridge University Press, 1991.
Campbell, R. Alastair. *The Elders: Seniority Within Earliest Christianity.* London: T&T Clark, 1994.
Campenhausen, Hans Von. *Ecclesiastical Authority and Spiritual Power in the Early Church.* London: Black, 1969.

Clark, Andrew D. *A Pauline Theology of Church Leadership*. London: T&T Clark, 2013.

Schweizer, E. *ABD* 4.835–42.

Selby, Andrew M. "Bishops, Elders, and Deacons in the Philippian Church: Evidence of Plurality from Paul and Polycarp." *Perspectives in Religious Studies* 39.1 (2012): 79–94.

*Strauch, Alexander. *Biblical Eldership: An Urgent Call to Restore Biblical Church Leadership*. Colorado Springs: Lewis and Roth Publishers, 1995.

4. Deacons (1:1)

Beyer, H. *TDNT* 2.81–93.

Hess, K. *NIDNTT* 3.544–49.

*Hiebert, D. Edmond. "Behind the Word 'Deacon': A New Testament Study." *BSac* 140 (1983): 151–62.

Merkle, Benjamin. *40 Questions About Elders and Deacons*. Grand Rapids: Kregel Academic, 2007.

Strauch, Alexander. *The New Testament Deacon: The Church's Minister of Mercy*. Colorado Springs: Lewis and Roth Publishers, 1992.

Weiser, A. *EDNT* 1.302–4.

5. The Fatherhood of God (1:2)

Bassler, Jouette. M. *ABD* 2.1,054–55.

Bruce, F. F. *NIDNTT* 2.655–56.

Burton, Ernest de Witt. *The Epistle to the Galatians*. Edinburgh: Clark, 1921. See pages 384–92.

Forsyth, Peter T. *God the Holy Father*. London: Independent, 1957.

Jeremias, Joachim. *The Prayers of Jesus*. Naperville, IL: Allenson, 1967. See pages 11–65.

*Manson, T. W. *The Teaching of Jesus*. Cambridge: Cambridge University Press, 1935. See pages 89–115.

Mawhinney, Allen. "God as Father: Two Popular Theories Reconsidered." *JETS* 31 (1988): 181–89.

Michel, O. *EDNT* 3.53–57.

Schrenk, G., and G. Quell. *TDNT* 5.945–1,022.

Spencer, Aida B. "Father-Ruler: The Meaning of the Metaphor 'Father' for God in the Bible." *JETS* 39 (1996): 433–42.

HOMILETICAL SUGGESTIONS

Introductory Greeting (1:1–2)

1. The writers: Paul (and Timothy) (v. 1a)
2. The addressees (v. 1b)
   a. All Christians in Philippi
   b. Overseers and deacons
3. The greeting: grace and peace (v. 2)

Paul's Apostolic Mind-set (1:1–2)

1. Refrains from honoring himself (v. 1a)
2. Affirms the status of others (v. 1b)
   a. Addresses believers as saints
   b. Addresses leaders by title
3. Sees God as the source of all that is worthwhile (v. 2)

B. THANKSGIVING AND PRAYER FOR PARTICIPATION IN THE GOSPEL (1:3–11)

3–4a   Εὐχαριστῶ τῷ θεῷ μου
        ἐπὶ πάσῃ τῇ μνείᾳ ὑμῶν
        πάντοτε
        ἐν πάσῃ δεήσει μου ὑπὲρ πάντων ὑμῶν,
4b–5   μετὰ χαρᾶς
        τὴν δέησιν ποιούμενος,
        ἐπὶ τῇ κοινωνίᾳ ὑμῶν εἰς τὸ εὐαγγέλιον
        ἀπὸ τῆς πρώτης ἡμέρας ἄχρι τοῦ νῦν,
6   πεποιθὼς αὐτὸ τοῦτο
        ὅτι ὁ ἐναρξάμενος ἐν ὑμῖν ἔργον ἀγαθὸν ἐπιτελέσει
                ἄχρι ἡμέρας
                Χριστοῦ Ἰησοῦ·
7   Καθώς ἐστιν δίκαιον ἐμοὶ τοῦτο φρονεῖν ὑπὲρ πάντων ὑμῶν
        διὰ τὸ ἔχειν με ἐν τῇ καρδίᾳ ὑμᾶς,
                ἔν τε τοῖς δεσμοῖς μου
                καὶ ἐν τῇ ἀπολογίᾳ
                καὶ βεβαιώσει τοῦ εὐαγγελίου
                συγκοινωνούς μου τῆς χάριτος πάντας
                ὑμᾶς ὄντας.
8   μάρτυς γάρ μου ὁ θεὸς
        ὡς ἐπιποθῶ πάντας ὑμᾶς
        ἐν σπλάγχνοις Χριστοῦ Ἰησοῦ.
9   Καὶ τοῦτο προσεύχομαι,
        ἵνα ἡ ἀγάπη ὑμῶν ἔτι μᾶλλον καὶ μᾶλλον περισσεύῃ
                ἐν ἐπιγνώσει
                καὶ πάσῃ αἰσθήσει
10a   εἰς τὸ δοκιμάζειν ὑμᾶς τὰ διαφέροντα,
10b–11   ἵνα ἦτε εἰλικρινεῖς καὶ ἀπρόσκοποι εἰς ἡμέραν Χριστοῦ,
        πεπληρωμένοι καρπὸν δικαιοσύνης
        τὸν διὰ Ἰησοῦ Χριστοῦ
        εἰς δόξαν καὶ ἔπαινον θεοῦ

Repeated ideas (dotted underline above) in the passage include the readers' participation in Paul's ministry (κοινων- word group [vv. 5, 7]), πᾶς and its derivatives (vss. 3, 4 [3x], 7 [2x], 8), a fourfold mention of Christ (vv. 6, 8, 10, 11 [vv. 6, 10 in an eschatological context]), and a consistent focus on the spiritual state of the Philippians, as evidenced by the plethora of second-pl. prons. (vv. 3–10).

Some compare Paul's thanksgivings with apparently similar sections from letters in the papyri (H-M 17; O'Brien 55, following Schubert [*Form*, 10–39]; H. Conzelmann, *TDNT* 9.412). Where parallels do exist, Paul has Christianized them in view of his commitment to the gospel. Thus, where a pagan letter reads, "I offer up thanks to all the gods, if you yourself are well" (cited by Fee 72 n. 6), Paul offers thanks to "my God" for the Philippians' involvement in the spread of the gospel (vv. 3–6).

VERSE 3

Εὐχαριστῶ τῷ θεῷ μου

Authors often thanked a deity in ancient letters, and Paul may be adapting a common formula since εὐχαριστέω is unattested in the OT, appearing only later, in apocryphal books (e.g., 3 Macc 7:16; 2 Macc 1:11, in a letter), presumably under Hellenistic influence (H.-H. Esser, *NIDNTT* 3.818; H. Patsch, *EDNT* 2.88a; H-M 17; Reumann 102). The intimately personal θεῷ μου contrasts sharply, however, with the "vague or casual reference to whatever gods there might be," characteristic of typical Greco-Roman letters (O'Brien 57; H-M 18; Reumann 148).

Εὐχαριστῶ means "to express appreciation for benefits or blessings" (BDAG 415c; "thank" or "give thanks" [EVV]). The word group is a favorite of Paul (37x of 54x in NT), approximating our word "praise," a somewhat broader notion than Eng. "thanksgiving." Paul regularly gives thanks for graces wrought in the lives of others by God, and his gratitude consistently finds outward, public expression (O'Brien 56–57).

The joint relationship with Timothy (v. 1) now gives way to the 1 sg. μου (cf. the pl., Col 1:3; 1 Thess 1:2; 2 Thess 1:3). The pron. (a) points to Paul's special relationship with God (Lightfoot 82; O'Brien 57; Reumann 101; cf. Acts 27:23; Gal 2:20), and (b) identifies the God in whom the Philippians had put their faith as Paul's—and Israel's—ancestral deity (Reumann 148).

ἐπὶ πάσῃ τῇ μνείᾳ ὑμῶν

Μνείᾳ is dat. sg. fem. from μνεία, -ας, ἡ, "mention (in prayer)" or "remembrance" (BDAG 654d; "remember" or "remembrance" [NRSV, NASB, NIV]; "think of" [NJB, CEV, NLT]). Ambiguity surrounding the mng. of ἐπί (H-M 19) and the gen. ὑμῶν (T 207) has generated two distinct readings of the prep. phrase:

1. Take ἐπί as causal; ὑμῶν as subj. gen., "because of your every remembrance of me"; either as a reference (a) to the Philippians' several gifts to Paul (R. Leivestad, *EDNT* 2.434b–c; O'Brien 58–61; Peterman 93–99; Witherington 36); or, more broadly, (b) to the readers general concern for Paul and commitment to his mission, including financial gifts and personnel sent from Philippi (Reumann 149).

   a. The context and the occasion of the letter favor this view. The Philippians had contributed to Paul's needs in "the beginning" (ἐν ἀρχῇ, 4:15, while Paul was in Thessalonica; cf. also 2 Cor 11:9). They have now renewed their gift giving (4:10, 18). Paul expresses gratitude for the readers' generosity in general in v. 3 (ἐπὶ πάσῃ τῇ μνείᾳ ὑμῶν) and then makes specific reference to the two occasions (with another causal ἐπί) in v. 5 (τῆς πρώτης ἡμέρας . . . τοῦ νῦν), where κοινωνίᾳ refers primarily to the Philippians' financial participation in Paul's ministry (O'Brien 61).

b. Taking ἐπί causally, and ὑμῶν as subj. gen., breaks up the otherwise awkward "accumulation of temporal phrases in direct succession" (O'Brien 60). The alternative way to break up the temporal phrases—taking πάντοτε ἐν πάσῃ δεήσει μου ὑπὲρ πάντων ὑμῶν (v. 4) with what follows—proves unworkable for other reasons (see below).

c. Ἐπί + dat. can function temp. ("very sparingly," R 604) or causally. Paul, however, rarely uses ἐπί + dat. to connote time (possibly in 2 Cor 1:4; 3:14; 7:4), and never in his opening thanksgiving, where (a) he uses ἐπί + gen. in a temporal sense (Rom 1:10; Eph 1:16; 1 Thess 1:2; Phlm 4), or (b) ἐπί + dat. in a causal sense (1 Cor 1:4; 1 Thess 3:9; cf. ἐπὶ τῇ κοινωνίᾳ [v. 5]) (R. Leivestad, *EDNT* 2.434b–c; O'Brien 59). But a causal ἐπί works adequately with ὑμῶν as obj. gen., as well (Reed 200–201).

d. "Remembering the poor" (Gal 2:10) is a characteristic Pauline sentiment (H-M).

*2. Take ἐπί temp.; ὑμῶν obj. gen., "every time I remember (or mention) you," i.e., in Paul's prayer (all EVV, except Moffat; Fee 78–80; H-M 19–20; Hansen 45–46; Silva 54; Reed 201).

a. In the other occurrences of μνεία + gen. in biblical Gk. (LXX: Job 14:13; Ps 111:4; Isa 23:16; Wis 5:14; etc.), the gen. is almost invariably the object of the remembering. This is to be expected since verbs and nouns denoting "memory" generally take the gen. as dir. obj. The only exception is Bar 5:5 ("rejoicing that God has remembered them" [τῇ τοῦ θεοῦ μνείᾳ]), but this is not analogous because of the enclosed gen. and the repetition of the def. art.; this leaves us with no known instance of μνεία + pers. pron. functioning as subj. gen. (Fee 79; Hansen 46). But this fails to distinguish between μνεία meaning "remembrance" when used with a prep. phrase and its connotation "mention" when used with ποιοῦμαι (O. Michel, *TDNT* 4.678; O'Brien 60). Since Paul has thrust μνεία earlier in the sentence for emphasis (leaving ποιούμενος with τὴν δέησιν), we cannot appeal to the usual idiom (μνείαν ποιεῖσθαι, "make mention"; Rom 1:9; Eph 1:16; 1 Thess 1:2; Phlm 4; MM 414d) for the meaning of μνεία here (Reumann 103).

b. The "remembrance" motif in Paul's letters invariably refers to his memory of the recipients of the letter (Fee 79).

c. Taking ὑμῶν as subj. gen. leaves μνεία without an expressed object (Fee 79; Hansen 46). But the allusion would have been clear to Paul and the Philippians; moreover, two gens. (μου [obj.]) and ὑμῶν [subj.]) would have been awkward (O'Brien 60).

d. The theme of Paul's intense feelings for the Philippians surfaces in vv. 7–8, suggesting that his gratitude for them is in view here, as well (Fee 79).

e. The art. τῇ after πάσῃ implies "in *all* (the whole of) my remembrance" (BDF §275[3]; T 200; R 772; BDAG 783d, "in all remembrance of you";

B. Reicke, *TDNT* 5.887). If "isolated, intermittent acts" (i.e., the Philippians' gifts to Paul) were in view, we would expect an anarthrous construction: πάσῃ μνείᾳ ὑμῶν, "your every remembrance." However such distinctions are "notoriously difficult" to carry through in Koine Gk. Grammatically possible are "in all remembrance," "in every remembrance," or "in any and every remembrance" (Reumann 103; Moule 93–95; Porter 119; Fee 79 n. 38). Note the parallel in 2 Cor 1:4 (ἐπὶ πάσῃ τῇ θλίψει), which BDF (§275[4]) renders "all tribulations actually encountered." Our expression could correspondingly be understood as "an allusion to the recent money gift as well as to their help on previous occasions" (O'Brien 59–60).

f. Intentional alliteration and verbal repetition across vv. 3–4 (πάσῃ . . . πάντοτε . . . πάσῃ . . . πάντων) suggest that Paul's prayer for the readers is at the forefront throughout (H-M 20). Yet alliteration and verbal repetition do not necessitate a common idea. Verses 3–5 could nicely be read as a set of two parallel prayers occasioned by the Philippian's generosity to Paul:

Εὐχαριστῶ τῷ θεῷ μου	ἐπὶ πάσῃ τῇ μνείᾳ ὑμῶν
πάντοτε ἐν πάσῃ δεήσει μου ὑπὲρ πάντων ὑμῶν	FOR THE PHILIPPIANS' GIFTS
PRAYER TO GOD	
μετὰ χαρᾶς τὴν δέησιν ποιούμενος	ἐπὶ τῇ κοινωνίᾳ ὑμῶν
PRAYER OF JOY	εἰς τὸ εὐαγγέλιον . . .
	FOR THE PHILIPPIANS' GIFTS

The arguments are finely balanced, and a decision is difficult. The second view—reading the gen. ὑμῶν as obj.—is to be preferred.

VERSE 4

πάντοτε ἐν πάσῃ δεήσει μου ὑπὲρ πάντων ὑμῶν

The clause can go

*1. with what precedes, Εὐχαριστῶ (Lightfoot 82; O'Brien 57; Silva 55); or
2. with what follows, μετὰ χαρᾶς τὴν δέησιν ποιούμενος (Fee 80; Reumann 104).

Several considerations favor the first option. (a) The repetitive alliteration (πάσῃ . . . πάντοτε . . . πάσῃ . . . πάντων, vv. 4–5) suggests that the terms should be kept together (Lightfoot 82). (b) The words μετὰ χαρᾶς τὴν δέησιν ποιούμενος seem to stand apart, as an explanatory clause defining the foregoing πάσῃ δεήσει; making one sentence of the two would be awkward: ἐν πάσῃ δεήσει . . . τὴν δέησιν ποιούμενος (Lightfoot 82). (c) Paul ties πάντοτε to εὐχαριστεῖν elsewhere (1 Cor 1:4; 1 Thess 1:2; 2 Thess 1:3; Eph 5:20; cf. also Eph 1:16) (Lightfoot 82).

Paul alliterates in πά- (vv. 3–4): πάσῃ . . . πάντοτε . . . πάσῃ . . . πάντων (H-M 20); Eng. equivalent might read, "every remembrance . . . every time . . . every prayer . . . every one of you" (Reumann 103). The "studied repetition" of πᾶς in the letter (used

9x of the Philippians) is related to "the strong and repeated exhortations to unity which the epistle contains" (Lightfoot 83; Fee 80–81).

Πάντοτε (adv., "always, at all times," BDAG 755c) does not refer to uninterrupted praying but means, rather, that on every occasion Paul does pray, he remembers the Philippians ("Whenever I pray" [NLT]; "In all my prayers" [NIV]; Fee 80; O'Brien 58; Reumann 104).

Ἐν πάσῃ δεήσει μου, lit., "in my every prayer" (Fee 80 n. 41). Δεήσει is from δέησις, -εως, ἡ, "urgent request to meet a need, exclusively addressed to God" (BDAG 213d). Words for prayer overlap semantically (Reumann 104), but δέησις, as a specific prayer in a specific situation, should probably be distinguished from προσευχή, prayer in general (H-M 20; U. Schoenborn, *EDNT* 1.287b; Fee 80 n. 41). Here δέησις reflects "that brotherliness which constrains one Christian to plead with God on behalf of another" (H. Schönweiss, *NIDNTT* 2.861).

Ὑπὲρ πάντων ὑμῶν exhibits the "weaker use" of ὑπέρ w. gen., "with reference to," here, "for" (R 629, 632; H. Riesenfeld *TDNT* 8.513–14).

μετὰ χαρᾶς τὴν δέησιν ποιούμενος

Example of μετά used as "marker of attendant circumstances [moods, emotions, etc.] of someth. that takes place" (BDAG 637b).

"Joy" (most EVV) pervades Philippians (χαρά/χαίρω occur 16x). Paul's joy is unaffected by imprisonment or the prospect of martyrdom since, for Paul, χαρά is more than an emotion: it is an overarching mind-set that allows him to look beyond his personal situation to "the sovereign Lord who stands above all events and ultimately has control over them" (H-M 21; "it makes me happy" [CEV] misses the mark). It is precisely in the midst of affliction and hardship that joy "gives proof of its power" (E. Beyreuther, G. Finkenrath, *NIDNTT* 2.359). Some identify an eschatological component, i.e., "a reference to the future experienced as joy in the present" (W. Zimmerli, *TDNT* 9.369). Although unaffected by his own circumstances, Paul's joy was conditioned, to some degree, by the spiritual state of his converts. Thus, the Philippians' positive response to Paul's plea for unity would make his joy complete (2:2; cf. 2:28; 4:1).

Ποιούμενος is nom. sg. masc. of pres. mid. ptc. of ποιέω, in mid., "make/do someth. for oneself" or "of oneself" (BDAG 841d). It modifies εὐχαριστῶ, either temp. ("when I make entreaty" [Wallace 627]) or manner ("by making entreaty") (Reumann 104).

VERSE 5

ἐπὶ τῇ κοινωνίᾳ ὑμῶν εἰς τὸ εὐαγγέλιον

Ἐπί with dat. here indicates the basis or ground of an action (Z §126; "causal" [Reumann 106]; Hansen 48 n. 39). Some connect ἐπὶ τῇ κοινωνίᾳ back to εὐχαριστῶ, v. 3, arguing that the verb otherwise lacks an obj. (O'Brien 61–63). It is better to take ἐπὶ τῇ κοινωνίᾳ with μετὰ χαρᾶς τὴν δέησιν ποιούμενος, immediately preceding (H-M 22). Since, however, ποιούμενος modifies εὐχαριστῶ, the result is much the same, so that ἐπὶ τῇ κοινωνίᾳ serves as the reason for both Paul's thanksgiving (εὐχαριστῶ, v. 3) and his joy (χαρᾶς, v. 4) (Fee 81).

Τῇ κοινωνίᾳ is dat. fem. sg. from κοινωνία, -ας, ἡ, "close association involving mutual interests and sharing" (BDAG 552d–553a; J. Hainz, *EDNT* 2.304a; "partnership" [RSV, NIV, NJB]; "sharing" [NRSV]; "participation" [NASB]). Ὑμῶν is subj. gen. (H-M 22; Reumann 106). Paul is not prone to confuse εἰς ("for the goal of an action" [Reumann 108]; Harris, *Prepositions*, 85) with ἐν, so that it is not (1) the Philippians' salvation (F. Hauck, *TDNT* 3.805) that is in view in τῇ κοινωνίᾳ ὑμῶν εἰς τὸ εὐαγγέλιον but, rather, (2) their participation in the spread of the gospel ("you have taken part with me in spreading the good news" [CEV]; sim. NLT; T 256; Z §107; Fee 81 n. 46)—primarily the Philippians' financial participation in Paul's ministry (Peterman 101; Silva 44). Paul twice uses the cognate vb. in precisely this sense later in the epistle (4:14–15). And in two other cases where κοινωνία is followed by εἰς (2 Cor 9:13; Rom 15:26), Paul has in mind the collection for the poor saints in Jerusalem (Fee 82 n. 50). If more is in view in τῇ κοινωνίᾳ ὑμῶν than the Philippians' monetary gifts (e.g., prayers or their own efforts at evangelism [H-M 22]), the contribution nevertheless remains at the forefront (O'Brien 61; Fee 84). It was, after all, the gift that occasioned the letter in the first place.

Paul uses εὐαγγέλιον (acc. sg. neut.; "gospel" [most EVV]; 9x in Philippians, more, proportionally, than any other letter [Fee 82]) (1) to refer to the content of the gospel (Gal 2:2; Col 1:23), or (2) as a noun of agency to describe the work of evangelism, so that εἰς τὸ εὐαγγέλιον τοῦ Χριστοῦ can mean "to proclaim the good news of Christ" (2 Cor 2:12). The latter is intended here, though the content of the gospel, of course, remains in view (O'Brien 62). As the fulfillment of OT prophetic hopes, where the εὐαγγελ- word group is used to herald Yahweh's return to Zion and his kingly rule (LXX Isa 40:9; 52:7 [= Rom 10:15]; 61:1), εὐαγγέλιον functions in Paul as "an eschatological, even apocalyptic, term, for what God has wrought at the end of the ages in Jesus' death and resurrection" (Reumann 150). Various images—justification, reconciliation, life, peace, love—suggest the content and result of the gospel, but Paul has no need to define "gospel" for the Philippians (Reumann 109–10, 150). Indeed, half of the occurrences of εὐαγγέλιον in Paul are absolute (no adj. or gen. noun), so clear was the concept for the apostle and his audience (G. Friedrich, *TDNT* 2.729). Εὐαγγέλιον also appeared in Roman imperial propaganda, where an emperor's birthday was associated with the dawn of a new era. The Priene inscription (9 BC; W. Dittenberger, *Orientis Graeci Inscriptiones*, 2:458) reads, in reference to Augustus (who is also called "savior"), "the birthday of the god was the beginning of good tidings (εὐαγγελί[ων]) for the world" (Reumann 108; U. Becker, *NIDNTT* 2.108). Whether intentional or otherwise, Paul's use of εὐαγγέλιον τοῦ Χριστοῦ represented a pointed challenge to political and religious claims (the two domains were not distinct in antiquity) about the emperor, particularly in an imperial colony like Philippi, which had been founded by Augustus himself (Hellerman 64–87).

ἀπὸ τῆς πρώτης ἡμέρας ἄχρι τοῦ νῦν

Ἄχρι + gen. (cf. v. 6) means "until" (BDAG 160d); νῦν is an adv. of time; with the art., subst., "the present time" (BDAG 681c; Wallace 232; G. Stählin, *TDNT* 4.1107). The phrase is not to be taken as a general reference to the Philippians' life in Christ (*pace* Reumann 150–51; Hansen 49) but, rather, as a twofold summary of their generous participation in Paul's missionary efforts, with particular focus on (a) their gifts when Paul was first in Macedonia and Greece (τῆς πρώτης ἡμέρας) and (b) the recent gift sent with Epaphroditus (τοῦ νῦν). The two temporal bookends appear again in 4:10–19. It was rare for Paul to accept gifts from a church for fear that he might be accused of charging for a gospel that was free (1 Cor 9:15–18; 2 Cor 11:7–9). The Philippians had apparently gained Paul's affection and confidence, so as to persuade him to accept gifts (H-M 23). Once in Corinth, Paul both worked for a living (Acts 18:3) and received help from Macedonia (2 Cor 11:9; cf. Acts 18:5).

VERSE 6

πεποιθὼς αὐτὸ τοῦτο

Πεποιθώς is nom. sg. masc. of pf. act. ptc. from πείθω; adv. ptc. of cause modifying εὐχαριστῶ (v. 3) (Wallace 820; H-M 23–24; Hansen 50 n. 52; O'Brien 63). A pf. with pres. force, "I have been persuaded and therefore am convinced" (Reumann 111; "sure" [BDAG 792a; RSV, HCSB, ESV]; "confident" [NASB, NIV, NRSV]; "certain" [CEV, NLT]; BDF §341; R 881; O. Becker, *NIDNTT* 1.591; "fully trust in" [A. Sand, *EDNT* 3.63b]). Confidence, like joy, surfaces often in Philippians (1:14, 25; 2:24; 3:3). Πέποιθα is common in the prayers of the Psalter (e.g., ὁ θεός μου. ἐπὶ σοὶ πέποιθα [LXX Ps 24:1–2]).

The αὐτός + οὗτος combination is "common in Paul" (R 705; "this very thing" [NASB] is better than "this" [NIV, ESV]). The neut. of certain prons. (τοῦτο) has a tendency to pass over to the acc. of general ref., "in just this confidence = I am sure" (BDF §154; alternately called a cognate acc. of inner content [R 478; T 246]). Although αὐτὸ τοῦτο could conceivably refer (a) back "to the constancy emphasized in v. 5" (BDF §290[4]), the ensuing ὅτι shows that it points (b) forward to what follows in v. 6 (Fee 85 n. 62; O'Brien 63; Reumann 111; Sumney 9).

ὅτι ὁ ἐναρξάμενος ἐν ὑμῖν ἔργον ἀγαθὸν ἐπιτελέσει

Subst. ὅτι-clause in appos. to αὐτὸ τοῦτο (R 699; Wallace 459), relating the object of Paul's certainty (H-M). Such cstrs. are common in Paul (T 45; cf. Rom 9:17; Eph 6:22; Col 4:8).

Ἐναρξάμενος is a nom. sg. masc. of aor. mid. ptc. from ἐνάρχομαι, "begin" (BDAG 331b; most EVV; "started" [HCSB]); subst. ptc. used of God (Reumann 111). Read ἐν ὑμῖν collectively, "among you" (NRSV; H-M 24–25; Reumann 112), rather than in an individualized sense, "in you" (KJV, RSV, NEB; A. Oepke, *TDNT* 2.539).

Ἔργον ἀγαθόν (adj. in attrib. position [R 776; Wallace 311]) means "a good work." A suggested allusion to God's work as Creator in Gen 2:2–3 (G. Bertram, *TDNT*

2.629–30; H-M 24) is probably "irrelevant at best and far-fetched at worst" (Fee 87 n. 73; Silva 45–46). The options for ἔργον ἀγαθόν are manifold, ranging from a highly generalized, soteriological reading to a narrowly contextual interpretation that views ἔργον ἀγαθόν as a reference to the Philippians' financial participation in Paul's ministry. The latter understanding continues the theme of partnership in the gospel in v. 5 (H-M 24; cf. the association of ἔργον ἀγαθόν with τῆς κοινωνίας in 2 Cor 9:8, 12, where financial gifts are also in view). But the expansive eschatological framework suggests that Paul has broadened his horizons (Fee 85; Hansen 50; O'Brien 64; Reumann 152). Had the gift been solely in view, moreover, we would expect διὰ ὑμῶν, rather than ἐν ὑμῖν, as well as an article with ἔργον ἀγαθόν (Fee 87 n. 69; cf. also θεός + the ἐργ- root in 2:13, where the readers' general spiritual life is in view). It is best to take the ἔργον ἀγαθόν in general terms, understanding the Philippians' participation in the gospel not as the "good work" itself but as "clear evidence of this work of salvation" (O'Brien 64).

Ἐπιτελέσει is 3 sg. fut. act. indic. of ἐπιτελέω, "to finish someth. begun" (BDAG 383c; "bring it to completion" [NRSV; cf. NIV]; "perfect it" [NASB]). In HGk. the intensified form cannot often be distinguished in usage and content from τελέω (R. Mahoney, EDNT 2.42a). The aspect of the fut. tense is external, "something of a temporal counterpart to the aorist indicative" (Wallace 566). The sense that ἐπιτελέσει is progressive comes not from the tense itself but, rather, from its placement "between the past (ἐναρξάμενος) and an end-point in the future (ἡμέρας Χριστοῦ Ἰησοῦ)" (Wallace 568; Sumney 10). Gr. economy will often omit a readily understood pron., ἐπιτελέσει (αὐτό) (T 38–39). God's activity is emphasized from beginning (ὁ ἐναρξάμενος) to end (ἐπιτελέσει) (Reumann 151; G. Bertram, TDNT 2.643).

ἄχρι ἡμέρας Χριστοῦ Ἰησοῦ

"By" (NRSV) is truer to the meaning of ἄχρι than "at" (RSV, ESV) since the ἔργον ἀγαθόν continues "until" (NASB, HCSB, NIV) the parousia but not "at" the judgment (Reumann 114).

The "day of Christ Jesus" is the goal of Christian existence, the future event central in Pauline eschatology (Reumann 115; G. Delling, TDNT 2.952). NT terminology varies: "day of the Lord" (1 Thess 5:2); "day of our Lord Jesus [Christ]" (1 Cor 1:8); "that day" (1 Thess 5:4); "day of Christ" (Phil 1:10; 2:16). The notion finds its origins in the OT concept of the day of Yahweh, which involved the idea of judgment (Joel 2:2; Amos 5:20). Much more often, however, the emphasis in Paul is not on judgment (cf. 1 Cor 3:13) but, rather, on "the eschatological consummation that has Christ's coming—and therefore his final exaltation and glorification, including those who are his—as its central focus" (Fee 86). If Paul has the OT prophetic sense in mind here, he certainly anticipated the day without alarm in the Philippians' case (H-M 25).

VERSE 7

Καθώς ἐστιν δίκαιον ἐμοὶ τοῦτο φρονεῖν ὑπὲρ πάντων ὑμῶν

The adv. καθώς ("as," "just as"), without a corresponding οὕτως, can be read (1) causally (BDF §453[2]; Hansen 51 n. 55; H-M 25; O'Brien 66; Reumann 115) or (2) in its normal correlative sense, with the whole of vv. 3–6 understood as the οὕτως: "[So] I give thanks in this way . . . just as it is fitting for me to feel this way about you" (Fee 88 n. 76). The result, semantically, is much the same. Take φρονεῖν subst., as subj. of ἐστιν, with the adj. δίκαιον (nom. sg. neut. from δίκαιος, -α, -ον) as a pred. nom (Wallace 600). Δίκαιος is used here in its conventional, nontheological sense (G. Schrenk, TDNT 2.188) and may be glossed as "right, fair, equitable" (BDAG 247a; "right" [EVV]; "natural" [CEV]).

Φρονεῖν is pres. act. inf. of φρονέω, "think or feel in a certain way about someone" (BDAG 1065c; "single-minded commitment . . . to the church" [H. Paulsen, EDNT 3.438d]). A distinctly Pauline word (26x in NT; 23x in Paul) with a broad semantic range, the vb. is of major importance for Philippians (10x). EVV that emphasize the mind ("think" [KJV, NRSV, HCSB]) or the emotions ("feel" [RSV, NASB, NIV]) only partially do justice to the term. In addition to thought and feeling, φρονεῖν includes an intentional, volitional component, "to set one's mind on" (H-M 26; "both interest and decision at the same time" [J. Goetzmann, NIDNTT 2.617]; "care in thought and act" [G. Bertram, TDNT 9.233]). A clue to the term's special nuance is found in the use of the cognate noun φρόνημα three times in Rom 8:6–7, in the sense "mind-set" (Fee 89, cf. n. 80).

The whole of vv. 3–6 (particularly the gratitude and joy Paul experiences for the Philippians' ongoing partnership in the ministry of the gospel [vv. 3–5]) functions as the antecedent of τοῦτο (acc. sg. neut., dir. obj. of φρονεῖν) (H-M 26; Fee 89).

In ὑπὲρ πάντων ὑμῶν, the prep. ὑπέρ connotes the general idea "about" or "concerning," encroaching on the province of περί (R 632; Moule 61; with φρονέω, ὑπέρ carries "the intensive sense 'to be concerned about someone'" [H. Riesenfeld, TDNT 8.508]).

διὰ τὸ ἔχειν με ἐν τῇ καρδίᾳ ὑμᾶς

διὰ τὸ + inf. is common in the NT (32x; esp. in Luke; only here in Paul) to denote cause (BDF §402[1]; R 966; T 143; Wallace 597; O'Brien 68). Since the inf. takes the acc. as subj., we have two options for the subj. of ἔχειν:

*1. με (most EVV; Fee 90; Hansen 53; O'Brien 68; Silva 27 n. 34)
  2. ὑμᾶς (NRSV; H-M 27; Reumann 153; Sumney 12)

Context is not decisive: The rest of v. 7 supports taking ὑμᾶς as the subj. of ἔχειν: "I am justified in thanking God for you because you have me in your heart, you being partakers with me in my imprisonment, etc." The explanatory γάρ which begins v. 8, however, makes the most sense with με as the subj. of ἔχειν in v. 7: "I have you in my heart . . . for God is my witness how I long for you, etc."

Lacking other syntactical markers, we would expect word order to clarify a writer's intention (O'Brien 68; the two examples H-M give to argue otherwise are not convincing; in both cases the subj. is contextually obvious and is, at any rate, otherwise syntactically marked [in Luke 18:5 the art. identifies τὴν χήραν as subj.; in Acts 4:2 the pron. αὐτούς marks the subj.]). Chrysostom, along with other Greek fathers, assumed, without comment, that με was the subj. of ἔχειν, showing that in this instance word order is "the factor that tips the scales" (Wallace 194, 196; Porter 203; Fee 90; Silva 27 n. 34; Jeffrey T. Reed, "The Infinitive with Two Substantival Accusatives: An Ambiguous Construction?" *NovT* 33 [1991]: 1–27).

Τῇ καρδίᾳ reflects Sem. pref. for a distributive sg., "your hearts" (T 23). The art. functions like a poss. pron. (Wallace 216). Καρδία reflects the Heb. *lēb*, "the center of inner life, including emotions, understanding and knowledge, and will" (Reumann 117). Not all aspects are equally present, however, in any given occurrence. Although some argue otherwise (Reumann 117–18; "the whole person" [O'Brien 68]), it is fair to view the affective component as dominant here (J. Behm, *TDNT* 3.612) since Paul reiterates his attitude in explicitly affective terms, with σπλάγχνοις, in v. 8 ("in the late writings of the LXX σπλάγχνα became interchangeable with καρδία" [A. Sand, *EDNT* 2.250c]).

ἔν τε τοῖς δεσμοῖς μου καὶ ἐν τῇ ἀπολογίᾳ καὶ βεβαιώσει τοῦ εὐαγγελίου

The extended prep. phrase goes with what follows (συγκοινωνούς μου . . . ὄντας) rather than with what precedes due to (a) the repetition of ὑμᾶς, (b) the development of thought as related to "fellowship," v. 4, and (c) the τε . . . καί (O'Brien 68).

The grammar is carefully crafted. The τε . . . καί cstr. ("both . . . and"; "not only . . . but also" [Reumann 118]), along with the repeated prep. + art. (ἐν . . . τοῖς . . . ἐν τῇ), mark out the phrases δεσμοῖς μου and ἀπολογίᾳ καὶ βεβαιώσει τοῦ εὐαγγελίου as two relatively distinct ideas in Paul's mind. The first is Paul's situation, the second his employment of that situation (Fee 91 n. 93; O'Brien 69). The one art. (τῇ) governing both ἀπολογίᾳ and βεβαιώσει shows that the two terms are "conceived as forming a certain unity" (R 566; 787; Z §184; O'Brien 69; Reumann 152). The art.-subst.-καί-subst. cstr. treats items that are more or less distinct as one for the purpose at hand.

Δεσμοῖς is dat. pl. masc. from δεσμός, -οῦ, ὁ, "bond, fetter" (BDAG 219b). Although "chains" could be a metonymy for imprisonment as such, some think Paul was literally chained to his guards (Fee 92; "chafed his skin, and severely restricted his mobility" [Hansen 53]; whether Paul was actually in chains remains "unclear" [Reumann 152]).

Ἀπολογίᾳ is dat. sg. fem. from ἀπολογία, -ας, ἡ, "the act of making a defense" (BDAG 117a; "defense" or "defending" [EVV]). Βεβαιώσει is dat. sg. fem, from βεβαίωσις, -εως, ἡ, "process of establishing or confirming something" (BDAG 173b; "confirmation," "confirming" [most EVV]; "establishment" [HCSB; cf. NJB]). Ἀπολογία "implies the negative or defensive side of the apostle's preaching," removing obstacles; βεβαίωσις "the positive or aggressive side, the direct advancement and establishment of the Gospel" (Lightfoot 85). Although ἀπολογία and βεβαίωσις are technical, legal terms from the law courts of Paul's day (U. Kellermann, *EDNT* 1.137b;

Acts 22:1; 25:16; 2 Tim 4:16), we should not limit the reference here to Paul's formal judicial proceedings in Rome (*pace* Hansen 53; H-M 28; H. Schlier, *TDNT* 1.603). The ἀπολογ- and βεβαιο- word groups are used elsewhere, in a broader sense, of defending and confirming both the gospel itself and Paul's gospel ministry (cf. Rom 15:8; 1 Cor 9:3; 2 Cor 12:19; Heb 2:2; 1 Pet 3:15; cf. F. F. Bruce, *The Defense of the Gospel in the New Testament* [Grand Rapids: Eerdmans, 1981]). In vv. 3–5, moreover, Paul has in view a partnership with the readers (cf. κοινωνία [v. 5] and συγκοινωνούς [here in v. 7]) that has extended over a significant period of time (ἀπὸ τῆς πρώτης ἡμέρας ἄχρι τοῦ νῦν [v. 5]). The long clause (ἔν τε τοῖς δεσμοῖς . . . ὄντας) thus indicates that whether Paul is in prison and arraigned before his judges or engaged in some other defense and confirmation of the gospel the Philippians are partakers with him in God's grace (O'Brien 69).

συγκοινωνούς μου τῆς χάριτος πάντας ὑμᾶς ὄντας

Συγκοινωνούς μου τῆς χάριτος means "sharers of the same grace as myself" (BDAG 952d). Some EVV (NRSV, HCSB, ESV) move the clause before ἔν τε τοῖς δεσμοῖς for clarity.

Paul uses χάρις (gen. sg. fem.) not only, generally, of God's saving grace (e.g., Rom 3:24; 5:15) but also of the special favor God granted Paul to preach the gospel to the Gentiles (Rom 1:5; 1 Cor 3:10; Gal 2:9; Eph 3:2, 7, 8). Either understanding is possible here:

1. God's saving grace (O'Brien 70).
   a. The pronoun μου is best taken with συγκοινωνούς, not τῆς χάριτος. When Paul speaks of the grace peculiar to himself he never says "my grace" but "the grace given to me." This, in turn, leaves τῆς χάριτος undefined (O'Brien 70; Sumney 13).
*2. Paul's apostolic ministry, with special reference to the hardship and opportunity Paul is presently experiencing as a result of his calling (Hansen 55; H-M 27; Reumann 119–20, 154; Silva 47; "his imprisonment as a χάρις" [G. Friedrich, *TDNT* 2.733]; K. Berger, *EDNT* 3.457d).
   a. The Philippians' participation in Paul's ministry has been at the forefront throughout (συγκοινωνούς μου τῆς χάριτος here thus alludes to τῇ κοινωνίᾳ ὑμῶν εἰς τὸ εὐαγγέλιον in v. 5), and Paul's imprisonment is a result of his apostolic commission. The Philippians share this "grace" by virtue of their financial involvement in Paul's ministry (H-M 27). It is in this sense that Paul later describes the recent gift as "participating in his suffering" (συγκοινωνήσαντές μου τῇ θλίψει [4:14]).
   b. The art. in τῆς χάριτος points to something specific in the situation just described in 7b, namely, τοῖς δεσμοῖς μου and τῇ ἀπολογίᾳ καὶ βεβαιώσει τοῦ εὐαγγελίου, something in which the Philippians also share (Reumann 119).
   c. Paul refers to financial support as a "grace" elsewhere (2 Cor 8:7) (Hansen 55).

View 2 makes the most sense of Paul's argument. Πάντας ὑμᾶς ὄντας is not acc. abs. but picks up ὑμᾶς from earlier in the verse (R 491). Ὄντας is acc. pl. masc. ptc. from εἰμί. Syntactically, ὄντας is an adj. ptc., in appos. to ὑμᾶς (which repeats the ὑμᾶς of 7a); semantically, the ptc. signifies cause, giving further justification for Paul's feeling about the Philippians (Hansen 54 n. 65; H-M 27; Silva 57; Sumney 12–13). In the adj. πάντας (cf. πάντας ὑμᾶς, again, v. 8) we encounter yet another echo of the emphasis on the whole church that permeates the letter (Hansen 52; Reumann 119).

VERSE 8

μάρτυς γάρ μου ὁ θεός

The γάρ explains "I have you in my heart," v. 7b (Fee 93). Μάρτυς (nom. sg. masc., pred. nom.) is "one who affirms or attests, testifier, witness" (BDAG 619d; "God is my witness" [NRSV, HCSB, ESV]; "God can/will testify" [NIV, NJB]). The art. marks ὁ θεός as subj. nom. (Wallace 243). The invocation of God as witness is a strong statement. Paul uses μάρτυς here not of a witness to observable facts, as in judicial proceedings, but, rather, of God as a witness to inner motives and intentions. These are matters of the heart, and only God knows the heart (H. Strathmann, *TDNT* 4.491; Fee 94; O'Brien 71).

ὡς ἐπιποθῶ πάντας ὑμᾶς ἐν σπλάγχνοις Χριστοῦ Ἰησοῦ

Ὡς functions like ὅτι, introducing a simple declarative clause, i.e., content, rather than degree of yearning (BDAG 1105c; BDF §396; O'Brien 71 n. 41; Sumney 11). The qualitative idea is expressed later in ἐν σπλάγχνοις Χριστοῦ Ἰησοῦ (H-M 28).

Ἐπιποθῶ is 1 sg. pres. act. indic. from ἐπιποθέω, "long for, desire" (BDAG 377c; "yearn for" [RSV, ESV]; "long for" [NASB, NIV, NJB]; "deeply . . . miss" [HCSB]; Spicq 2.58–60). A characteristic Pauline term (7x of 9x in NT), ἐπιποθέω "especially indicates that quality of affection which binds Paul to his brethren in Christ" (O'Brien 71). The verb implies a desire to be reunited with the Philippians ("God himself knows how much I want to see you" [CEV]; cf. 1:27; 2:26) (H-M 29; O'Brien 71). More is involved here, however, than a desire for physical proximity. Paul is also expressing a deep yearning for the Philippians to remain true to the gospel, as evidenced by the addition of the qualifiers πάντας ὑμᾶς and ἐν σπλάγχνοις Χριστοῦ Ἰησοῦ (Fee 94).

Σπλάγχνοις is dat. pl. neut. from σπλάγχνον, -ου, τό (almost always pl.), lit. "inward parts of the body" (Acts 1:18), fig., "affection of Christ" (BDAG 938d; most EVV; "compassion" [NRSV, NLT]). In Gk. τὰ σπλάγχνα most often refers to the nobler organs (heart, liver, lungs), not the intestines (τὰ ἔντερα), and were regarded as the seat and origin of deeply felt emotions, whether love or anger. The gen. Χριστοῦ Ἰησοῦ (subj. gen. [Sumney 13]) qualifies σπλάγχνοις here as "the love Christ has for you, which is also at work in me for you" (Fee 95; Reumann 122; N. Walter, *EDNT* 3.266a; "Christ mysticism" [H. Köster, *TDNT* 7.556]). The σπλαγχν- word group occurs thirteen times in the Gospels. In every case but one (Luke 10:33) the subject is either God (in the parables [Matt 18:27; Luke 15:20; etc.]) or Jesus himself (compassion toward the multitudes [Mark 6:34; etc.]; compassion toward individuals [Mark 1:41; 9:22; etc.]). Dunn is likely correct, therefore, to assume that "Jesus' emotional response at various point in his ministry" lies behind σπλάγχνοις Χριστοῦ Ἰησοῦ here in v. 8 (J. D. G. Dunn, *The Theology of Paul the Apostle* [Grand Rapids: Eerdmans, 1998], 193 n. 55).

VERSE 9

Καὶ τοῦτο προσεύχομαι

The καί is resumptive, (a) linking the prayer to follow directly with the affection expressed in v. 8, but also (b) picking up and expanding upon τὴν δέησιν ποιούμενος (v. 4) (Fee 98; O'Brien 73; Reumann 154; Silva 49).

Προσεύχομαι is 1 sg. pres. mid. indic. "to petition deity," "pray" (BDAG 879b), with dir. obj. τοῦτο (acc. sg. neut.). It is correct to see "continuing action" in the vb. (Reumann 122), understood iteratively, in view of the qualifiers in the surrounding context (cf. πάντοτε ἐν πάσῃ δεήσει [v. 4]).

ἵνα ἡ ἀγάπη ὑμῶν ἔτι μᾶλλον καὶ μᾶλλον περισσεύῃ

The ἵνα-clause is in appos. to τοῦτο (*pace* Reed 388, who sees τοῦτο as anaphoric), giving the content—not the purpose—of Paul's prayer (BDF §394; Moule 145–46; R 699; Fee 98; H-M 29; O'Brien 73; Reumann 123). Strikingly, Paul prays for the Philippians, not for his own difficult situation.

Ἀγάπη is rare among Gk. writers. It was chosen in the LXX to render the Heb. '*hb*, apparently to distinguish it from ἔρος ("desiring love") and φιλία ("natural sympathy" or "mutual affection"). It was used of both God's love for his people (e.g., Deut 7:8) and in the two love commands (for God [Deut 6:5] and neighbor [Lev 19:18]). This usage, which thus "fills an otherwise empty word full of theological grist," is the source of the NT idea of ἀγάπη, where it became "the ultimate theological word both to describe God's character and to articulate the essence of Christian behavior" (Fee 98 n. 11; G. Schneider, *EDNT* 1.10d). Accordingly the prayer that follows in Phil 1:9–11 emphasizes "love" not as "affection" (e.g., v. 8) but as behavior—behavior that is both "pure" (stemming from right motives) and "blameless" (lacking offense) (Fee 99). Candidates for the unexpressed obj. of ἡ ἀγάπη:

1. Paul means ἀγάπη in the broadest sense, including both love for God and one's fellow man (O'Brien 74; H-M 30).
2. Ἀγάπη refers to the Philippians' love for one another (Fee 98; Hansen 57–58; Reumann 123).
*3. Paul still has in view the Philippians' participation in the spread of the gospel, here identified as ἀγάπη.

View 1 has in its favor the expansive way Paul defines ἀγάπη in the clauses that follow (O'Brien 74). View 2 is supported by the emphasis on unity in the letter, as reflected in (a) the repeated "all" in vv. 1–8 (5x) and (b) the use of ἀγάπη of community relations in 2:2 (τὴν αὐτὴν ἀγάπην ἔχοντες). Note, as well, the expression of affection in v. 8 and the conceptual parallel to v. 9 at 1 Thess 3:12 (Fee 98).

It would seem odd, though, for Paul to depart from the theme of partnership in the gospel (vv. 3–8) to focus on either love in general (view 1) or community relations (view 2), only to return in v. 12 to the topic of the progress of the gospel. The ἀγάπη in view, moreover, is apparently a known commodity (the art. may be anaphoric) that Paul hopes will increase (ἔτι μᾶλλον καὶ μᾶλλον). The logical candidate in the previous context is the readers' participation in the gospel ministry. This is confirmed by the way in which καὶ τοῦτο προσεύχομαι (v. 9) picks up on Paul's comment about prayer in v. 4, where the Philippians' involvement in his ministry is clearly in view. In contrast, Paul has said nothing explicit about relations among the Philippians in vv. 3–8. It is preferable to assume, with view 3, that ἡ ἀγάπη refers primarily to the readers' sacrificial involvement in the spread of the gospel.

Περισσεύῃ is 3 sg. pres. act. subjunc. from περισσεύω, "to be in abundance, abound" (BDAG 805b). The pres. goes naturally with μᾶλλον καὶ μᾶλλον (Fee 95 n. 1). Περισσεύω is a Pauline word (26x of 39x in NT) that, perhaps as no other, characterized the new age inaugurated by the work of Christ, an age marked by "an overflowing and rich abundance of good things." Paul desires the Philippians to be "so rich in love that they have nowhere to store it" (H-M 30).

The adv. μᾶλλον is doubled for emphasis (R 663–64; "still more greatly" [T 29]; "that your love will keep on growing more and more" [GNB]). Ἔτι is used in a nontemporal sense, "in addition, more, also" (BDAG 400c; Reumann 123).

ἐν ἐπιγνώσει καὶ πάσῃ αἰσθήσει

The prep. ἐν marks the sphere (locat.) in which ἡ ἀγάπη operates (O'Brien 75). The single prep. governing both ἐπιγνώσει and πάσῃ αἰσθήσει suggests a close relationship between the nouns (Fee 99–100). Paul does not encourage "sentimental, undisciplined" love—ἐπιγνώσει and αἰσθήσει are "regulatory agents" guaranteeing "a discriminating love" (H-M 30–31). The nouns qualify ἀγάπη in ways that result in wise decision making in the practical arena of daily life (cf. εἰς τὸ δοκιμάζειν ὑμᾶς τὰ διαφέροντα, v. 10).

The meaning of αἰσθήσει (dat. sg. fem. from αἴσθησις, -εως, ἡ; "discernment" [BDAG 29b]) is relatively straightforward and will elucidate the more common but less transparent ἐπιγνώσει. Αἴσθησις signifies "wisdom and (moral) judgment" in the OT, where it occurs in Prov (22x out of 27x in LXX). It reflects "that practical understanding which is keenly aware of the circumstances of an action," e.g., discretion of speech (Prov 5:2; 14:7; 15:7) (O'Brien 77; Reumann 125; G. Delling, *TDNT* 1.188; cf. Heb 5:14). The adj. πάσῃ (dat. sg. fem.) is distributive ("in every situation") rather than elative ("full insight" [NRSV]) (O'Brien 77; Reumann 156). Αἰσθήσει in v. 9 denotes the application of discerning love to all sorts of situations that might arise in a mission church. "Discernment" (most EVV) properly brings out the "practical, less intellectual sense" of αἴσθησις [Reumann 125–26]).

'Επίγνωσις (EVV, "knowledge") is not primarily "knowledge about" something but rather the kind of "full" or "innate" knowing that comes from experience or personal relationship (cf. Rom 3:20, "through the Law comes the ἐπίγνωσις of sin," i.e., now people who were already sinners "know" sin for what it is [Fee 100 n. 17]; "grasping the full reality and nature of the object under consideration" [E. D. Schmitz, *NIDNTT* 2.393]). Compound forms (ἐπὶ + γνῶσις) can function in the same way as simple forms (Z §484; R. Bultmann, *TDNT* 1.707), or they can be intensive, as in 1 Cor 13:12 (ἄρτι γινώσκω ἐκ μέρους, τότε δὲ ἐπιγνώσομαι καθὼς καὶ ἐπεγνώσθην) (Fee 100 n. 17; H-M 30; O'Brien 76). The practical orientation of αἰσθήσει helps narrow the options for the unexpressed object of ἐπιγνώσει (dat. sg. fem. of ἐπίγνωσις, -εως, ἡ). If knowledge of God is primarily in view (O'Brien 76; E. Schütz, *NIDNTT* 2.391), it is a practical knowledge, "insight into the will of God" (Reumann 156). The tr. "perception" ("insight" [BDAG 29b]) helps to distinguish ἐπίγνωσις from overintellectual understandings that "knowledge" (EVV) might suggest (Reumann 125; "the guiding factor is not interest in Christian learning but the edification of the community" [R. Bultmann, *TDNT* 1.708], though a strict dichotomy between the two would be foreign to Paul's thought.). Reumann summarizes: "Where there is not full insight amid life's ambiguities, love decides, perceptively and discerningly. Such love that makes judgments with discernment must continue growing in the community" (Reumann 156).

VERSE 10

εἰς τὸ δοκιμάζειν ὑμᾶς τὰ διαφέροντα

The Philippians are to have an increasing and discerning gospel-centered love for two reasons: (a) to make the best possible choices (εἰς τὸ δοκιμάζειν κτλ.), and (b) to be the best possible people (ἵνα ἦτε κτλ.) (H-M 32; immediate purpose and ultimate purpose [Fee 101]).

Εἰς τό + inf. (pres. act. inf. from δοκιμάζω; inf. takes acc. ὑμᾶς as subj. [Z §393]) generally denotes purpose, more or less strong, in the NT (R 991, 1,071; T 143; O'Brien 77; Sumney 15; others opt for result [Reumann 126]). The pron. marks ὑμᾶς as the subj., τὰ διαφέροντα as the dir. obj., of δοκιμάζειν (Wallace 196).

BDAG offers two options for δοκιμάζειν in v. 10: (1) "make a critical examination of someth. to determine genuineness" (255c), or (2) "draw a conclusion about worth on the basis of testing" (255d). Τὰ διαφέροντα (acc. pl. neut. pres. act. ptc., used subst.) is similarly ambiguous (H-M 32; T 151) since διαφέρω can mean either (a) "to differ" (1 Cor 15:41) or (b) "to be superior" ("the things that really matter" [BDAG 239b]; "that which is fitting in a given situation" [W. Grundmann, *TDNT* 2.260]; L. Oberlinner, *EDNT* 1.315c; cf. Matt 6:26). The double ambiguity generates four possible understandings of the purpose clause (Reumann 126):

    1a. examine the things that differ;
    1b. examine the things that are superior;
    2a. approve the things that differ; or
  *2b. approve the things that are superior.

The last option is Paul's intended meaning ("approve the things that are superior" [HCSB]; "making proper assessments about what is absolutely essential regarding life in Christ" [Fee 101]; O'Brien 77; Reumann 127; Silva 57). This is precisely what Paul himself had learned to do (Phil 3:8, 13–14). But what, specifically, is in view? The ability to distinguish heresy from authentic doctrine (Reumann 126)? This is unlikely. Doctrine, as such, is emphasized nowhere in the context. Among those things which are to determine Christian priorities (τὰ διαφέροντα), for Paul the progress of the gospel was surely preeminent, as reflected in both the preceding (vv. 3–8) and ensuing (vv. 12–18) contexts. Thus the Philippians' partnership in the spread of the gospel likely remains in view here, as well.

ἵνα ἦτε εἰλικρινεῖς καὶ ἀπρόσκοποι εἰς ἡμέραν Χριστοῦ

῏Ητε is 2 pl. pres. act. subjunc. from εἰμί. It is unclear whether this purpose clause ("the nuance of result may also be present" [O'Brien 78]) should be taken

1. as parallel to the ἵνα-clause that began the prayer (v. 9), depending on προσεύχομαι (Reumann 127);
*2. as modifying (i.e., subordinate to) that previous ἵνα-clause, as a second ramification (along with εἰς τὸ δοκιμάζειν ὑμᾶς τὰ διαφέροντα) of Paul's prayer that the Philippians' love might abound (H-M 32); or
3. as modifying εἰς τὸ δοκιμάζειν ὑμᾶς τὰ διαφέροντα.

The second option seems best, understanding the ἵνα-clause in 10b to express the purpose of all included in vv. 9b–10a (ἵνα ἡ ἀγάπη . . . τὰ διαφέροντα).

Εἰλικρινεῖς is a nom. pl. masc. adj. (as is ἀπρόσκοποι) from εἰλικρινής, -ές, gen. -οῦς, meaning "sincere, without hidden motive or pretense" (BDAG 282c). Some cite etym. as informative: εἴλη, "the warmth/light of the sun" (cf. ἥλιος) + κρίνειν, "to judge." The image is of a garment brought out into the sunlight to confirm that it is free from stains. "Spotless" in the physical sense becomes "purity" in the moral realm (H-M 32). It is doubtful, however, that the Philippians were aware of such etym. since we find the moral sense as early as Plato (*Phaed* 66a, 81c; *Symp.* 211e) (Reumann 128). The idea is "'transparent' in character" (Reumann 157; "pure" [most EVV]; "sincere" [NASB]; "innocent" [NJB]; "moral purity" [F. Büchsel, *TDNT* 2.398]; cf. 2 Cor 1:12). Εἰλικρινεῖς may refer:

1. to sincerity of motive, horizontally, in terms of relationships in the Philippian church (Fee 102); or, more likely,
*2. to purity before God at the parousia (cf. εἰς ἡμέραν Χριστοῦ, v. 10c; cf. also ὡς ἐξ εἰλικρινείας in parallel with ὡς ἐκ θεοῦ κατέναντι θεοῦ in 2 Cor 2:17).

The second adj., ἀπρόσκοποι, can be (1) transitive, "not causing others to stumble," i.e., in the community (Fee 102–3; Hansen 61; H-M 33; cf. 1 Cor 10:32), or, more likely, (2) intransitive, "without stumbling" (BDAG 125d, "blameless for the day of Christ" [most EVV]; cf. Acts 24:16; "without failing in the faith" [G. Stälin, *TDNT* 6.756]; J. Guhrt, *NIDNTT* 2.707). Paul desires the Philippians to be "pure" or "sincere" (εἰλικρινεῖς) on the positive side, "blameless" (ἀπρόσκοποι) on the negative side (O'Brien 78). The community as a whole, not individual Christians, is primarily in view (Hansen 61). The prep. εἰς, in εἰς ἡμέραν Χριστοῦ, does not simply denote a time limit, "until" (Hansen 61; R 594). It is used here in a telic sense: the readers are to be pure and blameless "for the day of Christ," that is, with the day of Christ in view as their ultimate goal (Fee 102 n. 23; A. Oepke, *TDNT* 2.426–27; H-M 33; O'Brien 79).

VERSE 11

πεπληρωμένοι καρπὸν δικαιοσύνης

Πεπληρωμένοι is a nom. pl. masc. of the perf. pass. ptc. from πληρόω ("God" inferred as the One who fills [G. Delling, *TDNT* 6.291]). The perf. pass. generally emphasizes the present state, rather than the past action. Here the "present" is the future day of Christ, and the "past," viewed from the perspective of that day, is the current life orientation of the Philippians (Fee 103 n. 30).

The imagery pictures an orchard of trees loaded down with a full crop of good fruit (H-M 33; perhaps from Ps 1:3 [Hansen 62]).The ptc. phrase may (a) modify the ἵνα-clause preceding it (Fee 104; circumst. ptc. of cause [Reumann 129]), or (b) function in parallel with εἰλικρινεῖς καὶ ἀπρόσκοποι: Paul desires that they be not only acquitted on the last day but also filled with the fruit of godly deeds (T 89; O'Brien 80).

Καρπός was used lit., for "fruit" from trees or the earth (or offspring of animals or persons) and then metaphorically for the "product" or "result" of an action (Reumann 130); an instance of the acc. retained with a pass. verb (BDAG 828c; BDF §159[1]; "being filled with respect to the fruit of righteousness" [Porter 66]; R 483, 485, 510; T 232–33, 247; Wallace 197; Z §73; O'Brien 80). Paul has in view "all kinds of noble acts and worthwhile deeds" (H-M 34), including, perhaps, "the fruit of the Spirit" (Gal 5:22) (O'Brien 79).

Alternatives for δικαιοσύνης (gen. sg. fem.), and the function of the gen., generate several options. The third is best:

1. Read δικαιοσύνης ethically (G. Schrenk, *TDNT* 2.210), and the gen. as appos.: "fruit which is righteous behavior" ("produce of uprightness" [BDAG 248b]; "fruits of uprightness" [NJB]; "good deeds" [CEV]; Hansen 63; Silva 51–52).
   a. This a familiar biblical phrase for conduct pleasing to God (LXX: Prov 3:9; 11:30; Amos 6:12; cf. Jas 3:18) (Fee 103; H-M 33; attrib. gen., "righteous fruit," is also possible). But ethical uses of δικαιοσύνη are not common in Paul; the forensic usage predominates (Reumann 158).
   b. A parallel cstr. is found in 2 Cor 9:10 (τὰ γενήματα τῆς δικαιοσύνης ὑμῶν), where Paul alludes to Hos 10:12 (LXX), which clearly speaks of moral conduct (Silva 52).
2. Read δικαιοσύνης forensically (a right legal standing), and the gen. as appos.: "fruit which is righteousness."

*3. Read δικαιοσύνης forensically, and the gen. as source or origin: "fruit which comes from righteousness" ("fruit of your salvation" [NLT]; "filled with the result of justification" [Reumann 158]).

   a. Καρπός in NT generally refers to the result, outcome, or profit of an action (O'Brien 80–81). When Paul uses καρπός + gen. elsewhere, it is gen. of source (Phil 1:22; Rom 6:22; Eph 5:9; Gal 5:22) (Reumann 133).
   b. The modifier τὸν διὰ Ἰησοῦ Χριστοῦ supports this (Reumann 133).
   c. The forensic sense of δικαιοσύνη is "characteristic of Paul" (Silva 51).

τὸν διὰ Ἰησοῦ Χριστοῦ εἰς δόξαν καὶ ἔπαινον θεοῦ

Like the "fruit of the Spirit" (Gal 5:22), the "fruit of righteousness" can only come from Jesus Christ (διὰ Ἰησοῦ Χριστοῦ; causal use of διά + gen. with persons; "from" [A. Oepke, *TDNT* 2.68]), the source of all life and goodness (cf. John 15:4). The art. τόν is acc. sg. masc., identifying its antecedent as καρπόν, not δικαιοσύνης. As indicated by the EVV, the art., formally in 2 attrib. position, functions loosely as a rel. pron. ("which" [RSV, NASB]; "that" [NIV, HCSB, ESV]; cf. Wallace 213–14).

The preferred reading, εἰς δόξαν καὶ ἔπαινον θεοῦ (א A B Ψ 075 0150 6 33 *Byz* it[b. d. f. o. r] cop[sa, bo]; "little doubt" that it is original [Metzger 544]; UBS[5] = {A}), has generated three variants:

1. εἰς δόξαν καὶ ἔπαινον Χριστοῦ (D* 1962)
2. εἰς δόξαν καὶ ἔπαινον ἐμοί (F G it[g] Ambrosiaster)
3. εἰς δόξαν θεοῦ καὶ ἔπαινον ἐμοί (𝔓[46])

(1) represents a simple change toward the repeated use of Χριστοῦ in the passage; (2) and (3) likely reflect the influence of Paul's standard use of ἔπαινος as directed toward humans, not God (Fee 96 n. 3; Reumann 135).

The prep. εἰς is used of purpose (R 595), or both purpose and result (A. Oepke, *TDNT* 2.430). BDAG defines δόξαν here as "honor as enhancement or recognition of status or performance," glossed as "fame, recognition, renown, honor, prestige" (257d–258a). Both δόξα and ἔπαινος functioned semantically in the context of Rome's honor culture, where public recognition and acclamation served as preeminent social commodities (Reumann 136). Ἔπαινον signifies "the act of expressing admiration or approval" (BDAG 357b).

Understanding εἰς δόξαν καὶ ἔπαινον θεοῦ as glory and praise that accrues to God (θεοῦ as obj. gen.) seems self-evident (E. Stauffer, *TDNT* 3.333; H. Preisker, *TDNT* 2.588; O. Hofius, *EDNT* 2.17a; Hansen 64; H-M 34; O'Brien 82). Reumann, however, has recently marshaled a series of weighty arguments for seeing the Philippians as the ones who receive δόξα and ἔπαινος from God (θεοῦ as subj. gen.) on the day of Christ:

   a. Paul usually employs ἔπαινος as directed toward people rather than God (e.g., Rom 2:29; 13:3; 1 Cor 4:5; cf. 11:2, 17, 22; but see Eph 1:6, 12, 14). Though less common, Paul can also use δόξα in this sense, as well (Rom 2:7, 10) (Reumann 137).

b. Paul himself anticipated public acclaim at the eschaton for what God had wrought through him (1 Thess 2:20; cf. Phil 4:1). For Paul, his δόξα at the parousia consisted, in one sense, of his Gentile converts. To the degree that the Philippians participated in Paul's ministry, Paul's δόξα will be theirs, as well.

c. Most passages in the LXX involving εἰς (or πρός) δόξαν have human beings, or sites on earth, as the object of glory or honor from God (Exod 28:2, 40 [Aaron]; 2 Chr 3:6 [the temple]; Sir 45:23 [Phineas]). A warning to King Uzziah in 2 Chr 26:18 reads, "This will not be to you for honor from the Lord God" (εἰς δόξαν παρὰ κυρίου θεοῦ) (Reumann 136–37).

d. 1 Pet 1:7 uses the same pair of words to communicate this idea (εἰς ἔπαινον καὶ δόξαν καὶ τιμὴν ἐν ἀποκαλύψει Ἰησοῦ Χριστοῦ) (Reumann 137).

e. Ancient scribes apparently understood δόξα and ἔπαινος in Phil 1:11 as given by God (θεοῦ as subj. gen.); the var. readings (above) represent their efforts further to clarify this understanding (Reumann 137).

f. The focus has been on the Philippians' spiritual development and virtues throughout the prayer. Public affirmation from God makes sense as the response to a people who meet the day of Christ "filled with the fruit of righteousness" (Reumann 155).

g. The traditional view, which reads εἰς δόξαν καὶ ἔπαινον θεοῦ as a doxology directed godward, would leave Phil 1:11 as the only doxological conclusion in a Pauline introductory prayer (Reumann 136).

The decision is not easy. It remains the case that Paul generally uses δόξα of God's glory, often with εἰς (Rom 3:7 [εἰς τὴν δόξαν αὐτοῦ]; 1 Cor 10:31 [εἰς δόξαν θεοῦ]; 2 Cor 4:15 [εἰς τὴν δόξαν τοῦ θεοῦ]; Phil 2:11 [εἰς δόξαν θεοῦ πατρός]). Still, Reumann's interpretation is attractive. In addition to the arguments outlined above, the social world of Roman Philippi was particularly marked by preoccupation with public honors and recognition. Christians in the colony were to pursue, instead, "the things that really matter" (τὰ διαφέροντα, v. 10) to God. Paul assures the Philippians that their countercultural gospel priorities, though dishonorable in the eyes of their pagan contemporaries, will receive their proper recognition at the day of Christ.

FOR FURTHER STUDY

6. Thanksgiving (1:3)

Artz, Peter. "The 'Epistolary Introductory Thanksgiving' in the Papyri and in Paul." *NovT* 36 (1994): 8–46.

O'Brien, Peter T. "Thanksgiving and the Gospel in Paul." *NTS* 21 (1974–75): 144–55.

_____ . *Introductory Thanksgivings in the Letters of Paul.* Leiden: Brill, 1977. See pages 62–104.

*_____ . "Thanksgiving Within the Structure of Pauline Theology." Pages 50–66 in *Pauline Studies.* Edited by D. A. Hagner and M. J. Harris. Grand Rapids: Eerdmans, 1980.

Pao, David W. *Thanksgiving: An Investigation of a Pauline Theme.* Downers Grove: InterVarsity, 2003.

Peterman, Gerald W. *Paul's Gift from Philippi: Conventions of Gift-Exchange and Christian Giving.* SNTSMS 92. Cambridge: Cambridge University Press, 1997.

Schubert, Paul. *Form and Function of the Pauline Thanksgivings.* Berlin: Töpelmann, 1939.

7. Prayer (1:3, 9–11)

Brown, C. *NIDNTT* 2.882–86.

Carson, D. A. *A Call to Spiritual Reformation: Priorities from Paul and His Prayers.* Grand Rapids: Baker, 1992.

Coggan, F. Donald. *The Prayers of the New Testament.* New York: Harper and Row, 1967. See pages 87–167.

*Hunter, W. B. *DPL* 725–34.

Osborne, Grant. "Moving Forward on Our Knees: Corporate Prayer in the New Testament." *JETS* 53 (2010): 243–67.

Mullins, Terence Y. "Petition as Literary Form." *NovT* 5 (1962): 46–54.

Peterson, David G. "Prayer in Paul's Writings." Pages 85–101, 325–28 in *Teach Us to Pray: Prayer in the Bible and the Modern World.* Edited by D. A. Carson. Grand Rapids: Baker, 1990.

Wiles, Gordon P. *Paul's Intercessory Prayers.* SNTSMS 24. Cambridge: Cambridge University Press, 1974.

8. Joy (1:4)

Bloomquist, L. Gregory. "Subverted by Joy: Suffering and Joy in Paul's Letter to the Philippians." *Int* 61 (2007): 270–82.

Conzelmann, H. *TDNT* 9.359–72.

Berger, K. *EDNT* 3.454–55.

Beyreuther, E., and G. Finkenrath. *NIDNTT* 2.356–61.

Howard, David M. "Surprised by Joy: Joy in the Christian Life and in Christian Scholarship." *JETS* 47 (2004): 3–20.

Morrice, William G. *Joy in the New Testament.* Exeter: Paternoster, 1984.

*_____ . *DPL* 511–12.

Smalley, S. S. "Joy." Pages 608–10 in *NDBT.* Edited by T. D. Alexander and B. S. Rosner. Leicester/Downers Grove: InterVarsity, 2000.

Spicq 3.498–99.

9. Participation/Sharing (1:5, 8)

Campbell, J. Y. "Κοινωνία and Its Cognates in the New Testament." *JBL* 51 (1932): 352–82.

*Hainz, J. *EDNT* 2.303–5.

Hauck, F. *TDNT* 3.789–809.

McDermott, J. Michael. "The Biblical Doctrine of Κοινωνία." *Biblische Zeitschrift* 19 (1975): 64–77, 219–33.

O'Brien, P. *DPL* 293–95.

Panikulam, George. *Koinonia in the New Testament: A Dynamic Expression of Christian Life.* Rome: Biblical Institute, 1979.

Reumann, John. "Koinonia in Scripture: Survey of Biblical Texts." Pages 37–69 in *On the Way to Fuller Koinonia*. Edited by T. F. Best and G. Gassmann. Geneva: World Council of Churches, 1994.
Schlattenmann, J. *NIDNTT* 1.639–44.

10. Love (1:9)

Furnish, Victor. *The Love Command in the New Testament*. Nashville: Abingdon, 1972.
Günther, W., and W. G. Link. *NIDNTT* 2.538–47.
Moffat, James. *Love in the New Testament*. London: Hodder & Stoughton, 1930.
*Mohrlang, R. *DPL* 575–78,
Schneider, G. *EDNT* 1.8–12.
Spicq, Ceslaus. *Agape in the New Testament*. 2 vols. London: Herder, 1963, 1965.
Stauffer, E., and G. Quell. *TDNT* 1.221–54.

HOMILETICAL SUGGESTIONS

Paul's Attitude of Gratitude (1:3–11)

1. Past gratitude for the Philippians' participation in the gospel (vv. 3–6).
2. Present gratitude for the ongoing partnership (vv. 7–8).
3. Future prayer for continuing involvement in the priority of the gospel (vv. 9–11).

Paul's Prayer Is (1:4)

1. Intensely personal (δεήσει μου ὑπὲρ . . . ὑμῶν, "my prayer for you").
2. Constant (πάντοτε . . . ποιούμενος, "always . . . [constantly] making").
3. All inclusive (ὑπὲρ πάντων ὑμῶν, "for all of you").
4. Spontaneous (μετὰ χαρᾶς).

Partnership in the Gospel (1:4–8)

1. Partnership in the gospel is costly (vv. 4b–5).
2. Partnership in the gospel is evidence of genuine faith (v. 6).
3. Partnership in the gospel produces deep and lasting relationships (vv. 7–8).

An Effective Love (1:9–11)

1. An effective love is always increasing (v. 9a).
2. An effective love is carefully discerning (vv. 9b–10a).
3. An effective love is future oriented (vv. 10b–11).

II. Paul's Circumstances and the Gospel (1:12–26)

A. THE GOSPEL CONTINUES TO ADVANCE (1:12–18C)

... in the Face of Adverse Circumstances

12 Γινώσκειν δὲ ὑμᾶς βούλομαι, ἀδελφοί,
       ὅτι τὰ κατ᾽ ἐμὲ μᾶλλον εἰς προκοπὴν τοῦ εὐαγγελίου ἐλήλυθεν,
13   ὥστε τοὺς δεσμούς μου φανεροὺς ἐν Χριστῷ γενέσθαι
                   ἐν ὅλῳ τῷ πραιτωρίῳ
                   καὶ τοῖς λοιποῖς πᾶσιν,
14   καὶ τοὺς πλείονας τῶν ἀδελφῶν
                               ἐν κυρίῳ πεποιθότας τοῖς
                               δεσμοῖς μου
                               περισσοτέρως
                               τολμᾶν
                               ἀφόβως τὸν λόγον λαλεῖν.

... and in the Midst of Jealousy and Factionalism

15 [A] τινὲς μὲν καὶ διὰ φθόνον καὶ ἔριν,

      [B] τινὲς δὲ καὶ δι᾽ εὐδοκίαν
                   τὸν Χριστὸν κηρύσσουσιν.

16 [B'] οἱ μὲν ἐξ ἀγάπης,
                   εἰδότες
                   ὅτι εἰς ἀπολογίαν τοῦ εὐαγγελίου κεῖμαι,

17 [A'] οἱ δὲ ἐξ ἐριθείας τὸν Χριστὸν καταγγέλλουσιν,
                   οὐχ ἁγνῶς,
                   οἰόμενοι θλῖψιν ἐγείρειν τοῖς δεσμοῖς μου.

18 Τί γάρ; πλὴν ὅτι παντὶ τρόπῳ,
       εἴτε προφάσει
       εἴτε ἀληθείᾳ,
       Χριστὸς καταγγέλλεται,
       καὶ ἐν τούτῳ χαίρω.

There are several linguistic ties with previous context: (a) εὐαγγέλιον (vv. 5, 7 and vv. 12, 16); (b) δεσμός (v. 7 and vv. 13, 14, 17); (c) ἀπολογία (v. 7 and v. 16) (d) ἀγάπη (v. 9 and v. 16) (Fee 107). Nevertheless, a transition to a new section is indicated by (1) the switch to 1 sg. vbs., along with forms of ἐγώ, throughout vv. 12–18a (1 sg.: βούλομαι [v. 12], κεῖμαι [v. 16], χαίρω [v. 18]; forms of ἐγώ: vv. 12, 13, 14, 17); (2) voc. address ἀδελφοί; (3) change in topic, from prayer and gratitude (vv. 3–11) to imparting information (vv. 12–18a) (Reumann 191).

Thematically the passage constitutes a "massive unity" (Reumann 195) centered around the ways Paul's imprisonment (τὰ κατ᾽ ἐμέ [v. 12]; τοὺς δεσμούς μου [v. 13]; τοῖς δεσμοῖς μου [vv. 14, 17]) resulted in the progress and preaching of the gospel/Christ, a theme variously referenced eight times in the text: (1) v. 12 (προκοπὴν τοῦ εὐαγγελίου); (2) v. 13 (ἐν Χριστῷ); (3) v. 14 (τὸν λόγον λαλεῖν); (4) v. 15 (τὸν Χριστὸν κηρύσσουσιν); (5) v. 16 (ἀπολογίαν τοῦ εὐαγγελίου); (6) v. 17 (τὸν Χριστὸν καταγγέλλουσιν); (7) v. 18 (Χριστὸς καταγγέλλεται); (8) v. 18 (τούτῳ) (Reumann 188).

Much of the vocabulary is from the Greco-Roman world (no OT material or Christian liturgical traditions): προκοπήν (v. 12), φθόνον καὶ ἔριν (v. 15), ἐριθείας (v. 17), προφάσει (v. 18) (Reumann 188).

The Philippians knew Paul was in prison and would soon have his hearing: "How was he faring? . . . Were these events having an adverse effect on the progress of the gospel?" (O'Brien 86). The answer, in short, is Χριστὸς καταγγέλλεται, καὶ ἐν τούτῳ χαίρω (v. 18).

VERSE 12

Γινώσκειν δὲ ὑμᾶς βούλομαι, ἀδελφοί

V. 12 reflects a four-part "disclosure formula," common in the papyri (Mullins 44–50): (1) θέλω (or βούλομαι); (2) inf. vb. meaning "to know" (γινώσκειν or εἰδέναι); (3) the person(s) addressed, in the acc. (ὑμᾶς); (4) the information (frequently via a ὅτι-clause). An example from the papyri:

> "Apollinarius to Taesis, his mother and lady, many greetings. Before all, I pray for your health. . . . I wish you to know (γινώσκειν σε θέλω) . . . that I arrived in Rome in good health" (cited by H-M 41, from Hunt and Edgar, *Select Papyri*, 1:303).

Paul intentionally adapts the disclosure formula to his own concerns, and it is precisely at those places where Paul departs from the formula that the main idea of the passage comes to the forefront ("unconventional use of a conventional form" [Hansen

65]; Fee 106). According to the pattern (see above example), we would expect Paul to inform the Philippians about his suffering. Instead, we learn about Paul's circumstances only in passing, as he focuses, instead, on the progress of the gospel.

Γινώσκειν δὲ ὑμᾶς βούλομαι functions as a "metacomment," a discourse strategy whereby a writer stops saying what he is saying in order to comment on what is going to be said (Runge 101). Γινώσκειν δὲ ὑμᾶς βούλομαι could be removed "without substantially altering the propositional content" (Runge 102). Metacomments serve to draw special attention to what is about to be said. Here, γινώσκειν δὲ ὑμᾶς βούλομαι, along with the "redundant address" ἀδελφοί, markedly underscore what Paul is going to say about the surprising results of his imprisonment (Runge 121). The positioning of γινώσκειν + δέ at the beginning of the verse signals discontinuity and the start of a new thematic unit (Reed 118–19). "Now" (NIV, NASB, HCSB) marks the transition to the new discourse unit better than "and" (NLT). Some EVV omit δέ (NRSV, CEV, ESV).

Γινώσκειν is pres. act. inf. (with acc. subj. ὑμᾶς) from γινώσκω; a common use of inf. after vb. of wishing (BDF §392[1][a]; complementary inf. [Wallace 599]). Γινώσκω is used here in the sense "come to know" (BDAG 200d), or "learn," as in Phil 2:19 (R. Bultmann, *TDNT* 1.703; W. Schmithals, *EDNT* 1.248c). More than just news from Paul, it is interpreted news that the Philippians need to ponder ("I want you to realise" [NJB]; Reumann 192).

The vb. βούλομαι implies "conscious volition as a result of deliberate reflection" (BDAG 182c; "I want [you to know]" [most EVV]); in NT period βούλομαι (37x in NT) was crowded out by θέλω (208x) (Reumann 166).

Ἀδελφοί would have particularly resonated with Paul's readers. Due to the patrilineal orientation of kinship in the ancient world, "brothers and sisters" (NIV), who came from the same patriline, generally exhibited a higher degree of social solidarity than any other same-generation relationship—including spouses, who, of course, had different fathers. The voc. pl. masc. ἀδελφοί is commonly used generically in the NT to include both men and women. The importance of the surrogate sibling bond for Paul's ecclesiology highly problematizes gender-neutral renderings that sacrifice the metaphor ("My friends" [REB]; "beloved" [NRSV]). Paul uses ἀδελφός of his fellow Christians nine times in Philippians alone (1:12; 3:1, 13, 17; 4:1, 8 [voc.]; 1:14; 4:21 [Christians in Rome with Paul]; 2:25 [Epaphroditus]). Other religious groups and associations also adopted surrogate sibling terminology (MM 9a; J. Beutler, *EDNT* 1.29a). The early Christians, however, were particularly known for exhibiting family-like solidarity in their communities (see Joseph H. Hellerman, *The Ancient Church as Family* [Minneapolis: Fortress, 2001]).

ὅτι τὰ κατ᾽ ἐμὲ μᾶλλον εἰς προκοπὴν τοῦ εὐαγγελίου ἐλήλυθεν

The ὅτι-clause introduces the obj. of γινώσκειν ("recitative function" [Reumann 167]). A neut. pl. subj. (τὰ κατ᾽ ἐμέ) often takes a 3 sg. vb. (ἐλήλυθεν) (BDF §133).

Τὰ κατ᾽ ἐμέ, lit. "the things (nom. pl. neut. art. used as subst. [R 766]) concerning me," is a common expression to describe the situation of a person ("with respect to, in relation to" [BDAG 513c]; "what concerns me" [T 14–15]; "what has happened to me" [NRSV, NIV, HCSB]; "my circumstances" [NASB]); a general reference to Paul's imprisonment (= τοὺς δεσμούς μου, v. 13) (O'Brien 90). According to ancient epistolary convention, the Philippians will now expect Paul to expand upon his circumstances. Instead, he elaborates upon τὰ κατ᾽ εὐαγγέλιον.

Here the adv. μᾶλλον (comp. of μάλα) does not mean "more" (BDAG 613d) but "rather," in the sense "instead," pointing to an unanticipated result: "helping rather than hindering the advance of the gospel" (NJB; "actually" [NRSV, HCSB, NIV]; "really" [RSV, ESV]; M. Wolter, *EDNT* 2.382a; R 665; Fee 110–11 n. 18; H-M 43; O'Brien 90; Reumann 167–68).

Ἐλήλυθεν is 3 sg. perf. act. indic. from ἔρχομαι. With εἰς, the vb. relates the outcome of Paul's circumstances ("resulted in" [HCSB]; "served to" [RSV, NIV, ESV]; "turned out for" [NASB]; O'Brien 91). Reumann's reticence to see in the clause a "providential ordering of events" (167–68) fails properly to consider Paul's understanding of God's sovereignty, particularly where the advance of the gospel is concerned (1 Cor 16:9; 2 Cor 2:12; Col 4:3; J. Schneider, *TDNT* 2.674–75; T. Schramm, *EDNT* 2.56a).

Προκοπήν comes from προκοπή, -ῆς, ἡ, "progress, advancement, furtherance" (BDAG 871d; a Gk. term not found in the OT [G. Stählin, *TDNT* 6.713]). Paul may have intended a play on words: the Philippians anticipated that Paul's chains would result in προσκοπή, "hindrance," to the gospel (Hansen 67). The chapter has two of only three NT occurrences of προκοπή (cf. 1 Tim 4:15). In v. 12 Paul highlights the progress of the gospel (evangelism); in v. 25, the progress of the congregation (τὴν ὑμῶν προκοπὴν καὶ χαρὰν τῆς πίστεως) (spiritual formation). Verses 12–25 are thus "framed" by προκοπή (Fee 107; "inclusio" [111 n. 22]). The modifier τοῦ εὐαγγελίου (synonymous with τὸν λόγον [v. 14]) is a subj. gen., i.e., "the gospel progresses."

Etym. speculation proves unhelpful (e.g., προκοπή pictures "pioneers cutting a way before an army and so furthering its march" [H-M 43] or a ship making headway "in spite of blows" [G. Stählin, *TDNT* 6.704]). Contemporary writers used προκοπή in two key ways. Both potentially inform our understanding of the term in v. 12 (Reumann 194):

a. Προκοπή was a tech. term in Stoicism that denoted an individual's moral progress in virtue (Philo, Plut., and Epict.). Likely familiar with popular philosophy in the ancient world, the Philippians might have expected Paul to comment on his personal προκοπή in moral virtue through imprisonment and suffering—an expectation that would only have been reinforced by the use of a conventional "disclosure formula" at this point in the letter (see above). Strikingly, Paul speaks instead of the προκοπή of the gospel (Reumann 194).

b. The word group was also used to describe "the rise to power by Rome, progress based on Roman valor and divine fortune, part of a supposed administration (οἰκονομία) of the universe by Zeus and the gods for the good" (Reumann 194). The association of προκοπή with Roman expansion may have encouraged residents of Roman Philippi to interpret προκοπὴν τοῦ εὐαγγελίου as a counterimperial challenge to the progress of Caesar's "gospel" (see on εὐαγγέλιον [1:5]).

VERSE 13

ὥστε τοὺς δεσμούς μου φανεροὺς ἐν Χριστῷ γενέσθαι

The conj. ὥστε means "so that" (BDAG 1107b) and (with the parallel infs. γενέσθαι [v. 13] and τολμᾶν [v. 14]) marks the "actual results" of ἐλήλυθεν (v. 12) (R 1091; O'Brien 91). Cl. Gk. distinguished actual result (ὥστε + indic.) from possible outcome (ὥστε + inf.); the NT uses the inf. for both (but see indic. at Gal 2:13; Moule 141; BDF §391[2]; H-M 43). The ὥστε-clause elaborates upon the προκοπή of the gospel in two social contexts: (1) outside the Christian community (v. 13), and (2) within it (v. 14) (O'Brien 87, 91; Reumann 168, 194–95). Reumann suggests, from the sequence of tenses (ἐλήλυθεν [perf.], γενέσθαι [aor.], τολμᾶν, λαλεῖν [pres.]), that results related to outsiders (v. 13) have already come to fruition while those related to insiders (v. 14) continue to do so (Reumann 168–69).

Τοὺς δεσμούς explains τὰ κατ᾽ ἐμέ, v. 12 (Reumann 170). The noun is the acc. subj. of γενέσθαι (aor. mid. inf. from γίνομαι, "become," a change of state). The art. τούς distinguishes the subj. δεσμούς from its pred. adj. φανερούς. The nom. noun δεσμός can yield a neut. pl. acc. (δεσμά [Luke 8:29]) or a masc. pl. acc. (δεσμούς, as here) (R 262). The distinction between δεσμά, as actual bonds, and δεσμοί, as bondage, does not hold up for the NT.

Φανερούς is acc. pl. masc. from φανερός, -ά, -όν, "visible, clear, plainly to be seen . . . evident, known" (BDAG 1048a; with γενέσθαι "come to light, become known" [Reumann 170]).

There is some debate about whether ἐν Χριστῷ modifies

   1. τοὺς δεσμούς;
   *2. φανερούς; or
   3. the whole clause.

The alternatives have generated various interpretations, some more plausible than others. Fee's solution is attractive: take ἐν Χριστῷ with φανερούς (suggested by the word order), and assume an ellipsis: "so that my chains have become manifest [as being] in Christ" (Fee 112 n. 29; "I am in chains for Christ" [NIV; sim. CEV, NLT, NASB, HCSB]).

Paul generally uses ἐν Χριστῷ as a dat. of sphere, to characterize "one's realm of existence" (W. Elliger EDNT 1.448c), specifically, his conception of solidarity with Christ. Accordingly, some think that ἐν Χριστῷ in v. 13 expresses Paul's recognition that he is sharing in Christ's sufferings (Silva 62; "perhaps" [Campbell 125]). Though Paul certainly viewed his sufferings in this way (cf. 3:10; Rom 8:17), one wonders, in the present context, how Paul's union with Christ in his suffering could become "manifest" ἐν ὅλῳ τῷ πραιτωρίῳ καὶ τοῖς λοιποῖς πᾶσιν. Paul's point with ἐν Χριστῷ is more simple and straightforward: his imprisonment has to do with his Christian faith and missionary activities (Fee 112; a "causal" ἐν [M. Harris, *NIDNTT* 3.1,191–92]).

ἐν ὅλῳ τῷ πραιτωρίῳ καὶ τοῖς λοιποῖς πᾶσιν

Ἐν is locat., "in, among" (BDAG 326d; Fee 112 n. 25). The prep. governs either (1) both datives (ὅλῳ τῷ πραιτωρίῳ and τοῖς λοιποῖς πᾶσιν) (O'Brien 92), or (2) only ὅλῳ τῷ πραιτωρίῳ, with τοῖς λοιποῖς πᾶσιν functioning like an indir. obj. with the verbal noun φανερούς ("throughout . . . to" [most EVV]; Reumann 171).

The adjs. ὅλῳ and πᾶσιν represent hyperbole. Some—but surely not all—of the 9,000–10,000 praetorians in Rome would have encountered Paul through their supervisory duties (Fee 112 n. 25; O'Brien 93–94; Reumann 171), a point that would surely have been been self-evident to the letter's recipients.

Πραιτώριον, -ου, τό (dat. sg. neut.) is a Lat. loanword (BDF §5[1]) that originally denoted the tent of a Roman general in the field, then the area surrounding it. The term was later applied to those who guarded the general (*cohors praetoria*), thus "Praetorian Guard." After the battle of Philippi (42 BC), 8,000 veterans were organized into praetorian cohorts for Anthony and Octavian. In 27 BC, Augustus created a permanent corps of nine (later twelve) cohorts, 500 or 1,000 men each, a military elite. Under Tiberius all the cohorts were concentrated in a single barracks, northeast of Rome (Tac. *Ann.* 4.2). Praetorians made Claudius emperor in AD 41 and were emperor makers from then on (Reumann 171–72). The term continued to be used for the residence of a ruler or governor (so all other NT occurrences: Matt 27:27; Mark 15:16; John 18:28 [2x], 33; 19:9; Acts 23:35). So KJV here: "in all the palace, and in all other places." Most EVV read τῷ πραιτωρίῳ in v. 13, instead, as a reference to persons, i.e., the elite body of the Praetorian Guard (e.g., "the whole imperial guard" [HCSB]) due to: (a) abundant evidence for such usage in inscriptions, as well as in Tacitus, Pliny, Suetonius, and Josephus; (b) the reference to persons in the parallel expression (τοῖς λοιποῖς πᾶσιν, dat. pl. masc.; neut., "other places," is less likely [Reumann 172]) (Hansen 67 n. 113; O'Brien 93).

It is hard to tell what Paul meant with τοῖς λοιποῖς πᾶσιν (the adj. λοιποῖς is used as subst., "the others" [BDAG 602c]; "everyone else" [NIV, NRSV, HCSB], "all the rest" [RSV, ESV]). Clearly other non-Christians in Rome, apart from the Praetorians, are in view. Whether we can be more specific ("officials charged with preparing his case for hearing before the emperor" [Fee 114 n. 37]; "the bureaucracy of Rome" [Winter, *Seek the Welfare of the City*, 96]) is open to question. Paul seems to have in mind a ripple effect: his current imprisonment for the gospel is becoming apparent to wider circles of non-Christians, beginning with those involved in his imprisonment and trial. Paul is a "Trojan horse" in Caesar's system (Reumann 196; Fee 114 n. 38).

VERSE 14

καὶ τοὺς πλείονας τῶν ἀδελφῶν

The conj. καί introduces a second result (ὥστε), as well as a more precise statement of the nature of the gospel's progress. Paul piles up terms expressive of courage (πεποιθότας, περισσοτέρως, τολμᾶν, ἀφόβως) to make his point (O'Brien 94).

Πλείονας is from πλείων, πλεῖον, comp. of adj. πολύς, πολλή, πολύ, (subst. use, "the majority" [BDAG 848c]; "most" [EVV]; "many" [KJV] is inaccurate). Paul is drawing upon "popular language"; he had not "counted noses" in each house church (Fee 115 n. 45).

Τῶν ἀδελφῶν is a partitive gen. (Wallace 111 n. 104). It refers to fellow Christians who are in contact with Paul in Rome, including both groups of preachers mentioned in vv. 15–17.

ἐν κυρίῳ πεποιθότας τοῖς δεσμοῖς μου

Some take ἐν κυρίῳ with τῶν ἀδελφῶν ("brothers in the Lord" [HCSB]), following the Greek word order (one would expect an art. [τῶν] before ἐν κυρίῳ to mark attrib. position [Reumann 174], but this can be supplied [Moule 108; T 221–22]). The prep. phrase would then be tautological, however, since τῶν ἀδελφῶν already identifies those in view as Christians. Alleged parallels (Eph 6:21; Col 1:2; 4:7) do not hold up (Fee 116; O'Brien 94). Take ἐν κυρίῳ, instead, with πεποιθότας ("confident/ trusting in the Lord" [NRSV, NASB, ESV]; H. Von Soden, TDNT 1.144 n. 1; 145 n. 9; A. Sand, EDNT 3.63d; H-M 44; O'Brien 94–95; Reumann 174; cf. πέποιθα δὲ ἐν κυρίῳ [Phil 2:24]; Rom 14:14; Gal 5:10; Phil 3:3; 2 Thess 3:4). This is consistent with the fact that all modifiers in the clause stand in first position: (a) περισσοτέρως τολμᾶν, (b) ἀφόβως τὸν λόγον λαλεῖν, and now (c) ἐν κυρίῳ πεποιθότας. Paul placed ἐν κυρίῳ before πεποιθότας τοῖς δεσμοῖς μου to emphasize that the emboldened preachers' confidence "does not stem ultimately from his imprisonment but from the prior work of the Lord in their lives"; ἐν κυρίῳ thus refers to the ground of their confidence, τοῖς δεσμοῖς μου identifies the instrument (Fee 116).

Τοῖς δεσμοῖς can be read as instr. dat. ("by my imprisonment" [NRSV, ESV]; O'Brien 95), or dat. of cause ("because of my imprisonment/chains" [RSV, NLT, NIV]; Moule 45–46; T 242; Wallace 168; H.-G. Link, NIDNTT 3.592). The difference in meaning is negligible (Silva 66).

Πεποιθότας is acc. pl. masc. (agreeing with τοὺς πλείονας) of the perf. act. ptc. of πείθω (see on 1:6), an adv. ptc. of cause (modifying τολμᾶν), "because they have become confident" (Reumann 173; "made confident" or "gained confidence" [most EVV; R. Bultmann, TDNT 6.6]; "trusting" [NASB; O. Becker, NIDNTT 1.592; A. Sand, EDNT 3.63d]). The perf. tense here describes a conviction that began in the past and has continuing effects; with the pres. inf. τολμᾶν, the sense is "already convinced they now continue to dare" (O'Brien 95, author's italics).

περισσοτέρως τολμᾶν ἀφόβως τὸν λόγον λαλεῖν

The adv. περισσοτέρως (from the adj. περισσός) is the comp. of περισσῶς ("exceedingly, beyond all measure"). It modifies τολμᾶν intensively, "so much (the) more" (BDAG 806b; "dare even more" [HCSB]; "dare all the more" [NIV]). It is not that the majority were timid before but that "their courage had risen to new heights, when they might have been intimidated" (O'Brien 95). We would expect the opposite reaction (Reumann 196; cf. μᾶλλον [v. 12]).

Τολμᾶν is pres. act. inf. (with ὥστε [v. 13], denoting result) from the contract vb. τολμάω, "dare, have the courage, be brave enough" (BDAG 1010b; "the courage of confession" [G. Fitzer, *TDNT* 8.184]). The term is used elsewhere to describe the courage of Joseph of Arimathea in asking for the body of Jesus (Mark 15:43) and Paul's attitude toward opponents in Corinth (2 Cor 10:2). Τολμᾶν "presupposes danger" (O'Brien 95–96), perhaps "the historical situation in Rome in the early 60s, when Nero's madness was peaking and the church there had begun to fall under suspicion" (Fee 116).

Λαλεῖν functions, with τολμᾶν, as a complementary (pres. act.) inf. Speaking the word ἀφόβως (adv. "fearlessly" [H. Balz, *TDNT* 9.214]) is equivalent to speaking the word μετὰ παρρησίας (O'Brien 96).

Τὸν λόγον λαλεῖν is equivalent to λαλῆσαι . . . τὸ εὐαγγέλιον τοῦ θεοῦ (O'Brien 97). Ὁ λόγος was used absolutely ("no misunderstanding would be possible among Christians" [BDAG 600a]) as early as Gal 6:6 and 1 Thess 1:6, as a technical term for "divine revelation through Christ and his messengers" (BDAG 599d, 600a; "the totality of the Christian message" [H-M 45]; O'Brien 96; cf. Mark 8:32; John 12:48). Attempts to clarify (the likely original) τὸν λόγον λαλεῖν generated the following set of variants:

*1. τὸν λόγον λαλεῖν: 𝔓⁴⁶ (but most of [τὸν λόγο]ν must be supplied) D² K 6 739 *Byz* etc. ("the [M]essage" [NJB, CEV, HCSB]; "the word" [NRSV, ESV]; "the gospel" [NIV]);

2. τὸν λόγον τοῦ κυρίου λαλεῖν: F G Cyprian (H-M 39);

3. τὸν λόγον τοῦ θεοῦ λαλεῖν: ℵ A B D* Ψ 075 0150 33 itᵃʳ, ᵇ, ᶠ, ᵒ copˢᵃ, ᵇᵒ etc. ("the word of God" [RSV, NASB]; B. Klappert, *NIDNTT* 3.1110).

We cannot be dogmatic (UBS⁵ = {B} τὸν λόγον λαλεῖν), but the latter two vars. look like attempts to clarify τὸν λόγον, based on Paul's tendency elsewhere to add a genitive qualifier (Fee 109 n. 10; Hansen 70 n. 121; H-M 39; Metzger 544–45; cf. Rom 9:6; 1 Cor 1:18; 14:36; 2 Cor 2:17). There is "no discernable difference" in meaning among the vars. (G. Kittel, *TDNT* 4.114).

VERSE 15

τινὲς μὲν καὶ διὰ φθόνον καὶ ἔριν

Some see vv. 15–18c as a parenthetical aside that has nothing to do with τοὺς πλείονας τῶν ἀδελφῶν (v. 14) but reflects Paul's experiences with other people in various places over the years. Were this the case, however, Paul would surely have made it more clear (e.g., by introducing the clause not with τινές but with a differentiating word like ἄλλος [Fee 118]; H-M 45; Reumann 202). The groups in vv. 15–17 (τινές . . . τινές) are to be viewed, instead, as two subsets of τοὺς πλείονας τῶν ἀδελφῶν (Fee 118; Hansen 71; H-M 45; O'Brien 98).

Indef. pron. τινές (2x, both subj. of κηρύσσουσιν) is nom. pl. masc.-fem. from τις, τι, here = τις . . . ἕτερος, "someone . . . and another" (BDAG 1008b; R 743; "some . . . others" [EVV]). Paul often uses the indef. pron. to refer to those with whom he is not in agreement (Gal 1:7; 2:12; 2 Cor 2:5; 10:7; 11:21) (Reumann 198). The encl. pron. τις is usually found unaccented, in postpositive position, but here it begins the sentence, likely due to the μὲν-δέ (both postpositive) cstr. (R 235; BDF §301; Moule 125; Reumann 175).

Μὲν-δέ separates two groups ("some" . . . "others" [BDAG 630a]; R 1153) who do the same thing but with different motives (Reumann 175).

Καί appears three times in v. 15. The first καί (τινὲς μὲν καί) parallels not the second καί (καὶ ἔριν, which simply connects the two nouns, "envy and strife" [HCSB]) but, rather, the third καί (τινὲς δὲ καί). The common meaning for coordinate καί ("both . . . and") does not work, however, in this instance. Rather, take the first καί (τινὲς μὲν καί [v. 15a]) adv., with ascensive force, "even" or "indeed" (RSV, NEB, ESV; BDF §442.1; Fee 119 n. 9; "surprise at something unexpected or noteworthy" [H-M 45; cf. 1 Cor 5:2; Heb 3:9]). The coordinate καί (τινὲς δὲ καί [v. 15b]) can be rendered sim. ("others indeed") or be regarded as pleonastic and so omitted (RSV, ESV) (Reumann 176). Some EVV bring out a mildly concessive sense ("It is true that some . . . but others" [NIV, NLT]; "to be sure" [NASB, HCSB]; Silva 63).

Φθόνον is acc. sg. masc. from φθόνος, -ου, ὁ, "envy, jealousy" (BDAG 1054d; "envy" [NRSV, HCSB, ESV]; "jealous(y)" [CEV, NLT]; "malice" [NJB] fairly underscores the neg. connotations of φθόνος for the ancients). The causal sense of διά + acc. shades over into the idea of source (i.e., motive), "out of envy" (BDAG 1054d). A thoroughly Gk. term, the four LXX occurrences of φθόνος have no background in Heb. (Spicq 3.434–35). Aristotle distinguishes φθόνος, "the base passion of base people," from ζῆλος, "the honest passion of honest people" (Aristot. Rhet. 2.11.1,387b–88b). Ζῆλος is a desire to have what another person possesses without necessarily bearing a grudge against him because of it. Φθόνος is concerned more to deprive another of the desired thing than to gain it. It involves sadness when good things happen to others, joy at the evils they experience—thus the opposite of "rejoice with those who rejoice, weep with those who weep" (Rom 12:15).

Envy was a common theme in an honor culture in which males vigorously competed with one another for acclaim in the public arena. Those who excelled became targets of the φθόνος of others: "The envious are those who are annoyed only at their friends' successes" (Xenophon, cited by D. H. Field, NIDNTT 1.557). Jesus was delivered over to Pilate διὰ φθόνον (Matt 27:18). In Roman literature Julius Caesar—notoriously the first Roman figure to accumulate honors of a quasi-imperial nature—became a particular object of φθόνος among his senatorial peers: "Some, in order to please Caesar, heaped honors upon him, while others, in their perfidy, approved and proclaimed these extravagant honors only in order that envy (φθόνος) and suspicion might make Caesar hateful to the Romans" (*Vita Caesaris* by Nicolaus of Damascus [cited by Reumann 178]). Φθόνος often generated divisive factions in the city-state (and in the church), thus the common pairing φθόνος and ἔρις (Reumann 177–78). Φθόνος is one of the "works of the flesh" (Gal 5:21), a feature of life before conversion (Titus 3:3) that is to be put away by those who "grow up to salvation" (1 Pet 2:1–2) (O'Brien 99).

Ἔριν is acc. sg. fem. (Attic form, instead of ἔριδα [R 265]) from ἔρις, -ιδος, ἡ, "engagement in rivalry, esp. w. ref. to positions taken in a matter"; "strife, discord, contention" (BDAG 392c; "rivalry" [NRSV, ESV, NIV]; "strife" [NASB, HCSB]). Like φθόνος, it is a classic Gk. vice (esp. political strife and its causes) which persisted among the early Christians. Ἔριν is always used in NT of "disputes that endanger the church" (H. Giesen, *EDNT* 2.52d; all nine NT examples come from Paul, mostly in vice lists [Rom 1:29; 13:13; 1 Cor 1:11; 3:3; 2 Cor 12:20; Gal 5:20; 1 Tim 6:4; Titus 3:9]). The term also appears nine times in 1 Clement, where envy (φθόνος) and strife (ἔρις) result in replacing church elders with new ones (46.5).

The troubling idea that a group of Christians preaches Christ from impure motives has elicited a multitude of explanations. The preachers cannot be pagan detractors (or non-Christian Jews) pretending to preach Christ since they are a subset of τοὺς πλείονας τῶν ἀδελφῶν (v. 14). Nor is the group to be identified with any others in the epistle. Neither the "dogs, evil workers, who mutilate the flesh" (3:2), nor the intimidating "opponents" of 1:28–30, could be said to "proclaim Christ" in a way that would cause Paul to rejoice (*pace* P. W. Barnett, *DPL* 652). Nor are those criticized in 2:21 viable candidates. Unlike the preachers in 1:15, the coworkers in 2:21 are apparently at Paul's beck and call to send to Philippi; and they are referred to as "all" and not "some" (Reumann 202–03). The remaining options are equally unlikely:

1. preachers with a "divine man" theology;
2. gnostic Christians;
3. Judaizing Christians, like those in Galatians; or
4. zealot Christians preaching revolt against Rome.

Paul would not likely have affirmed the proclamation of any of these ideologies (on all this, see O'Brien 102–5 and Reumann 202–6).

For reasons that must remain unknown ("a desire to undermine Paul's evangelistic reputation" [D. H. Field, *NIDNTT* 1.558]; "personal animosity and rivalry" [H-M 47–48]; "personal rivalry" [O'Brien 105]), Paul was viewed as an intruder whose reputation has attracted the envy of some. Typical of ancient social relations, this envy resulted in a faction that opposed Paul's leadership but affirmed his gospel message. We can only speculate about the origins of the rivalry, which may have been reinforced by his letter to Rome a few years earlier, or, perhaps, by "effective preaching" that "won a bigger following" (Hansen 74). Paul did not feel compelled to explain. His primary concern was to assure his readers of the progress of the gospel.

Paul likely relates information regarding these divisions in Rome in order to caution against "internal unrest" in Philippi (Fee 123; cf. Phil 1:27; 4:2–3). The parallel terms ἐριθεία (1:17) and ἀγάπη (1:16) occur together again in Paul's appeal for unity at the beginning of the next chapter (2:1, 3), suggesting that 1:15–17 is intended to be paradigmatic.

τινὲς δὲ καὶ δι' εὐδοκίαν τὸν Χριστὸν κηρύσσουσιν

The second τινές ("still others" [BDAG 630b]; "others" [NIV, NRSV, HCSB, ESV]) may include persons mentioned in Rom 16, many of whom Paul commends for their faithful service to Christ (Fee 120).

Εὐδοκίαν is acc. sg. fem. from εὐδοκία, -ας, ἡ, "state or condition of being kindly disposed, good will"; with διά = "from good will" (BDAG 404d; most EVV; "whose intentions are good" [NJB], "because they want to help" [CEV], "with pure motives" [NLT]). The word group is almost completely restricted to Jewish and Christian lit. Two options:

1. God's goodwill toward Paul's ministry; or
*2. that of the friendly preachers (toward Paul).

View 1 is favored by: (a) both the LXX (εὐδοκέω [60x]; εὐδοκία [25x]) and the NT (cf. Matt 11:26; Luke 2:14; 10:21; Eph 1:5, 9; and esp. Phil 2:13; but cf. Rom 10:1), where εὐδοκία most often signifies divine favor; (b) the presence of the vb. κεῖμαι (v. 16); and (c) rabbinic parallels. The second group of preachers recognized the divine approval that rested on Paul's ministry and were motivated accordingly (O'Brien 99–101). In the immediate context, however, "envy," "strife," "selfish ambition," and "love" are all relational terms, and in each case Paul is the object. Εὐδοκίαν should therefore be taken as the preachers' "goodwill," directed toward Paul (view 2), as well (G. Schrenk, *TDNT* 2.746; H. Bietenhard, *NIDNTT* 2.81; Fee 120 n. 15; H-M 47; Hansen 72).

The vb. κηρύσσω (3 pl. pres. act. indic.; iterative pres. [Wallace 521]) means "make public declarations, proclaim aloud." The Philippians would have heard proclamations by a herald (κῆρυξ) in a public assembly, marketplace, or theater, announcing the victors at athletic games or, perhaps, relaying honors conferred on a patron or benefactor by the city's magistrates. The word group was also used of religious proclamation by both OT prophets and pagan philosophers (Jonah 1:2; 3:2 [LXX]; Epict. 3.13.12; cf. Jos. *Ant.* 9.214). Cynic preachers, for example, regarded themselves as messengers sent by Zeus (Reumann 175–76), and κῆρυξ in the papyri denotes "proclaimers of the great deeds of the gods" (BDAG 543c). What distinguished Christian preachers from their pagan counterparts was the content of their message: κηρύσσουσιν τὸν Χριστόν (Reumann 198; the "language of mission" [J. Schniewind, *TDNT* 1.71]). Here Χριστὸν κηρύσσουσιν takes up τὸν λόγον λαλεῖν (v. 14) and is virtually equivalent to τὸν Χριστὸν καταγγέλλουσιν (v. 17) (O'Brien 99).

VERSE 16

οἱ μὲν ἐξ ἀγάπης

The art. οἱ functions as a dem. pron. with μέν and δέ (BDAG 686b; "substantival art." [T 36]; Reumann 180). Ἀγάπης is love toward Paul (Fee 120). The prep. phrases (ἐξ ἀγάπης/ἐξ ἐριθείας) are to be taken not with the art. ("some who [act] out of love" . . . "others who [act] out of contention," in which case τὸν Χριστὸν καταγγέλλουσιν would awkwardly function as the whole predicate for οἱ ἐξ ἀγάπης) but, rather, with καταγγέλλουσιν (O'Brien 100; Reumann 180). Verses 15–17 form an ABB'A' chiasm built on antithetic parallelism (R 1200; Fee 118):

(A) τινὲς μὲν καὶ διὰ φθόνον καὶ ἔριν (v. 15)   (B) τινὲς δὲ καὶ δι᾽ εὐδοκίαν (v. 15)
(B') οἱ μὲν ἐξ ἀγάπης (v. 16)   (A') οἱ δὲ ἐξ ἐριθείας (v. 17)

The emphasis lies in the A-A' clauses, that is, with the wrongly motivated preachers (Fee 119).

εἰδότες ὅτι εἰς ἀπολογίαν τοῦ εὐαγγελίου κεῖμαι

Εἰδότες is nom. pl. masc. of the perf. (with pres. force) act. ptc. of οἶδα; adv. ptc. of cause (not reflected in most EVV), giving the underlying reason for their preaching (Reumann 181; O'Brien 101; adv. perf. ptcs. are almost always causal [Wallace 631]; a ὅτι-clause generally follows a vb. of perception [Porter 63–64]). The well-disposed preachers accurately perceive ("knowing" intentionally contrasts with "supposing" [οἰόμενοι, v. 17]) that Paul's imprisonment has to do with the gospel cause, indeed, that God's hand is in Paul's current circumstances (see on κεῖμαι, below) (Reumann 199).

Εἰς + acc. points to purpose or goal of Paul's imprisonment; "an unexpected opportunity for missionary proclamation" (Kellermann, *EDNT* 1.137b); τοῦ εὐαγγελίου is an obj. gen. (Sumney 23).

The vb. κεῖμαι is 1 sg. pres. pass. indic., "be appointed, set, destined" (BDAG 537d; cf. αὐτοὶ γὰρ οἴδατε ὅτι εἰς τοῦτο κείμεθα [1 Thess 3:3]). The vb. serves as a perf. pass. for τίθημι, "be placed, put, appointed" (R 316, 357, 813). Although some see military connotations ("like a soldier posted on duty" [H-M 46]), evidence for such usage is lacking, and the modifier ἀπολογίαν is a rhetorical or legal (not a military) term (Reumann 181). Commentators see God's sovereignty in κεῖμαι ("divinely appointed" [O'Brien 101]; "destined for (by God)" [H. Hübner, *EDNT* 2.280c; F. Büchsel, *TDNT* 3.654; Hansen 73; Silva 64). EVV downplay the idea ("I am/have been put here" [NRSV, NIV, ESV]; "I am here" [CEV]; but cf. "I am/have been appointed" [NLT, NASB, HCSB]).

VERSE 17

οἱ δὲ ἐξ ἐριθείας τὸν Χριστὸν καταγγέλλουσιν, οὐχ ἁγνῶς

Two options for ἐριθείας (gen. sg. fem. from ἐριθεία, -ας, ἡ):

1. "contentiousness, strife" ("partisanship" [RSV]; "rivalry" [HCSB]), tying the term etymologically to ἔρις, "strife, discord"; or,

*2. "selfish ambition" (most EVV; H. Giesen, *EDNT* 2.52b; Moulton Grammar 2:339; "What's in it for me?" [Spicq 2.70]; H-M 47; O'Brien 101; "base self-seeking," or simply "baseness" [F. Büchsel, *TDNT* 2.661]).

Most take view 2: (a) Ἔρις ("strife") and ἐριθεία occur together in vice lists (2 Cor 12:20; Gal 5:20), implying different meanings; (b) Aristotle uses ἐριθεία for "a self-seeking pursuit of political office by unfair means" (sole pre-NT occurrence); and (c) the term seems to mean "selfish ambition" in 2:3 (BDAG 392b–c; NIV, NRSV; the alternative meaning "cannot be excluded" [BDAG 392c]). "Selfish ambition" generally results in "strife" and "rivalry" in the church, so the two meanings ultimately intersect (Fee 121 n. 21; Reumann 182; Silva 66).

Καταγγέλλουσιν is 3 pl. pres. act. indic. from καταγγέλλω (a strengthened form of ἀγγέλλω); τὸν Χριστὸν καταγγέλλουσιν is equivalent to τὸν Χριστὸν κηρύσσουσιν (v. 15) and εὐαγγελίζεσθαι (J. Schniewind, *TDNT* 1.70–72).

The juxtaposition of οὐχ ἁγνῶς with τὸν Χριστὸν καταγγέλλουσιν is "jarring" (Reumann 200; O'Brien 101 n. 20). The adv. ἁγνῶς (only here in NT) comes from the adj. ἁγνός, "pure"; οὐχ ἁγνῶς means "not from pure motives" (BDAG 14a; NASB; Reumann 182; "not sincere(ly)" [most EVV; H. Baltensweiler, *NIDNTT* 3.101]). The term is used in Gk. inscriptions of the "blameless discharge of office" (F. Hauck, *TDNT* 1.122). Some link οὐχ ἁγνῶς to οἰόμενοι, but most take it independently, set off by commas (Reumann 182).

οἰόμενοι θλῖψιν ἐγείρειν τοῖς δεσμοῖς μου

Οἰόμενοι is the nom. pl. masc. pres. mid. ptc. of οἴομαι, "think, suppose, expect" (BDAG 701c), used causally (Reumann 182; Sumney 23). This purposely chosen word (only here in Paul) implies that what they "imagine" fails to happen. In the other two instances (John 21:25 and James 1:7), the suppositions prove to be false (O'Brien 102; cf. n. 21).

The pres. act. inf. ἐγείρειν (from ἐγείρω, "raise up, bring into being") functions as the obj. of οἴομαι, a typical CGk. cstr. (HGk. increasingly prefers a ὅτι-clause [T 137]). With the dir. obj. θλῖψιν, ἐγείρειν means "to cause" (BDAG 271d; CEV, NASB, HCSB; A. Oepke, *TDNT* 2.334).

Θλῖψις, -εως, ἡ (acc. sg. fem., lit. "pressure," fig. "oppression, affliction, tribulation") is frequently associated in the NT with persecution (1 Thess 1:6, 3:3; imprisonment [Acts 20:23; Eph 3:13]), or connected with God's judgment (Rom 2:9), often with eschatological overtones (Mark 13:19, 24). The word group gains added theological significance from the affliction of Israel or the righteous remnant (H. Schlier, *TDNT* 3.142, 144–46). It is difficult to know how much of this Paul intended here, where θλῖψιν may simply mean "trouble," as in papyri (MM 292b; Reumann 183). Θλῖψις can describe either:

*1. outward circumstances (persecution or imprisonment); or

2. mental and spiritual affliction (inner distress and sorrow [2 Cor 2:4; Jas 1:27]; anxiety and fear [2 Cor 7:5]).

View 1 assumes the rival preachers sought to cause harsher treatment for Paul by the Roman authorities (Winter, *Seek the Welfare of the City*, 95). Their hurtful intentions must have had something to do with Paul's incarceration and with the Romans because Paul doesn't say "θλῖψις for me" but, rather, "θλῖψις for my 'bonds' or 'imprisonment'" (Reumann 201). Most, however, prefer view 2 ("inward experience" [BDAG 457d]; "distress" [NASB], "anxiety" [HCSB]; H. Schlier, *TDNT* 3.147; Hansen 74). O'Brien suggests that the intention was to cause emotional anguish by displaying a freedom to preach that Paul now lacked (O'Brien 102). Most EVV allow for either interpretation ("suffering" [NRSV], "trouble" [NIV, CEV]; "afflict [me]" [RSV, ESV]).

Take the dat. τοῖς δεσμοῖς as an ind. obj. (R 538), or, perhaps better, as a dat. of ref. ("with regard to my imprisonment" [Reumann 183]).

VERSE 18A–C

The versification is potentially misleading. The first part of v. 18 (Τί . . . χαίρω) concludes one section of discourse; 18d (Ἀλλὰ καὶ χαρήσομαι) begins a new paragraph that runs through v. 26 (NA²⁸; Reumann 183).

Τί γάρ; πλὴν ὅτι παντὶ τρόπῳ

Τί is the nom. sg. neut. interr. pron. (from τίς, τί; "who?, which?, what?"); γάρ is a conj., generally indicating cause or reason ("for"), used here in an explanatory way (Fee 124 n. 36). Together the elliptical expression τί γάρ constitutes something of an exclamatory question: "What does it matter?" (BDAG 189c, 1,007c; BDF §299[3]; NIV, NRSV, HCSB; Fee 124, n. 36; O'Brien 105–6; "What then?" [RSV, NASB, ESV]). Paul raises it to answer it, a diatribal use of the interr. (Reed 348–49).

Πλήν breaks off the discussion and emphasizes Paul's conclusion (BDAG 826d; R 1187), an idea variously rendered in Eng. ("The important thing is" [NIV]; "all that matters is" [CEV]; "just this" [NRSV]; "just" [HCSB]; "in any case" [BDB §449(2)]; "except that" [H. Hübner, *EDNT* 3.106c]; "simply" [Reumann 183–84]).

Παντὶ τρόπῳ is a "stereotyped" phrase (T 241; Z §60) meaning "in any and every way" (BDAG 1017b); dat. of manner (R 530, cf. 487; BDF §198[4], cf. §160). Most EVV tr. "in every way"; some anticipate the twofold εἴτε προφάσει εἴτε ἀληθείᾳ ("either way" [NLT]; "both ways" [NJB]).

εἴτε προφάσει εἴτε ἀληθείᾳ, Χριστὸς καταγγέλλεται

Εἴτε is εἰ + the enclitic τέ (cf. BDF §446; 454[3]); the εἴτε . . . εἴτε cstr. can be either disjunctive, as here, or copulative (T 333). The two ways correspond to the two groups in vv. 15–17: they preach "either" in one way "or" in another (Reumann 184).

Both nouns are dat. sg. fem. (dat. of manner [R 530; Wallace 162]). With προφάσει (from πρόφασις, -εως, ἡ), Paul draws, once again, not from the LXX but from the thesaurus of CGk. and HGk. (common in the papyri [MM 555a]). The cognate vb. προφαίνω means "show forth, declare"; the noun πρόφασις denotes a "falsely alleged motive, pretext, ostensible reason, excuse," here "with false motives" ("in reality they have other interests") (BDAG 889c; NIV, NRSV, HCSB; "pretense" [RSV, NASB, ESV]; "under pretext" [Reumann 184]). Elsewhere Paul rejects the notion that his ministry was carried out "with a pretext for satisfying greed" (ἐν προφάσει πλεονεξίας [1 Thess 2:5]) (O'Brien 106).

Ἀλήθεια elsewhere means "truth" in opposition to falsehood (esp. as a designation for the gospel [cf. Gal 2:5, 14; 5:7]). Some find this meaning here ("a preaching . . . concerned only with the truth" [O'Brien 106]), but the content of the preaching is not at issue in vv. 15–17. Here ἀλήθεια is used of the preachers' motives, in the sense "reality . . . as opposed to mere appearance" (BDAG 42d; "true [motives]" [NIV, NJB, NRSV, HCSB]; "honestly," "with sincerity," "in reality" [Reumann 184]; R. Bultmann, *TDNT* 1.243).

The words Χριστὸς καταγγέλλεται are of "cardinal importance" in vv. 12–18a (O'Brien 91 n. 17). A sampling of EVV reveals the virtual synonymity of κηρύσσω and καταγγέλλω in the paragraph (J. Schniewind, *TDNT* 1.71; Fee, 120 n. 20; "rhetorical variation" [Reumann 181]):

	κηρύσσουσιν (v. 15)	καταγγέλλουσιν (v. 17)	καταγγέλλεται (v. 18)
RSV, HCSB, ESV	"preach"	"proclaim"	"proclaimed"
NIV, NLT	"preach"	"preach"	"preached"
NJB	"preaching"	"proclaiming"	"proclaimed"
NRSV	"proclaim"	"proclaim"	"proclaimed"

καὶ ἐν τούτῳ χαίρω

The conj. καί may have a stronger sense than "and" (KJV, NRSV) here (Reumann 185; perhaps "and so," to explain or comment on what has gone before [BDAG 495c; BDF §442(2)]; or to introduce something "surprising or unexpected or noteworthy" [BDAG 495b]).

Τούτῳ is dat. sg. neut. from οὗτος, referring back to Χριστὸς καταγγέλλεται (BDAG 741a; R 703; O'Brien 106). Ἐν + dat. with χαίρω can mean "rejoice over" ("over that" [I rejoice] [BDAG 1075a]; Reumann 185).

It is true that "the power of the gospel does not depend on the character of the preacher" (H-M 48). However, it is not the manner but, rather, the fact of the preaching that Paul affirms. The vocabulary Paul draws upon to describe these preachers is starkly negative—words frequently found in lists of vices that "always adversely affect, even endanger, the life of the church" (Rom 1:29; 2 Cor 12:20; Gal 5:20–21; 1 Tim 6:4) (H-M 48; the language "of *indictment*" [Fee 121 n. 22, author's italics]; G. Friedrich, *TDNT* 3.710).

FOR FURTHER STUDY

11. Christians as "Brothers" (1:12)

Bartchy, S. S. "Undermining Ancient Patriarchy: The Apostle Paul's Vision of a Society of Siblings." *BTB* 29 (1999): 68–78.

Hellerman, Joseph H. "Brothers and Friends in Philippi: Family Honor in the Roman World and in Paul's Letter to the Philippians." *BTB* 39 (2009): 15–25.

*_____. *The Ancient Church as Family*. Minneapolis: Fortress, 2001.

_____. *When the Church Was a Family*. Nashville: B&H, 2009.

Sanders, Karl O. "Equality Within Patriarchal Structures: Some New Testament Perspectives on the Christian Fellowship as Brother or Sisterhood and a Family." Pages 150–65 in *Constructing Early Christian Families*. Edited by H. Moxnes. London: Routledge, 1997.

12. Literary Structure (1:12)

*Mullins, Terence Y. "Disclosure: A Literary Form in the New Testament." *NovT* 7 (1964): 44–59.

Russell, Ronald. "Pauline Letter Structure in Philippians." *JETS* 25 (1982) 295–306.

13. Roman Imprisonment (1:12–18a)

Kittel, G. *TDNT* 1.195–97; 2.43.

Netzer, Ehud. "A New Reconstruction of Paul's Prison." *Biblical Archaeology Review* 35 (2009): 44–51, 71.

*Rapske, Brian. *The Book of Acts and Paul in Roman Custody*. Grand Rapids: Eerdmans, 1994.

_____. "The Importance of Helpers to the Imprisoned Paul in the Book of Acts." *Tyndale Bulletin* 42 (1991): 3–30.

Reid, D. G. *DPL* 752–54.

Rochman, Bonnie. "Imperial Slammer Identified: Caesarea Complex May Have Been Paul's Prison." *Biblical Archaeology Review* 24 (1998): 18.

Staudinger, F. *EDNT* 1.288–90.

Wansink, Craig S. *Chained in Christ: The Experience and Rhetoric of Paul's Imprisonments*. JSNTSup 130. Sheffield: Sheffield Academic Press, 1996.

14. Praetorian Guard (1:13)

Keppie, L. *ABD* 5.446–47.

15. Strife and Factionalism (1:15–17)

Marshall, Peter. *Enmity in Corinth: Social Conventions in Paul's Relations with the Corinthians*. WUNT 2.23. Tübingen: Mohr-Siebeck, 1987.

Walcot, Peter. *Envy and the Greeks: A Study of Human Behavior*. Warminster, England: Aris & Phillips Ltd., 1978.

16. The Identity of the Wrongly Motivated Preachers (1:15a, 17)

*Barnett, P. W. *DPL* 644–53.

Collange, Jean-François. *The Epistle of Saint Paul to the Philippians*. Translated by A. W. Heathcote. London, 1979. See pages 9–10, 51.

Jewett, Robert. "Conflicting Movements in the Early Church as Reflected in Philippians." *NovT* 12 (1970): 362–90.

Mearns, Chris. "The Identity of Paul's Opponents at Philippi." *NTS* 33 (1987): 194–204.

Sandes, Karl O. *Belly and Body in the Pauline Epistles*. SNTSMS 120. Cambridge: Cambridge University Press, 2002.

Sumney, Jerry. *Identifying Paul's Opponents*. Sheffield: JSOT, 1990.

HOMILETICAL SUGGESTIONS

The Gospel Advances (1:12–18c)

1. In the face of challenges from without: adverse circumstances (vv. 12–14).
2. In the face of challenges from within: jealousy and factionalism (vv. 15–18c).

Paul Finds Meaning in the Midst of Suffering (1:12–14)

1. Because he is committed to the advance of the gospel (God's purpose).
2. Because he sees God using his suffering to advance the gospel (God's providence).

The Fruit of Paul's First Roman Imprisonment (1:12–14)

1. Hundreds hear about Christ (v. 13).
2. Thousands hear about Christ (v. 14).
3. Millions read about Christ (Ephesians, Philippians, Colossians, Philemon).

Motives of Every Kind (1:15–18c)

1. Preachers with bad motives (jealousy, strife, selfish ambition) seek occasion to harm others who are gifted (vv. 15a, 17).
2. Preachers with good motives (goodwill, love) encourage others who are gifted because they see God at work (vv. 15b–16).
3. Preachers like Paul simply preach the gospel and rejoice when others—whatever their gifting or motives—preach Christ.

B. PAUL'S FUTURE EXPECTATIONS (1:18D–26)

18d Ἀλλὰ καὶ χαρήσομαι

19 οἶδα γὰρ ὅτι τοῦτό μοι ἀποβήσεται εἰς σωτηρίαν
        διὰ τῆς ὑμῶν δεήσεως
        καὶ ἐπιχορηγίας τοῦ πνεύματος Ἰησοῦ Χριστοῦ
20 κατὰ τὴν ἀποκαραδοκίαν
        καὶ ἐλπίδα μου,
        ὅτι ἐν οὐδενὶ αἰσχυνθήσομαι
        ἀλλ' ἐν πάσῃ παρρησίᾳ
            ὡς πάντοτε καὶ νῦν
            μεγαλυνθήσεται Χριστὸς
                ἐν τῷ σώματί μου
                εἴτε διὰ ζωῆς
                εἴτε διὰ θανάτου.

21 Ἐμοὶ γὰρ τὸ ζῆν Χριστὸς
        καὶ τὸ ἀποθανεῖν κέρδος.
22 εἰ δὲ τὸ ζῆν ἐν σαρκί,

        τοῦτό μοι καρπὸς ἔργου
        καὶ τί αἱρήσομαι οὐ γνωρίζω.
23 συνέχομαι δὲ ἐκ τῶν δύο
        τὴν ἐπιθυμίαν ἔχων εἰς τὸ ἀναλῦσαι
            καὶ σὺν Χριστῷ εἶναι
        πολλῷ [γὰρ] μᾶλλον κρεῖσσον·
24 τὸ δὲ ἐπιμένειν [ἐν] τῇ σαρκὶ ἀναγκαιότερον δι' ὑμᾶς.
25 καὶ τοῦτο πεποιθὼς
    οἶδα ὅτι μενῶ καὶ παραμενῶ πᾶσιν ὑμῖν
        εἰς τὴν ὑμῶν προκοπὴν
        καὶ χαρὰν τῆς πίστεως,
26   ἵνα τὸ καύχημα ὑμῶν περισσεύῃ
            ἐν Χριστῷ Ἰησοῦ
            ἐν ἐμοὶ
            διὰ τῆς ἐμῆς παρουσίας πάλιν
            πρὸς ὑμᾶς.

V. 18d begins a new paragraph (NA[28]; NRSV, HCSB, ESV; Reumann 209; but see RSV), transitioning from the progress of the gospel (vv. 12–18c) to Paul's own future (18d–26; cf. fut. vbs. χαρήσομαι [v. 18]; ἀποβήσεται [v. 19]; αἰσχυνθήσομαι and μεγαλυνθήσεται [v. 20]). Yet Christ (τοῦ πνεύματος Ἰησοῦ Χριστοῦ [v. 19]; μεγαλυνθήσεται Χριστός [v. 20]; τὸ ζῆν Χριστός [v. 21]; σὺν Χριστῷ εἶναι [v. 23]; ἐν Χριστῷ Ἰησοῦ [v. 26]) and the gospel (καρπὸς ἔργου [v. 22]; τὴν ὑμῶν προκοπὴν καὶ χαρὰν τῆς πίστεως [v. 25]) remain at the forefront (note the contrast between life and death and the continuing emphasis on Christ indicated by dotted underline above). The passage unfolds as follows:

1:18d–20—Paul voices his confidence that Christ will be magnified when he appears before the Roman tribunal. All the while, Paul is sure that he will be released. Nevertheless, the prospect of a trial that wields the power to determine one's earthly destiny compels Paul to include the phrase εἴτε διὰ ζωῆς εἴτε διὰ θανάτου, at the end of v. 20.

1:21–24—The inclusion of εἴτε διὰ ζωῆς εἴτε διὰ θανάτου, in turn, leads Paul to reflect on these two options, in a deeply personal "aside" (a soliloquy framed as a συγκρίσις). Verses 21–24, then, reveal Paul's personal outlook, conveyed as if the choice were actually his to make.

1:25–26—Paul now departs from his soliloquy (as indicated by the end of the συγκρίσις, and the fut. tense vbs.) to return to the actual expected outcome of his circumstances, namely, his imminent release, and the benefit of that outcome for the Philippians and for the gospel.

VERSE 18D

Ἀλλὰ καὶ χαρήσομαι

Χαρήσομαι is 1 sg. fut. mid. indic. of χαίρω (doubled, as at 2:17–18 and 4:4). The context suggests a durative ("I will continue to rejoice" [NIV, NJB, NRSV]), rather than punctiliar, sense (Moule 10; R 871; Reumann 209).

Ἀλλά with καί not adversative but "used to introduce an additional point in an emphatic way" (BDF §448; T 300; "Yes, and . . ." [most EVV]). Ἀλλά moves the focus from the advance of the gospel to the outcome of Paul's imprisonment, while καί underscores the continuation of his joyful attitude (Hansen 77).

VERSE 19

οἶδα γὰρ ὅτι τοῦτό μοι ἀποβήσεται εἰς σωτηρίαν

A γάρ-clause gives the ground for Paul's rejoicing: whatever happens at Caesar's tribunal, Paul will be vindicated by God in the heavenly court ("for" [most EVV]; "because" [HCSB; O'Brien 108]). The ὅτι of indir. discourse (on the Job verse apparently cited, see below) provides the content of what is known (Reumann 210).

Οἶδα (1 sg. perf. act. ind.) is the first of several noetic verbs in the passage (αἱρήσομαι . . . γνωρίζω [v. 22]; συνέχομαι [v. 23]; πεποιθὼς οἶδα [v. 25]). Distinctions traditionally proposed between οἶδα ("knowledge based on observation, complete and final") and γινώσκω ("knowledge incomplete and developing") (cf. A. Horstmann *EDNT* 2.494b) do not hold up. Paul prefers εἰδέναι to γινώσκειν but uses the verbs synonymously (H-M 48–49; Reumann 210).

Τοῦτό μοι ἀποβήσεται εἰς σωτηρίαν reproduces Job 13:16a LXX verbatim, where Job responds to his friends who chastised him. "Paul understood and interpreted his situation in terms of Job's experience" (H-M 49; Fee 130–31). Yet the citation cannot be pressed in every detail since what follows (αἰσχυνθήσομαι and μεγαλυνθήσεται v. [20]) points more generally to the plight of the "poor man" in the OT, who in his distress looks to God for vindication (Fee 130–31; O'Brien 108–9). The Job reference lacks a citation formula, so it is unlikely that the Philippians would have recognized it as Scripture (Reumann 233, 243).

Τοῦτο (nom. sg. neut.; subj. of ἀποβήσεται) refers back not to ἐν τούτῳ in v. 18 (i.e., to the preaching of the gospel, whatever the motives) but, rather, to Paul's current situation (τὰ κατ' ἐμέ [v. 12]), particularly the outcome of his trial (H-M 49; O'Brien 109; Reumann 210).

The pron. μοι (dat. sg. masc.) is a dat. of advantage, though often translated with σωτηρίαν as poss. ("to/for my deliverance" [most EVV]; Reumann 210).

Ἀποβήσεται is 3 sg. fut. mid. indic. of ἀποβαίνω, used fig., "to result in a state or condition," here "turn out to" (most EVV; BDAG 107c; O'Brien 109; "lead to" [HCSB]); εἰς + acc. = "with a view to, resulting in" (Moule 70; Reumann 210).

The meaning of σωτηρίαν is highly debated:

1. Eschatological salvation (BDAG 986b; J. Schneider, *NIDNTT* 3.214; W. Foerster, *TDNT* 7.993; O'Brien 110; Silva 70–71; "save me" [NJB]).
   a. This is the normal meaning of σωτηρία in Paul.
   b. This is the sense of σωτηρία in 1:28 and in 2:12.
   c. Paul focuses later in the letter on the ultimate vindication of Christ (2:9–11) and believers (3:20–21).
   d. This view gives full force (in a way view 2 does not) to the sweeping expression εἴτε διὰ ζωῆς εἴτε διὰ θανάτου (v. 20), which leaves open the possibility of Paul's execution. Attempts to overcome this objection by finding in εἴτε διὰ ζωῆς εἴτε διὰ θανάτου nothing more than an emphatic, stock expression that means "total" or "all-encompassing" (H-M 54; cf. Rom 8:38; 1 Cor 3:22; 2 Sam 15:21; Sir 11:14; 37:18 [LXX]) cannot account for the specific elaboration on life and death that follows in vv. 21–23 (Hansen 78; Sumney 27).
   e. In Job 13:16, which Paul is citing, Job's eternal destiny is in view (Silva 70). However, it is the context of Philippians 1, not that of Job, that should determine usage here (Reed 213).
   f. The expression κατὰ τὴν ἀποκαραδοκίαν καὶ ἐλπίδα μου is "(soteriologically) charged" and would hardly be used of release from prison (Silva 70–71; cf. Rom 8:19, 22).
2. Release from prison as the outcome of Paul's trial (Reumann 210; Winter, *Seek the Welfare of the City*, 96; "will keep me safe" [CEV]; implied by "deliverance" [NIV, HCSB, ESV]; K. Schelkle argues for both deliverance from prison and eschatological salvation [*EDNT* 3.328a]).

a. The meaning "deliverance" is attested in the NT (unambiguously in Acts 27:34 [in a speech by Paul]; Heb 11:7; possibly also in 2 Cor 1:6, where σωτηρίας coupled with παρακλήσεως could be taken to refer to the general welfare or profit of the Corinthians).

b. Σωτηρία commonly signifies "health" or "well-being" in the papyri (MM 622a). In epistolary contexts like this, σωτηρία almost always refers to the health or well-being of the author or recipients, and the same is true in Gk. inscriptions (Reed 213).

c. In the immediate context the Philippians' prayers are best understood not in reference to Paul's eschatological salvation but to deliverance from present straits.

d. In vv. 25–26, Paul expresses confidence that he will return to Philippi (also using οἶδα).

*3. The specific outcome described in v. 20, namely, that Paul will speak with such boldness before the Roman tribunal that Christ will be exalted, i.e., "a salvation of the Spirit of Christ in the present, an empowering to be a bold witness for Christ his Lord" (Hansen 80–81; Sumney 26; cf. Fee 131–32).

a. This is how Paul himself defines σωτηρίαν in the ensuing context.

b. This interpretation best accounts for the fact that the σωτηρία in view in v. 19 occurs (a) in the present (νῦν), (b) in his body (ἐν τῷ σώματί μου), and (c) whatever the outcome of the trial (εἴτε διὰ ζωῆς εἴτε διὰ θανάτου).

c. This does a better job than view 1 of accounting for the Philippians' prayers for this σωτηρία.

One hesitates to depart from Paul's normal use of σωτηρία (view 1), but the ensuing context seems to constrain the meaning to Paul's bold (ἐν πάσῃ παρρησίᾳ) and effective (μεγαλυνθήσεται Χριστός) witness before the Roman tribunal (view 3).

View 2 remains on the horizon, as well. Because the word meant "well-being" in virtually all ancient letters, the Philippians would have initially heard in σωτηρίαν "deliverance" from prison—an interpretation that might have encouraged them to anticipate relief from similar mistreatment at the hands of the pagan colonists at Philippi (1:28–30). Paul, well aware of this epistolary convention, problematized the interpretation by adding the phrase εἴτε διὰ ζωῆς εἴτε διὰ θανάτου, in order to "redirect the implied epistolary reader's MENTAL SCRIPT in a way that challenges their need for deliverance from physical suffering . . . what more striking way to do this than to manipulate conventions of language probably familiar to the reader" (Reed 215, author's emphasis).

διὰ τῆς ὑμῶν δεήσεως καὶ ἐπιχορηγίας τοῦ πνεύματος Ἰησοῦ Χριστοῦ

Δία + gen. means "by, via, through" (BDAG 224c), indicating "*how* Paul expects God to bring all this about" (Fee 132).

The single art. (τῆς) ties δεήσεως and ἐπιχορηγίας together, showing "how closely human prayers and God's provision are related" (Hansen 79; "the supply of the Spirit is the answer to his friends' prayer" [O'Brien 110]; R 787; Z §184). The poss. pron.

ὑμῶν (subj. gen. or gen. of source) stands between the art. and noun further to empha-size the Philippians' role in Paul's experiencing a fresh supply of the Spirit (Fee 132 n. 26; O'Brien 111). Δεήσεως (gen. sg. fem.) is a distributive sg. (Fee 132 n. 26, n. 27; "prayers" [most EVV]). Paul knew that God effected changes in history through prayer, so he often requests his churches to intercede for him in his gospel ministry (H-M 50; Rom 15:30–32; 2 Cor 1:11; Eph 6:19; Col 4:3; 1 Thess 5:25; 2 Thess 3:1–2; Phlm 22). The Philippians' prayers for Paul are part of "a mutual, reciprocal relationship" (cf. δέησις [1:4]) (Reumann 243).

Ἐπιχορηγίας is gen. sg. fem. from ἐπιχορηγία, -ας, ἡ, "assistance, support" (BDAG 387b; "provision" [NASB, NIV] is better than "help" [NRSV, HCSB; R. Mahoney, EDNT 2.45d]; Fee 133 n. 30). The term was used (a) in inscriptions, for "provision" out of temple proceeds for repair and fortification (BDAG 387b), (b) in marriage con-tracts, for "provision" for a spouse, (c) in medical contexts, to denote a "supporting" ligament (Eph 4:16), and (d) in Athenian drama festivals, to signify the "furnishing of the chorus" (O'Brien 111). The compound form (ἐπιχορηγία) may indicate a full or generous supply, but rare usage makes this hard to determine; in any case "all known uses do suggest 'full' or 'adequate' supply" (Fee 132 n. 28).

BDAG defines πνεῦμα (gen. sg. neut.) as "that which differentiates God fr. every-thing that is not God, as the divine power that produces all divine existence, as the divine element in which all divine life is carried on, as the bearer of every application of the divine will. All those who belong to God possess or receive this spirit and hence have a share in God's life" (BDAG 834b). The gen. τοῦ πνεύματος has been taken in two ways:

1. Subj. gen., the Spirit as supplier of the needed help or assistance ("from the Spirit" [CEV, HCSB; cf. NLT]; "by the Spirit" [E. Schweizer, *TDNT* 6.440 n. 650]; H-M 50; O'Brien 111–12). Jesus promises that the Spirit will assist believers who bear witness before their accusers and judges (Mark 13:11; Matt 10:20; Luke 12:12).

*2. Obj. gen., "I am provided with the Spirit" (Fee 133; Hansen 79; Silva 76).
   a. The verbal noun ἐπιχορηγία, like its cognate vb. (cf. the striking parallel ὁ οὖν ἐπιχορηγῶν ὑμῖν τὸ πνεῦμα [Gal 3:5]), is transitive in nature and expects an object in terms of what is supplied (Fee 133).
   b. In Luke 11:13, prayer is connected with the giving of the Spirit.

The second view is better. One might object that Christians, who already possess the Spirit, cannot be supplied with the Spirit, but this is a theological assumption that is out of touch with Paul, who can conceive of believers being "given" (1 Thess 4:8) or "supplied with" (Gal 3:5) the Spirit (Fee 134 n. 34).

Although τοῦ πνεύματος Ἰησοῦ Χριστοῦ is just another name for the Holy Spirit, the qualifier is hardly inconsequential. Πνεῦμα is modified by Ἰησοῦ Χριστοῦ only here in Paul (cf. Gal 4:6; Rom 8:9). The centrality of Christ in Philippians explains the unusual title (Fee 134–35). Ἰησοῦ Χριστοῦ is probably neither gen. of poss. nor source (*pace* BDAG 834c; O'Brien 111–12) since God the Father, not Christ, usually gives the Spirit in Paul (1 Cor 6:19; 2 Cor 1:21–22; 5:5; Eph 1:17; Gal 3:5; 1 Thess 4:8). Take the qualifier, instead, as a gen. of appos. (Reumann 212), not in a modalistic sense that blurs distinctions among the persons of the Godhead but, rather, as reflecting the Pauline notion that Christ is resident in the believer by the Spirit (O. Betz, *NIDNTT* 3.605; C. Brown, *NIDNTT* 3.703; Fee 135; Hansen 80; Reumann 212, 245).

VERSE 20

κατὰ τὴν ἀποκαραδοκίαν καὶ ἐλπίδα μου

Κατά (+ acc. = "in accordance with" [BDAG 512c]) introduces a second prep. phrase (par. with διὰ τῆς ὑμῶν δεήσεως κτλ.) modifying τοῦτό μοι ἀποβήσεται εἰς σωτηρίαν (O'Brien 112).

Ἀποκαραδοκία, -ας, ἡ (here acc. sg. fem.) is a colorful term. Preoccupation with questionable etym. ("to watch" [δοκεῖν] with "the head" [κάρα] "turned away from" [ἀπό] other interests, therefore, "outstretched" [H-M 51]) has given way to debate about whether a nuance of uncertainly or doubt is present in the term. Usage elsewhere (e.g., "await the hail of arrows" in battle [Jos. *J.W.* 3.264]) suggests a degree of anxious anticipation that is absent from the coordinated term ἐλπίδα (E. Hoffmann, *NIDNTT* 2.444–45). Two considerations argue against such a meaning here:

1. Ἀποκαραδοκίαν and ἐλπίδα are governed by a single article ("treated as one for the purpose at hand" [R 787]; "hendiadys" [H-M 51]). Ἐλπίδα thus "draws ἀποκαραδοκίαν into a more optimistic orbit" (Reumann 245; "hope-filled expectation" [Fee 135]).
2. Paul's only other usage (Rom 8:19, also with ἐλπίς [v. 20]) lacks negative connotations (Fee 135 n. 42).

Ἀποκαραδοκίαν and ἐλπίδα emphasize Paul's certainty that "the future is essentially guaranteed" (Hansen 80; H. Balz, *NIDNTT* 1.132). Thus, tr. ἀποκαραδοκίαν as "eager expectation" (NRSV, HCSB, ESV; BDAG 112c; "fully expect" [NLT]; "unreserved waiting" [G. Delling, *TDNT* 1.393]).

Ἐλπίδα is acc. sg. fem. from ἐλπίς, -ίδος, ἡ. BDAG places this occurrence under the activity of hoping (cf. R. Bultmann, *TDNT* 2.531, "sure confidence"), rather than the content of hope, "that for which one hopes" (BDAG 320c). If the ὅτι-clause that follows modifies τὴν ἀποκαραδοκίαν καὶ ἐλπίδα μου (see below), however, the latter view is preferred. Key elements of NT hope include (a) expectation of the future, (b) trust in God, and (c) patience in waiting (R. Bultmann, *TDNT* 2.521–23; J. M. Everts, *DPL* 415). "Boldness" (παρρησία [1:20]) and "boasting" (καύχημα [1:26]) are grounded in hope; hope itself is effected by the Spirit (cf. 1:19) (Reumann 213).

ὅτι ἐν οὐδενὶ αἰσχυνθήσομαι

Some connect the ὅτι-clause with οἶδα (v. 19), in par. to ὅτι τοῦτό μοι ἀποβήσεται, κτλ. (H-M 52; Reumann 213). Favoring this interpretation are the following considerations:

a. Ἐλπίς is often used without an object when it refers to Christian hope (e.g., Rom 5:5; 8:24; 1 Cor 13:13; 2 Cor 3:12; Col 1:5). When ἐλπίς does have an object, the object is almost always in the gen. case (e.g., Acts 16:19; Rom 5:2; 2 Cor 10:15; Gal 5:5; Col 1:27), even when the object is in verbal form (1 Cor 9:10). Ἐλπίς followed by ὅτι, to express the object of hope, occurs only once in the NT (Rom 8:20–21).

b. The notions expressed in ἐν οὐδενὶ αἰσχυνθήσομαι and the parallel μεγαλυνθήσεται Χριστός "so partake of the nature of certainty for the apostle" that οἶδα is a more appropriate term to govern these ideas than ἐλπίς (H-M 52).

For this to work, however, we would expect καί before the second ὅτι (Fee 129 n. 10; O'Brien 113 n. 35; cf. 1 Cor 8:4). The ὅτι-clause in v. 20 is better read as providing the content of τὴν ἀποκαραδοκίαν καὶ ἐλπίδα μου, by means of two antithetic parallel clauses: (1) ἐν οὐδενὶ αἰσχυνθήσομαι and (2) μεγαλυνθήσεται Χριστός (EVV; Fee 135; O'Brien 113; cf. 2 Cor 10:15, where the verb μεγαλυνθῆναι sim. provides the content of ἐλπίδα).

Ἐν with dat. sg. neut. οὐδενί (lit. "in nothing"; "not . . . in/about anything" [NASB, HCSB]) denotes "manner" (BDAG 33a; "not . . . in any way" [NRSV]). Some EVV loosely translate the cstr. as "never" (NJB, CEV).

Αἰσχυνθήσομαι is 1 sg. fut. pass. indic. from αἰσχύνω, "be put to shame, disgraced" (BDAG 30b). "Be ashamed" (most EVV; A. Horstmann, *NIDNTT* 1.42; "feeling shame" [R. Bultmann, *TDNT* 1.190]) is "altogether too Western" (Fee 136). The shame in view is public and social, not private and psychological ("being shamed" [Pilch and Malina, *Biblical Social Values and Their Meaning*, 180]; "put to shame" [NRSV, NASB]). In the Psalms and Prophets, as well as in the DSS, the αἰσχύνω word group describes "the humble pious" who trust in God not to let them be disgraced or brought by him into judgment, and thus be put to shame before their enemies (H-M 52; R. Bultmann, *TDNT* 1.189–90; cf. LXX [Pss 24:3; 34:26–27; 39:15–17; Isa 1:29; 45:17; 49:23]; 1QH IV, 23–24; V, 35; 1QS IV, 23).

The agent doing the shaming is left unexpressed in 1:20. Does Paul have in view the tribunal of Caesar or the tribunal of God? The honor culture of Mediterranean antiquity—where trials were as much about the honor of the defendant as the legality of his behavior—might suggest the former. In this case, however, Paul's confidence (τὴν ἀποκαραδοκίαν καὶ ἐλπίδα μου) could be hopelessly misplaced. For, from a Roman perspective, Paul will be publicly shamed if convicted of a capital crime and executed (cf. διὰ θανάτου [v. 20]). The ultimate agent of αἰσχυνθήσομαι, then, must be God, before whom Paul can be confident of vindication, whatever happens at Caesar's tribunal. By employing αἰσχύνω in this manner, Paul essentially redefines for the Philippians their widely held cultural values regarding honor and shame. For the shame Paul has in view is ultimately unrelated to public opinion. It has to do, instead, with his standing before God. Like Jesus, Paul may well experience public humiliation and shame from a Roman perspective (Hellerman 129–47). But by magnifying Christ—in life or death—Paul, like Jesus (2:9–11), will ultimately be vindicated and thus experience no shame whatsoever (ἐν οὐδενὶ αἰσχυνθήσομαι) according to the standards of God's radically alternative social economy.

ἀλλ᾽ ἐν πάσῃ παρρησίᾳ

Ἀλλ᾽ introduces a new clause, antithetically par. to ἐν οὐδενὶ αἰσχυνθήσομαι (Reumann 213); ἐν + dat. signifies manner; πάσῃ used in an elative (not distributive) sense, "all," "in the highest degree" ("full," "supreme," "total" [B. Reicke, *TDNT* 5.888]). The first of five phrases that qualify μεγαλυνθήσεται Χριστός: (1) ἐν πάσῃ παρρησίᾳ; (2) ὡς πάντοτε καὶ νῦν; (3) καὶ νῦν; (4) ἐν τῷ σώματί μου; (5) εἴτε διὰ ζωῆς εἴτε διὰ θανάτου (Reumann 246).

Παρρησίᾳ (dat. sg. fem., from παρρησία, -ας, ἡ) is difficult to render in English. Etym., πᾶν ("all") + ῥῆσις ("speech, word") = something like "(freedom) to say all." Such freedom encountered opposition at times, thus the further meaning "fearlessness, frankness" (H.-C. Hahn, *NIDNTT* 2.734). In v. 20 παρρησία is understood in two ways:

1. Subjectively, in terms of Paul's outlook, thus most EVV ("courage" [RSV, NIV, ESV]; "brave" [CEV]; cf. BDAG 781d).
*2. Objectively, as "outspokenness, frankness, and boldness of speech, especially in the presence of a person of high rank" (Hansen 80; "speaking with all boldness" [NRSV]; "openness to the public," "before whom speaking and actions take place" [BDAG 781c]; H. Balz, *EDNT* 3.46d; H. Schlier, *TDNT* 5.883; Fee 137 n. 57; "telling it like it is" [Osiek 43]).
   a. Παρρησία was prominent in the Greek political sphere for free and open speech by freeborn, male citizens, and among friends (Plut. *Adulator* 51C). The idea later became associated with the outspoken brazenness of popular Cynic philosophers, who defied the social conventions of elite society (Reumann 214).
   b. Ἐν πάσῃ παρρησίᾳ (a) modifies μεγαλυνθήσεται Χριστὸς ἐν τῷ σώματί μου and (b) contrasts with αἰσχυνθήσομαι (see above), both of which suggest that Paul has primarily in view "frankness of speech" at his public trial, not an inner virtue such as "fearlessness" or "courage."

Although a subjective element may be present secondarily (H-M 53; Reumann 246), the second view is clearly superior. V. 19 suggests that the πνεῦμα Ἰησοῦ Χριστοῦ effects this παρρησία.

ὡς πάντοτε καὶ νῦν

With ὡς, καί functions adv. as a comp. (BDAG 496a; "so," "so also"; "now as always" [EVV]). Note the alliteration, ἐν πάσῃ παρρησίᾳ ὡς πάντοτε (Reumann 215). The magnification of Christ has "always" (πάντοτε) been central to Paul's missionary efforts (Acts 9:20; 1 Cor 2:2) (Reumann 246).

μεγαλυνθήσεται Χριστός

Μεγαλυνθήσεται is 3 sg. fut. pass. indic. from μεγαλύνω (cf. μέγας, "great"), "exalt, glorify, magnify, speak highly of," here "the prestige of Christ will be advanced in connection with me" (BDAG 623b; "honored" [RSV; HCSB; ESV]; "exalted" [NIV, NRSV]; pass. "be glorified" [O. Betz, *EDNT* 2.399a]). The vb. is used often in the Psalms, of the Lord being "magnified" (e.g., LXX Pss 33:4; 34:26–27 [w/ αἰσχύνω]; 39:15–17 [w/ αἰσχύνω]; 56:11). Instead of retaining the 1 pers. (cf. αἰσχυνθήσομαι) with an act. form of μεγαλύνω, Paul changes to a 3 pers. pass. cstr. The change may be due to (a) rhetorical considerations (pairing one passive with another), or, perhaps, (b) the fact that the two vbs. in their pass. forms are coupled together in the Psalms (cf. LXX Ps 34:26–27). It may be the case, however, that (c) Paul cannot bring himself to write "*I* will magnify Christ," and thereby give undue prominence to himself. Christ becomes the subj. (requiring 3 pers.) since Paul is but an instrument to magnify Christ's greatness (the pass. voice implies the activity of God [H-M 53; O'Brien 115]). Both (a) the context (προκοπὴν τοῦ εὐαγγελίου [v. 12]; Χριστὸς καταγγέλλεται [v. 18]) and (b) the sole occurrence of μεγαλύνω elsewhere in Paul (2 Cor 10:15, of the expansion of Paul's mission) show that what is primarily in view in μεγαλυνθήσεται Χριστός is the spread of the gospel via Paul's testimony at the trial (H-M 53; Reumann 215).

ἐν τῷ σώματί μου

The prep. ἐν can be taken as instr., "through" (W. Grundmann, *TDNT* 4.543; cf. BDAG 328c) or, possibly, locat., the object in which something shows itself (cf. BDAG 329b; Reumann 215).

Σώματί (dat. sg. neut. from σῶμα, -ατος, τό) denotes "the living (physical) body," "the instrument of human experience and suffering" (BDAG 983d). The idea that σῶμα in Paul functions as an anthropological term, "person" or "life" (like ψυχή) (NEB, NLT; J. Stafford Wright, *NIDNTT* 2.566; E. Schweizer, *TDNT* 7.1,065–66; H-M 52), is no longer tenable (Fee 137 n. 57 cites R. H. Gundry, ΣΩΜΑ *in Biblical Theology with an Emphasis on Pauline Anthropology* [Cambridge: Cambridge University Press, 1976]; Silva 77). Paul is simply referring to what will happen to him physically, that is, whether his trial will result in physical life or death, as indicated by ἐν [τῇ] σαρκί in vv. 22 and 24 (Fee 137–38).

εἴτε διὰ ζωῆς εἴτε διὰ θανάτου

See 1:18 for εἴτε. Διά functions instr., "by life or by death" (Reumann 216; Fee 138 n. 60). The terms ζωῆς (gen. sg. fem. from ζωή, -ῆς, ἡ) and θανάτου (gen. sg. masc. from θάνατος, -ου, ὁ) denote physical life and death (BDAG 430a, 442d; R. Bultmann, *TDNT* 2.861 n. 242; H.-G. Link, *NIDNTT* 2.481; Reumann 216). The order (ζωῆς before θανάτου) indicates that Paul prefers the second alternative (see v. 21, below, on the *sygkrisis* form) (Reumann 246). Paul knows he will be released (vv. 25–26), but his imprisonment and impending trial confront him with the realities of life and death. The mention of ζωῆς and θανάτου in v. 20 generates a parenthetical soliloquy about the two options in vv. 21–24.

VERSE 21

Ἐμοὶ γὰρ τὸ ζῆν Χριστὸς καὶ τὸ ἀποθανεῖν κέρδος

Εἴτε διὰ ζωῆς εἴτε διὰ θανάτου (v. 20) launches Paul into a parenthetical soliloquy of sorts (vv. 21–24), where the 1 sg. dominates even more (ἐμοί [v. 21]; μοι, αἱρήσομαι, γνωρίζω [v. 22]; συνέχομαι [v. 23]; ἐπιμένειν [με implied, v. 24]; οἶδα, μενῶ, παραμενῶ [v. 25]; ἐμοί, ἐμῆς [v. 26]). Paul adopts an ancient rhetorical device known as σύγκρισις, "comparison," which compares and evaluates two persons or things. The pairing can be either antithetical (good versus bad) or comparative (good [τὸ ζῆν] versus better [τὸ ἀποθανεῖν]) (Reumann 235). Characteristics of σύγκρισις include (a) the idea of choice (αἱρήσομαι [v. 22]); (b) the use of comparatives (πολλῷ γὰρ μᾶλλον κρεῖσσον [v. 23]; ἀναγκαιότερον [v. 24]); (c) an ordering of the options, whereby the preferred option (τὸ ἀποθανεῖν [v. 21]) is listed second; and (d) personal evaluation (Ἐμοί [v. 21]) (Reumann 235–36). Even in this personal aside, everything remains subordinate to the gospel (O'Brien 117), and the soliloquy functions implicitly as a paradigm for the readers to emulate (Fee 127; cf. 3:15–17).

Ἐμοί ("to me" [most EVV]; "for me" [HCSB]; dat. of advantage [Reumann 217; Wallace 147]), emphatic in both form and position (H-M 54), marks the turn to purely personal reflection (Fee 139). No contrast with another group (e.g., the Philippians or the rival preachers) is intended. Personal evaluation is characteristic of the σύγκρισις form (Reumann 248).

The γάρ (a marker of inference, "certainly, by all means, so, then" [BDAG 190a]) most likely explains Paul's equanimity in the face of life and death (v. 20), as indicated by his elaboration upon the benefits of the two alternatives in vv. 22–24 (O'Brien 118).

The tenses of the infs. ζῆν (pres. act. from ζάω) and ἀποθανεῖν (aor. act. from ἀποθνήσκω) are lexically informed (Wallace 601; Silva 77): (a) ζῆν accentuates "the process of living" (H-M 55); (b) the act of death (aor. ἀποθανεῖν) is "neither progressive nor repetitive" (O'Brien 122; Fee 140–41 n. 9; Reumann 217). The subst. infs. function as subj. noms. of their respective clauses (ἐστιν understood) (Porter 195; R 1085; Wallace 235). The art. (τό [2x]) (a) distinguishes the subj. from the pred. nom., and (b) points back anaphorically to ζωῆς and θανάτου in v. 20 (BDF §399[1]). Since Χριστός is a proper name, the first assertion (τὸ ζῆν Χριστός) could conceivably be read as a convertible proposition (Z §174), leaving open the option of taking Χριστός as subj. (as in v. 20) and τὸ ζῆν as the pred. nom., "Christ is life" (cf. John 14:6). The parallelism with τὸ ἀποθανεῖν κέρδος, however, where the grammar is unambiguous, shows that τὸ ζῆν is the intended subj. Τὸ ζῆν Χριστός may have been heard by Greeks as a slogan, against the background of a Greek motto ζῆν χρηστός, "life is good" (H-M 55).

Ζῆν should not be decontextualized and understood as (1) the supernatural life of the new age in Christ ("to live in a transcendent sense") (BDAG 425d), nor (2) as the principle of life (for which we would expect ἐμοὶ γὰρ ζωὴ Χριστός). The contrast with ἀποθανεῖν (natural death), and the meaning of ζῆν in the v. 22, show that what is in view is (3) Paul's ongoing physical life (Z §173; Fee 141 n. 10; O'Brien 119–22).

Finally, τὸ ζῆν Χριστός is not to be read as broad gnomic assertion, i.e., "everything Paul does is done for Christ" (*pace* H-M 55). As vv. 15–20 (where gospel proclamation is central) and v. 22 (where τὸ ζῆν ἐν σαρκί = καρπὸς ἔργου) demonstrate, τὸ ζῆν Χριστός refers specifically to the ongoing mission opportunities that would result from Paul's release from prison ("Alive, I'm Christ's messenger" [*The Message*]; cf. CEV, NLT; Hansen 81; O'Brien 122).

Τὸ ἀποθανεῖν signifies physical death, without any of the theological freight Paul frequently associates with death (e.g., Rom 1:32; 6:23; 7:9–10) (Reumann 249). Some see Paul drawing upon contemporary sentiments that viewed death an escape from life's troubles (Palmer, "'To Die Is Gain,' (Philippians 1:21)," 203–18; C. Brown, *NIDNTT* 3.227; H-M 56; Reumann 217). Thus, Antigone: "Whoever lives in as many ills as I—how does this one not get gain (κέρδος) by dying?" (Sophocles, *Ant.* 463–64 cf. Plato, *Apol.* 29a–c; 40c–e). This uncritical appropriation of verbal parallels, however, ignores both the immediate context and Paul's theology of suffering more generally. Death is gain for Paul, not because it provides an escape from his troubles but because it means being "with Christ" (v. 23). Earthly life, moreover, far from being a set of dire circumstances from which to escape, offers further opportunity to serve Christ and the Philippians (vv. 22, 24–25). Finally, Paul views even the worst of life's circumstances as an opportunity to share Christ's sufferings and, thereby, to know Christ more fully (Phil 3:10; cf. 1:29; Rom 5:3–4). Paul thus gives the idea of death as κέρδος a "radically different sense" than the pagans did (Fee 142 n. 13; O'Brien 123; Hansen 83).

VERSE 22

εἰ δὲ τὸ ζῆν ἐν σαρκί, τοῦτό μοι καρπὸς ἔργου

H-M (cf. BDF §372[1]) take εἰ causally, "since," as an expression of Paul's confidence that he will be released (H-M 57). This, however, misses the reflective nature of the soliloquy, which deals with potentiality and not Paul's actual expectation. The εἰ-clause is the protasis of a cond. Paul reasons with himself about the alternatives of living and dying, according to the rhetorical demands of the συγκρίσις form (Hansen 85 n. 172). Two overlapping issues seek resolution: (a) the identification of the protasis and apodosis of the cond., and (b) whether to read τί αἱρήσομαι οὐ γνωρίζω as one sentence or two. Four options result:

*1. Take εἰ δὲ τὸ ζῆν ἐν σαρκί as protasis, τοῦτό μοι καρπὸς ἔργου as apodosis. What follows constitutes a new, declarative sentence: "If I am to live in the flesh, that means fruitful labor for me; and I do not know which I prefer" (NRSV; c.f. HCSB, ESV; Sumney 28–29);

*2. Take εἰ δὲ τὸ ζῆν ἐν σαρκί as protasis, τοῦτό μοι καρπὸς ἔργου as apodosis. What follows (καὶ τί αἱρήσομαι οὐ γνωρίζω) is then read as two sentences, the first a question (O'Brien 124): "If I am to go on living in the body, this will mean fruitful labor for me. Yet what shall I choose? I do not know!" (NIV);

3. Take all of εἰ δὲ τὸ ζῆν ἐν σαρκί, τοῦτό μοι καρπὸς ἔργου as the protasis, καὶ τί αἱρήσομαι οὐ γνωρίζω as a one-sentence apodosis: "If to be alive in the body gives me an opportunity for fruitful work, I do not know which I should choose" (NJB; H-M 57, adding another understood εἰ before τοῦτο; Silva 77); or

4. Take all of εἰ δὲ τὸ ζῆν ἐν σαρκί, τοῦτό μοι καρπὸς ἔργου as the protasis, καὶ τί αἱρήσομαι; οὐ γνωρίζω as a two-sentence apodosis: "But if to live in the flesh, this implying fruitful missionary labor for me, what then shall I choose? I do not know" (Reumann 250; BDF §442[8]).

The decision is difficult, as the EVV indicate. The breakdown of the cond. that is reflected in views 3 and 4 appears to have in its favor the adversative δέ, contrasting with τὸ ἀποθανεῖν κέρδος immediately previous ("*On the other hand again*, if to be alive in the body gives me an opportunity for fruitful work, I do not know which I should choose" [NJB, my italics]). But the δέ can also be taken as signaling "a progression of thought," expanding on what was said about life in vv. 20–21 ("Now" [HCSB]; omit [NIV, NRSV, ESV]; Fee 143–44; Reumann 220; Reed 327). The identification of καὶ τί αἱρήσομαι οὐ γνωρίζω as the apodosis, moreover, proves otherwise problematic: (a) there are no clear analogies in Paul for rendering καί as "then" (O'Brien 124; Fee 144 n. 25; Z §459 and Silva 77 offer 2 Cor 2:2, but the καί may be interpreted otherwise); (b) τοῦτο in the protasis is unnecessary and "cumbersome in the highest degree" (Fee 144 n. 25); (c) καρπὸς ἔργου makes more sense as a result of Paul's ongoing life (i.e., as an apodosis) than as an appositional restatement of τὸ ζῆν ἐν σαρκί (i.e., part of the protasis) (O'Brien 124). Either of the first two options, therefore, is acceptable.

Τὸ ζῆν is repeated from v. 21 ("clearly anaphoric" [Fee 143 n. 18]; Wallace 235). Ἐν σαρκί (σαρκί is dat. sg. fem.; ἐν means "in, in the sphere of" [T 264]) contains the first of five occurrences of σάρξ in the letter. Neither hostility to God (Rom 8:6–8) nor negative ethical aspects (Gal 5:19–21) are in view here—τὸ ζῆν ἐν σαρκί simply means "to remain alive" (E. Schweizer, *TDNT* 7.126; BDAG 915b; Hansen 85; H-M 57; O'Brien 125; Reumann 221).

Τοῦτο is nom. sg. neut. and refers back to the art. inf. τὸ ζῆν ἐν σαρκί ("calls attention to τὸ ζῆν ἐν σαρκί with special emphasis" [O'Brien 125]; R 698; Reumann 220). A vb. must be supplied in the clause. Take the pron. μοι as a dat. of advantage with implied vb., rather than as a dat. of poss. with καρπὸς ἔργου (Reumann 222; *pace* R 537).

Καρπός here means "advantage, gain, profit" (BDAG 510b). Ἔργον often refers to missionary or pastoral tasks (2:30; 1 Cor 16:10; 1 Thess 5:13; Rom 15:18; 2 Cor 10:11) (O'Brien 125). Paul has in view in καρπὸς ἔργου the productive future missionary work that would issue from τὸ ζῆν ἐν σαρκί (F. Hauck, *TDNT* 3.615; R. Hensel, *NIDNTT* 1.723; Hansen 85; H-M 57; O'Brien 125). The gen. ἔργου is variously interpreted (appos. [BDF §167]; source [BDAG 510b]; attributed gen., "fruitful labor/work" [most EVV; Wallace 91]), but the result is much the same.

καὶ τί αἱρήσομαι οὐ γνωρίζω

The καί means "and yet" (R 1182–83). Αἱρήσομαι is 1 sg. fut. mid. indic. from αἱρέω, "choose, prefer" (BDAG 28b; indir. mid., "I take/choose for myself" [R 801; Wallace 421]). In the act., αἱρέω is frequent in the LXX and secular Greek, meaning "to take into one's hands, seize." NT usage (3x in mid.) includes both (1) the specialized biblical meaning of God's choosing the Thessalonians εἰς σωτηρίαν (2 Thess 2:13), and (2) a weakened sense, "prefer," as here (G. Nordholt, NIDNTT 1.534; O'Brien 126; cf. Heb 11:25). It is unnecessary to interpret αἱρήσομαι in a concrete or realistic way (pace Reumann 250–51): "The question does not indicate that Paul actually has the power to choose life or death. Paul is asking himself a rhetorical question as he faces the possible alternatives before him" (Hansen 85; O'Brien 127; "prefer" [NRSV] brings this out better than "choose" [most EVV; BDAG 28b; Hansen 85 n. 172]).

Based on secular usage, some render γνωρίζω as simple act., "which I shall choose I do not know" (BDAG 203b; most EVV; R. Bultmann, TDNT 1.718). NT usage (26x; 18x in Paul) argues universally for a causative sense: "I do not reveal, make known" (BDF §108[3]; RSV, NEB, ESV; H-M 58; Hansen 86; O'Brien 127–28; O. Knoch, EDNT 1.256b, allows for either option). Paul may be reluctant to "make known" his own preference (ἀναλῦσαι καὶ σὺν Χριστῷ εἶναι) because he knows it conflicts with God's design (τὸ ἐπιμένειν ἐν τῇ σαρκί, cf. v. 25). The nature of the soliloquy allows for a bit of semantic elasticity. At this point in the process of reflecting on the alternatives of life and death, Paul "admits he is generally bewildered by the question of his own preference" (Hansen 86). The English idiom "I can't tell" (meaning, "in light of the alternatives, I don't know what to say") is probably close to Paul's intent with γνωρίζω (Fee 145 n. 28; Silva 77–78).

VERSE 23

συνέχομαι δὲ ἐκ τῶν δύο

The δέ is explicative, "indeed," not antithetical (pace NASB; most EVV omit δέ; Z §467; O'Brien 128; Reumann 223).

Συνέχομαι is 1 sg. pres. pass. indic. from συνέχω, "to cause distress by force of circumstances" (BDAG 971a; "hard pressed" [NRSV, NASB, ESV; A. Kretzer, NIDNTT 3.306]; "I am torn" [NEB, NIV, NLT]; "caught in this dilemma" [NJB]). In the NT the vb. has the sense "enclose, close" (e.g., crowds "pressing against" Jesus [Luke 8:45]; Jerusalem besieged [19:43]; the controlling power of a fever [4:38]), often with the idea of total control (Acts 18:5; ἡ γὰρ ἀγάπη τοῦ Χριστοῦ συνέχει ἡμᾶς [2 Cor 5:14]). Paul is like a traveler on a narrow road with walls of rock on both sides, unable to turn either way (O'Brien 129). The pass. generally takes a dat. indicating the agent; here the prep. phrase serves that function (ἐκ τῶν δύο ultimately refers back to ζωῆς and θανάτου [v. 20]).

τὴν ἐπιθυμίαν ἔχων εἰς τὸ ἀναλῦσαι καὶ σὺν Χριστῷ εἶναι

Usually neg. (e.g., ἐπιθυμίαν σαρκός [Gal 5:16]), Paul here uses ἐπιθυμία (acc. sg. fem.) with positive connotations, "desire for good things" (BDAG 372b; Reumann 223; cf. 1 Thess 2:17). The ptc. ἔχων is used causally (O'Brien 129).

Εἰς τὸ ἀναλῦσαι is an epex. inf. giving the content of ἐπιθυμίαν (BDF §402; R 1,072, 1,076; T 143; ἐπιθυμία + εἰς + acc. = "a desire for something" [BDAG 372b; most EVV]).

The inf. ἀναλῦσαι is aor. act. from ἀναλύω, "depart, return" (BDAG 67d; "depart" [most EVV]). Ἀναλύω was common as a euphemism for death "in kindly concealment of its terror" (O. Procksch, TDNT 4.337; cf. ὁ καιρὸς τῆς ἀναλύσεώς μου [2 Tim 4:6]). The vb. was also used (a) as a military term, of breaking up an encampment (2 Macc 9:1); (b) as a nautical expression, "weighing anchor" (Polyb. 3.69.14); and (c) to refer to the "solution" to some difficult problem (H-M 59). Paul has in view not Gk. ideas about the immortality of the soul and its release from the body at death but the hope of union with Christ, for which there was no adequate parallel in antiquity (O'Brien 130).

Σὺν Χριστῷ can signify (*view 1) simple association (e.g., 1 Thess 4:13–17) which, in the case of our relationship with Christ, would denote intimate, personal fellowship (BDAG 961d; R 628; W. Elliger, NIDNTT 3.291–92; "spatial proximity" and "active communion" [M. Harris, NIDNTT 3.1,206–7; Harris, Prepositions, 203–4]; W. Grundmann, TDNT 7.783–84; MM 600; H-M 60; O'Brien 132; cf. LXX Pss 138:18; 139:14); or (view 2) the more theologically charged idea of incorporation with Christ, as representative of the new humanity (e.g., Rom 6:4–8), here participation with Christ in his sufferings and death (Hansen 87–90; W. Schmithals, NIDNTT 1.440; K. Barth, Epistle to the Philippians, trans. J. Leitch [Richmond: Westminster John Knox, 2002], 38). *View 1 is better supported by:

a. Pauline Usage—Passages that unambiguously denote incorporation with Christ pair σὺν Χριστῷ/αὐτῷ not with εἰμί (as in Phil 1:23) but, rather, with vbs. formally associated with Christ's redemptive acts ([συν]ἐγείρω [2 Cor 4:14; Col 2:12]; [συ]ζάω [2 Cor 13:4; Rom 6:8]; συζωοποιέω [Col 2:13]; ἀποθνήσκω [Col 2:20; Rom 6:8]; cf. Col 3:3, 4). The only genuine parallel—where εἰμί does, in fact, occur—clearly denotes simple association and not theological incorporation: πάντοτε σὺν κυρίῳ ἐσόμεθα (1 Thess 4:17). For Paul εἶναι ἐν Χριστῷ signifies incorporative union with Christ (e.g., Rom 12:5; 1 Cor 1:30); εἶναι σὺν Χριστῷ, simple association (1 Thess 4:17; Phil 1:23). When Paul writes elsewhere of incorporation into Christ's death, moreover, he uses not ἀναλύω but, rather, ἀποθνήσκω and its cognates (e.g., Rom 6:3–5, 8; Phil 3:10; Col 2:20), or συσταυρόω (Gal 2:19; Rom 6:6). V. 23 wholly lacks the vocabulary that confirms the incorporation theme elsewhere in the letter (e.g., 3:10 [συμμορφίζω and θάνατος]) or in the rest of Paul's writings.

b. Context—Paul has turned his attention in the soliloquy directly to the consequences of physical life and death, so that the communion with Christ in the afterlife, not incorporation into his death, comes most naturally into view.

πολλῷ [γὰρ] μᾶλλον κρεῖσσον

The γάρ is in 𝔓⁴⁶ A B C (good evidence for inclusion [Fee 138 n. 1]), and in most editions of the Gk. NT. It is missing from ℵ D *Byz.* EVV vary ("for" [NRSV, NASB, ESV]; omit [NIV, HCSB]). Γάρ is causal, giving the reason for Paul's preference for death (Reed 324). The clause is elliptical, lacking both a subj. and a vb. ("that is" [NRSV, NASB, ESV]; "which is" [NIV, HCSB]; Reumann 225).

Πολλῷ μᾶλλον κρεῖσσον, lit. "by much more better" ("much better indeed" [BDAG 566b]; "far better" [NRSV, NLT, HCSB]; "very much better" [NASB]; "far, far better" [Porter 124]); an emphatic comp. cstr. (R 278, 546; Moule 98; T 29). Comparison is characteristic of the συγκρίσις form (Reumann 253). The expression can be broken down as follows:

a. Κρεῖσσον is nom. sg. neut. from κρείττων (Attic form), -ον, "more useful, more advantageous, better," the comp. form of the adj. ἀγαθός (BDAG 566b), here serving as pred. nom. of an understood τοῦτο [γάρ] ἐστιν.
b. The adv. μᾶλλον means "more" (BDAG 613d–614a).
c. The adj. πολλῷ (dat. sg. neut. from πολύς, πολύ, πολλή, "much, many") is used here as a subst. (BDAG 849b). The dat. of measure (not instr. [*pace* R 532]) functions adv. with κρεῖσσον ("better *by much*" [Wallace 167]).

VERSE 24

τὸ δὲ ἐπιμένειν [ἐν] τῇ σαρκὶ ἀναγκαιότερον δι᾽ ὑμᾶς

Some see τὴν ἐπιθυμίαν ἔχων εἰς (v. 23) governing both (a) τὸ ἀναλῦσαι καὶ σὺν Χριστῷ εἶναι and (b) τὸ δὲ ἐπιμένειν (H-M 62), but the adversative δέ ("but" [most EVV]) marks the beginning of a new sentence at v. 24, where the art. inf. has become the subj.; ἀναγκαιότερον the pred. nom., with another understood ἐστιν (BDF §399[1]; Moule 127; T 140). The pres. tense of ἐπιμένειν is lexically informed ("stay, remain" [BDAG 375d]), as the aor. ἀναλῦσαι is with the idea "depart" (v. 23).

𝔓⁴⁶ B D *Byz.* include the bracketed ἐν; ℵ A C omit it, perhaps by homoteleuton (ἐπιμένειν ἐν). But the dat. without ἐν can function with a verb prefixed with ἐπι, so it is preferable to see ἐν added as a "correction" (Reumann 225). For τῇ σαρκί see v. 22.

Ἀναγκαιότερον (nom. sg. neut.), "more necessary" (BDAG 60d; most EVV), is the comp. form of the adj. ἀναγκαῖος (for -οτερος as comp., see BDF §61[2]). The term denotes "necessity" or "compulsion" (O'Brien 131). Paul's ἐπιθυμία gives way to necessity, as he models what he will enjoin in 2:4 about considering the good of others (O'Brien 131). Serving the community takes priority over individual goals or desires, in anticipation of the self-emptying, other-centered character of Christ in 2:6–8 (Hansen 90).

VERSE 25

καὶ τοῦτο πεποιθώς

Verses 25–26 serve as the transition from τὰ κατ᾽ ἐμέ (v. 12) to τὰ περὶ ὑμῶν (v. 27), as Paul now begins to draw a connection between his circumstances and those of the Philippians (Fee 151). Τοῦτο looks backwards to v. 24 (most EVV; R. Bultmann, *TDNT* 6.6 n. 17; H-M 62; Reumann 226), not ahead to the ὅτι-clause that follows (NJB, NEB). Πεποιθώς is nom. sg. masc. of perf. act. ptc. from πείθω, used causally to modify οἶδα κτλ., "Since I am convinced of this" (NRSV, CEV, HCSB; Wallace 632; H-M 62; Reumann 225).

οἶδα ὅτι μενῶ καὶ παραμενῶ πᾶσιν ὑμῖν

Μένω and παραμένω (1 sg. fut. act. indics.; "remain . . . continue" [most EVV]) differ in meaning. Although παραμένω can mean simply "to remain, last, persist, continue to live" (cf. BDAG 631c), the prefixed vb. was also used in the sense "continue in an occupation or office," "serve" (BDAG 769a), e.g., of priests in Heb 7:23, and of slaves in the papyri (παραμένων was used as a slave's name [Reumann 227]). Thus, unlike μένω, the ideas of mission and service in ministry are at the forefront of παραμένω in v. 25, and the distinction should be preserved: "I will remain alive (μενῶ) so I can continue to help (παραμενῶ)" (NLT; "stay and stand by you all" [NJB]; R 828; F. Hauck, *TDNT* 4.578; Fee 152 n. 10; O'Brien 139; Reumann 255). To see behind πᾶσιν (versus ὑμῖν alone) friction in the congregation may be overinterpreting the adj. (*pace* Fee 152).

All the evidence (Phil 1:24–26; 2:24; Phlm 22) indicates that Paul expected to be released. But this seems to conflict with his reflections on the possibility of death in vv. 20–23 (θανάτου [v. 20]; τὸ ἀποθανεῖν [v. 21]; τὸ ἀναλῦσαι [v. 23]). Some downplay the assertion here (οἶδα ὅτι μενῶ κτλ.): Paul is "not expressing any definite opinion about the future. . . . [H]is presence will be a blessing to the Philippians in the future *if* he is released" (O'Brien 139, author's italics). The language in v. 25 is straightforward, however, and it makes more sense methodologically to begin with the fact that Paul expected to be released (reiterated in 2:24 [with sim. language, πέποιθα ἐν κυρίῳ]) (Fee 147 n. 37). Verses 21–24 are then read as a soliloquy "expressing his personal longing but unrelated to his actual expectation" (Fee 152).

εἰς τὴν ὑμῶν προκοπὴν καὶ χαρὰν τῆς πίστεως

Εἰς introduces the immediate purpose for Paul's ongoing ministry with the readers; the ἵνα clause in v. 26 then gives the ultimate purpose (Fee 151 n. 3). A single art. (τήν) closely connects προκοπήν and χαράν (R 787; Z §184; Reumann 227, 255). Ὑμῶν and τῆς πίστεως modify both nouns, as well (Fee 153 n. 14; O'Brien 140). Προκοπήν (see on v. 12), "advance" (NJB) or "progress" (most EVV), refers to the quality of the Philippians' faith, χαράν to their experience of it (Fee 153). Προκοπήν forms an *inclusio* with προκοπήν in v. 12—the gospel's progress there, the Philippians' here (O'Brien 140). Used in Gk. philosophy of the moral progress of the individual, προκοπή finds community application with Paul (ὑμῶν is emphatic by word order [Fee 153]), "a distinctive NT development" (G. Stählin, *TDNT* 6.714]; Reumann 168). Two options for πίστεως (gen. sg. fem. from πίστις, -εως, ἡ):

1. Subjectively, "the state of believing, trust" (BDAG 819d; R. Bultmann, *TDNT* 6.212 n. 283).
*2. Objectively, "the faith" (RSV, NASB, NIV, ESV; Z §184), i.e., in the sense of the Christian creed or, more broadly, as a metonymy for the Christian life (H-M 63; O'Brien 140). Paul uses πίστις like this two verses later (τῇ πίστει τοῦ εὐαγγελίου [v. 27]) (Fee 153).

Assuming that view 2 is correct, πίστεως is best viewed as a gen. of ref. (Fee 151 n. 51; "for your progress and joy in [the] faith" [most EVV]), rather than as a gen. of source or origin ("joy of your faith" [NLT]).

VERSE 26

ἵνα τὸ καύχημα ὑμῶν περισσεύῃ ἐν Χριστῷ Ἰησοῦ ἐν ἐμοὶ διὰ τῆς ἐμῆς παρουσίας πάλιν πρὸς ὑμᾶς

The ἵνα-clause may denote purpose or result (suggested by "so that" [most EVV; Porter 235]). For the pres. subjunc. περισσεύῃ see on 1:9.

Καύχημα (nom. sg. neut.) can mean (1) act of boasting ("take [great] pride" [NLT, CEV]) or (2) ground for boasting ("that which constitutes a source of pride" [BDAG 537a]; "cause to glory" [ESV, RSV]; O'Brien 141). The first view works best with ἐν Χριστῷ Ἰησοῦ as the expressed ground of boasting (cf. καυχώμενοι ἐν Χριστῷ Ἰησοῦ [3:3]). The word group does not signify "boasting" (NRSV, NIV) in the sense "brag about" or "be conceited about." Rather, "the motif of trust is inherent in Paul's use of the term" (J. Zmijewski, *EDNT* 2.278b), so that the idea "confidence" (NASB, HCSB), resulting in "glory[ing]" (RSV, ESV), is at the forefront. Negatively, people can place their confidence in the law (Rom 2:17) or in the flesh (Phil 3:3–4). Apart from God people actually have no secure basis for καύχημα (1 Cor 1:26–30; 4:7). Positively, believers can boast in God (Rom 5:11; 1 Cor 1:31; cf. Jer 9:23–24). Paul expected his churches to be the basis for such confidence at the parousia (1 Thess 2:19–20; 2 Cor 1:14; Phil 2:16). Here the apostle himself becomes the immediate cause of his con-verts' boasting.

The gen. ὑμῶν can be obj., Paul boasting about the Philippians (H.-C. Hahn, *NIDNTT* 1.229) or subj., "what you can be proud of" (BDAG 537a). The latter is clearly intended here (EVV; R. Bultmann, *TDNT* 3.651; H-M 63; O'Brien 141; Reumann 257).

Take ἐν Χριστῷ Ἰησοῦ (dat. of sphere) either (a) with περισσεύῃ (NASB, HCSB; O'Brien 141; Reumann 230) or (b) with καύχημα (NIV, NJB). In either case Christ is the ultimate reason for boasting; Paul's mission is the specific occasion (Hansen 92).

'Εν ἐμοί is causal: *"because of me* through my presence with you once again" (H-M 63, author's italics; O'Brien 141).

Διὰ τῆς ἐμῆς παρουσίας πάλιν πρὸς ὑμᾶς is connected with ἐν ἐμοί as a special instance, giving the particular ground of rejoicing that Paul has in mind (O'Brien 141). Paul may have chosen the poss. adj. (ἐμῆς, instead of μου) to generate the alliterative string of sigma endings (-ῆς . . . -ῆς . . . -ας . . . -ός . . . -ᾶς) (T 191).

Παρουσίας (gen. sg. fem.) is not intended eschatologically. It simply refers to Paul's "coming, presence" in Philippi (BDAG 780d; A. Oepke, *TDNT* 5.859; Reumann 231). In CGk. παρουσία could refer to the pomp and pageantry that accompanied the arrival of a king or governor in a city. This hardly proves, however, that Paul "expects to receive 'a king's welcome' from the Philippians when he arrives in town" (*pace* H-M 64).

Πρός + acc. ("by, at, near" you [BDAG 875c]) may (1) suggest motion toward ("coming to you" [ESV]), or (2) simply represent stylistic variation vis-à-vis the prefix παρά in παρουσία ("being with you" [NIV]). Perhaps both motion and the ensuing state of being are in view ("both coming again and staying" [B. Reicke, *TDNT* 6.722]).

FOR FURTHER STUDY

17. Job 13:16a Citation (1:19)

Bruno, Christopher R. "Readers, Authors, and the Divine Author: An Evangelical Proposal for Identifying Paul's Old Testament Citations." *WTJ* 71 (2009): 311–21.

Hays, Richard B. *Echoes of Scripture in the Letters of Paul.* New Haven, CT: Yale University Press, 1993. See pages 21–24.

Michael, J. Hugh. "Paul and Job: A Neglected Analogy." *ExpTim* 36 (1924): 67–73.

*Reumann, John. "The (Greek) Old Testament in Philippians 1:19 as Parade Example— Allusion, Echo, Proverb?" Pages 189–200 in *History and Exegesis: Essays in Honor of E. Earle Ellis on His Eightieth Birthday.* Edited by S. A. Son. New York: T&T Clark International, 2006.

Silva, M. *DPL* 630–42.

18. Honor and Shame in Paul's World (1:20)

De Silva, David. A. *Honor, Patronage, Kinship, and Purity: Unlocking New Testament Culture.* Downers Grove: InterVarsity, 2000.

Gupta, Nijay. "'I Will Not Be Put to Shame': Paul, the Philippians, and the Honorable Wish for Death." *Neot* 42 (2008): 253–67.

Hellerman, *Reconstructing Honor,* 34–62.

Malina, Bruce J. and Jerome H. Neyrey. "Honor and Shame in Luke-Acts: Pivotal Values of the Mediterranean World." Pages 25–65 in *The Social World of Luke-Acts.* Edited by Jerome H. Neyrey. Peabody, MA: Hendrikson, 1991.

Moxnes, Halvor. "Honor and Shame." Pages 19–40 in *The Social Sciences and New Testament Interpretation.* Edited by Richard Rohrbaugh. Peabody, MA: Hendrickson, 1996. See pages 19–40.

———. "Honor and Shame: A Reader's Guide." *BTB* 23 (1993): 167–76.

*Pilch, John J. "Honor/Shame." Pages 95–104 in *Biblical Social Values and Their Meaning*. Edited by John J. Pilch and Bruce J. Malina. Peabody, MA: Hendrikson, 1993.

19. Boldness (1:20)

Balz, H. *EDNT* 3.45–47.
Hahn, H.-C. *NIDNTT* 2.724–37.
*Marrow, Stanley. B. "Parrhesia and the New Testament." *CBQ* 44 (1982): 431–46.
Unnik, Willem C. van. "The Christian's Freedom of Speech in the New Testament." *Bulletin of the John Rylands Library* 44 (1961–62): 466–88.

20. Life and Death (1:20–24)

Dailey, Thomas F. "To Live or Die, Paul's Eschatological Dilemma in Philippians 1:19–26." *Int* 44 (1990): 18–28.
Grundmann, W. *TDNT* 7.766–97.
*Harris, Murray J. *Raised Immortal: The Resurrection and Immortality in the New Testament*. London: Marshall, Morgan, & Scott, 1983.
Kreitzer, L. J. *DPL* 438–41.
Lincoln, Andrew T. *Paradise Now and Not Yet: Studies in the Role of the Heavenly Dimension in Paul's Thought with Special Reference to His Eschatology*. SNTSMS 43. Cambridge: Cambridge University Press, 1981. See pages 103–6.
Palmer, D. W. "'To Die Is Gain,' (Philippians 1:21)." *NovT* 17 (1975): 203–18.
Vos, G. *The Pauline Eschatology*. Grand Rapids: Eerdmanns, 1961. See pages 136–50.

21. Faith (1:25)

Barth, G. *EDNT* 3.91–98.
Bultmann R. and A. Weiser. *TDNT* 6.174–228.
Lürhmann, D. *ABD* 2.749–58.
Michel, O. *NIDNTT* 1.593–606.
*Morris, L. *DPL* 285–91.
Yeung, Maureen W. *Faith in Jesus and Paul. A Comparison with Special Reference to "Faith That Can Move Mountains" and "Your Faith Has Healed/Saved You."* WUNT 2.147. Tübingen: Mohr Siebeck, 2002.

HOMILETICAL SUGGESTIONS

From Present Circumstances to Future Expectations (1:18b–26)

1. Magnifying Christ in prison and before the tribunal (vv. 18d–20).
2. A personal soliloquy (vv. 21–24).
3. Expectations for future ministry (vv. 25–26).

Surviving the Tough Times (1:19–20)

1. Ask for the prayers of others (v. 19).
2. Rely on the supply of the Spirit (v. 19).
3. Allow God to show his greatness in the midst of your trials (v. 20).

Living a Life that Makes God Famous (μεγαλυνθήσεται, 1:20)

1. Openly and boldly (ἐν πάσῃ παρρησίᾳ).
2. Faithfully and consistently (ὡς πάντοτε καὶ νῦν).
3. With all that we are (ἐν τῷ σώματί μου).
4. While we live and as we die (εἴτε διὰ ζωῆς εἴτε διὰ θανάτου).

Torn between Two Worlds (1:21–24)

1. Passionate about ministry ("to live" vv. 21–24).
2. Longing for more of Jesus ("to die" vv. 21–24).

The Simple Fruit of an Effective Life (1:25–26)

1. Bringing growth and joy to the lives of others (v. 25).
2. Bringing glory to God (v. 26).

III. Body of the Letter (1:27–4:9)

A. SUMMARY EXHORTATION TO UNITY AND STEADFASTNESS (1:27–30)

27 Μόνον   ἀξίως τοῦ εὐαγγελίου τοῦ Χριστοῦ
          πολιτεύεσθε,
          ἵνα   εἴτε ἐλθὼν καὶ ἰδὼν ὑμᾶς
                   εἴτε ἀπὼν
                   ἀκούω τὰ περὶ ὑμῶν,

                   ὅτι στήκετε
                       ἐν ἑνὶ πνεύματι,
                       μιᾷ ψυχῇ
                       συναθλοῦντες τῇ πίστει τοῦ εὐαγγελίου
28   καὶ μὴ πτυρόμενοι ἐν μηδενὶ ὑπὸ τῶν ἀντικειμένων,
                   ἥτις ἐστὶν αὐτοῖς ἔνδειξις ἀπωλείας,
                       ὑμῶν δὲ σωτηρίας,
                               καὶ τοῦτο
                               ἀπὸ θεοῦ·
29   ὅτι ὑμῖν ἐχαρίσθη τὸ ὑπὲρ Χριστοῦ,
                   οὐ μόνον τὸ εἰς αὐτὸν πιστεύειν
                   ἀλλὰ καὶ τὸ ὑπὲρ αὐτοῦ πάσχειν,
30   τὸν αὐτὸν ἀγῶνα ἔχοντες,
                              οἷον εἴδετε ἐν ἐμοὶ
                              καὶ νῦν ἀκούετε ἐν
                              ἐμοί.

    1:27–30 forms a discrete unit, a single sentence, with one main vb., πολιτεύεσθε (v. 27a). Asyndeton begins a new subject but one closely related to what has gone before: (a) εἴτε ἐλθὼν καὶ ἰδὼν ὑμᾶς εἴτε ἀπών (v. 27) recalls Paul's reflections about his future circumstances in vv. 25–26; (b) the account of Paul's own circumstances, and the fact that they served to advance the gospel (vv. 12–26), serve as the basis of his authority to challenge the Philippians in vv. 27–30 (Hansen 93; O'Brien 145; Reumann 287).

Though some see the beginning of an *inclusio* marked here, variously defined (e.g., πολιτεύεσθε [v. 27a] and πολίτευμα [3:20]; πάσχειν [1:29c] and παθημάτων [3:10]), it is preferable in each case to see a repetition of vocabulary rather than the framing of a unit (Reumann 276).

Repeated ideas within the passage include the gospel (v. 27 [2x]), suffering (vv. 28a, 29c), the Christian life as a struggle or athletic contest (vv. 27d, 30a), and the centrality of Christ in faith and hardship (vv. 27a, 29).

VERSE 27

Μόνον ἀξίως τοῦ εὐαγγελίου τοῦ Χριστοῦ πολιτεύεσθε

Μόνον is an acc. sg. neut. adj. from μόνος, -η, -ον, used adv. (BDAG 659a; "only" [many EVV]; "whatever happens" [NIV]; "but you must always" [NJB]). Μόνον has a limiting function that brings out the emphatic nature of the whole impv. cstr. that follows, ἀξίως τοῦ εὐαγγελίου τοῦ Χριστοῦ πολιτεύεσθε κτλ. ("Now, the important thing is this" [O'Brien 144–45]; "this point only" [Reumann 261]).

Ἀξίως is a prepositional adv. (from ἄξιος, -α, -ον) with the gen. τοῦ εὐαγγελίου, modifying πολιτεύεσθε (BDAG 94d; R 505, 637). One might have expected "in a manner worthy of citizens of Philippi." Instead, the gospel is the norm for community life, as εὐαγγέλιον surfaces as a recurring theme in the letter (1:5, 7, 12, 16; 2:22; 4:3, 15) (Reumann 286). Εὐαγγέλιον was used in public decrees to connote "good tidings" about an emperor's birthday (see on 1:5). The proclamation of Jesus as κύριος (2:11), along with πολιτεύεσθε here, may imply that Paul has this imperial background in view with εὐαγγελίου (2x) in 1:27.

The gen. τοῦ Χριστοῦ can be:

*1. obj., "the good news about Christ" (BDAG 403a; Sumney 35);
  2. subj., "from Christ" (G. Friedrich, *TDNT* 2.731 n. 70); or
  3. "comprehensive" (Spicq 2.89 n. 35; "Christ is both the subject and object of preaching" [G. Friedrich, *TDNT* 2.731]).

Paul unpacks the content of ἀξίως τοῦ εὐαγγελίου τοῦ Χριστοῦ πολιτεύεσθε in vv. 27c–28a: στήκετε . . . τῶν ἀντικειμένων.

Πολιτεύεσθε is 2 pl. pres. mid. impv. of πολιτεύομαι. The ἵνα-clause that follows shows that the tense signifies "continual, habitual action" (Reumann 262). Impv. force extends to στήκετε and its modifiers in vv. 27cd, 28a (Reumann 285). The lit. meaning, "to be a citizen" (BDAG 846a; "the political duties of citizens of a city" [Hansen 94]), has led some to find reference to Christians as citizens of Philippi: "Discharge your obligations as citizens and residents of Philippi faithfully as a Christian should" (Brewer, "The Meaning of *Politeuesthe*," 83; Winter, *Seek the Welfare of the City*, 85). Others see a double ref. to earthly and heavenly citizenship (H-M 68–69; Hansen 95; Reumann 285–86).

It is unlikely, however, that Paul is referring to Roman citizenship at all, except as a foil (nor is Jewish background, i.e., membership in the true Israel, in view [*pace* Miller, "Πολιτεύεσθε in Philippians 1.27," 86–96]). First, only about 36 percent of the Christians in the colony would have been Roman citizens (slanted for social accessibility; approximately 40 percent were citizens colony-wide [Oakes 61]). Second, the ensuing explanation of πολιτεύεσθε in vv. 27–28 says nothing about the civic duties of a Roman citizen (e.g., the work of a "jailer, pensioned military veteran, civil servant, in the forum, in business" [Reumann, 285]).

The political connotations of πολιτεύεσθε cannot be denied, however, so a purely fig. meaning, "live," "lead one's life" (so most EVV; BDAG 846a; "no political implications" [H. Strathmann, *TDNT* 6.534]) does not satisfy. For this Paul uses περιπατέω (e.g., Rom. 6:4; 8:4; 13:13; etc.), substituting πολιτεύομαι only in Philippians (one should not equate the two verbs [U. Hutter, *EDNT* 3.130c]). The change is likely due to the prevalence of the franchise in the colony (40% Roman citizens vs. 14% elsewhere in the empire). Only in Philippi, among Paul's three journeys, for example, does the issue of Roman citizenship arise in Acts (16:37–39; Hansen 94; Hellerman 112–13).

We conclude that Paul intentionally employs this politically charged term (subversively, in view of the pride of honors associated with Roman citizenship in the colony) in reference to another citizen body, namely, the Christian community in Philippi ("as citizens of heaven live" [NIV; sim. NLT]; Fee 162; Zerbe, "Citizenship and Politics"; cf. τὸ πολίτευμα ἐν οὐρανοῖς [3:20]). Paul intentionally marks out the church in the colony as an alternative society vis-à-vis the Roman imperial order. Readers are thereby prepared for the politically provocative acclamation of Jesus—not Caesar—as κύριος in 2:11.

ἵνα εἴτε ἐλθὼν καὶ ἰδὼν ὑμᾶς εἴτε ἀπὼν ἀκούω τὰ περὶ ὑμῶν

The ἵνα–clause (purpose) reminds the Philippians of Paul's plan to visit (1:26; cf. 2:24) and anticipates the announcement about sending Timothy in 2:19 (Hansen 95). With 1:30 the clause implies ongoing exchange of information between Paul and Philippians (Reed 308).

The 1 sg. pres. act. subjunc. ἀκούω, to be preferred to aor. var. ἀκούσω. The pres. is represented in the best mss. ($\mathfrak{P}^{46}$ ℵ* B D* P 629), and it is highly unlikely a scribe would have altered the more common ἀκούσω to ἀκούω (Fee 158). Εἴτε . . . εἴτε are coordinating conditional conjunctions, "whether . . . or" (Wallace 669).

The ptcs. ἐλθών and ἰδών are nom. sg. masc. aor. act. from ἔρχομαι and ὁράω, respectively; ἀπών is a pres. ptc. from ἄπειμι (cond. ptcs., modifying ἀκούω). The cstr. is irregular: if Paul does come and see them (as the first pair of ptcs. allows), then ἀκούω is not fitting (Sumney 35). We might expect, instead, εἴτε ἐλθὼν καὶ ἰδὼν ὑμᾶς εἴτε ἀπὼν καὶ ἀκούων, followed by a subjunc. (e.g., γνῶ) ("Whether I come and see you or am absent and hear about you, I will know" [NRSV]). The sense remains clear, however, and emendation is unnecessary (Fee 163; O'Brien, 148–49).

Τὰ περὶ ὑμῶν exhibits the characteristic use of the art. with a prep. phrase, "what concerns someone or something, his or its circumstances" (BDAG 798a; R 766; "of

you" [RSV, NASB, ESV]; "about you" [NIV, NRSV, HCSB]; "all about you" [NJB]
overdoes it [Reumann 265]).

ὅτι στήκετε ἐν ἑνὶ πνεύματι

The ὅτι-clause is in appos. to τὰ περὶ ὑμῶν, "(namely) that" (most EVV; O'Brien
149).

Στήκετε is 2 pl. pres. act. indic. from στήκω, a HGk. form based on ἔστηκα (cf.
στήκοντες [Mark 3:31] and εἱστήκεισαν [Matt 12:46]; John 1:26); lit., "to be in a standing position," here fig., "to be firmly committed in conviction or belief" (BDAG 944d;
BDF §73; Z §493). Commonly used by Paul to signify "stand firm" (most EVV),
"be steadfast" ("in the faith" [1 Cor 16:13]; "in the Lord" [Phil 4:1]; in the freedom
Christ has won [Gal 5:1]) (O'Brien 149). The vb. participates in the impv. force of
πολιτεύεσθε (Hansen 95 n. 200). Some see in στήκετε the image of "soldiers who deter-
minedly refuse to leave their posts irrespective of how severely the battle rages" (H-M
70; Geoffrion, *The Rhetorical Purpose*, 55; Krentz, "Military Language," 119–21).
Others question the notion that στήκω was a military term ("too new a word to have
an established history of meanings" [Reumann 287]). Philippi had been founded as a
veteran colony, however, and historically the citizen franchise was required of Roman
legionnaires. The settlement's location on the Egnatian Way would have exposed residents to Roman armies traveling east or west across the empire (Hellerman 141–42).
It is not unreasonable to see a military *topos* here.

Ἑνί is dat. sg. neut. from εἷς, μιά, ἕν, numeral, "one"; here, "one and the same"
(BDAG 292a). Πνεύματι is dat. sg. neut. from πνεῦμα. It is not easy to tell whether
Paul intends (view 1) the Holy Spirit ("one Spirit" [NIV]; *NIDNTT* 3.702; Fee 163–66;
Reumann 287), or (view 2) a part of the human personality, i.e., "one spirit" (NRSV,
HCSB, ESV; BDAG 833a; "anthropological pneuma" [E. Schweizer, *TDNT* 6.434–
35]; H-M 70–71; O'Brien 150; Silva 89). The carefully constructed chiasm—which
brings μιᾷ ψυχῇ immediately up against ἐν ἑνὶ πνεύματι—suggests that the two phrases
are synonymous (Silva 89). Also supporting "one spirit" is the appeal to unity throughout the letter (H-M 70; Sumney 35–36). View 1, "in one Spirit," however, has considerable support, as well:

a. The Eng. use of "one spirit" to refer to a "community spirit" or "common
   mind" has no analogy in Gk. Whereas ψυχὴ μία is often used to describe
   unity among two or more people, ἓν πνεῦμα is never so used (Fee 164).

b. Whenever Paul uses στήκετε + ἐν, the prep. phrase is invariably locative.
   This works with "one Spirit," but not with "one spirit," which would have
   to be read as manner (Fee 165).

c. Ψυχή and πνεῦμα appear together in what follows (κοινωνία πνεύματος . . .
   σύμψυχοι [2:1–2]), where the Spirit is clearly in view (Fee 166; Hansen
   96; cf. also ἐπιχορηγίας τοῦ πνεύματος Ἰησοῦ Χριστοῦ [1:19]).

d. Paul uses this language twice in Eph (ἐν ἑνὶ πνεύματι [2:18]; ἓν πνεῦμα
   [4:4]). In both cases the theme of unity is at the forefront (Fee 165; cf.
   1 Cor 12:13).

e. The close parallel στήκετε ἐν κυρίῳ (4:1) supports reading "Spirit" here (Hansen 96).

f. Ἑνὶ πνεύματι and μιᾷ ψυχῇ are not precisely parallel: ἐν ἑνὶ πνεύματι has the prep., μιᾷ ψυχῇ does not (G. D. Fee, *God's Empowering Presence: The Holy Spirit in the Letters of Paul* [Peabody, MA: Hendrikson, 1994], 744–46).

View 1 is somewhat stronger. However, since unity of purpose depends on the Holy Spirit, the two interpretations are closely linked (O'Brien 150).

μιᾷ ψυχῇ συναθλοῦντες τῇ πίστει τοῦ εὐαγγελίου

The ptcs. explain positively (συναθλοῦντες) and negatively (μὴ πτυρόμενοι) what στήκετε signifies, retaining the impv. force of πολιτεύεσθε (Reumann 267).

Ψυχῇ and its adj. μιᾷ are dat. sg. fem. (instr. dat. [Sumney 35]). Take the expression with συναθλοῦντες (most EVV), rather than in appos. to ἑνὶ πνεύματι ("one in spirit, one in mind" [NEB]) (O'Brien 151). Ψυχή, -ῆς, ἡ, is a multivalent word, the seat and center of the inner life in its many and varied aspects. Here the term is used not of feelings or emotions (BDAG 1,098d, 1,099b) but, rather, to denote unity of purpose ("as one person" [Fee 166; Hansen 97]), a notion variously reflected in EVV ("with one mind" [NRSV, HCSB, REB]; "a single aim" [NJB]; "one desire" [GNB]; "with one accord" [NIV]). Other examples: (a) the Israelites being "of a single mind to make David king" (1 Chr. 12:38 [RSV]; ψυχὴ μία [12:39 LXX]); (b) the early church in Jerusalem (καρδία καὶ ψυχὴ μία [Acts 4:32]). The communal/social use of ψυχὴ μία is also found in Gk. proverbs reported by Aristotle and in the Pythagorean concept of the ideal community (Reumann 288).

Συναθλοῦντες is nom. pl. masc. of pres. act. ptc. from συναθλέω (only here and 4:3 in the NT); adv. ptc. of means; "contend, struggle along with someone" (BDAG 964a; "working side by side" [HCSB] is weak). The συν- prefix reinforces the emphasis on unity ("side by side" [NRSV, ESV, *EDNT* 3.296d]; "together" [NASB, NIV]; O'Brien 151). Some see in συναθλοῦντες a continuation of the military imagery introduced by στήκετε ("soldiers fighting side by side" [Hansen 97]; "battling" [NJB]). More likely Paul now shifts to an athletic metaphor (H-M 71). The combination of συναθλοῦντες and ἀγών (v. 30) pictures Christians wrestling as gladiators in the arena of faith (O'Brien 150). A verbal link with συναθλέω in 4:3 is intentional. Euodia and Syntyche once "contended side by side with (Paul) in spreading the gospel" (ἐν τῷ εὐαγγελίῳ συνήθλησαν [4:3]). Now, however, they lack the unity (τὸ αὐτὸ φρονεῖν ἐν κυρίῳ [4:2]) associated with such a partnership. The situation surrounding the two women and their respective factions thus exemplifies the particulars toward which the challenge in 1:27 is directed (Fee 166; Hansen 97).

Τῇ πίστει, is (1) a dat. of advantage (BDAG 964a; Fee 166; Hansen 97 n. 212; H-M 71; O'Brien 152; "the gospel cause" [Reumann 268]), not (2) an instr. dat. (R 529; Spicq 1.336), or (3) a dat. of association (Lightfoot 106; the prep. prefix in συναθλοῦντες goes not with τῇ πίστει but, rather, with an understood ἀλλήλοις [H-M 71]).

Τοῦ εὐαγγελίου can be taken as:

1. an obj. gen., with τῇ πίστει denoting faith exercised by the Philippians, "faith in the gospel [good news]" (BDAG 403a; R. Bultmann, *TDNT* 6.204 n. 230; 208 n. 258; G. Barth, *EDNT* 3.93c; "faithfulness to the gospel" [Sumney 36]); or

*2. a gen. of appos. to τῇ πίστει, "the faith which is the gospel" (Fee 166; H-M 71; O'Brien 152).

Based on Paul's example, we may surmise that more than the personal faith of the Philippians is in view. Like Paul they are to struggle "for the cause of the faith—its spread and growth" (O'Brien 152; cf. προκοπὴν τοῦ εὐαγγελίου [1:12]). This would involve both sharing the gospel and conduct that is worthy of such a message (Hansen 98).

VERSE 28

καὶ μὴ πτυρόμενοι ἐν μηδενὶ ὑπὸ τῶν ἀντικειμένων

Πτυρόμενοι is nom. pl. masc. of the pres. pass. ptc. from πτύρω (only here in the Gk. Bible), "to let oneself be intimidated" (BDAG 895c, NRSV; "frightened" [RSV, HCSB, TNIV, *EDNT* 3.192c]; "alarmed" [NASB]). Μή + pres. does not mean "stop being afraid," as if the Philippians were already running scared (Reed 357). Πτύρω could denote the "uncontrollable stampede of startled horses" (O'Brien 152; Lightfoot 106; Geoffrion, *Rhetorical Purpose*, 67). Christians are not to be terrified and agitated on the battlefield as horses are (Hansen 98).

Μηδενί is dat. sg. neut. from μηδείς, μηδεμία, μηδέν (cf. οὐδείς), "no one," "nothing." Ἐν + neut. μηδενί = "in no way" (NRSV, NASB; "not in any way" [HCSB]); here, with μὴ πτυρόμενοι, a double neg. (a cstr. "beloved in Greek" [Reumann 269]). Ἐν μηδενί makes the clause emphatic ("without so much as a tremor" [NEB]).

Ἀντικειμένων is a gen. pl. masc. pres. mid. ptc. from ἀντίκειμαι, functioning subst., "opponents" (most EVV; "enemies" [F. Büchsel, *TDNT* 3.655]); the art. τῶν functions poss., "your opponents." The term is generic for "enemies" (Jesus' opponents [Luke 13:17; 21:15]; Paul's in Ephesus [1 Cor 16:9]; the Antichrist [2 Thess 2:4]; and Satan [1 Tim 5:14]). Geoffrion (*Rhetorical Purpose*, 70) cites as background Exod 23:22 (LXX): ἀντικείσομαι τοῖς ἀντικειμένοις σοι; thus, not primarily a military metaphor but, rather, "foes of God" (Reumann 288; cf. also 2 Macc 10:26; Isa 66:6).

The opponents in view are not the Judaizers referenced in 3:2–3 (*pace* H-M 72; Silva 82–83) but, rather, pagan residents of the colony. Reasons:

a. They are non-Christians, on the road to destruction (αὐτοῖς ἔνδειξις ἀπωλείας [v. 28]).

b. Paul likens their opposition to his struggle, when he brought the gospel to Philippi (v. 30). Paul faced pagan opposition, not Jewish or Jewish Christian (Fee 167; cf. Acts 16:16–24).

c. They are a present, not a future, threat (cf. 3:2; Fee 167; Hansen 98–99; O'Brien 153).

d. The opponents in 3:2–3 are more clearly defined; Paul "cautions" here; he is "passionate" in 3:2–3 (Reed 135).

The adversaries likely consisted of Roman officials and the local populace, motivated by the Christians' "withdrawal from the traditional Greco-Roman cults, especially from the Imperial cult" (De Vos, *Church and Community Conflicts*, 264–65). In Philippi the imperial cult was "emphasized more than in any city where Paul previously ministered" (Reumann 282).

ἥτις ἐστὶν αὐτοῖς ἔνδειξις ἀπωλείας, ὑμῶν δὲ σωτηρίας

Ἥτις is an indef. rel. pron. from ὅστις, ἥτις, ὅτι; nom. sg. fem. by attraction to pred. nom. ἔνδειξις (R 412; Fee 168 n. 53). The antecedent is in question. Some tie ἥτις to τῇ πίστει τοῦ εὐαγγελίου at the end of v. 27 (H-M 72–73; Sumney 37). The distance makes this unlikely (Fee 169 n. 53). Ἥτις may be indef. here precisely because it does not refer to a specific term in preceding context (though this is not always the case with the indef. rel. pron.) but, rather, to the whole idea in ὅτι στήκετε . . . ἀντικειμένων" (Fee 168; cf. οἵτινες in 1 Cor. 3:17). The opposition from enemies and the steadfastness of the Philippian Christians together constitute the ἔνδειξις Paul has in view (R 729; Fee 168; Hansen 99 n. 218; "which circumstance" [O'Brien 152–53]).

Αὐτοῖς is dat. pl. masc. from αὐτός, -ή, -ό referring back to τῶν ἀντικειμένων; a dat. of disadvantage (R 537), if we assume the opponents' destruction is in view (see below).

Ἔνδειξις is nom. sg. fem. (ἔνδειξις, -εως, ἡ), "a sign," "something that points to or serves as an indicator of something" (BDAG 332a), here with obj. gen. (Reumann 270) from ἀπωλεία, -ας, ἡ, "destruction, ruin, annihilation [both complete and in process]" (BDAG 127a; "eternal destruction" [A. Oepke, *TDNT* 1.397]). As an Attic law term, ἔνδειξις denoted "proof" obtained by appeal to facts (O'Brien 155); "(clear) sign" (most EVV; "evidence" [NRSV]; "clear omen" [RSV]). A "pointer" not "proof" (Reumann 270). "[P]roof . . . with the added touch of prophecy" is too strong (Reumann 270, cites Hendrikson 90 n. 70). Since an "omen" constituted proof for the ancients, and since Paul does not use the word "sign" (σημεῖον) here, "omen" is a good translation (Fee 168 n. 55).

Whose destruction (ἀπωλείας) is in view—the opponents or the Philippians—is debated ("sign of destruction for them" [HCSB, NASB] preserves the ambiguity of the Gk.).

*1. The destruction of the opponents is in view in ἀπωλείας (H. Paulsen, *EDNT* 1.450b; Fee 169; O'Brien 153–55; Reumann 289; Silva 89–90; Sumney 37; so, also, many EVV, either by paraphrase "a sign to them that they will be destroyed, but that you will be saved" [NIV, NJB], or by the addition of a poss. pron. "their destruction" [NRSV, ESV]).

   a. Paul normally uses ἀπώλεια eschatologically, of the "utter ruin of unbelievers" (Fee 169 n. 56). This is clearly the case here, as indicated by the parallel σωτηρία (Fee 169 n. 56; Reumann 271).

b. This interpretation makes the best sense of the grammar. View 2, in contrast, awkwardly takes ὑμῶν with both σωτηρίας and ἀπωλείας, across the advers. δέ (Reumann 271; "the syntax is barely defensible" [Silva 90]). In reply, ὑμῶν is placed between ἀπωλείας and σωτηρίας in a way that permits us to see it modifying both nouns; if the postpositive δέ were intended to limit the ὑμῶν to modifying σωτηρίας, one would expect the word order to have been, αὐτοῖς . . . ἀπωλείας . . . σωτηρίας δὲ ὑμῶν (H-M 73).

c. This view is strongly supported by 2 Thess 1:4–8, where ἔνδειγμα (v. 5) relates to the vindication of the Thessalonian Christians and the punishment of their persecutors (Silva 90).

2. The Philippian Christians are in view in both ἀπωλείας and σωτηρίας, from the perspective of the opponents and the readers, respectively (Hawthorne, "The Interpretation and Translation of Philippians 1²⁸ᵇ"; Fowl, "Philippians 1:28b"): "In no way let your adversaries strike terror in you. For although they see your loyalty to the truth as inevitably leading to your persecution and death (i.e., the ἀπώλεια of the Christians), you see it as leading through persecution to the salvation of your souls" (Hawthorne 60).

a. In a Roman colony founded by Augustus himself, uncompromising loyalty to Jesus (versus Caesar) as Lord, would have been "a concrete manifestation to the opponents of the Christians' impending destruction, a destruction that would have entailed not only physical death but also the judgment of the gods" (Fowl, "Philippians 1:28b," 176).

b. This is how some ancient scribes read the text, as indicated by variants that (a) supply μέν in the first clause, and (b) alter ὑμῶν to ὑμῖν in the second clause. Never, in contrast, was αὐτοῖς in the first clause altered to αὐτῶν, in order to find a parallel for ὑμῶν (i.e., "their" destruction contrasted with "your" destruction) (H-M 74).

c. View 1 makes little sense. How would the opponents see in the steadfastness of the Christians a sign of their own destruction? Proponents respond by asserting that Paul is simply stating the facts of the case (ἐστίν), while the persecutors may not have recognized in the circumstances a "sign" at all (O'Brien 155; Sumney 37). But this seems to devalue the meaning of Paul's words; it makes more sense to take ἔνδειξις (particularly preceded by the dat. αὐτοῖς) as an indicator of something that would be recognized (Hansen 100).

The decision is difficult. View 1 is preferred with some reservations.

Σωτηρίας, (obj.) gen. sg. fem. of σωτηρία, -ας, ἡ, is governed by head noun ἔνδειξις, in parallel to ἀπωλείας. The ref. is to the Philippians' eschatological salvation. "Standing steadfast shows [cf. ἔνδειξις] they are God's holy ones, to be vindicated at the End, on their way to what Paul prayed for them in 1:6 and 10b–11" (Reumann 289).

The change of case, from the dat. αὐτοῖς to the gen. ὑμῶν, suggests a shift of emphasis in Paul's mind "from the persons to their destinies" (Fee 169); ὑμῶν is emphatic at the start of the phrase; δέ is adversative (Reumann 270).

καὶ τοῦτο ἀπὸ θεοῦ

A verb (e.g., ἀπέρχεται) must be supplied (Reumann 271; "this is God's doing" [NRSV]). Options for interpreting τοῦτο:

1. Tie τοῦτο closely to σωτηρίας and see ἥτις . . . τοῦτο ἀπὸ θεοῦ as parenthetical. The ὅτι-clause that follows (v. 29) then picks up and expands upon the reference to opposition back in v. 28a (Fee 170, n. 58; cf. diagram, 160).
2. Take τοῦτο to refer to the preceding clause (ἥτις . . . σωτηρίας). God works both salvation and destruction (Reumann 290; Sumney 37).
*3. Trace τοῦτο back to "the whole episode of opposition in its double effect, leading the opponents to destruction and the believers to eternal salvation" (O'Brien 157).

View 3 is best. Paul normally employs sg. neut. τοῦτο to refer not to an individual term but, rather, to a clause or complex of clauses, denoting a general idea or set of circumstances (e.g., Phil 1:19, 22, 25; 2:5; 3:15). This allows us to see Paul refer back (a) to συναθλοῦντες τῇ πίστει and σωτηρίας (vv. 27–28), with τὸ εἰς αὐτὸν πιστεύειν (v. 29), and (b) to μὴ πτυρόμενοι ἐν μηδενὶ ὑπὸ τῶν ἀντικειμένων (v. 28), with τὸ ὑπὲρ αὐτοῦ πάσχειν (v. 29), although suffering (versus believing) now becomes the central focus.

Ἀπό with a passive verb (here perhaps anticipating ἐχαρίσθη) begins to take the place of ὑπό, meaning "by" (agency) instead of "from" (source) (Z §90).

VERSE 29

ὅτι ὑμῖν ἐχαρίσθη τὸ ὑπὲρ Χριστοῦ

Attempts narrowly to link the causal ὅτι back to a specific phrase or idea (e.g., μὴ πτυρόμενοι . . . τῶν ἀντικειμένων [Fee, 170 n. 58]) are unnecessary. Paul refers here in v. 29 both to the ongoing faithfulness of the Philippians (εἰς αὐτὸν πιστεύειν) and to their suffering at the hands of the opponents (τὸ ὑπὲρ αὐτοῦ πάσχειν), two key ideas that surfaced in the previous context and were then picked up and summarized by τοῦτο at the end of v. 28.

Ὑμῖν picks up ὑμῶν in the previous verse. The emphatically placed pron. (Fee 170; O'Brien 159), followed immediately by ἐχαρίσθη, calls attention to God's goodwill toward the Philippians in gifts their Lord gives them: "What gift(s) will he stress? Suspense is heightened by a tantalizing art. infin." (Reumann 291).

Ἐχαρίσθη is 3 sg. aor. pass. indic. of χαρίζομαι, "to give graciously"; here, "you have (graciously) been granted the privilege of suffering for Christ" (BDAG 1078c). The aor. does not signify "a single past divine action, at baptism" (pace Reumann 290) but simply the action viewed externally, in summary fashion (Reed 386 n. 120). The understood agent is God (O'Brien 159; Reumann 271; cf. καὶ τοῦτο ἀπὸ θεοῦ). Sumney (37–38) sees ἐχαρίσθη as a divine pass., a category that is currently being reevaluated as a distinct expression of the passive voice (Wallace 437–38). Some suggest that χαρίζομαι means simply "give." The Pauline element characteristic of the noun (i.e., "grace") must be found in the context (H. Conzelmann, *TDNT* 9.396). Most think otherwise. Suffering, like salvation, is evidence of God's favor toward the Philippians ("graciously granted" [NJB]; "granted the privilege" [NRSV]; "a grace to suffer for Christ" [J. Kremer, *EDNT* 3.51d]; Fee 171; Hansen 102; H-M 76). Paul may have a suffering-grace connection in view when he writes of the readers "sharing in God's grace with me" in 1:7 (Fee 171).

The art. in τὸ ὑπὲρ Χριστοῦ anticipates the twofold art. inf. cstr. that follows (R 777). Because πιστεύειν takes εἰς instead of ὑπέρ, the phrase τὸ ὑπὲρ Χριστοῦ is reiterated in the final clause. The result is an emphatic ἀλλὰ καὶ τὸ ὑπὲρ αὐτοῦ πάσχειν: "but also for him—*to suffer*" (O'Brien 159, author's italics).

Fee suggests that Paul began to dictate the subject (τὸ ὑπὲρ Χριστοῦ πάσχειν) immediately after the verb (ἐχαρίσθη). He only got as far as τὸ ὑπὲρ Χριστοῦ and interrupted himself with the οὐ μόνον phrase, intending to emphasize their suffering for Christ, but within the context of what he has just said about their salvation coming ἀπὸ θεοῦ. The interruption—whatever the cause—has resulted in the "Christocentric character" of the statement: ὑπὲρ Χριστοῦ . . . εἰς αὐτὸν . . . ὑπὲρ αὐτοῦ (Fee 171).

οὐ μόνον τὸ εἰς αὐτὸν πιστεύειν

Μόνος is used as an adv. (see on v. 27) with πιστεύειν, pres. act. inf. from πιστεύω, "to entrust oneself to an entity in complete confidence" (BDAG 817b); subst. inf., parallel to πάσχειν as subj. of ἐχαρίσθη (BDF §399[1]). The art. inf. is widely extended in HGk. (Z §382; 10x in Phil [R 1424]). Πιστεύειν with εἰς (in Paul only at Rom 10:14 and Gal 2:16; common in John), "a NT grammatical invention," is "the most emphatic way of expressing absolute trust in Christ" (H-M 76). The pres. tense signifies ongoing trust (cf. the parallel πάσχειν, along with ἀγῶνα ἔχοντες [v. 30]; "continue to believe" [Reumann 272]; "the Christian condition" versus εἰς Χριστὸν πιστεῦσαι [aor. inf.] as "entrance into that state" [Harris, *Prepositions*, 237]). God had graciously given to the Philippians the privilege of continuing to believe in his Son even while suffering and undergoing persecution (O'Brien 160–61; Reumann 291). The strong emphasis upon divine sovereignty—regarding both faith and suffering—should not be missed (cf. also καὶ τοῦτο ἀπὸ θεοῦ [v. 28]).

The presence of οὐ rather than μή is to be explained by the fact that οὐ negates not the inf. but, rather, the adv. μόνον (Porter 282). With a single exception (Gal 4:18), οὐ μόνον is the common combination in the NT (R 1162; Reumann 272).

ἀλλὰ καὶ τὸ ὑπὲρ αὐτοῦ πάσχειν

Michaelis reads ἀλλὰ καί ascensively: τὸ ὑπὲρ αὐτοῦ πάσχειν "is a privilege, a special grace (ὑμῖν ἐχαρίσθη) which surpasses even the grace of being able to believe in Christ" (*TDNT* 5.920).

Πάσχειν is pres. act. inf. from πάσχω, "to suffer, endure," with ὑπέρ + gen., "suffer for someone" (BDAG 785c). The suffering was continuous and current (O'Brien 159; "repeated action" [Reumann 272–73]). Paul saw suffering as an active, rather than a passive experience, as illustrated by the qualifier τὸν αὐτὸν ἀγῶνα ἔχοντες that follows ("to fight," perhaps "to fight an enforced fight" [W. Michaelis, *TDNT* 5.920]). The ancients viewed affliction as something to overcome. To Gk. ears any claim about πάσχειν as something good, or a divine gift, was alien. "To suffer for (the sake of the) god(s) was unthinkable" (Reumann 291–92).

Ὑπὲρ αὐτοῦ means "for the sake of him" ("for his sake" [RSV, ESV]; R 632). When used with verbs of suffering, ὑπέρ gives "the reason for it" (BDAG 1031a; "on account of" [O'Brien 159]; "because of" [E. Riesenfeld, *TDNT* 8.514]; Harris, *Prepositions*, 210; cf. ὑπὲρ τοῦ ὀνόματος [Acts 5:41]). Much less likely is the idea "in place of," according to the analogy of Col 1:24–25 (*pace* H-M 75–76). The topic is not suffering in general (cf. Rom 8:17–30) but, rather, suffering due to "public identification with Christ" (Hansen 102) "in a world that is openly hostile to God" (Fee 170). Ill treatment came in response to the Philippians' Christian way of life, not just from the proclamation of the gospel (O'Brien 160).

VERSE 30

τὸν αὐτὸν ἀγῶνα ἔχοντες

Αὐτόν here means "the same," a secondary but common usage of αὐτός (BDAG 153d); first attrib. position (Reumann 273).

The term ἀγῶνα is acc. sg. masc. from ἀγών, -ῶνος, ὁ, lit. "athletic competition," used fig. here, "struggle, fight" for the gospel, in the face of opposition (BDAG 17b; "struggle" [NIV, NRSV, HCSB]; "conflict" [RSV, NASB, ESV]; "to engage in competition or conflict" [E. Stauffer, *TDNT* 1.167]). It was Paul's characteristic word for the "intense wrestling and struggle" involved in the apostle's missionary work (O'Brien 161; cf. Col 2:1; 1 Thess 2:2; 1 Tim 6:12; 2 Tim 4:7). Some see in ἀγῶνα military imagery ("battle" [NJB]; Geoffrion, *Rhetorical Purpose*, 80–81; Krentz, "Military Language," 126). An athletic metaphor is more likely (Reumann 294). A contemporary author used identical terminology (ἀγών + the ἀθλε- word group) to describe the suffering of Jewish martyrs under Antiochus IV:

> Truly divine was the contest (ἀγών) in which they were engaged. . . . The first to enter the contest (προηγωνίζετο) was Eleazar, but the mother of the seven sons competed also (ἐνήθλει), and the brothers as well took part (ἠγωνίζοντο). The tyrant was the adversary, and the world and the life of men were the spectators. Piety won the victory and crowned her own contestants (τοὺς ἑαυτῆς ἀθλητάς) (4 Maccabees 17:11, 13–15 tr. H. Anderson, OTP 2:562–63).

In ancient moral discourse (Epictetus, Seneca, Plutarch, Marcus Aurelius) the ἀγών motif—complete with images of various athletic contests—was used of the struggle of the sage toward virtue. Paul has refashioned the motif into an ἀγών of faith for the gospel (Pfitzner, *Paul and the Agon Motif*; G. Dautzenberg, *EDNT* 1.26a). The communal emphasis of the Pauline mission marks out Paul's perspective as distinct from pagan moral discourse, which sought to bring people to "selfhood individually" (Reumann 294).

Ἔχοντες is the nom. pl. masc. pres. act. ptc. of ἔχω; used adv. of manner, or (loosely) cause, "since" (NIV; Reumann 273). The vb. can mean "experience (something)," here a struggle against opponents (BDAG 421d; NASB; "engaged in" [RSV, ESV]; "going through" [NIV]; "fighting" [NJB]). Semantically, ἔχοντες qualifies the inf. πάσχειν, giving the manner of the suffering, but the syntax is irregular (a "peculiar" nom. [Moule 31]; independent nom. [Porter 85–86]). We might have expected the dat., in agreement with ὑμῖν (v. 29). Paul likely had ὑμεῖς before his mind as the logical subject of the preceding clause (Fee 172 n. 66; O'Brien 161). One could conceivably connect ἔχοντες with στήκετε (v. 27), in parallel to συναθλοῦντες and πτυρόμενοι, and take ἥτις . . . πάσχειν (vv. 28b–29) as parenthetical. Paul's point is clear, though, and such attempts to smooth out the grammar are unnecessary.

οἷον εἴδετε ἐν ἐμοὶ καὶ νῦν ἀκούετε ἐν ἐμοί

The term οἷον is acc. sg. masc. from rel. pron. οἷος, -α, -ον, "being similar to someth.," "belonging to a class"; here "the same struggle . . . as you saw" (BDAG 701c; dir. obj. of εἴδετε and ἀκούετε). The point of comparison relates to a "Roman problem," not simply suffering in general (Zerbe, "Citizenship and Politics," 198). Paul's emphasis on Jesus as "lord" (see on 2:11) and "savior" (3:20) suggests that Christians would have suffered for refusing to partake in public assemblies dedicated to civic and Roman gods, particularly those that honored Caesar as lord. Economic marginalization from voluntary associations that worshiped pagan gods as patrons may also be in view (Zerbe, "Citizenship and Politics," 198). Paul likely saw both (a) his ill treatment by Roman magistrates in Philippi (εἴδετε ἐν ἐμοί; cf. Acts 16:19–40) and (b) his current incarceration in Rome (ἀκούετε ἐν ἐμοί) as analogous (Fee 167). Note the sg. ἀγών (versus pl. ἀγῶνες). Paul regards his treatment at Philippi and his present imprisonment as aspects of one and the same conflict (O'Brien 162).

Εἴδετε is 2 pl. aor. act. indic. of ὁράω. Persons still in the church who had witnessed Paul's beating and imprisonment in Philippi (Acts 16:19–40; ἐν πολλῷ ἀγῶνι [1 Thess 2:2]) may have included the jailer and his family, the slave girl who had been set free from Satan's tyranny, and Lydia, who hosted the missionaries (Fee 173).

Ἀκούετε is 2 pl. pres. act. indic. The vb. generally takes as dir. obj. the acc. of things (here οἷον) and the gen. of persons (but cf. Mark 14:64). Reumann sees an *inclusio*: (a) ἰδών and ἀκούω (information about the Philippians) in v. 27; εἴδετε and ἀκούετε (information about Paul) in v. 30 (Reumann 295).

The prep. ἐν (ἐν ἐμοί [2x]) can be used as a "marker denoting the object to which someth. happens" (BDAG 329b; "in me" [NASB; Reumann 274]; "to be mine" [RSV]; some EVV reframe ἐν ἐμοί as a subj., "that you saw I had" [NRSV, HCSB, NIV]).

FOR FURTHER STUDY

22. Military Imagery (1:27)

Geoffrion, Timothy C. *The Rhetorical Purpose and the Political and Military Character of Philippians: A Call to Stand Firm*. Lewiston: Mellon Biblical Press, 1993.

*Krentz, Edgar M. "Military Language and Metaphors in Philippians." Pages 105–27 in *Origins and Method: Towards a New Understanding of Judaism and Christianity*. Edited by B. H. McLean. Sheffield: JSOT Press, 1993.

23. Athletic Imagery (1:27, 30)

Dautzenberg, G. *EDNT* 1.25–27.
Esler, P. F. "Paul and the Agon. Understanding a Pauline Motif in Its Cultural and Visual Context." Pages 356–84 in *Picturing the New Testament: Studies in Visual Images*. Edited by A. Weissenrieder. WUNT 2/193. Tübingen: Mohr Siebeck, 2005.
*Pfitzner, Victor C. *Paul and the Agon Motif*. NovTSupp 16. Leiden: Brill, 1967.
Ringwald, A. *NIDNTT* 1.644–47.
Stauffer, E. *TDNT* 1.134–40, 167–68.

24. The Gospel (1:27)

Becker, U. *NIDNTT* 2.107–15.
Broyles, C. C. *DJG* 282–86.
Burrows, Millar. "The Origin of the Term 'Gospel.'" *JBL* 44 (1925): 21–33.
Fitzmyer, Joseph A. "The Gospel in the Theology of Paul." Pages 149–61 in *To Advance the Gospel*. New York: Crossroad, 1981.
Friedrich, G. *TDNT* 2.707–36.
Hall, David R. "Fellow-Workers with the Gospel." *ExpTim* 85 (1974): 119–20.
Keown, Mark J. *Congregational Evangelism in Philippians: The Centrality of an Appeal for the Gospel Proclamation to the Fabric of Philippians*. Paternoster Biblical Monographs; Milton Keynes: Paternoster, 2008.
*Luter, A. B. *DPL* 369–72.
Martin, R. P. *ISBE* 2.529–32.
O'Brien, Peter T. "The Importance of the Gospel in Philippi." Pages 224–26 in *God Who Is Rich in Mercy*. Homebush West: Grand Rapids, 1986.
Spallek, Andrew J. "The Origin and Meaning of Εὐαγγέλιον in the Pauline Corpus." *Concordia Theological Quarterly* 57 (1993): 177–90.
Stuhlmacher, Peter. "The Pauline Gospel." Pages 149–72 in *The Gospel and the Gospels*. Edited by P. Stuhlmacher. Grand Rapids: Eerdmans, 1991.

25. Roman Citizenship (1:27) *(see below, Church and State in Philippi)*

Ascough, Richard S. *Paul's Macedonian Associations: The Social Context of Philippians and 1 Thessalonians*. Tübingen: Mohr-Siebeck, 2003.
Cotter, Wendy. "Our Politeuma Is in Heaven: The Meaning of Philippians 3:17–21." Pages 92–104 in *Origins and Method: Towards a New Understanding of Judaism and Christianity*. Edited by B. H. McLean. Sheffield: JSOT Press, 1993.
*Hellerman, *Reconstructing Honor*, 113–16.
Hengel, Martin. *The Pre-Christian Paul*. Philadelphia: Trinity Press International, 1991. See pages 6–15.
Miller, Ernest C. "Πολιτεύεσθε in Philippians 1.27: Some Philological and Thematic Observations." *JSNT* 15 (1982): 86–96.
Minnen, Peter van. "Paul the Roman Citizen." *JSNT* 56 (1994): 43–53.
Oakes, 55–76.

Tellbe, Mikael. "The Sociological Factors Behind Philippians 3.1–11 and the Conflict at Philippi." *JSNT* 55 (1994): 97–121.

Zerbe, Gordon. "Citizenship and Politics According to Philippians." *Direction* 38 (2009): 193–208.

26. Suffering (1:29–30)

Bloomquist, L. Gregory. *The Function of Suffering in Philippians.* JSNTSup 78. Sheffield: Sheffield Academic, 1993.

_____ . "Subverted by Joy: Suffering and Joy in Paul's Letter to the Philippians." *Interpretation* 61 (2007): 270–82.

Gerstenberger, Erhard and Wolfgang Schrage. *Suffering.* Biblical Encounters Series. Nashville: Abingdon, 1980.

*Hafemann, S. J. *DPL* 919–21.

Pobee, John S. *Persecution and Martyrdom in the Theology of Paul.* JSNTSup 6. Sheffield: Sheffield Academic, 1985.

Simundson, D. J. *ABD* 6.219–25.

Talbert, Charles H. *Learning Through Suffering: The Educational Value of Suffering in the New Testament and Its Milieu.* Zacchaeus Studies. Collegeville, MN: Michael Glazier/ Liturgical Press, 1991.

27. Church and State in Philippi (1:28)

*Clarke, Andrew D. "God's Sovereignty over Roman Authorities: A Theme in Philippians." Pages 126–41 in *Rome in the Bible and the Early Church.* Edited by Peter Oakes. Grand Rapids: Baker Academic, 2002.

De Vos, Craig. *Church and Community in Conflict: The Relationships of the Thessalonian, Corinthian, and Philippian Churches to Their Wider Civic Communities.* SBLDS 168. Atlanta: Scholars Press, 1999.

Tellbe, Mikael. *Paul Between Synagogue and State: Christians, Jews, and Civic Authorities in 1 Thessalonians, Romans, and Philippians.* Stockholm: Almqvist and Wiksell International, 2001.

Wright, N. T. "Paul's Gospel and Caesar's Empire." Pages 160–83 in *Paul and Politics.* Edited by Richard A. Horsley. Harrisburg, PA: Trinity Press International, 2000.

28. αὐτοῖς ἔνδειξις ἀπωλείας (1:28b)

*Fowl, Stephen E. "Philippians 1:28b, One More Time." Pages 167–79 in *New Testament Greek and Exegesis: Essays in Honor of Gerald F. Hawthorne.* Edited by Amy Donaldson and Timothy Sailors. Grand Rapids: Eerdmans, 2003.

Hawthorne, Gerald F. "The Interpretation and Translation of Philippians 1[28b]." *ExpTim* 76 (1983): 80–81.

HOMILETICAL SUGGESTIONS

Living as Kingdom Citizens in the Light of God's Great Gifts (1:27–30)

1. The gift of suffering (vv. 28a, 29c)
2. The gift of perseverance (vv. 27d, 29b)

3. The gift of partnership (v. 30)
4. The gift of salvation (v. 28b)

To Conduct Myself in a Manner Worthy of the Gospel Is to (1:27–30)

1. Struggle like an athlete (vv. 27d, 30a)
2. Face formidable opponents (vv. 28a, 29c)
3. Be part of a team (v. 30b)
4. Emerge victorious (v. 28b)

Contending for the Faith (1:27–30)

1. The charge to stand fast (v. 27)
2. The challenge of opposition (vv. 28a, 29c)
3. The comfort of God's purposes now and in the future (vv. 28b–29)
4. The encouragement of fellow athletes (v. 30)

B. UNITY AMONG BELIEVERS (2:1–30)

1. PLEA FOR UNITY THROUGH HUMILITY (2:1–4)

1 a Εἴ τις οὖν παράκλησις ἐν Χριστῷ,
    b εἴ τι παραμύθιον ἀγάπης,
    c εἴ τις κοινωνία πνεύματος,
    d εἴ τις σπλάγχνα καὶ οἰκτιρμοί,
2 πληρώσατέ μου τὴν χαρὰν
      ἵνα τὸ αὐτὸ φρονῆτε,
        τὴν αὐτὴν ἀγάπην ἔχοντες,
        σύμψυχοι,
        τὸ ἓν φρονοῦντες,
3   A μηδὲν κατ' ἐριθείαν
           μηδὲ κατὰ κενοδοξίαν
        B ἀλλὰ   τῇ ταπεινοφροσύνῃ
           ἀλλήλους ἡγούμενοι ὑπερέχοντας ἑαυτῶν,
4   A' μὴ τὰ ἑαυτῶν ἕκαστος σκοποῦντες
        B' ἀλλὰ καὶ τὰ ἑτέρων ἕκαστοι.

The chapter division is unfortunate, as are attempts to distinguish too sharply between relations with outsiders (1:27–30) and relations in the church (2:1–4) (*pace* O'Brien 164). The charge in 1:27 (ἀξίως τοῦ εὐαγγελίου τοῦ Χριστοῦ πολιτεύεσθε) stands over all of 1:27–2:18, and Paul now directly expands upon a theme introduced in 1:27, where church unity was "deliberately placed within its real life setting in Philippi" (ἐν ἑνὶ πνεύματι, μιᾷ ψυχῇ) (Fee 175 n. 10; Hansen 105; H-M 81; Reumann 310, 319). The need for unity vis-à-vis opponents (1:27–30) naturally leads to the challenge to seek unity with those who have different interests within the church (2:1–4) (Hansen 106).

Unity depends on a distinct mind-set (cf. noetic verbs: φρονῆτε, φρονοῦντες [v. 2], ταπεινοφροσύνῃ, ἡγούμενοι [v. 3]), which is (a) is grounded in the prior work of God in the Philippians' lives (v. 1) and (b) finds tangible expression in the other-centered priorities of those who share Christ's mind-set (vv. 3–4). The result will be a community with a social ethos that contrasts markedly with the honor-seeking orientation of relational life in the broader culture of Roman Philippi.

Verbal parallels with 2:5–11 should not be missed: ἐν Χριστῷ (v. 1)/ἐν Χριστῷ Ἰησοῦ (v. 5); φρονῆτε (and φρονοῦντες) (v. 2)/φρονεῖτε (v. 5); ἡγούμενοι (v. 3)/ἡγήσατο (v. 6); κενοδοξίαν (v. 3)/ἐκένωσεν (v. 7) and δόξαν (v. 11); ταπεινοφροσύνη (v. 3)/ἐταπείνωσεν (v. 8) (R. Tuente, *NIDNTT* 3.597; O'Brien 166).

Attempts to identify a poetic structure for 2:1–4 have failed to satisfy (cf. Fee 176; H-M 81; O'Brien 165). What is clear is that "Paul puts the force of fine rhetoric to work to impress upon his audience the importance of fundamental Christian ideas— unity based on humility and self-sacrifice" (H-M 81). Factions represented by Euodia and Syntyche (4:2–3) may be in view here (Fee 187).

VERSE 1

Although the general ideas in v. 1 are clear enough, two problems challenge the interpreter: (1) ambiguity surrounding the meaning of specific words in each of the four clauses, and (2) questions about agency, i.e., "Who is doing what to whom?" The lexical issues will be addressed on a case-by-case basis, below. Solutions to the question of agency fall broadly into three categories:

*1. The four εἰ-clauses each describe an aspect of the work of God in the readers' lives, e.g., παραμύθιον ἀγάπης is a reference to the encouragement or consolation provided by God's love for the Philippians (O'Brien 174–76; Park 165); or,

 2. Mutual relations among the readers are in view, so that παραμύθιον ἀγάπης would refer to the comfort that comes from love among believers in Philippi (cf. G. Braumann on παράκλησις ἐν Χριστῷ: "Paul encourages the Philippians to exhort one another" [NIDNTT 1.570]); or,

 3. The clauses describe the relationship between Paul and the Philippians.

The three approaches have, in turn, generated further, variegated options. Thus, H-M see Paul encouraging and consoling the Philippians in 1ᵃᵇ, whereas God becomes the acting agent in 1ᶜᵈ (H-M 82–83, 85). For Fee, 1a is "Christ's comfort," shared by Paul and the Philippians; 1ᵇᶜ focus on "God's love and their participation in the Spirit"; 1d, on their relationship with Paul (Fee 178–79). Hansen finds both divine and human agency (views 1 and 2) in play in each clause (e.g., 1a, Christ is the source of encouragement, which, in the community, flows from one member to another [Hansen 106]). Some preserve the ambiguity in polyvalent translations. Thus, Reumann renders κοινωνία πνεύματος as "sharing in the Spirit and the fellowship brought about by the Spirit" (Reumann 297; cf. H-M 81).

Although relations among the Philippians are surely not far from Paul's mind (they become central in vv. 2–4), lexical considerations (see below, on κοινωνία πνεύματος and οἰκτιρμοί) argue in favor of taking all of v. 1 to refer to God's work in the lives of the Philippians (view 1 above) (O'Brien 174–76; Reumann 319). This accords with Paul's common practice of grounding ethics (the imperative) securely upon the bedrock of God's work in Christ (the indicative). View 2 makes less sense, in this regard, since it assumes (see on Εἴ below) healthy relations in the community (v. 1) as the basis for exhorting the Philippians to pursue the same (vv. 2–4). Further supporting view 1 is the apparent presence of a Trinitarian substructure in the first three εἴ-clauses: Christ (1a); God (1b, implied); Spirit (1c) (Fee 179–80; Reumann 321).

Εἴ τις οὖν παράκλησις ἐν Χριστῷ

Εἴ introduces the protasis of a first class cond. (apodosis = πληρώσατέ μου τὴν χαράν [v. 2]), assumed to be true for sake of argument. Here the εἰ-clauses correspond to reality (sometimes not, cf. Mark 3:26), and may be translated "since" (BDAG 277b; BDF §372; H-M 82; Moule 148; "if . . . as indeed there is" [Fee 178]; Hansen 106; O'Brien 165; Reumann 320).

The indef. prons. τις/τι are generally taken adj. with the noun(s) in each clause, with ἐστίν understood (Wallace 347; EVV impers., "if there is" [NRSV, NASB, HCSB], or paraphrasing, "if you have" [NIV, cf. CEV]). Lack of concord in the fourth clause (sg. masc. τις with pl. neut./masc. σπλάγχνα/οἰκτιρμοί), along with a textual var. in the second clause, has led some to postulate τι throughout (BDF §137[2]; T 316), and to take the prons. as preds.: "if παράκλησις in Christ (amounts to) something" (Reumann 298; cf. NJB). But after τις three times, a scribe could have easily written τις in the fourth clause, perhaps even mistaking σπλάγχνα for a fem. sg. (R 410). And although the neut. form τι is used indeclinably in papyri, a fourfold τι is "surely too great a modification of the text" (Z §9).

Οὖν stands third in its clause, rather than in its usual second position, because Εἴ τις was "felt to be one word" (BDF §475[2]). The inferential conj. ("so" [RSV, NJB, ESV]; "then" [NRSV, HCSB]; "therefore" [NASB, NIV]) is resumptive, taking up the main point of the previous paragraph, after the parenthetical remarks of 1:29–30. The exhortation to unity (2:2–4) with its fourfold basis (2:1) is a "concrete expression" of ἀξίως τοῦ εὐαγγελίου τοῦ Χριστοῦ πολιτεύεσθε . . . ἐν ἑνὶ πνεύματι, μιᾷ ψυχῇ (1:27) (O'Brien 164).

BDAG offers two options for παράκλησις:

1. "Exhortation, encouragement" (BDAG 766a; Schmitz, *TDNT* 5.795; G. Braumann, *NIDNTT* 1.570; H-M 82–83).
   a. Paul consistently uses the cognate παρακαλέω to exhort his churches (Rom 12:1; 15:30 [with διά . . . Ἰησοῦ Χριστοῦ]; 16:17; 1 Cor 1:10 [with διὰ . . . Ἰησοῦ Χριστοῦ]; 4:16; 16:15; Phil 4:2; 1 Thess 2:12; 5:14).
   b. This understanding is supported by the use of παράκλησις in extrabiblical Gr. ("primary meaning" in the papyri [MM 485b]) and in LXX texts that lack a Heb. original (O. Schmitz, *TDNT* 5.776, 799).
   c. "Exhortation" best suits the context, where a charge to unity is at the forefront (2:2–4), and where walking in a manner worthy of the gospel is the overarching theme (1:27).
*2. "Comfort, consolation" (BDAG 766b; Fee 179–80; Hansen 107–8; Oakes 179–80; O'Brien 170).
   a. ἡ παράκλησις in this case comes from God, not Paul, so the appeal to the cognate παρακαλέω is appreciably weakened (*pace* H-M 83; see above, for God as agent in v. 1).
   b. "Comfort, consolation" is the common meaning of the word group in the LXX where there is a Heb. original, particularly in the prophets (e.g., Isa 40:1; 51:18a) (O'Brien 170).
   c. "Comfort" is a frequent meaning of the noun in Paul (cf. esp. 2 Cor 1:3–7, where παράκλησις and cognates occur no fewer than ten times; 2 Cor 7:4, 7, 13; 2 Thess 2:16; Phlm 7; perhaps Rom 15:4–5).
   d. A reference to Christ's comfort would naturally follow the discourse on suffering in 1:29–30. The chapter division unfortunately obscures the connection (Fee 179–80; Hansen 107; Reumann 298). The link between

suffering and comfort in 2 Cor 1 mirrors the connection here, including several verbal parallels: ὅτι καθὼς περισσεύει τὰ παθήματα τοῦ Χριστοῦ εἰς ἡμᾶς, οὕτως διὰ τοῦ Χριστοῦ περισσεύει καὶ ἡ παράκλησις ἡμῶν (v. 5; cf. πάσχειν [Phil 1:29] and παράκλησις [2:1]; compare, as well, ὁ πατὴρ τῶν οἰκτιρμῶν [2 Cor 1:3] with οἰκτιρμοί [Phil 2:1] [Fee 180; Hansen 107–8]).

  e. Paul's exhortation begins later, in 2:2. V. 1 constitutes the fourfold basis of that exhortation, not the exhortation itself. "Comfort" is, therefore, a better fit at this point in the discourse (O'Brien 170).

  f. The parallel terms inform the meaning of παράκλησις; paired with παραμύθιον, παράκλησις becomes "more friendly" (J. Thomas, *EDNT* 3.25a).

The decision between "exhortation" and "comfort" is not an easy one, in part because the two meanings are not wholly unrelated—"comfort" implies a degree of "(ethical) encouragement" or "exhortation" (Reumann 301). Most EVV retain the ambiguity by translating παράκλησις as "encouragement," an Eng. term that, like its Gk. counterpart, can denote either (view 1) an "act of emboldening another in belief or course of action" (BDAG 766a), or (view 2) the "lifting of another's spirits" (BDAG 766b). The above arguments strongly suggest, however, that "encouragement" in the latter sense—"comfort"—is at the forefront in v. 1.

Ἐν Χριστῷ ("in Christ" [most EVV]; "being united with Christ" [NIV]) formally modifies only παράκλησις, but the remaining blessings are experienced in union with Christ, as well ("So if in Christ there is anything that will move you, any incentive in love, any fellowship in the Spirit, any warmth or sympathy" [NJB]).

εἴ τι παραμύθιον ἀγάπης

The semantic range of παραμύθιον (nom. sg. neut.) is sim. to παράκλησις, so that attempts sharply to distinguish the two are not convincing (H-M 83; Reumann 301]), as the EVV indicate ("incentive" [RSV, NJB]; "comfort" [NIV, NLT, ESV]; "consolation" [NASB, NRSV, HCSB]). In CGr. the word group (like παράκλησις/παρακαλέω) could signify either "comfort" (philosophy "comforts" the soul [Plato, *Phaedo* 70b]) or "exhortation" ("the others too I would kindly exhort to sail home" [Homer *Il.* 9, 417]) (G. Braumann, *NIDNTT* 1.328).

Παραμύθιον, however, seems to be "a 'friendly' word of support," rather than "a command to 'buck up'" (Reumann 322). The term denotes "comfort" or "consolation" at Wis 3:18 (it is not used in LXX where there is a Heb. original), while the few instances of the cognate vb. signify "soothe, comfort," rather than "exhort" (O'Brien 171 n. 37; G. Stählin, *TDNT* 5.820; but cf. the ptc. in 2 Macc 15:9, "Encouraging" [NRSV]). The neut. is found only here in NT (cf. fem. [παραμυθίαν] at 1 Cor 14:3; vb. παραμυθέομαι 4x [John 11:19, 31; 1 Thess 2:12, 5:14]). BDAG translates παραμύθιον ἀγάπης as "solace afforded by love" (BDAG 769c; sim. papyri [MM 488c]; Fee 180). The theme of suffering in the context (1:12–30) supports the meaning "comfort, consolation" (Hansen 109; H. Balz, *EDNT* 3.32d; G. Stählin, *TDNT* 5.821; H-M 83; O'Brien 172).

Though the παραμυθ- word group is elsewhere used in the NT not of divine but, rather, human comfort (H-M 83), contextual considerations (see above, on God as agent throughout v. 1) suggest that God is the source of the comfort here (NIV, NLT, CEV; Reumann 321; "the consolation which Christ's love for them has brought in their dangers and suffering" [O'Brien 172]). The modifier ἀγάπης (gen. sg. fem. [gen. of source or subj. gen.]) supports this reading, since "'love,' in keeping with Paul's OT roots, is most often expressed as from God" (Fee 181). Other options—that the comforting agent(s) is/are (1) Paul, (2) the Philippians ("mutual consolation" [G. Stählin, *TDNT* 5.822–23]), or (3) the apostle and the readers mutually, or that (4) ἀγάπης refers to the *agape* table fellowship—are possible but less likely (O'Brien 172; Reumann 322).

εἴ τις κοινωνία πνεύματος

The suggestion that πνεύματος refers to the human spirit, so that κοινωνία πνεύματος simply means "mutual harmony," is to be rejected, as indicated by the context and by the par. at 2 Cor 13:13: ἡ κοινωνία τοῦ ἁγίου πνεύματος (Fee 180; H-M 84; O'Brien 174).

The identity of the participants is unclear. The phrase can refer to:

1. "fellowship" among the Philippians, produced by the Holy Spirit ("fellowship together in the Spirit" [NLT; cf. CEV]; E. Schweizer, *TDNT* 6.434; H-M 84; πνεύματος taken as gen. of source).

*2. the readers' "participation in the Spirit" itself (RSV, ESV, cf. NRSV; F. Hauck, *TDNT* 3.807; J. D. G. Dunn, *NIDNTT* 3.702; O'Brien 174; πνεύματος as obj. gen.).

3. both 1 and 2 ("common sharing in the Spirit" [NIV]; Fee 181 n. 40; Reumann 303).

The second view is strongly supported by:

a. the use of κοινωνία + gen. outside the Bible to signify that of which one partakes;

b. the context, where divine, not human, activities form the basis for the paraenesis that follows;

c. the par. in 1 Cor 1:9 (κοινωνίαν τοῦ υἱοῦ αὐτοῦ Ἰησοῦ Χριστοῦ), which can only refer to participation in Christ;

d. the Pauline notion that the believer possesses and experiences the Holy Spirit (Gal 3:2; 1 Cor 12:13); and

e. the early church's understanding of the phrase in question as "participation in the Spirit" (O'Brien 174).

Paul's third ground of appeal, then, is the gift of the Holy Spirit, and the Philippians' knowledge of his indwelling and activity. Paul emphasizes the experience of the entire community rather than the idea that each individual possesses the Spirit (Hansen 110).

"Participation in the Spirit" should put an end to all factiousness and party spirit, for it is by this one Spirit that they were all baptized into one body (O'Brien 174).

εἴ τις σπλάγχνα καὶ οἰκτιρμοί

Τὰ σπλάγχνα, "the viscera," were thought of in the ancient world as the seat of one's deep feelings (see on 1:8; H-M 84; "affection" [NASB, HCSB, ESV]; "compassion" [NRSV]).

BDAG defines οἰκτιρμοί as "display of concern over another's misfortune," glossing the term as "pity, mercy, compassion" (BDAG 700c). Some take σπλάγχνα καὶ οἰκτιρμοί as a hendiadys, since the words describe similar feelings of pity, mercy, and compassion (BDAG 700c; "heartfelt sympathy" [R. Bultmann, *TDNT* 5.161; H.-H. Esser, *NIDNTT* 2.598]; H-M 85). This is not likely, however, since both terms appear in virtue lists and have somewhat different meanings (H. Koester *TDNT* 7.555–56; Fee 182). Σπλάγχνα have to do with feelings of mercy, οἰκτιρμοί the manifestation of those feelings in compassionate actions ("the root and the fruit" [Fee 182 n. 41]; Lightfoot 108; Reumann 303). Thus, for οἰκτιρμοί, "mercy" (HCSB) is a better tr. than "sympathy" (NRSV, NJB, ESV), since "mercy" more naturally implies activity of some sort.

Σπλάγχνα καὶ οἰκτιρμοί are best taken to refer to God's (or Christ's) affection and mercies (H-M 85; O'Brien 175–76; Reumann 323), not to the mutual affections of the Philippians ("kindness and compassion for one another" [GNB, cf. NLT, CEV]; R. Bultmann, *TDNT* 5.161; H.-H. Esser, *NIDNTT* 2.598; H. Balz & G. Schneider, *EDNT* 2.505a; Fee 182; Hansen 110):

    a. Οἰκτιρμοί is a characteristic word for the mercy of God (23 of 26 occurrences) in the LXX. A familiar synagogue prayer addressed God as "our Father, merciful Father" (cf. the expression "God of mercies" at Qumran [1QH X, 14; XI, 29]).

    b. Paul elsewhere uses οἰκτιρμοί of God's mercies (Rom 12:1; 2 Cor 1:3; but cf. Col 3:12). In Romans 12:1 the phrase τῶν οἰκτιρμῶν τοῦ θεοῦ summarizes Paul's gospel, as set forth in the first eight chapters of the letter, and provides the basis for the paraenesis that follows (cf. Παρακαλῶ [12:1]) (Reumann 323).

    c. Σπλάγχνον and its cognate vb. σπλαγχνίζομαι are also used of divine compassion: (1) of the attitude of Jesus as God's representative (Matt 9:36; 14:14; Mark 1:41; 9:22; Luke 7:13); and (2) of the actions of key persons in Jesus' parables who make the mercy of God visibly plain (Matt 18:27; Luke 10:33; 15:20).

Σπλάγχνα καὶ οἰκτιρμοί denote "the 'tender mercy and compassion' of Christ experienced by the Philippians when they became Christians through the preaching of the gospel" (O'Brien 176; the phrase serves as "a summary of the three preceding clauses" [H. Köster, *TDNT* 7.555]).

O'Brien's summary of 2:1 warrants full citation: "The fourfold basis of Paul's exhortation is grounded in divine certainties: the Philippians know God's comfort and salvation in Christ. They have experienced the consolation that Christ's love for them has brought in their sufferings and dangers. Theirs is a participation, a common sharing, in the Holy Spirit, and they have been blessed through his gracious ministry to their hearts and lives. When God began his good work in their midst through the preaching of the gospel, they were recipients of his tender mercies and compassion. Since they have been blessed with such riches in a magnificent way, let them hear Christ's exhortation through their beloved apostle" (O'Brien 176).

VERSE 2

πληρώσατέ μου τὴν χαράν

Πληρώσατε is 2 pl. aor. act. impv., from πληρόω, "bring to completion that which was already begun" (BDAG 828d; "complete" [most EVV; G. Delling, *TDNT* 6.297]; "fulfill" [HCSB]). The clause functions as the apodosis to the par. εἰ–clauses of v. 1 (R 1019). Attempts to assign emphatic force to μου (Fee 184 n. 52) are not convincing (Reumann 305; T 189). There is a degree of skewing here between syntax and semantics. Syntactically πληρώσατε functions as the main verb of a long sentence (vv. 2–4). But πληρώσατέ μου τὴν χαράν is not the main idea. It is a metacomment serving to highlight what is about to be said (Runge 278; see on 1:12). Paul is primarily concerned in 2:1–4 with unity among the Philippians, not with the fulfillment of his own joy (χαράν is acc. sg. fem.).

Nevertheless, the notion that πληρώσατέ μου τὴν χαράν is "simply prefatory" to the idea of unity (H-M 85) too easily dismisses an important, though admittedly secondary, point in the discourse, related to Paul's pastoral heart. Paul's life was already characterized by the Christian grace of joy, even in prison. Yet his joy was not wholly unrelated to external circumstances, especially the spiritual state of his churches. So, although Paul is already taking joy in the Philippians (1:4; 4:1), "his cup of joy will only be filled to the brim when the well-being of the congregation, currently troubled by strife and self-interest, is fully restored . . . then his joy will be complete" (O'Brien 177; Fee 183–84; Hansen 111).

ἵνα τὸ αὐτὸ φρονῆτε

The ἵνα-clause is usually taken epex., giving the content of πληρώσατέ μου τὴν χαράν (most EVV; Moule 145 n. 3; Porter 239; R 992; Wallace 476; Z §410; Reumann 305; O'Brien 177), or as the obj. of an implied vb., e.g., παρακαλῶ (BDF §392 [1c]). The result is much the same. The ἵνα-clause participates in the impv. force of πληρώσατε ("be of the same mind" [NRSV]; T 3:94–95).

Αὐτό is acc. sg. neut. from αὐτός, αὐτή, αὐτό, used subst., "the same (thing)." The idea is not "think the same thing as Paul" (though semantically possible, and Paul would certainly agree with the Christ-like mind-set in view) but, rather, "think the same thing as each other." Paul desires a single mind-set among the Philippians (implied in EVV, explicit in NLT, CEV; Reumann 305).

Φρονῆτε is 2 pl. pres. act. subjunc. from φρονέω, "think, form/hold an opinion, judge" (BDAG 1065c). BDAG glosses τὸ αὐτὸ φρονῆτε (a Pauline idiom [cf. Rom 12:16; 15:5; 2 Cor 13:11; Phil 4:2]) as "be in agreement" or "live in harmony" (1065d). Neither gloss is adequate for what Paul is doing with φρονέω in Philippians 2. Cognition and volition are both in view—"not merely an activity of the intellect, but also a movement of the will; it is both interest and decision at the same time" (J. Goetzmann, *NIDNTT* 2.617). Paul's point, then, is not simply that all should be "thinking the same way" (HCSB; cf. "agreeing wholeheartedly with each other" [NLT]), but, rather, that all should share the same comprehensive mind-set (H-M 86; "being of the same mind" [RSV, NASB, ESV]; "maintaining a Christian disposition in all things" [G. Bertram, *TDNT* 9.233]; H. Paulsen, *EDNT* 3.439b). Φρονῆτε here anticipates vv. 6–11, where Paul directs the Philippians to the mind-set of Christ (Τοῦτο φρονεῖτε [2:5]), and where the primary issue, again, is not mutual agreement but, rather, a Christlike attitude toward privileges of power, authority, and social capital (see below on vv. 5–11).

τὴν αὐτὴν ἀγάπην ἔχοντες, σύμψυχοι

῎Εχοντες is nom. pl. masc. of the pres. act. ptc. of ἔχω, "experiencing (something), have," when used of characteristics, capabilities, emotions (BDAG 421c). The ptc. formally modifies φρονῆτε (manner or means [Wallace 630]; "by showing love" [CEV]), though most EVV tr. as par. to τὸ αὐτὸ φρονῆτε (e.g., "being of the same mind, having the same love" [ESV]). Semantically, ἔχοντες and the following ptcs. take on the impv. force of the discourse (Hansen 112 n. 29; H-M 86).

The intensive pron. αὐτήν points back to v. 1, where παραμύθιον ἀγάπης describes the comfort provided by God's love. The Philippians are to have "the same love" toward one another as God has toward them (BDAG 6b; Wallace 350; Fee 185; O'Brien 178; Reumann 305).

Σύμψυχοι is nom. pl. masc. of σύμψυχος (lit. "souls together" [Hansen 112]), "harmonious" (BDAG 961c; "united in spirit" [C. Brown, *NIDNTT* 3.687]; "unity of the Church in feeling as well as in thought and action" [H. Balz & G. Schneider, *EDNT* 3.291a]). EVV vary ("in full accord" [NRSV, ESV]; "one/united in spirit" [NIV/NASB]; "sharing the same feelings" [HCSB]). The compound σύμψυχοι picks up and reinforces μιᾷ ψυχῇ in 1:27 (Fee 185 n. 60; Hansen 112). A similar compound (ἰσόψυχον) is used of Timothy at 2:20. Σύμψυχοι is sometimes set off with commas (UBS⁵, NASB, HCSB). Some EVV coordinate σύμψυχοι and τὸ ἓν φρονοῦντες ("being in full accord and of one mind" [NRSV, ESV; cf. NIV]). It is perhaps best to tie together σύμψυχοι and φρονοῦντες τὸ ἓν grammatically, so that σύμψυχοι describes how the Philippians can set their minds on the one thing (Fee 183 n. 47; Silva 91).

τὸ ἓν φρονοῦντες

Φρονέω (nom. pl. masc. of the pres. act. ptc.) is reintroduced. Paul does not specify the content of τὸ ἕν (acc. sg. neut., with the art. "the one [thing]"). Zerwick suggests some definite "one thing" known to Paul and to the Philippians (Z §170; "the one thing which would make me completely happy" [Reumann 306]). For O'Brien, that "one thing" ("one purpose" [NASB]; "one goal" [HCSB]) is the gospel, as indicated by the broader context (1:27; cf. v. 12): the Philippians are to be "'gospel oriented' as they relate to and care for one another" (O'Brien 179). The idea is an attractive one, but we would expect a clearer statement to that effect in the near context of 2:2. Ultimately, Paul explains what he means by τὸ ἓν φρονοῦντες in 2:5–11, with the challenge to share Christ's mind-set (Hansen 113). In the near context (a) the presence of the art. τό (anaphoric, picking up τὸ αὐτό [Fee 183 n. 47]), and, especially, (b) the repetition of φρονέω, suggest that τὸ ἓν φρονοῦντες is virtually synonymous with τὸ αὐτὸ φρονῆτε, earlier in v. 2 ("of one mind" [BDAG 292a; NRSV, ESV, NIV]; H. Paulsen, *EDNT* 3.439b; H-M 86). Reading the phrase closely with σύμψυχοι (see above), the argument unfolds as follows: the Philippians are to "share the same mind-set (of Christ)" (ἵνα τὸ αὐτὸ φρονῆτε); this they do by "having the same love" (τὴν αὐτὴν ἀγάπην ἔχοντες); it is with their very lives thus harmoniously united together (σύμψυχοι) that they can share such a (Christlike) mind-set (τὸ ἓν φρονοῦντες).

VERSE 3

μηδὲν κατ' ἐριθείαν μηδὲ κατὰ κενοδοξίαν

A vb. form must be supplied, either (a) a ptc. (ποιοῦντες or φρονοῦντες [from v. 2]) or (b) an impv. (most EVV; "the phrase has the force of a moral imperative" [Hansen 113; H-M 87]). The elliptical twofold expression "forcibly draw(s) attention to its absoluteness" (O'Brien 179). Κατά + acc. frequently function like an adv. (BDAG 513b; cf. κατὰ λόγον, "reasonably" [Acts 18:14]).

For ἐριθείαν (acc. sg. fem.) see on 1:17. The noun can mean (a) "selfish(ness)" (RSV, NLT, NASB; "selfish ambition" [NRSV, NIV, ESV]; "base self-seeking" [F. Büchsel, *TDNT* 2.661]), or (b) "rivalry" (HCSB). The ideas are not unrelated. Individuals in Philippi's highly stratified honor culture were deeply embedded in patronage networks that operated across the social classes. An ambitious local aristocrat would expect support from his friends, clients, and persons in his extended household. Preoccupation with one's own social advantage naturally led, therefore, to factions and rivalry (Oakes 181–82). Ἐριθεία is "a party spirit generated by selfish ambition" (H-M 87; O'Brien 180).

Κενοδοξίαν (acc. sg. fem.) (only here in NT) derives from κενός ("empty") + δόξα ("glory," "honor"). The word denotes "a vain or exaggerated self-evaluation" (BDAG 538d; not simply "conceit" [NRSV, HCSB] but, rather, "empty/vain conceit" [NASB/ NIV]; the grounds for boasting are altogether baseless [H-M 87; S. Aalen, *NIDNTT* 2.47]). It is not by accident that the two parts of the compound (κενός + δόξα) appear in vv. 6–11: ἐκένωσεν (v. 6) to describe the kind of self-emptying that is the precisely opposite of κενοδοξία; δόξαν (v. 11) to express the glory that accrues to God, when the self-emptying One receives divine vindication and the worship of all creation (Fee 186–87 n. 68; Hansen 114).

ἀλλὰ τῇ ταπεινοφροσύνῃ

Ταπεινοφροσύνη (here dat. sg. fem.) means "humility, modesty" (BDAG 989d; "humility" [most EVV]); dat. of manner (O'Brien 181) or "dat. of the motivating cause" (BDAG 989d; "instrumental dat." [Sumney 42]). The tr. "humility of mind" (NJB, NASB) preserves Paul's emphasis on a particular mind-set (cf. -φροσύνη). Clarified in context by its opposites (ἐριθείαν and κενοδοξίαν), and by the two ptc. clauses that follow, ταπεινοφροσύνη has nothing to do with self-disparagement but is "the resolution to subject oneself to others and to be more concerned about their welfare than one's own" (W. Grundmann, *TDNT* 8.21–22; H.-H. Esser, *NIDNTT* 2.262). As such, it is "the lynchpin that guarantees the health of the Christian community" (H-M 87). Humility became a defining concept for Christian ethics, the singular virtue that—more than any other—distinguished Christian social values from their pagan counterparts. A brief history of the idea proves highly illuminating:

a. Secular Greek: Ταπεινός ("humble") was used negatively in ancient literature to describe the mentality of a slave, or the servile nature of inferior social classes (H-M 88; "servile" [Aristot., *Eth. Eud.* 3.3]; "not free" [Plato, *Leg.* 4.774c]; "low-born, ignoble" [Arrian, Epict. 1.3]). The negative associations related primarily to social rank. The evaluation of persons according to social class was exacerbated among the Romans, particularly in a colony like Philippi, where humility would have been anything but a virtue. Ταπεινός was generally related to birth status, although a people or state could be "made lowly" (enslaved) by the military force of others (W. Grundmann, *TDNT* 8.1–2).

b. Judaism: The same negative connotations of ταπεινός and its cognates surface at times in the LXX (e.g., Gen 15:13; 31:50; Exod 1:12; Judg 6:15), but a new note is struck: God chooses the unimportant and insignificant for his plans (1 Sam 18:23; Ps 118:67; Jdt 9:11); God saves the lowly and humble (Job 5:11; Ps 17:28); God looks upon the lowly (Ps 112:4–6); God pays attention to the prayers of the lowly (Ps 101:18); God gives grace to the lowly while he opposes the scoffers (cf. Isa 2:11; Ezek 17:24). In later Judaism (e.g., Sirach and the DSS) humility is increasingly connected with communal values such as unity and love among the people of God. Thus, Qumran is to be a "community of truth and virtuous humility and loving charity and scrupulous justice" (1QS II, 24; cf. IV, 3; V, 3, 25) (H-M 88). Paul is heir to these ideas since for Paul, like Qumran, humility connotes "a practice of living together in community before God in such a way that other people are given a dignity and respect as they too are seen in God's sight" (R. P. Martin, *NIDNTT* 3.928).

c. Paul: Paul's contribution to the Jewish reframing of ταπεινός as a positive virtue is to situate humility preeminently in the mind-set and behavior of Christ Jesus (vv. 6–8). In this regard the connection between ταπεινοφροσύνη (v. 3) and its etym. components (ταπεινός + φροσύνη) elsewhere in the text must not be missed (the φρονέω word group [vv. 2, 5]; ἐταπείνωσεν [v. 8]) (O'Brien 166). Hansen's assertion that the humility of Christ "is not the same as the humility scorned by the Greeks" is only partially true (115). The basic sense is, in fact, the same, i.e., abject social status. To take on the form of a slave (v. 7) was to assume the lowest social rank in the Greco-Roman world. And crucifixion (v. 8) was the most degrading act of public humiliation conceivable. The striking difference is that the humiliation of Christ did not issue from passive inability, as in the case, for example, of the oppressed poor, or of a powerless slave who had no other option. Christ willingly chose weakness, servility, and subjection, and he did so in the service of others—a choice at odds with ancient social sensibilities. God's vindication of Christ's choice (vv. 9–11), in turn, affirms for the followers of Jesus in Philippi a radically alternative relational ethos vis-à-vis the honor culture of Roman Philippi.

Some cite our passage as the first occurrence of the compound ταπεινοφροσύνη in Gk. lit. (cf. Epictetus 3.24.56; Josephus, *Jewish War* 4.494). Perhaps Paul coined the term precisely to subvert the cultural values and social codes of the relational context in which the Philippians found themselves.

Reumann interprets τῇ, governing ταπεινοφροσύνῃ, possessively, referring not to a mind-set Paul wants the Philippians to adopt but, rather to "the social-world humiliation that the Philippian Christians [already] experience in daily life from their 'betters' in Roman social structures" (perhaps related to the suffering of 1:29–30) (Reumann 315). For this, however, we would expect ταπείνωσις, "lowliness, humble station" (BDAG 990c). The interpretation makes little sense, moreover, in the surrounding context. The art. points, instead, to "that humility proper to Christians which Paul has so often inculcated and on which he is about to insist once more, appealing to the example of God incarnate" (Z §170; O'Brien 181).

ἀλλήλους ἡγούμενοι ὑπερέχοντας ἑαυτῶν

Humility is now more precisely defined (H-M 88). Ἀλλήλους is acc. pl. masc. of gen. pl. ἀλλήλων (reciprocal pron. with no nom.), "each other, one another, mutually" (BDAG 46b)—one of the most significant words in Paul (40x) concerning relationships among believers (H. Krämer, *EDNT* 1.63c). To translate ἀλλήλους as "others" (NRSV, HCSB, ESV), rather than "one another" (NASB, GNB), is to "tone down the community significance of this exhortation" (Fee 189 n. 77).

Ἡγούμενοι is nom. pl. masc. of the pres. dep. ptc. of ἡγέομαι, "think, consider, regard" (BDAG 434b; "a consciously sure judgment resting on carefully weighed facts" [H-M 88]). A ptc. of manner with πληρώσατε (v. 2), ἡγούμενοι shows how the Philippians can make Paul's joy full (Reumann 307; or, taken with ἵνα τὸ αὐτὸ φρονῆτε, how unity is achieved [Fee 189]); impv. force (EVV; BDF §468[2]; Moule 179–80). Note, again, the verbal link with Paul's story of Christ (cf. ἡγήσατο [v. 6]). There may be a certain irony in Paul using a vb. that has, as a primary meaning, "to be in a supervisory capacity" (BDAG 434a), for an attitude of status inferiority and servant-hood vis-à-vis others in the community.

Ὑπερέχοντας is acc. pl. masc. of the pres. act. ptc. of ὑπερέχω (subj. = ἀλλήλους), used as a ptc. of indir. discourse (after vbs. of perception or communication) (R 1123; Wallace 646). Ὑπερέχω, common in CGk. for political or social position, refers in the NT to either

*1. superiority in status or authority (Rom 13:1; 1 Pet 2:13; "to be in a controlling position," "have power over, be in authority [over], be highly placed" [BDAG 1033b]; Park 164); or

2. superiority in quality or value (Phil 3:8; "be better than, surpass, excel"; here "each one should consider the others better than himself" [BDAG 1033b]; "excelling themselves" [G. Delling, *TDNT* 8.524]; T 52).

The honor culture of Roman Philippi commends the first option ("above your-selves" [NIV]; "more important" [NASB, CEV, HCSB]), rather than the second ("bet-ter" [NRSV, NLT]; *pace* BDAG 1033b). It is not that others in the community are to be thought of as "better than I am" but that others are to be thought of as those whose rank—and, therefore, whose needs and concerns—take precedence over my own (Fee 189). The sentiment is revolutionary, for Paul is essentially charging a church member with Roman citizen status (estimated at ca. 36% of the congregation at Philippi), for example, to treat a brother who is a slave as if the latter occupied a more prestigious rank than he, thus directly subverting the pride of honors that marked social life in the colony.

The refl. pron. ἑαυτῶν is gen. (of comp. [R 591; Sumney 43]) pl. masc., from ἑαυτοῦ, -ῆς, -οῦ (no nom. form; pers. must be determined from context [here 2]). This is the first in a series of alliterative prons. in vv. 3–4 (ἑαυτῶν, ἑαυτῶν, ἕκαστος, ἑτέρων, ἕκαστοι) that highlights the contrast between self-exaltation and self-denial (Black, "Paul and Christian Unity," 302).

VERSE 4

μὴ τὰ ἑαυτῶν ἕκαστος σκοποῦντες

V. 3 had to do with inner attitude. V. 4 now addresses behavior vis-à-vis one's fellow Christian, explaining how one considers others superior to himself (Fee 190; Reumann 317). The art. in τὰ ἑαυτῶν is acc. pl. neut., used subst., "the things of (your)selves" (see above, v. 3, on the refl. pron.), glossed in EVV as "your/his own interests."

Ἕκαστος (cf. ἕκαστοι, below) emphasizes the involvement "of each individual" and makes the exhortation "more direct and personal" (F. G. Untergassmair, *EDNT* 1.404a; Reumann 316). The tr. "each of you" (NRSV, NIV, ESV) is better than "everyone" (NJB, HCSB). The emphasis is on the community, but obedience begins with the indi-vidual (Fee 190).

Σκοποῦντες is nom. pl. masc. of the pres. act. ptc. of σκοπέω, another ptc. of manner; rightly interpreted as impv. in most EVV ("look . . . to" [NRSV, ESV]; "look out for"

[NASB, HCSB; BDAG 931a]; "care about" [CEV]). In CGk., σκοπέω meant "look critically," as a judge (Plato *Leg.* 11.925A), philosopher (Plato *Cra.* 440D), or historian (Thuc. 1.1.3), also to discover a propitious time (Thuc. 4.23.2). LXX use is minimal (Reumann 315). Some see Paul encouraging the readers not to focus on their own spiritual gifts or manifestations but, instead, to appreciate and value the spirit-inspired manifestations of others, so that σκοπέω here means "to hold something as a model before one's eyes" (Hansen 117; H-M 89). This is highly unlikely. Τὰ ἑαυτῶν σκοπεῖν is essentially synonymous with τὰ ἑαυτῶν ζητεῖν (2:21), so the normal meaning of σκοπέω, "to look at attentively," "fix one's attention on" (one's own interests) is to be retained (O'Brien 185).

ἀλλὰ [καὶ] τὰ ἑτέρων ἕκαστοι

Supply the ptc. σκοποῦντες from the previous clause (Porter 283). The καί is textually disputed. External evidence for inclusion is early and widespread ($\mathfrak{P}^{46}$ א A B C D² *Byz*; [lacking in D* F G K Tertullian]; omitted [NRSV, NIV]). Scribes may have omitted καί for the same reason that some EVV add "only": καί was perceived as awkward without μόνον in the first clause (Fee 175 n. 8; O'Brien 185). Others suggest καί was added to soften the injunction (Reumann 316). If καί is original, it either (a) softens the contrast ("also, likewise" [NASB, HCSB, ESV; O'Brien 185]), or (b) further strengthens it ("but actually, rather" [Bockmuehl 113–14; cf. LXX Job 21:17; Isa 39:4; 48:6; Ezek 18:11; Wis 14:22]). The preoccupation with the meaning of καί must not obscure the main idea: "Paul is rebuking self-interest in 2:3–4, not inviting his readers to have regard to their own interests" (H-M 80).

Τὰ ἑτέρων (acc. pl. neut. art. [subst.] + gen. pl. masc. adj. [also subst.] from ἕτερος, -α, -ον, "other") serves as a contrasting dir. obj. with τὰ ἑαυτῶν (Reumann 316). The pl. ἕκαστοι is emphatic, an earnest repetition signifying "each and all" (O'Brien 185) or, perhaps, "each without exception."

FOR FURTHER STUDY

29. Unity (2:2)

Allen, David M. "Philippians 4:2–3: 'To Agree or Not to Agree? Unity Is the Question." *ExpTim* 121 (2010): 533–38.
*Black, David A. "Paul and Christian Unity: A Formal Analysis of Philippians 2:1–4." *JETS* 28 (1985): 299–308.
Kinnamon, Michael. "Christian Unity: Recapturing the Passion." *Impact* 24 (1990): 1–11.
Malherbe, Abraham. "The Unity of the Church in Paul." *ResQ* 2 (1958): 187–96.
Moreton, Dorothea. "'Unity': Philippians 2:1–11." *Unitas fratrum* 10 (1981): 104–10.

30. Humility (2:4)

Boer, Willem. "*Tapeinos* in Pagan and Christian Terminology." Pages 143–62 in *Tria corda. Scritti in onore di Arnaldo Momigliano*. Edited by E. Gabba. Como: Edizione New Press, 1983.
*Dawes, Stephen B. "Humility: Whence This Strange Notion?" *ExpTim* 103 (1991): 72–75.

Dickson, John P., and Brian S. Rosner. "Humility as a Social Virtue in the Hebrew Bible."
    VT 54 (2004): 459–79.
Essler, H.-H. *NIDNTT* 2.259–64.
Giessen, H. *EDNT* 3.333–35.
Grundmann, W. *TDNT* 8.1–26.
Leivestad, Ragnar. "The Meekness and Gentleness of Christ." *NTS* 12 (1965–66): 156–64.
Spicq 3.369–71.
Wengst, Klaus. *Humility: Solidarity of the Humiliated: The Transformation of an Attitude
    and Its Social Relevance in Graeco-Roman, Old Testament, and Early Christian
    Tradition.* Translated by J. Bowden. Philadelphia: Fortress, 1988.

HOMILETICAL SUGGESTIONS

Unity Among Believers (2:1–4)

1. The basis for unity: God's blessings in our lives (v. 1)
2. The charge to unity: the right mind-set (v. 2)
3. The way of unity: a proper view of self and others (vv. 3–4)

Appreciating God's Blessings (2:1)

1. The comfort we have in Christ
2. The encouragement that comes from love
3. The gift of the Holy Spirit
4. The mercies of God

Sharing in the Mind-set of Christ: A Call to Unity (2:2–4)

1. The charge to unity (v. 2)
2. The way of unity (vv. 3–4)
   a. A proper view of self
   b. A proper view of others

2. CHRIST OUR EXAMPLE (2:5–11)

5   τοῦτο <u>φρονεῖτε</u> ἐν ὑμῖν

   |
   ὃ καὶ ἐν <u>Χριστῷ Ἰησοῦ</u>,

6   ἐν <u>μορφῇ θεοῦ</u> ὑπάρχων

            ὅς . . . οὐχ ἁρπαγμὸν ἡγήσατο τὸ εἶναι ἴσα θεῷ,

7   ἀλλὰ ἑαυτὸν ἐκένωσεν

            <u>μορφὴν</u> δούλου λαβών,

            ἐν ὁμοιώματι ἀνθρώπων γενόμενος·

            καὶ σχήματι εὑρεθεὶς ὡς ἄνθρωπος

8   ἐταπείνωσεν ἑαυτὸν

            γενόμενος ὑπήκοος μέχρι <u>θανάτου</u>,

                         <u>θανάτου</u> δὲ σταυροῦ.

9   διὸ καὶ ὁ <u>θεὸς</u> αὐτὸν ὑπερύψωσεν

        καὶ ἐχαρίσατο αὐτῷ τὸ <u>ὄνομα</u>

            τὸ ὑπὲρ πᾶν <u>ὄνομα</u>,

10   ἵνα   ἐν τῷ <u>ὀνόματι Ἰησοῦ</u>

        πᾶν γόνυ κάμψῃ

            ἐπουρανίων

        καὶ ἐπιγείων

        καὶ καταχθονίων

11   καὶ πᾶσα γλῶσσα ἐξομολογήσηται

            ὅτι κύριος <u>Ἰησοῦς Χριστὸς</u>

        εἰς δόξαν <u>θεοῦ</u> πατρός.

The literature on Philippians 2:5–11 has become virtually unmanageable. Scholars have produced whole books on single terms in the passage (e.g., Fabricatore on μορφή, below). The limitations of the EGGNT format necessitate a highly abbreviated treatment of this central Christological passage. Readers are referred to the commentaries (cf., especially, O'Brien and Reumann) and bibliography for further study and support for alternative views. The exegesis that follows assumes that Paul has leveraged Christology—conceived in terms of status and prestige—in the service of ecclesiology.

Traditional interpretations of Philippians 2:5–11 focus upon ontological Christology (v. 6 and v. 7 highlighting, respectively, Christ's divine and human natures), drawing upon theological categories fully articulated only later, at the ecumenical councils of Nicaea and Chalcedon (reflected in some EVV, e.g., "in very nature God" [NIV tr. ἐν μορφῇ θεοῦ, v. 6]). Paul's agenda, however, is primarily sociological, not ontological (*pace* Park 36). To be sure, one can effectively argue from Christ's status of "equality with God" to his divine nature. The acclamation of Jesus as κύριος (OT YHWH) in v. 11 points in the same direction (Wallace 474; Silva 114). Indeed, it could be fairly asserted that prior ontological assumptions, on Paul's part, stand behind and legitimate much of what the apostle says about Christ's status throughout our passage. But this argument is not Paul's, not explicitly, at any rate. His interests relate, rather, to Christ's position in the pecking order of the universe, so to speak. Paul focuses throughout not upon Christ's essential nature (οὐσία) but, rather, upon what Christ chose to do with his status (and corresponding authority) as the preincarnate Son of God. Paul appropriates Christ, so conceived, as a model for relationships among members of the Philippian church (v. 5). Philippians 2:5–11 is Christology in the service of ecclesiology, therefore, and will be treated as such in the discussion that follows.

The poetic language of the passage (Hansen 122–24; cf. Wallace 340–41) has led most to characterize Philippians 2:6–11 as a pre-Pauline hymn that the apostle adapted for the epistle (G. Delling, *TDNT* 8.500–501; Hansen 130–31; H-M 99–104; cf. the essays in Martin and Dodds, *Where Christology Began*). It is possible, however, that Paul composed 2:6–11 himself (Fee 193; Hellerman 155–56; Park 16; Oakes 208–10; cf. Wright, "ἁρπαγμος," 352; for bibliography, see Hellerman, "μορφῇ θεοῦ," 779 n. 1). In the final analysis little is at stake exegetically. For even if Paul appropriated an earlier source, he did so because (a) he thought the material perfectly advanced his argument in its present context in the letter and (b) he was in full agreement with the theology of the piece (see Fee's sensible comments along these lines [43–46]). The discussion that follows assumes Pauline authorship for vv. 6–11.

The term "hymn," moreover, is used rather loosely in the literature, and for good reason, since no agreement has been reached on the poetic structure of vv. 6–11 (Park 12–13). A more promising formal candidate is the Greco-Roman encomium, or "speech of praise." The encomium typically extolled its subject's "(divine) origins; deeds or acts, service on earth; and fame, including any titles bestowed" (Reumann 364). Identifying Philippians 2:6–11 as an encomium contributes little to the interpretation of the text, but it does show that the Philippians would have been in familiar territory when they heard this portion of the letter for the first time.

Paul's encomium to Christ, however, unfolds in a way that would have directly subverted the expectations of a Roman colonial audience. Elites in Rome competed with one another to ascend what was known as a *cursus honorum*, an "honors' race" that marked an aristocrat's social climb through a series of prestigious public offices. The titles accumulated along the way were, in turn, publicly proclaimed, in order of importance, by means of inscriptions erected either (a) by grateful recipients of elite benefaction or (b) by the aristocratic benefactors themselves. The *cursus honorum* was replicated throughout the empire, where local aristocrats competed for offices and honors in the smaller confines of their own provincial towns and municipalities. Still further down the pecking order, nonelites mimicked their social betters by adopting a race of honors in their various trade associations and religious groups.

Cursus ideology was particularly central to the cultural values and social codes of Philippi since the settlement had been established as a Roman colony in 42 BC and, again, under Augustus, in 30 BC. The following inscription presents the career of a second-century Philippian aristocrat:

Publius Marius Valens, son of Publius, from the tribe Voltinia, honored with the decorations of a decurion, aedile, also decurion of Philippi, priest of the divine Antoninus Pius, duumvir, sponsor of games (395/L780).

Publius was a Roman citizen from birth ("Voltinia" was his citizen tribe). Because he was born into a family that included persons who served as decurions (Philippi's town council), he was "honored with the decorations of a decurion," likely while still a child. Publius became a "decurion" himself as an adult, and soon won two important civic honors: the office of "aedile" and a priesthood in the imperial cult ("priest of the divine Antoninus Pius"). Finally, Publius became "duumvir" of Philippi, the highest civic office in the colony (the στρατηγοί of Acts 16:20 ff.). It was in that role, presumably, that he financed a display of public entertainment for the municipality ("sponsor of games").

The honors in Publius's *cursus* are listed in ascending order. In his encomium to Christ, Paul inverts the normal direction of the *cursus honorum*, by portraying Jesus descending through three stages of what we might label a *cursus pudorum*, or "race of ignomies." Instead of using his social capital to gain more honors and public recognition, Christ leveraged his status in the service of others. Such a utilization of power— indeed, a voluntary relinquishing of rank and prestige—would have struck Roman elites as abject folly. The esteemed senator Pliny pointedly observed, "It is more uglifying to lose, than never to get, praise" (*Ep.* 8.24.9). Christ lost it, and he did so willingly (ἑαυτόν [2x, vv. 7–8]). God's positive response to Christ's pilgrimage (vv. 9–11), in turn, strikingly affirms an approach to human relations radically contrary to that which characterized the dominant culture in the colony at Philippi, a way of life that Paul wished to see reflected in relationships among the Philippian Christians (v. 5).

Expressions from the semantic fields of public honor, shame, and social status include ἐν μορφῇ θεοῦ (v. 6), τὸ εἶναι ἴσα θεῷ (v. 6), ἐκένωσεν (v. 7), μορφὴν δούλου (v. 7), ἐταπείνωσεν (v. 8), ὑπήκοος (v. 8), σταυροῦ (v. 8), ὑπερύψωσεν (v. 9), ὄνομα (v. 9 [2x]), πᾶν γόνυ κάμψῃ (v. 10), πᾶσα γλῶσσα ἐξομολογήσηται (v. 11), κύριος (v. 11), and δόξαν (v. 11).

VERSE 5

τοῦτο φρονεῖτε ἐν ὑμῖν ὃ καὶ ἐν Χριστῷ Ἰησοῦ

Most Gk. mss. add γάρ after Τοῦτο (𝔓⁴⁶ ℵ² D F G 075 0150 *Byz* etc. [2492 has οὖν]; γάρ is absent from ℵ* A B C Ψ 33 81 etc.), "an unnecessary attempt" to link this section with the preceding vv. (H-M 99; Reumann 339); "one cannot imagine the reasons for omitting the conjunctions, if either were original" (Fee 197 n. 17; *pace* O'Brien 203; UBS⁵ = {B} τοῦτο).

As usual for Paul, τοῦτο (acc. sg. neut., dir. obj.) points back to the attitude described in vv. 2–4, not forward to the story of Christ (BDF §290[3]; R 703; Fee 199 n. 25; O'Brien 204; Reumann 340; *pace* H-M 107).

Φρονεῖτε is 2 pl. pres. act. impv. from φρονέω (cf. 1:7 and 2:2) and refers to a mind-set or a "kind of thinking" (BDAG 1,066a; "Have this mind/attitude" [RSV, NASB, ESV]). The vb. links what follows (vv. 6–11) with vv. 1–4 (cf. φρονέω 2x in v. 2).

The prep. modifier ἐν ὑμῖν can be taken distributively ("in yourselves" [NASB]) or collectively ("among yourselves" [RSV]; "in your relationships" [NIV]; H-M 108; Reumann 340). Given the emphasis upon relations in the church in 2:2–4 and 2:12–18, the latter interpretation is surely intended. The collective reading assumes a necessar-ily prior individual response, but Paul's focus is upon the community.

Καί (omit [NRSV, ESV]) here means "also" (NASB; "the same" [NIV, NLT]; Fee 201 n. 33), rather than an intensive "which indeed" (pace Reumann 340; Z §465).

The rel. clause (ὃ καὶ ἐν Χριστῷ Ἰησοῦ) has received two markedly different inter-pretations, depending upon how ἐν Χριστῷ Ἰησοῦ is read:

*1. Take the prep. phrase to refer to Christ's mind-set, as expressed in the incar-nation and crucifixion (vv. 6–8): "Have this attitude in yourselves which was also in Christ Jesus" (NASB; "let the same kind of thinking dominate you as dominated Christ Jesus" [BDAG 1066a]; cf. NIV, NRSV, CEV, NLT, HCSB; G. Bertram, TDNT 9.233 n. 75; M. Harris, NIDNTT 3.1192; Harris, Prepositions, 127; Fee 200; O'Brien 205, 253–62; Sumney 45).

   a. The interpretation flows most naturally into vv. 6–8, where Christ's self-humiliation, during his earthly ministry, becomes the model for the proper use of status and authority among Christians at Philippi (Fee 200 n. 29; O'Brien 200–201, 204).

   b. The reading makes good sense of both Τοῦτο and καί (v. 5). View 2 must interpret Τοῦτο and καί in ways that, although grammatically possible, are not in accord with normal Pauline usage.

2. Take ἐν Χριστῷ Ἰησοῦ to refer to the believer's union with Christ: "Have the same thoughts among yourselves as you have in your communion with Christ Jesus" (BDAG 1066a; "which is yours in Christ Jesus" [RSV, ESV; cf. NEB, "out of your life in Christ"]; J. Goetzmann, NIDNTT 2.618–19; H-M 104–9; Hansen 121; Reumann 333).

   a. Ἐν Χριστῷ is Paul's favorite formula for union with Christ (cf. 4:2, where the same vb. is followed by a reference to union in Christ [τὸ αὐτὸ φρονεῖν ἐν κυρίῳ]). But, the addition of Ἰησοῦ, and the mention of the incarnation and crucifixion that follows (vv. 7–8), likely point, in this instance, to the example of the historical Jesus (O'Brien 258).

   b. In Rom 15:5 Paul prays for the readers τὸ αὐτὸ φρονεῖν ἐν ἀλλήλοις κατὰ Χριστὸν Ἰησοῦν. The parallel expressions line up as follows:

Philippians 2:5	Romans 15:5
Τοῦτο φρονεῖτε	τὸ αὐτὸ φρονεῖν
ἐν ὑμῖν	ἐν ἀλλήλοις
ὃ καὶ ἐν Χριστῷ Ἰησοῦ	κατὰ Χριστὸν Ἰησοῦν

c. View 1 must insert an understood "was," ἦν, in the second clause, but there is nothing in the first clause to suggest any vb. other than φρονέω (Silva 96). However, this results in a tautology. Why challenge the Philippians to have the mind-set among themselves that they already have (indic. φρονεῖτε understood in the second clause) in Christ? In response, one might appeal to the structure of Pauline ethics, where the imperative is grounded in the doctrinal indicative (Hansen 121). This, however, fails to satisfy: (a) where Paul grounds the imperative in the indicative elsewhere, he is much more clear; Paul has been in the imperative throughout vv. 2–4, so that an opaque allusion to the Philippians' position in Christ would be particularly surprising; (b) the use of φρονέω in the second clause does not accord with Paul's normal presentation of the indicative in his theology as "an already given condition" (O'Brien 257–58); nowhere else is Paul's indicative framed in terms of the noetic activity of those who are "in Christ Jesus."

d. This allows both ἐν-phrases in v. 5 to refer to the new community of believers in union with Christ (Hansen 121; Silva 95–96). View 1, in contrast, must interpret ἐν in two different ways: (1) "among (you)" (demanded by φρονεῖτε) and (2) "in (Christ Jesus)." But the parallelism does not necessitate that ἐν be interpreted in the same way in each clause (O'Brien 256). The collective reading of ἐν ὑμῖν assumes a necessarily prior individual response, moreover, so that the understanding of the sg. ἐν Χριστῷ Ἰησοῦ advocated in view 1 does not irretrievably betray the parallelism.

e. The ethical understanding advocated by view 1 is a non sequitur: "How can one imitate, in any sense, an act that is unique, unrepeatable, and salvific?" (H-M 107). This objection completely misses the point. The Philippians (φρονεῖτε [v. 5]) are to emulate the mind-set of Christ (ἡγήσατο [v. 6]) by how they choose to leverage their social capital, not by imitating Christ's singular salvific act (Fee 196 n. 14, 201 n. 33).

The decision between the two interpretations of ἐν Χριστῷ Ἰησοῦ is not an easy one. Pauline usage of ἐν Χριστῷ (Ἰησοῦ) favors view 2, but the other arguments for the reading are quite weak. Paul's paraenetic aims in vv. 6–11 can be preserved on either reading (Hansen 121; Silva 97), but view 1 more pointedly reinforces the transparently ethical orientation of the context in which the debated expression is found (vv. 1–18) (see O'Brien 253–62, for an extended discussion). View 1 is preferred with some reservations.

VERSE 6

ὃς ἐν μορφῇ θεοῦ ὑπάρχων

The phrase ἐν μορφῇ θεοῦ presents the first crux in our passage. Μορφή (here dat. sg. fem.) is best tr. "form" (most EVV; BDAG 659c). The NIV's "in very nature God" ("truly God" [CEV]; "God" [NLT]; "possessed of the very nature of God" [H-M 114]) constitutes an interpretation that is not directly supported by the usage of the term in HGk. and which emphasizes, at best, a secondary implication of ἐν μορφῇ θεοῦ in its present context. Although the term can be used substantially (Plato *Phaed.* 103e; *Resp.* 381c; Aristotle *Met.* 11.1060b; *Phys.* 2.1.193b; Plut. *Quaest. plat.* 1003b; *Def. orac.* 429a; Philo *Spec.* 1.327–28), there is no semantic component in μορφή that necessitates a corresponding "nature" (NIV) or ontology (*pace* Fee 204; H-M 114). In the great majority of instances where μορφή and its cognates occur in HGk., the word group simply denotes "outward appearance" (Fabricatore, *Form of God, Form of a Servant*; "form, outward appearance, shape" [BDAG 659c]; that "which may be perceived by the senses" [J. Behm, *TDNT* 4.745–46]).

Jesus changed his appearance at the transfiguration (μετεμορφώθη ἔμπροσθεν αὐτῶν [Matt 17:2; Mark 9:2]), for example, but one would be hard-pressed to maintain that he underwent an ontological transformation during his experience on the mountain. Some texts use μορφή and its cognates in a manner that directly contradicts the inward reality of the object in view, e.g., 2 Tim 2:5: "holding to the outward form of godliness (μόρφωσιν εὐσεβείας) but denying its power." Plutarch compares uneducated rulers to "colossal statues which have a heroic and godlike form (μορφήν) on the outside but inside are full of clay, stone, and lead" (Plut. *Ad Princ. Inerud.* 780a). In each case outward appearance is solely in view. Examples of μορφή employed in this way abound.

How, then, are we to understand Paul's reference to Christ "being in the outward appearance of God"? We do not lack for proposals. The most persuasive takes into consideration the following:

a. A pronounced preoccupation with honor and status in Roman Philippi (Hellerman 88–109).

b. The importance of clothing as a public mark of social status in the Roman world (Hellerman 12–19).

c. The association between glory, clothing, and outward appearance in biblical literature (Luke 9:28–32; 12:27; cf. Matt 6:29; Job 40:10; Sirach 50:11).

d. A similar grammatical construction in Luke 7:25 (οἱ ἐν ἱματισμῷ ἐνδόξῳ καὶ τρυφῇ ὑπάρχοντες), where royal clothing is in view.

e. The meanings of τὸ εἶναι ἴσα θεῷ (v. 6), ἁρπαγμόν (v. 6), and the par. expression μορφὴν δούλου (v. 7).

In view of these factors, ἐν μορφῇ θεοῦ ὑπάρχων most likely presents a "picture of the preexistent Christ clothed in the garments of divine majesty and splendour" (O'Brien 209; J. Behm, *TDNT* 4.751; Hansen 136–38). Paul draws attention to Christ's preincarnate (a better term than "preexistent") social status, publicly marked out by clothing appropriate to his divine rank (Hellerman, "μορφῇ θεοῦ," 779–97; cf. John 17:5). The image was particularly fitting in a letter intended for a group of Christians in status-conscious Philippi (Hellerman 131–33).

This is not to say that an argument for the deity of Christ cannot be made, secondarily, from ἐν μορφῇ θεοῦ ὑπάρχων. As J. Behm notes, the expression portrays Christ clothed in "the garment by which His divine nature may be known" (*TDNT*

4.752; O'Brien 211; Hansen 138). Commentators who stress this theological corollary, however, tend to underemphasize the sociological thrust of Paul's argument. Μορφὴ θεοῦ may very well connote "the expression of the divine state" (W. Pölmann, *EDNT* 2.443d), but it is the "expression"—not the "state"—that is central to the meaning of the text. Paul focuses in ἐν μορφῇ θεοῦ ὑπάρχων on Christ's outward appearance and its implications for rank and status (a theme ignored in most treatments of the phrase), not upon Christ's inner or essential nature. See below, on τὸ εἶναι ἴσα θεῷ (v. 6), ἁρπαγμόν (v. 6), and μορφὴν δούλου (v. 7), for further support for reading μορφῇ θεοῦ as a signifier of social status.

The adv. ptc. ὑπάρχων is nom. sg. masc. pres. act. from ὑπάρχω, and is to be read concessively ("though he was" [NRSV, NLT, ESV]; "although he existed" [NASB]; BDAG 659c; Wallace 634–35; Silva 113; Sumney 45). This is preferable to a causal reading of the ptc., which has gained supporters (O'Brien 216), since concession better preserves the sharp contrast between v. 6 and v. 7 (H-M 116). Ὑπάρχω was widely used in HGk. as a substitute for εἶναι, "to be in a state or circumstance." A more robust meaning, "to be inherently (so)" or "be really," is possible (BDAG 1,029d–30a; Fee 202 n. 40). Except for εἶναι (v. 6), ὑπάρχων is the only pres. in vv. 6–11. Some suggest that the tense may signify "'continuing to be' (divine)" during the humiliation that follows in vv. 7–8 (Reumann 341). As attractive as this is theologically, it reads too much into the tense of the ptc. and contradicts the meaning of ἐν μορφῇ θεοῦ, as outlined above.

οὐχ ἁρπαγμὸν ἡγήσατο τὸ εἶναι ἴσα θεῷ

The vb. ἡγήσατο (3 sg. aor. mid. indic. from ἡγέομαι, "think, consider, regard" [BDAG 434b]; see on ἡγούμενοι [2:3]) anchors a double acc. obj.-complement cstr. The art. (acc. sg. neut.) identifies τὸ εἶναι ἴσα θεῷ as the dir. obj., ἁρπαγμόν as the complement (R 1059; Porter 197; Wallace 220). Τό also functions anaphorically ("this divine equality" [O'Brien 216]), so that εἶναι ἴσα θεῷ repeats in essence the sense of ἐν μορφῇ θεοῦ ὑπάρχων from the previous clause ("both point to the same reality" [Fee 207]; BDF §399[1]; G. Kittel, *TDNT* 2.395; Hellerman, "μορφῇ θεοῦ," 788; Hansen 145; H-M 114). Curiously, Wallace disallows the double function of the art. here (Wallace 186, 602 n. 41; cf. 220, where he sees μορφῇ θεοῦ referring to "essence," τὸ εἶναι ἴσα θεῷ to "function"), but readily acknowledges it at Phil 1:22, where the art. (τὸ ζῆν) is used both as a "substantiver of the infinitive and anaphorically" (Wallace 210).

Εἶναι is a pres. act. inf. from εἰμί, used subst. The neut. pl. ἴσα (like the neut. sg. ἴσον) functions as an adv., "equal" (BDAG 481a; BDF §434[1]; R 407; T 21, 226; E. Beyreuther, *NIDNTT* 2.498). Like μορφῇ θεοῦ, the phrase τὸ εἶναι ἴσα θεῷ ("equality/equal with God" [EVV]; "on par with" God [T. Holtz, *EDNT* 2.201d]) "should not be pressed ontologically" (Reumann 345; *pace* G. Stählin, *TDNT* 3.353; G. Braumann, *NIDNTT* 1.706). A variety of ancient sources specifically associate the idea of equality with God with the rank or position of a king or emperor, using language similar to Paul's. Given the centrality of the imperial cult in the social and religious life of the colony at Philippi, it is quite likely that Paul has emperor veneration directly in view in τὸ εἶναι ἴσα θεῷ in v. 6 (see on κύριος [v. 11]). In each of the conceptual parallels, more-over, the ruler-to-god comparison relates to the rank of the individual, which entitles him either (a) to receive public honor or (b) to exercise authority. Substance or essential nature are generally not in view. For example, a second-century AD papyrus reads τὶ θεός; τὸ κρατοῦν. τὶ βασιλεύς; ἰσόθεος ("What is a God? Exercising power; What is a king? One who is equal with a God" [Pap. Heid. 1716.5]). The point is that a king is in a position to exercise Godlike power; ontology is nowhere on the author's horizon (cf. 2 Macc 9:12). Even more often, when humans are equated with deity, Godlike public honors are in view (Appian BCiv. 2.148; Diod. Sic. 1.2.4; 10.9.9; Cass. Dio. 51.20). Osiek properly concludes the following, regarding τὸ εἶναι ἴσα θεῷ in Philippians 2:6:

> When applied to persons in this very status-conscious culture, it is more likely to mean equality of status or importance in a hierarchical order. It is not likely to mean what modern interpreters would want to read into the hymn, namely, equality of nature or substance with God. In other words, it is not a metaphysical but a social statement (71).

This understanding of εἶναι ἴσα θεῷ is confirmed, in turn, by the most likely meaning of the notorious crux ἁρπαγμόν.

Ἁρπαγμός broadly connotes "something to which one can claim or assert title by gripping or grasping," either:

1. in a neg. sense, "booty" (BDAG 133c); or
2. more positively, "a piece of good fortune, windfall, prize, gain" (BDAG 133c; nouns ending in -μος generally denote the action of the vb.; those ending in –μα, the result of the action, though the distinction cannot be pressed here [BDF §109(1–2); R 152; W. Foerster, *TDNT* 1.473]).

In either case, it remains unclear whether ἁρπαγμόν refers to:

a. something Christ already possessed in his preincarnate state, i.e., something that has "already been seized and is waiting to be used" (cf. "something to cling to" [NLT; cf. CEV]); or
b. something that "has not yet been appropriated" (BDAG 133d; potentially implied in the Eng. tr. "a thing to be grasped" [RSV, NASB, ESV, cf. NJB]).

Although there remain a few vocal dissenters, current scholarly consensus takes ἁρπαγμόν in our passage in sense 2a: Christ's equality with God (to which ἁρπαγμόν refers in the obj.-complement cstr.) is something positive that Christ possessed and chose not to exploit (unlike Roman aristocrats and emperors [Reumann 368–69]), not something that he lacked and chose not to acquire (W. Trilling, *EDNT* 1.156c; Fee 206–7; Hansen 145–46; O'Brien 214–16; Silva 102–4; *pace* C. Brown, *NIDNTT* 3.604; T. Holtz, *EDNT* 2.201d). This understanding of ἁρπαγμόν is increasingly reflected in our EVV: "something to be exploited" (NRSV); "something to be used to/for his own advantage" (NIV, HCSB; "something of which to take advantage" [Reumann 344, 367]; "a gain to be utilised" [W. Foerster, *TDNT* 1.474]). Paul emphasized Christ's attitude, in this regard, in order to challenge a "Philippian tendency to use status and privilege to one's own advantage" (Bockmuehl 131).

This interpretation of ἁρπαγμόν nicely accords with a nonsubstantial understanding of τὸ εἶναι ἴσα θεῷ (above) in terms of status or prestige. For it is difficult to discern how Christ could potentially have regarded "equality with God," understood metaphysically, as "something to be used for his own advantage" (HCSB). How does one exploit one's essence? The problem is immediately resolved by taking τὸ εἶναι ἴσα θεῷ (and, by extension, μορφῇ θεοῦ), as argued above, in a nonsubstantial sense, referring to rank or status. For it is easy to see how Christ could have regarded his position of power and prestige as "something to be used for his own advantage." The above interpretations of (a) ἐν μορφῇ θεοῦ ὑπάρχων, (b) τὸ εἶναι ἴσα θεῷ, and (c) ἁρπαγμόν are, therefore, mutually informing.

Some suggest, however, that the above interpretation of ἁρπαγμόν—which sees τὸ εἶναι ἴσα θεῷ as something Christ already possesses in v. 6—irretrievably compromises the text's dramatic quality, since the story ends (vv. 9–11) with Christ occupying the same position (τὸ εἶναι ἴσα θεῷ) he held at the outset. It is argued that understanding τὸ εἶναι ἴσα θεῷ, instead, as a prize yet to be acquired would allow the Christ to ascend to new heights at the end of the narrative. This, however, misses the central point of Paul's story: it is the universal public acclamation of Christ's status—not the acquisition of a new position previously declined—that serves as the crescendo of the Christ narrative (see, below, on vv. 9–11).

The expression τὸ εἶναι ἴσα θεῷ has encouraged some to assume that Paul intentionally contrasts Adam and Christ in 2:6–11 (see the chart in H-M 105; Hansen 138). Enthusiasm for the alleged contrast has produced parallels where none exist and, in some cases, distorted the meaning of the text. Thus, Dunn eliminates a preincarnate stage from v. 6, arguing that Christ, like Adam, begins his story as a human being, in "the image of God" (ἐν μορφῇ θεοῦ) (J. D. G. Dunn, *Christology in the Making*, 2nd ed. [Grand Rapids: Eerdmans, 1997], 113–21). Equating "form of God" (v. 6) with "image of God" (Gen 1:26–27), however, is linguistically untenable (Fee 209 n. 73). More to the point, the notion that Paul's story begins in v. 6 with Christ in the human realm is directly contradicted by ἐν ὁμοιώματι ἀνθρώπων γενόμενος (v. 7) (Hansen 134; H-M 111–12; Reumann 360). Other suggested parallels also prove to be asymmetrical (e.g., Adam sought after equality with God [Gen 3:4–5]; Christ possessed it but chose not to exploit it [v. 6]). If Paul intended an Adam-Christ contrast, it is, at best, a loose one, since there is not a single linguistic parallel with the Genesis story (Fee 209; "doubtful" [O'Brien 197, 263–68]; "attractive" but "no overt evidence" [Reumann 368]).

VERSE 7

ἀλλὰ ἑαυτὸν ἐκένωσεν

The contrast marked by οὐχ (v. 6) and ἀλλά (v. 7) is forceful ("Not this . . . *but* this!" [H-M 116]). Ἐκένωσεν is 3 sg. aor. act. indic. from κενόω. The lit. meaning, "to make empty" (BDAG 539c; "emptied himself" [NRSV, NASB, HCSB, ESV]; cf. the play on κενοδοξίαν [2:3], which contrasts Christ's self-emptying with the "empty glory" of those who live for themselves), has misled interpreters unnecessarily to assume the presence of an unspecified gen. modifier, that is, that Christ must have emptied himself "of something" ("he gave up everything" [CEV] is potentially misleading). This, in turn, has generated a lively debate over the metaphysical implications of the incarnation. Has the deity of Christ somehow been compromised in the kenosis? Or has the preincarnate Son simply "divested himself of his prestige or privilege" (BDAG 539c; NLT)?

The idea that ἐκένωσεν needs a modifier of some sort—that Christ has emptied himself "of something"—is a false assumption to begin with (Fee 210; H-M 117). As the ensuing ptc. modifiers demonstrate, ἐκένωσεν is intended metaphorically to signify a lowering of rank (vis-à-vis v. 6) by means of the incarnation ("in contrast to 'enriching' or 'making full' oneself" [Reumann 348]; M. Lattke, *EDNT* 2.282c): "The hearer will undoubtedly compare [μορφὴν δούλου] with ἐν μορφῇ θεοῦ and conclude that the content of ἐκένωσεν is some sort of lowering of position—in fact, a lowering of position which is about the most extreme that the Universe could offer" (Oakes 194; "there is no position higher than being God and there is no position lower than being a slave" [Park 122]). The NIV's "made himself nothing" nicely reflects Paul's status concerns in the passage. H-M's sharp criticism of the NIV as an "impossible, dehumanizing sentiment" (117) misses the point entirely. Paul (along with the NIV translators, we may presume!) is speaking of public status and prestige, not intrinsic human worth or dignity.

μορφὴν δούλου λαβών, ἐν ὁμοιώματι ἀνθρώπων γενόμενος

Each clause contains a nom. sg. masc. aor. ptc.: λαβών is act. (from λαμβάνω), γενόμενος is mid. (from γίνομαι). Both ptcs. portray action simultaneous with ἐκένωσεν (H-M 118; BDF §339[1]; R 1,114; Fee 211 n. 83). Some find in μορφὴν δούλου compelling evidence to interpret the parallel expression, μορφῇ θεοῦ (v. 6), metaphysically. Christ became "an actual servant," so "the ontological associations that attach to the phrase μορφὴν δούλου must attach equally to μορφῇ θεοῦ" (Jowers, "The Meaning of ΜΟΡΦΗ in Philippians 2:6–7," 760; cf. "the very nature of a servant" [NIV]; H-M 118). We are not constrained, however, to read either occurrence of μορφή ontologically (see above for μορφῇ θεοῦ). Consideration of the grammar of v. 7 will demonstrate why this is the case.

Both (a) μορφὴν δούλου λαβών and (b) ἐν ὁμοιώματι ἀνθρώπων γενόμενος modify ἐκένωσεν by elaborating upon the manner in which Christ "emptied himself" ("*by* taking/assuming" [HCSB, ESV, NIV]; Porter 192; Wallace 630; H-M 118; O'Brien 217; Reumann 367; Sumney 46). The relationship between these two subordinate clauses is not as clear. The preferred reading assumes that Paul intended for the second clause (ἐν ὁμοιώματι ἀνθρώπων γενόμενος) to explain the first (μορφὴν δούλου λαβών) (K. Rengstorf, *TDNT* 2.278; Fee 196, 213; Silva 106). This can be effectively argued grammatically, with the second ptc. clause formally modifying the first, or semantically, taking both ptc. clauses as defining more precisely the expression ἑαυτὸν ἐκένωσεν (O'Brien 224).

In what sense, then, did Christ take "the form of a slave"? In a relative sense—relative, that is, to his preincarnate status (v. 6). Christ took the form (μορφήν = "outward appearance," as in v. 6) of a slave by becoming a human being (γενόμενος as adv. ptc. of means). That is, for Christ, ἐν ὁμοιώματι ἀνθρώπων γενόμενος was tantamount to assuming slave status ("the humble position of a slave" [NLT]), vis-à-vis his former position as equal to God. Oakes summarizes: "Between being like God and being like a slave, there is the widest status gap imaginable by Paul's hearers. Paul is saying that for Christ to become human meant that deep a drop in status" (196). Christ did not, therefore, become "an actual servant," to adopt Jowers' terminology. He became an actual human being (ἐν ὁμοιώματι ἀνθρώπων γενόμενος). The second participial phrase, then, is the one that should be read ontologically.

Only here in his letters does Paul use δοῦλος to refer to Christ. The tr. "slave" (NJB, NRSV, HCSB, CEV; BDAG 659c) is far superior to "servant" (RSV, NIV), since Paul uses δοῦλος specifically because of the negative status connotations of slavery in the Roman world (O'Brien 223; Reumann 349). Δούλου is not intended as evidence that Christ willingly enslaved himself to the demonic powers, τὰ στοιχεῖα τοῦ κόσμου (G. Braumann, *NIDNTT* 1.707; sim. R. Tuente, *NIDNTT* 3.597). A good argument can be made, however, for echoes of Isaiah's Suffering Servant imagery in Phil 2:5–11 (J. Jeremias, *TDNT* 5.711–12; Hansen 150; see esp. Wright 681–83; Richard Bauckham, *Jesus and the God of Israel: "God Crucified" and Other Studies in the New Testament's Christology of Divine Identity* [Grand Rapids: Eerdmans, 2009], 205–6), though some would demur ("dubious" [Reumann 360; sim. K. Rengstorf, *TDNT* 2.278; O'Brien 269–71]). Whatever the intertextual OT allusions, to Paul's audience δοῦλος simply meant "slave," the lowest legal rank in the Roman world, "a term of extreme abasement" (H-M 119; Fee 212–13; O'Brien 223–24). And it is the shame associated with slave status—not the restriction of personal liberty—that ancient writers consistently emphasize. Thus, "slavery is the most shameful and wretched of states" (Dio Chrysostom, *Or.* 14.1; slaves are the "dregs of society" [Tacitus, *Ann.* 14.45]). Descendants of the Roman soldiers who had established the colony at Philippi decades earlier would have been particularly attuned to the social stigma of slavery. Slaves were excluded from Rome's citizen army except in those regrettable instances when necessity forced the senate to conscript slaves. Even then slaves were formally manumitted before joining the ranks, and they fought in separate units. The notion of a Being of equal rank to God willingly (ἑαυτὸν ἐκένωσεν [v. 7]) "taking on the form of a slave" would have struck residents of Roman Philippi as abject folly (Hellerman 141–42).

Ἐν ὁμοιώματι ἀνθρώπων γενόμενος is a straightforward reference to the incarnation, explaining how Christ "took on the form of a slave"; γενόμενος signifies "to experience a change in nature and so indicate entry into a new condition" (BDAG 198b–d; "being made" [NIV, NASB]; "being born" [NRSV, ESV]; "taking on" [HCSB]). This contrasts sharply with the previous verse: "There it was claimed that Christ *always existed*

116

PHILIPPIANS 2:8

(ὑπάρχων) 'in the form of God.' Here it is said that he *came into existence* (γενόμενος) 'in the likeness of human beings'" (H-M 120; O'Brien 224). Although ὁμοίωμα (dat. sg. neut.) technically connotes "likeness" (most EVV) and not identity ("Jesus in his earthly career was similar to sinful humans yet not totally like them" [BDAG 707d]; T. Holtz, *EDNT* 2.513b; K. Rengstorf, *TDNT* 1.335 n. 15; J. Schneider, *TDNT* 5.197; Fee 213; Hansen 153; H-M 120; cf. Rom 8:3), it is the similarity between Christ and humans that is emphasized here (Bockmuehl 137; O'Brien 225; cf. Rom 6:5). The pl. ἀνθρώπων implies "the whole human race" (Fee 213 n. 94).

καὶ σχήματι εὑρεθεὶς ὡς ἄνθρωπος

Καὶ σχήματι εὑρεθεὶς ὡς ἄνθρωπος does not advance the imagery of the previous clause (the incarnation is still in view) but expresses it in different terms. Whereas ἐν ὁμοιώματι ἀνθρώπων γενόμενος emphasized Christ's human nature as such, σχήματι εὑρεθεὶς ὡς ἄνθρωπος describes how Christ appeared to others. The shift from essential nature to outward appearance carries the point forward to the final stage of Christ's self-humiliation that follows in v. 8 (O'Brien 226; Silva 106).

Εὑρεθείς is nom. sg. masc. of the aor. pass. ptc. from εὑρίσκω, "to find" ("being found" [NRSV, ESV, NIV]), taken fig., "discover intellectually through reflection observation, examination or investigation" (BDAG 412b; H. Preisker, *TDNT* 2.769; "he was seen to be" [Fee 215 n. 4]). The versification is skewed. The temp. ptc. clause ("when" [NLT, HCSB]; BDAG 412b) modifies ἐταπείνωσεν ἑαυτόν (v. 8), not ἐκένωσεν (v. 7; *pace* H-M 122), as indicated by καί, which connects ἐταπείνωσεν to ἐκένωσεν, as the final stage in Christ's social descent (EVV; Fee 214; O'Brien 226).

The dat. σχήματι (sg. neut. from σχῆμα, -ατος, τό) functions somewhat synonymously with μορφῇ (v. 6), meaning "outward appearance, form, shape" (BDAG 981b; "appearance" [NASB, NIV]; "(external) form" [NRSV, ESV, NLT, HCSB]; G. Harder, *NIDNTT* 1.703–14, treats both μορφή and σχῆμα under "form"; "what anyone could see" [709]; J. Schneider, *TDNT* 7.956). The case is most likely a dat. of respect/ref. (T 220; Wallace 146; W. Pölhmann, *EDNT* 3.318a]), rather than locat. (R 523) or instr. (O'Brien 227).

VERSE 8

ἐταπείνωσεν ἑαυτόν γενόμενος ὑπήκοος μέχρι θανάτου

BDAG defines ταπεινόω (3 sg. aor. act. indic.; echoing ταπεινοφροσύνη [v. 3]) as "to cause someone to lose prestige or status" (BDAG 990a). "Humiliated" is perhaps a better tr. than "humbled" (most EVV), since "humble" in Eng. generally denotes an attitude or state of mind, while "humiliate" signifies action performed in a social context. In vv. 7–8, Paul has moved beyond attitude (ἡγήσατο [v. 6]) to a series of actions (ἐκένωσεν and ἐταπείνωσεν + modifiers) with profound social implications. The Philippians were all too familiar with "humiliation by superiors in their social, political, and economic worlds" (Reumann 352). The reflexive pron. ἑαυτόν ("himself" [most EVV]) emphasizes that the humiliation was freely self-imposed.

Γενόμενος is used modally to describe how Christ humiliated himself (*"by* becoming" [NASB, HCSB, ESV]; Fee 215; H-M 122; Reumann 352). The clause marks the final step in Christ's social descent from equality with God to the publicly degrading experience of crucifixion.

The adj. ὑπήκοος is a pred. nom. ("obedient" [BDAG 1035a; EVV]; anticipating ὑπηκούσατε [v. 12] [Fee 216]). The obj. of Christ's obedience is left unstated (one may infer "God" [F. Büchsel, *TDNT* 1.127; Hansen 156]), in order to emphasize the fact— rather than the object—of the obedience (O'Brien 229). The placing of δοῦλος (v. 7) and ὑπήκοος (v. 8) in close proximity should be noted. Due to the stigma that slavery cast upon relationships that were based upon the obedience of one party to another, Roman aristocrats intentionally avoided obedience terminology (e.g., ὑπήκοος) in their mutual interactions. Where functional hierarchy did obtain, other metaphors were employed ("father-son," etc.). Even the emperor Trajan, in his correspondence with lesser officials, avoided all mention of obedience. This background renders "obedience" on the part of the One who possessed status equal to God all the more striking and culturally anomalous.

The prep. μέχρι + gen. can denote "space," "time," or "degree." With θανάτου, μέχρι marks the degree of Christ's obedience ("to the point of death" [most EVV; BDAG 644d]; "all the way to death" [GNB]; Fee 216 n. 9; O'Brien 230; Reumann 352; not temp., "as long as he lived").

θανάτου δὲ σταυροῦ

The appos. modifier θανάτου δὲ σταυροῦ (gen. of "production," death "produced by . . . a cross" [Wallace 105]) is strongly emphatic ("and . . . at that" [BDF §447(8)]; Wallace 105 n. 90; Z §467; "sharpest climax" [W. Grundmann, *TDNT* 8.18]; Fee 215; H-M 122; O'Brien 230). The arresting cstr. is reflected in the EVV ("even [to] death on a cross[!]" [NRSV, NASB, ESV, NIV]) and makes good sense in a portrayal of Christ that centers around the themes of status and prestige. Western Christians traditionally highlight (a) the physical suffering involved in crucifixion (often mentioned in Good Friday sermons but not a theme in Scripture), or (b) the spiritual anguish Jesus experienced bearing the sins of the world (clearly a biblical emphasis [Mark 14:32–34; 15:34]). Paul's concern in v. 8 is with neither of these but, rather, with (c) the social stigma of crucifixion, as a status-degradation ritual designed publicly to shame the crucified individual and all who would associate with him. "No experience was more loathsomely degrading" (O'Brien 231). "Let the very name of the cross," Cicero proclaimed, "be far away not only from the body of a Roman citizen, but even from his thoughts, his eyes, his ears" (*Rab. Perd.* 5.10.16). The shame of the cross rendered the idea of a crucified God an oxymoronic affront to contemporary social sensibilities: "Where can anything be found more paradoxical than this? This death was the most shameful of all" (John Chrysostom, *Homily on Philippians* 2.5–11).

The connection between δούλου (v. 7) and σταυροῦ (v. 8) would not have escaped Paul's audience since crucifixion was explicitly identified as a punishment fit for a slave. The association of slavery with the cross was so widespread that it served as material for Plautus's comedies as early as the third century BC. A slave named Sceledrus, for example, proclaims, "I know the cross will be my tomb. There's where my ancestors rest—father, grandfather, great-grandfather, and great-great-grandfather" (*Mil.* 372). Roman authorities crucified slaves so often that the expression *servile supplicum* ("slaves' punishment") came to be used as a technical expression for death by crucifixion. The juxtaposition of slavery and crucifixion in the Roman psyche thus served to compound the social stigma associated with the terms δοῦλος and σταυρός in the ancient world. As a crucified slave, Christ has reached the utter nadir of his apparent descent into social oblivion. Although Paul may be alluding, secondarily, to the saving significance of Christ's death (cf. τὰ ἑτέρων, v. 4 [Hansen 156]), it is what Christ's obedience meant to *him*—not to *us*—that is in view in θανάτου δὲ σταυροῦ (J. Schneider, *TDNT* 7.575 n. 28; O'Brien 232).

Hansen's summary of Christ's *cursus pudorum* ("race of ignomies") is on target: Philippians 2:6–8 "take us down, down, down to the deepest darkest hellhole in human history to see the horrific torture, unspeakable abuse, and bloody execution of a *slave* on a *cross*" (Hansen 159, author's italics).

VERSE 9

διὸ καὶ ὁ θεὸς αὐτὸν ὑπερύψωσεν

Διό (from διά + ὅ [acc. neut. rel. pron.], lit. "on account of which") is an inferential conj., "therefore, for this reason" (BDAG 250c). The addition of καί shows the inference is "self-evident," "therefore . . . also" (BDAG 250c; NRSV; "For this reason also" [NASB]; "Therefore" [NIV, ESV]; Fee 220 n. 10; H-M 124; O'Brien 233; Reumann 372). There is a bit of irony here, however, since God's response to Christ's self-humiliation (αὐτὸν ὑπερύψωσεν) would be self-evident only to those who shared Paul's perspective on God's subversive social economy. The honoring of a crucified δοῦλος would have been anything but self-evident to pagans steeped in the social realities of Roman Philippi.

At one level Christ's exaltation represents the natural outworking of the biblical principle that self-humbling inevitably leads to exaltation (cf. Matt 16:25–26; 23:12), so that the transition to vv. 9–11 cannot be read solely in terms of recompense or reward (G. Bertram, *TDNT* 8.609). Yet it is Christ—a personal agent—who is at the center of the narrative, not "an inexorable law of God's kingdom" (H-M 124; Hansen 161). The exaltation expresses "divine affirmation of Christ's way of expressing his 'equality with God'" (Fee 197; "vindication and approval" [O'Brien 234]; "not as compensation for Christ's work, but as proof of divine approval" [Hansen 161]). God's response to Christ, in this regard, implicitly promises the Philippians future vindication, as well (O'Brien 261–62; Silva 108–9; note the verbal parallels in 3:20–21).

The subject shifts sharply from Christ to God at this crucial transition in the story of Jesus (cf. also the shift from ptcs. to the use of the subjunc. with finite vbs. [Reumann 372]), as Paul draws upon a cultural script that informed the way in which one aristocrat effectively honored another in the Roman world. Among Roman elites, to be honored by another aristocrat augmented one's own status "in proportion to that aristocrat's prestige" (Lendon 48). The ideal, in every case, was "to be praised by a praised man" (Symmachus, *Ep.* 9), that is, to be honored by someone of the highest possible social rank. The concern is reflected in inscriptions from Philippi, where several individuals specifically cite the emperor as the one who bestowed an honorific title or office upon them, in order to emphasize the legitimacy of the claim. There was a reason for this. Status was a public commodity in the Roman world, and a grant of honor had to be publicly recognized to count for anything: "To claim honor that the community does not recognize is to play the fool" (B. Malina and R. Rohrbaugh, eds., *Social Science Commentary on the Synoptic Gospels* [Minneapolis, Fortress: 1992], 213). Everything depended, in this regard, upon the rank of the person bestowing the honor. For when one man honored another in the ancient world, his ability to mobilize the public to affirm that grant "was proportional to his own honor" (Lendon 48).

Against this background Paul now dramatically introduces ὁ θεός, with an arresting switch of subjs. at v. 9 (Porter 296; the dir. obj. αὐτόν is emphatic, as well). The utterly unexpected status reversal of Jesus comes at the hands of the most exalted Being in the universe. The status of ὁ θεός, in turn, guarantees the efficacy of the honor he has granted to his crucifed δοῦλος. Given the indisputable rank of the Bestower, Paul leaves his Philippian audience with little doubt that God's grant of honor is such that all sentient creatures will publicly acknowledge the glorious "name" of Jesus of Nazareth (vv. 10–11) (Hellerman 149–51).

Ὑπερύψωσεν is 3 sg. aor. act. indic. from ὑπερυψόω, "to raise to a high point of honor," "raise τινά someone to the loftiest height" (BDAG 1034d; "elevated him to the place of highest honor" [NLT]; "highly exalted" [NRSV, NASB, HCSB]). The compound (ὑπέρ, "beyond, much more" + ὑψόω, "exalt") has lost none of its intended composite force ("to super-exalt" [H-M 125]; G. Bertram, *TDNT* 8.609; Reumann 354). Ὑπερ- compounds in Paul almost always connote excess, not position (i.e., elative, not comp. force) ("perfective" [R 629]). The point is not that Christ has been exalted "above" a position previously held, e.g., his preincarnate state. Rather, God has exalted him "to the highest possible degree" (Fee 221; Hansen 161–62; O'Brien 236; Silva 115). The vb. is used in the LXX of Yahweh who is exalted above all gods (Ps 96:9 [MT 97:9]) (H-M 125). Since v. 8 ended with the death of Christ, we may assume that ὑπερύψωσεν includes both the resurrection and the ascension (cf. Acts 2:32–33; 5:30–31; O. Michel, *TDNT* 5.212), though Paul's focus in vv. 9–11 lies elsewhere, namely, on the public acknowledgement of Jesus' universal lordship.

καὶ ἐχαρίσατο αὐτῷ τὸ ὄνομα τὸ ὑπὲρ πᾶν ὄνομα

The καί should be read epex., and the two vbs. as a hendiadys, "by granting him" (Fee 221 n. 15; Hansen 162; O'Brien 237; Reumann 354). Ἐχαρίσατο (with indir. obj. αὐτῷ, and dir. obj. τὸ ὄνομα) is 3 sg. aor. mid. indic. from χαρίζομαι, "to give freely as a favor," "give graciously" (BDAG 1,078b–c; "bestowed" [NASB, ESV]; "gave him" [NIV, NRSV, HCSB]; "conferred on him in an act of grace" [H-M 126]).

The phrase τὸ ὑπὲρ πᾶν ὄνομα is in second attrib. position; the art. functions as a rel. pron. ("the name which/that is above every name" [EVV]; "exalted above all other names" [H. Riesenfeld, *TDNT* 8.515]). Most see τὸ ὄνομα as a reference to a "name" or, perhaps better, a title (Reumann 372). The art. (2x), it is assumed, points to "the well-known name," drawing upon "the OT phenomenon where 'the name' was a periphrasis for Yahweh" (Fee 221; W. Foerster, *TDNT* 3.1088; Hansen 163; H-M 126; O'Brien 238; taking Ἰησοῦ in τῷ ὀνόματι Ἰησοῦ, below, as poss. gen.). Though an allusion to OT YHWH (cf. κύριος [v. 11]) is surely in view, Paul's primary emphasis in the ὄνομα terminology lies elsewhere. The word ὄνομα can refer not only to the name by which a person is called. It can also mean "fame" or "reputation," much as we might say in Eng. that a person has made a "name" for himself (cf. Mark 6:14; Rev 3:1). In an important discussion of the language of honor in Latin and Greek, Lendon, in fact, squarely situates the ὄνομα word group in the semantic field of honor discourse (278). Thus, BDAG cites as one of the possible meanings of the word "recognition accorded a person on the basis of performance" and glosses the meaning as follows: "(well-known) name, reputation, fame" (BDAG 741b). The omission of the art. from τὸ ὄνομα in numerous Gk mss. (D F G Ψ *Byz* many Fathers) suggests that some scribes and church fathers may have understood ὄνομα in precisely this way, though the art. is likely original (included in 𝔓⁴⁶ ℵ A B C 33 1175 1739 cop^{sa, bo}; UBS⁵ = {B} τὸ ὄνομα).

Like ὄνομα in Greek, the Heb. *šēm*, when associated with God, commonly signifies "fame," "reputation," and it often does so when contextually juxtaposed with YHWH (Exod 9:16 [cf. YHWH, v. 13]; 2 Sam 7:22–23; Isa 12:4, 26:8, 55:13, 63:12–14; Jer 10:6, 14:7, 32:20 [cf. v. 17]; Ezek 20:39; 36:20–23; Mal 1:6; Dan 9:14–15; Neh 9:10 [cf. v. 6]). Interestingly enough, most of these texts recall the "name" or "reputation" YHWH made for himself among the nations when he delivered Israel from Egypt. We will not be surprised, then, to find Christ gaining a corresponding grant of public recognition and esteem for the marvelous act of salvation (Phil 2:7–8) by which he inaugurated the new covenant. Thus, while the phrase τὸ ὄνομα τὸ ὑπὲρ πᾶν ὄνομα in Phil 2:9 allusively anticipates κύριος in v. 11, as the OT citation (vv. 10–11) clearly shows, in v. 9 the emphasis falls decidedly upon the public status associated with that name: God has granted Jesus "the reputation that is above every reputation."

There is yet another reason to read τὸ ὄνομα τὸ ὑπὲρ πᾶν ὄνομα (v. 9) in terms of public acclaim. To read it otherwise (as a reference to YHWH/κύριος [v. 11]) is to imply that Jesus was not YHWH/κύριος before his humiliation and subsequent exaltation, that is, that a significant Christological change somehow occurs at vv. 9–11, when Jesus receives a name that he did not possess before. We have good reason to believe, however, that the confessors in Phil 2:10 publicly acknowledge a title (YHWH/κύριος) that Christ has possessed all along. The Scriptures explicitly associate Christ with Yahweh before his exaltation. Most remarkable, in this regard, is John 12, where the author claims that Isaiah saw Christ's glory in the familiar OT theophany in Isaiah 6, where the figure in view is specifically identified in the Heb. Scriptures as YHWH (Isa 6:3, 5; cf. John 12:41). The "I am" statements in John's Gospel point in the same direction (cf. esp. 8:58). The title "Lord" is, in fact, applied to Jesus throughout the Gospels, not often, to be sure, with the connotations suggested here, but there are representative instances even in the Synoptics where the evangelists (and/or various tradents who may have preceded them) associate Jesus with κύριος/YHWH well before the exaltation (Mark 1:3, Luke 1:43, 11; less directly Luke 5:8, 10:17). Paul himself could talk about the crucifixion of "the Lord of glory" (1 Cor 2:8; cf. Gal 6:14; 1 Thess 2:15; note also 1 Cor 7:10 and 9:14, where Paul relates Jesus traditions that "the Lord" [ὁ κύριος] gave during his earthly ministry; cf. 11:23, 26). Particularly relevant in the present connection is 2 Cor 8:9, which (like Phil 2:6–11) describes the preexistence and the humiliation (though not the exaltation) of Christ and which appears to assume that Christ possessed the title κύριος throughout: "For you know the generous act of our Lord Jesus Christ, that though he was rich, yet for your sakes he became poor, so that by his poverty you might become rich." We cannot interpret ἐχαρίσατο αὐτῷ τὸ ὄνομα to imply, therefore, that Jesus somehow receives a new "name" or title during his vindication in Phil 2:9–11. What Jesus receives is not a new name but, rather, a new reputation. It is the public acclamation of Jesus as κύριος/YHWH—and the effective exercise of his universal dominion—that represents the heart of what transpires in the exaltation of Christ, as portrayed by Paul in the text.

VERSE 10

ἵνα ἐν τῷ ὀνόματι Ἰησοῦ

Generally taken to connote purpose ("that" [RSV, NIV, NLT]; Reumann 373), it is probably best to read ἵνα as result (Fee 223), or, perhaps, purpose and result (Wallace 473–74; cf. "so that" [NRSV, HCSB, ESV]; see below on ἐξομολογήσηται).

'Εν with the dat. τῷ ὀνόματι has been variously understood. Κάμπτω generally takes the dat. of indir. obj. (Rom 11:4; or πρός + acc. [Eph 3:14]) to signify the obj. of homage ("to") (O'Brien 240). 'Εν + dat. is a different cstr. Some assign ἐν a temp. significance ("when the name of Jesus is mentioned" [BDAG 713b–c]; Moule 78; Reumann 356). More than time is in view, however, since the proclamation of Jesus' name is not simply "the accompanying circumstance of the submission but its efficient cause" (O'Brien 240). Finally, more than simply Jesus' "name" (i.e., "Lord" [v. 11]) is meant, as well, given the status connotations of τὸ ὄνομα τὸ ὑπὲρ πᾶν ὄνομα, above. The tr. "in honor of the name of Jesus" (GNB) communicates this a bit better than the more lit. "at the name of Jesus" (most EVV).

The gen. Ἰησοῦ is best taken as poss. ("Jesus' name/reputation"), rather than appos. ("the name [which is] Jesus" [Silva 110]; or, sim., reading Ἰησοῦ as dat., "the name Jesus") (F. F. Bruce, NIDNTT 2.654; L. Hartman, EDNT 2.521a; O'Brien 240; Reumann 356). Ἰησοῦς pointedly signifies that it is the humiliated one of vv. 6–8—the crucified Jew whose earthly name was "Jesus"—who has been exalted to the highest place (H-M 127).

πᾶν γόνυ κάμψη

The vb. κάμψη is 3 sg. aor. act. subjunc. from κάμπτω, "to assume a bending posture" (BDAG 507a; "bend/bow" [EVV]; see below, on ἐξομολογήσηται, for whether to tr. the par. subjuncs. with "will" [NASB, CEV] or "should" [most EVV]). Since the posture for prayer was often standing (e.g., Jer 18:20; 1 Kgs 18:15; Luke 18:11, 13), kneeling denotes "great reverence and submission" (O'Brien 241). Paul draws here on Isa 45:23 but with a striking change. In the LXX every knee will bow "to me" (ἐμοί, i.e., God) and every tongue confess "to God" (τῷ θεῷ). Paul substitutes ἐν τῷ ὀνόματι Ἰησοῦ (v. 9) and ὅτι κύριος Ἰησοῦς Χριστός (v. 11), respectively, thereby equating Ἰησοῦς in Phil 2:9–11 with θεός in Isaiah 45:23 (but cf. εἰς δόξαν θεοῦ [v. 11]). The citation also implicitly anticipates a status reversal for Christ's followers since the ensuing context of Isa 45:23 in the LXX promises vindication and glory (δικαιωθήσονται καὶ ἐν τῷ θεῷ ἐνδοξασθήσονται [v. 25]) for those who turn to God (cf. v. 22) and publicly confess him.

ἐπουρανίων καὶ ἐπιγείων καὶ καταχθονίων

The gen. pl. adjs. are used subst., modifying both γόνυ (v. 10) and γλῶσσα (v. 11). Decline as masc., designating rational beings, rather than neut., as a personification of all creation (O'Brien 244). Ἐπουρανίων (from ἐπουράνιος, -ον) refers to "heavenly beings" (BDAG 388b). Ἐπιγείων is from ἐπίγειος, -ον, and pertains to "what is characteristic of the earth as opposed to heavenly" (BDAG 368d; "on earth" [EVV]). Καταχθονίων comes from the adj. καταχθόνιος, -ον, "under the earth, subterranean," here "beings or powers under the earth" (BDAG 530a; "in the underworld" [NJB]; "under the earth" [most EVV]). Those who limit ἐπουρανίων καὶ ἐπιγείων καὶ καταχθονίων to the spirit world (H. Traub, TDNT 5.541; H. Sasse TDNT 3.634) interpret the comprehensive expression too narrowly. Among the remaining proposals for identifying the three groups, the following is the "least objectionable" (Silva 116 n. 39; Fee 224; O'Brien 245):

    a. ἐπουρανίων—angels and demons in heaven
    b. ἐπιγείων—persons alive on earth (including oppressive secular authorities, the emperor and local elite decurions in Philippi [Reumann 345])
    c. καταχθονίων—the dead, along with demons in the underworld

Such specificity, however, may be reading too much into Paul's language. In antiquity people believed in a three-storied universe, and Paul likely chose the threefold comprehensive expression simply to communicate the boundless extent of Christ's lordship (J. Guhrt, NIDNTT 1.522–23; H-M 128; cf. Rev 5:3). The list thus includes every intelligent being in the universe, "all the principalities and powers," as well as "all people" (H-M 127–28; Hansen 165; Silva would include even the natural world [116]).

VERSE 11

καὶ πᾶσα γλῶσσα ἐξομολογήσηται

Both πᾶσα γλῶσσα (nom. sg. fem., lit., "the tongue of every person") and the parallel πᾶν γόνυ are used poetically to signify "everyone," "all" (H-M 129; "everyone" [CEV]; "all beings" [NJB]).

Ἐξομολογήσηται is 3 sg. aor. mid. subjunc. from ἐξομολογέω. Although the vb. came to mean "confess, admit (wrongdoing)" in certain instances, and "praise" or "give thanks" in the LXX, ἐξομολογήσηται is to be understood here according to its basic meaning in CGk., "to declare openly or confess publicly" (BDAG 351b). Public acknowledgement—not praise or personal confession—is in view (O'Brien 246–50). Not all will respond willingly. The tr. "acknowledge" (NJB) and "openly agree" (CEV) are less ambiguous, in this regard, than "confess" (most EVV).

Many mss. (A C D F G Ψ 075 0150 *Byz*^pt etc.) read the fut. indic. ἐξομολογήσεται. The earliest witnesses have the subjunc. (𝔓^46 ℵ B 256 263 424 1852 it^ar, b, d, f, g, o *Byz*^pt etc.; UBS⁵ = {C} ἐξομολογήσηται). The subjunc. reflects Paul's ordinary style. The slight change to the fut. was likely accidental or, perhaps, a scribal attempt to harmonize the text with Isa 45:23 (Fee 218 n. 2; H-M 99; O'Brien 203).

There are two alternatives for the sense of the ἵνα-clause in vv. 10–11:

*1. All creatures *will* publicly acknowledge the lordship of Christ, either voluntarily or under compulsion (= ἵνα result, or purpose and result; "will bow . . . confess" [NASB]; "will bow down . . . openly agree" [CEV]).

    a. Paul's LXX citation (Isa 45:23) reflects the familiar OT theme, that at the consummation of the age all creatures will bow down and worship Yahweh: ἐμοὶ κάμψει πᾶν γόνυ καὶ ἐξομολογήσεται (fut. indic.) πᾶσα γλῶσσα τῷ θεῷ. Included are those who give homage unwillingly, who are put to shame during the acclamation: καὶ αἰσχυνθήσονται πάντες οἱ ἀφορίζοντες ἑαυτούς (v. 24).

    b. The comprehensive expression ἐπουρανίων καὶ ἐπιγείων καὶ καταχθονίων (v. 10) includes both good and evil beings that will acknowledge Jesus' lordship.

    c. The use of the same passage in Rom 14:11, where the predictive fut. of Isa 45:23 is retained, suggests that Paul understood the LXX passage in this sense, and simply changed it to ἵνα + subjunc. in Phil 2:10–11 due to the constraints of grammar in the subordinate clause (Wallace 474).

2. The universal public affirmation of Christ status is to be understood as a divine purpose that remains contingent upon the response of creatures exercising their own volitional capacities (= ἵνα purpose; implied in "should bow . . . confess" [most EVV]; "worship of the community . . . made in the Holy Spirit" [O. Michel, *TDNT* 5.214]).

View 1 is clearly superior. The ἵνα-clause governing κάμψῃ and ἐξομολογήσηται points to an eschatological future, when every rational creature will acknowledge

Jesus' status as sovereign Lord, whether willingly or unwillingly (D. Fürst, *NIDNTT* 1.347; Hansen 165; Silva 111). (The textual var. does not inform the decision. Even the fut. ἐξομολογήσεται can be read with a degree of contingency [with view 2], since it remains subordinated to ἵνα, in par. with the subjunc. κάμψῃ [H-M 129]).

ὅτι κύριος Ἰησοῦς Χριστός

Ὅτι (dir. speech) introduces the exact words of what was likely the earliest confessional formula of the church (Acts 2:36; Rom 10:9; 1 Cor 11:23; 12:3; 16:22–23) (H-M 129; "the eschatological acclamation" [G. Schrenk, *TDNT* 5.1,011 n. 394]). Κύριος (first for emphasis [Hansen 166]; ἐστιν understood [T 302]) permeates the letter to the Philippians (15x). The origin of κύριος as a designation for Jesus on the part of Aramaic-speaking Christians in the East has been generally acknowledged (H. Bietenhard, *NIDNTT* 2.514), and the link in our text between Jesus as κύριος and OT Yhwh can hardly be disputed (the LXX tr. Yhwh with κύριος "at least 6,156 times" [Hansen 167]). With the title κύριος, Jesus is obliquely declared to be "on par with Yahweh" (J. A. Fitzmyer, *EDNT* 2.330c), with all the rights and privileges of God (H-M 130; *pace* Reumann 359).

Pertinent to the setting in Roman Philippi is the emperor cult, through which homage was paid to the imperial family. The confession of Jesus as κύριος tacitly but inescapably elicits comparison to the affirmation "Gaius (or Nero) Caesar is *dominus*" (Reumann 374; "subverts the Roman imperial cult" [Hansen 163]). Under Nero, the acclamation of Caesar as Lord became widespread (on the ubiquity of the imperial cult, see Wright 311–43). In a 67 AD inscription from Corinth, for example, Nero is called ὁ τοῦ παντὸς κόσμου Νέρων, αὐτοκράτωρ μέγιστος and ὁ κύριος Σεβαστός (SIG 2.814.30–31, 55). The association of κύριος terminology with the ruler of the Roman world would have played a key part in the Philippians' political and social reality (on the ruler cult in Philippi, see Hellerman 80–86).

εἰς δόξαν θεοῦ πατρός

The phrase is to be taken in a final sense ("purpose and result merge, for a result may be a *designed* consequence" [M. Harris, *NIDNTT* 3.1187]) with κάμψῃ and ἐξομολογήσηται (EVV; Harris, *Prepositions*, 93), not tied to κύριος Ἰησοῦς Χριστός, as part of the confession itself (*pace* O'Brien 250; Z §108). Paradoxically, for all that occurs during the exaltation, Jesus neither rivals nor displaces God. Christ's status and authority remain derived: God exalted him, enthroned him, conferred on him τὸ ὄνομα τὸ ὑπὲρ πᾶν ὄνομα, and purposed that Jesus would be universally acclaimed. Hence, only God the Father has ultimate authority and sovereignty (ἵνα ᾖ ὁ θεὸς πάντα ἐν πᾶσιν [1 Cor 15:28]; cf. John 13:31; Rev 3:21) (H-M 130). In the final analysis Paul's is a theocentric Christology (Reumann 374).

BDAG properly defines δόξαν here as "honor as enhancement or recognition of status or performance," glossed as "fame, recognition, renown, honor, prestige" (BDAG 257d–58a; "to the glory of God the Father" [EVV]; Reumann 359). Paul carries the themes of status, honor, and prestige through to the end of the narrative, where, through the exaltation of Jesus, God finally receives the public recognition that is his due.

FOR FURTHER STUDY

31. μορφῇ θεοῦ *(2:6)*

Bockmuehl, Markus. "The Form of God (Phil 2:6): Variations on a Theme of Jewish Mysticism." *JTS* 48 (1997): 1–23.

Fabricatore, Dan. *Form of God, Form of a Servant: An Examination of the Greek Noun Morphe in Philippians 2:6–7*. Lanham, MD: University Press of America, 2009.

*Hellerman, Joseph. "μορφῇ θεοῦ as a Signifier of Social Status in Philippians 2:6." *JETS* 52 (2009): 779–97.

Jowers, Dennis. "The Meaning of ΜΟΡΦΗ in Philippians 2:6–7." *JETS* 49 (2006): 739–66.

Martin, Ralph, and Brian Dodds, eds. *Where Christology Began: Essays on Philippians 2*. Louisville, TN: Westminster/John Knox, 1998.

32. ἁρπαγμόν *(2:6)*

Hoover, Robert. "The HARPAGMOS Enigma: A Philological Solution." *HTR* 64 (1971): 95–119.

*Martin, Ralph, and Brian Dodds, eds. *Where Christology Began: Essays on Philippians 2*. Louisville, TN: Westminster/John Knox, 1998.

*Wright, N. T. "ἁρπαγμός and the Meaning of Philippians 2:5–11." *JTS* 37 (1986): 321–52.

33. The Cross and Crucifixion in the Roman World *(2:8)*

Chapman, David W. *Ancient Jewish and Christian Perceptions of Crucifixion*. Grand Rapids: Baker, 2010.

Cook, John G. "Crucifixion as Spectacle in Roman Campania." *NovT* 54 (2012): 68–100.

Hellerman, *Reconstructing Honor*, 144–48.

*Hengel, Martin. *Crucifixion in the Ancient World and the Folly of the Message of the Cross*. Philadelphia: Fortress, 1977.

Samuelsson, Gunnar. *Crucifixion in Antiquity: An Inquiry into the Background of the New Testament Terminology of Crucifixion*. Tübingen: Mohr Siebeck, 2011.

Schneider, J. *TDNT* 7.572–80.

Tzaferis, Vassilios. "Crucifixion: The Archaeological Evidence: Remains of a Jewish Victim of Crucifixion Found in Jerusalem." *Biblical Archaeology Review* 11 (1985): 44–53.

Williams, Demetrius. *Enemies of the Cross of Christ: The Terminology of the Cross and Conflict in Philippians*. London: Sheffield Academic, 2002.

34. Jesus Christ as Lord *(2:11)*

Bietenhard H., and C. Brown. *NIDNTT* 2.508–19.

Capes, David B. *Old Testament Yahweh Texts in Paul's Christology*. WUNT 2.47. Tübingen: Mohr Siebeck, 1992.

Fitzmyer, J. A. *EDNT* 2.328–31.

_____. "The Semitic Background of the New Testament *Kyrios*-Title." Pages 115–42 in *A Wandering Aramaean: Collected Aramaic Essays*. SBLMS 25. Missoula, MT: Scholars Press, 1979.

Foerster, W., and G. Quell. *TDNT* 3.1039–98.

*Hurtado, L. *DPL* 560–69.

_____. *Lord Jesus Christ: Devotion to Jesus in Earliest Christianity*. Grand Rapids: Eerdmans, 2005.

35. The Story of Christ in Philippians 2:5–11

Fee, Gordon. "Philippians 2:5–11: Hymn or Exalted Prose?" *BBR* 2 (1992): 29–46.

Feinberg, Paul. "The Kenosis and Christology: An Exegetical-Theological Analysis of Phil 2:6–11." *TJ* 1 (1980): 21–46.

Hellerman, *Reconstructing Honor*, 129–56.

Hurtado, Larry. "Jesus as Lordly Example in Philippians 2:5–11." Pages 113–26 in *From Jesus to Paul: Essays in Honour of Francis Wright Beare*. Edited by P. Richardson and J. C. Hurd. Waterloo: Wilfrid Laurier University Press, 1984.

Martin, Ralph P. *Carmen Christi: Philippians 2:5–11 in Recent Interpretation and in the Setting of Early Christian Worship*. Grand Rapids: Eerdmans, 1983.

*Martin, Ralph, and Brian Dodds, eds. *Where Christology Began: Essays on Philippians 2*. Louisville, TN: Westminster/John Knox, 1998.

Moule, C. D. F. "Further Reflexions on Philippians 2.5–11." Pages 264–76 in *Apostolic History and the Gospel. Biblical and Historical Essays Presented to F. F. Bruce*. Edited by W. W. Gasque and R. P. Martin. Exeter: Paternoster, 1970.

Strimple, Robert B. "Philippians 2.5–11 in Recent Studies: Some Exegetical Conclusions." *WTJ* 41 (1979): 247–68.

HOMILETICAL SUGGESTIONS

Reflecting the Mind-set of Christ (2:5–8)

1. Status and authority not used for personal advantage (v. 6)
2. Status and authority willingly relinquished in the service of others (vv. 7–8)

The Countercultural Pilgrimage of Christ Jesus (2:6–11)

1. From divine status: preexistence (v. 6)
2. To slave status: incarnation (v. 7)
3. To no status: crucifixion (v. 8)
4. To ultimate status: vindication (v. 9–11)

The Vindication of Christ (2:9–11)

1. The highest of honors (v. 9)
2. Public recognition by all (v. 10)
3. Identity with OT Yahweh (v. 11)

3. HUMILITY LIVED OUT IN COMMUNITY WITH OTHERS (2:12–18)

12 Ὥστε, ἀγαπητοί μου,
  καθὼς πάντοτε ὑπηκούσατε,
   μὴ ὡς ἐν τῇ παρουσίᾳ μου μόνον
   ἀλλὰ νῦν πολλῷ μᾶλλον ἐν τῇ ἀπουσίᾳ
   μου,
   μετὰ φόβου καὶ τρόμου
  τὴν ἑαυτῶν σωτηρίαν <u>κατεργάζεσθε</u>·
13 <u>θεὸς</u> γάρ ἐστιν ὁ ἐνεργῶν ἐν ὑμῖν καὶ τὸ θέλειν
  καὶ τὸ ἐνεργεῖν
   ὑπὲρ τῆς εὐδοκίας.

14 Πάντα ποιεῖτε χωρὶς γογγυσμῶν καὶ διαλογισμῶν,
15–16   ἵνα γένησθε ἄμεμπτοι καὶ ἀκέραιοι,
   τέκνα <u>θεοῦ</u> ἄμωμα
    μέσον γενεᾶς σκολιᾶς καὶ διεστραμμένης,
    ἐν οἷς φαίνεσθε
     ὡς φωστῆρες ἐν κόσμῳ,
     λόγον ζωῆς ἐπέχοντες,
     εἰς καύχημα ἐμοὶ εἰς
      ἡμέραν Χριστοῦ,
      ὅτι οὐκ <u>εἰς κενὸν</u>
      ἔδραμον
      οὐδὲ <u>εἰς κενὸν</u>
      ἐκοπίασα.

17–18 Ἀλλὰ
   εἰ καὶ σπένδομαι ἐπὶ τῇ θυσίᾳ καὶ λειτουργίᾳ τῆς πίστεως ὑμῶν,
  <u>χαίρω</u> καὶ <u>συγχαίρω</u> πᾶσιν ὑμῖν·
  τὸ δὲ αὐτὸ καὶ ὑμεῖς <u>χαίρετε</u> καὶ <u>συγχαίρετέ</u> μοι.

The passage concludes the larger paraenetic section (1:27–2:18) over which stands the comprehensive injunction of 1:27 (O'Brien 272). The text is dominated by impvs. (κατεργάζεσθε [v. 12]; ποιεῖτε [v. 14]; γένησθε [w/impv. ἵνα, v. 15]; and χαίρετε καὶ συγχαίρετε [v. 18]), and maintains Paul's twofold focus on (a) relationships among Christians (2:2–4/2:14) and (b) relations between the church and outsiders (1:27/2:15–16). Paul also revisits the themes of presence/absence (1:27/2:12) and eschatology (1:28/2:16) (O'Brien 272 n. 2, 274; Reumann 407).

The exhortation is steeped in LXX phrases and OT allusions: (1) μετὰ φόβου καὶ τρόμου (v. 12e par. several OT passages); (2) γογγυσμῶν καὶ διαλογισμῶν (v. 14 par. the "murmuring" tradition in the wilderness [cf. Exod 16:12, Num 14:2]); (3) τέκνα θεοῦ ἄμωμα . . . γενεᾶς σκολιᾶς καὶ διεστραμμένης (v. 15a par. Deut 32:5); (4) φαίνεσθε ὡς φωστῆρες (v. 15b par. Dan 12:3a); λόγον ζωῆς ἐπέχοντες (v. 15c par. Dan 12:3b); (4) εἰς κενὸν ἐκοπίασα (16b par. Isa 49:4; 65:23) (Reumann 402). The OT imagery is scattered, however, and inconsistently applied. Initially, the Philippians are warned against grumbling and complaining, like Israel in the wilderness. In the verse immediately following, however, it is the residents of Roman Philippi who are identified with rebellious Israel, as a crooked and perverse generation. Some phrases appear to be cited intentionally (v. 15a par. Deut 32:5; v. 15b–c par. Dan 12:3). Others (v. 16b par. Isa 49:4; 65:23) are not employed by Paul elsewhere and may simply reflect "the overflow of a mind steeped in Scripture" (Fee 242). The allusions may well be sermonic material Paul used in his teaching (Fee 243). One wonders whether the Philippians would have recognized the OT background (Reumann 404, 407).

VERSE 12

Ὥστε, ἀγαπητοί μου

Paul resumes the exhortation begun in 1:27. Ὥστε is an inferential conj. introducing an independent sentence (Moule 144; O'Brien 274; "Therefore" [NRSV, NIV, ESV]; "So" [NJB]; "So then" [NASB, HCSB]). Paul uses ὥστε especially when applying an argument to a local situation (Fee 231 n. 7). Ὥστε, ἀγαπητοί μου is to be connected with the main impv. command (τὴν ἑαυτῶν σωτηρίαν κατεργάζεσθε), twenty-three Gk. words later (Reumann 407).

The voc. pl. masc. form of the adj. ἀγαπητός ("dear, beloved, prized, valued" [BDAG 7b]) functions as a voc. subst.: "beloved" (NASB, NRSV, ESV), "dear friends" (NIV, NJB, HCSB). Ἀγαπητός is a favorite of Paul's (at times associated with God's love in the context of election [e.g., Rom 1:7]) to introduce earnest appeals to his readers (1 Cor 10:4; 15:58; 2 Cor 7:1; 12:19; Phil 4:1). The implication may be twofold: "You are a people especially loved by God, but also by me (μου)" (H-M 139). Ἀγαπητοί μου and καθὼς πάντοτε ὑπηκούσατε frame Paul's appeal in an affirming, not accusing, way (Hansen 170).

καθὼς πάντοτε ὑπηκούσατε

The lengthy καθώς ("as" [RSV, NIV, ESV]; "just as" [NRSV, NASB, HCSB]) clause (καθώς . . . τῇ ἀπουσίᾳ μου) constitutes the basis for the impv. κατεργάζεσθε (Reumann 385).

Ὑπηκούσατε is 2 pl. aor. act. indic. of ὑπακούω, "obey, follow, be subject to" (BDAG 1028d; "have . . . obeyed" [EVV]; "followed . . . instructions" [NLT]). The etym. is transparent: ὑπό- adds the "idea of subjection" to ἀκούειν (R 634). The context marks ὑπηκούσατε as a constative aor., denoting ongoing or repeated action(s) regarded as a whole (Reumann 384; cf. BDF §332). Paul returns here to the leitmotif of obedience that marked vv. 6–11 (cf. ὑπήκοος [v. 8]) (G. Kittel, TDNT 1.224; H-M 138).

The obj. of ὑπηκούσατε is left unspecified (with most EVV). Some see Paul as the obj. ("obeyed me" [NRSV]; "followed my instructions" [NLT]). The verbal link with Christ's obedience (ὑπήκοος [v. 8]), along with the immediately preceding imagery of Jesus as sovereign Lord (vv. 10–11), suggest, instead, that God is the implied obj. of ὑπηκούσατε (Fee 232–33; H-M 139). Paul is the authoritative apostle through whom God speaks, however, so a sharp wedge should not be driven between the two options (Hansen 171; O'Brien 275).

Πάντοτε ὑπηκούσατε is not hollow rhetoric but "genuine commendation of the Philippians, if with some hyperbole" (Reumann 409). Paul likely has in view the Philippians' initial response to his preaching (Acts 16:14, 32–33) (H-M 139; O'Brien 275–76). The temp. adv. πάντοτε suggests more recent instances of obedience, as well, though we have no record of these (O'Brien 275–76).

μὴ ὡς ἐν τῇ παρουσίᾳ μου μόνον

The "presence"/"absence" clauses (μὴ ὡς ἐν τῇ παρουσίᾳ . . . τῇ ἀπουσίᾳ μου) can modify:

1. ὑπηκούσατε, in which case τῇ παρουσίᾳ μου would refer to earlier ministry in Philippi ("when I was with you" [NLT, CEV]; Runge 236–37).
   a. Word order supports this view (Reumann 385, 409).
   b. Παρουσία is listed before ἀπουσία here, thus pointing to a visit to Philippi before Paul's current absence. However, at 1:27, where a future visit is clearly in view, the order is exactly the same (O'Brien 281).
*2. κατεργάζεσθε (RSV, ESV), interpreting τῇ παρουσίᾳ μου to refer to a future visit (note the absence of temporal indicators in the clauses): "Work . . . not only in light of my anticipated coming to you again, but all the more now while I am absent from you" (H-M 141; O'Brien 276, 281; G. Braumann, NIDNTT 2.899).
   a. The neg. μή is almost always used with nonindic. moods (κατεργάζεσθε = impv.) (BDF §426; R 1,162; T 281–82; H-M 140–41; O'Brien 281).
   b. The term παρουσία has already been used to speak of a possible future visit (1:26), also mentioned in 2:23–24.
   c. The ὡς before ἐν τῇ παρουσίᾳ (problematic on any interpretation) is hard to explain (thus its omission in some mss.), unless it is given its less frequent meaning "when" (cf. BDF §455[2]), "in light of," or "in view of," in which case παρουσία then points to the future (H-M 141; O'Brien 281).

The adv. ὡς ("as" [RSV, NASB, ESV]; "when" [NJB, NLT, CEV]) is found in 𝔓⁴⁶ ℵ A C D G Ψ 075 0150 6 81 Byz etc. It is omitted by B 33 1241 (with NRSV, NIV, HCSB), perhaps to smooth out the grammar (O'Brien 272), or to avoid implying that "they might be obedient only when he was present" (Fee 230 n. 3). The text with ὡς is clearly the harder and best attested reading: UBS⁵ = {A} ὡς.

Παρουσία (derived from πάρειμι, "be present") can mean "coming, advent," or "presence"; the latter meaning is clearly in view (NRSV, ESV, HCSB; BDAG 780d; A. Oepke, TDNT 5.859; W. Radl, EDNT 3.44a).

Μόνον (see on 1:27) is acc. sg. neut., used adv., in the sense "only" (K.-H. Bartels, NIDNTT 2.724).

ἀλλὰ νῦν πολλῷ μᾶλλον ἐν τῇ ἀπουσίᾳ μου

Most EVV keep ἀλλὰ νῦν together ("but now" [NIV, HCSB, NASB]), but RSV and ESV move νῦν to beginning of the par. παρουσίᾳ/ἀπουσίᾳ clauses ("as you have always obeyed, so now, not only as in my presence but much more in my absence"), thereby explicitly connecting both clauses with κατεργάζεσθε, not ὑπηκούσατε (see above).

For πολλῷ μᾶλλον ("much more" [NASB, NIV, ESV]; "even more" [HCSB, CEV]; πολλῷ is dat. of measure [Wallace 167]) see on 1:23. Paul's absence is heightened by νῦν πολλῷ μᾶλλον (Reumann 385).

The term ἀπουσία (from ἄπειμι, "be absent" [cf. ptc. 1:27]) is dat. sg. fem. from ἀπουσία, -ας, ἡ; "absence" (NIV, ESV, HCSB).

μετὰ φόβου καὶ τρόμου

Μετά + gen. is here used in the sense "with" = "having" (Harris, *Prepositions*, 163). Φόβου καὶ τρόμου ("fear and trembling" [most EVV]) is best taken as a stock phrase since the terms occur in tandem throughout the Bible (13x in the LXX to indicate an "appropriate response to God's mighty acts," generally on the part of Israel's enemies [Exod 15:16, Canaanites; Isa 19:16, Egyptians; cf. Deut 2:25; 11:25]; O'Brien 282). The single LXX occurrence where Israel's response to God is in view paradoxically enjoins God's people to exult or rejoice in the context of "fear and trembling" (δουλεύσατε τῷ κυρίῳ ἐν φόβῳ καὶ ἀγαλλιᾶσθε αὐτῷ ἐν τρόμῳ [Ps 2:11]). In our passage, too, fear is "only one side of the motivation" (cf. v. 13; W. Mundle, *NIDNTT* 1.623; Fee 237). Most, therefore, interpret φόβος καὶ τρόμος as "reverence and awe" (BDAG 1062c; G. Wanke, *TDNT* 9.197), closely tied to obedience ("a part of faith that characterizes Christian obedience" [H. Balz, *EDNT* 3.433c]; "an attitude of obedience" [H-M 142]; Reumann 386).

Paul elsewhere uses φόβος καὶ τρόμος in the context of human relations (1 Cor 2:3; 2 Cor 7:15; Eph 6:5). Accordingly, some suggest that the expression in v. 12 refers to mutual respect among the Philippians. God is the ultimate object of φόβος καὶ τρόμος in 2 Cor 7:15 and Eph 6:5, however, and both (a) the γάρ-clause in v. 15 (θεὸς γάρ ἐστιν ὁ ἐνεργῶν) and (b) God's response to Jesus in vv. 9–11 suggest Paul has God in view, here, as well (Hansen 176; O'Brien 283–84; Reumann 410).

τὴν ἑαυτῶν σωτηρίαν κατεργάζεσθε

Until recently the theological problem raised by Paul's charge had polarized commentators into two camps:

1. The so-called "theological" reading understands the injunction in terms of individual, eschatological salvation. This is then carefully qualified by interpreting the command in a way that does not conflict with Paul's teaching on justification by faith in Romans and Galatians (e.g., by highlighting θεὸς γάρ ἐστιν ὁ ἐνεργῶν ἐν ὑμῖν [v. 13]).

2. The "sociological" interpretation takes σωτηρίαν to mean not "salvation" but "deliverance," understood to refer to the relational health of the church at Philippi. Eschatological salvation is not in view.

The semantic range of κατεργάζεσθε is broad enough to support either view. Both interpretations have much in their favor, and a general consensus on the following two points has led recent commentators to avoid a strict dichotomy between the two views:

a. Lexicography—Although used in the papyri and LXX (occasionally in the NT [Mark 3:4; Acts 4:9; 14:9; 27:34]) to convey the idea of health or well-being (H-M 140), σωτηρία and cognates are consistently employed by Paul to denote eschatological salvation (cf. 1:28; 3:20–21). Σωτηρίαν (v. 12) is situated in an eschatological framework, between 2:9–11 and 2:16. Nearly all scholars read the term here in its traditional Pauline sense, "salvation" (EVV; BDAG 986b; W. Foerster, *TDNT* 7.992; J. Schneider, *NIDNTT* 3.214; K. H. Schelkle, *EDNT* 3.328a; Hansen 174; O'Brien 278–79; Reumann 387; Silva 119–20).

b. Context—The whole of 1:27–2:18 is concerned with a united body of believers free from all disputes and dissensions, each member sacrificing individual desires and ambitions to promote the good of the whole. After speaking out sharply against caring for their own personal interests (note ἑαυτῶν in vv. 3–4 [cf. v. 21]), Paul can hardly be urging each individual member to concentrate on his or her own salvation with τὴν ἑαυτῶν σωτηρίαν (H-M 138). The passage is clearly "an ethical text" on "how saved people live out their salvation," not "a soteriological text" about "people getting saved" (Fee 235; Hansen 172; Reumann 409). The context strongly supports a sociological reading of Paul's injunction in 2:12.

Recent treatments seek to retain both (a) the traditional meaning of σωτηρία and (b) the ethical orientation of the exhortation. Paul's challenge, then, relates to "the *present* outworking of their *eschatological salvation* within the *believing community* in Philippi" (Fee 235, author's italics; Hansen 172–74; "work with fear and trembling to discover what it really means to be saved" [CEV]). Σωτηρίαν is thus read eschatologically; κατεργάζεσθε refers to interpersonal behaviors and attitudes that would contribute to unity in the church (e.g., Πάντα ποιεῖτε χωρὶς γογγυσμῶν καὶ διαλογισμῶν [v. 14]). NT writers commonly draw upon eschatology as a basis for ethical paraenesis (Reumann 387). O'Brien reminds us, moreover, that "to speak of believers being responsible for the outworking of their personal salvation in their day-to-day living in no way denies that this σωτηρία is an act of God. . . . In precisely the same way 'make your calling and election sure' (2 Pet 2:10) does not suggest that election is not God's act" (O'Brien 279).

For ἑαυτῶν ("your own" [NRSV, ESV, HCSB], "your" [NIV, NJB, NASB]) see on 2:3.

Κατεργάζεσθε, is 2 pl. pres. dep. impv. of κατεργάζομαι, "cause a state or condition" (BDAG 531c; κατά has "perfective force" [R 606]). The vb. appears 20 times in Paul (only here with σωτηρία), negatively (Rom 2:9; Rom 7:13, 17) and positively (Rom 15:18). Although appearing more in Romans (11x) than any other letter, Paul does not use κατεργάζομαι in discussing "works of the law" or "the person who works" for wages (Rom 4:5) (Reumann 387). BDAG glosses the vb. "bring about, produce, create" (531c). EVV prefer "work out" (NRSV, NASB, HCSB), presumably to avoid the impression that Paul views salvation as a human achievement. Compared to ἐργάζομαι ("doing work"), κατεργάζομαι "accents the carrying of the work through . . . the outworking or development" (R 564). The NIV's emphasis on ongoing action ("continue to work out") finds support in the surrounding context (πάντοτε . . . νῦν) (Hansen 171; H-M 140; Reumann 387). The pl. should be noted (cf. also ἑαυτῶν), since Western interpreters "tend to individualize Paul's corporate imperatives" (Fee 231).

VERSE 13

θεὸς γάρ ἐστιν ὁ ἐνεργῶν ἐν ὑμῖν

Verses 12–13 reflect the fundamental unity of the indic. and the impv. in Paul's theology (O'Brien 285; Reumann 406).

The cstr. is periph. for the simple θεὸς γάρ ἐνεργεῖ, making θεός (pred. nom. [Moule 115; Wallace 602–3; pace Sumney 53]) emphatic (Fee 238; O'Brien 286; Runge 198). EVV bring out emphasis with impers. cstr., "It is God who" (NIV, HCSB, ESV). The anarthrous θεός is qualitative (cf. John 1:1), stressing God's power, i.e., "the how of sanctification, not the who" (Wallace 46, 264, author's italics).

Γάρ ("for" [NRSV, NIV, HCSB]) gives the ground for the entire exhortation in v. 12 (Reumann 387; O'Brien 284). God does not work because man works. Rather, man can and must work because God has worked and is working (H-M 142). The tension between the indic. and the impv. (cf. the "already" and "not yet" of NT eschatology) is variously construed by Paul. Those who have been incorporated in Christ's death, for example (ἀπεθάνετε [Col 3:3]), are nevertheless exhorted to "put to death" (Νεκρώσατε [Col 3:5]) their earthly members, i.e., to strive to become what they already are. Christians, who have "put on Christ" (ἐνεδύσασθε [Gal 3:27]), are commanded to "put on the Lord Jesus Christ" (ἐνδύσασθε [Rom 13:14]). The distinct feature in Phil 2:13 is that the indic. is expressed not in terms of incorporation with Christ (Col 3:3), or having put on Christ (Gal 3:27), but, rather, as the ongoing activity of God in the Philippians' lives (ὁ ἐνεργῶν ἐν ὑμῖν) (O'Brien 285). God's work and the believer's efforts are coextensive, thereby excluding, as non-Pauline, any kind of synergism whereby some "division of labor" might come into play between God and the Philippians: "θεὸς γάρ ἐστιν ὁ ἐνεργῶν ἐν ὑμῖν stands behind all κατεργάζεσθαι" (G. Bertram, TDNT 3.635).

Ἐνεργῶν is nom. sg. masc. of the pres. act. ptc. of ἐνεργέω, used subst., "the one who produces" (BDAG 335d; "work(s)" [most EVV]; "at work, enabling" [NRSV]; "The Great Energizer" [H-M 142]; D. Müller, NIDNTT 3.1021]). Ἐνεργέω is a special Pauline word (18x out of 20x in NT; "fixed theological meaning" [H. Paulsen, EDNT 1.453b]), usually (like cog. ἐνέργεια) describing supernatural activity, either the mighty work of God (Gal 3:5; Eph 1:11, 20; Col 1:29) or the activities of Satan (2 Thess 2:7; Eph 2:2). Note, especially, 1 Cor 12:4–6: χαρισμάτων, διακονιῶν, and ἐνεργηημάτων correlate, respectively with πνεῦμα, κύριος, and θεός, but in v. 11 it is the Spirit who ἐνεργεῖ "all these things." It is likely the case that ἐνεργῶν denotes "continuous activity" (O'Brien 286; "always at work" [GNB]). This should be argued, however, from context and lexeme, not from the tense of the ptc., since Paul often uses an arthrous pres. ptc. subst. without any such nuance (e.g., Rom 2:1, 3, 21; 3:5, 11; 1 Cor 11:29; 14:2–5, 11; 2 Cor 2:2; etc.; Wallace rightly notes that the adj. nature of the ptc. "tends to dilute the strength of the aspect" [615]).

Some interpret ἐν ὑμῖν ("in you" [EVV]) collectively, "among you," that is, of God's work in the community, rather than in the individual. But ἐνεργέω + ἐν ἡμῖν/ὑμῖν clearly means "in us/you" (not "among us/you,") in 2 Cor 4:12, and probably also in Rom 7:5 and 1 Cor 12:6 (Silva 119). It is clear, nevertheless, that the tangible evidence of ἐνεργῶν ἐν ὑμῖν is to be understood in terms of community relations (cf. v. 14) (Hansen 177 n. 323; O'Brien 287; Reumann 388).

καὶ τὸ θέλειν καὶ τὸ ἐνεργεῖν ὑπὲρ τῆς εὐδοκίας

Θέλειν and ἐνεργεῖν are pres. ("an ongoing or lengthy process" [O'Brien 287]) act. infs., used subst. as dir. objs. of ἐνεργῶν (Porter 196–97). The subj. (the Philippians) is unexpressed. When a subst. inf. is used as subj. or obj., the art. is generally anaphoric (here pointing back to κατεργάζεσθε) (BDF §399[1]). The art. (2x) thus grounds the impv. of v. 12 in the indic. of v. 13.

EVV variously render θέλω in v. 13 as "will" (NRSV, NIV), "desire" (HCSB, NLT), and "intention" (NJB) ("will, wish, want, be ready" [BDAG 448a]). The vb. is widely used (208x in NT; 61x in Paul), with human and divine subjs. Although "wish" is sometimes appropriate (Gal 4:20), θέλω commonly denotes "a resolve or purposeful determination" (Rom 7:15, 18, 19; 2 Cor 8:10), here a "persistent resolution . . . due to divine activity" (O'Brien 287; "purpose, opp. ἐνεργεῖν [BDAG 448b]; G. Schrenk, *TDNT* 3.30).

See above on ἐνεργεῖν ("to work [out]" [NRSV, NASB, HCSB]; "to act" [NIV]; with τὸ θέλειν, "the will and the action" [BDAG 335b]). Only here in the NT is the vb. is used to describe human activity in a context where it is still God's power that is at work (O'Brien 287).

The coordinated conjs. (καὶ . . . καί) signify "both . . . and" (NRSV, HCSB; BDAG 495d; R 1182; NIV omits "both").

Attempts to connect ὑπὲρ τῆς εὐδοκίας with what follows (Πάντα ποιεῖτε, v. 14) are to be rejected (*pace* BDF §231[2]; Moule 65). Ὑπέρ + gen. "suggests the object at which one is aiming" (R 632; "with a view to" [Moule 65]; "for" [ESV]; "in order to fulfill" [NIV]; "for the sake of" [Fee 239 n. 42]).

Εὐδοκία (here gen. sg. fem.) is the "state or condition of being kindly disposed" (BDAG 404c; "good pleasure" [NASB, NRSV, ESV]; "good purpose" [NIV, HCSB]). When used of God the noun is "loaded with heavy theological emphasis" (H-M 143; cf. Eph 1:5, 9; Matt 11:26; Luke 10:21; a synonym for "God's redemptive plan" [O'Brien

289]; "His gracious resolution to save" [G. Schrenk, *TDNT* 2.747]). EVV universally interpret εὐδοκίας in terms of God's goodwill. Some commentators interpret εὐδοκίας, instead, to denote goodwill among the Philippians ("by and among human beings" [Reumann 410]; cf. BDAG 404c):

a. Εὐδοκία is used of human relations in 1:15 (of the goodwill of Christian preachers).
b. The surrounding context of 2:13 has to do with relationships among believers.
c. The term lacks the poss. pron. αὐτοῦ (added for clarity in EVV).

The arguments fail to persuade. The emphasis in v. 13 on God's sovereign activity (θεὸς γάρ ἐστιν ὁ ἐνεργῶν) shows that God's good pleasure is in view in εὐδοκίας, rendering the addition of αὐτοῦ as unnecessary (Hansen 178–79; O'Brien 288; Silva 131; cf. Rom 2:18). The art. τῆς, moreover, is likely poss., referring anaphorically back to θεός (Hansen 178; Fee 239 n. 39). Finally, a further reference to the will of human beings after τὸ θέλειν καὶ τὸ ἐνεργεῖν would be "tautologous, even banal" (O'Brien 288; G. Schrenk, *TDNT* 2.774 n. 33; Hansen 178).

VERSE 14

Πάντα ποιεῖτε χωρὶς γογγυσμῶν καὶ διαλογισμῶν

Πάντα ποιεῖτε is asyndetic (no connecting particle or conj.), reflecting "the closest possible tie" to vv. 12–13, as a more specific injunction (Fee 243; O'Brien 289). The vb. is 2 pl. pres. act. impv. from ποιέω, "do" (EVV; "Let your behavior be free of" [NJB]). Πάντα (neut. pl. acc.; "everything mentioned from 1:27 on" [Reumann 411]), along with the pres. ποιεῖτε, adds emphasis to the command.

Χωρίς with the gen. means "without" (most EVV; "free of" [NJB]).

Γογγυσμῶν is gen. pl. masc. from γογγυσμός, "complaint, displeasure, expressed in murmuring, behind-the-scenes talk" (BDAG 204c; "complaining" [NLT]; "grumbling" [ESV, NASB, NIV]; like Eng. "murmuring" [NJB], γογγυσμός is onomatopoetic). The noun is found only here in Paul (cognate vb. 2x [1 Cor 10:10]) but was used in the LXX of Israel grumbling in the wilderness (e.g., Exod 16:7–8, 12; Num 17:25).

More common is διαλογισμός, used in CGk. of "conversation," especially philosophical dialogue (G. Schrenk, *TDNT* 2.93–98). Although occasionally neutral (Luke 2:35), NT use is generally negative: (a) thoughts that are opposed to God's designs (Matt 15:19; Rom 1:21); (b) "doubts" (Luke 24:38 [NRSV]); and (c) interpersonal disputes (Luke 9:46). The latter sense is intended here ("arguing" [NRSV, NIV, HCSB]; "disputing" [ESV, NASB]; BDAG 233a; Fee 243–44; H-M 144; Reumann 389). Although γογγυσμῶν καὶ διαλογισμῶν "made sense in the Greco-Roman world" (Reumann 411), the use of the cognate vb. at 1 Cor 10:10 (the only other place Paul employs the word group) of Israel in the wilderness shows that Paul draws upon the wilderness experience here in v. 13, as well (K. Rengstorf, *TDNT* 1.736; A. J. Hess, *EDNT* 1.256d; Fee 243; O'Brien 291–92).

Paul does not identify the object(s) of the grumbling. Perhaps, like the Israelites, the Philippians were complaining against their leaders about the suffering they were experiencing. There is no evidence to this effect in the epistle, however, so the allusion to Israel's behavior should probably not be pressed in every detail. The emphasis on unity in the paraenesis (1:27–2:18) argues, rather, for the presence of discord in the broader community (O'Brien 291). Paul likely explains the OT allusion (γογγυσμῶν) with the term that follows (διαλογισμῶν), thus putting Israel's grumbling into the Philippians' context. The Israelites "grumbled" against Moses and Yahweh. The Philippians "grumbling" consists of their "disputes" with one another (Fee 243–44).

VERSE 15

ἵνα γένησθε ἄμεμπτοι καὶ ἀκέραιοι

The ἵνα-purpose clause participates in the impv. force of ποιεῖτε (Fee 244; Reumann 390; "so that" [NRSV, NIV, HCSB]); γένησθε is 2 pl. aor. mid. subjunc. of γίνομαι. Though some render the vb. "become" (NIV), "be" (= εἰμί) is more common (NRSV, ESV, HCSB). Glossing γένησθε as "prove yourselves to be" (NASB)—as though the Philippians were already "blameless and flawless" in God's eyes (i.e., positionally) and were now to demonstrate it in their behavior—reads into the text theological subtleties that are nowhere in view (O'Brien 293).

Ἄμεμπτοι and ἀκέραιοι are pred. noms. Ἄμεμπτοι ("blameless" [EVV; H. Balz, *EDNT* 1.69b]; "blameless, faultless" [BDAG 52d]) comes from μέμφεσθαι, "to blame." One described as ἄμεμπτος stands above accusation or blame, either by people or God (H-M 144). The noun is used sixteen times in the LXX (11x in Job), always of persons. The word group in Paul has (1) a eschatological meaning (usually with temporal modifiers, e.g., ἐν τῇ παρουσίᾳ τοῦ κυρίου [1 Thess 3:13]) and (2) a present, ethical sense (1 Thess 2:10; Phil 3:6). The latter is in view here, as shown by the dependent clauses (O'Brien 293).

Related to the vb. κεραννύμι ("to mix," "to mingle"), ἀκέραιος was used in Paul's day to describe undiluted wine or unalloyed metal. Applied to people, it conveyed the idea of simplicity of character, purity, guiltlessness, or innocence (H-M 144; "innocent" [NRSV, ESV]; "pure" [NIV, NJB, HCSB]; "pure, innocent" [BDAG 35d]; "that which is still in its original state of intactness, totality or moral innocence" [G. Kittel, *TDNT* 1.209]). The noun appears only twice elsewhere in NT ("innocent as doves" [Matt 10:16]; "guileless, unsophisticated" with respect to evil [Rom 16:19]).

It is not advisable to make subtle distinctions among ἄμεμπτοι, ἀκέραιοι, and ἄμωμα (e.g., that the first two adjs. denote the external appearance of the Christian community and its true, inner nature, respectively [H-M 144]). Paul piles up semantically related terms simply to emphasize the importance of the Philippians' testimony before an unbelieving world (Reumann 391; "stylistic reinforcement" [Silva 132]). The adjs. refer, moreover, not to the moral state of the individual vis-à-vis God but, rather, to the Philippian church's public testimony, specifically, to "the way Christians talk with and about each other," as the negative alternative, γογγυσμῶν καὶ διαλογισμῶν, clearly indicates (Hansen 181).

τέκνα θεοῦ ἄμωμα μέσον γενεᾶς σκολιᾶς καὶ διεστραμμένης

Ἄμωμα modifies τέκνα, which is in simple appos. to ἄμεμπτοι καὶ ἀκέραιοι (H-M 145; an alliterative series of α-privatives). The description alludes to Deut 32:5: ἡμάρτοσαν οὐκ αὐτῷ τέκνα μωμητά, γενεὰ σκολιὰ καὶ διεστραμμένη (lit., "they sinned; not his children; blemished, a crooked and perverted generation"). Paul applies the LXX description of Israel, however, to two different groups: (1) "blemished" Israel becomes the "unblemished children of God" (τέκνα θεοῦ ἄμωμα) at Philippi, while (2) γενεᾶς σκολιᾶς καὶ διεστραμμένης describes the pagan residents of the colony. The "artful reworking" of Deut 32:5 may reflect prior teaching or sermonic material (Reumann 412).

The term ἄμωμος ("without blemish" [NRSV, ESV]; "without fault" [NIV; cf. HCSB]; "being without fault and therefore morally blameless" [BDAG 56a]) was widely used in the LXX of "unblemished" sacrificial animals (Lev 1:3, 10) and then, by extension, in a moral sense, of God (Ps 17:31), the Law (Ps 18:8), or a faithful Israelite (Ps 14:2). The twofold meaning is reflected in the NT (cultic [Heb 9:14; 1 Pet 1:19]; moral [Eph 1:4; 5:27; Phil 2:15; Col 1:22; Jude 24; Rev 14:5]).

Τέκνα (nom. pl. neut. from τέκνον, -ου, τό) is cognate with τίκτειν, "to give birth to," and stresses the idea of family resemblance, of sharing the nature of the parent, in this case, God. Thus BDAG defines the term here broadly, as "one who has the characteristics of another being" (BDAG 995a). Combined with ἄμωμα, "Paul's aim is that the Philippians, like God, would be morally unblemished" (H-M 144–45).

Μέσον (acc. sg. neut. from μέσος, -η, -ον), "in (the midst of)" (EVV), is an adv. acc. used as improper prep. with the gen. (BDAG 635b; BDF §215[3]; Moule 85; Porter 180; R 488, 775).

The noun γενεᾶς (gen. sg. fem. from γενεά, -ᾶς, ἡ), usually translated "generation" (NRSV, NIV, HCSB), generally denotes "all those living at the same time" (BDAG 191d), often (as here) with a pejorative adj. (μοιχαλίς [Matt 12:39]; ἄπιστος [Mark 9:19]). The temporal, "genealogical" element is absent here, where "[t]he emphasis lies entirely on the sinfulness of this class, this type of people" (R. Morgenthaler, NIDNTT 2.36; F. Büschel, TDNT 1.662; "people" [NLT, CEV]).

The adj. σκολιᾶς (gen. sg. fem. from σκολιός, -ᾶς, -όν), "crooked, twisting," was used (a) lit., of roads, rivers, and snakes, and (b) fig., of speech, actions ("crooked, unscrupulous, dishonest" [BDAG 930d]). The term is common in LXX for "the nature of the man who does not walk in the straightness and uprightness which God has ordained for him but . . . is crooked, cramped, distorted and hence corrupt" (G. Bertram, TDNT 7.406). The Philippians would have understood "harsh masters" of slaves (σκολιοῖς [1 Pet 2:18]) (Reumann 392). Peter employs nearly identical language to describe fellow Jews in Acts 2:40 (τῆς γενεᾶς τῆς σκολιᾶς ταύτης).

Διεστραμμένης is gen. sg. fem. of the perf. pass. ptc. of διαστρέφω, "make crooked, pervert" (BDAG 237b; here in a moral sense "perverse" [NRSV, NLT, NASB];

"perverted" [HCSB]; by extension, "evil" [CEV]). The adj. ptc. modifies γενεᾶς. The perf. is intensive, emphasizing the state resulting from the action. In both LXX and NT, διαστρέφω describes the person who is "perverse" or who seeks to "pervert" the straight ways of God (perverting justice [Exod 23:6]; Elymas [Acts 13:10]; false prophets at Ephesus [Acts 20:30]) (O'Brien 295). Διαστροφή became a technical term in Hellenistic and Stoic ethics for "the moral corruption of the empirical man. The nature of man, which is originally good and oriented to the good, is 'twisted' (διαστρέφεται) by bad teaching and example and by environmental influences of all kinds" (G. Bertram, *TDNT* 7.717; by "empirical" Bertram appears to mean man as conditioned only by human factors and not by divine revelation or grace). For Paul, of course, the problem is much more profound since, apart from God's grace, corruption is not merely "environmental" but endemic to the fallen human condition.

ἐν οἷς φαίνεσθε ὡς φωστῆρες ἐν κόσμῳ

The rel. pron. οἷς is not in concord with its antecedent but is constructed according to sense: οἷς (dat. pl. masc.) = the persons who make up γενεᾶς (H-M 145; BDF §296; R 714).

Φαίνεσθε is 2 pl. pres. pass. indic. from φαίνω. The pass. is used, with φωστῆρες, in an act. sense, "shine, flash" (BDAG 1046d; EVV; P.-G. Müller, *EDNT* 3.411d [but see NASB, "appear"]; H-M 145; O'Brien 295; cf. Matt 2:7; 24:27). Some take the vb. as impv. (CEV; H-M 146), but the indic. (most EVV) is more likely in a rel. clause that is further subordinated to a ἵνα-clause (Fee 246; O'Brien 296; Reumann 392; Silva 126). The objection that Paul would not remind the Philippians of what they are already doing (H-M 146) overlooks the function of the clause, namely, to provide motivation for responding to the nearby impvs. (Hansen 184; Reumann 392).

Paul likely alludes to Dan 12:3 (LXX), where the resurrected righteous φανοῦσιν ὡς φωστῆρες τοῦ οὐρανοῦ. The "already" of Paul's "not yet"/"already" schema may be in view (cf. Col 3:1; H. Conzelmann, *TDNT* 9.345; Fee 242). Both φωστῆρες (nom. pl. masc. from φωστήρ, -ῆρος, ὁ; the -τήρ ending expresses agency [BDF §109(8)]) and κόσμῳ can be used lit. ("stars in the universe/sky" [NIV; BDAG 561d; 1073d]) or fig. ("lights among the people of this world" [CEV]; cf. "lights in the world" [RSV, NASB, ESV]). Paul's point, in any case, is clear: the Philippians shine among their pagan neighbors like stars shine in the sky.

VERSE 16

λόγον ζωῆς ἐπέχοντες

'Επέχοντες is nom. pl. masc. of the pres. act. ptc. of ἐπέχω. Take as an adv. ptc. of manner or means ("by your holding fast" [NRSV]; "holding" [ESV, NASB]; Hansen 184; O'Brien 297), rather than impv. ("Hold firmly" [HCSB, NLT]; H-M 146). Some press the significance of the pres. ("continue to hold fast" [Reumann 394]), but we would expect a pres. ptc. in conjunction with φαίνεσθε at this point in the discourse, so little should be made of the tense of ἐπέχοντες. Due to the evangelistic flavor of φαίνεσθε ὡς φωστῆρες, some think ἐπέχοντες means "hold forth," i.e., to others ("proffering" [NJB]). Most opt for "hold fast" (BDAG 362c; most EVV; H. Hanse, *TDNT* 2.816 n. 1; H. Balz, *EDNT* 2.21d; Hansen 184; H-M 146; O'Brien 297–98; Reumann 394). The latter is supported by:

a. The broader context of 1:27–2:18.
b. The ensuing clause, εἰς καύχημα ἐμοί, which makes more sense when understood as a result of the Philippians' steadfastness, rather than their evangelistic zeal.
c. The lack of comparable evangelistic use of ἐπέχω elsewhere.

In Dan 12:3b (LXX), the MT's "those who lead many to righteousness" (NRSV) is glossed as οἱ κατισχύοντες τοὺς λόγους μου, making it likely that Paul continues the allusion to Dan 12:3 with λόγον ζωῆς ἐπέχοντες (Fee 247–48).

The dir. obj. λόγον ζωῆς ("word/message of life" [most EVV]) occurs first for emphasis (H-M 146). The phrase suggests a corpus of teaching (C. Brown, *NIDNTT* 3.61). Of the options for the gen. ζωῆς, either (1) obj. ("message that gives life" [CEV]; Reumann 413; cf. G. Kittel, *TDNT* 4.118) or (2) source/origin (O'Brien 297–98) makes good sense.

εἰς καύχημα ἐμοὶ εἰς ἡμέραν Χριστοῦ

The first εἰς is telic, "with a view to" (A. Oepke, *TDNT* 2.427; "(so) that" [NRSV, ESV]; BDAG 290c; Moule 70; Fee 248; Reumann 395). The clause can be taken with the broader context (ἵνα γένησθε, κτλ.) (NIV, NJB; Hansen 185 n. 359; O'Brien 298; Reumann 413), or tied closely to λόγον ζωῆς ἐπέχοντες ("It is by your holding fast to the word of life that I can boast" [NRSV, cf. HCSB]; H-M 146). Since Paul shifts focus from the Philippians to himself, some EVV begin a new sentence here (NIV, NJB, HCSB).

Καύχημα can denote the "act of taking pride" (BDAG 537a; most EVV), or a "ground for boasting" or "a source of pride" (O'Brien 298; "my pride" [BDAG 537a]). The former is more likely, since ὅτι (which follows) more often introduces indir. discourse (appropriate following καύχημα as a *nomen actionis*) than epexegesis (required after καύχημα as "ground for boasting"). The cstr. does not allow for formal equivalency, so most EVV tr. ἐμοί (dat. of advantage [H-M 147]) as subj. and καύχημα as vb. ("I may be proud" [RSV, ESV]; "I can boast" [HCSB]).

Ἡμέραν Χριστοῦ marks the day of "final judgment," when Paul must stand before the tribunal of Christ (2 Cor 5:10), not to discover his eternal destiny but to give an account of his stewardship to his Lord (1 Cor 4:1–5) (H-M 147; Reumann 395; cf. BDAG 438b). The idea is not of a present boasting "in view of" or "up to" (cf. εἰς in Gal 3:24) the day of Christ but a future boasting "on" or "in" the day of Christ (cf. εἰς in Acts 13:42; BDAG 537a; O'Brien 299).

ὅτι οὐκ εἰς κενὸν ἔδραμον οὐδὲ εἰς κενὸν ἐκοπίασα

The ὅτι clause introduces the obj. of the verbal idea contained in καύχημα (indir. discourse; "that" [most EVV]; not causal [*pace* NASB, NJB]).

Κενόν is acc. sg. neut. from κενός, -ή, -όν, lit. "empty"; fig. "without purpose or result"; "in vain" (most EVV; BDAG 539b; adv. force with εἰς [R 550]). Sim. language is used in Gal 2:2 (μή πως εἰς κενὸν τρέχω ἢ ἔδραμον; cf. 1 Thess 2:1; 3:5; 1 Cor 15:10). Most see in ἔδραμον (1 sg. aor. act. indic. from τρέχω, lit. "to run"; fig. "to make an effort to advance spiritually or intellectually," "exert oneself" [BDAG 1015b]) imagery from the athletic arena (W. Grundmann, *TDNT* 7.629; A. Ringwald, *NIDNTT* 1.649; Fee 250; H-M 147), although, unlike 1 Cor 9:24–26 and Heb 12:1, associated terms are missing. The metaphor must not be overly pressed, at any rate, since there are no competitors to beat in the Christian race (O. Bauernfeind, *TDNT* 8.232). Ἔδραμον and ἐκοπίασα (also 1 sg. aor. act. indic.) look back from the standpoint of the Day of Christ, an instructive example of the aor. used for action that may have occupied a long time or was repeated (Reumann 395).

The κοπιάω word group ("exert oneself physically, mentally, or spiritually" [BDAG 558c]) is a favorite of Paul's (κοπιάω or κόπος 25x) to signify both (a) manual labor, self-support while preaching (1 Thess 2:9; 2 Thess 3:8; 1 Cor 4:12), and (b) the hard work of ministry (himself [1 Cor 15:10] others [1 Cor 15:58; 2 Cor 10:15]). Paul antic-ipated a final eschatological testing of all mission work (1 Cor 3:10–15). Ἔδραμον and ἐκοπίασα tell of "toil and training, pain, striving, and suffering" (H-M 147; "rough, persevering labors" (Spicq 2.329).

VERSE 17

Ἀλλὰ εἰ καὶ σπένδομαι ἐπὶ τῇ θυσίᾳ καὶ λειτουργίᾳ τῆς πίστεως ὑμῶν

Cultic imagery dominates v. 17. Σπένδομαι ("libation" [NRSV, NJB]; "drink offer-ing" [NIV, ESV, HCSB]) is 1 sg. pres. pass. indic. from σπένδω. The vb. was com-mon in extrabiblical Gk. for "pouring out" a (portion of a) drink on the ground at meals in honor of gods, heroes, or the dead, and for libations of wine or oil offered to a god in formal religious ceremonies (alone or with some other sacrifice [Reumann 398]). Σπένδω and its cognate σπονδή often appear in the LXX (86x) to describe drink offerings (e.g., Num 28:7, 14, 24, 31). These were "ancillary offerings," almost never an independent sacrificial act (C. Dohmen, *TDOT* 9.458–59). Paul likely has OT, rather than pagan, background in view (Fee 251 n. 51), but the terminology would have been immediately familiar to Paul's audience from their own religious back-ground (Reumann 398).

Most EVV separate τῇ θυσίᾳ καὶ λειτουργίᾳ ("the sacrifice and service" [NIV, HCSB, NASB]). However, the cstr. (two dat. sg. fem. nouns governed by a single prep. + art.) is best read as a hendiadys, taking λειτουργίᾳ as basic and θυσίᾳ as adj. ("sacrificial offering" [RSV, ESV]; "sacrificial service" [BDAG 591c; Z §184; H-M 148; O'Brien 309; Reumann 401]; hendiadys is "more frequent in examples where a genitive occurs also" [τῆς πίστεως ὑμῶν here; R 787]).

NT usage (28x) supports reading θυσίᾳ not as a verbal noun, denoting the act of sacrificing ("as you offer your faith" [BDAG 462c]), but, rather, to designate the sacrifice itself (BDAG 463a) (O'Brien 308). The word is used in the NT of (a) animal sacrifices (Matt 9:13; 12:7); (b) the sacrificial death of Christ (Eph 5:2; Heb 9:26); and (c) the spiritual sacrifices of Christians, including the offering of oneself (Rom 12:1), whether in gifts (Phil 4:18), or praise and good works (Heb 13:15–16). Θυσία was also used in the LXX both lit. and fig. (a broken spirit [Ps 50:19]; praise [Ps 49:8, 14, 23]).

The λειτουργ- word group ("offering" [NRSV, ESV, NJB]; "service" [BDAG 591c; NIV, HCSB, NASB]) was used in a secular sense in the Greco-Roman world but in an almost exclusively cultic sense in the LXX (140x). Paul likely has both in view with λειτουργία in v. 17. Paul's Jewish background virtually guarantees that the imagery of ὁ λειτουργός as a priest ministering to Yahweh remains close at hand. In Rom 15:16, the apostle is "a minister (λειτουργόν) of Christ Jesus to the Gentiles in the priestly service (ἱερουργοῦντα) of the gospel of God." In Phil 2:17, λειτουργία occurs with other cultic terminology (σπένδομαι and θυσίᾳ), so that "sacred ministry" is clearly in view (H. Strathmann, *TDNT* 4.227). In Paul's social world, however, λειτουργία most often described services that local elites provided for their municipality or city-state (BDAG 591b; "service of a formal or public type" [BDAG 591b–c]). Local aristocrats served in a variety of offices (including priesthoods), paying from their own funds the costs of the construction or maintenance of public buildings and the production of dramas and games. In return for such services, aristocrats received public recognition as benefactors or persons of exceptional merit. The linguistic payoff, for our purposes, is the "aura of high status" that Paul's audience associated with λειτουργία and its cognates (BDAG 591a–b; Hansen 190). Romans, in particular, competed vigorously for the social status and honor associated with public office (see Introduction), so it is no accident that six of the seven times Paul uses the word group, he does so in letters to churches in a markedly Roman setting (Rom 13:6; 15:16; 15:27; Phil 2:17, 25, 30). Paul thus frames the Philippians' priestly ministry in the service of the gospel as a counter-λειτουργία of sorts—one boasting an "aura of high status" that ultimately exceeds anything associated with public services rendered by the elite luminaries of Philippi's local aristocracy.

Some think Paul's λειτουργία is in view (cf. v. 16 and Rom 15:16): Paul serves the faith of the Philippians (τῆς πίστεως as obj. gen.) (K. Hess, *NIDNTT* 3.552; H. Balz, *EDNT* 2.348). As the other two occurrences of the word group indicate (2:25, 30), however, Paul has in view here the "priestly service" of the Philippians, represented by Epaphroditus, who risked his life to minister to Paul (O'Brien 309; Silva 129; cf. 4:18, where the gift is described with cultic terminology). Accordingly, τῆς πίστεως works best as a gen. of source (NIV; Hansen 189; H-M 148; Reumann 401), or, perhaps, appos. (BDAG 463a; "that is, your faith" [O'Brien 310]).

Scholars read σπένδομαι in two distinct ways:

1. Paul's ongoing missionary work, including his present suffering (Fee 254; H-M 148–49; Reumann 398).

a. The σπένδ- word group was not used of sacrifice that involved the death of an animal (H-M 148). In reply Paul uses the term fig., in a transferred sense (as in 2 Tim 4:6), not lit., of spilling his blood in martyrdom (cf. Ign. *Rom.* 2.2) (O'Brien 306).

b. The note of joy in vv. 17–18 is odd, if martyrdom (view 2) is intended with σπένδομαι (H-M 148–49). But Paul's joy is not over death as such, but over what his death would accomplish in completing the Philippians' "sacrificial service" (Hansen 190; O'Brien 312).

c. The pres. tense of σπένδομαι describes what is currently happening to the apostle, not what is about to happen. But the tense can be read as a futuristic pres., or Paul could simply be viewing his imprisonment-trial-martyrdom as a single idea. The protasis of the cond. concessive cstr. (εἰ καὶ + indic.) assumes the reality of this possibility for the sake of argument, a reasonable assumption, given what is at stake in Paul's impending trial (O'Brien 305; Hansen 188; cf. εἴτε διὰ ζωῆς εἴτε διὰ θανάτου [1:20], where the same possibility surfaces).

d. Paul expects to return to Philippi when he gets out of prison (2:24) (H-M 149).

e. The previous two metaphors (ἔδραμον and ἐκοπίασα) refer to Paul's apostolic labors. It is likely that the metaphor of sacrifice does, as well (H-M 149). But this would generate a tautology. After the forceful references to Paul's apostolic labors in ἔδραμον and ἐκοπίασα, it is hard to see how σπένδομαι can refer to the same thing (O'Brien 305).

*2. Potential martyrdom at the hands of the Romans ("am to be poured out" [RSV, NJB]; BDAG 937a; C. Brown, *NIDNTT* 3.432; O. Procksch, *TDNT* 1.108; O. Michel, *TDNT* 7.535; H. Balz, *EDNT* 2.348d; Hansen 187 n. 368; O'Brien 305–6; Silva 128–29).

a. The Ἀλλὰ εἰ καί cstr. strongly favors this view. Proponents of view 1 connect Ἀλλά not with εἰ καί but with ἐπὶ τῇ θυσίᾳ . . . χαίρω and take it in an adversative sense to correct any wrong idea that might arise from εἰς κενόν (v. 16 [2x]) (H-M 148; Reumann 414). This is highly unnatural. It is best to take Ἀλλὰ with εἰ καί, ascensively (cf. 1 Cor 7:21; 1 Pet 3:14). This understanding of Ἀλλὰ εἰ καί, in turn, favors the potential martyrdom reading of σπένδομαι. For of the two metaphors in v. 16, ἐκοπίασα amplifies the meaning of ἔδραμον. The Ἀλλά takes the point further: "But why talk of labors? I am ready even if the worst comes, i.e., being condemned to death" (O'Brien 303; Hansen 187; BDAG 278d).

View 2 seems better, though one cannot be dogmatic.

Some connect ἐπὶ τῇ θυσίᾳ καὶ λειτουργίᾳ τῆς πίστεως ὑμῶν to χαίρω that follows (taking ἐπί as causal [Reumann 397, 399]). Word order favors connecting the prep. phrase to σπένδομαι, as does the imagery, since the reading keeps the series of three cultic terms together. Paul envisions his death as a drink offering "being poured" upon, or in addition to, the Philippians' "sacrificial offering," as in Num 15:5, "You shall offer one-fourth of a hin of wine as a drink offering with (LXX ἐπί) the burnt offering." Ἐπί can be taken to mean "in addition to" (Fee 254 n. 2; Hansen 189; O'Brien 306–7; "together with" [BDAG 367b]), or, in a local sense, "on" (NIV, HCSB; "upon" [RSV, ESV]). Note the relative importance of the sacrifices. The Philippians offer the main sacrifice. Paul's death would add but a modest drink offering to the their θυσία (O'Brien 310).

χαίρω καὶ συγχαίρω πᾶσιν ὑμῖν

It is not the absence of suffering that generates joy in Paul but, rather, the presence of sacrifice, inspired by faith in Christ, whether his own or that of others (Hansen 190). Some who read σπένδομαι in terms of martyrdom render χαίρω and συγχαίρω as futures ("If this happens, I will be glad and rejoice with you" [CEV]). This seems unnecessary, as the point is clear when the pres. is retained in tr. (NRSV, NIV, HCSB). See below, on v. 18, for the meaning of the fourfold occurrence of the χαίρω word group.

VERSE 18

τὸ δὲ αὐτὸ καὶ ὑμεῖς χαίρετε καὶ συγχαίρετέ μοι

The pron. αὐτό is an acc. of content (also called adv. acc.) (BDF §154; Moule 34; R 487; T 246; Reumann 402); "in the same way" (NRSV, NJB, HCSB); "likewise" (RSV, ESV); "so you too" (NIV).

The pres. tense of the 2 pl. impvs. χαίρετε and συγχαίρετε signifies iterative, repeated action (Reumann 401). The vbs. could be indic., but τὸ δὲ αὐτό calls for impv. (Reumann 402). The fourfold (συγ)χαίρειν may be understood as follows (Hansen 190; O'Brien 312):

χαίρω (v. 17)—Paul is glad at the possibility of being "poured out as a drink offering."

συγχαίρω (v. 17)—Paul rejoices with the Philippians over their own sacrificial service since it is an offering acceptable to God (Hansen 190; O'Brien 312). This assumes the Philippians are, in fact, rejoicing over their service to Paul.

χαίρετε (v. 18)—Paul is not content to be joyful about his own situation and to share the Philippians' joy over theirs (v. 17). He wants them to share his joy, as well. If they are able to be joyful over their sacrificial service to Paul (συγχαίρω, v. 17), they should also be able to rejoice in anticipation of the possibility that Paul will be poured out as a drink offering to complete their sacrifice (Hansen 190; O'Brien 312).

συγχαίρετε (v. 18)—The fourth instance of the word group is pleonastic, serving to balance the twofold χαίρω in v. 17 with a parallel cstr. in v. 18. As the Philippians respond by rejoicing over Paul's situation (χαίρετε), they will, of course, be joining Paul in the joy that he has already expressed (cf. χαίρω [v. 17]).

Nowhere else in his letters does Paul so pointedly emphasize joy in the midst of suffering for the gospel.

FOR FURTHER STUDY

36. Fear of God (2:12)

Balz, H. *EDNT* 3.432–34.
Balz, H., and G. Wanke. *TDNT* 9.189–219.
Downs, Perry. "What Ever Happened to the Fear of God?" *Christian Education Journal* Series 3. No. 1 (2004): 152–57.
Jindo, Job Y. "On the Biblical Notion of Human Dignity: Fear of God as a Condition for Authentic Existence." *Biblical Interpretation* 19 (2011): 433–53.
Mundle, M. *NIDNTT* 1.621–24.
*Waltke, Bruce K. "The Fear of the Lord: The Foundation for a Relationship with God." Pages 17–33 in *Alive to God: Studies in Spirituality Presented to James Houston*. Edited by J. I. Packer and L. Wilkinson. Downers Grove: InterVarsity, 1992.
Yancey, Philip. "A Bow and a Kiss: Authentic Worship Reveals Both the Friendship and Fear of God." *Christianity Today* 49 (2005): 80.

37. Work Out Your Own Salvation (2:12)

Bertram, G. *TDNT* 3.635–55.
Green, E. M. B. *The Meaning of Salvation*. London: Hodder, 1965.
Hahn, H.-C. *NIDNTT* 3. See pages 1,147–52.
Hill, David. *Greek Words and Hebrew Meanings: Studies in the Semantics of Soteriological Terms*. SNTSMS 5. Cambridge: Cambridge University Press, 1967.
*Marshall, I. Howard. *Kept by the Power of God: A Study of Perseverance and Falling Away*. London: Epworth, 1969. See pages 122–25.
Michael, J. H. "Work Out Your Own Salvation." *Expositor* Series 9, no. 12 (1924): 439–50.
Morris, L. *DPL* 858–62.
Parsons, Michael. "Being Precedes Act: Indicative and Imperative in Paul's Writings." *EvQ* 60 (1988): 99–127.
Stanley, Alan P., ed. *Four Views on the Role of Works at the Final Judgment*. Counterpoints: Bible and Theology. Grand Rapids: Zondervan, 2013.
Wagner, J. R. "Working Out Salvation: Holiness and Community in Philippians." Pages 257–74 in *Holiness and Ecclesiology in the New Testament*. Edited by K. E. Brower and A. Johnson. Grand Rapids: Eerdmans, 2007.
Warren, J. "Work Out Your Own Salvation." *EvQ* 16 (1944): 125–37.

38. Sacrifice (2:17)

Behm, J. *TDNT* 3.180–90.
*Ferguson, Everett. "Spiritual Sacrifice in Early Christianity and Its Environment." Pages 1,151–89 in *Aufstieg und Niedergang der Römischen Welt* 2.23.2. Berlin: Walter De Gruyter, 1997.
Kendall, Edith L. *A Living Sacrifice*. London: SCM, 1960.
Morris, L. *DPL* 856–58.
Thyen, H. *EDNT* 2.161–63.

HOMILETICAL SUGGESTIONS

The Philippians and Their Apostle (2:12–18)
1. A faithful church (vv. 12–16a) . . .
2. gives Paul hope for the future (v. 16b) . . .
3. and joy in the midst of suffering (vv. 17–18)

Faith that Works (2:12–16a)
1. Responds to the example of Jesus (v. 12, cf. vv. 5–11)
2. Is not "people pleasing" (v. 12)
3. Rejoices that God is at work within us (v. 13)
4. Presents a united family to a broken world (vv. 14–16a)

Living Out the Mind-set of Christ (2:14–16a)
1. With other believers (v. 14)
2. In the midst of a challenging world (v. 15a)
3. Before a watching world (vv. 15b–16a)

A Window into the Heart of a Gospel-Centered Apostle (2:16b–18)
1. He focuses on tomorrow (v. 16b).
2. He sacrifices for today (v. 17).
3. He is joyful throughout (v. 18).

4. PAUL COMMENDS TIMOTHY AS AN EXAMPLE OF HUMILITY (2:19–24)

19 Ἐλπίζω δὲ ἐν κυρίῳ Ἰησοῦ Τιμόθεον ταχέως πέμψαι ὑμῖν,
    ἵνα κἀγὼ εὐψυχῶ γνοὺς τὰ περὶ ὑμῶν.
20 οὐδένα γὰρ ἔχω ἰσόψυχον,
    ὅστις γνησίως τὰ περὶ ὑμῶν μεριμνήσει·
21–22 οἱ πάντες γὰρ τὰ ἑαυτῶν ζητοῦσιν,
       οὐ τὰ Ἰησοῦ Χριστοῦ.
    τὴν δὲ δοκιμὴν αὐτοῦ γινώσκετε,
    ὅτι ὡς πατρὶ τέκνον
       σὺν ἐμοὶ
             ἐδούλευσεν
             εἰς τὸ εὐαγγέλιον.
23 τοῦτον μὲν οὖν ἐλπίζω πέμψαι
             ὡς ἂν ἀφίδω τὰ περὶ ἐμὲ ἐξαυτῆς·
24 πέποιθα δὲ ἐν κυρίῳ ὅτι καὶ αὐτὸς ταχέως ἐλεύσομαι.

Letters of recommendation in antiquity typically included (a) an introduction of some sort (vv. 19, 24), (b) credentials, praise for the person, relationship of person to author of letter (vv. 20–22), and (c) instructions for the recipient(s) (not here, but cf. v. 29) (Reumann 436; cf. 2 Cor 3:1) (Fee 259 n. 3).

Verbal and conceptual parallels between 2:19–30 and 2:2–11 suggest that Paul presents Timothy and Epaphroditus as "godly examples of the way the Philippians should imitate Christ" (O'Brien 315; H-M 152; Fee 261 n. 8, cautions against overemphasis; *pace* Reumann 437, 439): (1) Timothy illustrates the altruistic attitude enjoined in 2:4, namely, concern for τὰ ἑτέρων (= τὰ περὶ ὑμῶν [v. 20] and τὰ Ἰησοῦ Χριστοῦ [v. 21]), because he is enslaved to the gospel (ἐδούλευσεν echoes μορφὴν δούλου λαβών [2:7]); (2) Epaphroditus came close to death, mirroring Christ, as portrayed by Paul in 2:8 (μέχρι θανάτου [cf. 2:30]) (Hansen 192).

Ancient friendship themes in vv. 19–30 include (a) the presence/absence *topos* (v. 24); (b) a longing and affection for friends (v. 26); (c) contrasting models (v. 21); (d) the father-son metaphor (v. 22); (e) συν- terminology (vv. 22, 25b); and (f) joy (2:28–29) (Reumann 437). There is no OT or Jewish material in 2:19–30.

VERSE 19

Ἐλπίζω δὲ ἐν κυρίῳ Ἰησοῦ Τιμόθεον ταχέως πέμψαι ὑμῖν

Ἐλπίζω ("I hope" [EVV]) is used in a nontheological sense, as in travel plans (1 Cor 16:7; Rom 15:24) (Spicq 1.482; Reumann 419). Yet the qualifier ἐν κυρίῳ Ἰησοῦ (vv. 19, 24), plus the change to πέποιθα in reference to his own arrival (v. 24), suggests that "hope" here "moves much closer to certainty" (Fee 264; Hansen 193).

Commentators differ on the significance of δέ (omitted in most EVV):

1. Contrastive to vv. 17–18 ("but" [NASB]). Paul has mentioned the possibility that his life might be poured out like a drink offering (v. 17), but against (δέ) such a possibility, which he knows would trouble the Philippians, he informs them of his plans to send Timothy (v. 19) and come to Philippi himself (v. 24) (O'Brien 316).

*2. Resumptive or transitional ("now" [HCSB]; omit [NIV]), "moving the letter along to the next item" by picking up where the narrative left off with Paul's circumstances in 1:26 (Fee 263 n. 15).

The latter view is likely what Paul intended since he does not mention his own travel plans until v. 24.

Ἐν κυρίῳ Ἰησοῦ could be a stock phrase, allowing for the sovereignty of God in Paul's travel plans ("If the Lord Jesus is willing" [NLT; cf. CEV]; Hansen 193). For this idea, however, Paul generally prefers a more straightforward expression (ἐὰν ὁ κύριος θελήσῃ or ἐπιτρέψῃ [1 Cor 4:19; 16:7, also with ἐλπίζω]). Most, therefore, find more significance in ἐν κυρίῳ Ἰησοῦ in v. 19. Perhaps echoing 2:9–11 (Fee 262 n. 9), the phrase reminds the Philippians of Paul's overarching outlook: "All his hopes and aspirations, his plans and expectations, were subject to the lordship of Jesus Christ" (H-M 153; "grounded in the Lord Jesus" [Harris, *Prepositions*, 130]; O'Brien 317). The repetition of ἐν κυρίῳ in v. 24 supports this understanding, forming an *inclusio* that extends the shadow of Jesus' lordship over all of vv. 19–24 (Reumann 419).

Τιμόθεον is the acc. dir. obj. of the aor. act. inf. πέμψαι, "to send," from πέμπω. Timothy, a half-Gentile convert, is the fourth most frequently mentioned missionary in the NT (after Paul, Peter, and Barnabas) (Reumann 440). He was with Paul in Macedonia (Acts 16:1–3; 1 Thess 3:2). He is not mentioned in the Philippian narrative itself (Acts 16:1–35), but Paul's assertion in v. 22 (τὴν δὲ δοκιμὴν αὐτοῦ γινώσκετε) likely alludes to some part Timothy played in Philippi, either during the founding of the church or, perhaps, during a later visit (Acts 19:21–22; 20:3–4).

The adv. ταχέως (from adj. ταχύς, -εῖα, -ύ) focuses either on the speed of an action ("quickly") or, as here, on the shortness of interval between two points in time, "soon" (BDAG 992d; most EVV; "shortly" [NASB]; Hansen 193, n. 392; "as soon as possible" [Fee 264]).

ἵνα κἀγὼ εὐψυχῶ γνοὺς τὰ περὶ ὑμῶν

Ἵνα ("[so] that" [most EVV]) introduces a purpose clause (Reumann 419). Κἀγώ is crasis for καί + ἐγώ. The καί ("also" [NIV, NASB, HCSB]; "too" [ESV]) hints that the Philippians, too, will benefit from Timothy's coming: they will be heartened with good news about Paul, just as he will be encouraged when he hears about them (Fee 265 n. 24; H-M 153; O'Brien 317; Reumann 419).

Εὐψυχῶ is 1 sg. pres. act. subjunc. from εὐψυχέω. Although cognates (εὐψυχία and εὔψυχος) are used of "courage" in military contexts (1 Macc 9:14; 2 Macc 14:18), the vb. here means "be glad," with the implication of "release from anxiety" (BDAG 417b; "cheered" [NRSV, NIV, ESV]; "encouraged" [NASB, HCSB]; H. Balz, *EDNT* 2.90a). A father to his son: "Write me soon (ταχέως) so that I may be encouraged (ἵνα εὐψυχῶ)" (P.Oxy. 2860.17) (Reumann 419). Εὐψυχέω in the impv. occurs in letters of condolences, and in burial inscriptions, in the sense "Take heart!" "Be it well with your soul!" "Have courage!" (Spicq 2.155–56; Reumann 419).

Γνούς is nom. sg. masc. of the aor. act. ptc. of γινώσκω, used here in the sense "learn (of)" (BDAG 200a; R. Bultmann, *TDNT* 1.703; W. Schmithals, *EDNT* 1.248d); ingressive aor. ("come to know" [O'Brien 318]); the ptc. is temp. ("when" [NIV, NASB, HCSB]), or even causal ("by" [NRSV, CEV, ESV]) (Reumann 419). Paul does not specify when he expects to hear back from Timothy, though some have speculated, based on various reconstructions of Pauline chronology (Fee 265 n. 26).

For τὰ περὶ ὑμῶν ("news of/about you" [most EVV]; "how you are getting along" [NLT]; "your condition" [NASB]), cf. τὰ κατ' ἐμέ (v. 12); art. used subst., with a prep. and pron. The cstr. refers not to general circumstances but, rather, the specifics addressed in 1:27–2:18. Paul still has in mind the progress of the gospel in Philippi, as verified by the ensuing context, where concern for τὰ Ἰησοῦ Χριστοῦ (v. 21, syntactically echoing τὰ περὶ ὑμῶν) finds tangible expression in the description of Timothy "slaving in the gospel" with Paul (v. 22) (Fee 265).

VERSE 20

οὐδένα γὰρ ἔχω ἰσόψυχον

Οὐδένα ("no one/nobody [else]" [EVV]) signals a problem that Paul will expand upon in v. 21 and marks out Timothy as unique (Reumann 419). Οὐδένα + ἰσόψυχον forms a double acc. of obj. and complement (Wallace 187).

The γάρ explains why Timothy—and not someone else—was sent (Reumann 419). We are not sure why Paul felt the need "elaborately to justify his decision" to send Timothy, but given the commendation that follows, it is unlikely that Timothy made a poor impression on the Philippians during the initial mission to Philippi (*pace* H-M 153).

The vb. ἔχω is used here to signify those Paul has at his disposal, not to denote all those whom he knows (Reumann 420; BDAG 420b).

Ἰσόψυχον (etym. ἴσος, "equal" + ψυχή "soul" [cf. BDF §118(1)]; a NT hapax) is acc. sg. masc. from ἰσόψυχος, -ον, "of like soul/mind" (BDAG 481b; "fully like-minded" [E. Beyreuther, *NIDNTT* 2.499]; "of the same excellence" [H. Balz, *EDNT* 2.202b]; describes "the spiritual state of man" [E. Schweizer, *TDNT* 9.666]). The one occurrence in the LXX (Ps 54:14) has the sense "my equal." Paul likely intends wordplay on εὐψυχῶ (2:19) and σύμψυχοι (2:2) (MM 307c; Fee 266), subtly reinforcing the directive in 2:2 to be σύμψυχοι (Hansen 194). It is left to the reader to decide whether ἴσο- signifies:

*1. "like me (Paul)" ("who sees things like I do" [NEB]; Fee 266 n. 28; Hansen 194; H-M 154; O'Brien 318; Reumann 420; Silva 140);
2. "like Timothy" (most EVV; H. Balz, *EDNT* 2.202b); or
3. "like the Philippians."

Some EVV leave the referent unspecified ("like-minded" [HSCB]). Supporting view 1 (cf. the loose parallel in 1 Cor 16:10) are:

a. ὅστις γνησίως τὰ περὶ ὑμῶν μεριμνήσει (v. 20), which harkens back to Paul's own concern for the Philippians in v. 19 (τὰ περὶ ὑμῶν);
b. the father-child metaphor in v. 22; and
c. the unexpressed obj., suggesting that the obj. is Paul, the subj. of the sentence.

ὅστις γνησίως τὰ περὶ ὑμῶν μεριμνήσει

Ὅστις introduces a "qualitative-consecutive clause" (BDF §379) building on ἰσόψυχος (O'Brien 319; R 961, 996). The indef. rel. pron. ὅστις (nom. sg. masc., "who" [EVV]) often takes the place of ὅς when "an undetermined person (cf. οὐδένα) belonging to a class or having a status" is in view. Paul uses ὅστις here "to emphasize a character quality" (BDAG 729d–30a).

The adv. γνησίως comes from the adj. γνήσιος, -α, -ον, "legitimate, true" (e.g., of offspring) or "genuine," thus "sincerely, genuinely" (BDAG 202c; "genuine(ly)" [NRSV, HCSB, ESV; H. Balz, EDNT 1.255c]; "sincerely" [NJB]). The notion of paternal legitimacy in γνησίως may imply that Timothy has inherited the priorities of his spiritual father ("like father, like son" [cf. ὡς πατρὶ τέκνον [v. 22]). Timothy "legitimately" cares for the Philippians because he is Paul's "legitimate" son (H-M 154; Hansen 194; supported by ἰσόψυχον and the twofold τὰ περὶ ὑμῶν [vv. 19, 20]).

Μεριμνήσει is 3 sg. fut. act. indic. from μεριμνάω, "care for, be concerned about" (BDAG 632b; "concerned" [NASB, NRSV, ESV]; "care(s)" [NJB, HCSB]). The root "refers to that which is existentially important, that which monopolizes the heart's concerns" (D. Zeller, EDNT 2.408c). The vb. is used negatively or positively, depending on the obj. Anxiety about self-related issues is discouraged (Matt 6:25; Phil 4:6). Concern directed toward others is commendable (1 Cor 7:32–34; 12:25; Phil 2:20) (J. Goetzmann, NIDNTT 1.278; O'Brien 319). Here μεριμνάω retains "overtones of the pressure or weight of anxiety that grows out of true concern for the welfare of others" (H-M 154). Paul uses the fut. to describe what Timothy will do when he arrives in Philippi (NRSV, HCSB, NIV; Fee 266 n. 30; O'Brien 319; pace NLT, CEV).

With μεριμνάω, the dir. obj. τὰ περὶ ὑμῶν means something like your "welfare" (BDAG 632c), understood, again, in relation to Paul's gospel priorities outlined in 1:27–2:18.

VERSE 21

οἱ πάντες γὰρ τὰ ἑαυτῶν ζητοῦσιν, οὐ τὰ Ἰησοῦ Χριστοῦ

Πάντες, nom. pl. masc. from πᾶς, is used with the art. as a subst., "all (of them)" (BDAG 784b; most EVV; "everyone" [NIV]; "the others" [CEV, NLT]). The art. is demonstrative ("they all" [B. Reicke, TDNT 5.888]). Paul could have intended the sweeping condemnation in one of several ways:

*1. Rhetorically, to praise Timothy by comparison, through the use of a sweeping, negative hyperbole.

2. As a straightforward reference to those persons Paul had available to him at the time (H-M 155; Reumann 441). Οἱ πάντες corresponds to the οὐδένα of the preceding verse, which is the object of ἔχω and refers not to all whom Paul knows, or to all Christians generally, but to those who might have been available at the time (Hansen 195; O'Brien 321). But Paul elsewhere expresses high regard for those in his company (οἱ σὺν ἐμοὶ ἀδελφοί [4:21], those who preach Christ δι᾿ εὐδοκίαν and ἐξ ἀγάπης [1:15–16]) (Fee 267).

*3. Οἱ πάντες are simply people who came to mind, as Paul was dictating (perhaps prompted by the wrongly motivated preachers mentioned in 1:15, 17) (Fee 267–68).

The first and last options are best. At any rate the focus remains upon Timothy, not upon οἱ πάντες, who are mentioned only for the sake of contrast.

The γάρ is continuative and explanatory, giving the reason why Paul has no one like Timothy, not a second reason why Paul is sending Timothy (O'Brien 320–21; Reumann 421; pace H-M 154).

Ζητοῦσιν (3 pl. pres act. indic. from ζητέω, "to devote serious effort to realize one's desire or objective" [BDAG 428c]) can mean (a) lit. "looking for" something (Luke 15:8); (b) "investigating, examining, considering" something (Mark 11:18; John 16:19); (c) "striving for, aiming at, desiring" (1 Cor 10:24; 13:5). The latter sense is intended here: "strive for [their] own advantage" (BDAG 428c; E. Larson, EDNT 2.103a; "seek" [ESV, HCSB]; "want to work for" [NJB]; "look after/out for" [RSV, NIV]).

Verses 20–21 likely alludes to Jesus' teaching in Matt 6:25–33, where concern for/seeking (μεριμνᾶτε [v. 25]/ἐπιζητοῦσιν [v. 32]) the necessities of life is contrasted with seeking (ζητεῖτε [v. 33]) the kingdom of God. Using sim. vbs. (μεριμνάω and ζητέω), Paul has substituted τὰ ἑαυτῶν for Matthew's τί φάγητε . . . τί πίητε . . . τί ἐνδύσησθε (6:25; cf. v. 31), and τὰ Ἰησοῦ Χριστοῦ for Matthew's τὴν βασιλείαν τοῦ θεοῦ (6:33) (Reumann 420).

Τὰ ἑαυτῶν (neut. pl. art. + gen. [here ἑαυτῶν versus Ἰησοῦ Χριστοῦ; an echo of 2:4?]) connotes "someone's things, affairs, circumstances" (BDAG 688d; R 767). Most EVV render τὰ ἑαυτῶν as "their/his own interests" ("for themselves" [NJB, NLT]), and τὰ Ἰησοῦ Χριστοῦ as "those of Jesus Christ" ("what concerns Christ Jesus" [CEV]; "what matters to Jesus Christ" [NLT]).

VERSE 22

τὴν δὲ δοκιμὴν αὐτοῦ γινώσκετε

The δέ contrasts Timothy with οἱ πάντες in v. 21 and links v. 22 back to v. 20 (Fee 268 n. 37; Reumann 421), providing the second reason Paul sends Timothy (O'Brien 323).

Δοκιμήν is acc. sg. fem. from δοκιμή, -ῆς, ἡ and signifies "the experience of going through a test with special ref. to the result" (BDAG 256a; H. Haarbeck, *NIDNTT* 3.809–10). Seven Pauline occurrences variously emphasize (1) the process (2 Cor 8:2; cf. vb. δοκιμάζω in Phil 1:10) or, most often (as here), (2) the result of being tested (Rom 5:4; 2 Cor 9:13); "proven worth/character" (NASB, HCSB, ESV; "proved himself" [NIV, NJB, NLT]; BDAG 256a; "reliability" [G. Schunack, *EDNT* 1.341d]; Fee 268; O'Brien 323; Reumann 421). The cognate δόκιμος is typically used by Paul in the sense "recognized, approved, accepted" (Rom 14:18; 16:10; 1 Cor 11:19).

Γινώσκετε is 2 pl. pres. act. indic. (not impv. [O'Brien 323 n. 55; Reumann 421]) from γινώσκω ("you know" [EVV]). The Philippians knew of Timothy's character and his relationship with Paul from the days of the founding of the church in Philippi (Acts 16).

ὅτι ὡς πατρὶ τέκνον σὺν ἐμοὶ ἐδούλευσεν εἰς τὸ εὐαγγέλιον

The ὅτι-clause can be taken:

1. with γινώσκετε to introduce indir. discourse ("that . . . he served" [NASB]);
*2. epex., giving the content of δοκιμήν ("how . . . he has served" [NRSV, ESV]); or
3. in a causal sense ("because he has served" [NIV, HCSB]; Fee 262; Reumann 422).

The second option is preferable, but the resultant meaning is much the same.

An intentional lack of symmetry marks the imagery. Paul initially portrays Timothy as his subordinate (πατρὶ τέκνον) but quickly adjusts the cstr. to σὺν ἐμοὶ ἐδούλευσεν, which presents Timothy as an associate who "slaved for the gospel together with Paul" (Reumann 440; cf. 1:1; R 441, 1,199; H-M 156).

A filial relationship between master and disciple (πατρὶ τέκνον) occurs as early as 2 Kgs 2:12 (Elijah and Elisha), and was common among rabbis during the NT period. Of the two terms for offspring, υἱός underscores the status of sonship, while τέκνον emphasizes ("more tenderly" [H-M 156]) the father-son relationship (Fee 268 n. 39). Paul most often uses the imagery of spiritual parenthood in the sense of apostolic teacher and convert(s) (1 Cor 4:14–17; 2 Tim 1:2; Titus 1:4; Reumann 440). Here, however, it is not Paul's role in Timothy's conversion that is in view but, rather, the universal assumption of filial likeness and imitation: "like father, like son" (Fee 269; see on γνησίως [v. 20]; cf. μιμηταὶ τοῦ θεοῦ ὡς τέκνα ἀγαπητά [Eph 5:1]).

Ἐδούλευσεν is 3 sg. aor. act. indic. from δουλεύω, "perform the duties of a slave, serve, obey" (BDAG 259b; Fee 269 n. 40; "he has slaved with me" [Reumann 418]). "[S]erved" (most EVV; BDAG 259d; "working" [NJB, CEV]) fails to communicate the social stigma associated with slave status in antiquity and obscures the intended allusion to two earlier occurrences of the word group. Paul portrays Timothy patterning himself after Christ, who assumed slave status (μορφὴν δούλου [2:7]) for the sake of others (Hansen 197; O'Brien 325). Ἐδούλευσεν also echoes 1:1, where Paul and Timothy are introduced as δοῦλοι Χριστοῦ Ἰησοῦ (Fee 269 n. 40). Though the aor. may refer to Timothy's service during the founding of the church at Philippi, it is probably "complexive . . . viewing Timothy's ongoing service εἰς τὸ εὐαγγέλιον and summing it up as a whole" (O'Brien 325; gnomic aor., continual, habitual service [Reed 224; Reumann 421]).

Εὐαγγέλιον functions as a noun of action, denoting "the work of evangelism," rather than the content of the message ("in the furtherance of the gospel" [NASB]; "in spreading the good news" [CEV]; H-M 156; O'Brien 325; Reumann 422).

VERSE 23

τοῦτον μὲν οὖν ἐλπίζω πέμψαι

The οὖν ("therefore" [most EVV]) is resumptive (Moule 162–63), as v. 23 proceeds to draw upon much of the language of v. 19: (a) ἐλπίζω + πέμψαι are repeated; (b) ἐξαυτῆς corresponds to ταχέως; (c) τοῦτον picks up Τιμόθεον (Fee 269; O'Brien 325; Reumann 422). Unlike v. 19, however, (but sim. to vv. 20 and 22) the dir. obj. (τοῦτον) is in first position for emphasis: "This one who is of proven worth and so well qualified for the task" (O'Brien 326; Reumann 422).

Μέν begins a μέν . . . δέ cstr. (with πέποιθα δέ [v. 24]; "on the one hand . . . on the other hand" [BDAG 629d]).

ὡς ἂν ἀφίδω τὰ περὶ ἐμὲ ἐξαυτῆς

Ὡς ἄν (here = ὅταν, a temporal conj.) + subjunc. points to the time of an uncertain future event, "when, as soon as" (BDAG 1106a; BDF §455[2]; R 974; O'Brien 326).

The vb. ἀφίδω is 1 sg. aor. act. subjunc. from ἀφοράω, "to develop more precise knowledge about someth. in the offing," "determine, see" (BDAG 158c). The prep. prefix has variously been interpreted to mean "look away," from the pres. to the fut. (Reumann 423), or "view something from a distance" (cf. Jonah 4:5 [LXX]) (O'Brien 326).

The adv. ἐξαυτῆς (= ἐξ αὐτῆς τῆς ὥρας) means "at once, immediately, soon thereafter" (BDAG 346d). Both ἐξαυτῆς and ὡς ἂν ἀφίδω τὰ περὶ ἐμέ modify the aor. inf. πέμψαι. This generates some grammatical dissonance, since the ὡς ἄν clause indicates an uncertain future point in time, while ἐξαυτῆς emphasizes present action. The semantics are straightforward, however, if ὡς ἂν ἀφίδω τὰ περὶ ἐμέ is interpreted as qualifying ἐξαυτῆς (O'Brien 326; Reumann 423; "immediately, as soon as I see" [NASB]; cf. "just as soon as I see/find out" [RSV, ESV, NLT]).

Some suggest that τὰ περὶ ἐμέ ("how things go with me" [NASB, NIV, NRSV]; "what is going to happen to me (here)" [NJB, CEV, NLT]) involves more than just the outcome of Paul's trial, since the expression must somehow be connected to the sending of Timothy, and Paul seems already to know "what is going to happen" where the trial is concerned (v. 24; cf. 1:25). Perhaps some general, personal matters required Timothy's presence, such as "the gathering of essential data for [Paul's] final defense, or perhaps, more importantly, the working toward reconciling differences among local Christians" (H-M 156–57; O'Brien 326–27). In 1:12, however, Paul used τὰ κατ᾽ ἐμέ

more narrowly, of his imprisonment and the impending trial, so τὰ περὶ ἐμέ should
probably be taken in the same way here (the two expressions are interchangeable [cf.
Col 4:7–8]) (Fee 269 n. 42). Note that τὰ περί + acc. functions in the same way as τὰ
περί + gen. (older Attic cstr.) in v. 20 ("my circumstances," not "my surroundings"
[T 14, 270]; Moule 62–63).

VERSE 24

πέποιθα δὲ ἐν κυρίῳ ὅτι καὶ αὐτὸς ταχέως ἐλεύσομαι

Πέποιθα is 1 sg. perf. act. indic. from πείθω, with pres. force (R 895), "I have been
persuaded," therefore "I trust" (NRSV, NASB, ESV; "I am confident/convinced" [NIV,
NJB, HCSB]; "confident conviction" [R. Bultmann, TDNT 6.6]; O Becker, NIDNTT
1.591). The perf. tense of πείθω is a favorite device in Philippians to express certainty
or conviction (1:6, 14, 25; 2:19) (O'Brien 327). The shift from ἐλπίζω (vv. 19, 23)
to πέποιθα is "Paul's way of subtly assuring the Philippians that his own coming to
them again, in spite of immense obstacles, is more certain than the expected arrival of
Timothy" (repeats 1:24–26 "more emphatically" [Fee 270]; H-M 153; O'Brien 327;
"a new tone of faith" [Reumann 442]).

For ἐν κυρίῳ see on v. 19. The ὅτι introduces indir. discourse (as in 1:6), giving the
content of Paul's assurance (Reumann 423; O'Brien 327). The cstr. with καί + the
intensive pron. (αὐτός) is emphatic ("I myself . . . also" [NASB, HCSB, ESV]), showing that Timothy's visit will not be a substitute for Paul's presence (Hansen 198 n. 418;
O'Brien 327).

For ταχέως see on v. 19. Eng. tr. such as "shortly" (RSV, NASB, ESV), or "quickly"
(HCSB), need to be qualified, in light of v. 19. The sending of Timothy to Philippi
and his (implied) subsequent return with good news for Paul (κἀγὼ εὐψυχῶ γνοὺς τὰ
περὶ ὑμῶν) point to an interval of some weeks, at least, possibly months, before Paul
himself will go Philippi (O'Brien 327).

FOR FURTHER STUDY

39. Paul and His Coworkers (2:19–30)

Banks, Robert. *Paul's Idea of Community*. Rev. Ed. Peabody, MA: Hendrickson, 1994. See
  pages 149–58.
Bruce, F. F. *The Pauline Circle*. Grand Rapids: Eerdmans, 1985.
Culpepper, R. Alan. "'Co-workers in Suffering,' Philippians 2:19–30." *RevExp* 77 (1980):
  349–58.
*Ellis, Edward E. *DPL* 183–89.
_____. "Paul and His Co-workers." *NTS* 17 (1970–71): 437–52.
Filson, Floyd V. *Pioneers of the Primitive Church*. New York: Abingdon, 1940.
Furnish, Victor P. "'Fellow Workers in God's Service' (1 Cor 3:9)." *JBL* 80 (1961):
  364–70.
Gerberding, K. A. "Women Who Toil in Ministry, Even as Paul." *Currents in Theology and
  Mission* 18 (1991): 285–91.

Gillman, J. *ABD* 6.558–60.
Harrington, Daniel J. "Paul and Collaborative Ministry." *New Theology Review* 3 (1990) 62–71.
Hellerman, Joseph H. *Embracing Shared Ministry*. Grand Rapids: Kregel, 2013.
Redlich, E. B. *S. Paul and His Companions*. London: Macmillan, 1913.

HOMILETICAL SUGGESTIONS

A Faithful Junior Partner in Ministry (2:20–23)

1. Genuinely concerned for the well-being of others (v. 20)
2. Seeks the things of Christ (v. 21)
3. Accountable to his mentor in a father-son relationship (v. 22a)
4. Known to the Philippians as a true servant of the gospel (v. 22b)
5. Willing to travel when and where he is needed (vv. 20, 23)

The Priorities of a Proven Minister (2:20–22)

1. A proven minister is other centered (v. 20)
2. A proven minister is Christ centered (v. 21)
3. A proven minister is gospel centered (v. 22)

5. PAUL COMMENDS EPAPHRODITUS AS AN EXAMPLE OF HUMILITY (2:25–30)

25 Ἀναγκαῖον δὲ ἡγησάμην Ἐπαφρόδιτον
τὸν ἀδελφὸν
καὶ συνεργὸν
καὶ συστρατιώτην
μου,
ὑμῶν δὲ
ἀπόστολον
καὶ λειτουργὸν τῆς χρείας μου, πέμψαι πρὸς ὑμᾶς,
26 ἐπειδὴ ἐπιποθῶν ἦν πάντας ὑμᾶς καὶ ἀδημονῶν,
διότι ἠκούσατε
ὅτι ἠσθένησεν.
27 καὶ γὰρ ἠσθένησεν παραπλήσιον θανάτῳ·
ἀλλὰ ὁ θεὸς ἠλέησεν αὐτόν,
οὐκ αὐτὸν δὲ μόνον
ἀλλὰ καὶ ἐμέ,
ἵνα μὴ λύπην ἐπὶ λύπην σχῶ.
28 σπουδαιοτέρως οὖν ἔπεμψα αὐτόν,
ἵνα ἰδόντες αὐτὸν πάλιν χαρῆτε
κἀγὼ ἀλυπότερος ὦ.
29 προσδέχεσθε οὖν αὐτὸν ἐν κυρίῳ μετὰ πάσης χαρᾶς
καὶ τοὺς τοιούτους ἐντίμους ἔχετε,
30 ὅτι   διὰ τὸ ἔργον Χριστοῦ
μέχρι θανάτου
ἤγγισεν
παραβολευσάμενος τῇ ψυχῇ,
ἵνα ἀναπληρώσῃ τὸ ὑμῶν ὑστέρημα τῆς πρός με λειτουργίας.

The commendation of Epaphroditus continues the theme of Christlike examples (cf. Timothy [vv. 19–24]), playing directly, in this case, on the preoccupation with social status and honorific titles that characterized life among the pagan population of Roman Philippi. Paul honors Epaphroditus with five such titles (v. 25) and instructs the Philippians to honor him, as well (v. 29). Honor is awarded to citizens of God's countercultural commonwealth, however, for behavior that would have been seen as wholly dishonorable by the dominant culture: risking one's life after the pattern (cf. μέχρι θανάτου [2:8])—and in the service—of a crucified Messiah (v. 30).

Reconstructions of Epaphroditus's travels problematize the idea of a Roman provenance for Philippians, due to the distance between Rome to Philippi. Some maintain the need for five journeys:

a. Someone brings news of Paul's imprisonment from Rome to Philippi (1:12).

b. The Philippians send Epaphroditus to Paul, where he becomes seriously ill (2:27).

c. News of Epaphroditus's illness is brought from Rome to Philippi (2:26b).

d. Someone travels from Philippi to Rome to inform Epaphroditus that the Philippians are concerned about him (2:26a).

e. Paul sends Epaphroditus back to Philippi (2:25, 28).

The distance and time involved in these five trips, it is argued, makes an Ephesian imprisonment more likely.

Journey "d" can be eliminated, however, since Epaphroditus would hardly have needed someone to tell him that his illness would concern back home (Fee 278; Hansen 204 n. 443; O'Brien 335). Trip "c" is questionable, as well. Implied in v. 30 (ἵνα) is "a causal connexion between the bringing of the gift and the risking of his life" (B. S. Mackay, "Further Thoughts on Philippians," NTS 7 [1960–61], 169). Epaphroditus likely became ill on the way to Rome. Given the fact that he was carrying money, he was probably not traveling alone (cf. 1 Cor 16:3; 2 Cor 11:9; Acts 20:4). A likely scenario sees one of his traveling companions returning to Philippi—or, perhaps, someone traveling in the opposite direction—with news of Epaphroditus's condition. The result is a reconstruction of events that well allows for a Roman imprisonment and provenance for Philippians.

VERSE 25

Ἀναγκαῖον δὲ ἡγησάμην Ἐπαφρόδιτον . . . πέμψαι πρὸς ὑμᾶς

Ἀναγκαῖον ("necessary" [EVV; BDAG 60d]; "essential" [NJB]) is first for emphasis (Fee 274 n. 10; Reumann 442). Neither Paul nor Timothy was free to travel (2:19, 24), and Epaphroditus's illness caused concern at Philippi, which, in turn, distressed Epaphroditus himself (H-M 161–62), thus the need (Ἀναγκαῖον) to send Epaphroditus.

The conj. δέ ("But" [NIV, NASB, HCSB]; "Nevertheless" [NJB]; "Still" [NRSV]; omit δέ [ESV]) introduces a new section (vv. 25–30) that both (a) contrasts with (Paul sent Epaphroditus but not Timothy) and (b) parallels ("sending pericopes") what was said about Timothy in vv. 19–24 (Reumann 424).

Ἡγησάμην is 1 sg. aor. mid. indic. from ἡγέομαι, "think, consider, regard" (BDAG 434a). The vb. commonly occurs with the inf. + ἀναγκαῖον/δίκαιον as a "fixed expression" (T. Schramm, EDNT 2.113c; cf. 2 Cor 9:5; 2 Pet 1:13). Ἡγησάμην is an epistolary aor. and can be tr. as pres. ("I think" [NIV, NRSV, CEV]) or past ("I thought" [RSV, NASB]; "I considered" [HCSB]), depending on whether the time frame is Paul's or the Philippians, respectively (Fee 274 n. 1; cf. BDF §334; Moule 12; O'Brien 330). The implication (cf. also vv. 29–30) is that Epaphroditus was the bearer of the letter (H-M 161; O'Brien 330).

Ἐπαφρόδιτον (acc. sg. masc.) occurs only in Philippians (cf. 4:18). Common in antiquity, Ἐπαφρόδιτος came from Aphrodite, the Greek fertility goddess worshipped throughout the Greco-Roman world ("the personification of the sexual instinct" [H-M 162]; Lat. Venus). Ἐπαφρόδιτος came to mean "lovely," "charming," or "amiable."

Perhaps named by Gentile parents in honor of Aphrodite, Epaphroditus became a follower of Christ (Fee 274 n. 11; O'Brien 329). Given the symbolism of names in antiquity, it is interesting to note that upon becoming a Christian, persons with overtly pagan names were not required to change or otherwise Christianize them (Reumann 424).

τὸν ἀδελφὸν καὶ συνεργὸν καὶ συστρατιώτην μου, ὑμῶν δὲ ἀπόστολον καὶ λειτουργὸν τῆς χρείας μου

The string of five titles (acc. sg. masc., dir. objs. of aor. act. infin. πέμψαι) is unparalleled in Paul. Passages cited as analogous contain at most three, usually two, epithets (1 Thess 3:2; 1 Cor 4:17; Rom 16:1; Col 4:7). Some think Paul felt compelled to assure the Philippians that Epaphroditus has not somehow failed or fallen short in his mission. A better explanation for the anomalous commendation is to be found in the social orientation of Roman Philippi, where persons prized the various titles won in the military or civic *cursus honorum* ("race of honors") and publicly displayed those titles in inscriptions erected throughout the colony (J. Hellerman, "Brothers and Friends in Philippi: Family Honor in the Roman World and in Paul's Letter to the Philippians," *BTB* 39 [2009]: 15–25; *Reconstructing Honor*, 88–109). As noted below, at least two of the terms in the list—συστρατιώτης and λειτουργός—were honorary epithets not only among Christians (cf. ἀδελφός and συνεργός) but in the broader Greco-Roman world, as well.

Ἀδελφὸν καὶ συνεργὸν καὶ συστρατιώτην are bracketed together by the shared τόν and μου (H-M 163; O'Brien 330). Reading the terms as an "ascending sequence" (O'Brien 330; Reumann 433) works better as one moves from ἀδελφόν to συνεργόν, than from συνεργόν to συστρατιώτην (Fee 275 n. 13).

Although ἀδελφός ("brother" [most EVV]) is applied to all Christians ("a follower . . . of the Lord" [CEV]), (a) μου (rare when ἀδελφός in the sg. refers to an individual [cf. 2 Cor 2:13]) and (b) the συν-prefixed words that follow underscore a special surrogate sibling bond between Paul and Epaphroditus, one forged in the shared work and conflict of the gospel ministry ("a person deep in [Paul's] affections" [H-M 162]; W. Michaelis, *TDNT* 7.742 n. 290; O'Brien 330–31). The order of ἀδελφός and συνεργός is not incidental. For Paul effective team ministry assumes the prior context of a "deeply personal relationship" (Hansen 201–201; Hellerman, *Embracing Shared Ministry*, 173–98).

Συνεργόν (acc. sg. masc.) is a favorite of Paul's (12x of 13x in NT) to identify a "co-worker" (HCSB, NIV; "fellow worker" [RSV, NJB; BDAG 969c]; "mission colleague" [W.-H. Ollrog, *EDNT* 3.304a]; but not unconditional equality with the apostle [G. Bertram *TDNT* 7.874]). Συνεργός, unlike ἀδελφός, is not used of believers in general. Since Paul uses συνεργός primarily of associates on his mission team, its appearance here may imply that he knew Epaphroditus previously, perhaps as one of the founding members of the Philippian church, who later joined the Pauline mission (H-M 163). "Paul explicitly calls no less than sixteen persons 'fellow workers,' and his usage, along with circumstantial evidence, suggests that he would have so identified another twenty to twenty-five women and men. Acts and the Pastorals have picked up this evidence and added another fifteen names. Paul's association with so many fellow workers has no parallel in early Christian missionary activity" (W.-H. Ollrog, *EDNT* 3.304b).

Συστρατιώτην (acc. sg. masc. from συστρατιώτης, -ου, ὁ; cf. BDF §19) elicits the image of "a wounded comrade-in-arms, who is being sent back home for rest" (Fee 276; "fellow soldier" [EVV]; "companion in arms" [NJB]). Originally a military term describing those who fight side by side, συστρατιώτην here speaks of conflict or persecution, possibly even imprisonment, that Epaphroditus faced with Paul, as they labored together in the gospel (H-M 163; O'Brien 331; Reumann 425). Paul elsewhere speaks of his ministry as a military campaign (2 Cor 10:4), in which he and his colleagues are waging spiritual warfare (1 Cor 9:7; 2 Cor 10:3). Martial imagery would have resonated strongly at Philippi, which had been established as a colony of veterans. Paul intends συστρατιώτην as a "term of honor" (BDAG 979a; H. Balz, *EDNT* 3.314b), since Roman generals used the term to portray their soldiers as equal to their commander in chief (συστρατιῶται, Polyaenus *Stratagems*, 8.23.22). Thus, Caesar honors his troops by addressing them as *commilitones* (Suetonius, *Divus Iulius* 67).

The final two terms mark Epaphroditus's relationship with the Philippians (ὑμῶν goes with ἀπόστολον καὶ λειτουργόν). The syntax (μου, ὑμῶν δέ) sharply distinguishes the last two titles from the first three (R 418, 502; H-M 163; O'Brien 332; Reumann 443). It is possible to take ἀπόστολον καὶ λειτουργὸν τῆς χρείας μου as a hendiadys, "whom you sent to take care of my needs" (NIV; [cf. NJB, CEV]; "the one whose service supplied my need" [BDAG 1088c]; O'Brien 331), but we should not, thereby, downplay the import of the anomalous string of five honorary titles.

Etym. ἀπόστολος is "one sent" ("messenger" [most EVV]). The term was used in extrabiblical Gk. for someone sent on a naval or military expedition, including colonists for a settlement, and also for Cynic-Stoic philosophers, as messengers of Zeus (K. H. Rengstorf, *TDNT* 1.407–11). Two extremes should be avoided: (1) elaborate taxonomies that identify three or more distinct ways in which ἀπόστολος is used in the NT, and (2) interpretations that efface such distinctions entirely, as if Epaphroditus is "equally an 'apostle' with Paul" (H-M 163). Although some occurrences defy facile classification (Timothy and Silas [1 Thess 2:7]; Andronicus and Junia [Rom 16:7]), we can distinguish broadly between (1) apostles who had been commissioned by the risen Lord as his authoritative representatives, and (2) "messengers without extraordinary status," commissioned by congregations for specific purposes (BDAG 122b; K. H. Rengstorf, *TDNT* 1.422; 2 Cor 8:23; highlights the functional nature of ἀπόστολος [Fee 276 n. 18; Hansen 202]). Epaphroditus is called the Philippians' apostle, not an apostle of Jesus Christ (Silva 141).

As in v. 18, λειτουργόν ("one engaged in administrative or cultic service" [BDAG 591d]) has a twofold resonance. The cultic imagery (spiritualized) is central, so that "minister" (NRSV, HCSB, ESV) remains a good tr. for λειτουργόν (H. Balz, *EDNT* 2.348d–49a; "'priestly service' (to God, is implied)" [Fee 276]; *pace* H. Strathmann, *TDNT* 4.231; Reumann 426, 443). The Philippians, however, would have been more familiar with the λειτουργός as a person of some wealth who served as a benefactor (perhaps in the official capacity of gymnasiarch, priest, or civic leader) for his local municipality. Such persons boasted relatively high social status, moreover, so that Paul is consciously "heightening the status" of Epaphroditus with the designation λειτουργόν (BDAG 592a; D. Peterlin, *Paul's Letter to the Philippians*, 200).

Χρείας is gen. sg. fem. from χρεία, -ας, ἡ, "need, lack, want, difficulty" (BDAG 1088c; "my need(s)" [EVV]); the gen. is obj. This is the first explicit mention of the gift, which is likely alluded to in 1:3–5.

VERSE 26

ἐπειδὴ ἐπιποθῶν ἦν πάντας ὑμᾶς καὶ ἀδημονῶν

Ἐπειδή is a causal conj. ("for" [NIV, ESV]; "because" [NJB, NASB]; "since" [HCSB]) introducing the reasons Paul sent Epaphroditus back sooner than expected (O'Brien 333).

The vb. ἐπιποθέω (nom. sg. masc. pres. act. ptc.) means "to have a strong desire for someth., with the implication of need" (BDAG 377c; "longing for" [most EVV]), not "the painful experience of homesickness" (*pace* H-M 164; "bad psychologizing" [Fee 277 n. 22]; Hansen 203; the vb. cannot mean "homesickness" in 1:8). Ἐπιποθῶν and ἀδημονῶν can be interpreted as adjs. or, better, with the 3 sg. impf. ἦν as a twofold periph. cstr., though Paul seldom employs periphrasis (O'Brien 334; R 888). The notion of "a persistent continuance" (H-M 164; R 888, but see 1,120; Fee 277 n. 22) is possible, but details regarding the duration of Epaphroditus's illness are otherwise nowhere in sight. Whether we tr. as a pres. (NIV, CEV) or a past (NRSV, HCSB, NASB) will depend on how the epistolary aor. ἡγησάμην (v. 25) has been rendered.

UBS[5] assigns the text a {C} level of certainty (Metzger 613–14) because some important witnesses (ℵ* A C D 33 81 104 etc.) add ἰδεῖν τὸ ἐπιποθῶν ἦν, probably under the influence of 1 Thess 3:6; Rom 1:11; and 2 Tim 1:4. The idea that Epaphroditus simply "longs for them"—which included a desire "to see" them but is not limited to such (as in 1:8)—best fits the immediate context (Fee 271 n. 1, 277 n. 26; H-M 159; O'Brien 328; Reumann 427).

Ἀδημονῶν (nom. sg. masc. pres. act. ptc.) continues the periph. cstr. with ἦν. The vb. ἀδημονέω ("be in anxiety, be distressed, troubled" [BDAG 19b–c; H. Balz, *EDNT* 1.30d]; "distressed" [most EVV]; "worrying/worried" [NJB, CEV]) is a strong word, used elsewhere in the NT only of the anguish that gripped Jesus in Gethsemane (Matt 26:37 [with λυπεῖσθαι]; Mark 14:33 [with ἐκθαμβεῖσθαι]). Fanciful etym. is to be avoided (e.g., δῆμος + α-privative, "not at home, away from home," therefore, "beside oneself" with "homesickness") (Fee 277 n. 22; Reumann 427). Ancient parallels include a letter from a soldier to a mother who had somehow heard he was ill: "So do not grieve about me. I was much grieved to hear that you had heard about me, for I was not seriously ill" (P.Oxy. 12.1481.4, cited by MM 382a; H-M 164). Although ἀδημονῶν may simply amplify ἐπιποθῶν (Epaphroditus's yearning was prompted by his anxiety of their welfare), the intervening words (πάντας ὑμᾶς) suggest that ἀδημονῶν should be read, instead, as a separate idea with the διότι-clause that follows (O'Brien 334).

διότι ἠκούσατε ὅτι ἠσθένησεν

The causal conj. διότι ("because" [EVV]; R 964) introduces a clause that explains ἀδημονῶν. The 2 pl. aor. act. indic. ἠκούσατε (with ὅτι of indir. discourse) may be rendered in Eng. as a simple past ("you heard" [NIV]) or a pluperf. ("you had heard" [NASB]), depending, again, on the temporal perspective the translator assigns to the epistolary aor. ἡγησάμην (v. 25).

ἠσθενέω (3 sg. aor. act. indic.) lit. signifies "weakness or powerlessness" (α-privative + σθένος, "strength"), here in the sense "be sick," "suffer a debilitating illness" (BDAG 142c; "he was ill/sick" [EVV]; J. Zmijewski, EDNT 1.170d). Some interpret ἠσθένησεν as an ingressive aor. ("he became sick") (Sumney 65), but in light of v. 27, where the vb. is repeated, it is best to regard the aor. as constative, simply portraying Epaphroditus's illness as a simple fact (O'Brien 335). We are told neither the cause nor the nature of Epaphroditus's illness.

VERSE 27

καὶ γὰρ ἠσθένησεν παραπλήσιον θανάτῳ

"For indeed" (NASB; "certainly . . . in fact" [NLT]) accounts for both conjs. in the καὶ γάρ cstr. The combination confirms (γάρ) and intensifies (καί) what was said about Epaphroditus's illness in v. 26 (BDF §452[3]; Fee 279 n. 32; O'Brien 336; Reumann 428; "indeed" [NRSV, NIV, HCSB]).

Παραπλήσιον is acc. sg. neut. of the adj. παραπλήσιος, -ία, -ιον, "coming near," used adv., as an improper prep. + dat. (Porter 180; "approaching" [H. Balz, EDNT 3.33b]; Moule 86; R 646; Reumann 428). Lit. "a near neighbor to death" (ὁ πλησίον ["neighbor"] + παρά ["alongside"]) (H-M 165; O'Brien 336). Epaphroditus "nearly died" (NJB, NRSV, HCSB; BDAG 770b; "near to death" [ESV]). Paul adds this data (a) to highlight God's mercy in restoring him (ἀλλὰ ὁ θεὸς ἠλέησεν αὐτόν), and (b) to present Epaphroditus as an imitator of Christ in anticipation of the explicit verbal parallel in v. 29 (μέχρι θανάτου [cf. 2:8]) (O'Brien 336).

ἀλλὰ ὁ θεὸς ἠλέησεν αὐτόν

Ἀλλά functions here as a strong contrastive conj. to highlight "the wonder of God's mercy" (O'Brien 336; Reumann 428). The juxtaposition of θανάτῳ with ἀλλὰ ὁ θεός gives God all the glory for Epaphroditus's recovery (Hansen 205).

The vb. ἠλέησεν is 3 sg. aor. act. indic. of ἐλεέω ("had mercy on" [EVV; BDAG 314d]; "was kind to him" [CEV] is weak). In the LXX, God demonstrates mercy in his saving benefactions to Israel. Paul, too, uses the word group primarily in a salvation-historical sense (e.g., Rom 11:30; 15:9; Eph 2:4; cf. τοῦ ἐλεῶντος θεοῦ [Rom 9:16]). From this comes the use of the vb. to describe Paul's call to ministry (2 Cor 4:1; 1 Tim 1:13). Only here does Paul employ the word group of physical healing (common in the

Gospels [e.g., Matt 9:27; 15:22]). Stoic philosophers regarded mercy as a sickness of the soul (Reumann 428). Surviving a life-threatening illness was uncommon in antiquity, so God likely had a direct hand in Epaphroditus's recovery (Fee 279; cf. n. 34). The focus, however, is on neither the fact nor the manner of the healing but, rather, on the mercy of God. The healing itself is simply implied (H-M 165; O'Brien 336).

οὐκ αὐτὸν δὲ μόνον ἀλλὰ καὶ ἐμέ

For the adv. use of the neut. μόνον, see on 1:27 (also 1:29; 2:12). The δέ (slightly adversative [Reumann 429]; with καί a "marker of heightened emphasis" [BDAG 213c]) indicates that not all has been said in the previous clause about God's mercy ("and" [most EVV]). The οὐκ . . . μόνον ἀλλὰ καί ("not only . . . but also" [BDAG 659b]) introduces, in an emphatic way, the additional point that Paul, too, has been the recipient of divine mercy (O'Brien 337).

ἵνα μὴ λύπην ἐπὶ λύπην σχῶ

Most see in ἵνα ("[so] that" [EVV]) both purpose and result (O'Brien 337 n. 52; Reed 325; Reumann 429).

BDAG defines λύπην (acc. sg. fem. [2x]) as "pain of mind or spirit," variously glossed as "grief, sorrow, affliction" (BDAG 604d; "sorrow" [NIV, ESV]; "grief" [NJB, HCSB]). The λύπη in v. 27 is not the ἡ κατὰ θεὸν λύπη that "produces a repentance that leads to salvation" (2 Cor 7:10; cf. vv. 9–11) (R. Bultmann, TDNT 4.32; Reumann 429). Rather, it is the grief that is common to all humankind: "You must rejoice and grieve, for you are a mortal" (Eur. Iph. Aul. 31–32). To live without joy or grief is "to live like stone" (Plato, Gorg. 494A) (Reumann 429). For all his eschatological optimism (cf. 1:23), Paul is realistic about the heartache involved in the potential loss of a dear brother like Epaphroditus this side of eternity. The second λύπην (ἐπί denotes "addition" here [Harris, Prepositions, 138; BDAG 365b; BDF §235[3]]; cf. the comparative ἀλυπότερος [v. 28]) likely alludes to Paul's imprisonment, along, perhaps, with the opposition of rival preachers mentioned in 1:14–17 (Fee 280; O'Brien 338).

Σχῶ is the 1 sg. aor. act. subjunc. of ἔχω; when used of emotions, the vb. means "experience something" (BDAG 421c). EVV tr. "have" (NRSV, NLT, HCSB) or paraphrase (with μή) "(so as) to spare me" (NIV, NJB, CEV).

VERSE 28

σπουδαιοτέρως οὖν ἔπεμψα αὐτόν

BDAG (939d) gives two meanings for the adv. σπουδαίως (from adj. σπουδαῖος [R 298]):

1. "with haste," in reference to time ("as promptly as I can" [NJB]; "with special urgency" [BDAG 939d]; G. Harder, TDNT 7.566; H-M 166; O'Brien 339).

*2. "diligently, earnestly, zealously," in reference to manner ("more/very eager(ly)" [most EVV]; "especially eager" [H. Balz, *EDNT* 3.267a]; Fee 280 n. 38; Reumann 429).

Since the form of σπουδαιοτέρως is comp., those who opt for view 1 feel compelled to explain why Paul sent Epaphroditus back sooner than planned. Some suggest a two-fold mission. The Philippians sent Epaphroditus not only to deliver the gift. They also intended for him to remain in Rome to minister to Paul's ongoing needs. Epaphroditus has become ill, and he returns home earlier than anticipated (H-M 166; O'Brien 333, 339). Paul seeks to deflect anticipated criticism, and he does so by profusely commending Epaphroditus to the Philippians (vv. 25, 29–30), and by emphasizing the fact that the early return was his (Ἀναγκαῖον δὲ ἡγησάμην)—not Epaphroditus's—idea (O'Brien 330).

This reconstruction of events is not unreasonable, but it is less than convincing. First, Paul normally uses the σπουδαί- word group of manner (view 2), rather than time (cf. 2 Cor 8:17, 22) (Fee 280 n. 38). Second, the comp. in HGk. can be used as a positive ("hastily" or "eagerly") or a superlative ("as quickly as possible" [G. Harder, *TDNT* 7.566] or "most zealously"), obviating any need to explain why Paul sent Epaphroditus back "sooner" (view 1) than anticipated (*TDNT* 7.566; Spicq 3.281 n. 20; T 30; but see R 665; H-M 166; O'Brien 339; Reumann 430). Finally, the letter itself seems to imply a single, successful mission (v. 29; cf. 4:14–19, especially v. 18) (Fee 273 n. 8). The commendation of Epaphroditus—and Paul's earnest desire (view 2) to return him to the Philippians—should be taken at face value. Epaphroditus really has been full of concern for his brothers and sisters in Philippi, and his Christlike behavior on their behalf, in the face of life-threatening illness, adequately explains Paul's warm commendation (Hansen 201; Fee 273).

Although οὖν picks up the thought of v. 25 (the sending of Epaphroditus), the conj. is inferential, not simply resumptive, pointing back to the reasons Paul sends Epaphroditus back, as outlined in vv. 26–27 (Fee 280; O'Brien 339).

Ἔπεμψα is an epistolary aor., like ἡγησάμην in v. 25, implying the letter is going with Epaphroditus (R 846; T 73; Wallace 563; O'Brien 339).

ἵνα ἰδόντες αὐτὸν πάλιν χαρῆτε κἀγὼ ἀλυπότερος ὦ

The ἵνα-clause ("so that" [NIV, NJB, HCSB]; "in order that" [NRSV]) introduces a final twofold purpose for the sending of Epaphroditus: the joy of the Philippians and the partial amelioration of Paul's sorrow. The ἵνα governs both χαρῆτε (2 pl. aor. pass. subjunc. from χαίρω) and ὦ (1 sg. pres. act. subjunc. from εἰμί).

Ἰδόντες (nom. pl. masc. of the aor. act. ptc. of ὁράω) can be taken as an adv. temporal ptc. modifying χαρῆτε ("when you see" [NIV, NASB, HCSB]), or as a pred. ptc. with a vb. of emotion ("rejoice at seeing" [NRSV, ESV]; "have the joy of seeing" [NJB]; T 158–60; Reumann 430). The meaning is much the same.

Although most EVV take πάλιν with ἰδόντες (e.g., "when you see him again" [HCSB]), the adv. should be taken with χαρῆτε ("you will be glad again" [GNB]; O'Brien 339; Reumann 430), since Paul almost always places the adv. before the vb.

(Fee 280, cf. n. 39). This is consistent with Paul's other admonitions to the church to rejoice again and again (Hansen 207 n. 453). Curiously, the pred. nom. ἀλυπότερος (nom. sg. masc. comp. adj. from ἄλυπος, -όν) is consistently glossed as "less anxious" (NRSV, HCSB, NIV; BDAG 48c; "without anxiety" [H. Balz, *EDNT* 1.64d]; "less concerned" [NASB]; "not . . . so worried" [NLT]). The word, however, is formed from λυπή (+ α-privative) and means to be "without sorrow" ("the less sorrowful" [KJV]). The notion of anxiety (we would expect the μέριμνα- word group) has "no lexical basis whatever" (Fee 281 n. 40; Hansen 207; Reumann 430). We are not told how Epaphroditus's return will ease Paul's sorrow. Perhaps Paul identifies with concerns in Philippi over Epaphroditus's illness. When he returns home, both they and Paul will be at ease on this point (H-M 166; O'Brien 339).

VERSE 29

προσδέχεσθε οὖν αὐτὸν ἐν κυρίῳ μετὰ πάσης χαρᾶς

Προσδέχεσθε is 2 pl. pres. mid. impv. from προσδέχομαι. Some interpret the pres. as "ongoing action" (Reumann 448; "give an enduring welcome" [O'Brien 340]), though one wonders how the reception of Epaphroditus upon his arrival at Philippi could be an "ongoing" event. The pres. is probably used simply to underscore the importance of the admonition in Paul's eyes. Προσδέχομαι can mean either "receive in a friendly manner" or "wait for, expect" (BDAG 877a–b). The first meaning is clearly in view, as the adv. qualifiers (ἐν κυρίῳ μετὰ πάσης χαρᾶς) indicate. "Welcome" (NIV, NRSV, NLT, HCSB; BDAG 877a; "offer hospitality" [A. Palzkill, *EDNT* 3.162d]) brings out the positive connotations of the term better than "receive" (NASB, ESV), which can sound grudging in Eng.

The conj. οὖν is "another inferential 'therefore'" (Fee 281).

The phrase ἐν κυρίῳ ("in the Lord" [most EVV]; "in the sphere of Christ's lordship" [Reumann 431]) adds weight to Paul's directive, but the intended nuance is hard to pin down. Some suggest "as the Lord would receive him," but for that we would expect a comp. clause of some kind. More likely in view is the mutual relationship of the Philippians and Epaphroditus as fellow Christians, so that ἐν κυρίῳ means something like "as a brother in the Lord" ("as a believer in the Lord" [GNB]; Fee 282; Hansen 208; O'Brien 340–41). Harris finds ἐν κυρίῳ here equivalent to the adj. χριστιανός, -ή -όν ("Give him a very joyful Christian welcome" [*Prepositions*, 130]).

Μετὰ πάσης χαρᾶς implies not "every kind of joy" but "with fullness of joy" (Fee 281 n. 42; "with all/great joy" [EVV]; "a joyfulness that is unmixed and unreserved" [O'Brien 341]).

καὶ τοὺς τοιούτους ἐντίμους ἔχετε

The forward position of τοιούτους ties it closely to αὐτόν. Τοὺς τοιούτους ἐντίμους is an obj.-complement cstr.; τοὺς τοιούτους is the dir. obj., ἐντίμους is the complement (pred. adj.) (BDAG 421b; BDF §157[3]; R 480–81; O'Brien 341 n. 79; Reumann 431). Some EVV collapse ἐντίμους ἔχετε into the single vb. "honor" (NIV, NRSV, ESV).

Others preserve the grammar, variously translating ἔχετε: "hold in high regard/honor" (NASB, HCSB); "give the honor" (NLT). The adj. τοιούτους (acc. pl. masc. from τοιοῦτος, -αύτη, -οῦτον; "of such a kind, such as this" [BDAG 1009d]) functions with the art. as a subst. and designates "a class or group (of congregational leaders) whom Philippian house church members are to hold in honor" (Reumann 448; O'Brien 341).

With ἐντίμους (from ἔντιμος, -ον, "honored, respected" [BDAD 340a]), Paul draws upon the honor discourse of the Roman world. That Epaphroditus is to be publicly esteemed for risking his life in the service of a crucified Messiah (v. 30), however, represents an utter inversion of the social values of the dominant culture. Paul's sentiments are, however, consonant with the teachings of Jesus (Mark 10:42–45) and, especially, with the portrait of Christ in 2:6–11, where God's crucified δοῦλος receives the public acclaim reserved in the Hebrew Scriptures for Yahweh alone.

῎Εχετε is 2 pl. pres. act. impv. In such a cstr. ἔχω means "consider, look upon, view"; with τινὰ ἔντιμον, "hold someone in honor" (BDAG 421b; H. Balz, *EDNT* 1.458d).

Paul's command (v. 29) and commendation (v. 30) clearly position Epaphroditus positively vis-à-vis the Philippians (Reumann 448). To assume from this, however, that there is a subtext of trouble (see above, on σπουδαιοτέρως) is to read too much into vv. 29–30 ("unconfirmed theories" [Hansen 207]; Fee 281). Such commendations are common in Greco-Roman letters.

VERSE 30

ὅτι διὰ τὸ ἔργον Χριστοῦ μέχρι θανάτου ἤγγισεν

V. 30 is framed as a chiasm:

A   διὰ τὸ ἔργον Χριστοῦ
   B   μέχρι θανάτου ἤγγισεν
   B'   παραβολευσάμενος τῇ ψυχῇ
A'   ἵνα ἀναπληρώσῃ τὸ ὑμῶν ὑστέρημα τῆς πρός με λειτουργίας

The ὅτι is causal, most immediately qualifying the second command of v. 29 (τοὺς τοιούτους ἐντίμους ἔχετε), not the first (προσδέχεσθε κτλ.) (Fee 282 n. 46).

The causal adv. modifier, διὰ τὸ ἔργον Χριστοῦ ("for the work of Christ" [EVV]; A. Oepke, *TDNT* 2.70), is emphatically placed at the beginning of the clause (O'Brien 342). The general statement finds specific elaboration in the final clause of v. 30. Τὸ ἔργον [τοῦ] Χριστοῦ, occurring only here, is well attested (𝔓⁴⁶ B F G 6 1175 1739 etc.; D *Byz* add the art.; UBS⁵ = {B} Χριστοῦ; Metzger 614) and "surely the original reading" (Fee 271 n. 3), since the var. τὸ ἔργον τοῦ κυρίου (א A P Ψ 075 0150 33 81 104 365 etc.) evidences assimilation to common Pauline usage (cf. 1 Cor 15:58; 16:10) (Fee 271 n. 3; H-M 160).

Μέχρι with the gen. signifies "to the point of" and is used "to note degree" (BDAG 644d; H. Balz, *EDNT* 2.422a; "nearly/almost died" [RSV, ESV, NIV]; "close to death" [NRSV, NASB, HCSB]). Μέχρι θανάτου occurs only here and in 2:8 in Paul. The "striking echo" of Christ's humiliation is intentional (Hansen 205; Fee 282 n. 47; O'Brien 343; *pace* Reumann 432, 438). The vb. ἤγγισεν is 3 sg. aor. act. indic. from ἐγγίζω, meaning "to draw near in a temporal sense" (with μέχρι θανάτου, tr. "come close to dying" [BDAG 270c]).

παραβολευσάμενος τῇ ψυχῇ

Παραβολευσάμενος is nom. sg. masc. of the aor. mid. ptc. of παραβολεύομαι, "expose to danger, risk" (BDAG 759b; "risking/risked" [EVV]; "venture, risk" [H, Balz, *EDNT* 3.15b]). The modal ptc. describes how Epaphroditus came close to death (O'Brien 343). A second-century AD inscription refers to a lawyer who had "risked danger" (παραβολευσάμενος) for the sake of friendship in legal strife (Reumann 432). It was the illness that had brought Epaphroditus close to death (vv. 26–27). Παραβολεύομαι may have been a term associated with gambling, now used metaphorically (Fee 282 n. 48). Dice players cried out, "Epaphroditos!" ("favorite of Aphrodite!") when hoping for a lucky throw, and some suggest that Paul intended a pun on Ἐπαφρόδιτος: Epaphroditus gambled with his life but won because God was there (H. C. Lees, "Epaphroditus, God's Gambler," *ExpTim* 37 [1925]: 46; H-M 167–68). There is little evidence, however, for either the association of παραβολεύομαι or for the cry "Epaphroditos!" in dice playing (Hansen 209; Silva 142).

Ψυχῇ (dat. of ref., used adv. [T 239]) denotes not the immaterial part of a person (the popular Eng. sense) but, rather, physical life. It was not Epaphroditus's "soul" that was at risk but his present life on earth (Fee 202 n. 48; E. Schweizer, *TDNT* 9.648).

ἵνα ἀναπληρώσῃ τὸ ὑμῶν ὑστέρημα τῆς πρός με λειτουργίας

Ἀναπληρώσῃ is 3 sg. aor. act. subjunc. from ἀναπληρόω, "to supply what is lacking" (BDAG 70d); ὑστέρημα refers to a "need, want deficiency" (BDAG 1044a).

The purpose clause (E. Stauffer, *TDNT* 3.332 n. 85) formally situates the "lack" (ὑστέρημα) in the Philippians' "service" or "ministry" to Paul, taking τῆς πρός με λειτουργίας as a subj. gen. (NASB, HCSB, ESV; BDF §168(1); R 503; T 218). This does not mean, however, that the gift was somehow inadequate, much less that Epaphroditus made up for the financial deficit from his own funds (*pace* D. Peterlin, *Paul's Letter to the Philippians*, 181–84). The vb. ἀναπληρόω + the acc. ὑστέρημα is a stylized expression meaning "to make up for the absence by representing others who could not be present" (W. L. Lane, *NIDNTT* 3.955; Fee 282 n. 49; O'Brien 343–44; Reumann 433, 449; cf. 1 Cor 16:17). The presence of the Philippians themselves—not the content of the gift itself—is lacking. Fee paraphrases: "So that he might make up for your absence, and thus 'minister' to my needs as you have not had opportunity to do recently" (284; "doing for me what you couldn't do from far away" [NLT]).

Λειτουργίας is commonly rendered "service(s)" (NRSV, NASB, ESV; "help" [NIV]; "help, assistance, service" [BDAG 591c]). The idea that in serving Paul the Philippians are ministering to God remains in view ("ministry" [HCSB]; see on λειτουργόν [v. 25]; *pace* H. Strathmann, *TDNT* 4.227).

Parallel expressions in vv. 25 and 30 form an *inclusio* of sorts:

v. 25	v. 30
συνεργόν	τὸ ἔργον Χριστοῦ
συστρατιώτην	παραβολευσάμενος τῇ ψυχῇ
ἀπόστολον	ἀναπληρώσῃ τὸ ὑμῶν ὑστέρημα
λειτουργὸν τῆς χρείας μου	τῆς πρός με λειτουργίας

FOR FURTHER STUDY

40. Apostle and Apostleship (2:25)

Agnew, F. H. "On the Origin of the Term *Apostolos*." *CBQ* 38 (1976): 49–53.
_____ . "The Origin of the New Testament Apostle-Concept: A Review of Research."
   JBL 105 (1986) 75–96.
Ashcroft, Morris. "Paul's Understanding of Apostleship." *RevExp* 55 (1958): 400–412.
*Barnett, P. *DPL* 45–51.
Barrett, C. K. *The Signs of an Apostle*. Philadelphia: Fortress, 1972.
Bühner, J.-A. *EDNT* 1.142–46.
Geldenhuys, J. Norval. *Supreme Authority*. London: Marshall, 1953. 46–97.
Kirk, J. Andrew. "Apostleship Since Rengstorf: Towards a Synthesis." *NTS* 21 (1974–75):
   249–64.
Müller, D., and C. Brown. *NIDNTT* 1.126–37.
Rengstorf, K. H. *TDNT* 1.407–47.
Schmithals, Walter. *The Office of Apostle in the Early Church*. Nashville: Abingdon, 1969.
Schnackenburg, Rudolf. "Apostles Before and During Paul's Time." Pages 287–303 in
   Apostolic History and the Gospel. Edited by W. W. Gasque and R. P. Martin. Grand
   Rapids: Eerdmans, 1970.
Spicq 1.186–94.
Turner, *Words*, 23–25.

HOMILETICAL SUGGESTIONS

Character Traits of a Faithful Church Emissary (2:25–30)

1. He is strategically engaged in ministry (v. 25).
2. He is deeply connected to his brothers and sisters in Christ (vv. 26–28).
3. He is willing to risk his life to fulfill his God-given mission (vv. 29–30).

Epaphroditus as a Highly Honored Christian (2:25)

1. He is "brother."
2. He is "co-worker."
3. He is "fellow soldier."
4. He is "messenger."
5. He is "minister" to the needs of the church.

Reasons Publicly to Commend a Brother (2:29–30)

1. He risked his life for the work of Christ.
2. He risked his life to minister to an imprisoned apostle.
3. He acted like Jesus.

C. STEADFASTNESS TOWARD OPPONENTS (3:1–4:1)

1. RESISTING THE OPPONENTS' FLESHLY CONFIDENCE (3:1–16)

a. PAUL'S RELATIONSHIP WITH JUDAISM (3:1–11)

3:1 Τὸ λοιπόν, ἀδελφοί μου, χαίρετε ἐν κυρίῳ.
τὰ αὐτὰ γράφειν ὑμῖν ἐμοὶ μὲν οὐκ ὀκνηρόν,
ὑμῖν δὲ ἀσφαλές.
2 βλέπετε τοὺς κύνας,
βλέπετε τοὺς κακοὺς ἐργάτας,
βλέπετε τὴν κατατομήν.
3 ἡμεῖς γάρ ἐσμεν ἡ περιτομή,
οἱ πνεύματι θεοῦ λατρεύοντες
καὶ καυχώμενοι ἐν Χριστῷ Ἰησοῦ
καὶ οὐκ ἐν σαρκὶ πεποιθότες,
4 καίπερ ἐγὼ ἔχων πεποίθησιν καὶ ἐν σαρκί.
Εἴ τις δοκεῖ ἄλλος πεποιθέναι ἐν σαρκί, ἐγὼ μᾶλλον·
5 περιτομῇ ὀκταήμερος,
ἐκ γένους Ἰσραήλ,
φυλῆς Βενιαμίν,
Ἑβραῖος ἐξ Ἑβραίων,
κατὰ νόμον Φαρισαῖος,
6 κατὰ ζῆλος διώκων τὴν ἐκκλησίαν,
κατὰ δικαιοσύνην τὴν ἐν νόμῳ γενόμενος ἄμεμπτος.
7 [Ἀλλὰ] ἅτινα ἦν μοι κέρδη†,
ταῦτα ἥγημαι* διὰ τὸν Χριστὸν ζημίαν†.
8 ἀλλὰ μενοῦνγε καὶ ἡγοῦμαι* πάντα ζημίαν† εἶναι
διὰ τὸ ὑπερέχον τῆς γνώσεως Χριστοῦ Ἰησοῦ τοῦ κυρίου μου,
δι' ὃν τὰ πάντα ἐζημιώθην†,
καὶ ἡγοῦμαι* σκύβαλα,
ἵνα Χριστὸν κερδήσω†
9 καὶ εὑρεθῶ* ἐν αὐτῷ,
μὴ ἔχων ἐμὴν δικαιοσύνην
τὴν ἐκ νόμου
ἀλλὰ   τὴν διὰ πίστεως Χριστοῦ,
τὴν ἐκ θεοῦ δικαιοσύνην ἐπὶ τῇ
πίστει,
10 τοῦ γνῶναι αὐτὸν
καὶ τὴν δύναμιν τῆς ἀναστάσεως αὐτοῦ
καὶ [τὴν] κοινωνίαν [τῶν] παθημάτων
αὐτοῦ,
συμμορφιζόμενος* τῷ θανάτῳ* αὐτοῦ,
11 εἴ πως καταντήσω εἰς τὴν ἐξανάστασιν
τὴν ἐκ νεκρῶν.

The text is marked by (1) verbal parallels with 2:6–11 (*), (2) a generous use of various literary devices (see below, on v. 2), (3) vocabulary from the semantic fields of accounting and commerce (†), and (4) the centrality and preeminence of Christ, who is mentioned ten times in vv. 7–11 alone, by name (vv. 7, 8 [2x], 9) or pronoun (vv. 8, 9, 10 [4x]) (underlined above). Additionally, Paul has structured his catalogue of Jewish privileges (vv. 4–6) like the honor inscriptions found in the forum and cemeteries of Philippi, thereby setting up his Roman audience for the startling rejection of honor seeking and social posturing reflected in the verses that follow (vv. 7–8).

VERSE 1

Τὸ λοιπόν, ἀδελφοί μου, χαίρετε ἐν κυρίῳ

Τὸ λοιπόν is acc. sg. neut. of the adj. λοιπός, -ή, -όν, used adv. to mark a transition to new material (R 487, 550; Wallace 201, 293): "as far as the rest is concerned, beyond that, in addition" (BDAG 602d–3a; W. Günther, *NIDNTT* 3.252). Since the term can signal the end of a letter (cf. 2 Cor 13:11), some see 3:1 concluding one of several earlier epistles that now constitute Philippians. Χαίρετε is then taken to mean not "rejoice" but "farewell" (cf. BDAG 1075b; H. Conzelmann, *TDNT* 9.367 n. 68; Reumann 452). Silva (144) suggests that Paul may have intended to end the letter and then decided against it, in order to include the warnings in ch. 3. This is unnecessary. Λοιπόν is used often in the NT to mark a transition to a new topic (1 Cor 7:29; esp. 1 Thess 4:1; 2 Thess 3:1; "a connective sense" [Porter, *Idioms*, 122]). It is unlikely, moreover, that χαίρω—"rejoice" elsewhere in Philippians (cf. the same impv. in 2:18; 4:4 [2x])—should suddenly acquire a new meaning at this point in the letter (O'Brien 348; Reed 242 n. 315). Tr. Τὸ λοιπόν as "Further" (NIV; "Whatever happens" [NLT]; "and now" [H-M 172–73]; Moule 161–62; Wallace 493 n. 114; Fee 290; Hansen 214), rather than "finally" (most EVV; H. Fendrich, *EDNT* 2.360c; cf. BDAG 603a).

The 2 pl. pres. act. impv. χαίρετε runs like a friendly refrain throughout the letter (2:18; 3:1; 4:4 [2x]), a subset of some fourteen occurrences of the word group in Philippians. Not a "superficial cheerfulness" that ignores life's realities but a joy that takes into account the Philippians' hardships and "recognizes God's mighty working in and through those circumstances to fulfill his own gracious purposes in Christ" (O'Brien 349).

For the first time in the letter Paul adds ἐν κυρίῳ to χαίρω. The phrase can:

1. mark the obj. of χαίρω, echoing a common exhortation in the Psalms (31:11; 32:1 [LXX]; cf. Phil 1:18, ἐν τούτῳ χαίρω); or
*2. be taken in an incorporative sense, referring obliquely to the Philippians' union with Christ, i.e., either "the ground of their rejoicing" or "the sphere in which it thrives" [O'Brien 350]).

Most prefer the second alternative (H-M 173; Reumann 452).

τὰ αὐτὰ γράφειν ὑμῖν ἐμοὶ μὲν οὐκ ὀκνηρόν

Αὐτά is acc. pl. neut. from the adj. αὐτός, -ή, -ό, used subst. ("the same things" [most EVV]) as dir. obj. of γράφειν. The tr. "what I have already written before" (NJB; cf. CEV) assumes too much since the emphasis in the word order is on τὰ αὐτά, not γράφειν (Fee 292 n. 30). Paul may be writing "the same things" he had previously taught in person (see below).

Some take τὰ αὐτά to refer back to χαίρετε ἐν κυρίῳ since Paul has already (a) charged the Philippians to receive Epaphroditus μετὰ πάσης χαρᾶς (2:29) and (b) used (συγ)χαίρω four times in 2:17–18 (Hansen 213; Guthrie, *Cohesion Shifts*, 43–44). Additionally, "cross-linguistic studies show that anaphora is more frequent than kataphora in most languages because it is easier on the interpretative faculties of the reader" (Reed 255). It is doubtful, however, that a simple and natural summons to rejoice, which occurs twice again in 4:4, would have called forth an apology for repetition (O'Brien 351). It is also hard to see how the command to rejoice would in any sense be "safe" (ἀσφαλές) for the readers (O'Brien 351; Reumann 457). Read τὰ αὐτά, instead, as pointing ahead to what follows in vv. 2–11 (Fee 288 n. 11, 293). Paul may have (a) written a previous letter on the topic (Polycarp mentions "letters" [ἐπιστολάς] to the Philippians [*Ep. Phil.* 3:2]), or, more likely, (b) instructed the Philippians about the common themes of righteousness, the law, and faith in Christ while among them during the second missionary journey (Silva 167, 171–72). The reference in 3:18 to previous verbal instruction that is now repeated in the letter is analogous (O'Brien 352).

The pres. act. inf. γράφειν (from γράφω) is subst., functioning as the subj. of the sentence; ὀκνηρόν and ἀσφαλές are pred. noms. (ἐστίν understood). Μέν . . . δέ connects and contrasts ἐμοὶ μὲν οὐκ ὀκνηρόν with ὑμῖν δὲ ἀσφαλές (R 1,058, 1,153; Wallace 601; Reumann 453–54).

The first dat. pron. (ὑμῖν) is the indir. obj. of γράφειν ("to you" [EVV; omitted in NASB]); the two that follow are dats. of interest (ἐμοί = disadvantage; ὑμῖν [second occurrence] = advantage, "for you" [most EVV]; Hansen 215 n. 16).

'Οκνηρόν is nom. sg. neut. of the adj. ὀκνηρός, -ά, -όν, "causing hesitation, reluctance" (BDAG 702a). 'Οκνηρός means "hesitating" (not "burdensome" or "bothersome") in secular Gk. (Reumann 454). Thus, the combination γράφειν + ὀκνηρός + μή commonly occurs in papyri letters in the sense "I do not hesitate to write" (Jeffrey T. Reed, "Philippians and the Epistolary Hesitation Formulas: The Literary Integrity of Philippians, Again," *JBL* 115 [1996]: 63–90). The term is used of the "slothful" person in the wisdom books of the LXX, however, and is always pejorative in biblical lit. (cf. τῇ σπουδῇ μὴ ὀκνηροί, "do not be slothful/lag in zeal" [Rom 12:11]), so the tr. "troublesome" (BDAG 702a; NRSV; "trouble" [NASB, NIV, HCSB]; "arousing dislike or displeasure" [F. Hauck *TDNT* 5.167]) is appropriate here (Fee 292 n. 32). "Reluctant" (H. Balz, *EDNT* 2.506a) is broad enough to include ideas of both hesitation and displeasure.

ὑμῖν δὲ ἀσφαλές

The δέ (μὲν . . . δέ) here has adversative force (BDAG 630a). The adj. ἀσφαλές (nom. sg. neut., from ἀσφαλής, -ές) means "safe, secure"; with ὑμῖν, "(a) safe (course) for you" (BDAG 147b; RSV, ESV; "a safeguard" [NASB, NIV; NRSV; Reumann 458]; "a protection" [NJB; HCSB]; "security" [G. Schneider, *EDNT* 1.176b]). From α-privative + σφάλλω ("trip up"), ἀσφαλής signifies etym. "not slipping or falling" (Reumann 455; "a basis of stability" [Hansen 215]).

VERSE 2

Βλέπετε τοὺς κύνας, βλέπετε τοὺς κακοὺς ἐργάτας, βλέπετε τὴν κατατομήν

The vigor of Paul's emotions in vv. 2–3 is moderated by the EVV, which cannot consistently reproduce Paul's rhetoric (v. 2. is "as contemptuous a line as anything he ever wrote" [Wright 362]). Literary devices include (a) the repetition of words (βλέπετε 3x [v. 2]) and sounds (β. τ. κ., β. τ. κ., β. τ. κ. [v. 2]) in v. 2, (b) a clever play on similar sounding words (κατατομή/περιτομή [vv. 2–3]) and a chiasm in which the noun phrases alternate position in a crisscross fashion with the participles (v. 3) (H-M 172; O'Brien 367).

Βλέπετε (3x) is 2 pl. pres. act. impv. from βλέπω. Each clause describes the same people from a different angle (O'Brien 353). Most commentators interpret the familiar vb. ("to see") in its stronger sense, "watch, look to, beware of" (BDAG 179a–d; K. Dahn, *NIDNTT* 3.517; "Beware" [NRSV, NASB]; "Watch/Look out for" [RSV, NIV, HCSB, ESV]). Others maintain that the syntax disallows this meaning. Βλέπω generally means "beware of" only when followed by (a) an obj. clause introduced by μή ("lest"), or (b) the prep. ἀπό. The idea is not that the Philippians are to "beware of" a Judaizing challenge. Rather, they must "take proper notice of" (or "consider") the Jews as a cautionary example. First Corinthians 10:18 (βλέπετε τὸν Ἰσραὴλ κατὰ σάρκα) is offered as a parallel (H-M 174). In this instance, however, semantics trumps syntax since the meaning "consider" fails to account for the threefold repetition of the vb. or for the strong language in the dir. objs. (Fee 293 n. 36; Hansen 215; O'Brien 354; Reumann 461; Reed 245–46; *pace* Park 54). Unlike 1 Cor 10:18, the context is highly polemical. "Beware" also better accounts for the causal γάρ in v. 3 (Fee 293 n. 36).

Κύνας ("dogs" [EVV]) is acc. pl. masc., from κύων, κύνος, ὁ, "dog," used fig., "an infamous pers[on]" (BDAG 579d; "those people who behave like dogs" [CEV]). Except for hunting, herding, and watchdogs, dogs in the ancient world were generally held in contempt, not esteemed as "man's best friend" ("despicable, insolent" [O. Michel, *TDNT* 3.1101]; Reumann 460). The dog evoked for Jews the image of uncleanness since dogs fed on carrion, filth, and garbage. Dogs and Gentiles are found juxtaposed in various contexts (Matt 15:21–28; cf. 7:6; cf. "dogs" used for the enemies of Israel in Pss 22:16, 20; 59:6, 14). The Mishnah says that flesh torn in the field could be used to feed dogs or Gentiles (*m. Ned.* 4:3; *m. Bek.* 5:6, interpreting Exod 22:31). According to tradition, R. Aqiba named his two dogs Rufus and Rufina because Gentiles are like dogs in their manner of life (Tanch 107b; cited in Str-B 1.725 [Fee

295 n. 44]). Judaizers likely viewed Paul's uncircumcised Gentile converts as "dogs," outside the circle of the holy people of God. Paul gives his opponents "a bitter taste of their own poisonous prejudice," by turning the Judaizers' epithet back against them: as it turns out, it is the Judaizers who are the "Gentile dogs" that stand outside the covenant blessings (Hansen 217). The ensuing wordplay on circumcision (κατατομή/ περιτομή [vv. 2–3]) communicates the same "amazing reversal" (O'Brien 355).

The noun ἐργάτας is acc. pl. masc., from ἐργάτης, -ου, ὁ, "worker, laborer" (BDAG 390b). An adj. (κακούς) in the first attributive position (art.–adj.–noun) "receives greater emphasis than the substantive" (R 776; Wallace 306). The adj. modifies the persons in view (ἐργάτας), "evil workers" (RSV, NASB, HCSB; E. Achilles, *NIDNTT* 1.564)—not their implied deeds ("those people who do evil" [NLT]). Paul's intentions in τοὺς κακοὺς ἐργάτας are disputed:

1. Paul simply draws upon imagery from the Psalms (5:5 [LXX v. 6]; 6:8 [LXX v. 9]), changing ἀνομία (LXX) to κακός to preserve the alliteration (Fee 296).
   a. In response the LXX cstr. is different ("workers of iniquity" [οἱ ἐργαζόμενοι τὴν ἀνομίαν]), and the noun ἐργάτης does not appear in the canonical books (cf. 1 Macc 3:6, οἱ ἐργάται τῆς ἀνομίας).
2. Τοὺς κακοὺς ἐργάτας is a deliberate pun on the opponents' claim to be doing the works of the law (H-M 174; Silva 147).
   a. But the phrase does not occur in Paul's treatment of τὰ ἔργα νόμου in Galatians or Romans (Reumann 472).
   b. And the ἔργ- root is conspicuously absent from the discussion of ἡ δικαιοσύνη ἡ ἐν νόμῳ/ἐκ νόμου in vv. 6, 9 (Reumann 472).
*3. Paul uses ἐργάτας here as a technical term for "apostles and teachers" (BDAG 390b; O'Brien 356; Reumann 462; Sumney 71).
   a. Ἐργάται functions as a missionary term elsewhere in Paul (esp. 2 Cor 11:13, where Paul's Judaizing opponents are described as ἐργάται δόλιοι, "deceitful workers"; cf. 1 Tim 5:17–18; 2 Tim 2:15).
   b. The use of ἐργάτης for Christian workers likely finds its origins in the teachings of Jesus (Matt 9:37–38; 20:1–16; cf. Paul's picture of the church: θεοῦ γάρ ἐσμεν συνεργοί, θεοῦ γεώργιον [1 Cor 3:9]).

Presumably, the Judaizers styled themselves ἐργάται. Paul calls them κακοὶ ἐργάται because, in his eyes, their efforts to circumcise Gentile converts seriously compromised Paul's gospel of justification by faith in Christ alone.

Κατατομήν is acc. sg. fem. from κατατομή, -ῆς, ἡ, lit. "cutting down, mutilating (the penis)" (Reumann 462; "mutilation, cutting in pieces" [BDAG 528d]; "those who mutilate the flesh" [NRSV, HCSB, ESV]; here, "those for whom circumcision results in [spiritual] destruction" [BDAG 528d]). In the LXX the cognate vb. κατατέμνω is used of the pagan rite of slitting the skin, a practice forbidden to Israel (Lev 21:5; cf. 19:28; Deut 14:1) and graphically illustrated in the context Baal worship (1 Kgs 18:28). Reumann's tr. "incision" (a) preserves the "ironic play on words" (H. Koester, *TDNT* 8.110–11) with περιτομή ("circumcision") in v. 3 and (b) reflects the likely LXX background (Reumann 463). Greek Christians at Philippi may have heard κατατομή

against their own cultural convictions, according to which "to circumcise was to mutilate the body" (Reumann 473 n. 12).

The identity of the opponents in v. 2 has elicited a variety of proposals (see Reumann
469–70). Other groups mentioned in the letter are not in view: (1) the rival preachers
of 1:14–18 exhibit poor motives but preach an orthodox gospel; (2) the opponents
mentioned in 1:27–30 are local Roman authorities, while those in view here are clearly
Jewish (Reumann 469). Nor would Paul use such harsh invectives to describe Jews
in general or Jewish Christians who continued to circumcise their sons according to
ancestral tradition. The κακοὶ ἐργάται are, rather, "an aggressive Jewish-Christian missionary group stressing circumcision (and therefore the Law)" for Gentile converts to
Christianity (as in Galatians), in order to be justified in God's sight and become part
of the eschatological people of God (S. Pedersen, *EDNT* 2.332c; Fee 294; H-M 172;
O'Brien 357; Reumann 468; Sumney 71). Paul may have heard that such persons were
targeting Philippi for their work. Or, perhaps, he simply thought it wise to include a
word of warning about this vexing issue that had become highly problematic during
his ministry elsewhere (Fee 294–95).

VERSE 3

ἡμεῖς γάρ ἐσμεν ἡ περιτομή

The sentence is a convertible proposition where both subj. nom. (ἡμεῖς) and pred.
nom. (ἡ περιτομή) are "definite, treated as identical, one and the same, and interchangeable" (R 768–69).

The pron. is emphatic (Reumann 463; "it is we who are" [NIV, NRSV]; "we . . . are
the ones who are" [NLT, cf. CEV]). Paul at times shifts from the second or third pers.
to an inclusive first pl. when he wishes to emphasize an important soteriological reality (Fee 298; cf. 1 Thess 1:9–10; Gal 4:5; Rom 8:15). Ἡμεῖς refers not just to Jewish
Christians but includes "all Christians, believing Jews and Gentiles alike" (O'Brien
359; Reumann 474).

Περιτομή formally refers to the rite of "circumcision," whereby, on the eighth day
after a male's birth, the foreskin was cut off as a sign of the covenant between God
and Israel. So highly was the sign valued that the term came to be used, via metonymy,
for the persons who were circumcised, either Jews (Rom 3:30) or Jewish Christians
(Gal 2:12). Only here are Gentiles included, where ἡ περιτομή designates "believers
in Jesus Christ (as truly circumcised people of the promise)" (BDAG 807d; O. Betz,
EDNT 3.79b). The groundwork for such a meaning was laid in the OT (appropriated at
Qumran [1QS 5:5]), where the cognate vb. was used in a transferred and ethical sense,
e.g., the "circumcision of the heart" (LXX Deut 10:16; Jer 4:4; Ezek 44:7). Περιτομή
(v. 3) is yet another "Israel term" that Paul adopts for the church (K. L. Schmidt,
TDNT 3.517; H-M 175; O'Brien 358; Reumann 474–745; cf. "Israel of God" [Gal
6:16], "seed of Abraham" [Gal 3:29]; "sons of Abraham" [Gal 3:7], "the saints" [Phil
1:1, etc.], "the elect" [Rom 8:33], "the called" [1 Cor 1:1], "remnant" [Rom 11:5],
"God's field" [1 Cor 3:9]). It is important to note, however, that the contrast Paul

draws (κατατομήν/περιτομή) is not between Israel and the church but, rather, between Judaizing Messianists (a subset of ethnic Israel) and the church. A wholesale replacement motif cannot, without qualification, be read into the passage (Hansen 220–21).

οἱ πνεύματι θεοῦ λατρεύοντες καὶ καυχώμενοι ἐν Χριστῷ Ἰησοῦ

א² D* P ψ 365 1175 and a few other mss. read the dat. θεῷ instead of the gen. θεοῦ, clearly a secondary attempt to find an expressed obj. for λατρεύοντες (λατρεύω takes the dat.), in order to avoid the possibility that a reader might think Paul meant to say, "We worship the Spirit of God" (Fee 288 n. 10; H-M 171; O'Brien 346; Reumann 464; {B} θεοῦ [UBS⁵]). The obj. of service is not at issue—Paul and the Judaizers served the same God of Israel, who had revealed himself in Messiah Jesus—but, rather, the manner. Translations that depart from the Gk. syntax by supplying an obj. for λατρεύοντες ("serve God by his Spirit" [NIV; cf. RSV]) somewhat obscure Paul's emphasis.

The art. οἱ, in appos. to ἡμεῖς in the previous clause is best rendered in Eng. as a rel. pron. (most EVV). The one art. closely links the three ptc. clauses, indicating that the groups are identical (R 785; Wallace 283; O'Brien 359).

The adj. ptcs. are descriptive, not causal (cf. "since we worship" [NJB]). They simply amplify the opening statement of v. 3 by describing spiritual orientation of ἡμεῖς ἡ περιτομή (O'Brien 360). Some see an "implicit Trinitarianism" here (πνεύματι–θεοῦ–Χριστῷ Ἰησοῦ) (Fee 302), but the terms are not grammatically equivalent as, for example, in 2 Cor 13:13. Trinitarian imagery should probably not be pressed (Reumann 475).

The Spirit is "the fundamental mark of belonging to Christ . . . the power of the new age already broken into the old" (J. D. G. Dunn, *NIDNTT* 3.700–701). The dat. πνεύματι θεοῦ is variously interpreted. Although a dir. obj. is possible (λατρεύω takes the dat. as dir. obj.), the Spirit in Paul is seldom the obj. of service or worship (Reumann 464). Reading πνεύματι as adv. dat. ("whose divine service is of a spiritual [and not of a material] sort" [Moule 46]; T 239; cf. "worship God in spirit" [RSV]) (a) fails adequately to account for the gen. modifier θεοῦ, (b) and overlooks the obvious, namely, that "the reference is surely to the eschatological significance of the Holy Spirit's outpouring" (Silva 149; Hansen 221 n. 46; Fee 300). More viable options for πνεύματι include:

1. dat. of sphere ("in the Spirit of God" [NASB, NRSV]; "in the sphere of, dominated by, the Spirit" [Reumann 476]); or,
*2. dat. of instr. ("by the Spirit of God" [NJB, NLT, HCSB, ESV]; Moule 46; R 540; E. Schweizer, *TDNT* 7.131–32; Fee 300 n. 62; Hansen 221 n. 46).

View 2 is more likely, given the sense "serve" for λατρεύοντες (see below). Λατρεύοντες is nom. pl. masc. of the pres. act. ptc. of λατρεύω. The vb. is widely used in the LXX as a cultic term, where it is applied to the people as a whole, versus λειτουργέω, which is restricted to priestly functions (H. Strathmann, *TDNT* 4.61; K. Hess, *NIDNTT* 3.550). In both OT and NT, λατρεύω signifies divine service (never human relations or secular service), either to the true God (e.g., Exod 23:25; Deut

6:13; 10:12, 20; Luke 2:37; 4:8) or to pagan deities (e.g., Exod 20:5; Rom 1:25) (H. Strathmann, *TDNT* 4.62; O'Brien 360). Here λατρεύοντες functions in a broadly metaphorical sense, "the whole of Christian existence" ("cultic concept is now spiritualized" [H. Strathmann, *TDNT* 4.64]; H. Balz, *EDNT* 2.345b; cf. λατρεία in Rom 12:1). "Serve" (HCSB, NIV; Reumann 476) is more accurate than "worship" (BDAG 587c; most EVV), which is too limiting ("quite misleading" [Fee 300]). Some narrow down the meaning of λατρεύοντες to "work(ing) as a missionary" (cf. BDAG 587c), but if Paul intended that meaning, he would have likely been more explicit (cf. Rom 1:9, where the qualifier ἐν τῷ εὐαγγελίῳ is added to λατρεύω) (Fee 299–300; Reumann 464). With λατρεύοντες (cf. Rom 9:4) Paul has co-opted another Israel term (cf. περιτομή [v. 3]) for the Christian church (O'Brien 361).

The vb. καυχάομαι (καυχώμενοι is nom. pl. masc. of the pres. mid. ptc.) means "to take pride in someth(ing)" (BDAG 536c; CEV; "glory" [RSV, NASB, ESV]; "boast" [NIV, NRSV, HCSB, cf. NJB; H-M 176]). Prominent are connotations of "trust" or "confidence" (Fee 301; "trust . . . is primary" [R. Bultmann, *TDNT* 3.649]; cf. "rely on" [NLT]; parallel to πεποιθότες). The negative sense of the vb. surfaces frequently in polemical contexts in the LXX (1 Kgs 21:11; Prov 25:14; 27:1), where boasting is not simply a casual fault but is a characteristic mark of the foolish and the ungodly, who depend upon themselves instead of God (Pss 51:1 [LXX 51:3]; 94:4 [93:3]). Positively, καυχάομαι denotes a God-confident boasting that humbles one before God (Jer 9:23–24). Such a person "looks away from himself, so that his glorying is a confession of God" (R. Bultmann, *TDNT* 3.467). The qualifier ἐν Χριστῷ Ἰησοῦ is, therefore, crucial.

Ἐν Χριστῷ Ἰησοῦ can read as "in the sphere of Christ Jesus" (M. Harris, *NIDNTT* 3.1192) or, more likely, acc. to LXX usage (reflected in Paul's citation of Jer 9:23 at 1 Cor 1:31 and 2 Cor 10:17), as the obj. of καυχώμενοι, "We boast in Christ Jesus" (O'Brien 362; "about what Christ Jesus has done" [Harris, *Prepositions*, 132]).

καὶ οὐκ ἐν σαρκὶ πεποιθότες

Paul reiterates the meaning of the previous clause (note chiasm) negatively (O'Brien 362). The presence of οὐ (instead of the expected μή) with a ptc. means that "the negative is clear-cut and decisive" (R 1,137–38; reflects older practice [BDF §430]; Reumann 465).

Πεποιθότες is the nom. pl. masc. of the perf. act. ptc. from πείθω (a favorite vb. of Paul's in Philippians [6x]; see above, on 1:6, 14, 25; 2:24). The perf. has pres. force: "put/have . . . confidence" (most EVV; "rely(ing)" [NJB, NLT]; "depend on, trust in" [BDAG 792a]; BDF §341; R 881).

Σάρξ is used differently here than in 1:22, 24, where it referred simply to physical existence. With ἐν σαρκὶ πεποιθότες, Paul purposefully advances the focus of the discourse from (a) the Judaizers' central expression of Torah observance, circumcision, to (b) the theological implications of Gentiles yielding to the rite. Σάρξ in v. 3 thus refers at once to both (a) the actual "flesh" cut away during circumcision (A. Sand, *EDNT* 3.231a) and (b) "life before and outside of Christ" (Fee 301–2; Silva 149).

Dynamic renderings invariably sacrifice the former to highlight the latter ("what we have done" [CEV]; "human effort" [NLT]; "place one's trust in earthly things or physical advantages" [BDAG 916a]). The tr. "flesh" (most EVV) preserves the polysemy. Some would limit the second of the above two nuances of σάρξ ("human effort") to the apostle's Jewish privileges (vv. 4–6). Paul's πνεῦμα-σάρξ contrast, however, transcends issues of Jewish national identity. Πνεῦμα and σάρξ stand juxtaposed as "eschatological realities that describe existence in the (present) overlap of the ages" (Fee 302). The sweeping nature of Paul's πνεῦμα-σάρξ contrast suggests that the apostle already has in mind, in v. 3, the futility of placing one's confidence in "anything outside Christ," a sentiment he will return to later in the passage (ἡγοῦμαι πάντα ζημίαν εἶναι [v. 8]) (E. Schweizer, TDNT 7.130–31; 6.428; O'Brien 364; Reumann 512). When the flesh (so understood) is the object of one's trust (πεποιθότες), then σάρξ becomes, according to Paul's understanding, "the subject on which, and through which, Sin acts . . . the base for operations by Sin, the bastion for human pride and improper boasting" (Reumann 465).

VERSE 4

καίπερ ἐγὼ ἔχων πεποίθησιν καὶ ἐν σαρκί

The conj. καίπερ occurs five times in the NT, always with a ptc., to clarify the participle's concessive sense ("[al]though" [EVV; BDAG 497c]; BDF §425[1]; R 1129; T 157; Wallace 635; O'Brien 367; etym. πέρ intensifies καί, "and, 'in spite of opposition'" [R 1154]).

Paul switches from the pl. to the nom. sg. masc. of the pres. act. ptc. of ἔχω, with an expressed subj., ἐγώ ("I myself" [most EVV; HCSB omits "myself"]; O'Brien 367). The sg. continues to v. 15, where the pl. appears again. Paul now becomes "intensely personal" (O'Brien 366). It is unnecessary to press the pres. for a markedly durative meaning (e.g., "continue to possess" [Reumann 478]). Although ἔχων is concessive (cf. on καίπερ, above), there is no sense of contingency, as might be implied by "although I myself might/could have confidence" (NASB/NJB). Paul claims that he does, indeed, have whatever it takes to boast in or rely upon himself ("I myself have reason" [ESV; cf. NRSV]; H-M 183; O'Brien 367).

Πεποίθησιν, -εως, ἡ (acc. sg. fem.) is cognate to the vb. πείθω, formed off the perf. stem. The general idea is that of "trust" or "confidence"; ἔχειν πεποίθησιν ἐν σαρκί means to "put one's trust in physical matters" (BDAG 796b–c). Πεποίθησις can denote "ground for confidence" or simply "confidence" (H-M 183; Reumann 466). The former meaning ("reason for/to put confidence" [most EVV]) is intended here. Paul enumerates several grounds for confidence in the vv. that follow.

The καί is a bit opaque. Had Paul intended the sense "I also" (i.e., like the Judaizers), one would expect καί to occur earlier in the vs. The sense "also in the flesh" (i.e., as well as in Christ) is possible (O'Brien 367; "also" [NRSV, HCSB]). A final option takes the conj. intensively with ἐν σαρκί ("even/indeed in the flesh" [NASB; cf. NIV]; Reumann 467).

Εἴ τις δοκεῖ ἄλλος πεποιθέναι ἐν σαρκί, ἐγὼ μᾶλλον

Εἴ introduces a first-class cond. (BDF §372), inviting dialogue (Reumann 482). BDAG defines δοκέω (here 3 sg. pres. act. indic.) as "to consider as probable" (BDAG 254d; "think(s)" [RSV, NIV, ESV, HCSB]; "has a mind" [NASB]; "does claim" [NJB]). O'Brien finds the transitive use of δοκέω ironical, given its common intransitive meaning "seem" (O'Brien 368).

The perf. act. inf. πεποιθέναι introduces an inf. obj. sharing the same subj. as δοκεῖ. The repetition of πεποιθ- + ἐν σαρκί underscores the central problem Paul here addresses, namely, "arrogant boasting in one's own achievement as a basis for a saving relationship with God" (O'Brien 368).

The adv. μᾶλλον is used in its basic sense, "to a greater or higher degree" ("I can do so even more" [BDAG 613d]; "I have (even) more" [NRSV, NIV; HCSB]; "I far more" [NASB]; "my claim is better" [NJB]). Ἐγὼ μᾶλλον is elliptical, δοκῶ πεποιθέναι ἐν σαρκί is understood (O'Brien 368).

VERSES 5–6

περιτομῇ ὀκταήμερος, ἐκ γένους Ἰσραήλ, φυλῆς Βενιαμίν, Ἑβραῖος ἐξ Ἑβραίων

Paul structures his list of Jewish privileges in the form of a Roman *cursus honorum* ("honors race") (see above on 2:5–11). Honor inscriptions in the ancient world were necessarily economical in style. The medium of hammer, chisel, and stone required short words and abbreviations. In similar fashion Paul abruptly departs in vv. 5–6 from sentential syntax to craft a short, staccato-like catalog of his Jewish honors. Although the content of Paul's *cursus honorum* is Jewish, the framework is unmistakably Roman. Just like Philippi's honor inscriptions, for example, Paul lists ascribed honors (inherited at birth) first, followed by achieved honors (adult accomplishments). Agonistic honor encounters between males were the norm for ancient (especially Roman) social life. Paul plays the honor game (cf. Εἴ τις δοκεῖ ἄλλος πεποιθέναι ἐν σαρκί, ἐγὼ μᾶλλον), only finally to dismiss all such posturing as "rubbish" (vv. 7–11). In view of the surpassing value of knowing Christ, Paul regards as ζημία and σκύβαλα not only (a) the contents of his Jewish *cursus honorum*, but also (b) the Roman cultural values and social codes that encouraged males in Philippi to compete with one another for honor in the public arena (Hellerman 121–27).

Ὀκταήμερος is nom. sg. masc. from the adj., ὀκταήμερος, -ον (ὀκτα ["eight"] + ἡμέρα ["day"]), here used subst. ("an eight-day-er" [R 657, 549–50; H-M 184]); περιτομῇ is dat. of ref./respect; lit. "a person-of-eight-days relative to circumcision" (BDAG 702b; BDF §197; R 523; T 220; H-M 184). The cstr. makes for awkward Eng., thus the loose equivalent, "circumcised on the eighth day" (most EVV). For background see Gen 17:12; Lev 12:3; Luke 1:59; 2:21. A male child not circumcised on the eighth day "has broken my covenant" (*Jubilees* 15:11–14). The circumcision of adult Gentile converts championed by the Judaizers is, by implication, "a second-rate circumcision" (Hansen 223).

"Nation" (NASB, HCSB; BDAG 194d) and "people" (RSV, NIV, ESV) are not wholly accurate renderings of γένους (gen. sg. neut., from γένος, -ους, τό). Paul's point here is to claim Israelite blood kinship ("genealogical purity" [Hansen 223]), not simply membership in a "people" (cf. λαός), which could include nonethnic Jews (proselytes), as well (O'Brien 370). Although technically more accurate, the way "race" (NJB) is used in contemporary discourse renders it somewhat problematic as a tr. for γένος.

Ἰσραήλ, a gen. of appos., is indeclinable. "Israel" and "Israelite" were terms of special significance for Paul's compatriots, while the name "Jew" was uttered by Gentiles in a rather derogatory manner (O'Brien 370). Paul's point is straightforward: "I am an Israelite by birth" (H-M 184).

Φυλῆς is gen. sg. fem., from φυλή, -ῆς, ἡ, "a subgroup of a nation characterized by a distinctive blood line" (BDAG 1069a; "tribe" [EVV]). Βενιαμίν (indeclinable) is the name of Paul's Israelite tribe (BDAG 174b). Paul's parents may have named him "Saul" after Israel's first king, the most famous Benjamite (O'Brien 371). Commentators have expended unnecessary effort to explain the reference, extolling the superiority of Benjamin over other Israelite tribes (Hansen 224; H-M 184–85; more balanced is N. Hillyer, who recalls Benjamites involved in "atrocity" [Judg 19:16–30], "rape" [Judg 21], and "insult to David" [2 Sam 16:5–13] [*NIDNTT* 3.873–74]; nor was Saul a paragon of kingly virtue). It is unlikely, however, that Paul's audience possessed the OT background necessary to understand Βενιαμίν in the subtle ways suggested by scholars who highlight the tribe's alleged preeminence. The term is to be accounted for, instead, by Philippi's social values. Romans, like Israelites, were divided into citizen tribes. More than half of the Latin inscriptions from Philippi contain the abbreviation *VOL*, which boasts of membership in the Roman tribe *Voltinia*. At issue in every instance is not tribal superiority but, rather, a desire to proclaim one's citizen status. Residents of Philippi who could do so publicly proclaimed their tribal membership because it marked them out as Roman citizens. The phrase φυλῆς Βενιαμίν is no more intended to highlight Benjamin's superiority among the tribes of Israel than *VOL* in the Philippian inscriptions is meant to imply the superiority of *Voltinia* vis-à-vis Rome's remaining citizen tribes. Paul uses φυλῆς Βενιαμίν simply to underscore his identity as a true Israelite. By drawing attention to his membership in the tribe of Benjamin and then dismissing it as "rubbish" in the ensuing context (v. 8), Paul pointedly challenges those who would privilege their Roman citizen status vis-à-vis their fellow believers in the church in Philippi (Hellerman 126).

The nouns in Ἑβραῖος ἐξ Ἑβραίων are from Ἑβραῖος, -ου, ὁ (4x in NT), which can either (1) identify an ethnic Israelite, "Hebrew" (BDAG 270a; EVV), or (2) distinguish a Hebrew or Aramaic-speaking Israelite from one who speaks Greek (BDAG 270a). The latter is probably intended, since (a) the expression likely means something more than ἐκ γένους Ἰσραήλ; (b) Paul differentiates between "Israelite" and "Hebrew" in 2 Cor 11:22; and (c) Ἑβραῖος is used to distinguish Aramaic-speaking Jews in Acts 6:1. Ἑβραῖος is rare in the LXX (Gen 40:15; 43:32; Exod 1:15) but became more frequent in later Jewish literature, where it was preferred to Ἰουδαῖος, which Gentiles used in a derogatory sense (J. Wanke, *EDNT* 1.369c; Reumann 483). Because Heb. lacks comp. and superl. forms. (cf. Ἅγια Ἁγίων, "the holiest of all holy places" [Heb 9:3]), Ἑβραῖος ἐξ Ἑβραίων may signify "the most Hebrew person of all" (Wallace 298). The prep. ἐξ, however, points to descent (W. Gutbrod, *TDNT* 3.390; "origin or source" [R 598]; "a Hebrew, the son of Hebrews," not "a thorough Hebrew" [Harris, *Prepositions*, 104]). Thus, Ἑβραῖος ἐξ Ἑβραίων may imply that Paul's parents, who had brought him up to speak Hebrew and Aramaic, avoided assimilation to the Gentile environment at Tarsus. From Acts 22:3 we may surmise that Paul's parents arranged for him to spend his boyhood years in Jerusalem prior to entering the school of Gamaliel during his teens (O'Brien 372; Paul apparently had a sister and nephew in Jerusalem [Acts 23:16]). Despite his diaspora background, therefore, Paul's Pharisaic origins (Acts 23:6) and education in Jerusalem made him a Hebrew (cf. Acts 22:2–3), not a Hellenist (Hansen 225; H-M 185).

κατὰ νόμον Φαρισαῖος, κατὰ ζῆλος διώκων τὴν ἐκκλησίαν, κατὰ δικαιοσύνην τὴν ἐν νόμῳ γενόμενος ἄμεμπτος

A change of cstr. marks a shift from inherited honors to personal achievements. The prep. κατά + acc. here (3x) means "with respect to, in relation to" (BDAG 513b–c; O'Brien 372). EVV vary ("as to" [NRSV, ESV]; "as for" [NJB]; "regarding" [HCSB]; "in regard to . . . as for . . . as for" [NIV]).

Νόμον refers to the Law of Sinai. Attempts to distinguish "law" from "the Law" in Paul, based on the presence or absence of the art., produce "no firm rule" (BDF §258[2]; Moule 113; T 177; O'Brien 373 n. 38; Reumann 484). Jewish sects took different positions "with respect to the Law." Paul's approach had been conditioned by his Pharisaic convictions.

Φαρισαῖος is a HGk. form of an Aram. word meaning "separated one" (i.e., from sin and impurity [O'Brien 373]; 98x in NT, only here outside of Gospels and Acts). The rabbis commented on Lev 19:2 ("You shall therefore be holy, for I the Lord your God am holy") as follows: "As I am holy, so you also must be holy; as I am separate (Heb. *pārûš*), so you must also be separate (Heb. *perûšîm*)" (*Lev. Rab.* 24:4). Separation from ethical and ritual impurity inevitably generated a corresponding set of social boundaries (cf. Mark 2:15–16). The Pharisees became "the fundamental and most influential religious movement within Palestinian Judaism between 150 B.C. and 70 A.D." (Deines, "The Pharisees Between 'Judaisms' and 'Common Judaism,'" 503). Their 6,000 or so members engaged in various occupations, usually in Palestine. Not content merely to obey the law of Moses, the Pharisees bound themselves also to observe every one of the myriad of commandments contained in the oral law, the interpretive traditions of the scribes. For Paul, a disciple of the great Pharisee Gamaliel, Φαρισαῖος was not a term of reproach but a title of honor. In Acts 23:6 he continues to claim Pharisee status even as a Christian missionary: ἐγὼ Φαρισαῖός εἰμι. Paul would have added, "Not a converted Pharisee, but a completed one" (H-M 186). Paul's Judaizing opponents may have been Pharisees, as well (Fee 308; cf. Matt 23:15; Acts 15:5).

The noun ζῆλος (here acc. sg. neut. from ζῆλος, -ους, τό) can be used positively ("zeal, ardor" [BDAG 427a]) or negatively ("jealousy, envy" over another's achievements [BDAG 427b]). The former meaning is clearly intended. The ζῆλος tradition (echoing Yahweh's zeal for his people [Exod 20:5; Deut 4:24; Isa 9:7]) goes back to Phinehas (Num 25:1–18), who killed an Israelite man and a Midianite woman who were having sex. Phinehas stopped a plague, and ἐλογίσθη αὐτῷ εἰς δικαιοσύνην (LXX Ps 105:31; cf. ἡ δικαιοσύνη ἡ ἐν νόμῳ that follows in Phil 3:6 [O'Brien 375]). Phinehas was later extolled as "third in glory" after Moses and Aaron for zeal (Sirach 45:23–24). Phinehas was particularly esteemed by Maccabean freedom fighters because he had purified the camp of Israel by slaying a non-Israelite and a fellow countryman who was compromising the integrity of God's people. Thus the Hasmonean patriarch Mattathias "burned with zeal for the law, just as Phinehas did," when he killed a fellow Jew who was sacrificing on a pagan altar, along with the Syrian official who was enforcing the apostasy (1 Macc 2:26; cf. vv. 23–25). The popular and widespread stories of Phineas and Mattathias legitimated for many the use of violence in the exercise of "zeal for the law," against Jews or Gentiles who were perceived as compromising or subverting the Torah (Hansen 226 n. 67; Wright 86–89). "Hence, not because Paul was evil, but precisely because he was 'good,' an ardent Pharisee, zealous for God, inflamed with zeal for the law and committed to keeping the community of God pure, he did what he later came to lament, namely, persecute the church" (H-M 186).

Διώκων (nom. sg. masc. of the pres. act. ptc. from διώκω, "persecute" [BDAG 254a]) is generally taken as an anar. subst. ptc., "a persecutor," in par. with Φαρισαῖος (NRSV, NASB, ESV; T 151; Z §371; Reumann 487; but "persecuting" [NIV, HCSB]). The basic idea of the vb. is "to cause something to run," "to pursue or chase." It pictures an army setting to flight and pursuing its enemy, or a hunter tracking down his quarry and putting it on the run (H-M 186; O'Brien 376). The CEV ("made trouble for the church") is too mild (Reumann 486). Paul engaged in a pogrom against Jewish Messianist communities in Jerusalem and Damascus (Gal 1:13–14, 23), and viewed this activity, in retrospect, as "the sin of all sins" (O'Brien 376; cf. 1 Cor 15:9; 1 Tim 1:13–15). The inclusion of διώκων τὴν ἐκκλησίαν underscores how utterly blind and at cross-purposes with God ἡ πεποίθησις ἐν σαρκί can be.

The term ἐκκλησία (here acc. sg. fem., dir. obj. of διώκων) is used 100 times in the LXX, almost exclusively for the people of God, the congregation of Israel (but cf. LXX Ps 25:5). Some see Paul co-opting yet another Israel term for the church, which, in turn, generates a bitter irony: while Paul was an ardent young Pharisee, a new Phineas attempting to preserve the purity of the ἐκκλησία, he was, instead, persecuting the ἐκκλησία (H-M 187).

Δικαιοσύνην (acc. sg. fem., from δικαιοσύνη, -ης, ἡ, "righteousness" [most EVV]; "everything the Law demands" [CEV]) refers here not to τὴν ἐκ θεοῦ δικαιοσύνην, which is imputed to the believer ἐπὶ τῇ πίστει (v. 9) but, rather, to "upright behavior" (BDAG 248a–d). The prep. phrase ἐν νόμῳ is locat., "in the law," "rooted in the law," "which rests in the law" (O'Brien 379).

Γενόμενος is nom. sg. masc. of the aor. mid. ptc. of γίνομαι. For ἄμεμπτος, "blame-less, faultless" (BDAG 52d), see on 2:15. The ptc. clause is not to be taken ironically, nor in the sense "I thought or felt myself blameless" (i.e., a pre-Christian, versus a post-Christian, perspective). It is a straightforward assertion of an objective reality, just like the other qualifications on the list (O'Brien 380; Hansen 229). The claim represented in κατὰ δικαιοσύνην τὴν ἐν νόμῳ γενόμενος ἄμεμπτος must be read in the context of early Judaism and Paul's purposes at this point in Philippians, not against the backdrop of theological convictions about human inability to keep the law. The Pharisaic claim was not to be sinless but, rather, scrupulously to keep the written and oral Torah. When a person "missed the mark," or the whole nation did, Judaism had a divinely given system of temple sacrifices to expiate sin, along with the related prac-tices of prayer and repentance (Reumann 487). Paul's intention here, at any rate, is not to argue that he had satisfied God's demands, but, rather, to demonstrate that he has more reason for "confidence in the flesh" than his contemporaries. The focus in v. 6 is horizontal ("manward"), not vertical ("Godward"): ἄμεμπτος "implies no more than what passed for 'blameless' among the Jews" (C. Brown, *NIDNTT* 2.282; cf. Luke 1:6). No one who had known the pre-Christian Paul could contradict the statement that he was "blameless" with respect to outward adherence to the Law's moral and ritual commandments.

VERSE 7

[Ἀλλὰ] ἅτινα ἦν μοι κέρδη

Most find ἀλλά (attested in B D Ψ *Byz*) to be the easier reading ("the context cries out for such a contrastive particle" [Fee 311 n. 1]) and, therefore, secondary to the text of 𝔓⁴⁶ ℵ* A G 0282 33 81, which omit the conj. (Hansen 230 n. 82; H-M 181; "an addition . . . though a 'correct' one" [Reumann 488]).

The pron. ἅτινα (nom. pl. neut. [takes sg. vb. ἦν] from ὅστις) functions as a pendent nom. that is picked up later in v. 7 by the acc. pron. ταῦτα. The indef. rel. pron. gen-erally identifies things belonging to a certain class (BDAG 729d), so that ἅτινα may imply a wider scope to Paul's gains than those listed in vv. 4–6, i.e., not just those things but "whatever things" (NASB; "whatever" [NIV, ESV]; "everything" [HCSB]; Fee 315 n. 9; Hansen 232). It is questionable, however, whether a distinction between the def. ὅς and the indef. ὅστις can be pressed in every instance in the NT, so the pron. should probably be strictly understood to refer back to Paul's Jewish honors in vv. 5–6 (R 698; O'Brien 384 n. 4; Reumann 488). Paul will expand the scope of his potential gains to include πάντα in v. 8.

Κέρδη is nom. pl. neut. from κέρδος, -ους, τό, "a gain" (most EVV) or "profit" (BDAG 541b). Κέρδος and ζημία are accounting terms, picturing a balance sheet with columns for "assets" and "liabilities"; the imagery was also used by the rabbis and Jesus (Matt 16:26) (H-M 188; O'Brien 383); μοι is dat. of advantage (BDF §188; O'Brien 384 n. 8; Reumann 488).

ταῦτα ἥγημαι διὰ τὸν Χριστὸν ζημίαν

Ten times, by name (vv. 7, 8 [2x], 9) or pronoun (vv. 8, 9, 10 [4x]), Christ is referenced in vv. 7–10. Paul's life is completely consumed with Christ (Hansen 231).
Ταῦτα is resumptive of ἅτινα (R 698). The vb. ἥγημαι is 1 sg. perf. mid. indic. from
ἡγέομαι, "think, consider, regard" (BDAG 434b). Ἡγέομαι is often found with a double acc. of obj. (ταῦτα) and complement (ζημίαν) (R 480; T 246; Wallace 186). The vb.
denotes "an intellectual process" (BDAG 434b). Paul's conversion was "not an escape
from reason but an illumination of reason" (Hansen 233). The perf. should be given its
full force: "I have come to regard" (NRSV; "have considered, counted" [BDF §341]),
in order to underscore "the present significance of Paul's change of attitude" (tr. not
as pres., "I now consider" [NIV]; nor simple past, "I counted" [RSV, ESV]) (O'Brien
384; H-M 188; Reumann 488).

Commentators differ over whether διὰ τὸν Χριστόν (and διὰ τὸ ὑπερέχον and δι' ὅν
[v. 8]) means:

*1. "because of the fact or work of Christ," i.e., retrospective, looking back to
Paul's recognition on the Damascus road that Jesus was Lord and Messiah,
and his experiences since, as Christ's apostle (H-M 189; "because of Christ"
[NRSV, HCSB]; R 583–84; Fee 315 n. 8; Reumann 489, 517); or

2. "for the sake of Christ" (RSV, NASB, NIV), i.e., prospective, with a view
ahead to the goal of "gaining Christ" (v. 9) (O'Brien 385).

The first alternative better accords with the common meaning of διά + the acc. and
makes the best sense of the cstr. in 3:7–8 (Fee 315 n. 8; 316 n. 18; 319 n. 22).

Ζημίαν is acc. sg. fem., from ζημία, -ας, ἡ. The word means "damage, disadvantage, loss, forfeit" (BDAG 428a; "loss" [EVV]). Paul views his previous gains "not
simply as indifferent or unimportant, but as positively harmful," as liabilities that were
working to destroy him (O'Brien 385). The natural tendency would be for κέρδη (pl.)
and ζημίαν (sg.) to agree in number. Paul effectively bundles up his many gains and
treats them all as "one great loss" (O'Brien 384 n. 5, 385; H-M 188–89). Paul likely
draws upon the Jesus tradition: τί γὰρ ὠφελεῖ ἄνθρωπον κερδῆσαι τὸν κόσμον ὅλον καὶ
ζημιωθῆναι τὴν ψυχὴν αὐτοῦ (Mark 8:36). In addition to the appropriation of the gain-
loss vocabulary (cf. κερδῆσαι and ζημιωθῆναι), Paul's πάντα and τὰ πάντα (v. 8) may
reflect the Jesus tradition's τὸν κόσμον ὅλον (O'Brien 390–91; cf. also the parables in
Matt 13:44–46).

VERSE 8

ἀλλὰ μενοῦνγε καὶ ἡγοῦμαι πάντα ζημίαν εἶναι

Paul now heightens the sense of v. 7 in three ways: (1) An "extraordinary accumulation of particles" that is powerfully emphatic (Reumann 489; H-M 189); (2) a
change to the pres. tense, "I do consider" (or "continue to consider" [O'Brien 386]);
and (3) the use of the universal πάντα ("all things"), instead of the particular ἅτινα/
ταῦτα ("which things"/"these things"; ἅτινα/ταῦτα referred narrowly to Paul's Jewish

privileges [vv. 4–6], while πάντα includes everything and anything in which Paul is tempted to trust in apart from Christ) (H-M 190; O'Brien 387).

Commentators group ἀλλὰ μενοῦνγε καί together in various ways. For example, ἀλλά + καί introduces "an additional point in an emphatic way" ("not only this, but also" [BDF §448(6)]; BDAG 45b–c; R 1,145, 1,185–86; cf. 1:18), while μενοῦνγε accentuates, in turn, the progressive sense of ἀλλά + καί (BDAG 630d; BDF §450[4]; Moule 163–64; T 338; O'Brien 386). Grammarians specializing in discourse find significance in each conj. and particle (Runge 99):

- Ἀλλά marks the shift from counting just Paul's potential list as loss (v. 7) to counting all things as loss.
- οὖν (μεν<u>οῦν</u>γε) instructs the reader to view v. 8 as an inferential development building directly on v. 7.
- μεν (<u>μεν</u>οῦνγε) has "its normal forward-pointing constraint, signaling a counterpoint correlation with some related element that follows" (here v. 8d: καὶ ἡγοῦμαι σκύβαλα).
- The combination of an ascensive καί with γε (μενοῦν<u>γε</u>) strengthens the connection with v. 7 by creating yet another thematic link.

A lit. tr. of ἀλλὰ μενοῦνγε καί ἡγοῦμαι is hopelessly unwieldy ("Furthermore, I do indeed therefore continue to consider" [Reumann 489]). EVV vary ("more than that" [NASB, NRSV, HCSB; BDAG 630d]; "what is more" [NIV]; "yes, I will go further" [NJB]; "indeed" [RSV, ESV] is a bit understated).

Ἡγοῦμαι is 1 sg. pres. mid. indic. from ἡγέομαι. Although Robertson lists ἡγέομαι as a dep., he sees here "intensive force" and "the personal interest of the subject" (R 812; sim. Porter 71). The change from perf. to pres. is intentional. The settled evaluation Paul came to in the past must be reinforced in the present by continuous conscious moral choices (H-M 190; Silva 157). In πάντα ζημίαν we have another double acc. of obj.-complement, this time with an expressed εἶναι.

διὰ τὸ ὑπερέχον τῆς γνώσεως Χριστοῦ Ἰησοῦ τοῦ κυρίου μου

This prep. phrase expands upon διὰ τὸν Χριστόν (v. 7) (O'Brien 387). Tr. διά "because of" (NRSV, ESV, NIV), or "in view of" (NASB, HCSB), not "compared with" (NLT). Comparison is not strictly at issue here (H-M 190).

Ὑπερέχον is acc. sg. neut. of the pres. act. ptc. of ὑπερέχω, used subst., "the surpassing greatness" (BDAG 1033 b–c; O'Brien 387; "surpassing worth/value" [NRSV, HCSB, NIV]; "supreme advantage" [NJB]; "infinite value" [NLT]; lit. "surpassingness" [Reumann 489]). The subst. ptc. is "more concrete and graphic" than the cognate ὑπεροχή (BDF §263[2]; T 14). The tr. "worth" or "value" preserves the commercial metaphor (Fee 317 n. 19).

The case of τῆς γνώσεως (gen. sg. fem. from γνῶσις) has elicited a number of interpretations. Likely options include:

*1. a gen. of appos., equating τὸ ὑπερέχον and τῆς γνώσεως ("what is so much more valuable, the knowledge" [GNB]; Hansen 235 n. 101; H-M 190; O'Brien 387; Sumney 78); or

2. an attributed gen., in which the head noun functions like an attributive adj., e.g., καρπὸς ἔργου ("fruitful labor" [Phil 1:22]); τὸ ὑπερέχον τῆς γνώσεως = "the surpassingly great knowledge" ("the unsurpassable knowledge" [H. Balz, *EDNT* 3.398d]; cf. Wallace 90).

The other gens. are straightforward. Χριστοῦ Ἰησοῦ is obj. (cf. τοῦ γνῶναι αὐτόν [v. 10]) (H-M 190; O'Brien 387; Reumann 491); τοῦ κυρίου is in simple appos. to Χριστοῦ Ἰησοῦ. It is not the doctrinal confession of "Christ Jesus as Lord" (τοῦ κυρίου ≠ pred.) that Paul has in mind but, rather, personal knowledge of, and intimate acquaintance with, "Christ Jesus, the one who is my Lord" (H-M 191).

The sg. pron. is highly significant. Elsewhere (53x) Paul uses ἡμῶν (pl.) with κύριος ("our Lord"). Only here does he pair κύριος with the μου (sg.) ("intensely personal" [O'Brien 387]; W. Foerster, *TDNT* 3.1,092; cf. Gal 2:20; 2 Tim 1:12).

Γνῶσις (here "personal acquaintance w. Christ Jesus" [BDAG 203d]; "knowing" [EVV]) is a slippery term with a multiplicity of potential backgrounds, a "buzzword" in the religious and philosophical discourse of Paul's day (Reumann 518; O'Brien 387–88). Two points are relatively certain. First, Paul has in view in v. 8 the act of knowing (γνώσεως as a *nomen actionis* [Reumann 490]; cf. τοῦ γνῶναι [v. 10]), not a body of knowledge (Fee 317 n. 20). Second, whatever additional nuances γνῶσις might have acquired from Hellenism and current Jewish conceptions of knowledge, we can assume that OT ideas about knowledge formed the basis of Paul's conception (E. D. Schmitz, *NIDNTT* 2.398–401; Fee 318 n. 21; Hansen 235; cf. n. 104). Knowledge in the OT begins with God's knowledge in the election of his people (Exod 33:12, 17; Amos 3:2). When knowledge is used to describe Israel's relationship to God, ideas of obedience and covenant loyalty on the part of the nation as a whole are at the forefront (Hos 4:1; 6:6; cf. Jer 2:8; 4:22; 22:16; H-M 191). Personal, affective intimacy receives little emphasis. Paul, too, generally views the relationship between God and humans—and, by extension, the knowledge of God—primarily in collectivist (κύριος + ἡμῶν [53x in his letters]) rather than individualistic (κύριος + μου [only 1x]) terms. In the OT, however, Jeremiah's new covenant promised an increased level of personal intimacy in the experiential knowledge of God, thus anticipating the kind of relationship reflected in τῆς γνώσεως Χριστοῦ Ἰησοῦ τοῦ κυρίου μου, here in Phil 3:8 (Jer 31:33–34; O'Brien 388).

δι' ὃν τὰ πάντα ἐζημιώθην

Ὅν is an acc. sg. masc. of the rel. pron. (ὅς, ἥ, ὅ); its antecedent is Χριστοῦ Ἰησοῦ τοῦ κυρίου μου.

The vb. ἐζημιώθην is 1 sg. aor. pass. indic. from ζημιόω (cognate of ζημία), "to experience the loss of someth[ing], with implication of undergoing hardship or suffering" (BDAG 428a; the pass. takes the acc. of thing lost [τὰ πάντα] [R 485]; "acc. of respect" [Porter 66]). Since ζημιόω occurs only in the pass. in the NT, some read it as a dep., so that Paul was not stripped of his Jewish advantages but, rather, voluntarily renounced them ("I have discarded" [NLT]; "I forfeited" [BDAG 428a]). The focus on personal conviction and volition in the context (ἤγημαι . . . ἡγοῦμαι [vv. 7–8]) would seem to support this interpretation (H-M 192; BDF §159[2]). More likely, however, the pass. points to loss at the hands of an external agent ("I have suffered the loss" [NRSV, NASB, HCSB]; "accepted the loss" [NJB]). Ζημιόω is used in the pass. in the papyri, for example, of persons who have been "fined," i.e., deprived of money, by creditors and others (MM 273; cf. the accounting imagery reflected in ζημίαν and κέρδη [v. 7]).

Paul not only considered all things loss but actually experienced the loss of τὰ πάντα (pace A. Stumpff, TDNT 2.890). By placing the art. before πάντα, and τὰ πάντα before the vb., Paul emphasizes that he lost everything (H-M 192). The losses may have included disinheritance by family, with the corresponding loss of property, and alienation from friends (haverim, "companions, associates," as the Mishnah refers to those who are scrupulous in keeping the law), as well as the loss of status in Judaism, which he had formerly prized (O'Brien 389–90). Some see in the aor. specific reference to the Damascus road experience (K. Rengstorf, TDNT 1.437; Hansen 235–36; O'Brien 389). Perhaps so, but "the bill kept coming in for years thereafter" (Reumann 519).

καὶ ἡγοῦμαι σκύβαλα, ἵνα Χριστὸν κερδήσω

Supply τὰ πάντα with σκύβαλα, as a double acc. cstr. (Reumann 491). Σκύβαλα (acc. pl. neut., from σκύβαλον, -ου, τό) is a NT hapax. The word was used for "excrement, manure, garbage, kitchen scraps," in each case, "useless or undesirable material that is subject to disposal" (BDAG 932d; "a coarse, ugly, violent word" [J. I. Packer, NIDNTT 1.480]). Two notions, worthlessness and filth, are present in σκύβαλον (O'Brien 390). Tr. ἡγοῦμαι σκύβαλα "I consider everything garbage/crud" (BDAG 932d; "refuse" [RSV]; "rubbish" [NASB, NRSV, ESV]; "garbage" [CEV, NLT, NIV]; "filth" [NJB, HCSB]; "crap" [Reumann 491–92; Silva 157]). "The choice of the vulgar term stresses the force and totality of this renunciation" (F. Lang, TDNT 7.446; "the climax of a crescendo" [H-M 192]). Paul may be taking a parting shot at the Judaizers, scavengers whose Jewish advantages Paul here relegates to "'foul-smelling street garbage' fit only for 'dogs'" (v. 2)" (Fee 319).

Κερδήσω is 1 sg. aor. act. subjunc. from κερδαίνω, "to acquire by effort or investment," "gain Christ, make him one's own" (BDAG 541a; "gain" [most EVV] "win" [H. Schlier, TDNT 3.673]). The tr. "that Christ may be my wealth" (NAB) preserves the accounting imagery (H-M 193; Reumann 492). When will Paul "gain Christ"? The ἵνα-clause governing both κερδήσω and εὑρεθῶ (purpose [Reumann 492]; most see a hendiadys; "gain Christ" = "being found in him" [BDF §442(9)]; Fee 320; O'Brien 392; Reumann 519–20]) suggests future judgment; Paul appears before God's tribunal "in him," "having the righteousness that comes from God" (v. 9) (H-M 193; O'Brien 384, 393). What follows (v. 10), however, qualifies the twofold ἵνα-clause in a way that problematizes an exclusively eschatological time frame for κερδήσω/εὑρεθῶ since to know Christ (τοῦ γνῶναι αὐτόν) means to know the power of his resurrection and fellowship of his sufferings "in the everyday events of [Paul's] own life" (O'Brien 402; C. Brown, *NIDNTT* 3.278). Paul does not normally use "in Christ" (cf. εὑρεθῶ ἐν αὐτῷ), moreover, of the parousia and thereafter. Hence εὑρεθῶ ἐν αὐτῷ can mean "found united to" or "incorporate in" Christ now (Reumann 519). Most commentators resolve the dilemma by recourse to Paul's familiar "already but not yet" eschatology (Fee 320–21; H-M 193 O'Brien 391; Reumann 519). Δικαιοσύνη (v. 9 [2x]), for example, is a term of continuity, involving "God's judgment at the End and a verdict moved up through faith to the present" (Reumann 521; cf. Rom 2:13; and 3:21; 5:1, 9). Wherever one finally lands on the time element in the vbs. (F. W. Beare suggests Paul had no particular moment in view [O'Brien 392 n. 61]), the application of broader theological categories nicely allows us to read (a) κερδήσω/εὑρεθῶ in terms of justification, (b) τοῦ γνῶναι αὐτόν, sanctification, and (c) εἴ πως καταντήσω εἰς τὴν ἐξανάστασιν τὴν ἐκ νεκρῶν (v. 11), glorification (Hansen 213; Silva 159). It is not enough for Paul to be right with God forensically (v. 9). He longs to know Christ intimately, as well (v. 10).

VERSE 9

καὶ εὑρεθῶ ἐν αὐτῷ

Paul elaborates on what he means by "gain Christ" with καὶ εὑρεθῶ ἐν αὐτῷ ("namely, to be found in him" [Reumann 519–20]; Hansen 237; epexegetic καί [Silva 150]). Εὑρεθῶ is 1 sg. aor. pass. subjunc. from εὑρίσκω, "find, come upon," here "that I might be found in Christ" (BDAG 411c; most EVV; "belong to him" [CEV]; "become one with him" [NLT]). As in Eng., the idea of "finding" has virtually disappeared from the vb., which means something like "prove to be, be shown to be," "turn out to be," or simply "to be in him" (cf. on 2:7) (O'Brien 393). The pass. voice here refers to divine, not human, assessment of Paul (Hansen 237). A forensic element is likely present since εὑρίσκω often "relates the conclusion of an investigation into the facts of a charge," as in the trials of Jesus and Paul's defense before Claudius Lysias (Luke 23:4, 14, 22; John 19:4, 6; Acts 23:29) (S. Pedersen, *EDNT* 2.84b).

Ἐν αὐτῷ denotes incorporation in Christ ("incorporate in him" [NEB]), and thus to stand before the Judge not presenting his own claims to God's favor but—because Paul is ἐν αὐτῷ—presenting Christ and his all-prevailing merits (H-M 194).

μὴ ἔχων ἐμὴν δικαιοσύνην τὴν ἐκ νόμου

Though the pres. act. ptc. ἔχων could be causal, it is best taken in a modal sense (O'Brien 393; BDF §418[5]), contemporaneous with the time of εὑρεθῶ ἐν αὐτῷ (Wallace 497–98; 614–15; BDF §339[2–3]). "Christianity is a religion of having as distinct from other religions of seeking and expecting" (H. Hanse, *TDNT* 2.826).

The poss. adj. ἐμήν is acc. sg. fem., from ἐμός, -ή, -όν; "of my own" (most EVV). We would expect an art. with ἐμήν, since "we hardly ever find a prepositional phrase used as attribute to an anarthrous noun" [T 221; BDF §272]). The anar. ἐμὴν δικαιοσύνην serves, in turn, "to focus attention strongly on the quality of this righteousness, that is, it is Paul's own" (O'Brien 394; T 191; Z §180). See below on δικαιοσύνην. The art. in τὴν ἐκ νόμου functions as a rel. pron. (as also in the contrastive clause that follows [Wallace 215]); νόμου with ἐκ is a gen. of source or origin (Reumann 494; "derivation" [BDAG 296d]).

ἀλλὰ τὴν διὰ πίστεως Χριστοῦ, τὴν ἐκ θεοῦ δικαιοσύνην ἐπὶ τῇ πίστει

Πίστις is not simply "intellectual assent to a series of propositions . . . but the act of personal trust . . . self-surrender" (H-M 195; Reumann 494). The phrase διὰ πίστεως Χριστοῦ finds itself at the center of a vigorous debate among NT scholars. Is Χριστοῦ to be taken (traditionally) (*view 1) as an obj. gen., "faith in Christ" (EVV; R. Bultmann, *TDNT* 6.210 n. 267; Fee 325–26; Hansen 241)? Or did Paul intend Χριστοῦ as (view 2) subj., "the faithfulness of Christ" (O'Brien 399–400; Sumney 80; cf. Wallace 114–16)? The arguments are finely balanced. The subj. gen. (view 2) is favored by the following:

a. "Faithfulness, fidelity, reliability" is the normal meaning for πίστις in HGk. and in the LXX; πίστος describes God's faithfulness to his covenant promises in the OT (Deut 7:9) (O'Brien 399).

b. Apart from the debated phrase πίστις Χριστοῦ (or its equivalent), Paul uses πίστις + gen. of a person (either a noun or pronoun) twenty-four times. In every instance the reference is to faith (or faithfulness) exercised by the individual, not the individual as the obj. of faith. Moving to the debated cstr., the expression ἐκ πίστεως Ἰησοῦ [Χριστοῦ] (Rom 3:26; Gal 3:22) has an exact parallel in Rom 4:16, ἐκ πίστεως Ἀβραάμ, where Ἀβραάμ is clearly a subj. gen. (O'Brien 399). In Hellenistic Jewish literature, πίστις + the personal gen. is rare. When it does occur, however, it is "virtually always subjective." Where an object is in view, the cstr. πίστις πρὸς τὸν θέον is preferred (O'Brien 399). In reply, there are three clear examples of πίστις + obj. personal gen. in the NT (Mark 11:22; Jas 2:1; Rev 2:13), as well as two clear instances in Paul that involve an impersonal gen. noun (Col 2:12; 2 Thess 2:13) (Wallace 116).

c. Jesus' faithful obedience plays a central role in Paul's theology (Rom 5:18–19), not least in Philippians, where Paul portrays Jesus exhibiting faithfulness to the point of death on the cross (2:8). However, the language in 2:8 is of "obedience," not strictly "faithfulness" (Reumann 496).

The obj. gen. interpretation of Χριστοῦ (view 1) finds formidable support, as well:

a. Verbal articulation of the "faithfulness of Christ" is noticeably absent from Paul and the Gospels. Nowhere is Jesus the subject of the vb. πιστεύω, while there are many examples of believers so used. Paul, on his part, never speaks unambiguously of Jesus as faithful (πίστος) or believing (πιστεύω), while he regularly speaks of individuals believing in Christ (Silva 161; Reumann 496).

b. Τῇ πίστει, later in v. 9, refers to the believer's faith. We should expect the first occurrence of πίστις to carry the same meaning (τῇ is anaphoric [Hansen 242]). But if πίστις is taken to refer to the believers' faith in both instances, (a) Paul has left the objective ground of God's action unspecified, and (b) he has unnecessarily repeated the statement about man's trust (διὰ πίστεως + ἐπὶ τῇ πίστει) (O'Brien 400). In response the objective ground of God's action is adequately represented in τὴν ἐκ θεοῦ δικαιοσύνην, and the rhetorical demands of the argument of the passage fully account for the repetition "in slightly different language, so as to reinforce the point" (Fee 325–26). With respect to the subj. gen. interpretation, one wonders how the Philippians could "possibly have caught on to such a radical shift of subject and object in a clause that seems so clearly designed to repeat the first for emphasis" (Fee 325 n. 45).

c. Elsewhere in Philippians the word group signifies the Philippians' faith in Christ (πίστις 3x [1:25, 27; 2:17]; πιστεύω [1:29]). Paul's assertion that God has gifted the Philippians with both τὸ εἰς αὐτὸν πιστεύειν and τὸ ὑπὲρ αὐτοῦ πάσχειν has prepared the readers for mention here of Paul's "faith in Christ" (πίστεως Χριστοῦ [v. 9]) and "participation in his sufferings" (κοινωνίαν παθημάτων αὐτοῦ [v. 10]) (Hansen 241).

The decision is difficult. The lack of conceptual parallels to the idea of Jesus exercising faithfulness seriously compromises the subj. gen. interpretation of Χριστοῦ. Although theologically and contextually attractive, it is prudent provisionally to retain the traditional understanding of πίστεως Χριστοῦ in v. 9 as "faith in Christ."

The twofold use of δικαιοσύνη in v. 9 presents another challenge. Recent attempts to read δικαιοσύνη solely in terms of faithfulness to the covenant badges of circumcision and the food laws—not self-achieved, moral righteousness—properly remind us of the social implications of Paul's gospel and of the centrality of debates over social boundaries in formative Christianity. To limit the occurrences of δικαιοσύνη in v. 9 to "membership language," however, does not satisfy the demands of Paul's argument (Park 41–47). His reasons for confidence in the flesh involve personal achievements that far surpassed those of fellow Jews with whom Paul shared national identity—thus the augmentation, in Paul's Jewish *cursus honorum* (vv. 5–6), of ascribed (birth) honors (v. 5) with achieved (adult) honors (v. 6). It is these personal achievements that Paul refers to as ἐμὴν δικαιοσύνην in v. 9 (Hansen 239).

Most, therefore, interpret the first occurrence (ἐμὴν δικαιοσύνην τὴν ἐκ νόμου) in terms of ethical righteousness ("righteousness" [most EVV]; "uprightness" [NJB]; "righteousness in conduct" [Reumann 521]), as in v. 6 but with a different orientation. The legal righteousness which Paul claimed in v. 6 had to do with "confidence in the flesh" vis-à-vis the Torah achievements of Paul's contemporaries (cf. Εἴ τις δοκεῖ ἄλλος πεποιθέναι ἐν σαρκί, ἐγὼ μᾶλλον [v. 4]). Here in v. 9 Paul turns Godward, as he reflects upon his "own moral achievement, gained by obeying the law (τὴν ἐκ νόμου) and intended to establish a claim upon God, particularly in view of the final judgment" (O'Brien 394). That which had positioned the apostle at the top of the social pecking order among his Torah-minded Jewish contemporaries gains Paul no status whatsoever in God's judicial economy.

All this makes good sense until the second occurrence of δικαιοσύνη in v. 9 is taken to denote "righteousness" not as upright behavior (vv. 6, 9a) but, rather, as a "quality or state of juridical correctness with focus on redemptive action" (BDAG 247c–d; "righteousness imputed to the believer" [Silva 160]), as indicated by the emphatic gen. modifier ἐκ θεοῦ. No longer is δικαιοσύνη a "kind of moral achievement." It is now "a relational term," having to do with "'the status of being in the right' . . . God's way of putting people right with himself" (O'Brien 396; Hansen 240). This, however, demands two different meanings for δικαιοσύνη in the same ptc. clause, an unlikely scenario, particularly since the two occurrences are contrasted as to their sources.

A more promising approach situates the ethical component surrounding the first occurrence of δικαιοσύνη not in the term itself but, rather, in the qualifiers ἐμήν and τὴν ἐκ νόμου. This is supported by the chiastic structure, which emphasizes τὴν ἐκ νόμου and τὴν ἐκ θεοῦ δικαιοσύνην as its innermost elements (see below, on ἐπὶ τῇ πίστει). In each instance δικαιοσύνη retains its basic sense, "the status of being in the right," a status which, in the biblical framework, is at once both forensic and relational in nature (C. Brown, NIDNTT 3.373). The contrasting qualifiers then serve to distinguish between (a) a status that can be sought (but never finally achieved [Gal 2:16; Rom 3:20]) through one's own moral efforts at Torah keeping (ἐμὴν . . . τὴν ἐκ νόμου), versus (b) a status received from God on the basis of faith (ἐκ θεοῦ . . . ἐπὶ τῇ πίστει).

Finally, δικαιοσύνη—the status of being in the right before God, and therefore in a right relationship with him—is granted to those who meet God's ethical demands, who exhibit covenant faithfulness, broadly conceived (thus blurring somewhat the sharp distinction in the lexicons between δικαιοσύνη as status and δικαιοσύνη as ethic [cf. BDAG 247b–248a]). Human beings have universally failed in this regard (Rom 3:1–20, 23). Jesus alone remained faithful to God's will for his life (Mark 14:36). It is Christ's δικαιοσύνη—his status of being in the right, earned by "obedience to the point of death" (2:8)—which becomes, in turn, ἡ ἐκ θεοῦ δικαιοσύνη that is imputed to the believer (2 Cor 5:21).

The prep. phrase ἐπὶ τῇ πίστει could be taken with ἔχων and read in a causal sense (BDF §235[2], cf. ἐφ᾽ ᾧ [3:12]). More likely, however, ἐπί marks the "basis for a state of being, action, or result," and amplifies the meaning of τὴν ἐκ θεοῦ δικαιοσύνην (BDAG 364d; "on the basis of/based on faith" [NASB, HCSB, NIV]; "(that) depends on faith" [RSV, NLT, ESV]). The objs. in the ptc. clause (μὴ ἔχων κτλ.) are structured chiastically:

ἐμὴν δικαιοσύνην   τὴν ἐκ νόμου

τὴν διὰ πίστεως Χριστοῦ   τὴν ἐκ θεοῦ δικαιοσύνην

The chiasm does not account for ἐπὶ τῇ πίστει ("a non-chiastic pendant" [Reumann 498]). This has led some to take the prep. phrase with τοῦ γνῶναι, which follows, but this is unlikely and may be taken as an appropriate caution against overemphasizing the importance of chiastic structures for syntactical analysis.

VERSE 10

τοῦ γνῶναι αὐτόν

The art. inf. τοῦ γνῶναι (aor. act., from γινώσκω) expands upon the meaning of τῆς γνώσεως Χριστοῦ Ἰησοῦ (v. 8). The knowledge Paul has in view includes both "understanding and experience" (O'Brien 402; Park 71). Τοῦ + inf. here can signify (1) *purpose (BDAG 688c; Hansen 242; H-M 196; O'Brien 400; Reumann 498), (2) result ("so as to know" [Moule 128–29; T 136, 141–42]), or be (3) epexegetical (Moule 128–29). The gen. art. (τοῦ) + inf. was standard in CGk. for purpose, and the cstr. also occurs widely in this sense in the LXX. Paul prefers εἰς or πρός + the art. inf. in the acc., but he does use τοῦ + inf. for purpose at least once (Rom 6:6) (R 1088). The goal expressed in τοῦ γνῶναι is syntactically connected to what precedes in one of two ways:

    1. It is parallel to the twofold ἵνα-clause ("that is, to know him" [BDF §400(8)]; cf. T 136; Z §392; Silva 163); or
  *2. It relates the ultimate goal of a penultimate ἵνα-clause in vv. 8c–9 (Fee 327; see diagram).
    a. Τοῦ γνῶναι αὐτόν, as defined by the dir. obj. clause that follows (καὶ τὴν δύναμιν κτλ.), appears to move beyond justification (εὑρεθῶ ἐν αὐτῷ . . . ἐπὶ τῇ πίστει) to portray the process of sanctification. To be "found in Christ" positionally becomes the basis for "knowing Christ" relationally (Fee 314).
    b. When Paul intends coordinate purpose clauses elsewhere, both clauses are introduced by ἵνα (1 Cor 7:5; Gal 3:14; 4:5). When he changes conjs. (here), the second clause is typically dependent on—not parallel to—the first (2 Thess 1:11–12; 1 Cor 1:28–29; 2 Cor 8:14; Rom 7:4; 15:16) (Fee 327 n. 50).

καὶ τὴν δύναμιν τῆς ἀναστάσεως αὐτοῦ καὶ [τὴν] κοινωνίαν [τῶν] παθημάτων αὐτοῦ

The tr. "and" (most EVV) for the initial καί wrongly assumes three distinct objs. for τοῦ γνῶναι: (1) αὐτόν, (2) τὴν δύναμιν τῆς ἀναστάσεως αὐτοῦ, and (3) κοινωνίαν παθημάτων. The καί functions, rather, epexegetically, "that is," explaining what Paul means in τοῦ γνῶναι αὐτόν (H-M 197; Hansen 243; Silva 163; "I want to know Christ—yes, to know the power of his resurrection and participation in his sufferings" [NIV]).

The vars. are exegetically significant. The bracketed arts. are lacking in 𝔓⁴⁶ ℵ* B, present in ℵ² D F G Ψ Byz. It appears that scribes, understanding κοινωνίαν as a distinct entity parallel to τὴν δύναμιν, added the article to clarify the perceived relationship between the terms (H-M 181; Fee 311 n. 2; Reumann 500; pace Silva 195). "The shorter reading, which was both widespread and early, is more difficult on the grounds of symmetry and parallelism" (O'Brien 382). The two concepts (δύναμιν τῆς ἀναστάσεως αὐτοῦ and κοινωνίαν παθημάτων αὐτοῦ)—now governed by a single art. and joined by καί—are to be taken closely together, as alternate aspects of the same experience ("You cannot have one without the other" [Reumann 522]; Fee 328). Paul amplifies τοῦ γνῶναι αὐτόν (cf. καί, above) "in terms of knowing the power of his resurrection as he participates in Christ's sufferings." Resurrection power enables Paul to endure suffering (O'Brien 383, 404; Hansen 243; Sumney 81–82).

The order—"resurrection" first, then "suffering"—is striking, since Jesus first suffered and was afterwards resurrected. The order parallels Paul's own experience, however, where he first encountered the risen Christ and subsequently learned that suffering would be his lot as Christ's apostle (Acts 9:16).

Δύναμιν, -εως, ἡ (acc. fem. sg.) generally connotes "potential for functioning in some way" (BDAG 262b; "potency in contrast to ἐνέργεια" [W. Grundmann, TDNT 2.285–90]; "power" [EVV]; "mighty power" [NLT]; "the effectiveness of his resurrection" [BDAG 263a]). In the OT, God's power is at work in salvation history (e.g., the Exodus), as well as in creation; in the NT, in the resurrection of Jesus (Rom 1:4; 2 Cor 13:4; Phil 3:10). The often-preached etym. connection between δύναμις and "dynamite" is completely unwarranted. In addition to the obvious anachronism (dynamite was invented in the nineteenth century), the association is utterly inappropriate, since dynamite is a destructive force, while the δύναμις τῆς ἀναστάσεως αὐτοῦ is constructive, restorative power.

The gen. τῆς ἀναστάσεως (sg. fem. from ἀνάστασις, -εως, ἡ; the word group is one of two [cf. ἐγείρω] for resurrection in the NT) is not to be taken as appos. ("the power that his resurrection is" [Reumann 500]), nor as source ("the power that emanates from his resurrection") but, rather, loosely, as a descriptive gen., "the power that characterized (or "was active in") his resurrection." What is in view is not strictly resurrection power but the more expansive "life-giving power of God" that he manifested in raising Christ, and which now also operates in the life of the believer, a common theme in the prison epistles (cf. Eph 1:19–20) (O'Brien 404–5; O. Betz, NIDNTT 2.606). Resurrection was inconceivable in Gk. world (cf. the scorn Paul received when he mentioned the resurrection in Athens [Acts 17:32]). At best it was an isolated event in stories about the physician Aesculapius or Apollonius of Tyana. After death one faced a shadowy existence in the abode of Hades; other incorporeal notions of the afterlife included the immortality of the soul and "transmigration" of souls (Plato Resp. 10). Resurrection is absent from most of the OT, as well (but cf. Isa 26:19 and Dan 12:2), but gained popularity during the Second Temple period. Jesus (Matt 22:29–32) and the Pharisees (Acts 23:8) shared a belief in the resurrection. Samaritans and Sadducees (Matt 22:23) did not.

Take κοινωνίαν in an active sense, "participation, sharing" (BDAG 553b) and παθημάτων (gen. pl. neut. from πάθημα, -ατος, τό, "suffering, misfortune" [BDAG 747d]) as an obj. gen., denoting that in which one participates ("share his sufferings" [RSV, ESV]; "participation in his sufferings" [NIV]; Hansen 245; O'Brien 405; less clear is "fellowship of His sufferings" [NASB, HCSB]). The pron. αὐτοῦ is subj. gen. (H. Schlier, TDNT 3.144). In view of συμμορφιζόμενος τῷ θανάτῳ αὐτοῦ, which follows, some see in v. 10 not Paul's physical suffering, rather, a spiritual "dying-and-rising-with-Christ," as in the baptismal imagery of Romans 6 (H-M 198–99). The emphasis on suffering in 1:28b–30, however, and the fact that this is a personal (1 sg.) narrative (cf. 2 Cor 11:23–27), point to physical suffering ("daily afflictions" [J. Kremer, *EDNT* 3.2a]; W. Michaelis, *TDNT* 5.932; Hansen 245–46; Reumann 524). The parallel in 2 Cor 1:7 (κοινωνοί ἐστε τῶν παθημάτων) confirms this understanding. Paul sees these sufferings as part of "the messianic woes of Jewish apocalyptic thought, the birth pangs of the Messiah (cf. αὐτοῦ)." All Christians participate in these sufferings and through them enter the kingdom of God (Acts 14:22; cf. 1 Thess 3:3, 7) (O'Brien 406; G. Delling, *TDNT* 6.307).

συμμορφιζόμενος τῷ θανάτῳ αὐτοῦ

Συμμορφιζόμενος is nom. sg. masc. of the pres. pass. ptc. of συμμορφίζω, "be conformed to" (NASB, HCSB), "be like [Christ in his death]" (BDAG 955a; NRSV, NIV, ESV; "fashioned like" [G. Stählin, *TDNT* 5.435 n. 373]); possibly coined by Paul (R 150; O'Brien 408). The ptc. can be temporal ("while" [Reumann 502]) or modal ("by being moulded to the pattern of" [NJB]; "by becoming like him" [NRSV]; Fee 333 n. 65). The nom. is a cstr. according to sense with the inf. γνῶναι, which would normally take the acc. (O'Brien 406; Reumann 502). O'Brien suggests that the pres. tense "emphasizes continuity" (408), but contextual constraints would seem to limit Paul's choice to the pres. Here Paul does, in fact, transition from physical sufferings (see, above, on παθημάτων) to "a metaphor of incorporation" (unless martyrdom is in view, an unlikely alternative that would require συμμορφιζόμενος to be read as a futuristic pres.). The vb. συμμορφίζω is one of a series of compounds with συν- that Paul employs to describe "the momentous truth that he and other believers have been incorporated into Christ and indissolubly joined with him so that they share in the events of his death, resurrection, ascension, and future glory" (O'Brien 408; see, esp., W. Grundmann, *TDNT* 7.786–87; C. Brown, *NIDNTT* 3.278). Union with Christ in his death is both a past event (Rom 6:4–6; Gal 2:19) and an ongoing experience (Rom 8:13; Col 3:5).

VERSE 11

εἴ πως καταντήσω εἰς τὴν ἐξανάστασιν τὴν ἐκ νεκρῶν

Ἐξανάστασιν is acc. sg. fem., from ἐξανάστασις, -εως, ἡ. Elsewhere Paul uses ἀνάστασις (8x; cf. 3:10). Though possibly rhetorical variation ("The two words are equivalent" [A. Oepke, *TDNT* 1.371]; Reumann 503), the repetition of the prep. later in the clause (τὴν ἐκ νεκρῶν) suggests otherwise. Paul may, in fact, have coined the hapax ἐξανάστασιν to reinforce the significance of the following ἐκ, "out from among the dead ones" [O'Brien 14–15]), in order to counterbalance an overly realized eschatology of opponents in Philippi (Hansen 248; H-M 201).

The vb. καταντήσω (1 sg. act. from καταντάω) can be read as aor. subjunc. or fut. indic. (εἰ + subjunc. is found elsewhere in the NT and in extrabiblical κοινή [R 1017]). Καταντάω, used lit. of arriving at a place or a town (cf. Acts 16:1; 18:19, 24), functions here metaphorically (W. Mundle, *NIDNTT* 1.325) to denote "the attainment of an objective" (O'Brien 414; "to reach a condition or goal" [BDAG 523a]; cf. Eph 4:13). Εἴ πως can be:

1. read as the final note in a series of statements about Paul's relationship with Christ (vv. 8c–10), beginning with the ἵνα-clause in v. 8c;
2. connected to τοῦ γνῶναι κτλ. (v. 10); or, most likely,
*3. taken closely with συμμορφιζόμενος τῷ θανάτῳ αὐτοῦ, in which case συμμορφιζόμενος τῷ θανάτῳ αὐτοῦ becomes a prerequisite for participation in ἡ ἐξανάστασις ἡ ἐκ νεκρῶν.
   a. Paul says much the same in Rom 8:17 (εἴπερ συμπάσχομεν ἵνα καὶ συνδοξασθῶμεν) and 2 Tim 2:12 (εἰ ὑπομένομεν, καὶ συμβασιλεύσομεν) (Fee 336; O'Brien 413; cf. Acts 14:22).

The apparent note of uncertainty in εἴ πως ("if perhaps, if somehow" [BDAG 279a]) is problematic in light of Paul's robust eschatological confidence elsewhere. In all ten instances of εἴ πως in biblical Gk., elements of hope and doubt seem to be involved, so that "total elimination of uncertainty for εἴ πως is hard to pull off" (Reumann 502–3, 525; *pace* O'Brien 411–13). Yet Paul elsewhere presents participation in the resurrection as a certainty for the Christian (1 Cor 15:20; 2 Cor 5:1), and he is optimistic about his own future, as well (Phil 3:9, 20–21; cf. esp. 1:23, where union with Christ after death is a given). The dilemma is vividly reflected in the variety of EVV ("that if possible" [RSV]; "in order that" [NASB]; "and so, somehow" [NIV]; "striving towards" [NJB]; "if somehow" [NRSV]; "so that somehow" [CEV]). An appealing solution situates Paul's uncertainty not in the *fact* of attaining the resurrection but in the *manner* by which he will attain it ("so that one way or another I will" [NLT]; "assuming that I will somehow" [HCSB]; "that by any means possible I may" [ESV]; C. Brown, *NIDNTT* 3.279). The cond. particle (πώς always occurs in the NT with εἰ [4x] or μή [11x] [W. Schenk, *EDNT* 3.202b]), however, underscores the idea of indefiniteness in the εἴ πως cstr. The idea of manner is present secondarily, if at all (Silva 192). A better explanation takes the grammar at face value, as either:

*1. emphasizing that the resurrection of believers is conditioned upon our first "being conformed to his death" (connecting εἴ πως closely to συμμορφιζόμενος τῷ θανάτῳ αὐτοῦ [see above]) (Fee 335–36); or
*2. reflecting "a humility [on Paul's part] that recognizes that salvation is a gift from God from start to finish and that as a consequence he dare not presume on this divine mercy" (H-M 200; Hansen 248; Reumann 526).

The two options are not mutually exclusive. It may be the case, as well, that the tentativeness of the construction anticipates his challenge to the perfectionist tendencies in the congregation that Paul will proceed to address in vv. 12ff. (Silva 167).

FOR FURTHER STUDY

41. Judaizers (3:2)

Barnett, Paul. "Opposition in Corinth." *JSNT* 22 (1984): 3–17.
*Campbell, W. S. *DPL* 513–16.
Ellis, Earle E. "Paul and His Opponents." Pages 264–89 in *Christianity, Judaism, and Other Graeco-Roman Cults*. Studies in Judaism in Late Antiquity 12. Edited by J. Neusner. Leiden: Brill, 1975.
Elmer, Ian J. *Paul, Jerusalem and the Judaisers: The Galatian Crisis in its Broadest Historical Context*. WUNT 2.258. Tübingen: Mohr Siebeck, 2009.
Grayston, Kenneth. "The Opponents of Paul in Philippians 3." *ExpTim* 97 (1986): 170–72.
Lea, Thomas D. "Unscrambling the Judaizers: Who Were Paul's Opponents?" *SwJT* 37 (1994): 23–29.
Tellbe, Mikael. "The Sociological Factors Behind Philippians 3:1–11 and the Conflict at Philippi." *JSNT* 55 (1994): 97–121.

42. Circumcision (3:3, 5)

Barclay, John. "Paul, the Gift and the Battle over Gentile Circumcision: Revisiting the Logic of Galatians." *Australian Biblical Review* 58 (2010): 36–56.
Borgen, Peder. "Paul Preaches Circumcision." Pages 37–46 in *Paul and Paulinism: Essays in Honour of C. K. Barrett*. Edited by M. D. Hooker and S. G. Wilson. London: SPCK, 1982.
Ferguson, Everett. "Spiritual Circumcision in Early Christianity." *SJT* 41 (1988): 485–97.
Marcus, Joel. "The Circumcision and the Uncircumcision in Rome." *NTS* 35 (1989): 67–81.
McEleney, Neil J. "Conversion, Circumcision, and the Law." *NTS* 20 (1974): 319–41.
Robinson, D. W. B. "'We Are the Circumcision' (Phil 3:3)." *Australian Biblical Review* 15 (1967): 28–35.
*Schreiner, T. *DPL* 137–39.

43. Pharisees (3:5)

*Deines, Roland. "The Pharisees Between 'Judaisms' and 'Common Judaism.'" Pages 443–504 in *Justification and Variegated Nomism. Volume I. The Complexities of Second Temple Judaism*. Edited by D. A. Carson, P. T. O'Brien, and M. A. Seifrid. Grand Rapids: Baker Academic, 2001.
Meier, John. *A Marginal Jew: Rethinking the Historical Jesus*. Vol. 3. New York: Doubleday, 2001. See pages 289–388.
Neusner, Jacob, and Bruce Chilton, eds. *In Quest of the Historical Pharisees*. Waco, TX: Baylor University Press, 2007.
Overman, J. Andrew. "Kata Nomon Pharisaios: A Short History of Paul's Pharisaism." Pages 180–93 in *Pauline Conversations in Context: Essays in Honor of Calvin J. Roetzel*. JSNTSS 221. Edited by J. C. Anderson. London: Sheffield Academic, 2002.
Wright. See pages 80–90.

44. The Law (3:6, 9)

Donaldson, T. L. "Zealot and Convert: The Origin of Paul's Christ-Torah Antithesis." *CBQ* 51 (1989): 655–82.

Hübner, Hans. *Law in Paul's Thought*. Edinburgh: T&T Clark, 1973.

Räisänen, Heiki. *Paul and the Law*. Philadelphia: Fortress, 1983.

Rosner, Brian. *Paul and the Law: Keeping the Commandments of God*. New Studies in Biblical Theology. Downers Grove: InterVarsity, 2013.

Sanders, E. P. *Paul, the Law, and the Jewish People*. Minneapolis: Fortress, 1983.

Schreiner, Thomas R. "Paul and Perfect Obedience to the Law: An Evaluation of the View of E. P. Sanders." *WTJ* 47 (1985): 245–78.

*Thielman, Frank. *DPL* 529–42.

————. *Paul and the Law: A Contextual Approach*. Downers Grove: InterVarsity, 1995.

Westerholm, Stephen. *Israel's Law and the Church's Faith: Paul and His Recent Interpreters*. Grand Rapids: Eerdmans, 1988.

Wright, N. T. *The Climax of the Covenant: Christ and the Law in Pauline Theology*. Edinburgh: T&T Clark, 1991.

45. Righteousness (3:9)

Cosgrove, Charles H. "Justification in Paul." *JBL* 106 (1987): 653–70.

Käsemann, Ernst. "The Righteousness of God in Paul." Pages 168–82 in E. Käsemann, *New Testament Questions of Today*. Philadelphia: Fortress, 1969.

Koperski, Veronica. "The Meaning of δικαιοσύνη in Philippians 3:9." *Louvain Studies* 20 (1995): 147–69.

*McGrath, Alister E. *DPL* 517–23.

Onesti, K. L., and M. T. Brauch. *DPL* 827–16.

Piper, John. *The Future of Justification: A Response to N. T. Wright*. Wheaton, IL: Crossway, 2007.

Plevnik, Joseph. "Recent Developments in the Discussion Concerning Justification by Faith." *Toronto Journal of Theology* 2 (1986): 47–62.

Williams, Sam K. "'The Righteousness of God' in Romans." *JBL* 99 (1980): 241–90.

Wright, N. T. *Justification: God's Plan and Paul's Vision*. London: SPCK, 2009.

46. Πίστις Χριστοῦ (3:9)

*Dunn, J. D. G. "Once More, ΠΙΣΤΙΣ ΧΡΙΣΤΟΥ." Pages 61–81 in *Pauline Theology*. Vol. 4. Edited by E. E. Johnson and D. M. Hay. Atlanta: SBL Literature, 1997.

Harrisville, Roy A. "ΠΙΣΤΙΣ ΧΡΙΣΤΟΥ: Witness of the Fathers." *NovT* 36 (1994): 233–41.

Hays, Richard B. "ΠΙΣΤΙΣ and Pauline Christology: What Is at Stake?" Pages 35–60 in *Pauline Theology*. Vol. 4. Edited by E. E. Johnson and D. M. Hay. Atlanta: SBL Literature, 1997.

————. *The Faith of Jesus Christ: An Investigation of the Narrative Substructure of Galatians 3:1–4:11*. Society of Biblical Literature Dissertation Series 56. Chico, CA, Scholars, 1983.

Hooker, Morna. "ΠΙΣΤΙΣ ΧΡΙΣΤΟΥ." *NTS* 35 (1989): 321–49.

Howard, George. "The Faith of Christ." *ExpTim* 85 (1973–74): 212–14.

Hultgren, Arland J. "The ΠΙΣΤΙΣ ΧΡΙΣΤΟΥ Formulation in Paul." *NovT* 22 (1980): 248–63.

Matlock, R. Barry. "Demythologizing the ΠΙΣΤΙΣ ΧΡΙΣΤΟΥ Debate: Cautionary Remarks from a Lexical Semantic Perspective." *NovT* 42 (2000): 1–23.

47. Resurrection (3:11)

Coenen, L. *NIDNTT* 3.259–309.

Cullmann, Oscar. *Immortality of the Soul or Resurrection of the Dead?* London: Epworth, 1958.

Ellis, Earle E. "II Corinthians V.1–10 in Pauline Eschatology." *NTS* 6 (1959–60): 211–24.

Harris, Murray J. *Raised Immortal: The Relation Between Resurrection and Immortality in New Testament Teaching.* Grand Rapids: Eerdmans, 1983.

*Kreitzer, L. *DPL* 805–12.

Lincoln, Andrew T. *Paradise Now and Not Yet.* SNTSMS 43. Cambridge: Cambridge University Press, 1981.

Nickelsburg, George. *Resurrection, Immortality, and Eternal Life in Intertestamental Judaism.* HTS 26. Cambridge, MA: Harvard University Press, 1972.

Otto, Randall E. "'If Possible I May Attain the Resurrection from the Dead' (Philippians 3:11)." *CBQ* 57 (1995): 324–40.

Wright, N. T. *The Resurrection of the Son of God.* Minneapolis: Fortress, 2003.

HOMILETICAL SUGGESTIONS

Trading Up (3:1–11)

1. Exchanging a righteousness that comes from being Jewish and obeying Torah (vv. 1–6).
2. For the righteousness of God that is found in Christ (vv. 7–11).

Characteristics of the True People of God (3:3)

1. They serve by means of the Spirit of God.
2. They place their confidence in Christ.
3. They do not trust in the works of the flesh.

All for Jesus (3:7–11)

1. Exchanging all things (vv. 7–8).
2. To be found in him (v. 9).
3. To know him (v. 10).
4. To be with him forever (v. 11).

The Surpassing Value of Knowing Christ (3:9–11)

1. From justification (v. 9).
2. To sanctification (v. 10).
3. To glorification (v. 11)

What It Means to Know Christ (3:10)

1. It means to experience the power of his resurrection.
2. It means to participate in his sufferings.
3. It means to be conformed to his death.

b. Pressing Toward the Goal (3:12–16)

12   Οὐχ ὅτι ἤδη ἔλαβον
      ἢ ἤδη τετελείωμαι,
      διώκω δὲ εἰ καὶ καταλάβω, ἐφ' ᾧ καὶ κατελήμφθην ὑπὸ Χριστοῦ ['Ιησοῦ].
13   ἀδελφοί, ἐγὼ ἐμαυτὸν οὐ λογίζομαι κατειληφέναι·
      ἓν δέ,
         τὰ μὲν ὀπίσω ἐπιλανθανόμενος
         τοῖς δὲ ἔμπροσθεν ἐπεκτεινόμενος,
14   κατὰ σκοπὸν
         διώκω εἰς τὸ βραβεῖον τῆς ἄνω κλήσεως τοῦ θεοῦ ἐν Χριστῷ 'Ιησοῦ.
15   Ὅσοι οὖν τέλειοι,
         τοῦτο φρονῶμεν·
            καὶ εἴ τι ἑτέρως φρονεῖτε,
         καὶ τοῦτο ὁ θεὸς ὑμῖν ἀποκαλύψει·
16   πλὴν εἰς ὃ ἐφθάσαμεν,
         τῷ αὐτῷ στοιχεῖν.

Lit. devices include (a) wordplay on a common root (ἔλαβον . . . καταλάβω . . . κατελήμφθην . . . κατειληφέναι), (b) doublets (διώκω/διώκω; ἤδη/ἤδη; τετελείωμαι/ τέλειοι; φρονῶμεν/φρονεῖτε), (c) a carefully structured pair of ptc. clauses, each with four terms in antithetical parallelism,

τὰ	μὲν	ὀπίσω	ἐπιλανθανόμενος
τοῖς	δὲ	ἔμπροσθεν	ἐπεκτεινόμενος

and (d) a foot race metaphor (κατὰ σκοπὸν διώκω εἰς τὸ βραβεῖον [v. 14]).

Most find the athletic imagery beginning with the first occurrence of διώκω (v. 12; "I keep on running" [CEV]) and continuing at least through 14a (κατὰ σκοπὸν διώκω εἰς τὸ βραβεῖον [A. Oepke, TDNT 2.229; G. Ebel, NIDNTT 2.807; H-M 207, 210; Reumann 545, 551–52]). Fee limits the imagery solely to v. 14a (340). The ptc. clauses in 13b clearly portray an athlete's manner of running, however, so the metaphor is in play at least from 13b through 14a (τὰ μὲν ὀπίσω . . . τὸ βραβεῖον) (O'Brien 419, 424). Like all such images the analogy breaks down: all runners who finish this race receive the prize (O. Bauernfeind, TDNT 8.232).

Verses 12–14 consist of two disclaimers each followed by an affirmation of Paul's intention to stay the course and reach his goal. The reason for the disclaimers, and the ensuing interpretation of vv. 12–16, fall into two broad camps:

1. There is a change of subject matter at v. 12. Paul turns now to address claims of moral or spiritual perfectionism in the Philippian church, adopting the terminology of his opponents (e.g., τετελείωμαι) to challenge their convictions.
   a. The strong disclaimers cry out for explanation. It is fair to assume that influential persons in Philippi were making claims to the contrary (Reumann 542, 546, 560).

b. Greek aversion to the idea of bodily resurrection, coupled with Paul's more appealing teaching on present justification and a spiritual rising with Christ, likely resulted in an overly realized eschatology that encouraged opponents to postulate the possibility of a life of spiritual perfection in the here and now (cf. τετελείωμαι, τέλειοι [vv. 12, 15]) (1 Cor 15:12–19; Acts 17:32; cf. 2 Tim 2:18; cf. the problems in 1 Thess 4:13–5:11; 2 Thess 3:10; and the injunction in 1 Cor 15:58) (Reumann 554, 558). But there is no data in Philippians to suggest the kind of resistance to the doctrine of bodily resurrection that Paul ran into elsewhere (but note the striking expression τὴν ἐξανάστασιν τὴν ἐκ νεκρῶν [v. 11]). Nor is there evidence, anywhere in Paul's churches, for opponents promoting spiritual perfectionism (Fee 344).

c. Terms unparalleled earlier in Philippians—along with an atypical Pauline emphasis on human achievement—were likely occasioned by the opponents' particular ideologies, the "perfectionism that they taught" (Reumann 554; G. Delling, TDNT 8.76 n. 52).

d. The use of the cognate τέλειοι in v. 15 clearly refers to a maturity or perfection in this life of some sort. We would expect τετελείωμαι to be similarly intended.

2. Verses 12–16 are to be taken closely with vv. 8–11, and the passage is to be read eschatologically. Paul is not disclaiming moral perfection (though he would certainly do so in the proper context). He is asserting that he has not yet gained the full knowledge of Christ that will only come with the future resurrection. Perfectionist opponents are hardly (if at all) in view.

a. Nowhere else in the NT does οὐχ ὅτι (v. 12) mark a paragraph break (see, e.g., Phil 4:11, 17; Fee 339). The unexpressed obj. of ἔλαβον, and Paul's intended sense for τετελείωμαι, should, therefore, be determined by the preceding context, not by mirror reading the text in search of alleged opponents (Fee 344 n. 24).

b. An eschatological reading of the text is supported both by what precedes (εἴ πως καταντήσω εἰς τὴν ἐξανάστασιν τὴν ἐκ νεκρῶν [v. 11]) and by what follows (τὸ βραβεῖον τῆς ἄνω κλήσεως τοῦ θεοῦ ἐν Χριστῷ Ἰησοῦ [v. 14]). In reply, the reference to future resurrection in v. 11 is subordinate to the ptc. phrase συμμορφιζόμενος τῷ θανάτῳ αὐτοῦ (see on v. 10). The main idea in vv. 8–11 remains the experience of knowing Christ this side of the eschaton (τοῦ γνῶναι αὐτόν, explained by τὴν δύναμιν τῆς ἀναστάσεως αὐτοῦ καὶ κοινωνίαν παθημάτων αὐτοῦ, συμμορφιζόμενος τῷ θανάτῳ αὐτοῦ; see on v. 10).

c. The use of the cognate ἐπιτελέσει, in reference to the Day of Christ Jesus (1:6), suggests that future eschatology is in view in τετελείωμαι here.

The views are not mutually exclusive. The ensuing context (vv. 13–14), where Paul clarifies the meaning of the more obscure expressions (ἔλαβον and τετελείωμαι [v. 12]), suggests that Paul has eschatological consummation primarily in view. Yet the terminology and the emphatic disclaimers likely indicate that Paul is correcting wrong assumptions. The exegesis that follows adopts a mediating position: Paul emphasizes that full and complete apprehension of Christ comes only at the eschaton, in order to challenge overly enthusiastic claims to the contrary. The details surrounding those claims remain obscure. An overly realized eschatology (view 1) would nicely explain Paul's language, but the amount of mirror reading required to reconstruct such background renders the notion speculative, at best. Perhaps the opponents taught that Torah observance somehow made one more complete in Christ, in the sense of having achieved "ultimate status in the people of God" (Fee 342; Hansen 249; H-M 205; O'Brien 418). This view has the context in its favor (cf. 3:2–6, and also τὰ μὲν ὀπίσω ἐπιλανθανόμενος [v. 13], if taken to refer to Paul's former life in Judaism), but Paul does not typically challenge Judaizers (e.g., in Galatians) with the approach taken in vv. 12–16.

VERSE 12

Οὐχ ὅτι ἤδη ἔλαβον ἢ ἤδη τετελείωμαι

Οὐχ ὅτι is an ellipsis for "I don't mean to say that" (NLT [supplying λέγω]) or "It is not that" (Reumann 533 [supplying ἐστίν]), designed to prevent the readers from drawing wrong inferences from vv. 7–11 ("Not that" [most EVV]; "not that, not as if" [BDAG 732a]; Fee 342; Reumann 533). Οὐχ ὅτι disallows separating vv. 12–16 from the vv. 7–11 (*pace* CEV, ESV, HCSB), since in no other instance in the NT does οὐχ ὅτι mark a paragraph break (Fee 339; Sumney 84).

The adv. ἤδη ("already" [EVV]; "now, already, by this time" [BDAG 434c]) shows that ἔλαβον (1 sg. aor. act. indic. from λαμβάνω) does not denote a single past event, e.g., Paul's Damascus road encounter. Rather, the vb. sums up Paul's past experiences (particularly those described in vv. 8–11) and views them as a whole. Tr. ἔλαβον with an Eng. perf. (most EVV; O'Brien 422; R 845). The vb. has no dir. obj. (see O'Brien 420–22 and Reumann 533). Most EVV supply an ambiguous pron. ("this" [NRSV]; "all this" [NIV]; "it" [NJB]). The implied obj. is best understood as "the full 'knowing' of Christ," an idea later expressed by the athletic metaphor τὸ βραβεῖον in v. 14 (τὸ βραβεῖον serves as the obj. of διώκω, repeated from v. 12). Paul will acquire this only when Christ returns, at the resurrection from the dead (v. 11, the obj. of ἔλαβον linguistically [Silva 175]) (E. Stauffer *TDNT* 1.638–39; A. Ringwald, *NIDNTT* 1.648–49; A. Kretzer, *EDNT* 2.337d; Fee 341–42; Hansen 250; O'Brien 421–22). The tr. "have . . . reached the/my goal" (HCSB, CEV; cf. "I have . . . obtained" [NRSV, NIV, ESV]) retains the eschatological thrust of the context better than "have made (him) my own" (= "the mystical apprehension of Christ" [BDAG 584b]; Fee 343 n. 20).

A striking var. occurs after ἔλαβον, where 𝔓⁴⁶ D* Irenaeus^lat Ambrosiaster insert ἢ ἤδη δεδικαίωμαι (F G have δικαίωμαι). Reumann (534–35) thinks ἢ ἤδη δεδικαίωμαι is original:

    a. Δικαιοσυνή occurs in the previous context (v. 9).

    b. The principle that the shorter reading is more probable has been qualified in recent years. In papyri like 𝔓⁴⁶, for example, it is now known that scribes tended to omit, rather than add, material (Reumann 534).

c. The phrase could have been omitted because of perceived theological difficulty vis-à-vis Paul's teaching elsewhere (O'Brien 417). But a lack of scribal analogies (particularly this early) to such "theologically astute" omissions, especially one that would fit so well with vv. 8–11, suggests otherwise (Fee 337 n. 1; Sumney 84).

d. The phrase could have been omitted due to homoiarcton (ἢ ἤδη) (Reumann 535), or homoioteleuton (H-M 203; O'Brien 417; Silva 187).

e. The later introduction of this apparently un-Pauline idea is difficult to explain (O'Brien 417). Paul generally viewed justification as a past act (cf. Rom 5:1). Οὐχ . . . ἤδη δεδικαίωμαι would be more akin to a view like Ignatius's (e.g., Ign. Rom. 5:1), who implies with δεδικαίωμαι that he will finally be justified when he is martyred (O'Brien 421 n. 7). However, this could also explain why a later scribe, influenced by patristic views of justification, might add the phrase.

f. Paul may have intended paronomasia between δεδικαίωμαι and διώκω (H-M 203).

Those who reject ἢ ἤδη δεδικαίωμαι as a scribal gloss note the following:

a. Such additions are typical of the Western text (Fee 337 n. 1).

b. The phrase may have been added by analogy with 1 Cor 4:4 (οὐκ ἐν τούτῳ δεδικαίωμαι) (H-M 203; Reumann 535).

c. The addition may have arisen to compensate for the lack of objects and corresponding clarity in the verse (Reumann 534).

d. The strongest textual evidence is for the omission of ἢ ἤδη δεδικαίωμαι (O'Brien 418; Sumney 84; originality "doubtful at best" [Silva 187]).

The disjunctive particle, ἤ ("or" [NRSV, NASB, NIV, ESV]; "nor" [NJB]; "nor, or" [BDAG 432c]) here connects two similar processes, not distinct or alternative ones; ἤ ἤδη τετελείωμαι parallels and further explains ἤδη ἔλαβον: Paul has not yet arrived at the full, eschatological knowledge of Christ (ἔλαβον); he has not yet been made perfect (τετελείωμαι) (O'Brien 423; cf. 1 Cor 15:50–53; 1 John 3:2).

Τετελείωμαι is 1 sg. perf. pass. indic. from τελειόω, used only here by Paul (he prefers τελέω or ἐπιτελέω). Suggested meanings include:

1. Moral perfection ("make perfect" [BDAG 996d]; "am/have become/have been made perfect" [ESV, NASB]; "am . . . fully mature" [HCSB; Reumann 535, 554]; a key theme in Gk. philosophy).

2. Initiation into a mystery religion ("be consecrated, become a τέλειος" [BDAG 996d]). The Philippian audience was no stranger to the mysteries. There was an Eleusis cult near Athens, and we have evidence for Dionysian initiation rites in Philippi. We cannot rule out an ironic swipe at the mystery cults here (Reumann 553).

*3. Eschatological consummation ("have . . . arrived at/reached the/my goal" [NRSV, NJB, NIV]; G. Delling TDNT 8.84; H. Hübner, EDNT 3.344d; "been brought to completion" [Fee 344]; Hansen 251; Silva 175; Sumney 84). The cognate noun, τέλος, bears the primary sense of a "goal" or "aim" toward which something is pointing. Τετελείωμαι thus clarifies the previous ἔλαβον (with its implied obj.), in terms of the future, when Paul arrives at his final goal (via the resurrection) of "the ultimate apprehension of Christ" (Fee 346; cf. ἐπιτελέω in 1:6).

View 3 works best in context. Most agree, however, that Paul here takes over the terminology of his opponents for the purpose of correcting their false views, so the erroneous teachers in Philippi may well have used τελειόω in senses 1 or 2 above (O'Brien 423).

διώκω δὲ εἰ καὶ καταλάβω

The δέ is strongly adversative, highlighting Paul's "unrelenting determination to press on despite the limitations caused by his present imperfection" (Hansen 251).

The primary sense of διώκω is "to move rapidly and decisively toward an objective" (BDAG 254a; "hasten (toward the goal)" [A. Oepke, *TDNT* 2.229]). The objective can be bad (e.g., "persecute" [v. 6]) or good ("I press on" [most EVV]; "I make every effort" [HCSB]; "hasten, run, press on" [BDAG 254a]; Fee 354 n. 28). O'Brien (424) sees in the pres. "an ongoing pursuit," but one wonders what other tense Paul could have used. After the twofold ἤδη and the perf. pass. τετελείωμαι, one would hardly anticipate an aor. The "continual action" *Aktionsart* of the pres. should not be pressed where the choice of tense is constrained by other factors.

Εἰ + subjunc. introduces an indir. question, "I press on (to see) whether I can capture" (BDAG 278b; BDF §368, 375; R 916, 1024; expresses "an uncertain expectation associated with an effort to attain something" [Z §403]; Fee 345 n. 30; H-M 207).

Some take εἰ καί together, "if indeed" (O'Brien 424). The two conjs. (καὶ καταλάβω ... καὶ κατελήμφθην) are better taken in parallel, with their respective verbs ("both/ and" or "also/also"), expressing a reciprocal relationship: "I on my part, Christ on his part" (Reumann 537). Paul's point is not to express doubt (implied by taking εἰ καί together) but precisely the opposite, to communicate "expectancy" (Fee 345 n. 30).

Καταλάβω is 1 sg. aor. act. subjunc., the first of three forms of καταλαμβάνω in the passage (brought out in NRSV ["make it my own/made me his own/made it my own"] and NIV ["take hold/took hold/have taken hold"; cf. HCSB]). The compound vb. means "to take aggressively," hence, "grasp" or "seize" (Fee 345 n. 29; "make someth[ing] one's own" [BDAG 519d; NRSV, ESV]; "lay/take hold" [NASB, NIV, HCSB]), positively (Rom 9:30; 1 Cor 9:24) or negatively (Mark 9:18; 1 Thess 5:4). The lit. connotation "grasp" passes over to the sense "understand" or "grasp an idea with one's mind" (H-M 207; O'Brien 425). The same pair of vbs. occurs in Herodot. 9.58, where enemies are "pursued" (διώκ- root) until "overtaken" (καταλημφθέντες) (Reumann 537).

ἐφ' ᾧ καὶ κατελήμφθην ὑπὸ Χριστοῦ ['Ιησοῦ]

The prep. + rel. pron. (ἐφ' ᾧ; dat. sg. neut.) has been understood in several ways:

1. As an obj. that serves both καταλάβω and κατελήμφθην (= τοῦτο ἐφ᾽ ᾧ, "that with a view to which") ("aim or purpose" [R 605]; Fee 346 n. 31; "that for which" [NASB, NIV, cf. NJB, NLT]). But there is no obj. for ἔλαβον (v. 12) or for κατειληφέναι (v. 13). We would not expect an obj. here (Silva 176).

*2. To signify cause, as in Rom 5:12 and 2 Cor 5:4 (ἐφ᾽ ᾧ = ἐπὶ τούτῳ ὅτι, "for this reason that, because" [BDAG 365 b]; "because" [NRSV, ESV, HCSB]; BDF §235[2]; Moule 50, cf. 132; Wallace 342; Z §127; Harris, *Prepositions*, 140; Hansen 252 n. 168; O'Brien 425; Silva 176). This view takes ἐφ᾽ ᾧ only with κατελήμφθην, leaving καταλάβω without an obj. (cf. ἔλαβον, above, and κατειληφέναι [v. 13]), though EVV supply one (O'Brien 425).

3. Adv., "the way I was successfully taken hold of by Christ Jesus" (Reumann 538).

The first alternative finds some support in the use of the cstr. at 4:10, where ἐφ᾽ ᾧ looks both backwards (picking up ἐμοῦ) and forwards (as the obj. of ἐφρονεῖτε), though the use of ἐπί + dat. as an obj. after καταλαμβάνω "needs proving" (Reumann 538). View 2 is probably best.

The καί is hard to render accurately ("also" [NASB]; omit [NIV]), likely focusing on the past event as the basis for Paul's hope ("already" [Silva 187]).

See above, on καταλάβω, for the basic meaning of κατελήμφθην (1 sg. aor. pass. indic.), which changes slightly here. Instead of mental or spiritual apprehension, the reference is to Paul's Christ encounter on the Damascus road, the point at which Christ "laid hands on him, so to speak, forcefully arresting him and setting him off in a new lifelong direction" (H-M 208; Fee 346 n. 32; O'Brien 425). This was the point in time at which Paul encountered "the upward call of God" (v. 14) (W. Grundmann, *TDNT* 9.552 n. 376).

Vars. surrounding Χριστοῦ Ἰησοῦ are common; 𝔓⁴⁶ 𝔓⁶¹ ℵ A Ψ *Byz* read Ἰησοῦ; B D* F G 33 and early Fathers omit Ἰησοῦ. Omission could have occurred via homoteleuton, especially since our earliest mss. have the abbreviations ΧΥ ΙΥ for the divine names. But unintentional addition is possible, as well, since scribes would often write the full name without even thinking about it. The shorter reading is likely original, but one has no guarantee (Fee 338 n. 5; UBS⁵ = {C} Χριστοῦ Ἰησοῦ).

VERSE 13

ἀδελφοί, ἐγὼ ἐμαυτὸν οὐ λογίζομαι κατειληφέναι

Paul repeats his disclaimer and emphatically reinforces it by means of (a) two expressed prons. (ἐγὼ ἐμαυτόν), (b) a switch to pres. tense, and (c) the arresting voc. ἀδελφοί (Fee 346; O'Brien 425–26).

That this is all being told for the Philippians' sake is evidenced by "the sudden—and surprising—appearance of the vocative," ἀδελφοί (lit., "Brothers" [NJB, HCSB, ESV], but semantically including both genders, "Brothers and sisters" [NIV, cf. NLT]). Paul addresses the Philippians directly for the first time since vv. 2–3, in the middle of his own personal story (Fee 346–47). The elimination of the sibling metaphor in the

service of a gender neutral rendering ("Beloved" [NRSV] and "My friends" [CEV])
blunts the paraenetic force of Paul's address (see on 1:12).

The expressed ἐγώ provides further emphasis, as does the "syntactically unnecessary" ἐμαυτόν (O'Brien 426; "I (Paul) in contrast to others," "I, for my part" [Reumann
538]; R 811). The contrast is not with opinions others have of Paul but, rather, with
opinions others have of themselves (Hansen 252).

Several significant witnesses have οὔπω (𝔓¹⁶ᵛⁱᵈ 𝔓⁶¹ᵛⁱᵈ ℵ A D* P 33 81 etc.) instead
of οὐ (𝔓⁴⁶ B D² F G Ψ *Byz* it etc.). Οὔπω is clearly secondary (UBS⁵ = {B} οὐ) since
it fits the context so well, making early omission highly unlikely (Fee 338 n. 5; H-M
204; O'Brien 418). The difference is inconsequential, if the passage is interpreted
eschatologically, as argued above. The addition of "yet" to our EVV (e.g., NIV, NASB,
NJB) becomes highly problematic, however, on a moral perfectionist reading of vv.
12–13. For, in spite of the apostle's plain assertions to the contrary, the presence of this
"nefarious adv." opens the door to the assumption that Paul expected to become τέλειος
during his lifetime on earth, a notion with potentially devastating ramifications for
Christians who would seek to pattern their lives after the apostle (Reumann 552–53;
Fee 338, cf. n. 5).

Λογίζομαι is 1. sg. pres. mid. indic., "to hold a view about someth[ing]" (BDAG
598a; "draw a logical conclusion" [J. Eichler, *NIDNTT* 3.823]). Commonly rendered
"consider" (NIV, NRSV, HCSB; BDAG 598a; "regard" [NASB]), the subject's cogni-
tive faculties are at the forefront of the vb., which was used (a) in commercial transactions and (b) for the "nonemotional" reflections of the philosopher (O'Brien 426; "I
don't feel" [CEV] is potentially misleading).

For κατειληφέναι (perf. act. inf., w/subj. acc. ἐμαυτόν [BDF §406(2); T 147–48]; "to
attain definitively" [G. Delling, *TDNT* 4.10]), see on καταλάβω (v. 12). The vb. has no
obj., though most EVV supply "it."

ἓν δέ, τὰ μὲν ὀπίσω ἐπιλανθανόμενος τοῖς δὲ ἔμπροσθεν ἐπεκτεινόμενος

Ἕν is the neut. sg. of the numeral "one" (εἷς, μία, ἕν). Most EVV (NIV, HCSB,
ESV) supply ποιῶ (making ἕν acc.) to this "short but forceful interjection" (O'Brien
427; BDF §481). But this reduces the strength of Paul's rhetoric, which lies precisely
in the ellipsis and leaves the rest of the sentence to define the ἕν (Fee 347 n. 38; "just
one thing!" [BDAG 292d]; Hansen 253).

Τὰ μὲν ὀπίσω ἐπιλανθανόμενος is the first of two contrasting (μὲν . . . δέ), parallel
ptc. clauses ("what lies/is behind . . . what lies/is ahead" [most EVV; H. Seesemann,
TDNT 5.290]). The clause introduces an athletic metaphor that continues in v. 14
(O'Brien 428). The arts. (τά [acc. pl. neut.] and τοῖς [dat. pl. neut.]) are used subst.
with two advs. (ὀπίσω and ἔμπροσθεν [cf. BDAG 688d; BDF §215; R 765]). The advs.
(a) have spatial connotations at the level of the image (ὀπίσω = "the part of the course
already covered" [BDAG 716a]; O'Brien 428), but (b) are temporal with respect to the
metaphor's referent, i.e., Paul's progress in the spiritual life. The Christian life is lived
"between the 'no longer' and the 'not yet'" (W. Günther, *NIDNTT* 2.129).

Τὰ μὲν ὀπίσω points either to (1) Paul's heritage and accomplishments in Judaism (cf. 3:4–8 [Reumann 539, 555]), (2) "what Paul has already achieved in his apostolic service" (O'Brien 429; Hansen 253–54), or (3) both "wrongs done" and "attainments achieved" (H-M 209). The first view makes the best sense in the broader context of Paul's argument, the second in the immediate context of vv. 12–13. Τοῖς δὲ ἔμπροσθεν refers to the remainder of Paul's life as a missionary, which lies between him and the eschaton, when he will receive τὸ βραβεῖον, consisting of the full and complete apprehension of Christ.

ʼΕπιλανθανόμενος and ἐπεκτεινόμενος are each nom. sg. masc. of the pres. mid. ptc. (though ἐπεκτεινόμενος may be a direct mid., "stretching myself forward" [R 807]). Both ptcs. anchor "circumstantial clauses of manner," explaining how Paul is able to press on (O'Brien 428; Hansen 255; H-M 209). The first is from ἐπιλανθάνομαι, which most EVV render as "forgetting" (cf. BDAG 374d; O'Brien 428). Like the Eng. vb. "forget," ἐπιλανθάνομαι can also mean being "inattentive to," here "disregard, put out of mind" (BDAG 374d; "Not amnesia, but what Paul concentrates on" [Reumann 539]; Fee 347 n. 40; Sumney 86). Paul still remembers past experiences and achievements, of course, but pays no attention to them in order to concentrate on what lies ahead. Some see in the pres. tense of ἐπιλανθανόμενος "continuous and ceaseless" activity (O'Brien 428).

The second ptc., a double compound found nowhere else in the Gk. Bible, comes from ἐπεκτείνομαι, "to exert oneself to the uttermost" (BDAG 361b). The tr. "straining" (NRSV, NJB, ESV, NIV) is properly more forceful than "reaching" (NASB, HCSB). The metaphor pictures a runner extending himself or herself by leaning toward the goal (Fee 347 n. 41; Reumann 555).

VERSE 14

κατὰ σκοπὸν διώκω

Σκοπός means "goal" or "mark" (BDAG 931b; "goal-marker" [H-M 210]), and was used of an archer's target (Job 16:12; Lam 3:12) or of a goal or marker that controls a person's life (Plato, *Gorg.* 507d). Here σκοπόν refers to the post at the end of the race upon which a runner fixed his gaze (O'Brien 430; Reumann 540). Κατά + acc. is used in the sense "toward, to, up to" (BDAG 511d; R 608; "toward the goal" [NRSV, NASB, NIV; BDAG 254a]).

For διώκω see v. 12. Some EVV reflect the metaphor ("I am racing" [NJB]; "I run" [CEV]). Context encourages us to read the pres. tense as "I continue my pursuit" (Reumann 556).

εἰς τὸ βραβεῖον τῆς ἄνω κλήσεως τοῦ θεοῦ ἐν Χριστῷ Ἰησοῦ

Εἰς is telic, indicating purpose or goal, rather than simply directional (Fee 348 n. 45; O'Brien 430; Sumney 87).

Βραβεῖον is acc. sg. neut. from βραβεῖον, -ου, τό, "an award for exceptional performance," a "prize" (EVV; BDAG 183a). It occurs elsewhere in the NT only at 1 Cor

9:24, where it also signifies the "prize" in a foot race, typically a wreath of wild olive or celery branches given to a winning runner. The cognate βραβεύς was used of an umpire or official at the games (βραβεύω means "to order, rule, control" [cf. Col 3:15]) (Reumann 540). The imagery would have been familiar in Philippi for champions at the games and, perhaps, for awards granted to civic benefactors (Reumann 556). The "prize" in v. 14 consists of what Paul will gain at the return of Christ, whether understood, narrowly, as the resurrection (cf. v. 11; E. Stauffer *TDNT* 1.638–39), or, more broadly, as the full apprehension of Christ and his benefits (O'Brien 433). Verses 20–21 will fill out the picture (Reumann 558).

Τῆς ἄνω κλήσεως ("the upward/heavenly call" [NRSV, NASB, ESV, cf. NJB]) has been understood in three different ways:

1. The τῆς ἄνω κλήσεως continues the athletic metaphor. The Panhellenic games were organized and presided over by officers called *Hellenodikai*. The victorious athlete was called up to receive his prize from their hands. The summons included the public announcement of the victor, his father's name, and his country (H-M 210–11). But there is no concrete evidence that κλῆσις was ever used in this context (O'Brien 432 n. 76; "fanciful" [Fee 349 n. 49]). The addition of τοῦ θεοῦ ἐν Χριστῷ Ἰησοῦ further problematizes this interpretation.

2. Τῆς ἄνω κλήσεως was an expression Paul's opponents used to refer to being "called up to God" to attain a heavenly existence in this life. Paul counters by asserting that the upward call consists of the prize that comes at the end of the race. Κλήσεως is interpreted as a gen. of appos. ("the [eschatological] prize that is God's call to the life above" [NEB; cf. CEV]), so that what was first described via metaphor (βραβεῖον) is now described without the imagery (τῆς ἄνω κλήσεως).

   a. A parallel is found in Philo: πρὸς γὰρ τὸ θεῖον ἄνω καλεῖσθαι (*Plant.* 23). But the single parallel from Philo (which could be differently interpreted) is insufficient to establish this meaning for Paul's opponents (O'Brien 431).

   b. Also, κλῆσις and καλέω generally look at the believer's calling from the perspective of its beginnings rather than its completion (e.g., 1 Cor 1:9, 26; 1 Thess 2:12; 2 Thess 2:13–14; Eph 4:1; 1 Tim 6:12). It would be odd for Paul to equate the "call" with the "prize" at the end of the race (Fee 349 n. 47; O'Brien 433).

*3. The κλήσεως is the believer's initial call to faith, which promises an ultimate "prize" that will be received only at the eschaton ("the prize promised by God's heavenly call in Christ Jesus" [HCSB; cf. NIV]; "the prize that is the object of (and can only be attained in connection with) the upward call" [BDAG 183a; J. Eckert, *EDNT* 2.243b; Fee 349; Hansen 256; O'Brien 433; Reumann 540; God's call to "the whole work of salvation—with all its implications" [Silva 177]). The gen. is (loosely) subj. (Hansen 256; "indicative of belonging" [O'Brien 432]) or, perhaps, a gen. of "result-means," the call being the means that has brought about the promised result, the prize

(Fee 349 n. 47). This view retains the common Pauline meaning of κλῆσις, "a nearly technical term for God's call of the believer to himself" (Fee 349 n. 49; K. L. Schmidt, *TDNT* 3.492), which occurs at the beginning of the race, when God "brings the one called into fellowship with Christ (1 Cor 1:9) and at the same time into fellowship with other members of his body" (L. Coenen, *NIDNTT* 1.275).

View 3 is clearly superior.

The adv. ἄνω means "heavenward," i.e., "upward," not "from above" (O'Brien 432; "extension toward a goal which is up" [BDAG 92b]; cf. ἐν οὐρανοῖς [3:20]). Reflects common cosmology, still used in popular parlance, which pictures heaven as "above" the earth (Fee 350 n. 50; cf. Acts 2:19, ἐν τῷ οὐρανῷ ἄνω).

Τοῦ θεοῦ (τῆς ἄνω κλήσεως τοῦ θεοῦ) is a subj. gen.; God does the calling (Fee 349 n. 47; Reumann 541).

VERSE 15

Ὅσοι οὖν τέλειοι, τοῦτο φρονῶμεν

Ὅσοι is nom. pl. masc. of the quantitative rel. pron. ὅσος, -η, -ον, "how much (many), as much (many) as" (BDAG 729a; "as many as are" [NASB]; often expressed in Eng. with a rel. pron., "[A]ll/those . . . who are" [most EVV]; ἐσμέν understood [R 395]). Fee rejects the notion that the cstr. with ὅσοι is partitive (i.e., implying that some are τέλειοι and some are not). "Paul intends to include all of them with himself in this imperative." Rom 8:14 (ὅσοι γὰρ πνεύματι θεοῦ ἄγονται, οὗτοι υἱοὶ θεοῦ εἰσιν) is offered as a parallel, where Fee finds the ὅσοι cstr. to be all-inclusive, i.e., all of God's children are led by the Spirit of God (Fee 356). This, however, is to miss the comparative force of ὅσοι (cf. "pert. to a comparative quantity" [BDAG 729b]), which has in view in Rom 8:14 not only οὗτοι υἱοὶ θεοῦ εἰσιν, but also an implied group who are not led by the Spirit of God (cf. vv. 13, 15). In Romans 8, some are led by the Spirit; some are not. In Phil 3:15, some are τέλειοι; some are not. Paul (a) leaves it up to the reader to decide whether he or she fits the category of τέλειοι, (b) includes himself in this group, and (c) proceeds to instruct the τέλειοι accordingly (Reumann 559).

The inferential conj. οὖν (regrettably omitted in RSV, NLT, ESV) and the shift to the 1 pl. mark a turning point in the argument, as Paul now transitions toward the application of the 1 sg. narrative in vv. 4–14 (Fee 355 n. 14; Reumann 541; "therefore" [NASB, HCSB]; "so" [NJB]; "then" [NRSV, NIV]).

BDAG connects τέλειοι (nom. pl. masc. from τέλειος, -α, -ον) with "the mystery religions"; those "initiated into mystic rites" (BDAG 995d–996a; "maybe" [Reumann 559]). It is far better to take τέλειοι in its normal Pauline sense, "mature" (most EVV; "perfect" [NASB]; "pert. to being mature" [BDAG 995c]; G. Delling, *TDNT* 8.76; R. Schippers, *NIDNTT* 2.62; H. Hübner, *EDNT* 3.343b; Hansen 258; 1 Cor 2:6; 14:20; Eph 4:13; Col 1:28; 4:12). The word group that was used in v. 12 to connote "that perfection which occurs at the eschatological consummation" (τετελείωμαι) here means "spiritually mature" (O'Brien 436). A wordplay is clearly intended. By exhorting the τέλειοι to "have this mind-set" (τοῦτο φρονῶμεν [τοῦτο = the content of vv. 12–14]), Paul essentially says, "Let ὅσοι οὖν τέλειοι recognize that οὐ τετελειώμεθα" (F. Selter, C. Brown, *NIDNTT* 2.741; Fee 355; Hansen 258; Wright, *Paul and the Faithfulness of God*, 551; *pace* O'Brien 436).

Φρονῶμεν is 1 pl. pres. act. hortatory (= volitive) subjunc. (R 931; Wallace 465; for φρονέω, see on 1:7; 2:2). The vb. "has to do with a person's whole disposition or direction of life" (O'Brien 437; "be thus minded" [RSV]; "have this attitude" [NASB]; "think this way" [HCSB; ESV]). The 1 pl. shows goodwill toward the Philippians ("No gruff 2nd per. command" [Reumann 559]; "gentle tone of exhortation" [H-M 211]; O'Brien 437). Paul used the same vb. to apply the Christ narrative to the Philippians in 2:5. It seems hardly coincidental that Paul's story corresponds at several crucial points with Christ's (Fee 354; Hansen 258; cf. also Stephen E. Fowl, *The Story of Christ in the Ethics of Paul: An Analysis of the Function of the Hymnic Material in the Pauline Corpus.* JSNT Supplement Series [Sheffield: Sheffield Academic Press, 1990]). The indic. var. φρονοῦμεν (א L 1241, etc.: "As many as are mature, we think this way") represents an attempt to smooth out the text (Fee 352 n. 5) or is, perhaps, an error of sound or sight (H-M 204) ({A} φρονῶμεν [UBS⁵]).

The pron. τοῦτο can be read as a dir. obj. ("have this attitude" [NASB]; "take such a view of things" [NIV]) or adv. acc. ("be thus minded" [RSV]; "think this way" [HCSB]) (Reumann 542). Though some suggest that Paul has in view his whole first-person narrative (vv. 4–14) (Fee 354–57), the τετελείωμαι/τέλειοι wordplay shows that τοῦτο refers primarily to what Paul has emphasized in vv. 12–14, namely, that the full apprehension of Christ and his benefits constitutes a "prize" to be awarded only at the eschaton, at τὴν ἐξανάστασιν τὴν ἐκ νεκρῶν (Reumann 559).

καὶ εἴ τι ἑτέρως φρονεῖτε, καὶ τοῦτο ὁ θεὸς ὑμῖν ἀποκαλύψει

Καὶ εἴ is to be read in a conj. sense ("[and if" [EVV]; common in Paul [e.g., Rom 11:16; 13:9; 1 Cor 6:2]; or adversative [H-M 212, see below]), not concessively (the only two instances in Paul [1 Cor 8:5; Gal 1:8] have contextual indicators indicating concession) (Fee 357 n. 24).

The τι (indef. pron.) can function as (1) an adv. acc. ("in some way") (τι ἑτέρως φρονεῖτε = "you have a somewhat different attitude" [H-M 212]; cf. BDF §137; Reumann 542), or as (2) a dir. obj. ("think differently about anything" [NRSV, HCSB]; "on some point you think differently" [NIV]; "think of" or "regard someth[ing] differ-ently" [BDAG 1065d]).

Ἑτέρως is found only here in the NT and may carry neg. connotations, i.e., not sim-ply "differently" but "otherwise than should be, badly, wrongly" (Silva 187–88, cites LSJ; Epict. *Diss.* 2.16.16; Jos. *Ant.* 1.26).

Commentators differ over the significance of καὶ εἴ τι ἑτέρως φρονεῖτε, καὶ τοῦτο ὁ θεὸς ὑμῖν ἀποκαλύψει:

*1. The cond. sentence continues to address the main point raised in 15a (F. Selter, C. Brown, *NIDNTT* 2.741; Reumann 560):

a. The repetition of φρονέω points not to minor matters but "the right Christian mind-set" (Reumann 560; H-M 212).

b. The adv. ἑτέρως is naturally taken to mean "differently" (1) from what Paul wrote in vv. 12–14 (= τοῦτο [15a]) or, perhaps, (2) from the sentiments outlined in vv. 4–14 (H. W. Beyer, *TDNT* 2.703). In either case a key issue is in view.

c. Divine revelation (ὁ θεὸς ὑμῖν ἀποκαλύψει) would be unnecessary to solve minor disagreements. Ἀποκαλύψει represents a "theologically-important word group" that is never used in the NT to describe human activity or communication (O'Brien 439; Reumann 560; cf. the association of ὁ θεός and ἀποκαλύψεως in Eph 1:17–18, where minor matters are scarcely in view).

d. A "throw away" sentence would make little sense in a context in which Paul has so emphatically rejected wrong conclusions that might be drawn from his personal narrative (note the three disclaimers in vv. 12–13: Οὐχ ὅτι ἤδη ἔλαβον ἢ ἤδη τετελείωμαι . . . οὐ λογίζομαι κατειληφέναι).

2. Καὶ εἴ . . . ἀποκαλύψει is "a kind of aside," "a 'throw away' sentence" (Fee 355, 358) treating minor "inadequacies or inconsistencies" (O'Brien 437–40; Hansen 259). This view is favored by the grammar:

a. We would expect a stronger adversative (e.g., ἀλλ' εἰ καί [1 Cor 7:21; 2 Cor 4:16; Phil 2:17] or εἰ καί [2 Cor 5:16]) if major matters were in view. But the initial καί may be read as an adversative conj. "emphasizing a fact that is surprising but nevertheless true"; tr. "but," rather than "and" (H-M 212; cf. BDAG 495b).

b. There is a switch to the second person here, followed immediately by a return to the first person in v. 16, which makes the direct address sound like "a parenthetical aside" (Hansen 260).

c. Καὶ τοῦτο (v. 15b; the καί has adv. force, "too" [NRSV, NIV]; "also" [RSV, NASB, ESV]; Reumann 543) points to something beyond what was discussed in vv. 12–14 and summarized in the previous τοῦτο (v. 15a). The τοῦτο in καὶ τοῦτο refers, therefore, to the preceding τι, not to the τοῦτο in τοῦτο φρονῶμεν (v. 15a) (O'Brien 437–38).

The evidence is finely balanced, and a decision is not easy. The context tips the scales slightly in favor of view 1. Paul has in mind a major issue.

Ἀποκαλύψει is 3 sg. fut. act. indic. from ἀποκαλύπτω (used 26x in NT, 13x in Paul; the cognate ἀποκάλυψις occurs 18x NT, 13x in Paul). It means "reveal" (NRSV, ESV, HCSB; "make clear/plain" [NIV, NJB]; "divine revelation of certain transcendent secrets" [BDAG 112a]). The word group occurs in the NT in connection with (a) revelation of the righteousness and wrath of God (Rom 1:17, 18), (b) things revealed through the Spirit (1 Cor 2:10), (c) revelations when house churches assemble (1 Cor 14:6, 26, 30), and (d) the revealing of the man of lawlessness (2 Thess 2:3, 6, 8). Paul does not specify how the revelation will occur. The pl. ὑμῖν suggests the ministry of the Spirit through the prophets at house church gatherings (Reumann 561). It may have occurred, however, "in a quiet way as they reflected on the contents of the apostle's letter" (O'Brien 440).

VERSE 16

πλὴν εἰς ὃ ἐφθάσαμεν, τῷ αὐτῷ στοιχεῖν

The adv. πλήν is used as a conj., "breaking off a discussion and emphasizing what is important" (BDAG 826c; BDF §449[2]; R 1187; O'Brien 440; Reumann 543). EVV that begin a new sentence ("Only" [RSV, NIV, ESV]; "In any case" [HCSB]) are to be preferred to those that do not ("however" [NASB]).

The logic is a bit opaque: the rel. clause (εἰς ὃ ἐφθάσαμεν) seems to speak of a point already attained, whereas the main clause (τῷ αὐτῷ στοιχεῖν) implies a "rule" whereby it is reached (G. Fitzer, *TDNT* 9.90; Reumann 543). The point is clear, at any rate: "The Philippians must behave in a manner consistent with what truth they have already received" (Silva 178).

Εἰς ὃ functions as an acc. of reference, "with respect to what we have attained" (Reumann 543; or take εἰς as "toward," indicating "the direction of the Christian's moral movement" [H-M 213]). Since the pronouns ὃ and αὐτῷ have the same referent, most EVV include both in a single expression ("what" [NRSV, NIV, ESV]; "whatever truth" [HCSB]; "the point" [NJB]; but cf. "that same *standard* to which" [NASB], retaining each pron.).

Ἐφθάσαμεν is 1 pl. aor. act. indic. from φθάνω, "to come to or arrive at a particular state" (BDAG 1053d; "attained" [NRSV, ESV, NASB; V. Hasler, *EDNT* 3.422a]). Φθάνω originally meant "to come before, precede" (1 Thess 4:15) but came to be used also in the sense "arrive, come" (2 Cor 10:14) (O'Brien 441).

What is it (ὅ) that "we have attained?" Some suggest the righteousness by faith that comes through the gospel (G. Fitzer, *TDNT* 9.90; cf. Rom 9:31); others, "The stage of their spiritual experience that they have reached" (O'Brien 441). Read in light of the disclaimers of vv. 12–14 and the clause that follows (cf. τῷ αὐτῷ στοιχεῖν), however, εἰς ὃ ἐφθάσαμεν points not to a stage or goal reached but, rather, to a way of life ("how they have already followed Christ" [Fee 360; Reumann 562]). Contextually, ὅ and τῷ αὐτῷ denote "an understanding of the gospel in which the life of the Crucified one is the paradigm for those who would be his followers" (Fee 361; cf. συμμορφιζόμενος τῷ θανάτῳ αὐτοῦ [v. 10]).

The pres. act. inf. στοιχεῖν (from στοιχέω) functions with impv. force ("we must hold on" [BDAG 946d]; BDF §389; Moule 126; Porter 202; R 944, 1,092; T 75, 78; Wallace 608; Reumann 544; cf. Rom 12:15). The pres. tense is rightly understood in context to mark ongoing action ("let us continue" [Reumann 544; R 1,081; T 75]). Στοιχέω means "to be in line with a pers. or thing considered as a standard for one's conduct" (BDAG 946c; "hold true to" [RSV, ESV; E. Plümacher, *EDNT* 3.278d]; "keep living by" [NASB]; "live up to" [NIV]). Originally a military term, "to be in a rank, or series" (suggesting yet another appeal to unity in the letter [H-M 213; O'Brien 442]), στοιχέω would have resonated among the descendents of the military veterans who had established the colony at Philippi (Delling *TDNT* 7.666–67; Reumann 562). Στοιχεῖν marks a progression from mind-set (φρονεῖν [v. 15]) to practice, which v. 17 takes up with περιπατεῖν (O'Brien 442).

The terse clause τῷ αὐτῷ στοιχεῖν (attested in 𝔓¹⁶·⁴⁶ ℵ* A B 6 33 1739 etc.) has generated vars. that add κανόνι (cf. Gal 6:16) and τὸ αὐτὸ φρονεῖν (cf. Phil 2:2) in different configurations (ℵ² D G Ψ 075 *Byz* etc.). Though "obviously secondary" (Fee 352 n. 6; H-M 204; O'Brien 418; Silva 188; UBS⁵ = {A} τῷ αὐτῷ στοιχεῖν), the additions "capture the meaning here in an appropriately Pauline manner" (Bockmuehl 228). Some kind of "rule" or "standard" is implied (cf. ὅσοι τῷ κανόνι τούτῳ στοιχήσουσιν [Gal 6:16]; O'Brien 441–42; τῷ αὐτῷ = dat. of norm or rule [H-M 213; Wallace 158]; H.-H. Esser, *NIDNTT* 2.451–52).

Paul does not specify the content of τῷ αὐτῷ. Some EVV fill in the blank ("that same *standard*" [NASB]; "the progress" [NLT]; "truth" [HCSB]); others do not (RSV, ESV, NIV). See above for the meaning of τῷ αὐτῷ.

FOR FURTHER STUDY

48. Christian Perfection (3:12–16)

Beet, Joseph A. "Christian Perfection. I. The Word 'Perfect' in the New Testament." *Exp* 5th Series. 5 (1897): 30–41.

Dieter, Melvin E., et al. *Five Views on Sanctification*. Grand Rapids: Zondervan, 1987.

Du Plessis, Paul J. *TELEIOS: The Idea of Perfection in the New Testament*. Kampen: Kok, 1959.

Flew, Robert N. *The Idea of Perfection in Christian Theology*. Oxford: Oxford University Press, 1934; New York: Humanities, 1968.

Klein, W. W. *DPL* 699–701.

Schippers, R. *NIDNTT* 2.59–66.

Schnackenburg, Rudolph. "Christian Adulthood according to the Apostle Paul." *CBQ* 25 (1963): 354–70.

*Turner, *Words* 324–39.

49. Athletic Imagery (3:13–14)

See on 1:27–30.

HOMILETICAL SUGGESTIONS

Perfect like an Apostle (3:12–16)

1. We have not yet arrived (vv. 12a & 13a).
2. We press on to reach the goal (vv. 12b & 13b–14).
3. We maintain a mature mind-set (v. 15).
4. We stay the course we are on (v. 16).

People Who Make Progress (3:12–14)

1. People who make progress acknowledge that they are "in process" (vv. 12a & 13a).
2. People who make progress focus on the future instead of the past (v. 13b).
3. People who make progress keep their eyes on the goal (v. 14).

2. RESISTING THE OPPONENTS' FLESHLY BEHAVIOR (3:17–4:1)

17 Συμμιμηταί μου γίνεσθε, ἀδελφοί,
καὶ σκοπεῖτε τοὺς οὕτω περιπατοῦντας
καθὼς ἔχετε τύπον ἡμᾶς.
18 πολλοὶ γὰρ περιπατοῦσιν
οὓς πολλάκις ἔλεγον ὑμῖν, νῦν δὲ καὶ κλαίων λέγω,
τοὺς ἐχθροὺς τοῦ σταυροῦ τοῦ Χριστοῦ,
19 ὧν τὸ τέλος ἀπώλεια,
ὧν ὁ θεὸς ἡ κοιλία καὶ ἡ δόξα ἐν τῇ αἰσχύνῃ αὐτῶν,
οἱ τὰ ἐπίγεια φρονοῦντες.
20 ἡμῶν γὰρ τὸ πολίτευμα ἐν οὐρανοῖς ὑπάρχει,
ἐξ οὗ καὶ σωτῆρα ἀπεκδεχόμεθα
κύριον Ἰησοῦν Χριστόν,

21 ὃς μετασχηματίσει τὸ σῶμα τῆς ταπεινώσεως ἡμῶν
σύμμορφον τῷ σώματι τῆς δόξης αὐτοῦ
κατὰ τὴν ἐνέργειαν τοῦ δύνασθαι αὐτὸν
καὶ ὑποτάξαι αὐτῷ τὰ πάντα.
4:1 Ὥστε, ἀδελφοί μου,
ἀγαπητοὶ καὶ ἐπιπόθητοι,
χαρὰ καὶ στέφανός μου,
οὕτως στήκετε ἐν κυρίῳ, ἀγαπητοί.

Asyndeton begins the paragraph, but the direct exhortation in v. 17 to imitate Paul (as outlined in vv. 7–14) has already been implied by the switch to the 1 pl. at vv. 15–16 (Ὅσοι οὖν τέλειοι, τοῦτο φρονῶμεν . . . εἰς ὃ ἐφθάσαμεν, τῷ αὐτῷ στοιχεῖν) (O'Brien 443).

VERSE 17

Συμμιμηταί μου γίνεσθε, ἀδελφοί

Συμμιμηταί is nom. pl. masc. of συμμιμητής, -οῦ, ὁ, "fellow-imitator" (BDAG 958a; H. Balz, EDNT 3.287c), used only here in Gk. literature. Paul's normal use of the word group lacks the συν- prefix. Possible interpretations:

1. There is no significance in the συν- prefix; συμμιμητής is equivalent to μιμητής ("I want you to follow my example" [CEV]; "pattern your lives after mine" [NLT]; W. Michaelis, TDNT 4.667 n. 13). The prefix seems to be an intentional addition, however, in a term placed in emphatic position at the beginning of the sentence. The contrast with Pauline usage elsewhere (μιμητής [1 Thess 1:6; 2:14; 1 Cor 4:16; 11:1; Eph 5:1]) demands explanation.
2. Συμ- refers to Paul. The Philippians are to join with Paul in imitating Christ.

    a. The other συν- compounds in Philippians include Paul and the readers
      (e.g., συγκοινωνούς [1:7]; συγχαίρω [2:17]).

    b. But for this we would expect the dat. pron. μοι. The gen. μου functions
      more naturally as the obj. of the verbal noun Συμμιμηταί (most EVV;
      H. Balz, *EDNT* 3.287c; Reumann 566; always so with μιμηταί [Hansen
      261 n. 222]).

  *3. The idea is "join with others in following my example" (BDAG 958a; Wallace
     130; Silva 188; Sumney 92).

    a. The emphasis on unity throughout the letter strongly suggests that those
      in view in συμ- are the Philippians themselves ("Join together in follow-
      ing my example" [NIV]; "be united in imitating me" [NJB]; Fee 364–65;
      Hansen 261; H-M 217; O'Brien 445; Reumann 567).

    b. Paul is the obj. of imitation as the sentence proceeds to unfold (cf. καθὼς
      ἔχετε τύπον ἡμᾶς).

View 3 has the most in its favor.

The earliest Christians, coming out of paganism and lacking an easily accessible
body of sacred literature, relied for ethical direction upon the living examples of those
who brought them the gospel (cf. Acts 16:12–40; 1 Thess 2:2, 14) (H-M 219). The pattern in view in συμμιμηταί μου is to be found in vv. 4–16, in summary, Paul's "burning
ambition to know Christ fully in the power of his resurrection and the fellowship of his
sufferings, together with his determination to press on so as to finish the race and win
the prize" (O'Brien 444).

That a person of Paul's stature would exhort others to imitate him has become a
stumbling block among postmodern interpreters, numbers of whom work with a her-
meneutic of suspicion toward power and authority. Feminist and postcolonial readings
of Paul's imitation theme are stridently negative, seeing Paul valorizing sameness over
difference and shoring up power via "the hierarchy Christ–Paul–Christians" (Castelli,
Imitating Paul, 96; obedience to Paul's apostolic authority is "primarily" in view
[W. Michaelis, *TDNT* 4.668, 671–72]).

These interpretations should not be summarily dismissed since they serve to remind
us of the potentially dark side of power and authority, the bitter fruits of which surface
far too often in our churches today (Hellerman, *Embracing Shared Ministry: Power
and Status in the Early Church and Why It Matters Today* [Grand Rapids: Kregel,
2013]). With respect to Paul, however, these negative readings of the imitation *topos*
prove to be overly reductionistic since they ignore much evidence to the contrary (see
Park's extended critique of Castelli's methodology and conclusions [82–116]):

    a. Paul emphatically reiterates that he himself is still "a work in prog-
      ress" (ἐγὼ ἐμαυτὸν οὐ λογίζομαι κατειληφέναι [v. 13]). The mind-set (cf.
      φρονῶμεν . . . φρονεῖτε [v. 15]) in view in συμμιμηταί μου γίνεσθε is one
      that passionately pursues the knowledge of Christ along the characteristi-
      cally Christian road of perseverance through suffering (vv. 10, 14–15).

    b. The assertion that Paul's imitation theme serves to reinscribe hierarchies
      of power stumbles over (1) the presence of the markedly nonhierarchical

sibling metaphor, ἀδελφοί, in the same sentence (and 8x elsewhere in Philippians; "a term of affection" [Reumann 590]; a "humble term" [Silva 179]), and (2) the fact that Paul includes others, along with himself, as examples to follow (imitation is still in view in v. 17b: "notice those who conduct themselves thus, i.e., in order to imitate them" [BDAG 931a, on σκοπέω]).

  c. Finally, the Pauline archetype ultimately goes back to the mind-set of Christ (2:5–11), a mind-set that places power, status—indeed, all personal resources—in the service of the needs of one's fellow-human beings.

Γίνεσθε is 2 pl. pres. mid. impv. from γίνομαι. The idea that the pres. tense "strikes the note of continuing on" (Reumann 590) should not be pressed since Paul uses the 2 pl. impv. of γίνομαι in the pres. exclusively (17x; but cf. 1 Pet 1:15).

καὶ σκοπεῖτε τοὺς οὕτω περιπατοῦντας καθὼς ἔχετε τύπον ἡμᾶς

The vb. σκοπεῖτε is 2 pl. pres. act. impv., from σκοπέω, "pay careful attention to" (BDAG 931a; "observe" [NRSV, HCSB]; "keep your eyes on" [ESV, NIV]; "close observation, fixed attention" [H-M 218]). The vb. could be used negatively (e.g., σκοπεῖν τοὺς τὰς διχοστασίας . . . ποιοῦντας [Rom 16:17]) or positively ("to consider something critically and then to hold something before one as a model on the basis of inspection" [E. Fuchs, *TDNT* 7.415]; Reumann 567). Paul may intend a contrast with the threefold βλέπετε in v. 2 (Silva 179).

Περιπατοῦντας is acc. pl. masc. of the pres. act. ptc. of περιπατέω, lit., "to walk around," fig., "to conduct one's life," "live" (BDAG 803b–c); subst. ptc. dir. obj. (Porter 183; Wallace 661; "those who walk/live" [most EVV]; "those who act" [NJB]). Περιπατέω is Paul's primary vb. (32x) for paraenesis ("the walk of life" [Reumann 568]; cf. περιπατοῦσιν [v. 18]), deriving from his Jewish heritage, where God's people are to "walk in the ways of the Lord" (G. Bertram, *TDNT* 5.942–43; the LXX often uses πορεύομαι for this idiom [but cf. 2 Kgs 20:3; Prov 8:20]). The fig. meaning is rare in nonbiblical Gk. (Fee 365 n. 13). Those in view likely include itinerants traveling along the Egnatian Way. Philippi was a full day's walk from Neapolis along this east-west thoroughfare, so the Philippians likely provided Christian hospitality for numbers of travelers (Fee 366). Their religious credentials might impress members of the Philippian church. Paul emphasizes the way they "live" or "act" (περιπατοῦντας)—not "letters of recommendation" (2 Cor 3:1–3)—as the test of a model to be emulated.

The form οὕτω is only here in Paul (usually οὕτως [BDF §21]). The οὕτω-καθώς cstr. can be understood in one of two ways:

  1. Take καθώς as causal ("since, in so far as" [BDAG 494a]; cf. BDF §453[2]; cf. Phil 1:7; Silva 188). Οὕτω then looks backwards, and the καθώς clause supplies the reason for two things the Philippians are supposed to do: "Imitate me and mark those who *thus* walk (i.e., in imitation of me), *because* you have an example in us (i.e. in them and me)."

*2. Take οὕτω and καθώς together: "Imitate me, and mark those who *thus* walk *as* you have an example in us" (cf. EVV; O'Brien 448–49; Reumann 568).

View 2 preserves the common correlative sense of οὕτω(ς)-καθώς.

The vb. ἔχω (2 pl. pres. act. indic.) is follwed by a dir. obj. (ἡμᾶς) and predicate acc. (τύπον) (also called an obj.-complement cstr. [Wallace 184]); ἔχω τινὰ τύπον means "have someone as an example" (BDAG 420d; cf. BDF §157 [1]).

The complement is acc. sg. masc., from τύπος, -ου, ὁ, glossed by BDAG as "example, pattern" (1020b; "example" [most EVV; L. Goppelt, *TDNT* 8.249]; "model" [NIV]; in ethics a "model" = an "example" [Spicq 3.384–87]). Τύπος and μιμηταί also occur together in 1 Thess 1:6–7. *Exempla* (examples, models, patterns, prototypes) were a necessary part of ancient rhetoric. They were taken from myth, history, drama, family ancestors, and superiors in government (Reumann 585).

The pl. obj. ἡμᾶς (acc. masc.; "us" [most EVV]) can be read (1) as a literary pl., referring solely to Paul (supported by the sg. τύπον [H-M 218]; cf. "the example you have from me" [NJB]), or, more likely, (2) to include both Paul and associates such as Timothy and Epaphroditus (Fee 365 n. 14; O'Brien 450). Although common in ancient Gk. (BDF §280), Paul does not often use the literary pl. (Moule 118–19; O'Brien 450). The change from sg. (μου) to pl. (ἡμᾶς), moreover, suggests a corresponding change in referents, and Paul elsewhere associates his colleagues with himself in his ministry (Phil 1:1; 2:23; 2:25–30) (O'Brien 450; Sumney 92). Since most of us study the letter in small pieces, it is easy to forget that just a few minutes earlier—in the actual reading of the letter—both Timothy and Epaphroditus were set before the Philippians as associates who share Paul's Christlike mind-set (Fee 362 n. 3; Hansen 263).

VERSE 18

πολλοὶ γὰρ περιπατοῦσιν οὓς πολλάκις ἔλεγον ὑμῖν

A detailed profile of those described in vv. 18–19 continues to elude interpreters (see below, on v. 19). We can, however, note the following with some confidence:

    a. They are not part of the Philippian church. Paul would not so sharply castigate "many" (πολλοί) in a small congregation, after he has prayed for and commended "all" of them earlier in the letter (1:4 [πάντων ὑμῶν], 7 [πάντων ὑμῶν . . . πάντας ὑμᾶς], 8 [πάντας ὑμᾶς]). The repeated warnings (πολλάκις + impf. ἔλεγον), moreover, and the contrast between οὓς and ὑμῖν serves to distinguish the πολλοί from the community itself (Fee 368; O'Brien 452; Reumann 570; Paul normally refers to those within a church with an indef. rel. pron. [Fee 368 n. 4]).

    b. The πολλοί claimed to be Christians. Neither pagan opponents nor non-Christian Jews are in view: (1) Paul uses the characteristic vb. περιπατέω to describe the lifestyles of both positive (v. 17) and negative (v. 18) examples (O'Brien 452); (2) it is unlikely that Paul would have been moved to tears by the fate or behavior of pagan opponents (cf. 1:28). He generally

reserves weeping for professing Christians (Fee 369; Hansen 265; O'Brien
452 [1 Cor 7:30; Rom 12:15; 2 Cor 2:4; 2 Tim 1:4; Acts 20:19, 31]).

c. The opposition of the πολλοί to τοῦ σταυροῦ τοῦ Χριστοῦ (v. 18) appears
to be ethical, not ideological (unless, as is unlikely, Judaizers are in view
[see below, on v. 19]) (Hansen 264–65). Although ethics and theology are
mutually informing categories for Paul, the περιπατέω terminology (v. 18),
as well as the more specific descriptions in v. 19 (ὧν ὁ θεὸς ἡ κοιλία καὶ
ἡ δόξα ἐν τῇ αἰσχύνῃ αὐτῶν), relate more immediately to behavior than to
theological issues, e.g., "antipathy to atonement" (pace Reumann 593).

Πολλοί is nom. pl. masc., from πολύς, πολλή, πολύ, used subst., "'many,' i.e., persons" (cf. BDAG 848a). If πολλοί is somewhat rhetorical, the threat is nonetheless
real (Silva 188). Reumann attempts to capture the alliterative paronomasia (πολλοὶ
. . . περιπατοῦσιν . . . πολλάκις) in Eng.: "the lot of them, how they live, lots of time"
(Reumann 593).

The γάρ ("For" [EVV]) is a "marker of clarification," explaining the "why" of v. 17:
they need to imitate Paul and those who live like him precisely because there are others
who walk contrary to that pattern (BDAG 189d; H-M 220; Reumann 569); "negative
examples clamor for attention and lead to destruction" (Hansen 263).

EVV generally gloss περιπατοῦσιν (3 pl. pres. act. indic.) the same as περιπατοῦντας
(v. 17): "walk"/"walk" (NASB, ESV); "live"/"live" (NRSV, NIV, HCSB); but
"act"/"behave" (NJB).

The rel. pron. οὕς (acc. pl. masc.) serves as the obj. of both ἔλεγον and λέγω and
anticipates the acc. τοὺς ἐχθρούς (Reumann 569; R 718; Wallace 183). Πολλάκις
("often" [EVV]) is an adv. meaning "many times, often, frequently" (BDAG 846b).

The vb. λέγω is used two times in v. 18 (1 sg. imperf. act. indic. and 1 sg. pres. act.
indic.) in the sense "inform" or "bring a report," i.e., about οὕς/τοὺς ἐχθρούς to ὑμῖν
(dat. pl. masc. indir. obj.) (BDAG 590a; "have . . . told" [NRSV, NIV, HCSB]; "have
warned" [NJB; cf. CEV]). The cstr. (impf. ἔλεγον + πολλάκις) emphasizes repeated
past action (O'Brien 451 n. 31; Reumann 569). The warnings may have been given in
person, in lost letters, or both (O'Brien 451).

νῦν δὲ καὶ κλαίων λέγω

Νῦν is a temp. adv. ("now" [EVV]). The δέ can be taken as a simple coordinating
conj. ("and" [most EVV]), or in an adversative sense, contrasting νῦν + pres. λέγω
with πολλάκις + impf. ἔλεγον in the previous clause (Reumann 569); καί is generally
read ascensively ("even" [NRSV, NASB, NIV, ESV]), rather than in an additive sense
("again" [NLT, HCSB]).

The nom. sg. masc. pres. act. ptc. κλαίων (from κλαίω; "weeping" [NASB]; lam-
entation and audible grief [H-M 222]; "strong inner emotion" [K. Rengstorf, TDNT
3.722]) is a ptc. of manner (Wallace 628). Most tr. as adv. prep. phrase: "with tears
(in my eyes)" (EVV; BDAG 545d; cf. BDF §418; H. Balz, EDNT 2.294b; Reumann
569). Paul seldom shows his emotions, especially when dealing with adversaries.
Where strong emotions do surface, they show (a) Paul's tenderness in dealing with

his converts (Acts 20:31; 2 Cor 2:4), or (b) his concern for the people of Israel (Rom 9:1–5; 10:1). Paul weeps here for the perilous condition of πολλοί who claimed to be followers of Jesus but lived as "enemies of the cross of Christ," and for the potential threat they posed to the church in Philippi (O'Brien 451).

τοὺς ἐχθροὺς τοῦ σταυροῦ τοῦ Χριστοῦ

The adj. ἐχθρός, -ά, -όν (acc. pl. masc.) can be used pass., "hated," or (here) actively, "hating, hostile," with the "gen. of that which is the obj. of the enmity" (BDAG 419b–d; "enemies" [EVV]; M. Wolter, *EDNT* 2.94a). The art. turns the adj. into a subst. and makes the group definite (Reumann 570; "marks the class of people represented" [O'Brien 451]; "*the* enemies" [H-M 223]). Though formally in appos. to οὕς (and thus acc.), EVV trans. according to sense, reading τοὺς ἐχθρούς as if it is in appos. to the nom. πολλοί ("many live as enemies" [NIV, HCSB]; "many . . . walk as enemies" [ESV]).

Some see in τοῦ σταυροῦ "a colorful way of saying Christ suffered and died for sins." Τοὺς ἐχθρούς are then understood as enemies "on theological issues," who reject the idea of Jesus' sacrifice of atonement (Reumann 593, 595). Both (a) the way Paul draws upon σταυρός imagery elsewhere (1 Cor 1:18; Gal 6:12), and (b) the description to follow (v. 19), suggest, instead, that behavior—not theology—is at stake in vv. 18–19. The enemies "spurn the cross" by walking (περιπατοῦσιν) contrary to the pattern Paul set for them in 3:7–14 (J. Schneider, *TDNT* 7.576; Fee 370; Hansen 264–65). In particular, the obj. gen. τοῦ σταυροῦ likely indicates that those in view are unwilling to embrace suffering as a key component of the Christian life (Hansen 265; cf. θανάτου δὲ σταυροῦ [2:8] and συμμορφιζόμενος τῷ θανάτῳ αὐτοῦ [3:10]). For Roman attitudes toward crucifixion, see on σταυροῦ (2:8).

VERSE 19

ὧν τὸ τέλος ἀπώλεια

The rel. pron. ὧν is gen. pl. masc. ("whose" [NASB]). Most EVV retain the poss. but start a new sentence ("Their" [NRSV, NIV, HCSB]). Others recast the cstr. ("They are destined to be lost" [NJB]; "[T]hey are headed for destruction/hell!" [CEV; NLT]).

Τὸ τέλος ἀπώλεια (supply a copulative vb.) is the first of four characteristics of "the enemies." The first three are linked to v. 18 by a gen. rel. pron. (2x); the fourth reverts to the nom. (οἱ τὰ ἐπίγεια φρονοῦντες), changing the cstr. (Fee 372 n. 37; Reumann 570).

The noun τέλος, -ους, τό means "end" (NASB, HCSB, ESV), and is used either (a) of simple "termination, cessation, close, conclusion," or, as here, (b) in a telic sense, "the goal toward which a movement is being directed," "goal, outcome" (BDAG 998a-d; "destiny" [NIV; cf. CEV, NLT]; "end result," "final destiny" [G. Delling, *TDNT* 8.55; H. Hübner, *EDNT* 3.348a]; O'Brien 455; Reumann 570). Some suggest wordplay with τέλειοι (v. 15) (Fee 370 n. 34; Hansen 265; O'Brien 455; Reumann 570).

PHILIPPIANS 3:19

The pred. nom. ἀπώλεια (nom. sg. fem.) means "destruction, ruin, annihilation" (BDAG 127a; "destruction" [most EVV]; "eternal destruction" [A. Oepke, *TDNT* 1.397]) and is Paul's normal antonym for σωτηρία (see on 1:28) ("the eternal destiny of those outside of Christ" [Fee 371 n. 35]; "hell" [CEV]). The term is rare in secular Gk. but common in the LXX (A. Oepke, *TDNT* 1.396–97). Paul places the description of their destiny first in his fourfold list for rhetorical effect (Fee 371). Their τέλος is the same as that of the pagan adversaries of 1:28.

ὧν ὁ θεὸς ἡ κοιλία καὶ ἡ δόξα ἐν τῇ αἰσχύνῃ αὐτῶν

The professing Christians introduced with πολλοί, and subsequently identified as τοὺς ἐχθροὺς τοῦ σταυροῦ τοῦ Χριστοῦ (v. 18) are now described by a series of expressions, two of which (κοιλία and αἰσχύνη) continue to elude scholarly consensus.

The meaning of δόξα is relatively straightforward: "fame, recognition, renown, prestige" (BDAG 257d; "their/they glory [is] in their shame" [most EVV]; "repute, honor" [G. Kittel, *TDNT* 2.237]; Sumney 94). Some see irony: Paul uses δόξα in anticipation of the phrase σύμμορφον τῷ σώματι τῆς δόξης αὐτοῦ (v. 21). Not only are the πολλοί not destined for glory (rather, ἀπώλεια), what glory they have in the present lies precisely in what should be for them a matter of shame (Fee 373).

The debated expressions κοιλία and αἰσχύνη are best taken together, as mutually informing (Fee 372 n. 37). See the treatments in O'Brien (454–57) and Reumann (571–74) for various nuances of (and less likely alternatives to) the following views:

1. Paul has Judaizers in view. Κοιλία is a swipe at their preoccupation with table fellowship and the food laws (H-M 224; so most church fathers; "bitter scorn on Judaizers with their belly god" [J. Behm, *TDNT* 3.788]). Αἰσχύνη refers to the circumcised penis (cf. 1 Cor 12:23) (H-M 224).

   a. But nowhere is κοιλία so used in Jewish or Greco-Roman literature (Reumann 572).

   b. Also, Paul never considers circumcision shameful—just irrelevant (Fee 373 n. 46; O'Brien 457; Reumann 573).

   c. Finally, Paul is "forthright about this issue elsewhere" (Fee 372).

*2. Κοιλία and αἰσχύνη characterize a libertine party who interpreted freedom in Christ as license to gratify the lusts of the flesh, either narrowly, in terms of gluttony, or, more broadly, i.e., fleshly desires in general ("imprisonment to the particular nature and constraint of bodily existence in this world" [F. G. Untergassmair, *EDNT* 2.301c]; cf. "appetite" [NASB, NLT]).

   a. Κοιλία lit. denotes "the digestive tract in its fullest extent," especially "the body's receptacle for aliments," thus, "belly" (NRSV, ESV) or "stomach(s)" (NIV, NJB, CEV, HCSB) (BDAG 550d). The "stomach" (usually γαστήρ) is used by Greco-Roman writers as a metonymy for gluttony and the like; so Seneca refers to people who are "slaves of their bellies" (*Ben.* 7.26) (Fee 372 n. 38). The closest ancient parallel comes from Euripides, where Cyclops says, "I offer sacrifice . . . to this belly (γαστρί) of mine, the greatest of deities" (Reumann 571).

b. Aristocratic excess at the table was a common practice in the Greco-Roman world, one which Paul himself had to address in Corinth, where the rich feasted on delicacies before workers or slaves could get there (Reumann 571; cf. 1 Cor 11:17–34).

c. Κοιλία includes the "womb, uterus" (BDAG 550d), so sexual immorality may be in view, in addition to gluttony ("unbridled sensuality, whether gluttony or sexual licentiousness" [J. Behm, *TDNT* 3.788 citing but rejecting this view]; O'Brien 456 n. 72; Christians who "have taken Paul's view of 'justification by faith' to a libertine conclusion" [Fee 375]).

d. Αἰσχύνη (dat. sg. fem., from αἰσχύνη, -ης, ἡ) can mean either (a) public "shame" or "disgrace" that a person experiences (BDAG 30a; R. Bultmann, *TDNT* 1.189), or (b) "a shameful deed" (BDAG 30a; A. Horstmann *EDNT* 1.42d; Reumann 573). The latter idea is in view here ("they glory in what they should think shameful" [NJB]; cf. ἐφ' οἷς νῦν ἐπαισχύνεσθε [Rom 6:21]), perhaps with special reference to sexual immorality ("disgrace, but in such a way that there is a play on the sexual sense of αἰσχύνη" [R. Bultmann, *TDNT* 1.190]; "Most likely" [Reumann 595]). The word group is used in the LXX of nakedness, uncovered sexual organs, of which one should be ashamed (e.g., Gen 2:25; Exod 20:26; Lev 20:17; cf. 1 Cor 12:23). An alternative reading, which takes τῇ αἰσχύνῃ αὐτῶν to refer to shame at final judgment (common in the LXX), conflicts with the fact that current behavior is emphasized in the present context (ὁ θεὸς ἡ κοιλία; οἱ τὰ ἐπίγεια φρονοῦντες; περιπατέω terminology) (*pace* O'Brien 457; Silva 181–82).

e. The progression in Philippians 3—from (1) the rejection of legalistic righteousness (vv. 4–8), to (2) trust in Christ (vv. 9–11), to (3) a warning against licentiousness (vv. 18–19)—is a familiar one in Pauline theology (Bockmuehl 232; cf. Galatians).

f. In reply the letter lacks any indication elsewhere of a libertine threat (Fee 372).

View 2 is arguably superior, though the lack of antilibertine polemic elsewhere in Philippians should give us pause. Where we land on κοιλία and αἰσχύνη, moreover, directly informs our understanding of the identity of "the enemies of the cross." We may at the outset dismiss readings of 3:2, 12–16, and 18–19 that refer all three passages to a single party (*pace* H-M 221). Problems surrounding a Judaizing interpretation of κοιλία and αἰσχύνη (view 1, above) suggest a different group in vv. 18–19 than those mentioned in v. 2. Nor can vv. 15–19 be read as characterizing a single group of opponents. Paul addresses insiders in vv. 15–16 (cf. 1 pl. φρονῶμεν and ἐφθάσαμεν), outsiders in vv. 18–19. The rest of Philippians 3, then, offers little help for further identifying those in view in vv. 18–19.

A bit of historical imagination readily allows us to envision a social context that might have supported the libertine behaviors reflected in v. 19. The church in Philippi was one among a number of nonelite religious associations in the colony that shared meals together as part of their regular meetings. The pagan gatherings were known to involve gluttony and immorality, including sexual license (cf. κοιλία and αἰσχύνη; Reumann 576–77, 594). And because the associations replicated, in miniature, the *cursus honorum* of the broader municipality in Philippi, they also provided opportunity for those of relatively superior social status to flaunt their δόξα (Hellerman 100–106). In 1 Corinthians 11, for example, Paul confronts both social posturing (vv. 18–19) and bodily indulgence (v. 21) at community gatherings. It is not hard to imagine one of the house churches at Philippi adopting such practices and justifying them by means of a libertine interpretation of the gospel.

Most EVV read ἡ κοιλία and ἡ δόξα as distinct subjs., each with an understood copula (e.g., "their god is their stomach; their glory is in their shame" [HCSB]). It is also possible to take (a) ἡ κοιλία καὶ ἡ δόξα together (they are governed by a single rel. pron.) as a single subj., (b) ὁ θεός as pred., and (c) ἐν τῇ αἰσχύνῃ αὐτῶν as modifier (H-M 225; "artificial" [Silva 189]): "whose stomach and glory are their god in their shameful activities"—an apt description of the practices of a typical Greco-Roman association in the colony.

οἱ τὰ ἐπίγεια φρονοῦντες

Φρονοῦντες (nom. pl. masc. pres. act. ptc.) contrasts with φρονῶμεν (v. 15a), as τὰ ἐπίγεια with ἐν οὐρανοῖς (vv. 20–21) (O'Brien 457). Again, φρονέω points to "basic aims and inward disposition" (O'Brien 458). "They do not simply 'think about' earthly things; their 'minds are set on' such things" (Fee 374; most EVV). The subst. ptc. clause can be taken (with little difference in meaning):

1. as a disconnected nom. with explanatory force, a cry of disappointment to climax Paul's description: "Men whose minds are set on earthly things!" (Lightfoot 156);
2. as a cstr. according to sense, referring to the logical subj. for what immediately precedes ("I am talking about those who are set upon the things of this world" [NAB]; BDF §136[1]; 137[3]; O'Brien 458); or
3. as syntactically connected to πολλοί (v. 18) (R 413; Fee 368 n. 26).

The dir. obj. ἐπίγεια (acc. pl. neut. adj., used subst.) "pert[ains] to earthly things, with implication of personal gratification," i.e., "worldly things" (BDAG 369a; "earthly things" [most EVV]; "that which is temporal and transient" [O'Brien 458]). "To the degree that the earth is the place of sin, ἐπίγειος acquires a subsidiary moral sense" (H. Sasse, *TDNT* 1.681). The ἐπίγεια/οὐρανοῖς (vv. 19/20) contrast closely resembles Paul's Spirit-flesh contrast elsewhere (O'Brien 458; see esp. Rom 8:5–6, where the φρον- word group also occurs; τὰ ἐπίγεια = τὰ τῆς σαρκός [E. Schweizer, *TDNT* 7.131 n. 264]). Given the wordplay elsewhere in the passage, this fourth and final characterization may be an ironic reversal of the enemies' claim to be heavenly minded. They may have boasted, τὰ ἄνω τὰ ἐπουράνια φρονοῦμεν. Instead, they are οἱ τὰ ἐπίγεια φρονοῦντες (O'Brien 459).

VERSE 20

ἡμῶν γὰρ τὸ πολίτευμα ἐν οὐρανοῖς ὑπάρχει

Verses 20–21, which contrast Paul and the Philippians with "the enemies of the cross," contain a series of striking verbal and conceptual parallels to 2:6–11 (H-M 229; Fee 382):

3:20–21	2:6–11
σύμμορφον (3:21)	μορφῇ/μορφήν (2:6, 7)
ὑπάρχει (3:20)	ὑπάρχων (2:6)
μετασχηματίσει (3:21)	σχήματι (2:7)
ταπεινώσεως (3:21)	ἐταπείνωσεν (2:8)
δύνασθαι . . . ὑποτάξαι . . . τὰ πάντα (3:21)	πᾶν γόνυ κάμψῃ (2:10)
κύριον Ἰησοῦν Χριστόν (3:20)	κύριος Ἰησοῦς Χριστός (2:11)
δόξης (3:21)	δόξαν (2:11)

Language from the semantic field of honor and shame permeates both passages. The theme of "abasement" and "exaltation," for both the believer and for Christ, is at the heart of the parallel (H-M 230). Some see vv. 20–21 as a Christological hymn inserted by Paul at this point in the letter (H-M 228–29). Few are convinced, however, that vv. 20–21 are pre-Pauline.

The 1 pl. gen. pron. ἡμῶν is emphatic by position ("the strongest kind of contrast" [Fee 378 n. 14]; "τὸ γὰρ ἡμ. πολ. was not sufficient" [BDF §284(2)]; T 190; H-M 231; Reumann 575; Silva 189; cf. the "them-us" contrast in vv. 2–3 [ἡμεῖς γάρ ἐσμεν ἡ περιτομή]).

The contrast introduced in v. 20 had led most EVV to render γάρ as "But." There is no evidence, however, for an adversative γάρ (Fee 377–78 n. 13; Runge 51–54), so we should tr. "for" (NASB). O'Brien connects γάρ to v. 19, but it is hard to see how "our commonwealth . . . in heaven" can in any sense explain the worldly mind-set (οἱ τὰ ἐπίγεια φρονοῦντες) of the πολλοί. A better solution takes γάρ with v. 17 (note the return to the first pl. with ἡμῶν), providing a second reason why the Philippians should pattern their lives after Paul and those like him. This clause (ἡμῶν γάρ [v. 20]) thus further explains Paul's command in the primary clause (v. 17), by way of an ἐπίγεια/ οὐρανοῖς contrast with the intervening γάρ clause (πολλοὶ γάρ [v. 18]) (Fee 378, cf. n. 13; Hansen 268; Silva 183):

17   Συμμιμηταί μου γίνεσθε . . . καθὼς ἔχετε τύπον ἡμᾶς.
18–19   πολλοὶ γὰρ περιπατοῦσιν . . . οἱ τὰ ἐπίγεια φρονοῦντες
20   ἡμῶν γὰρ τὸ πολίτευμα ἐν οὐρανοῖς ὑπάρχει κτλ.

Πολίτευμα is nom. sg. neut. from πολίτευμα, -ατος, τό; only here in the NT. The tr. "citizenship" (NIV, NRSV, HCSB) is one of the least attested meanings for the term (O'Brien 460; Reumann 576). Πολίτευμα is commonly used, instead, of a political entity, a "commonwealth, state" (BDAG 845d; RSV; MM 525d; H. Strathmann, *TDNT* 6.535; U. Hutter, *EDNT* 3.130a; Fee 378–79; O'Brien 460). Appeal is made by some to πολίτευμα as a term for "Jewish political enclaves in Greco-Roman cities like Alexandria," with which Paul was certainly familiar (Reumann 576). The background for πολίτευμα here, however, is Roman, not Jewish. Founded as a Roman colony, with Latin as its official language, Philippi was a miniature Rome, with an administration that reflected that of the mother city in almost every way. Citizens of Philippi were citizens of Rome and proud of it (see on πολιτεύεσθε [1:27]). Paul reminds the Philippians that they belong, instead, to "a heavenly commonwealth, that is, their state and constitutive government is in heaven, and as its citizens they are to reflect its life" (O'Brien 461; Hansen 269).

Πολίτευμα ἐν οὐρανοῖς ὑπάρχει has been interpreted by some to refer to a "colony of heaven" that has been established on earth, in Philippi (BDAG 845d cites Dibelius). Paul, however, explicitly situates τὸ πολίτευμα not on earth but "in heaven" (ἐν οὐρανοῖς). Were it otherwise, we might expect πολίτευμα οὐρανῶν ἐπὶ τῆς γῆς ("a colony of heaven on earth") (O'Brien 460; MM 526a; H. Strathmann, *TDNT* 6.535; Fee 378 n. 17). Although the tr. "colony" no longer attracts serious adherents, the effects of the imagery are close to Paul's point in the passage: "Just as Philippi was a colony of Rome, whose citizens thereby exemplified the life of Rome in the province of Macedonia, so the citizens of the 'heavenly commonwealth' were to function as a colony of heaven in that outpost of Rome" (Fee 379).

The pl. οὐρανοῖς ("heaven" [EVV; BDAG 738c; BDF §141(1); R 408]) is a Semiticism, via the LXX. Here the concept is sg., as indicated by the sg. rel. pron., which most likely goes with οὐρανοῖς, not with τὸ πολίτευμα (H. Traub, *TDNT* 5.513; 523 n. 207; Fee 378 n. 15; O'Brien 461). Οὐρανός signifies the dwelling place of God in both OT and Gk. thought (Reumann 575). Note the parallel in 1 Thess 1:10: ἀναμένειν τὸν υἱὸν αὐτοῦ ἐκ τῶν οὐρανῶν.

Ὑπάρχει ("is" [most EVV]; "[We] are" [CEV, NLT]) is 3 sg. pres. act. indic., from ὑπάρχω (see on 2:6), "to exist, be present" (BDAG 1029d; does not simply = εἰμί, but "emphasizes the actual existence" [Fee 379 n. 18]; "really exists" [Reumann 597]). This is the "already" of Paul's eschatology. The contrast between this clause and the preceding (οἱ τὰ ἐπίγεια φρονοῦντες [v. 19]) is between earthly and heavenly spheres of present existence (cf. Col. 3:1–2), not between the present and the future. The next clause (ἐξ οὗ καὶ σωτῆρα ἀπεκδεχόμεθα κτλ.) moves to the "not yet" (Fee 379–80; O'Brien 461).

ἐξ οὗ καὶ σωτῆρα ἀπεκδεχόμεθα κύριον Ἰησοῦν Χριστόν

The prep. phrase ἐξ οὗ (ἐκ + gen. sg. masc. rel. pron.; ἐκ becomes ἐξ before rough breathing) is variously tr. ("from it" [RSV, ESV]; "from which" [NASB, HCSB]; "from there" [NIV, NJB, NRSV, CEV]). For the pl. antecedent, see above on οὐρανοῖς. The καί is generally rendered "and" (most EVV; "also" [NASB, HCSB]), but may, instead, mean "indeed," intensifying the emphasis on heaven (Reumann 577, 597).

Σωτῆρα (-ῆρος, ὁ, acc. sg. masc.) means "savior, deliverer, preserver" (BDAG 985b; "Savior" [most EVV]) is used only of God (8x) or Christ (16x) in the NT. Elsewhere σωτήρ is used (1) as a title of honor for deserving individuals (e.g., Josephus is εὐργέτης καὶ σωτήρ of Galilee [Jos. Vit. 244, 249]); (2) in the LXX of various "saviors" the Lord raised up for Israel (Judg 3:9, 15) but, especially, of the Lord himself, the ultimate source of deliverance (Deut 32:15; 1 Chr 16:35; Isa 45:15; often in Psalms); (3) as a common title for Greek gods who deliver, protect, or heal a πόλις and its citizens; (4) of (deified) rulers, first in the Greek East (e.g., Ptolemy 1 Soter [323–285 BC]: Πτολεμαῖος καὶ Βερενίκη Θεοὶ Σωτῆρες); later, Roman emperors in the imperial cult (on Rome and emperor worship, see Wright, *Paul and the Faithfulness of God*, 279–346). One inscription from 9 BC from Priene in Asia Minor, for example, identifies "the birthday of the god Augustus" as "the beginning of the good tidings for the world," claiming that "Providence . . . sent him as savior (σωτήρ), both for us and for our descendants." An AD 48 inscription in Ephesus designates Julius Caesar as visible "god and political savior of human life"; Nero is "savior and benefactor of world" (MM 621d; H-M 233). Paul rarely uses σωτήρ in his earlier letters (elsewhere only in Eph 5:23 and 10x in the Pastorals). Given the centrality of the imperial cult in Roman Philippi, and the reference to τὸ πολίτευμα ἐν οὐρανοῖς in the previous clause, an "anti-Caesar overtone" is almost certainly intended (Reumann 598; Fee 381; Hansen 270; Witherington 99–102; *pace* K. H. Schelkle [*EDNT* 3.326c–d]). Paul, drawing upon his Jewish heritage, thus employs a rich OT title for Yahweh (see meaning 2, above) that at once "echoes, and hence deeply subverts, language in common use among Roman imperial subjects to describe Caesar" (N. T. Wright, *What Saint Paul Really Said* [Grand Rapids: Eerdmanns, 1997], 88).

The lack of art. does not mean "a savior," as if any would do, but is to be understood in a qualitative sense, "he will come *as* Savior" (H-M 232; cf. BDF §252[2]). Fee sees here "a variation" of Colwell's rule, that "a definite predicate noun that precedes the verb is usually anarthrous (in this case a definite direct object, followed by an apposition, seems to function analogously)" (Fee 380–81 n. 23).

Ἀπεκδέχομαι (1 pl. pres. mid. indic.) appears for the first time in Gk. literature in 1 Cor 1:7. It was probably coined by someone in the early church (Fee 380 n. 22). The rare compound (intensifying ἐκδέχομαι with ἀπό) means to "eagerly await/wait for" (NIV, NASB, HCSB; BDAG 100d; less satisfying are "await" [RSV, ESV] and "are expecting" [NJB, NRSV]). It describes the "earnest desire for the second coming of Christ" (H-M 232; M. E. Glasswell, *EDNT* 1.407c–d; 6x in this sense in Paul: Rom 8:19, 23, 25; 1 Cor 1:7; Gal 5:5). The prevalence of the theme in the letter (cf. 1:6, 10, 20–24, 26; 2:9–11, 16; 3:11, 12–19) is likely intended to remind a suffering church (cf. 1:28–30) of the certainty of future vindication, which may have been compromised by "an ebb in their eschatological anticipation" (Fee 376).

For κύριον Ἰησοῦν Χριστόν ("the Lord Jesus Christ" [EVV]) see on 1:1–2. With anarthrous κύριος, any appositives can dispense with the art. (Reumann 577; cf. BDF §254[1]; 268[2]; T 206). This is Paul's normal order for the terms when all three appear (e.g., Rom 1:7; 1 Cor 6:11; etc.).

VERSE 21

ὃς μετασχηματίσει τὸ σῶμα τῆς ταπεινώσεως ἡμῶν

Μετασχηματίσει is 3 sg. fut. act. indic. (nom. sg. masc. rel. pron. ὅς = subj.), from μετασχηματίζω, "to change the form of someth[ing]" (BDAG 641d; "transform" [most EVV]; "change" [RSV, NLT]; "transform," "transfigure" [J. Schneider, *TDNT* 7.957]). Conceptual parallels are found at Rom 8:29 and 1 Cor 15:42–47. The statement "emphasizes the great 'eschatological reversal' that they (and we) shall experience at his coming, that Christ himself experienced at his resurrection and exaltation" (Fee 380).

The dir. obj. phrase τὸ σῶμα τῆς ταπεινώσεως ἡμῶν can be understood in two ways, depending on what the gen. ἡμῶν modifies:

1. Take ἡμῶν with σῶμα, and τῆς ταπεινώσεως as an attributive gen. (= gen. of quality), "our lowly body/bodies" (BDAG 641d, 990c; NIV; "these poor bodies of ours" [CEV]; BDF §165; R 496; T 214; Wallace 87; Z §41); or
*2. Take ἡμῶν with τῆς ταπεινώσεως, and τῆς ταπεινώσεως as a poss. gen. (or ref. [Sumney 96]), "the body that belongs to our humiliation" (Fee 382 n. 28; "the body of our humble state/condition [NASB, HCSB; cf. NRSV]; Sumney 96).

The second alternative is better. The body itself is not "lowly" (much less "wretched" [NJB]). Rather, τὸ σῶμα is "the locus of present suffering and weakness" (Fee 382 n. 28; ταπείνωσις is the sphere or realm to which our body now belongs [Reumann 599]). Similarly, τῷ σώματι τῆς δόξης αὐτοῦ, later in v. 21, means "the body that belongs to (the realm of) his glory," not "his glorious body" (*pace* ESV, HCSB, CEV). Τὸ σῶμα is a collective sg., the body of each individual Christian (O'Brien 464; Reumann 579; σῶμα as "man in his whole existence" is too broad [*pace* W. Grundmann, *TDNT* 7.788]).

For the ταπεινο- word group (here gen. sg. fem., from ταπείνωσις), see on 2:3, 8. Unlike ταπεινοφροσύνη, which denotes an attitude or mind-set, ταπείνωσις signifies a "state or condition" (BDAG 990c). Paul is thinking not only theologically ("the state of humiliation caused by sin and is thus always characterized by physical decay, indignity, weakness, and finally death" [O'Brien 464]; W. Grundmann, *TDNT* 8.21), but also socioeconomically ("humble station" [BDAG 990c]; Reumann 599). The status connotations of ταπείνωσις would have resonated among the Philippians, who lived in a Roman settlement marked by a sharply vertical social hierarchy (Hellerman 88–109). Rank and resources went hand in hand in Roman antiquity, for better or for worse, depending on one's place in the social hierarchy. Paul elsewhere describes the economic situation of the churches in Macedonia in stark terms: ἡ κατὰ βάθους πτωχεία (2 Cor 8:2).

σύμμορφον τῷ σώματι τῆς δόξης αὐτοῦ

The adj. σύμμορφον (σύμμορφος, -ον) is acc. sg. neut. in appos. to τὸ σῶμα (τῷ σώματι is an associative dat. [R 528]; "conformity with the body" [NASB]). It means "having a similar form, nature, or style" (BDAG 958a; "like" [RSV, ESV, NIV]; "likeness" [HCSB]; "conformity/conformed" [NASB, NRSV]). Like Christ we will have "spiritual bodies—not bodies consisting of spirit merely but bodies with a new determining or motivating force" (H-M 233). The presence of σῶμα in both phrases shows continuity between the present and future (Fee 383; "a non-somatic life is inconceivable to Paul" [A. Oepke, *TDNT* 2.869]).

Most take δόξης as "radiant, glorious body" (BDAG 257a; Reumann 580), but given (a) the status connotations of the parallel ταπεινώσεως ("humble state or condition") and (b) the intended contrast with the pseudo-glory of those who set their minds on earthly things (Fee 383 n. 30; Reumann 599), the meaning "fame, recognition, renown, prestige" (cf. BDAG 257d) is probably better. The gen. αὐτοῦ is poss. with δόξης, "the body belonging to his prestigious condition" ("his glorified state" [Fee 383 n. 30]; "body of his glory" [NASB, NRSV]), not attrib. with σώματι ("his glorious body" [RSV, ESV, HCSB, NJB; BDAG 257a]) (Reumann 599; see above, on τὸ σῶμα τῆς ταπεινώσεως ἡμῶν).

κατὰ τὴν ἐνέργειαν τοῦ δύνασθαι αὐτὸν καὶ ὑποτάξαι αὐτῷ τὰ πάντα

Κατά never functions instr. but, rather, conveys the norm or standard in relation to which something is done ("in keeping with," not "by" [*pace* EVV]; Fee 383 n. 31). "[T]he norm is at the same time the reason, so that 'in accordance with' and 'because of' are merged" (O'Brien 465 n. 139; cf. BDAG 512d; Reumann 580). The language of the κατά clause is striking since what is said of Jesus here (αὐτόν = ὅς [v. 21] = κύριον Ἰησοῦν Χριστόν [v. 20]) is elsewhere ascribed to God the Father (Fee 384; Z §210):

a. κατὰ τὴν ἐνέργειαν τοῦ δύνασθαι αὐτόν is similar to Eph 1:19; 3:20, which portray God's power tangibly at work in the world (both texts use the ἐνέργ- and δύνα- word groups);

b. ὑποτάξαι αὐτῷ τὰ πάντα is reminiscent of Ps 8:7, where God will "subject all things" to his Messiah (cf. 1 Cor 15:25–28).

Ἐνέργεια, -ας, ἡ, is "the state or quality of being active" ("working, operation action" [BDAG 335b]; "activity" [G. Bertram, *TDNT* 2.652]; "effective action" [H. Paulsen, *EDNT* 1.453d]). Δύνασθαι (pres. dep. inf., subst. with gen. art.), in contrast, connotes power as potential or ability ("can, am able, be capable" [BDAG 261d–262a], usually with a complementary inf. [here ὑποτάξαι]; Reumann 581; see on δύναμιν [3:10]). The tr. "the working of the power which he has" (NJB; sim. "the exertion of the power" [NASB]; "the outworking of his ability" [O'Brien 466]) properly reflects the different nuances of the two terms.

The art. inf. (τοῦ δύνασθαι with acc. subj. αὐτόν) is to be taken "as a real substantive" (R 1061). Regarding the gen. τοῦ δύνασθαι, BDF (§400[2]) notes: "Certain passages exhibit a very loose relationship between the substantive and infinitive and tend toward the consecutive sense" ("the outworking of his ability" [O'Brien 466]; T 141). An epexegetical gen. ("power, namely his ability to" [Reumann 581]; Moule 129) is "possible" (Wallace 607), but the different nuances of ἐνέργεια (power in action) versus δύναμαι (power as potential) suggest that τοῦ δύνασθαι be interpreted, instead, as a gen. of source or subj. gen.

The καί that precedes ὑποτάξαι (aor. act. inf. from ὑποτάσσω, "subject, subordinate" [BDAG 1042a; NRSV, HCSB, ESV]; "bring . . . under control/mastery" [NIV/NJB]) should not be overlooked (*pace* NIV, HCSB). Paul assures the Philippians that not only will Christ transform "the bodies of their humble condition." He will use the same power "also" (NRSV; "even" [RSV, NASB, ESV]) to subject τὰ πάντα ("the universe" [BDAG 784b]; "the totality of all created things" [H. Sasse, *TDNT* 3.884; B. Reicke, *TDNT* 5.888]) to himself, including Rome and all those who in the emperor's name who are causing the Philippians to suffer (Fee 384).

The pron. αὐτῷ can be reflexive in function ("himself" [most EVV]; Reumann 581; Moule 119; T 41; Wallace 325; Z §210).

VERSE 4:1

Ὥστε, ἀδελφοί μου ἀγαπητοὶ καὶ ἐπιπόθητοι

Paul now shifts from theology and polemics to final exhortations, expressions of gratitude, and words of farewell (H-M 238). 4:1 functions as a hinge: (a) Ὥστε ("Therefore" [most EVV]; "So then" [NJB, HCSB]) draws consequences from vv. 17–21, while (b) the six terms of address, along with a shift to the impv. (στήκετε), point forward to Paul's concluding remarks (Reumann 605).

Ἀδελφοί is the first and most important in "an extraordinary, long series of appellatives" (H-M 239) reflecting a "flood of affection" (Fee 388; "unparalleled in his other letters" [O'Brien 474]). Ἀδελφοί reminds the Philippians that they and Paul belong to the same divine family and hold equal status in relation to God the Father (H-M 239; "equality and mutuality" [Hansen 279]).

The voc. ἀγαπητοί means "beloved, prized, valued" (BDAG 7c; "humble way of saying 'I love you'" [H-M 239]). It is a verbal adj. with pass. force, used subst. (cf. BDF §112; H-M 239). Most EVV vary their tr. of the two occurrences of ἀγαπητοί in v. 1 ("[whom] I love"/"my beloved" [NRSV]; "whom I love"/"dear friends" [NIV]; "dearly loved"/"dear friends" [HCSB]). The NASB ("beloved" 2x) and NJB ("dear friends" 2x) opt for consistency over stylistic variation.

Also voc. pl. masc., ἐπιπόθητοι (only here in NT) is from ἐπιπόθητος, -ον (verbal adj. with pass. force), "earnestly desired" (BDAG 377d; "long(ed) for/to see" [most EVV; H. Balz, *EDNT* 2.33a]; "miss so much" [NJB]). See on ἐπιποθέω (1:8; 2:26). This exemplifies ancient friendship language: "[F]riends yearn to be with friends and rejoice together" (Reumann 606). Included are ideas of longing and "pain of separation" (H-M 239; O'Brien 475]).

χαρὰ καὶ στέφανός μου

With the second set of vocs. ("joy and crown" [EVV]; "pride and joy" [CEV]) Paul looks to the future (Fee 338, cf. n. 19; Reumann 631; *pace* Hansen 280; H-M 240), as indicated by (a) the connection, via Ὥστε, of 4:1 to 3:20–21, and (b) the striking

parallel at 1 Thess 2:19, where the same language is used of the parousia (τίς γὰρ ἡμῶν
ἐλπὶς ἢ χαρὰ ἢ <u>στέφανος</u> καυχήσεως . . . ἔμπροσθεν τοῦ κυρίου ἡμῶν Ἰησοῦ ἐν τῇ αὐτοῦ
παρουσίᾳ).

Χαρά is a striking way of saying that the Philippians are the cause of Paul's joy
(O'Brien 475). Στέφανος here is not a king's diadem (cf. the use of the term for Jesus'
"crown" of thorns [Matt 27:29; Mark 15:17; John 19:2, 5]). It is a victor's crown or
wreath (made of laurel, olive, ivy, or oak [W. Grundmann, *TDNT* 7.616–17]) presented
by judges to the winner in the Olympian games. Στέφανος is used eighteen times in the
NT, most often metaphorically, for the eternal reward of the faithful (e.g., 1 Cor 9:25;
2 Tim 4:8; 1 Pet 5:4; 6x in Rev). BDAG defines στέφανος as either (1) "that which
serves as adornment or source of pride" (here), or (2) an "award or prize for exceptional service or conduct" (BDAG 944b; "the crown I receive for my work" [NLT];
W. Grundmann, *TDNT* 7.630). The latter meaning preserves the eschatological flavor
of στέφανος in v. 1, but either connotation will work since the imagery is not strictly
lit. to begin with (i.e., the Philippians are not the actual crown; rather, they are the fruit
of Paul's labors that qualify him to receive the crown).

οὕτως στήκετε ἐν κυρίῳ, ἀγαπητοί

The adv. οὕτως ("thus" [RSV, ESV]; "in this way/manner" [NRSV, NIV, HCSB])
has been read to point (1) backwards (Fee 388 n. 23; Silva 186), (2) forwards ("vv 2–9
state precisely how Christians are to stand firm" [H-M 239]), or (3) both (Hansen 282;
O'Brien 476). The first option is best:

   a. When not functioning as a correlative, Paul normally uses οὕτως retrospec-
      tively (2 Thess 3:17; 1 Cor 7:17; 9:24; 11:28; 15:11; Gal 6:2).
   b. Without the extended vocs., Ὥστε and οὕτως occur adjacent to one another
      (Ὥστε . . . οὕτως στήκετε ἐν κυρίῳ). Paul uses ὥστε like this only to apply
      a preceding argument. To take οὕτως as pointing forward misses the force
      of Ὥστε and the link (στήκετε) with 1:27.

Στήκετε is 2 pl. pres. (BDF §73) act. impv. from στήκω, "be firmly committed in
conviction or belief" (BDAG 944d; see on 1:27; "stand firm" [NIV, HCSB]; "keep on
being faithful" [CEV]).

The prep. phrase ἐν κυρίῳ ("in the Lord" [most EVV]) is to be read either as (1) locat. of
sphere ("believers are to remain securely fixed within the domain of Christ" [Campbell
162]; Fee 388 n. 22; "Stand in obedience to the Lord" [W. Grundmann, *TDNT* 7.637]);
or as (2) marking agency, "through the Lord's help" (Harris, *Prepositions*, 129).

FOR FURTHER STUDY

50. Paul's Opponents (3:2, 18–19)

See on 1:12–18a.

51. Imitating Paul (3:17)

Brandt, Jo-Ann A. "The Place of *Mimesis* in Paul's Thought." *Studies in Religion* 22 (1993): 285–301.

Castelli, Elizabeth A. *Imitating Paul: A Discourse of Power.* Louisville: Westminster, 1991.

De Boer, W. P. *The Imitation of Paul: An Exegetical Study.* Grand Rapids: Eerdmans, 1962.

Fiore, Benjamin. *The Function of Personal Example in the Socratic and Pastoral Epistles.* Rome: Pontifical Biblical Institute, 1986.

*Fowl, S. E. *DPL* 428–31.

Kurz, William S. "Kenotic Imitation of Paul and of Christ in Philippians 2 and 3." Pages 103–26 in *Discipleship in the New Testament.* Edited by F. F. Segovia. Philadelphia: Fortress, 1985.

Lindars, Barnabas. "Imitation of God and Imitation of Christ." *Theology* 76 (1973): 394–402.

Reinhartz, Adele. "On the Meaning of the Pauline Exhortation: 'mimetai mou ginesthe—become imitators of me.'" *Studies in Religion* 16 (1987): 393–403.

Sanders, Boykin. "Imitating Paul: 1 Cor 4:16." *HTR* 74 (1981): 353–63.

Stanley, David M. "Become Imitators of Me: The Pauline Conception of Apostolic Tradition." *Bib* 40 (1958): 859–77.

HOMILETICAL SUGGESTIONS

Following the Right People (3:17–4:1)

1. Who we should follow (3:17)
2. Who we should avoid (3:18–19)
3. Reasons to follow the right people (3:20–21)
4. Following in action (4:1)

Who Are Our Role Models? (3:17–21)

1. Follow the right role models to end up in the right place (3:17, 21–22).
2. Follow the wrong role models to end up in wrong right place (3:18–19).

An Apostle Considers His Converts (4:1)

1. God dearly loves them.
2. Paul deeply longs for them.
3. They are Paul's hope for the future.

D. FINAL WORDS OF EXHORTATION (4:2–9)

1. RESTORING A BROKEN RELATIONSHIP (4:2–3)

2 Εὐοδίαν παρακαλῶ [τὸ αὐτὸ φρονεῖν ἐν κυρίῳ]
   καὶ Συντύχην παρακαλῶ τὸ αὐτὸ φρονεῖν ἐν κυρίῳ.
3 ναὶ ἐρωτῶ καὶ σέ, γνήσιε σύζυγε,
   <u>συλλαμβάνου</u> αὐταῖς,
             αἵτινες ἐν τῷ εὐαγγελίῳ <u>συνήθλησάν</u> μοι
             μετὰ καὶ Κλήμεντος
             καὶ τῶν λοιπῶν συνεργῶν μου,
   ὧν τὰ ὀνόματα ἐν βίβλῳ ζωῆς.

Paul addresses a specific problem in the Philippian church, under the broader rubric of the selfless mind-set (τὸ αὐτὸ φρονεῖν [cf. 2:2, 5]) and evangelistic priorities (ἐν τῷ εὐαγγελίῳ συνήθλησάν [cf. 1:27]) that have been central to the letter throughout. The language is marked (a) by a striking number of personal references (Εὐοδίαν, Συντύχην, γνήσιε σύζυγε, Κλήμεντος) and (b) by σύν-prefixed terms designed to emphasize unity and teamwork in the ministry of the gospel.

VERSE 2

Εὐοδίαν παρακαλῶ καὶ Συντύχην παρακαλῶ

Παρακαλῶ ("encourage," to "appeal to," to "urge" [BDAG 765a]), which elsewhere emphasizes the authoritative word of the apostle, here reflects an appeal of a more personal kind. The word choice and repetition, however, underscore the "earnestness" of the appeal (H-M 240; "urge strongly" [BDAG 765a]; "urge" [NRSV, NASB, HCSB]; "exhort" [O'Brien 477 n. 2; Reumann 607]), making the tr. "I beg" less than adequate (CEV, NEB; cf. "I plead with" [NIV]). The twofold παρακαλῶ suggests that Paul refused to take sides, as he equally addresses both women with the parallel cstr. (Hansen 282; O'Brien 477–78).

Εὐοδία and Συντύχη (acc. sg. fem.) appear frequently in inscriptions (H-M 241). The former comes from εὐ ("well") + ὁδός ("way, road"), thus, "Prosperous Journey" or, more generally, "Success" (Fee 390; Reumann 607; cf. vb. εὐοδόω, "go well, succeed" [Rom 1:10; 3 Jn 2]). Συντύχη etym. means "with luck," "Lucky." Tyche (Lat. *Fortuna*) was a deity governing human affairs, who became prominent as traditional Gk. gods and goddesses declined in importance, post-fourth century BC (Reumann 607; cf. Fee 390 n. 30). Names derived from the Gk. and Lat. roots were common in antiquity (e.g., Tychichus [Acts 20:4; Col 4:7]; Eutyches [Acts 20:9]; Fortunatus [1 Cor 16:17]). Macedonian women apparently played a larger role in civic life and religious devotion in the public arena than was the case elsewhere in the empire (Fee 390; cf. n. 31). Women were certainly at the forefront of Paul's ministry in Macedonia (at Philippi, Lydia and the slave girl [Acts 16:14, 16–18, 40]; cf. also 17:4, 12).

Scholars differ over the seriousness of the dispute. Fee downplays the discord: "one of the marks of 'enmity' in polemical letters is that the enemies are left unnamed, thus denigrated by anonymity" (Fee 389–90). Paul certainly does not view the women as enemies, and Fee's comment is a bit off point to begin with, since the dispute is between Euodia and Syntyche, not between the women and Paul. Two considerations suggest that the problem was serious enough to threaten church unity:

a. Paul does not correct people by name in letters to be read publicly to the church. The only clear instance occurs in a letter addressed not to a congregation but to an individual ("Hymenaeus and Alexander" [1 Tim 1:20]; cf. 2 Tim 2:18). Interpersonal conflict in an otherwise unified congregation (e.g., "stop arguing with each other" [CEV]) would not have elicited such an approach (Hansen 282). The women must have been prominent members of the community, perhaps two church leaders (patrons of two house churches? [Reumann 626–27]) engaged in a power struggle to expand their spheres of influence (Hansen 284; O'Brien 478).

b. Paul intentionally draws upon the language that elsewhere articulates his foundational appeal to church unity (cf. τὸ αὐτὸ φρονῆτε [2:2]; τοῦτο φρονεῖτε ἐν ὑμῖν ὃ καὶ ἐν Χριστῷ Ἰησοῦ [2:5]; τὸ αὐτὸ φρονεῖν [4:2]). Thus, D. E. Garland notes, "Paul carefully and covertly wove his argument to lead up to the impassioned summons of 4:2" ("The Composition and Unity of Philippians," *NovT* 27 [1985]: 173).

At the same time, Paul honors the disputants by reminding the Philippians that the women had contended alongside him in the work of the gospel (v. 3). Again the choice of words (ἐν τῷ εὐαγγελίῳ συνήθλησάν) intentionally echoes the activity Paul enjoins at the heart of the letter's paraenesis in 1:27: συναθλοῦντες τῇ πίστει τοῦ εὐαγγελίου. The prominence of Εὐοδία and Συντύχη, in this regard, made settling the potentially divisive dispute all the more urgent.

τὸ αὐτὸ φρονεῖν ἐν κυρίῳ

Φρονεῖν (pres. act. inf.) bears impv. force since it functions in an obj. clause connected with παρακαλῶ (Reed 349). The term denotes a shared mind-set, involving the "aim, direction, and orientation of their behaviour" (O'Brien 478; "be of the same mind" [NRSV, NIV]; see on 1:7; 2:2, 5; 3:15, 19). Such an outlook serves, of course, as the point of departure for coming to "agreement" (NJB; cf. RSV, HCSB, ESV) on specific issues.

The qualifier ἐν κυρίῳ ("in the Lord" [most EVV]; "[because] you belong to the Lord" [CEV, NLT]) is used broadly to "characterise an activity or state [here = τὸ αὐτὸ φρονεῖν] as Christian" (A. Oepke, *TDNT* 2.541). The specific emphasis in 4:2 may be that of (1) submission to Christ's lordship (H-M 240; "the ecclesial sphere where the Lord Jesus rules" [Reumann 608]; cf. 2 Cor 10:5; "under the Lordship of Christ"), or (2) the common bond the women share with one another "in the Lord" (O'Brien 478; "by recognizing their oneness in the Lord" [Harris, *Prepositions*, 129]).

VERSE 3

ναὶ ἐρωτῶ καὶ σέ, γνήσιε σύζυγε

Ναί denotes "affirmation, agreement, or emphasis" (BDAG 665b; "yes" [NIV, NRSV, HCSB]; "indeed" [NASB]), used here to emphasize the repetition of a previous assertion ("yes, and I ask you" [BDAG 665c]; R 1150) and thereby strengthen the appeal (O'Brien 479).

The switch from παρακαλῶ to ἐρωτῶ ("I ask" [EVV]) is likely an indication of status. Even though the two women contended by Paul's side in the gospel (v. 3), they remained his subordinates, for which παρακαλῶ (v. 2) was appropriate. The "loyal yoke-fellow" here addressed is at some level to be regarded as Paul's equal (Fee 391 n. 33).

The καί ("also," not "and" [BDAG 395c; Reumann 608]) is best taken with the pron. σέ, as ascensive ("you also" [NRSV, NASB, ESV]; Fee 392 n. 39; "in addition to the two women directly exhorted" [O'Brien 479–80]), rather than with the vb. ("I also ask you" [HCSB; cf. NIV]).

For γνήσιε, see on γνησίως (2:20). The adj. (voc. sg. masc. from γνήσιος, -α, -ον) lit. denotes "one who is considered a valid member of a family," hence "legitimate, true" (BDAG 202b–c; most EVV; F. Büchsel, TDNT 1.727). The rendering "loyal" (NRSV; cf. "faithful" [GNB]) is "hard to justify," since γνήσιος has to do with legitimacy not faithfulness (Fee 392 n. 40).

The term σύζυγε (voc. sg. masc.) derives from σύν ("with") + ζυγός ("yoke"), lit. "in the same yoke" (H. Balz, EDNT 3.284d; "yokefellow" [RSV]; "comrade" [BDAG 954d]; "companion" [NRSV, NASB, NIV]; "partner" [NJB, CEV, NLT; Reumann 609]). The image was widely used. The cognate συζυγέω portrayed soldiers standing in one rank (Polyb. 10.23.7; cf. Arr. Tact. 7.2, 8.2 [Reumann 609]). The ζυγός topos also surfaced in connection with friendship. Plutarch (De Am. mult. 93E) describes famous pairs like Achilles and Patroclus as being under the "yoke of friendship" (ζυγός φιλίας). Friendship is "sweetest" when "yoked together with (coniugavit) congeniality of character" (Cicero, Off. 1.58).

Attempts to identify the person addressed with γνήσιε σύζυγε stumble over (a) a lack of evidence (a proper name [NJB]; the entire church at Philippi [H-M 242]) or (b) evidence to the contrary (Paul's wife [Clem. Alex. Strom. 3.53.1]; Timothy; Epaphroditus [Reumann 629]) (see BDAG 954d; G. Delling, TDNT 7.749; O'Brien 480–81; Reumann 608). Most intriguing is Fee's suggestion that γνήσιε σύζυγε = Luke (Fee 392–94):

a. Paul elsewhere uses the qualifier γνήσιος/γνησίως of coworkers in his itinerant ministry (Phil 2:20; 1 Tim 1:2; Titus 1:4).

b. Luke likely remained in Philippi between Acts 16 and 20:1–5 (where the "we-passages" drop out between the two Philippian visits).

c. The public nature of the letter assumes the person in view would have been well known to the Philippians.

This, however, would require Luke to have returned to Philippi from Rome (a) after the apostle wrote Colossians and Philemon (cf. Col 4:14; Phlm 24) but (b) before he wrote Philippians ("certainty" is "no longer possible" [BDAG 954d; Hansen 285]).

συλλαμβάνου αὐταῖς

Συλλαμβάνου, 2 sg. pres. mid. impv. of συλλαμβάνω ("help" [EVV]; lit. "take hold of together" [H. Balz, EDNT 3.285c; Reumann 609]) has a broad semantic range, including (a) (physically) "capture," "apprehend"; (b) "become pregnant"; (c) (here) "support, aid, help," w/dat. of the one to whom help is given (BDAG 955d). The combination of ἐρωτῶ + impv. (versus an inf. or a ὅτι-clause) "intensifies the sense of urgency" (H-M 242). The nuance "along with someone," from the prep. prefix σύν-, "still lingers" (H-M 242; cf. Luke 5:7), leading O'Brien to assume that "the women were already attempting to overcome their discord" (O'Brien 481).

αἵτινες ἐν τῷ εὐαγγελίῳ συνήθλησάν μοι

The indef. rel. pron. αἵτινες (from ὅστις, ἥτις, ὅτι) is nom. pl. fem. It denotes "a characteristic quality, by which a preceding statement (in this case a command) is to be confirmed" (BDAG 729d; "these women" [NJB, CEV]). Here αἵτινες functionally introduces a subordinate causal clause ("for" [NRSV, NLT]; R 728; H-M 242; O'Brien 481; Reumann 610).

Συνήθλησάν is 3 pl. aor. act. indic. from συναθλέω, a metaphor drawn from the gladiatorial arena or the battlefield (E. Stauffer, TDNT 1.167; "fight together, assist in battle" [H. Balz, EDNT 3.296d]; "fought at my side in [spreading] the gospel" [BDAG 964a]). The vb. here "implies a united struggle in preaching the gospel, on the one hand, and a sharing in the suffering that results from the struggle, on the other" (H-M 243). The tr. "contended" (NIV, HCSB; "struggled" [NRSV, NJB]) is better than "worked hard" (NLT; "labored" [RSV, ESV]). The imagery emphasizes the bravery of Euodia and Syntyche (Malinowski, "The Brave Women of Philippi," 60–64; cf. the contrast with μὴ πτυρόμενοι ἐν μηδενὶ ὑπὸ τῶν ἀντικειμένων in 1:27–28). The women are put forth as examples of what Paul commanded earlier in the letter (συναθλοῦντες τῇ πίστει τοῦ εὐαγγελίου [1:27]).

Εὐαγγελίῳ denotes "the work of the gospel" (NRSV; "spreading the good news" [CEV]) rather than simply the gospel itself (Reumann 610; cf. Rom 1:9; 1 Thess 3:2).

μετὰ καὶ Κλήμεντος καὶ τῶν λοιπῶν συνεργῶν μου

Most EVV omit the first καί as pleonastic with a prep. (BDAG 496b; BDF §442[13]). Some retain the conj. and interpret μετὰ καί to mean "along also with" (Reumann 610; T 335).

Κλήμεντος is gen. sg. masc. from Κλήμης, the Gk. form of a common Lat. name, Clemens (BDAG 547c). He may be the descendent of an army veteran who had settled in the colony. "Valerius Clemens" is attested on a second-century AD inscription from Philippi (Reumann 610). No evidence links Κλήμεντος with (a) the author of

1 Clement or (b) the Clement who later became the third bishop of Rome (H-M 243; cf. Eusebius, *HE* 3.4; 5.6).

For συνεργῶν ("fellow-workers" [NASB, ESV] and "co-workers" [NRSV, HCSB, NIV]), see on 2:25. It is the fourth σύν- compound in the passage (σύζυγος, συλλαμβάνω, συναθλέω, συνεργοί), underscoring the idea of partnership (O'Brien 482; the compounds function "in the orbit of friendship" [Reumann 610]; perhaps Συντύχη heard an echo of her own σύν-prefixed name in the compounds).

For λοιπῶν (gen. pl. masc. attrib. adj.), see on 1:13. Two important mss. (א 𝔓[16vid]) read καὶ τῶν συνεργῶν μου καὶ τῶν λοιπῶν, two groups ("patently secondary" [Fee 385 n. 4; H-M 237; Metzger 617; UBS⁵ = {A} τῶν λοιπῶν συνεργῶν μου]).

ὧν τὰ ὀνόματα ἐν βίβλῳ ζωῆς

Most EVV supply a vb: "whose names <u>are</u> in the book of life" ("written" [NJB, CEV, NLT]). The gen. pl. masc. rel. pron., ὧν, is to be taken generically, referring back not just to τῶν λοιπῶν συνεργῶν, but to Εὐοδίαν, Συντύχην, and Κλήμεντος, as well (H-M 243; O'Brien 482).

Omission of the art. (βίβλῳ ζωῆς) is not uncommon for def. nouns governed by a preposition (T 180). Ζωῆς (gen. sg. fem.) here denotes "future glory" (BDAG 431a). With ζωῆς, βίβλῳ (dat. sg. fem.) is "a book of accounts," a "record-book" (BDAG 176d). The idea goes far back in Israel's history (βίβλου ζώντων [Ps 68:29 LXX; cf. τῆς βίβλου σου in Moses's prayer in Exod 32:32]), and the concept was likely reinforced by the genealogies and family lists of those who belonged to God's people in the OT. "Book of life" imagery became common in apocalyptic lit. to denote those who are admitted to eternal life (Dan 12:1; cf. *1 Enoch* 47:3; 1QM 12:3; Luke 10:20; Heb 12:23; Rev 3:5; 13:8; 17:8; 20:12, 15; 21:27). Paul's reference to a "heavenly commonwealth" earlier in the letter (3:20) suggests an intended contrast with a civic register of Roman citizens in the colony at Philippi, i.e., the archives of the *tribus Voltinia*, documented also in Aquae Sextiae and Nemausus (Reumann 611).

FOR FURTHER STUDY

52. Women in Paul's Churches (4:2)

Abrahamsen, Valerie. "Women at Philippi: The Pagan and Christian Evidence." *Journal of Feminist Studies in Religion* 3 (1987): 17–30.

Beck, James R. *Two Views on Women in Ministry.* Rev. ed. Grand Rapids: Zondervan, 2005.

Cotter, Wendy. "Women's Authority Roles in Paul's Churches: Countercultural or Conventional?" *NovT* 36 (1994): 350–72.

D'Angelo, Mary Rose. "Women Partners in the New Testament." *Journal of Feminist Studies in Religion* 6 (1990): 65–86.

Gillman, Florence M. "Early Christian Women at Philippi." *Journal of Gender in World Religions* 1 (1990): 59–79.

Keener, Craig. *Paul, Women and Wives: Marriage and Women's Ministry in the Letters of Paul.* Peabody, MA: Hendrickson, 1991.

Lamoreaux, Jason T. *Ritual, Women, and Philippi: Reimagining the Early Philippian Community.* Eugene, OR: Cascade Books, 2013.

Luter, Boyd. "Partnership in the Gospel: The Role of Women in the Church at Philippi." *JETS* 39 (1996): 411–20.

Malinowski, Francis X. "The Brave Women of Philippi." *BTB* 15 (1985): 60–64.

Pierce, Ronald W., and Rebecca M. Groothius, eds. *Discovering Biblical Equality: Complementarity Without Hierarchy.* 2nd ed. Grand Rapids: InterVarsity Academic, 2005.

Piper, John, and Wayne Grudem, eds. *Recovering Biblical Manhood and Womanhood: A Response to Evangelical Feminism.* Redesigned. Wheaton, IL: Crossway, 2012.

Trebilco, Paul. "Women as Co-workers and Leaders in Paul's Letters." *Journal of the Christian Brethren Research Fellowship* 122 (1990): 27–36.

HOMILETICAL SUGGESTIONS

Keys for Restoring Broken Relationships (4:2–3)

1. Challenge the disputants (v. 2).
2. Engage a mediator (v. 3a).
3. Affirm earlier accomplishments (v. 3b).

2. THE JOY AND PEACE OF KNOWING CHRIST (4:4–7)

4   <u>Χαίρετε</u> ἐν <u>κυρίῳ</u> πάντοτε·
    πάλιν ἐρῶ, <u>χαίρετε</u>.
5   τὸ ἐπιεικὲς ὑμῶν <u>γνωσθήτω</u> πᾶσιν ἀνθρώποις.
    ὁ <u>κύριος</u> ἐγγύς.
6   μηδὲν <u>μεριμνᾶτε</u>,
    ἀλλ᾽
            ἐν παντὶ
            τῇ προσευχῇ καὶ τῇ δεήσει
            μετὰ εὐχαριστίας
            τὰ αἰτήματα ὑμῶν <u>γνωριζέσθω</u> πρὸς τὸν <u>θεόν</u>.
7   καὶ ἡ εἰρήνη τοῦ <u>θεοῦ</u> ἡ ὑπερέχουσα πάντα νοῦν φρουρήσει τὰς καρδίας ὑμῶν
            καὶ τὰ νοήματα ὑμῶν
            ἐν Χριστῷ Ἰησοῦ.

The passage is marked by a series of apparently unrelated impvs. with no connecting words except ἀλλ᾽ [v. 6] and καί [v. 7]). The grammar raises two questions:

1. Are the commands specifically relevant to the Philippians, or is Paul simply reiterating standard requirements for living the Christian life that surface elsewhere in his letters?

Only the command to "rejoice" is distinctly Philippian. However, (a) the call to rejoice (v. 4), (b) the forbearance command, with the assurance that the Lord is near (v. 5), and (c) the instructions about anxiety (vv. 6–7) can be viewed together as particularly appropriate to the two key challenges facing the Philippians: opposition from without (1:27–30) and disunity within (2:2–4; 4:2–3) (Fee 404, 408; Hansen 287, 289–90). The relevance becomes transparent on a properly corporate reading of vv. 4–7, as addressed to a gathered community, not just individual Christians.

2. Are the asyndetic injunctions (χαίρετε . . . γνωσθήτω . . . μεριμνᾶτε) logically related or unrelated to one another?

Commentators who emphasize the asyndetic syntax view the impvs. as unrelated (O'Brien 484). Those who look beyond syntax to semantics find some connections ("aphoristic dicta but linked at points" [Reumann 634]), but conclusions differ. Few argue for a logical link between the twofold χαίρετε (v. 4) and the preceding admonition in vv. 2–3 (but cf. Hansen [287]). Most agree, however, that the statement ὁ κύριος ἐγγύς (v. 5b) grounds either:

1. the preceding impv. (v. 5a) (Hansen 289),
2. the following impv. (v. 6) ("The Lord is near; have no anxiety" [NEB]; J. Goetzmann, *NIDNTT* 1.278–79); or, most likely,
*3. both v. 5a and v. 6 (Fee 407–8; O'Brien 490; Silva 194–95).

The exhortations of vv. 4–7 also share common ground as a "threefold expression of Jewish piety—rejoicing in the Lord, prayer, and thanksgiving—which are basic to the Psalter" (Fee 402–3).

Finally, recent commentators are rightly sensitive to the danger of misinterpreting vv. 4–7 as a series of injunctions primarily addressed to individual Christians. Rather, "As always in Paul, 'joy, prayer, and thanksgiving,' evidenced outwardly by their 'gentleness' and inwardly by God's 'peace' in their midst, first of all have to do with the (gathered) people of God" (Fee 403).

VERSE 4

Χαίρετε ἐν κυρίῳ πάντοτε· πάλιν ἐρῶ, χαίρετε

Χαίρετε (2x) is 2 pl. pres. act. impv. from χαίρω ("rejoice" [most EVV]; "be joyful" [NJB]; "be glad" [CEV]). Ἐρῶ is 1 sg. fut. act. indic. of λέγω (functionally equivalent to a hortatory subjunc., "let me say anew" [Reumann 611]). The assonance and chiastic structure of the doublet would have been readily apparent to hearers: Χαίρετε ἐν κυρίῳ πάντοτε—πάλιν ἐρῶ, χαίρετε (Fee 404 n. 19; Reumann 611).

Other references to joy in Philippians seem to respond to specific circumstances (e.g., 1:18; 2:2, 17–18, 29), but it is difficult to connect χαίρετε . . . χαίρετε to the appeal to the women in vv. 2–3. The notion that Paul assumes communal joy will either (a) contribute to or (b) result from the reconciliation of Euodia and Syntyche is not convincing (pace Hansen 287). It is possible, however, that the mention of "the book of life" (βίβλῳ ζωῆς), at the end of v. 3, may have elicited the ensuing charge to rejoice if Paul at this point recalled the Jesus tradition in Luke 10:20b: χαίρετε δὲ ὅτι τὰ ὀνόματα ὑμῶν ἐγγέγραπται ἐν τοῖς οὐρανοῖς (O'Brien 486).

The connection between χαίρετε . . . χαίρετε and the broader setting of the letter is easier to discern. Paul writes from prison to Christians who are suffering for their faith. Christian joy is not temporal and fleeting, depending on circumstances, but is predicated, instead, on the fact that they are "in the Lord" (ἐν κυρίῳ). Rejoicing is to mark the Philippians' individual and corporate lives "at all times" (πάντοτε), just as it did in the case of Paul and Silas, who had rejoiced in the Lord while imprisoned in the colony a decade earlier (Acts 16:25; cf. Phil 2:17).

VERSE 5

τὸ ἐπιεικὲς ὑμῶν γνωσθήτω πᾶσιν ἀνθρώποις

Ἐπιεικές is nom. sg. neut. from the adj. ἐπιεικής, -ές, used as an abstract subst. w/ art. (BDF §263[2]; R 763; T 14; Z §140). The adj. means "not insisting on every right of letter of law or custom" (BDAG 371b; fits well with Philippians 2 [Jesus] and Philippians 3 [Paul] [Wright 449]). Aristotle contrasted ἐπιεικής with ἀκριβοδίκαιος, "strict justice," and used it to describe a person "who does not stand on his rights unduly, but is content to receive a smaller share although he has the law on his side" (Aristotle, Eth. nic. 5.10.8). The term is elsewhere sandwiched between μὴ πλήκτην and ἄμαχον, as a qualification for church leaders (1 Tim 3:3), and between εἰρηνική and εὐπειθής, as a description of ἡ . . . ἄνωθεν σοφία (Jas 3:17). Ἐπιεικές has generated a remarkable variety of Eng. translations in 4:5, some of which seem somewhat removed from the definition cited above (e.g., "gentle(ness)" [NIV, NRSV, CEV, cf. NASB]; "good sense" [NJB]; "considerate" [NLT]; "reasonableness" [ESV]; "a very elusive term" [MM 238c]).

   Since the word group often describes the superior party, where uneven power relations obtain (Felix [Acts 24:4]; Christ [2 Cor 10:1]; slave owners [1 Pet 2:1]), some see Paul enjoining the Philippians to exhibit ἐπιεικεία from a position of relative power. "The Lord is at hand," so the Philippians should feel free to exercise "magnanimity" (NEB; cf. "graciousness" [HCSB]) toward all, given their anticipated position of future δόξα (H. Preisker, TDNT 2.589–90; H-M 244). The application of the word group is hardly limited, however, to those in a position to dispense favors, e.g., "Let us test him with insult and torture, so that we may find out how gentle he is (τὴν ἐπιείκειαν αὐτοῦ), and make trial of his forbearance" (Wisdom 2:19; cf. Titus 3:2). It is preferable to see Paul commanding the Philippians to exhibit ἐπιεικές from a position of relative weakness vis-à-vis Roman opposition to the Christians in the colony ("forbearance" [RSV; H. Giesen, EDNT 2.26d]; "spirit of forbearance" [BDAG 371c]; "gentle forbearance" [Fee 406]; "patient steadfastness" [O'Brien 487]; Reumann 613; Ragner Leivestad, "'The Meekness and Gentleness of Christ' II Cor. X.1," NTS 13 [1965–66]: 158).

   Γνωσθήτω is 3. sg. aor. pass. impv. from γινώσκω, "to know," here probably "be recognized by" (Fee 406 n. 26; "Let . . . be known/evident/obvious" [most EVV]). Some EVV change the cstr., taking as subj. either the Philippians ("have a reputation for" [Philipps]) or those who observe them ("Let all men know" [RSV]; "Let everyone see" [NLT]).

   The adj. πᾶσιν is dat. pl. masc., "all people/men, everyone" (BDAG 782c; "all sorts of people" [Reumann 611]), including—perhaps especially—those who are hostile to the faith (cf. 1:27–30 and Wisdom 2:19, above). Paul regularly points outward with the combination πάντες ἄνθρωποι, to the whole of humankind (e.g., 1 Thess 2:15; 2 Cor 3:2; Rom 5:18 [2x]; 12:17–18, etc.) (Fee 406 n. 27; O'Brien 488).

ὁ κύριος ἐγγύς

'Ο κύριος is the Lord Jesus (Reumann 613). Three options present themselves for ἐγγύς (pred. use of the adv., supply ἐστίν [R 546; T 226; Reumann 613]; "at hand" [RSV, ESV]; "near" [NIV, NRSV, HCSB]):

1. "Being in close proximity spatially," "near, close to" (BDAG 271b).
   a. The interpretation finds support in the Psalter, where we read ἐγγὺς κύριος πᾶσιν τοῖς ἐπικαλουμένοις αὐτόν, πᾶσι τοῖς ἐπικαλουμένοις αὐτὸν ἐν ἀληθείᾳ (Ps 144:18 [LXX]; cf. 33:19; 118:151). Yahweh in the Pss. is now none other than the Lord Jesus.
   b. A spatial reading of ἐγγύς leads naturally to the admonition that follows (μηδὲν μεριμνᾶτε κτλ. [vv. 6–7]).

2. "Being close in point of time," "near" ("coming soon" [NLT, GNB cf. CEV]; BDAG 271b; H. Preisker, *TDNT* 2.331; W. Foerster *TDNT* 3.1091; A. Oepke, *TDNT* 5.868; W. Bauder, H.-G. Link, *NIDNTT* 2.54; Hansen 289 n. 42; Silva 198).

    a. This echoes the apocalyptic language of Zeph 1:7, 14 ("the Day of the Lord is near"; cf. Rom 13:12; Jas 5:8), and finds support in the threefold mention in Philippians of "the Day of Christ" (1:6, 10; 2:16) (Fee 408; Reumann 635).

    b. A temporal understanding of ἐγγύς—implying imminent deliverance and vindication—is most suitable after the command to exercise forbearance toward opponents (v. 5a).

  *3. Take ἐγγύς to include both ideas of time and space: "as close to intentional double entendre as one finds in the apostle" (Fee 407; H-M 245; O'Brien 489).

The third view is best: "Since their present suffering is at the hands of those who proclaim Caesar as Lord, they are reminded that the true 'Lord' is 'near.' Their eschatological vindication is close at hand. At the same time, by using the language of the Psalter, Paul is encouraging them to pray in the midst of their present distress, because 'the Lord is near' in a very real way to those who call on him now" (Fee 408).

VERSE 6

μηδὲν μεριμνᾶτε

Μηδέν is acc. sg. neut. from μηδείς, μηδεμία, μηδέν, used subst. (Reumann 614); acc. of respect (O'Brien 491 n. 45) or cognate acc. (as if = μηδεμίαν μέριμναν [Moule 34]). The μηδέν-παντί contrast (vv. 6–7) , along with the disjunctive ἀλλ' (v. 7), underscores the comprehensive nature of Paul's twofold injunction: "The way to be anxious about nothing is to be prayerful about everything" (O'Brien 492 cites R. Rainy). EVV generally move the neg. part. (μη-) to the vb. ("Do not worry about anything" [NRSV]; but cf. NASB).

Μεριμνάω (2 pl. pres. act. impv.) can be used positively ("care for, be concerned about" [cf. 2:20]) or neg., "be apprehensive"; with μηδέν "have no anxiety" (BDAG 632b; RSV; "worry" [NRSV, NJB, HCSB; D. Zeller, *EDNT* 2.408d]; "anxious care" [J. Goetzmann, *NIDNTT* 1.278]). The asyndeton isolates the admonition, making it emphatic (O'Brien 491). Most think the neg. pres. impv. "indicates that the readers must stop doing what they are habitually doing" (Hansen 289; H-M 245; O'Brien 491; Reumann 614; cf. BDF §336[3]; R 851–54; cf. Z §246 for the cstr.). Wallace appropriately cautions against the universal application of this narrow "phenomenological" usage (i.e., a meaning affected by lexical, contextual, or other grammatical features)" of the neg. pres. impv. (Wallace 716; cf. 714–17). Μηδὲν μεριμνᾶτε seems to be an instance of just such a usage, however, so that "stop worrying" remains a reasonable translation. Since Paul uses μεριμνάω in a positive sense everywhere else (2:20; 1 Cor 7:32–34 [4x]; 12:25; noun in 2 Cor 11:28), some hear in v. 6 an echo of the gospel tradition (Matt 6:25–34, cf. μὴ οὖν μεριμνήσητε εἰς τὴν αὔριον [34a]; par. Luke 12:22 –32)

(H-M 245; Fee 408; O'Brien 636). As with similar epistolary requests in the papyri, μηδὲν μεριμνᾶτε is "not a timeless, theological exhortation but one occasioned by the threatening circumstances facing the Philippians" (Reed 270), which likely included the activities of pagan adversaries in the colony (1:27–30), Paul's situation (1:12), and Epaphroditus's illness (2:26).

ἀλλ' ἐν παντὶ τῇ προσευχῇ καὶ τῇ δεήσει μετὰ εὐχαριστίας

'Ἐν παντί (prep. + dat. sg. neut.), "in everything" (most EVV), signifies "in every situation" (NIV) or "circumstance," not "always" (O'Brien 492; Reumann 614). The adj. παντί does not modify the noun that follows (≠ "in all your prayers" [GNB; sim. NAB]), since προσευχῇ is fem., παντί neut.

The dat. sg. fem. nouns τῇ προσευχῇ and τῇ δεήσει are used instr. (Reumann 601; accompaniment [Moule 45]; manner [T 241]). Some argue for a difference in meaning for προσευχή versus δέησις (e.g., "prayer comprehensively, in contrast to petitionary prayer" [Reumann 614]; "general" versus "specific" [U. Schoenborn, *EDNT* 1.287b]; "prayer and supplication" [NRSV, NASB, ESV]; "prayer and petition" [NIV, NJB, HCSB]; "prayer and requests" [CEV]). Others are more cautious (Greeven, *TDNT* 2.807; "not significantly distinguishable" [Fee 409]; "perhaps even as a hendiadys" [O'Brien 492–93; cf. n. 63]; see on 1:4). Paul multiplies vocabulary throughout vv. 6–7: (1) προσευχῇ ... τῇ δεήσει ... εὐχαριστίας ... αἰτήματα; (2) νοῦν ... καρδίας ... νοήματα; (3) παντὶ ... πάντα. Whatever the distinct nuances of these terms, the main point of this lexical thesaurus is clearly "the great importance Paul attaches to the believer's prayer life" (Silva 195).

The def. art. τῇ is almost equivalent to a poss. pron. "your [prayer]" (O'Brien 493). The qualifier μετὰ εὐχαριστίας (prep. + gen. sg. fem.; "with thanksgiving/thankful hearts" [most EVV]; "with gratitude" [NJB]) reminds us that thanksgiving is "an explicit acknowledgment of creatureliness and dependence, a recognition that everything comes as a gift" (Fee 409; "the proper mode of eschatological vigilance" [H. Conzelmann, *TDNT* 9.414]). Loss of gratitude toward God opens the door to idolatry (Rom 1:21–23; cf. the juxtaposition of ἐδόξασαν and ηὐχαρίστησαν [v. 21]), which results in a world plagued with moral and relational chaos (cf. vv. 24–32). Paul modeled his admonition (εὐχαριστῶ [1:3]), even though he had good reason to be anxious about (a) the Philippians' response to persecution (1:27) and (b) disunity in their midst (2:2–4; 4:2–3), not to mention his own circumstances.

τὰ αἰτήματα ὑμῶν γνωριζέσθω πρὸς τὸν θεόν

Τὰ αἰτήματα, which functions as the subj. of the impv. γνωριζέσθω, is nom. pl. neut. (takes sg. vb.) from αἴτημα, -τος, τό, "request" (BDAG 30d). This third term for prayer in the passage refers to the "individual petitions which constitute a prayer" (G. Stählin, *TDNT* 1.193; H. Schönweiss, *NIDNTT* 2.858). "Paul encourages being specific in prayer to God—not mouthing vague generalities and amorphous meditation" (Hansen 291).

The vb. γνωριζέσθω is 3 sg. pres. pass. impv. from γνωρίζω, "make known" (BDAG 203b); "let your requests be made known" (most EVV; BDAG 30d and 203b; "present your requests" [NIV; cf. NLT]). Repeated action ("be constantly made known" [Reumann 614]) is likely, in view of the pl. αἰτήματα. The point, of course, is not the impartation of knowledge to a God who knows all (in the passage Paul echoes, Jesus explicitly says οἶδεν γὰρ ὁ πατὴρ ὑμῶν ὁ οὐράνιος κτλ. [Matt 6:32]) but, rather, "full self-disclosure in God's presence" (Hansen 291; "total dependence on God" [O'Brien 493]).

Not simply a dat. (τῷ θεῷ, "to God") but an "unusual turn of phrase" (Reumann 636) πρὸς τὸν θεόν denotes "movement or orientation toward" God (BDAG 874b; Hansen 291; Reumann 614).

VERSE 7

καὶ ἡ εἰρήνη τοῦ θεοῦ ἡ ὑπερέχουσα πάντα νοῦν

The καί is used with "consecutive force" to mark "result" (R 1183; cf. BDAG 495a; Hansen 291; H-M 246; O'Brien 495). The cstr. functions semantically as a cond., with v. 6 serving as the protasis, v. 7 as the apodosis (trans. καί "then" [NEB, CEV]; Reumann 615; cf. BDF §442[7] for Semitic background). The promise is not that God will answer all our prayers but that he will give us his peace if we pray in every situation with thankful hearts. "God's peace will be powerfully at work in their lives as a result (καί) of their pouring out their hearts in petition with thanksgiving, not because they have made requests that are perfectly in line with the will of God" (O'Brien 495).

Εἰρήνη ("peace" [EVV]) is rooted in the OT (see on 1:2), not in the sense "inward peace" but, rather, as "an emphatically social concept" (G. von Rad, TDNT 2.406; "health and harmony in personal relationships" [Hansen 292]). For Paul, too, peace is "primarily a community matter" (Fee 411–12). The apostle typically employs εἰρήνη in a relational sense, i.e., peace with God (Rom 5:1) or peace among people (Rom 14:17; 1 Cor 7:15; Eph 4:3; 2 Tim 2:22). It would seem odd for ἡ εἰρήνη τοῦ θεοῦ (v. 7) to denote inner peace (pace H-M 246), particularly since the closest parallel has church unity directly in view: καὶ ἡ εἰρήνη τοῦ Χριστοῦ βραβευέτω ἐν ταῖς καρδίαις ὑμῶν (Col 3:15) (E. Stauffer, TDNT 1.638). Accordingly, recent commentators see the community primarily in view in vv. 6–7. Corporate prayer (v. 6) will bring God's peace to troubled relationships (v. 7), resulting in the unity Paul desires (τὸ αὐτὸ φρονεῖν [v. 2]; τὸ αὐτὸ φρονῆτε [2:2]) (Hansen 293). Ἡ εἰρήνη τοῦ θεοῦ is, therefore, "God's 'peace' in their midst"—not "the well-arranged heart" (Fee 403, 411–12). Yet, as Fee notes, "the fact that 'the peace of God shall guard your hearts and minds' reminds us that what is to be reflected in the gathered community must first of all be the experience of each believer" (403, his italics).

The gen. τοῦ θεοῦ is not obj. ("peace with God" [cf. Rom 5:1] is presupposed) but, rather, subj. ("the peace that God has and gives" [R 499]), or perhaps, a gen. of source or origin ("peace from God") (Porter 93). Some take the gen. as loosely descriptive (H-M 246; O'Brien 496).

The adj. ptc. ὑπερέχουσα (modifying ἡ εἰρήνη) is nom. sg. fem. of the pres. act. ptc. of ὑπερέχω, "to surpass in quality or value," "be better than, surpass, excel" (BDAG 1033b; R 629; "being superior to/surpassing" H. Balz, *EDNT* 3.398d]). The term with its obj. πάντα νοῦν can be taken in either of two ways:

*1. God's peace cannot be comprehended by human reasoning ("exceeds anything we can understand" [NLT; implied in most EVV]; "completely 'exceeds' what we can grasp or think" [G. Delling, *TDNT* 8.524]; O'Brien 497; Silva 195–96; most early Gk. commentators). Supported by the obj. πάντα νοῦν, which does not mean "all planning" or "all cleverness, inventiveness" but, rather, "all understanding" or, possibly, "every thought" (O'Brien 497, cf. n. 89).

*2. God's peace is far superior to human reasoning (perhaps implied by "surpasses every thought" [HSCB]; Fee 410–11; Hansen 294). This, in turn, can be read either:

    *a. in the sense that God's peace is more effective for removing anxiety or addressing relational discord in the community, than any intellectual effort or power of reasoning (Hansen 293; H-M 247); or

    b. as anti-Roman polemic vis-à-vis (1) the propagandist expression *pax Romana*, which denoted the peace that Augustus and his heirs had purportedly brought to the peoples of the empire (a statue base in Philippi was dedicated to the *Quies Augusti*, "the quiet of Augustus" [Reumann 615]), and (2) the presence of a Roman garrison in Philippi to guard the peace of the colony (see on φρουρήσει, below).

This is a toss-up between view 1 and view 2a. View 2b has the least in its favor.

The obj. νοῦν is acc. sg. masc. from νοῦς, νοός, ὁ, and denotes "the faculty of intellectual perception" (BDAG 680a; "intellectual-rational understanding—with a pejorative accent" [A. Sand, *EDNT* 2.479b; "the reasoning power in each person, practical perception rather than the 'academic mind'" [Reumann 615]). EVV generally tr. "understanding" ("comprehension" [NASB]; "thought" [HCSB]; "power of thought" [BDAG 680a]).

φρουρήσει τὰς καρδίας ὑμῶν καὶ τὰ νοήματα ὑμῶν ἐν Χριστῷ Ἰησοῦ

Φρουρήσει is 3 sg. fut. ("a sure promise, not a wish" [O'Brien 498 n. 90]) act. indic. of φρουρέω, "guard, protect, keep" (BDAG 1,067a; "guard" [most EVV]; "'preserve,' i.e., both 'hold fast' and 'protect'" [H. Balz, *EDNT* 3.440c]; "control" or "rule" [E. Stauffer, *TDNT* 1.638; CEV; cf. Col 3:23]). The vb. lit. means "to maintain a watch or guard" over a city (2 Cor 11:32), or "to hold someone in custody" (BDAG 1,066d–1,067a).

Although καρδία ("hearts" [most EVV]) often refers to "the center and source of the whole inner life, with its thinking, feeling and volition" (Hansen 294; J. Behm, *TDNT* 3.612), the pairing with νοήματα ("thoughts")—and the fact that each noun has its own art. and poss. pron. to distinguish it from the other ("emphatically separated" [O'Brien 498])—suggests a narrower meaning here, "emotions" or "feelings" (H-M

247; or, perhaps [still excluding "mental aspects"] "emotions and volition" [O'Brien 498]; Sumney 104).

Νοήματα is widely attested ($\mathfrak{P}^{46}$ א A B D Ψ 075 0150 6 33 *Byz* etc.; UBS⁵ = {A} νοήματα). A few Western mss. (F G it^{ar, d, g, o}) read σώματα ("bodies") instead. $\mathfrak{P}^{16vid}$ has νοήματα καὶ τὰ σώματα (O'Brien 483). Haplography may account for the loss of καὶ τὰ σώματα, but it is more probable that (a) scribes changed νοήματα to σώματα, thinking, perhaps, that νοήματα (after καρδίας) was redundant, and (b) $\mathfrak{P}^{16}$ then conflated the two readings (O'Brien 483). A less likely scenario traces the addition of σώματα to 1 Thess 5:23 (τὸ πνεῦμα καὶ ἡ ψυχὴ καὶ τὸ σῶμα), with νοήματα later lost via haplography (Fee 402 n. 1).

Like νοῦς, above, νόημα, -ατος, τό (acc. pl. neut.) can mean "mind, understanding," i.e., "the faculty of processing thought" (G. Harder, *NIDNTT* 3.128; "minds" [NRSV, NIV, HCSB]; cf. BDAG 647a; O'Brien 498). Here, however, νοήματα more likely denotes the "product of intellectual process," i.e., "thoughts" (NJB; BDAG 674a; J. Behm, *TDNT* 4.960–61; H. Balz, *EDNT* 2.470b; MM 428a; Hansen 294; Fee 411 n. 59). Taken together τὰς καρδίας ὑμῶν καὶ τὰ νοήματα constitutes "a holistic summary of the interior life of the church and all its members" (Hansen 295).

Once again Paul adds a crucial qualifier, ἐν Χριστῷ Ἰησοῦ ("in Christ Jesus [most EVV]). It is "only in union with Christ" that anyone can have "the secure assurance that he is indeed the object of the protection of God's peace" (H-M 248; "because you belong to Christ Jesus" [CEV]; O'Brien 498–99).

FOR FURTHER STUDY

53. Joy (4:4)
See on 1:3–11.

54. Prayer (4:6)
See on 1:3–11.

55. Peace (4:7)
Beck, H., and C. Brown. *NIDNTT* 2.776–83.
Hasler, V. *EDNT* 1.394–97.
Kreider, Alan, et al. *A Culture of Peace: God's Vision for the Church*. Intercourse, PA: Good Books, 2005.
Minear, Paul S. "The Peace of God: Conceptions of Peace in the New Testament." Pages 118–31 in *Celebrating Peace*. Edited by L. Rouner. Notre Dame, IN: Notre Dame University Press, 1990.
Porter, S. E. *DPL* 695–99.
Reimer, R. H. "Living Out the Peace of God: The Apostle Paul's Theology and the Practice of Peace." Pages 91–101 in *Vital Christianity: Spirituality, Justice, and Christian Practice*. New York: T&T Clark, 2005.
Spicq 1.424–38.
Von Rad, G., and W. Foerster. *TDNT* 2.400–420.
Wengst, Klaus. *Pax Romana and the Peace of Christ*. Philadelphia: Fortress, 1987.

HOMILETICAL SUGGESTIONS

The Nearness of Christ and the Challenges of Life (4:4–7)

1. The return of Christ means we will one day be vindicated (v. 5b), so we can stop insisting upon our every right in this world (v. 5a).
2. The presence of Christ (v. 5b) means that the peace of God is just a prayer away, so we can be anxious for nothing (vv. 6–7).
3. The nearness of Christ is grounds for great and constant rejoicing (v. 4).

Peace-Producing Prayer (4:6)

1. Pray in every situation (ἐν παντί).
2. Employ every kind of prayer (τῇ προσευχῇ καὶ τῇ δεήσει).
3. Pray with gratitude (μετὰ εὐχαριστίας).
4. Pray consistently (pres. tense γνωριζέσθω).

The Powerful Peace of God (4:7)

1. The peace of God is superior to human reasoning.
2. The peace of God guards our emotions.
3. The peace of God guards our thoughts.
4. The peace of God is found only in Christ Jesus.

3. THE COMMON GOOD AND THE APOSTLE'S EXAMPLE (4:8–9)

Verse 8   Verse 9

Τὸ λοιπόν, ἀδελφοί,
(a) ὅσα ἐστὶν ἀληθῆ,   ἃ   καὶ ἐμάθετε
     ὅσα σεμνά,   καὶ παρελάβετε
     ὅσα δίκαια,   καὶ ἠκούσατε
     ὅσα ἁγνά,   καὶ εἴδετε
     ὅσα προσφιλῆ,
     ὅσα εὔφημα,
(b)   εἴ τις ἀρετή   ἐν ἐμοί,
     καὶ εἴ τις ἔπαινος,
(c) ταῦτα λογίζεσθε·   ταῦτα πράσσετε·
     καὶ ὁ θεὸς τῆς εἰρήνης ἔσται μεθ᾿ ὑμῶν.

Verses 8–9 consists of two sentences, each with a three-part structure: (a) a series of "whatever things," emphasized rhetorically by the repeated ὅσα in v. 8 and the repeated καί in v. 9; (b) a qualification: the εἴ-clauses in v. 8, and the prep. phrase ἐν ἐμοί in v. 9; (c) par. occurrences of an appos. ταῦτα + impv. (Fee 413 n. 5). Attempts to identify the material as "the 'stuff' of friendship" (Fee 413) fail to convince ("unsupported" [Bockmuehl 249]; Reumann 637).

VERSE 8

Τὸ λοιπόν, ἀδελφοί

Τὸ λοιπόν here means "finally" (most EVV; "and now . . . one final thing" [NLT]; "in conclusion" [GNB]; BDAG 603a; Moule 121), rather than "in addition" (O'Brien 503) or "it follows in this connection" ("almost = οὖν" [R 1146]). The adv. expression does not mark the end of the letter, however, but introduces the last in a series of impvs. that describe how the Philippians are to "stand firm in the Lord" (4:1) (Hansen 295; H-M 248).

ὅσα ἐστὶν ἀληθῆ, ὅσα σεμνά, ὅσα δίκαια, ὅσα ἁγνά, ὅσα προσφιλῆ, ὅσα εὔφημα

The six ὅσα clauses (nom. pl. neut. rel. pron. from ὅσος, -η, -ον; "all that" [BDAG 729b])—in synonymous parallelism and grammatically unconnected—produce "a vivid and impassioned effect" (BDF §460[3]; "very emphatic" [O'Brien 500; H-M 250]). The sixfold ὅσα functions as a lengthy pendant nom. cstr., summarized (along with εἴ τις ἀρετή καὶ εἴ τις ἔπαινος) in ταῦτα, the acc. dir. obj. of λογίζεσθε, in the main clause. EVV that reverse the syntax sacrifice the rhetorical effect (e.g., "let your minds be filled with everything that is true, etc." [NJB]). The ἐστίν occurs only in the first ὅσα–clause (sg. vb. w/neut. pl. subj. [BDF §133]; most EVV sg. throughout ["whatever is"]; cf. "everything that is" [BDAG 13d]).

Some have attempted to read v. 8 in terms of Jewish moral values (a "forced interpretation" [Reumann 638]; but cf. the par. in Jas 3:13–18, one of the least Hellenized books in the NT [Fee 415 n. 11]). The following considerations suggest, however, that Paul has moved beyond Judaism to affirm broadly Hellenistic virtues shared by the Philippians' pagan contemporaries ("current coin in popular moral philosophy, especially in Stoicism" [O'Brien 502]; Hansen 296; H-M 250; Reumann 638; Wright 236):

a. Προσφιλῆ and εὔφημα occur nowhere else in the NT (εὔφημα nowhere in the LXX) (O'Brien 502).
b. Paul uses ἀρετή nowhere else in the extensive paraenesis that marks his letters, in spite of the fact that the term was the "primary Greek word for 'virtue' or 'moral excellence'" (Fee 419; Hansen 296).
c. Paul uses δίκαια here in a broader sense than he generally does when he draws upon the δίκαι- word group (Reumann 638; see below).
d. Such virtue lists were common in the Greco-Roman world, though none contains the same particulars (H.-G. Link and A. Ringwald, NIDNTT 3.925–27; C. G. Kruse, DPL 962–63; Hansen 296). The Stoics elaborated upon Plato's list of four cardinal virtues (prudence, justice, fortitude, and temperance) with their own catalogs of virtues (e.g., "justice . . . piety . . . endurance . . . bravery . . . contempt of death" [Seneca, De tranq. anim. 3.4; LCL Moral Essays 2:224–25]). Aristotle had developed a lengthy virtue list, as well (Eth. nic. 2.6–9). Cicero extols "all that is lovely, honourable, of good report" (Tusc. 5.23.67; LCL 141:493).

Paul "obviously assumes a certain consensus in ethical judgment" (G. Delling, TDNT 8.30 n. 20). In the words of Justin Martyr, "The truth which men in all lands have rightly spoken belongs to us" (2 Apol. 2.13, cited by H-M 249). The sentiment is not unique to our passage. Paul elsewhere draws upon common ethical ground (Rom 2:14–15; 1 Cor 5:1) or identifies behavior that is in accordance with custom or broadly accepted morality (Rom 13:1; 1 Cor 11:4–6; cf. 9:7–8, 13) (O'Brien 503).

The commendation of pagan virtues is qualified in v. 9 (cf., also on εἴ τις, below), where Paul filters the virtues through his own instruction and example so that "[u]ltimately, life in Christ brings to fulfillment the highest moral aspirations in the surrounding culture" (Hansen 297; cf. the helpful contrast between Gk. and NT virtues in H.-G. Link and A. Ringwald, NIDNTT 3.927). The tension between v. 8 (Hellenistic virtues) and v. 9 (Paul's cruciform lifestyle) reflects the complex realities of the Philippians' own situation, as a people whose commonwealth and Lord are in heaven (v. 9) but who continue to live among their fellow colonists in Philippi under the earthly lordship of Caesar (v. 8).

Ἀληθῆ (the adjs. are all nom. pl. neut.) is from ἀληθής, -ές, "pert. to being in accordance with fact" (BDAG 43b; "true in fact" [MM 21d]; "true" [EVV]; "upright" [R. Bultmann, TDNT 1.248]; "true [honest]" [Spicq 1.82–83 n. 75]). Ἀληθῆ here does not mean "true" in the typical Pauline sense, "whatever conforms to the gospel" (pace Fee 417). The occurrence in a list of Hellenistic ethical qualities points to a more comprehensive meaning: "'true' in the sense of 'truthful,' and 'truthful' in every aspect of life, including thought, speech, and act" (H-M 251; Hansen 297; O'Brien 504; "true/ honest/genuine" in a Greco-Roman moral sense [Reumann 617]).

The second virtue, σεμνά (σεμνός, -ή, -όν), denotes "august qualities in a person that call forth respect, awe, and reverence" (Reumann 617; "pert. to evoking special respect" [BDAG 919a]; used of gods [e.g., Isis] and even cities [MM 572a]; "worthy of respect" [Fee 417]). The term has a richness that is impossible to equate with any single Eng. word (H-M 251); thus, "honorable, worthy, venerable, holy, above reproach" (BDAG 919b). Generally, "honorable" in EVV (P. Fieldler, *EDNT* 3.238b; "noble" [NIV], "pure" [CEV]). The adj. and noun are used in the Pastorals for church leaders (1 Tim 3:8; Titus 2:2, 7; "an ethical and aesthetic outlook resulting in decency and orderliness" [W. Günther, *NIDNTT* 2.95]) and the life of Christians (1 Tim 2:2).

Δίκαιος (-αία, -ον), used in the neut., "denotes that which is obligatory in view of certain requirements of justice"; "right, fair, equitable" (BDAG 247a; G. Schneider, *EDNT* 1.324c; "just" [NRSV, HCSB, ESV]; "right" [NIV, NLT, CEV, NASB]). The δίκαιος person in Greco-Roman tradition is "one who upholds the customs and norms of behavior, including esp. public service, that make for a well-ordered, civilized society" (BDAG 246b; H. Seebass, *NIDNTT* 3.353). For pagans such obligations encompassed realms both human and divine, and it is certainly the case that what is "right" for Paul is "always defined by God and his character" (Fee 417–18). Paul uses δίκαια here "in a broadly secular sense" (cf. 1:7; Col 4:1; cf. Matt 20:4), however, so that the covenant obligations between Israel's God and his people—most often associated with the δίκαι- word group in Paul—are not immediately in view (Hansen 298; G. Schrenk, *TDNT* 2.187–88; O'Brien 504).

Ἁγνά ("pure" [EVV; BDAG 13d]; "holy" [CEV]), originally a cultic word, here exhibits its transferred moral sense, "moral purity and sincerity" (F. Hauck, *TDNT* 1.122; "pure, undefiled" in conduct [H. Balz, *EDNT* 1.22c]). In Gk. civic life, ἁγνός (-ή, -όν) was "a term of honour denoting the blameless discharge of office" (F. Hauck, *TDNT* 1.122). In the LXX the word had the particular nuance of "integrity" (Ps 11:7; Pr 20:9; cf. 15:26; 21:8) (O'Brien 504). Ἁγνός and its cognates have broad application in the NT, e.g., "chaste" (2 Cor 11:2; Titus 2:5), "innocent" (2 Cor 7:11), "morally pure" (1 John 3:3), in summary, "whatever is not 'besmirched' or 'tainted' in some way by evil" (Fee 418). The adj. can describe every area of life, including one's motives (H-M 251; cf. Phil 1:17). "For Paul, purity in all of life begins in the thought life" (Hansen 298).

With προσφιλῆ (προσφιλή, -ές) we encounter a term denoting conduct that has little to do with morality in itself but is recognized as admirable by the world at large ("aesthetic appreciation" [Hansen 298]; "that which calls for love" [cf. προσ + φιλή] [O'Brien 505]). Προσφιλή broadly pertains to anything eliciting admiration and affection, "pleasing, agreeable, lovely, amiable" (BDAG 886d–887a; MM 552d; "lovely" [NIV, HCSB, ESV]; "pleasing" [NRSV], "admirable" [NAB, NEB]; "friendly" [CEV] is incorrect; H-M 251). "Here is where Mozart and Beethoven (not only Bach!) come under Christian embrace" (Fee 417 n. 17).

EVV assign to εὔφημα (εὔφημος, -ον) a pass. sense ("admirable" [NIV, NLT]; "that we . . . admire" [NJB]; "commendable" [NRSV, HCSB, ESV]; "of good repute" [NASB]; "honorable" [GNB]; "praiseworthy, commendable" [BDAG 414d]). The adj.

does not, however, appear to have been used elsewhere in the pass., so most commentators prefer an active meaning, "well-speaking," hence "winning, attractive," not "well-spoken of, well reputed" (H-M 251; cf. etym. εὖ ["well"]+ φημί- ["say"]; "hightoned" [Moffatt]; "fair-spoken, fair-sounding" [LJS 757]; "well-sounding" [H. Balz, *EDNT* 2.86c]; O'Brien 505; Reumann 618; cf. 2 Cor 6:8, where εὐφημίας means "good report" [Hansen 299]). Εὔφημος, like προσφιλή, transcends strictly moral categories (Fee 418).

εἴ τις ἀρετὴ καὶ εἴ τις ἔπαινος

The εἴ τις ("if there is any" + noun [NRSV, HCSB, ESV]; "if anything is" + adj. [NIV]) can be connected to what precedes in three ways:

1. Take εἴ τις as a rhetorical variation for ὅσα, resulting in eight parallel virtues (Reumann 619, 640).
2. Εἴ τις ἀρετὴ καὶ εἴ τις ἔπαινος "are inclusive of the preceding" and summarize the previous six virtues (O'Brien 500; e.g., "fill your minds with those things that are good and that deserve praise: things that are true, noble, right, pure, lovely, and honorable" [GNB]); the sg. nouns reinforce "the comprehensive nature of the exhortation" (O'Brien 505).
*3. The clauses function in their normal grammatical sense as the protases of simple first class conds.: "If there is anything morally excellent [to them], consider . . ." (Fee 416 n. 13). Paul intends the Philippians to select out what is ἀρετή and ἔπαινος from among the sixfold ὅσα list (Fee 416; Sumney 106).

The third option most naturally accounts for the grammar. The lack of inherent morality in the two immediately previous terms (προσφιλῆ and εὔφημα) likely called for this "interrupting double proviso" (Fee 419). The first class cond. assumes, for the sake of argument, the truth of the condition (Hansen 299; H-M 248; O'Brien 500).

Ἀρετή (nom. sg. fem., ἀρετή, -ῆς) was a key term in Gk. ethics. For Plato it took precedence over and included such virtues as σοφία ("wisdom"), ἀνδρεία ("courage"), σωφροσύνη ("prudence"), and δικαιοσύνη ("justice") (*Resp.* 4.433, 442 B-D). Ἀρετή later became a favorite in Stoic discussions of morality. The term denotes "consummate 'excellence' or 'merit' within a social context." "Exhibition of ἀρετή invites recognition, resulting in renown or glory" (BDAG 130b; proper to "an 'honor' culture" [Reumann 640]). The ideas surface in the Maccabean lit., where ἀρετή describes "the fidelity of the heroes of faith in life and death" ("the single basic meaning" is "eminence" [O. Bauernfeind, *TDNT* 1.458–59]). The two aspects of ἀρετή—moral and social ("excellence of character, exceptional civic virtue" BDAG 130b)—make it hard to translate: "excellence" (NRSV, NASB, ESV; "excellent" [NIV]) is too broad; "moral excellence" is better (HCSB; H-M 249; O'Brien 506), though still lacking the nuance of public recognition (conveniently supplied in our context by ἔπαινος).

Paul uses ἀρετή nowhere else in his letters (a "signal" that he is dealing with Hellenistic, not Jewish, virtues [Hansen 296]), and the meaning of the term as outlined above is absent from the OT, as well, perhaps because the Gk. concept of virtue "was far too anthropocentric" (O. Bauernfeind, *TDNT* 1.460; H-M 249). Isaiah used ἀρετή, instead, of God's "excellencies" (42:8, 12; 43:21; 63:7). Peter uses ἀρετή twice in that sense (God's "wonderful deeds" [1 Pet 2:9]; his praiseworthy "excellence" [2 Pet 1:3]), and twice of human virtue ("moral excellence" [2 Pet 1:5, 2x]).

Ἔπαινος can refer to the act of praise or, as here, to "a thing worthy of praise" (BDAG 357b; "the object of praise" [O. Hofius, *EDNT* 2.16d]; "worthy of praise" or "praiseworthy" [EVV]). Humans are most often the objects of praise in the NT (Rom 2:29; Rom 13:3; 1 Cor 4:5; 2 Cor 8:18; Phil 1:11 [see above]; 1 Pet 1:7; 2:14; God as object in Eph 1:6, 12, 14). Praise comes from both God (Rom 2:29; 1 Cor 4:5; Phil 1:11; 1 Pet 1:7) and men (Rom 13:3; 2 Cor 8:18; 1 Pet 2:14). The latter idea—"general human recognition . . . a concept of civic life"—is most immediately in view in v. 8, where ἔπαινος occurs among a catalog of Hellenistic virtues (H. Preisker, *TDNT* 2.587; H-M 249; Hansen 299; O'Brien 507). These pagan virtues will be qualified in v. 9, however, by the example of Paul's own cruciform life, so that approval of God cannot be wholly excluded (Fee 419).

Western mss. (D* F G it^{ar, d, f, g, o} vg^{cl}) added ἐπιστήμης, "praise of understanding," either (a) because scribes were unfamiliar with the pass. sense "worthy of praise" and added an obj. to its act. sense (Silva 199), or (b) as "an attempt to put the whole totality within the framework of the 'mind'" (Fee 413 n. 2; UBS^5 = {A} ἔπαινος).

ταῦτα λογίζεσθε

The pron. ταῦτα ("these things" [most EVV]; "such things" [NIV]) picks up the six ὅσα-clauses, along with their qualifiers, εἴ τις ἀρετὴ καὶ εἴ τις ἔπαινος (R 698; O'Brien 507).

Λογίζεσθε is 2 pl. pres. mid. impv. from λογίζομαι, clearly denoting "continuing activity" (O'Brien 507). Though λογίζομαι is generally parsed as dep., the personal interest of the subject persists in "verbs of mental action" (R 812; Porter 71). The vb., which meant "to hold a view about someth[ing]" in 3:13, here means "give careful thought to a matter" (BDAG 598a; "thinking as a reasoning process" [H.-W. Bartsch, *EDNT* 2.355b]; "think about" [NRSV, NIV, ESV]). The idea is not so much "think high thoughts" as "'take into account' the good that they have long known from their own past, as long as it is conformable to Christ" (Fee 415–16; "dwell on" [NASB, HCSB]; "fix your thoughts on" [NLT]). The vbs. λογίζεσθε (v. 8) and πράσσετε (v. 9) should not be too sharply contrasted, i.e., as thought versus action. Paul wants the Philippians to reflect on the virtues in v. 8 "so that their conduct will be shaped by them" (O'Brien 507 [cf. 511 n. 71]; H-M 250; Reumann 639).

VERSE 9

ἃ καὶ ἐμάθετε καὶ παρελάβετε καὶ ἠκούσατε καὶ εἴδετε ἐν ἐμοί

With v. 9 the letter's paraenesis concludes. Having already qualified the sixfold list of virtues with εἴ τις ἀρετὴ καὶ εἴ τις ἔπαινος (v. 8), Paul now expands upon that qualification by drawing, once again, on the motif of imitation. As it turns out, Paul is not embracing Stoicism or Hellenistic moralism, as such (cf. vv. 11–13, where Paul transforms the Stoic conception of self-sufficiency into Christ sufficiency). The list of virtues in v. 8 is to be read—and put into practice (πράσσετε)—in light of what "you have learned and received and heard and seen in me" (Fee 414–15, 419–20; Wright 449).

An acc. neut. pl. rel. pron. begins the sentence, to be summed up later with the demonstrative ταῦτα. The change from the quantitative (ὅσα) to the def. (ἅ) rel. pron. reflects a transition from general matters to "those particular things that [Paul] himself had taught and which the Philippians had learned from him" (H-M 252).

It is possible to read ἅ as retrospective, picking up the preceding ταῦτα and thereby formally reiterating the qualification in v. 8 (εἴ τις ἀρετὴ καὶ εἴ τις ἔπαινος) in terms of Paul's own life and teaching (Hansen 300; O'Brien 508). Sentences beginning with a def. rel. pron. do, in fact, generally "introduce a further and specific elaboration of the preceding subject at hand" (Bockmuehl 254; see 1 Cor 2:13; Gal 2:10; 1 Pet 3:21; Acts 11:30; 26:10), though the rule is not absolute (cf. Gal 1:20). In the present case, however, the par. grammatical cstrs. in v. 8 and v. 9 (see diagram) show that the ἅ in v. 9 goes with the ταῦτα that follows, just as the sixfold ὅσα went with the ταῦτα that followed the rel. cstr. in v. 8. (R 698; Fee 413 n. 5; Reumann 640). The qualifying relationship of v. 9 to v. 8, then, is semantic, not syntactical, and the EVV are correct to begin a new sentence with v. 9.

The four vbs. are each 2 pl. aor. act. indic. and are variously grouped together:

1. Take the first three to refer to Paul's teaching, the last to his behavior ("Do the things that you learned, received, and heard from me, and that you saw me do" [Goodspeed]).

2. See the second two vbs. expressing the content of the first two ("what you learned and received from me, both from my words and my actions" [GNB, cf. NLT]).

*3. Take ἐμάθετε καὶ παρελάβετε to refer to Paul's teaching, ἠκούσατε καὶ εἴδετε to his example (Hansen 300; O'Brien 509).

Of the three options listed, the last is superior. It may be best, however, to leave the issue open by simply stringing together the four vbs. (with most EVV), thereby preserving the staccato effect of the repeated καί ("polysyndeton produces the impression of extensiveness and abundance by means of an exhausting summary" [BDF §460[3]; R 1182).

The initial καί (omitted in most EVV) is problematic. Those who take ἅ to refer back to ταῦτα in v. 8 interpret the conj. to mean "also" (O'Brien 508). This, however, is unlikely (see, above, on ἅ). An adversative reading has been suggested (cf. "and yet, and in spite of that, nevertheless" [BDAG 495b]), but καί is rarely, if ever, used adversatively in the NT (we would expect ἀλλά or δέ [O'Brien 508]). It is improbable, moreover, that Paul wished to drive such a wedge between vv. 8 and 9 (cf. "Indeed" [Reumann 621]). The conj. is best interpreted, in conjunction with the second καί, as the first in a pair of correlatives: "both learned and received."

Ἐμάθετε (from μανθάνω; "[have] learned" [EVV; BDAG 615c]) refers to what Paul preached and taught while in Philippi (O'Brien 509; Reumann 620; "You know the teachings I gave you" [CEV, combining ἃ καὶ ἐμάθετε καὶ παρελάβετε]). Although μανθάνω can refer to simply acquiring new information (e.g., μαθὼν ὅτι Ῥωμαῖός ἐστιν [Acts 23:27]), it is more often used in the NT in the OT sense of learning and appropriating the will of God (Matt 9:13; 11:29; John 6:45; 1 Cor 4:6; "to gain knowledge or skill by instruction" [BDAG 615c]; "rejection of the old existence and beginning the new life of discipleship in him" [D. Müller, NIDNTT 1.486]; "consistently has an intellectual focus" but "includes also the conduct of one's life" [G. Nebe, EDNT 2.384c]).

The primary emphasis of παρελάβετε (from παραλαμβάνω) in v. 9 "lies not so much on receiving or taking over, as on the fact that the word implies agreement or approval," i.e., not "received" (EVV; "were told" [NJB]) but "accept[ed]" (BDAG 768b; cf. τὸ εὐαγγέλιον ὃ εὐηγγελισάμην ὑμῖν, ὃ καὶ παρελάβετε [1 Cor 15:1]). A secondary nuance relates to the semitechnical use of παραλαμβάνω to denote "the receiving of something delivered by tradition" (O'Brien 509; "a [technical term] for the apostolic paradosis" [A. Kreitzer, EDNT 3.30c]; cf. 1 Cor 15:3; 11:23). Paul inherited the idea of transmitting and safeguarding a tradition from rabbinic Judaism ("Moses received the Law from Sinai and committed it to Joshua, and Joshua to the elders, and the elders to the Prophets, and the Prophets committed it to the men of the Great Synagogue" [m. ʾAbot 1:1, Danby, 446]; G. Delling, TDNT 4.13; Hansen 300 n. 124). With παρελάβετε in v. 9, then, Paul (a) portrays himself as "a link in the chain of tradition" and (b) implicitly charges the Philippians with the task of guarding and carefully passing on the tradition to others (H-M 253). The Christian tradition for Paul comprised: (1) a summary of the gospel itself (1 Cor 15:1–5; 1 Thess 2:13); (2) various teachings of Jesus (1 Cor 11:23–36; 7:10–11; 9:14); and (c) ethical and procedural rules (1 Cor 11:2; 1 Thess 4:1; 2 Thess 3:6). The third category is in view here (O'Brien 510).

Ἠκούσατε ("heard" [most EVV]) may refer to Paul's teaching, i.e., "what you heard me preach." More likely, however, ἠκούσατε is to be taken closely with εἴδετε ("have . . . seen" [most EVV]; "saw" [NLT]) to refer to the "impression made on the Philippians by Paul's Christian character" (O'Brien 510; what they "heard" of Paul's lifestyle; Hansen 301; H-M 253). The vbs. ἀκούω and ὁράω were used in par. in this sense earlier in the letter (τὸν αὐτὸν ἀγῶνα ἔχοντες, οἷον εἴδετε ἐν ἐμοὶ καὶ νῦν ἀκούετε ἐν ἐμοί [1:30]), and teaching, as such, has already been mentioned in the present context (ἐμάθετε καὶ παρελάβετε). Paul felt obliged not only to teach but also to show others what it is to be a Christian—thus the "close connection between the word Paul preached and the life he lived" (H-M 253).

Ἐν ἐμοί formally modifies only εἴδετε but can be taken loosely with all four vbs. (O'Brien 511; cf. NJB). Paul placed ἐν ἐμοί after the four vbs. for rhetorical effect ("to say as forcefully as possible that everything he knew, believed, and taught was embodied in himself" [H-M 253]; Hansen 301).

ταῦτα πράσσετε

Πράσσετε is 2 pl. pres. act. impv. from πράσσω, "do, accomplish (oft. used without distinction betw. itself and ποιεῖν)" (BDAG 860b; "do" [RSV, HCSB]; "put into practice" [NIV]; "practice" [NASB, ESV]; "follow my example" [CEV]). Interpreting the *Aktionsart* as iterative ("repeated action" [Reumann 620]) is more accurate than labeling it "continuous" (O'Brien 511; "keep on doing" [NRSV, cf. NJB, NLT]). The term is always used of humans, never of God, in the NT, and usually (but not here) has negative connotations (C. Maurer, *TDNT* 6.635; G. Schneider, *EDNT* 3.145d–146a).

καὶ ὁ θεὸς τῆς εἰρήνης ἔσται μεθ᾽ ὑμῶν

Καί, like the Eng. "and/and" (NIV, HCSB, ESV), can be used in a consecutive sense (as in v. 7), "to introduce a result that comes from what precedes" (Hansen 303 n. 141; "then" [NJB, NLT]; "and so, so" BDF §442[2]; cf. BDAG 495a; "as a consequence" [O'Brien 511]). The καί + fut. indic. ἔσται (3 sg. mid. from εἰμί), occurring where it does in the context, indicates "a promise or word of assurance," not "a wish-prayer or earnest desire" (O'Brien 511 n. 73; Hansen 303).

The phrase ὁ θεὸς τῆς εἰρήνης ("the God of peace" [EVV]) is derived from the OT and is common with Paul (1 Thess 5:23; 1 Cor 14:33; 2 Cor 13:11; Rom 15:33; 16:20; 2 Thess 3:16 [ὁ κύριος τῆς εἰρήνης]). The gen. τῆς εἰρήνης signifies (1) that God is the source and origin of peace ("God, who gives peace, will be with you" [CEV]; "who along creates peace" [Spicq 1.432]; gen. of "product" [Wallace 107]), (2) that he himself is characterized by peace, or (3) "both at once" (H-M 254). The presence of God's Spirit is ultimately in view; "the fruit of the Spirit" is "peace" (Fee 421). Biblically "peace" is "nearly synonymous w. messianic salvation" (BDAG 288a), investing the phrase with application both to relations within the Christian community in Philippi and to relations with Rome and the emperor. For a church wrestling with disunity, Paul's promise offers hope for the restoration and renewal of broken relationships (Hansen 304; W. Foerster, *TDNT* 7.195). In every instance the phrase θεὸς τῆς εἰρήνης (or κύριος τῆς εἰρήνης) occurs in "contexts where there is strife or unrest close at hand" (Fee 420; e.g., 1 Cor 14:33; 2 Thess 3:16; Rom 16:20). On the Roman side, Augustus was called "the guardian of peace" (εἰρηνοφύλαξ), who ended warfare and brought order out of disorder (Philo, *Legat.* 143–47; Antony had earlier conferred the title "peacemaker" [εἰρηνοποιός] on Julius Caesar [*Dio Cass.* 44.49.2]). The *Res Gestae* (13, 25, 26) boasted that Augustus pacified land and sea (Caesar "seems to provide great peace for us" [*Epictet.* 3.13.9–10]). Paul may be intentionally applying an epithet expected in Philippi for Caesar (Reumann 622). Some see an advance in thought over the promise in v. 7 (God himself, who gives peace [v. 9] versus the peace of God [v. 7]) (H-M 254). More likely Paul is expressing the same idea in different words.

FOR FURTHER STUDY

56. Virtue and Vice Lists (4:8)

*Charles, J. Daryl. *DNTB* 1,252–57.

————. "The Language and Logic of Virtue in 2 Peter 1:5–7." *BBR* 8 (1998): 55–73.

————. *Virtue Amidst Vice: The Catalog of Virtues in 2 Peter 1*. JSNTSup 150. Sheffield: Sheffield Academic Press, 1997.

Easton, B. S. "New Testament Ethical Lists." *JBL* 51 (1932): 1–12.

Engberg-Pedersen, Troels. "Paul, Virtues, and Vices." Pages 608–33 in *Paul and the Greco-Roman World: A Handbook*. Edited by J. P. Sampley. Harrisburg, PA: Trinity Press International, 2003.

Fitzgerald, John T. *ABD* 6.857–59.

Kruse, Colin G. *DPL* 962–63.

Malherbe, Abraham J. *Moral Exhortation: A Greco-Roman Sourcebook*. Library of Early Christianity 4. Edited by Wayne Meeks. Westminster: John Knox, 1989. See pages 138–41.

Martin, Ralph P. *NIDNTT* 3.928–32.

McEleney, Neil J. "The Vice Lists of the Pastoral Epistles." *CBQ* 36 (1974): 203–19.

Schroeder, D. *International Dictionary of the Bible: Supplementary Volume* (Nashville: Abingdon, 1976), 546–47.

HOMILETICAL SUGGESTIONS

The God of Peace Will Be with Us (4:8–9)

1. As we focus our thoughts on the right things (v. 8)
2. As we do the right things (v. 9)

IV. Paul's Circumstances and the Philippians' Gift (4:10–20)

10 Ἐχάρην δὲ ἐν κυρίῳ μεγάλως
    ὅτι ἤδη ποτὲ ἀνεθάλετε τὸ ὑπὲρ ἐμοῦ φρονεῖν,
    ἐφ' ᾧ καὶ ἐφρονεῖτε, ἠκαιρεῖσθε δέ.
11   οὐχ ὅτι καθ' ὑστέρησιν λέγω,
    ἐγὼ γὰρ ἔμαθον ἐν οἷς εἰμι αὐτάρκης εἶναι.
12 οἶδα καὶ ταπεινοῦσθαι.
  οἶδα καὶ περισσεύειν·
    ἐν παντὶ καὶ ἐν πᾶσιν
  μεμύημαι,
    καὶ χορτάζεσθαι καὶ πεινᾶν
    καὶ περισσεύειν καὶ ὑστερεῖσθαι.
13 πάντα ἰσχύω
    ἐν τῷ ἐνδυναμοῦντί με.
14 πλὴν καλῶς ἐποιήσατε
        συγκοινωνήσαντές μου τῇ θλίψει.
15 οἴδατε δὲ καὶ ὑμεῖς, Φιλιππήσιοι,
    ὅτι   ἐν ἀρχῇ τοῦ εὐαγγελίου,
        ὅτε ἐξῆλθον ἀπὸ Μακεδονίας,
        οὐδεμία μοι ἐκκλησία ἐκοινώνησεν εἰς λόγον δόσεως καὶ λήμψεως
        εἰ μὴ ὑμεῖς μόνοι,
16   ὅτι καὶ ἐν Θεσσαλονίκῃ καὶ ἅπαξ καὶ δὶς εἰς τὴν χρείαν μοι ἐπέμψατε.
17 οὐχ ὅτι ἐπιζητῶ τὸ δόμα,
    ἀλλὰ ἐπιζητῶ τὸν καρπὸν τὸν πλεονάζοντα εἰς λόγον ὑμῶν.
18 ἀπέχω δὲ πάντα καὶ περισσεύω·
  πεπλήρωμαι
    δεξάμενος παρὰ Ἐπαφροδίτου τὰ παρ' ὑμῶν,
            ὀσμὴν εὐωδίας,
            θυσίαν δεκτήν,
            εὐάρεστον τῷ θεῷ.

19 ὁ δὲ θεός μου πληρώσει πᾶσαν χρείαν ὑμῶν
          κατὰ τὸ πλοῦτος αὐτοῦ
              ἐν δόξῃ ἐν Χριστῷ Ἰησοῦ.
20 τῷ δὲ θεῷ καὶ πατρὶ ἡμῶν ἡ δόξα εἰς τοὺς αἰῶνας τῶν αἰώνων, ἀμήν.

As noted by Guthrie (*Cohesion Shifts*, 45, 58), both 1:12–26 and 4:10–19 treat Paul's circumstances and thereby bracket the body of the letter (1:27–4:9). Two traditional ways of paragraphing the text (10–13, 14–20 [NA[26], NIV, GNB, NAB]; versus 10–14, 15–20 [UBS[5], NRSV, REB]) both wrongly break up what is in fact a single piece in Paul's letter (NASB, NJB) (Fee 426 n. 12).

Parallels with 1:3–11 (Peterman, *Paul's Gift from Philippi*, 91–93):

Εὐχαριστῶ (1:3), χαρᾶς (1:4)	Ἐχάρην (4:10)
κοινωνίᾳ (1:5)	ἐκοινώνησεν (4:15)
φρονεῖν (1:7)	ἐφρονεῖτε (4:10)
περισσεύῃ (1:9)	περισσεύειν (4:12 [2x]), περισσεύω (4:18)
πεπληρωμένοι (1:11)	πεπλήρωμαι (4:18), πληρώσει (4:19)
καρπόν (1:11)	καρπόν (4:17)
Ἰησοῦ (1:11)	Ἰησοῦ (4:19)
δόξαν (1:11)	δόξα (4:20)

VERSE 10

Ἐχάρην δὲ ἐν κυρίῳ μεγάλως

Ἐχάρην is 1 sg. aor. pass. indic. from χαίρω, the first of a series of 1 sg. vbs. (8x in vv. 10–13; 5x in vv. 17–18); a true past tense, "I rejoiced" (NASB, HCSB, ESV, NIV; Hansen 306; O'Brien 516; Reumann 647, Silva 208), not as an epistolary aor., "I rejoice" (*pace* NRSV, NJB; H-M 260). The reception of the gift occurred in the past from Paul's own perspective, not simply from that of the Philippians when they heard the letter (μεγάλως would makes less sense modifying an epistolary aor. [Fee 428 n. 17]).

Some make much of δέ ("important word" [H-M 260–61]; "But" [NASB]), as if Paul had said, "I must not forget to thank you for your gift" (Lightfoot 163). The conj. is properly omitted, however, in most EVV (NRSV, NIV, HCSB, ESV; Fee 428; O'Brien 516 n. 7). Paul had already alluded to the Philippians' generosity earlier in the letter (Phil 1:3–5; 2:25–30), so he has not actually forgotten anything. Δέ simply marks the transition to a new section (Fee 428 n. 16).

The adv. modifier ἐν κυρίῳ ("in the Lord" [EVV]) can be taken as the ultimate ground/basis of Paul's rejoicing ("the ultimate Provider of all good gifts" [Hansen 306]; H-M 261; O'Brien 517; see below on ὅτι), or simply to characterize an activity or state "as Christian" (Reumann 647).

The adv. μεγάλως ("greatly" [most EVV]; with χαρῆναι, "to be very glad" [BDAG 623b] or "full of joy" [NJB]) is a NT *hapax* (O'Brien 516). Only here does Paul quantify his experience of joy, thus intensifying the expression of the depth of his feeling (H-M 261; Paul "burst into joy" [Fee 428]; cf. "How I praise the Lord" [NLT]).

ὅτι ἤδη ποτὲ ἀνεθάλετε τὸ ὑπὲρ ἐμοῦ φρονεῖν

The ὅτι—taken by EVV ("that") as a noun clause, giving the content of Paul's rejoicing—functions semantically in a causal sense (cf. BDAG 732b; 1,075a; Fee 428 n. 21; Vg. *quoniam*). The ultimate cause of Paul's joy was the Lord (ἐν κυρίῳ); the more immediate cause (ὅτι) was the Philippians' concern for his welfare (H-M 261; O'Brien 517).

The adv. expression ἤδη ποτέ denotes the idea of culmination ("now at length/at last" [most EVV]; "once again" [HCSB; BDAG 434d]; R 1147; cf. Rom 1:10), not that of elapsed time. Paul is not chiding the Philippians for delay in sending help. The rest of v. 10 clearly indicates that Paul intends no reproach (O'Brien 517). We do not know how much time had elapsed since the Philippians last assisted Paul ("likely several years" [Fee 429]).

Ἀνεθάλετε is 2 pl. aor. act. indic. from ἀναθάλλω, "to (cause to) be in a state identical with a previous state" (BDAG 63a; "revived" [NRSV, NASB, ESV]; "renewed" [NIV, HCSB]). It was used of trees and flowers "bursting into bloom again," or plants "sprouting afresh" after a period of dormancy (ἀνα ["again"] + θάλλω ["grow, flourish"]) (H-M 262; BDAG 63a). Ἀνεθάλετε can function either of two ways (BDAG 63a; BDF §101; H. Balz, *EDNT* 1.80d): (1) transitively, in a causative sense ("cause to grow/bloom again" [BDAG 63a]; Silva 208), taking τὸ ὑπὲρ ἐμοῦ φρονεῖν (subst. inf.) as an acc. dir. obj. (most EVV; "you have revived your concern for me" [BDAG 63a]; Wallace 602; O'Brien 518; Reumann 648), or (2) intransitively, taking the inf. phrase as an acc. of ref. ("you have revived, as far as your care for me is concerned" [BDAG 63a]; Moule 33–34; R 476). The result is much the same (H-M 262; O'Brien 518).

Φρονέω (pres. act. inf.) + ὑπέρ means not simply "think about" but, intensively, "be concerned about" ("your care for me" [HCSB; BDAG 63a, cf. 1065a]; "your concern for me" [NRSV, NIV, ESV]). The repetition of "the key verb of this letter" is hardly an accident [H-M 261]). Through their gift the Philippians expressed the mind-set Paul enjoins elsewhere (φρονῆτε [2:2]; φρονεῖτε [2:5]; Hansen 307). Reumann (648) thinks the art. is anaphoric, identifying something well known to both parties, previously done and now revived. More likely, τό simply marks the inf. cstr. as the acc. obj. of ἀνεθάλετε.

ἐφ' ᾧ καὶ ἐφρονεῖτε, ἠκαιρεῖσθε δέ

Omitted in some EVV (NASB, NIV), ἐφ' ᾧ has occasioned a variety of explanations:

1. causal (BDF §235 [2]; R 963; Harris 140; H-M 262; but this "makes little sense" [O'Brien 518 n. 25]);
2. temporal (T 272);

*3. "about whom," taking ᾧ as masc. ("for me" [NRSV, ESV; cf. HCSB]; Reumann 650); or

*4. "with regard to which," taking ᾧ as neut. (Moule 132; Fee 430; O'Brien 518; antecedent = τὸ ὑπὲρ ἐμοῦ [Sumney 110]).

Views 3 and 4 make the best contextual sense of the construction. The καί emphasizes the repeated φρονέω (O'Brien 518 n. 28) and should be tr. "in fact" (HCSB) or "indeed" (NRSV, NIV, ESV; Fee 430; Reumann 649). The *Aktionsart* of ἐφρονεῖτε (2 pl. impf. act. indic.) and ἠκαιρεῖσθε (2 pl. impf. mid. indic.) denotes "a continual concern for Paul with a likewise ongoing lack of opportunity" (Fee 430; H-M 262; "(repeatedly) concerned" [Reumann 648]; O'Brien 518; "you were thinking about me all along" [CEV]).

Ἠκαιρεῖσθε (NT *hapax*) is from ἀκαιρέομαι (cf. α + καιρός), "have no opportunity, have no time" (BDAG 34b; RSV, NIV, ESV; "you didn't have the chance" [NLT, CEV]). Explanations vary, none of which can be fully supported (Reumann 701): (1) a lack of resources on the part of the Philippians (cf. 2 Cor 8:1–4); (2) no one to send on the long and difficult journey to Rome; (3) no need on Paul's part, until the imprisonment; (4) Paul's unwillingness to accept a gift.

VERSE 11

οὐχ ὅτι καθ᾽ ὑστέρησιν λέγω

Supply ἐστίν to οὐχ ὅτι: "(It is) not that" (T 303; R 965; Reumann 650). Paul vacillates throughout vv. 10–20 between affirmation of the Philippians' generosity (3x: vv. 10, 14–16, 18–20) and insistence on his own self-sufficiency (2x: vv. 11–13, 17), thus seeming to be a "reluctant recipient" of the gift (Hansen 305). Paul's equivocation—called by some a "thankless thanks"—finds explanation in two ancient social institutions:

a. Greco-Roman Friendship—The identification of Philippians as a Greco-Roman hortatory letter of friendship has not been universally accepted in recent scholarship (Bockmuehl 35; Reumann 678–83; Still, "More than Friends," 56–66). Friendship language is present, however, as a secondary theme of the epistle ("topoi of friendship rather than Gattung of friendship" [Reed 172]), and we find a significant concentration of such terms in 4:10–20. This, in turn, sheds light on Paul's strategy in the passage.

In antiquity friendship based on need was considered inferior to true friendship, which occurred between persons who were self-sufficient or content: "It is far from being true that friendship is cultivated because of need; rather it is cultivated by those who are most abundantly blessed with wealth and power and especially virtue, which is man's best defense; by those least in need of another's help; and by those most generous and most given to acts of kindness" (Cicero, *Amic.* 14.51; cf. 9.30, tr. Falconer, LCL, cited by Hansen 311; cf. Aristotle, *Eth. nic.* 8.3.1–5).

Additionally, among friends explicit expressions of gratitude (e.g., via the use of εὐχαριστεῖν) were apparently not the norm (Reumann 719). Thus a papyrus letter reads, "I may dispense with writing to you with a great show of thanks (μεγάλας εὐχαριστίας); for it is to those who are not friends that we must give thanks in words" (P. Merton 12 [AD 58] cited by Fee 446 n. 31). Instead, friends would express their gratitude by engaging in the "contest of benefits" that often characterized ὁ λόγος δόσεως καὶ λήμψεως (cf. v. 15, below) in the ancient world (Reumann 682). The person on the receiving end of a gift would feel obligated to respond ("he who does not repay a benefit sins" [Seneca *De ben.* 1.1.13]), likely with a larger gift, thereby placing the obligation back in the hands of the original benefactor. The result would be a "most honorable contest" of outdoing benefits with benefits (*De ben.* 1.4.4).

b. Patron-Client Relations—Expectations surrounding the institution of patronage also serve to explain Paul's apparent equivocation surrounding the gift. The unqualified acceptance of the Philippians' generosity on Paul's part would have tacitly placed Paul in the role of a client vis-à-vis the Philippians (particularly since Paul was unable to respond in kind), an arrangement that Paul had already risked by accepting Lydia's hospitality (Acts 16:15) and previous gifts from Philippi (4:15–16).

The apparent equivocation in vv. 10–20, therefore, makes good sense. With respect to "b," above, the apostle will not be co-opted as the Philippians' client, thus (1) Paul's insistence that, unlike a typical Roman client, he is not actually in need, since he is self-sufficient in Christ (vv. 11–13), and (2) his use of expressions of appreciation such as καλῶς ἐποιήσατε (v. 14), which sounds "like a teacher congratulating a student" (Peterman, *Paul's Gift from Philippi*, 145), rather than an explicit "thank you," which would have sounded like a client responding to the generosity of patron (Hansen 316–17). Regarding friendship language ("a," above), with ἀπέχω πάντα (v. 18), Paul does, in fact, acknowledge that "his 'receipt' of what they have 'given' puts the 'obligation' of friendship back on his side" (Fee 451). In a brilliant countermove ("adaptation of convention" [Reed 295]), however, Paul transfers this obligation to God (Fee 444; Reumann 705), who will ultimately prove the victor in any contest of benefits, whether as Paul's benefactor (v. 13) or the Philippians' (ὁ δὲ θεός μου πληρώσει πᾶσαν χρείαν ὑμῶν κατὰ τὸ πλοῦτος αὐτοῦ [v. 19]; Hansen 310).

Paul's alleged lack of gratitude has, in fact, been overemphasized. The expression of joy in v. 10, for example, "certainly communicates thankfulness" (Silva 208; "implicitly" [Hansen 308]), as does καλῶς ἐποιήσατε in v. 14 (F. Hauck, *TDNT* 3.807). On all this see the works of G. Hansen, P. Marshall, and G. Peterman cited in For Further Study 28.

Ὑστέρησιν (acc. sg. fem.) is from ὑστέρησις, -εως, ἡ, "the condition of lacking that which is essential" (BDAG 1044b). This form of the root, found only here in Paul, is to be compared with ὑστερήμα (2:30; cf. 1 Thess 3:10; 1 Cor 16:17; 2 Cor 8:14; 9:12; 11:9). The former (-ησις) emphasizes the verbal idea; -ήμα nouns denote a concrete expression. Thus, Paul is not referring to a specific expression of need but to "being in need" (Fee 431 n. 33). It is not necessary, therefore, to read καθ᾽ causally (*pace* BDAG 512d, 1,044b; H-M 263; O'Brien 520). The basic sense—"the standard by which something is measured"—works fine with the verbal noun ὑστέρησις: it is not "personal 'need' which sets the standard for what I say" (Fee 431 n. 3). Paul's joy is not that "of a poor person whose need has been met" (U. Wilckens, *TDNT* 8.599) but of a man whose Christian family has found renewed opportunity to tangibly express its Christlike mind-set of concern for him.

Λέγω is variously rendered: "complain(ing)" (RSV, CEV); "say(ing)" (NIV, NJB, HCSB); "speak(ing)" (NASB, ESV).

ἐγὼ γὰρ ἔμαθον ἐν οἷς εἰμι αὐτάρκης εἶναι

Some see little emphasis in ἐγώ (T 37). Paul likely singles himself out, however, to some degree: "I, for my part, whatever it may be with others" (O'Brien 520; H-M 263). The explanatory γάρ ("for" [most EVV; Fee 431]; omit [NJB, CEV]) gives the reason for the previous disclaimer.

Followed by an inf. (εἶναι), μανθάνω (1 sg. aor. act. indic.) means "to learn how," rather than "to learn that" (R 1,040–41; NLT; "to come to a realization, with implication of taking place less through instruction than through experience or practice" [BDAG 615c]; K. Rengstorf, *TDNT* 4.410; "learn by experience" [Reumann 651]). The consummative aor. is best rendered with an Eng. perf. ("have learned" [EVV]; O'Brien 520; R 835, 845; cf. BDF §322[1]).

᾽Εν οἷς εἰμι is not indef. but formally truncates ἐν τούτοις ἐν οἷς εἰμι and could therefore be read narrowly in terms of Paul's current situation: "in these (things) in which I am" (R 721; "with what I have" [TEV]; Reumann 651). The pl. οἷς (dat. neut. rel. pron.), however, along with the surrounding context (cf. ἐν παντὶ καὶ ἐν πᾶσιν [v. 12]), supports the more encompassing interpretation of the rel. pron. reflected in most EVV ("whatever state/circumstances/situation"; Fee 431 n. 36; O'Brien 521; Sumney 111).

Αὐτάρκης (nom. sg. masc. adj. from αὐτάρκης, -ες) "looks like a meteor fallen from the Stoic sky" (Fee 431; αὐτάρκης retains the nom. in the inf. obj. clause because εἶναι has a nominal predicate and shares the same subj. as ἔμαθον [T 146; R 1,037–38]). The meaning of the adj. (from αὐτός ["self"] + ἀρκέω ["suffice, be enough"]) ranges from a subj. sense, "satisfied, content" (EVV), to the more obj. notion, "self-sufficient" ("'content,' perh. 'self-sufficient'" [BDAG 152a]; "contented, in need of no support" [H. Balz, *EDNT* 1.179b]). Αὐτάρκης represented "the essence of all virtues" for Stoic and Cynic philosophers, who sought an inward state unaffected by external circumstances (O'Brien 520). Cynics pursued self-sufficiency through austerity (eliminating possessions), engaging in culturally anomalous (even scandalous) behavior, and often adopting an itinerant life. Stoics focused more on inner tranquility, whatever their circumstances might be. Paul in v. 11 sounds more Stoic than Cynic ("exactly like something Seneca or Epictetus could have written" [Fee 431–32 n. 37]). Seneca, a Stoic philosopher who was a contemporary of Paul's, claims that "the wise person will develop virtue" whether "in riches" or "in poverty," "in his own country" or "in exile," "as commander" or "as a soldier," "healthy" or "sickly" (*Ep. Mor.* 2.309; cf. 9.13). Seneca elsewhere asserts that "the happy man is content with his present lot, no matter what it is, and is reconciled to his circumstances" (*De Vita Beata* 6). Commentators differ over whether Paul has Stoicism directly in view. By Paul's time the technical meaning of αὐτάρκης, "self-sufficient," had given way to a general, nonphilosophical sense, "content" (G. Kittel, *TDNT* 1.466–67; Fee 431–32; O'Brien 521; Reumann 653; Silva 204). Paul uses the cognate αὐτάρκεια elsewhere twice in this nontechnical sense (2 Cor 9:8; 1 Tim 6:6). The appearance of the *hapax* αὐτάρκης here, however, in a context full of Stoic overtones, suggests a philosophical background (MM 93c; H-M 264; Hansen 311; "it is difficult to imagine the Philippians not having recognized it as such" [Fee 432]).

Paul's αὐτάρκεια, however, is ultimately not a "*self*-sufficiency" at all. No Stoic would have added πάντα ἰσχύω ἐν τῷ ἐνδυναμοῦντί με (v. 13). Nor would a Stoic philosopher have engaged in Paul's outburst of joy in v. 10 (for the Stoic "emotional detachment is essential" [Hansen 310]; ἐχάρην is "un-Stoic" [Fee 428 n. 20; Reumann 701], as is λύπην ἐπὶ λύπην [2:27]; cf. Wright 433–34, on Paul's different perspective on suffering). The contrast articulated by G. Findlay more than a century ago deserves citation: "The self-sufficiency of the Christian is relative: an independence of the world through dependence upon God. The Stoic self-sufficiency pretends to be absolute. One is the contentment of faith, the other of pride. Cato (a Roman Stoic) and Paul both stand erect and fearless before a persecuting world: one with a look of rigid, defiant scorn, the other with a face now lighted up with unutterable joy in God" (G. Findlay, *Christian Doctrine* [London: Charles Kelly, 1894], 31).

VERSE 12

οἶδα καὶ ταπεινοῦσθαι, οἶδα καὶ περισσεύειν

Paul now explains what he meant by αὐτάρκης. The first three finite vbs.—οἶδα + οἶδα + μεμύημαι—are parallel to one another and elaborate upon the circumstances in which Paul has learned αὐτάρκης εἶναι. The summary statement in v. 13 then reveals the ultimate source of Paul's contentment.

Οἶδα + inf. (2x, in antithetical parallelism) means "to know/understand how," "can, be able" (BDAG 694a; "to be able" [H. Seesemann, *TDNT* 5.117]). It is not simply that Paul has been exposed to the circumstances that follow ("I know what it is to" [NIV, NRSV, CEV]). Rather, Paul "knows how to live in an appropriate manner" in the midst of such contrasting circumstances (O'Brien 523; "I know how to" [NJB, HCSB, ESV]).

Some take the twofold καί as "even . . . also" (BDF §444[3]; Reumann 646, 654). A correlative interpretation of the conjs. is better ("both . . . and" [HCSB]; implied by omission of first καί in most EVV; R 1181), even though the intervening οἶδα ("emphatic" [O'Brien 524]) becomes a bit "peculiar" on such a reading (BDF §444[3]).

Ταπεινοῦσθαι is pres. pass. inf. of ταπεινόω (see on 2:8). Some maintain (from usage elsewhere [2:8; 2 Cor 11:7; 2 Cor 12:21]) that the vb. here means "to be humbled"

in a broad sense: "not only indicates 'poverty,' but embraces a way of life similar
to that of his Lord" (Fee 432–43]; "be abased" [RSV]; "be brought low" [ESV]).
In that case, however, we would expect it to be paired not with περισσεύειν but with
ὑψοῦν, "to exalt," the usual antonym of ταπεινόω (O'Brien 524). The context (cf. v.
12, where περισσεύειν is contrasted with ὑστερεῖσθαι; cf. καθ' ὑστέρησιν [v. 11]) points
more narrowly to ταπεινοῦσθαι as "economic deprivation" (O'Brien 523; most EVV;
BDAG 990b–c; W. Grundmann, *TDNT* 8.17–18; H.-H. Esser, *NIDNTT* 2.263; "financial humiliation" [Hansen 312]). The voice is likely pass., rather than mid., since the
discussion assumes the effect of external circumstances beyond Paul's control (not
"to live with renunciation" [H. Giesen, *EDNT* 3.335b]; this idea would more likely be
expressed by the act. + the refl. pron. [cf. 2:8] [Hansen 312]).

The pres. act. inf. περισσεύειν here means "have an abundance, abound, be rich"
(BDAG 805c; "live in prosperity" [NASB]; "have plenty" [NIV]; "have a lot" [HCSB];
Reumann 655). In light of the natural human propensity to covet more even in prosper-
ity, Paul's contentment in abundance is a notable virtue (Hansen 312).

ἐν παντὶ καὶ ἐν πᾶσιν μεμύημαι

Ἐν παντὶ καὶ ἐν πᾶσιν describes "the inclusive and varied spheres of Paul's 'initiation'" (O'Brien 525; "repetition for the sake of emphasis" [B. Reicke, *TDNT* 5.889];
Moule 75). The adv. modifier (take with μεμύημαι) is variously rendered: "[I]n any and
all circumstances" (NRSV, HCSB; cf. NASB; BDAG 660c; "in any and every situation" [NIV; cf. NLT]).

The *hapax* μεμύημαι (1 sg. perf. pass. indic. from μυέω) was a technical term from
the mystery religions to describe "the initiatory rites of a devotee who wished to enter
their secrets and privileges" (O'Brien 525; "initiate (into the mysteries)" [BDAG
660b–c]; MM 418d). Paul uses the term metaphorically (par. to οἶδα, above [Reumann
702]) to refer not to an esoteric rite of entry but, rather, to "moments of learning in
daily life" (Reumann 702). Paul may, indeed, have intended an "ironical" use of a technical term (G. Bornkamm, *TDNT* 4.828), but tr. that reflect this religious background
("learned the secret" [most EVV]) are potentially misleading to the Eng. reader. The
focus is on the result of an initiation process (cf. perf. tense [O'Brien 525]), not upon
a secret learned. Better is the NEB's "very thoroughly initiated into the human lot with
all its ups and downs" (cf. "I have lived . . . I know what it means" [CEV]; Fee 433).

καὶ χορτάζεσθαι καὶ πεινᾶν καὶ περισσεύειν καὶ ὑστερεῖσθαι

The two pairs of correlative conjs. (καί [4x]) are rendered in different ways: "(omit)
. . . and . . . (omit) . . . and" (NRSV, NJB, ESV); "whether . . . or . . . whether . . . or"
(NIV, HCSB); "(omit) . . . and . . . both . . . and" (NASB).

Χορτάζεσθαι is pres. pass. inf. from χορτάζω, "to fill with food" (BDAG 1087b;
"well fed" [NIV, HCSB, cf. NRSV]; "full stomach" [NJB, NLT]; "to eat or to satisfy
with food" [J. Baldwin, *NIDNTT* 1.743]). Πεινᾶν is pres. act. inf. from πεινάω, "to
feel the pangs of lack of food," "be hungry" (BDAG 792c, cf. 1,087b; most EVV;
"empty stomach" [NJB]). Paul is not referring to self-imposed spiritual discipline,

e.g., periods of indulgence alternating with periods of ascetic fasting. Rather, Paul's "concrete fiscal, economic situation" is in view (Reumann 656; J. Behm, *TDNT* 4.925; O'Brien 525). Paul repeats περισσεύειν, now in contrast with ὑστερεῖσθαι, a pres. mid. inf. from ὑστερέω, "lack, be lacking, go without, come short of" (BDAG 1044a; "being in/suffering/facing need" [NRSV, NASB HCSB, ESV]; W. Lane, *NIDNTT* 3.954–55). The two infs. denote, respectively, "[m]aterial abundance and dearth of resources" (Reumann 656; F. Hauck, *TDNT* 6.61).

VERSE 13

πάντα ἰσχύω ἐν τῷ ἐνδυναμοῦντί με

Now the grand paradox: "The secret of Paul's independence was his dependence on Christ" (H-M 266). While it is fair to interpret πάντα ἰσχύω (1 sg. pres. act. indic., "have power, be competent, be able" [BDAG 484c]) to include more than just the varied economic circumstances involved in Paul's apostolic ministry (Fee 343 n. 50), πάντα picks up the preceding ἐν παντὶ καὶ ἐν πᾶσιν (v. 12) and thus refers primarily to "all those circumstances of fullness and hunger, abundance and lack, which the apostle has experienced" (O'Brien 526; "I can do all this" [NIV]; Hansen 314). EVV which imply that nothing was beyond Paul's capabilities ("There is nothing I cannot do" [NJB]; "I can do everything/all things" [NRSV, NASB, NLT]), while grammatically correct, are contextually "misleading to the point of being false" (H-M 266) and make Paul "sound like a superman" (Reumann 703).

The prep. phrase ἐν τῷ ἐνδυναμοῦντί με is taken by many in an instr. sense ("through [H]im" [NIV, NRSV, HCSB]; ἐν as "marker of agency" [BDAG 329a]; BDF §219; M. Harris, *NIDNTT* 3.1210). It may be better to take the modifier in an "incorporative sense, that is, 'in vital union with the one who strengthens me,' with the implication that the One who so strengthens Paul is Christ" (O'Brien 527; "in him" [RSV]; "in the One who" [NJB]; W. Grundmann, *TDNT* 3.398; Fee 434 n. 48; H-M 266; Hansen 315; Moule [77] affirms either option).

Τῷ ἐνδυναμοῦντι is dat. sg. masc. (unless neut., referring to πνεῦμα) of the pres. act. ptc. of ἐνδυναμόω, "to cause one to be able to function or do someth." (BDAG 333b; BDF §148[3]; ἐν- suggests intensity [Moule 88]; "to endow with power" [W. Grundmann, *TDNT* 2.313]). In view of Paul's use of the aor. in 1 Tim 1:12, the pres. may denote "ongoing powerful activity" (O'Brien 527). The ptc. functions as a subst., and likely refers to Christ (ἐνδυναμόω is used of Christ in Eph 6:10; 1 Tim 1:12; 2 Tim 2:1; 4:17; but cf. Rom 4:20), as later scribes assumed (see below) ("Christ, who gives me strength" [NLT]; O. Betz, *NIDNTT* 2.604; H. Paulsen, *EDNT* 1.451b; Fee 434 n. 49; H-M 267; Hansen 315; O'Brien 527).

Some mss. (ℵ² D² Ψ *Byz* etc.) add Χριστῷ for clarity, perhaps due to "the preponderance of 'in Christ' language in the letter" (Fee 426 n. 13). The shorter reading, however, is more likely on internal grounds, and it has much stronger external support

(א* A B D* 1 33 629 ᶦᵗᵃʳ, ᵇ, ᵈ, ᶠ, ᵒ, ʳ copˢᵃ, ᵇᵒ etc.) (H-M 258; O'Brien 515; Reumann 656; USB⁵ = {A} με). If "Christ" were original, there would have been no reason to omit it.

VERSE 14

πλὴν καλῶς ἐποιήσατε συγκοινωνήσαντές μου τῇ θλίψει

The conj. πλήν ("Yet" [RSV, NIV, ESV]; "In any case" [NRSV]; "All the same" [NJB]; "Nevertheless" [NASB]; "Still" [HCSB]) is (a) "always adversative" (R 1187) and (b) serves the function of "breaking off a discussion and emphasizing what is important" (BDAG 826a). Here (a) the term obviates any potential misunderstanding of Paul's assertion of independence in vv. 11–13, and (b) returns to the theme of the section (vv. 10–20) that had been introduced in v. 10 (H-M 267; Hansen 315; Reumann 705). EVV that begin a new paragraph (RSV, NIV, NAB) obscure the unity of vv. 10–20 (Fee 437–38).

The adv. καλῶς is related to the adj. καλός, "good, beautiful, pleasant, noble, splendid" (Fee 438 n. 7). Ἐποιήσατε is 2 pl. aor. act. indic. With ποιεῖν, καλῶς means "be kind enough to do someth." (BDAG 506a; "it was kind of you" [NRSV, ESV]). Fee finds the Eng. equivalent "well" (NLT, NASB, HCSB) unacceptably weak and prefers the literal, if ungrammatical American slang "you did good" (Fee 438 n. 7; "it was good of you" [NIV, NJB, CEV]). More than mere acknowledgment, the idiom καλῶς ἐποιήσατε communicates "positive and generous praise" (O'Brien 528).

With συγκοινωνήσαντές μου τῇ θλίψει Paul returns to the language of 1:7, where he grounds his gratitude (1:3) in the Philippians' partnership together with him ἔν τε τοῖς δεσμοῖς μου καὶ ἐν τῇ ἀπολογίᾳ καὶ βεβαιώσει τοῦ εὐαγγελίου (Fee 438).

Συγκοινωνήσαντές, a key term from the word field of friendship (Reumann 706), is nom. pl. masc. of the aor. act. ptc. of συγκοινωνέω, "to be associated w. someone in some activity," here in the sense of "taking a sympathetic interest" (BDAG 952c; "share (with me)" [EVV]; "help me" [CEV]). The adv. modal ptc. ("by sharing" [HCSB; Fee 438 n. 8]) refers exclusively to the recent gift (H-M 267).

By means of their generosity, the Philippians shared with Paul in his "affliction" (NASB; "trouble(s)" [NIV, RSV, ESV]; συγκοινωνεῖν τῇ θ. = "show an interest in (someone's) distress" [BDAG 457b–c]; the συν- prefix serves "to intensify the emphasis on the mutuality and solidarity of the Philippians and Paul" [Hansen 316]). θλίψει (dat. sg. fem.) is not used here eschatologically (cf. Matt 24:29; Mark 13:19; 2 Thess 1:6) but, rather, of Paul's current imprisonment ("in my present difficulty" [NLT]; Fee 438–39 n. 9; H-M 267).

The grammar is odd. We might expect μοι τῆς θλίψεως, where the μοι naturally picks up the prefix of συγκοινωνήσαντες, and τῆς θλίψεως functions as the participle's gen. dir. obj. ("sharers together with me in the affliction"). Instead, Paul employs a "vernacular possessive" (μου) and places the obj. in the dat. The intended meaning is likely much the same, though now the case of τῇ θλίψει serves more pointedly to emphasize that the Philippians shared with Paul in the affliction itself (Fee 438–39 n. 9). In Paul's view, therefore, the monetary support was more than a gift intended to alleviate difficult circumstances. It was an expression of the Philippians' participation the broader task of proclaiming the gospel, including, especially (cf. 1:7), the θλῖψις Paul experienced as part of his apostolic mission (O'Brien 530 n. 107).

VERSE 15

οἴδατε δὲ καὶ ὑμεῖς, Φιλιππήσιοι

Οἴδατε is 2 pl. perf. (pres. force) act. indic. from οἶδα. The vb. can be taken as impv., "what the Philippians now need to recall" (Reumann 660), or, most likely, as indic. (EVV). The δέ is not adversative but simply transitional, carrying the discourse forward, while καί compares the Philippians with Paul (i.e., "you as well as I" [Hansen 317 n. 224; Reumann 660]), lit. "and you yourselves also know" (H-M 268; O'Brien 530). EVV tend to omit either the δέ (NRSV, NASB) or the καί (RSV, ESV, HCSB).

Καὶ ὑμεῖς + Φιλιππήσιοι "create the impression of strong emphasis . . . . 'sit up and take note of what I am about to say'" (Fee 439 n. 10; Hansen 317 n. 224). Φιλιππήσιοι can be read either as a voc. (NASB, CEV) or a nom. (NIV, ESV, HCSB). Paul uses a Latin spelling found nowhere in Gk. literature (Gr. Φιλιππεῖς or Φιλιππηνοί). The result is a reproduction of part of the official title of the colony (*Colonia Augusta Iulia Philippensis* [renamed by Augustus in 31 BC]), by which Paul "flatters the Philippians" (Reumann 660; "expression of affection" [Fee 439 n. 10]). There may be a bit of irony here, as well, since the Latinism brings to mind the Julio-Claudian patronage system that Paul disavows (Reumann 706), though this seems overly subtle.

ὅτι ἐν ἀρχῇ τοῦ εὐαγγελίου, ὅτε ἐξῆλθον ἀπὸ Μακεδονίας

The ὅτι ("that" [NRSV, HCSB, ESV]) introduces indir. discourse, giving the content of οἴδατε (Reumann 660).

Ἐν ἀρχῇ τοῦ εὐαγγελίου is to be understood with reference to Paul's time in Philippi ("in the early days of your acquaintance with the gospel" [NIV, sim. NLT]; cf. ἀπὸ τῆς πρώτης ἡμέρας [1:5]) and broadly describes Paul's initial ministry in Macedonia and Achaea during the second journey (Hansen 318). Εὐαγγελίου is verbal noun, "beginning (of the proclaiming) of the gospel" (BDAG 402d; *nomen actionis* [G. Friedrich, *TDNT* 2.729]; O'Brien 532).

The temp. clause ὅτε ἐξῆλθον ἀπὸ Μακεδονίας modifies ἐκοινώνησεν and further defines ἐν ἀρχῇ τοῦ εὐαγγελίου. The 1 sg. aor. act. indic. (from ἐξέρχομαι, "when/after I left/set out from" [EVV]) should not be pressed to mean "at the very moment I left Macedonia." It refers more generally to an unspecified period of time after Paul's departure from the province and functions (as aor. often does in narrative [Fee 441 n. 13]) much like an Eng. pluperfect ("after I had left" [O'Brien 533 n. 129; Reumann 660]). The phrase likely refers to Paul's ministry in Corinth, when Christians from Macedonia supported Paul (2 Cor 11:8–9; Acts 18:5) (Hansen 318). In v. 16 (below), Paul will backtrack to recall help provided yet earlier while Paul was still in Macedonia. The chronology of the narrative is "typically imprecise, as such personal recountings of 'history' often are" (Fee 442).

οὐδεμία μοι ἐκκλησία ἐκοινώνησεν εἰς λόγον δόσεως καὶ λήμψεως εἰ μὴ ὑμεῖς μόνοι

Οὐδεμία is nom. sg. fem. from οὐδείς, used adj. with subj. ἐκκλησία ("no church" [NRSV, NASB, HCSB; BDAG 552c]; "not one church" [NIV]); ἐκοινώνησεν is 3 sg. aor. act. indic. from κοινωνέω ("shared" NIV, NRSV, HCSB; "entered into partnership" [RSV, ESV]; "made me its partner" [BDAG 552c]; see on κοινωνία [1:5]). With οὐδεμία . . . εἰ μὴ ὑμεῖς μόνοι, Paul appears to be comparing the Philippians with house churches at Thessalonica or Berea (Reumann 661). Paul mentions "churches" (pl.), however, when he refers to the early gifts sent from Macedonia to Corinth (ἄλλας ἐκκλησίας ἐσύλησα [2 Cor 11:8]). Some suggest that, although Philippi alone contributed when Paul was in Thessalonica and Berea (= "at the beginning"), by the time he had reached Corinth, other churches participated, as well (Reumann 699). The modifier ὅτε ἐξῆλθον ἀπὸ Μακεδονίας speaks against this understanding, however, and it is probably better to take ἄλλας ἐκκλησίας (2 Cor 11:8) to refer, broadly, to "other believers," in accord with Paul's own emphasis in the passage (Fee 442 n. 17).

Εἰς λόγον is a technical phrase referring to the "settlement (of an account)" (BDAG 601a; B. Klappert, NIDNTT 3.1,106; G. Kittel, TDNT 4.104). Δόσεως is gen. sg. fem. from δόσις, -εως, ἡ, found only here and at James 1:17 in the NT. Lit., "act of giving" (generally distinguished from δόμα, "gift"), δόσις was used in commercial contexts for "debit" on a ledger (common for "installment, tax payment" [Reumann 661]). The NT hapax λήμψεως (gen. fem. sg., from λῆμψις, lit. "receiving") correspondingly denotes "credit" in a ledger (Reumann 662). Λόγον δόσεως καὶ λήμψεως is thus a commercial expression used to refer to "monetary transactions on two sides of a ledger" (O'Brien 534; "settlement of a mutual account" [BDAG 601a]; H. Ritt, EDNT 2.359d; MM 169b; H-M 269–70). Paul will return to the metaphor with τὸν καρπὸν τὸν πλεονάζοντα εἰς λόγον ὑμῶν ("the profit that is increasing to your account" [v. 17]) and ἀπέχω δὲ πάντα ("I have been paid in full" [v. 18]). The social context softens the commercial imagery, which might otherwise appear cold and calculative. Κοινωνεῖω εἰς λόγον δόσεως καὶ λήμψεως functioned in ancient literature as an idiomatic expression denoting "consensual friendship," where such gifts and services were understood as "'benefits' mutually given and received" (Fee 443; Marshall, Enmity in Corinth, 160–64). The imagery thus resonates with a positive tone that "reflects a warm and lasting relationship" (O'Brien 534).

It is not unreasonable to read δόσεως καὶ λήμψεως ("giving and receiving" [most EVV]; "expenditure and receipts" [NJB]; "payments and receipts" [NEB]) as a reference to the Philippians' gifts, on the one hand, and Paul's gospel ministry to them, on the other (F. Hauck, TDNT 3.808; Hansen 319; Reumann 662; cf. Κοινωνείτω δὲ ὁ κατηχούμενος τὸν λόγον τῷ κατηχοῦντι ἐν πᾶσιν ἀγαθοῖς [Gal 6:6; cf. 1 Cor 9:11; Rom 15:27]). Paul has, in fact, just mentioned his ministry (ἐν ἀρχῇ τοῦ εὐαγγελίου [v. 15]). Other contextual indicators, however, make this interpretation problematic. The Philippians' gift is not portrayed in vv. 10–20 as a response to Paul's gospel ministry. Rather, the Philippians are the initiators in λόγον δόσεως καὶ λήμψεως, to whom God will respond, in the apostle's place, by meeting all their needs (v. 19).

The particles εἰ (cond.) + μή (neg.) mean "if not, except" (BDAG 278d; 644d). Μόνοι (nom. pl. masc. adj. from μόνος, in appos. to ὑμεῖς; "you only/alone" [EVV]) is used pleonastically after the neg. οὐδεμία (BDAG 658d; "emphatically" [O'Brien 533]).

VERSE 16

ὅτι καὶ ἐν Θεσσαλονίκῃ καὶ ἅπαξ καὶ δὶς εἰς τὴν χρείαν μοι ἐπέμψατε

The ὅτι is causal, justifying what Paul said in v. 15 ("for" [NRSV, NIV, HCSB]; omit [NLT, CEV]; Fee 445 n. 25; O'Brien 535). The first καί is ascensive ("even" [EVV]), the next two are correlative, functioning as part of the idiom καὶ ἅπαξ καὶ δίς (R 1183; Fee 445 n. 26; Hansen 320 n. 238; Reumann 664).

Καὶ ἅπαξ καὶ δίς (lit. "once and twice" [BDAG 97b; 252a]) is an idiom to be rendered "more than once" (NRSV, NASB, NIV; "once and again" [RSV, ESV; H. Balz, EDNT 1.337a]) or "several times" (HCSB; cf. 1 Thess 2:18), rather than "again and again," "repeatedly" (G. Stählin, TDNT 1.381). The Thessalonian correspondence suggests that aid from Philippi fell short of meeting all Paul's needs (H-M 271; cf. 1 Thess 2:9; 2 Thess 3:8).

In the clause εἰς τὴν χρείαν μοι ἐπέμψατε ("send someth. to someone to supply his needs(s)" [BDAG 1088c]), εἰς + acc. denotes purpose, and τήν identifies Paul's particular need at that time (Fee 446 n. 30; H-M 270; O'Brien 536 n. 154). The vb. (2 pl. aor. act. indic. from πέμπω) lacks a dir. obj. (supplied in most EVV: "you sent me help/(a) gift(s)" [NRSV, ESV, CEV, HCSB]; "you sent me aid" [NIV]). The dat. pron. functions as the indir. obj. The notion of poss. ("my need(s)" [NASB, HCSB]) is understood from the context or reflected in the def. art.

The grammar generated a number of vars., though "little rides on the matter" (Reumann 664): (1) εἰς τὴν χρείαν μοι is the most difficult reading and boasts considerable external support: א B F G K Ψ 6 33 Byz etc. ("preferred" [Reumann 663; O'Brien 515]; UBS⁵ = {C} εἰς τὴν χρείαν μοι); (2) τὴν χρείαν μοι (omit εἰς) is also early (𝔓⁴⁶ A etc.) but can be explained by haplography or a desire to provide a dir. obj. (Metzger 617). Two remaining, poorly attested vars. alter μοι to μου in (1) and (2), respectively.

VERSE 17

οὐχ ὅτι ἐπιζητῶ τὸ δόμα

A second οὐχ ὅτι ("Not that" [most EVV]; cf. v. 11) expresses "strong denial" of another potential misunderstanding of what Paul has just said, i.e., that Paul coveted their gifts and is buttering them up for future favors ("I am not trying to get something from you" [CEV]; O'Brien 536–57; Reumann 710; Silva 209). Supply λέγω ("I don't say this because" [NLT]; BDF §480[5]) or ἐστίν to the ellipsis (T 303; Reumann 665). This disclaimer differs from vv. 11–12. The earlier passage described conditions in Paul's life, while v. 17 clarifies the aim of the apostle's work and conduct (O'Brien 536).

The prefix in ἐπιζητῶ (1 sg. pres. act. indic.) is intensive ("seek *eagerly*"; cf. H.-G. Link, *NIDNTT* 3.532) or directional ("seek *for*") or both ("to be seriously interested in or have a strong desire for" [BDAG 371c]; "I have my heart set on" [H-M 271]; "strive for" [Fee 447 n. 35]). EVV are a bit reserved ("I seek" [NRSV, HCSB, ESV]; "I desire" [NIV]; "I want" [NLT]).

Τὸ δόμα (acc. sg. neut. from δόμα, -τος, τό) may refer to the specific gift Paul has just received ("the gift" [NRSV, NJB, HCSB; BDAG 256d]) or, more generally, "to each particular instance of a gift being sent him" (O'Brien 538; "your gifts" [NIV]). The term was used for a wide range of gifts and services, particularly in the context of friendship (cf. Marshall, *Enmity in Corinth*, 223–24).

ἀλλὰ ἐπιζητῶ τὸν καρπὸν τὸν πλεονάζοντα εἰς λόγον ὑμῶν

The "strong adversative" ἀλλά ("but" [most EVV]; "rather" [NLT]) reinforces the denial expressed by οὐχ ὅτι (O'Brien 538).

Most EVV (not NLT, CEV) reflect Paul's return to the commercial metaphor in τὸν καρπὸν τὸν πλεονάζοντα εἰς λόγον ὑμῶν (e.g., "the profit which increases/that is increasing to your account" [NASB, HCSB]; "an accrual of 'interest' against your divine 'account'" [Fee 447]; W. Bauder and D. Müller, *NIDNTT* 2.131). The acc. dir. obj. τὸν καρπόν, lit. "fruit" (RSV, ESV), i.e., produce of the land, is used here metaphorically in a commercial sense, "advantage, gain, profit" (BDAG 510b–c; "profit" [NRSV, NASB, HCSB]; "interest" [NJB; O'Brien 538]; cf. cognates καρπεῖαι ["profits"] and καρπίζεσθαι ["to reap the return"]).

The adj. ptc. πλεονάζοντα (acc. sg. masc. pres. act.) is from πλεονάζω, "to become more and more, so as to be in abundance" (BDAG 824b). The commercial idea of "profit that accumulates to your account" (Reumann 666) comes not from the vb. itself but from the surrounding context (O'Brien 538).

For the technical commercial sense of εἰς λόγον ὑμῶν ("to/in your credit/account" [EVV]), see above on εἰς λόγον δόσεως καὶ λήμψεως. The Philippians themselves will be Paul's eschatological reward (2:16; 4:1). The gift has the effect of increasing the profit of the Philippians' reward (Fee 447).

VERSE 18

ἀπέχω δὲ πάντα καὶ περισσεύω

The δέ is neither sharply adversative, nor is it to be read as a simple connective following the ἀλλά clause immediately preceding (*pace* O'Brien 539). Rather, δέ is "slightly contrastive" (Fee 450), setting what follows in contrast to οὐχ ὅτι ἐπιζητῶ τὸ δόμα κτλ. in v. 17 ("But" [NASB, HCSB, NEB]; "But in fact" [Fee 450 n. 5]). EVV that omit the conj. wrongly imply a paragraph break (RSV, NIV, ESV).

The ἀπό prefix gives the pres. tense of ἀπέχω a perf. meaning (Reumann 666; "I have been paid back everything" [CEV]). Ἀπέχω πάντα recalls one of two themes from the immediate context:

1. The vb. meant "to receive in full what is due" (cf. NRSV, NIV, ESV) and was used in a commercial sense (cf. εἰς λόγον δόσεως καὶ λήμψεως [v. 15, above]), "provide a receipt for a sum paid in full" (BDAG 102c; "Here, then, is my receipt for everything you have given me" [GNB]; H. Hanse, *TDNT* 2.828; A. Hortsmann, *EDNT* 1.121a; O'Brien 540]).

2. The combination ἀπέχω πάντα was used among Stoic writers, as a near equivalent for αὐτάρκεια (see on αὐτάρκης [v. 12]). The "wise man," who is "self-sufficient" thereby "has all things." The image thus recalls vv. 11–13. Paul, who has learned contentment in all situations, can say, "I have all things; indeed, I have more than enough" (Fee 451; cf. 450 n. 7).

View 1 has the closest conceptual antecedent, in the commercial imagery of v. 15, but view 2 cannot be ruled out. Perhaps Paul intended ἀπέχω πάντα to elicit both themes.

With περισσεύω ("and more" [RSV, NJB, ESV, cf. NRSV]; "and (I) have an abundance" [NASB, HCSB]; "have more than enough" [BDAG 805c]), Paul is not "pleading for no more gifts" (*pace* H-M 272). Rather, he anticipates God's generosity, as promised in v. 19, as he echoes the language of v. 12 (περισσεύειν [2x]) (Hansen 323).

πεπλήρωμαι δεξάμενος παρὰ Ἐπαφροδίτου τὰ παρ᾽ ὑμῶν

Πεπλήρωμαι is 1 sg. perf. pass. indic. from πληρόω, "to make full," "fill" (BDAG 828a; "πληροῦν τινα = supply someone fully" [BDAG 828c]; "I am amply/fully/well supplied" [NIV, HCSB, ESV]; "I have enough" [G. Delling, *TDNT* 6.294 n. 49]). The perf. points to "a state of being full" (O'Brien 540). Parallels with Paul's prayer in 1:9–11 may indicate an *inclusio*:

1:9–11	4:17–20
πεπληρωμένοι (v. 11)	πεπλήρωμαι (v. 18; cf. v. 19)
καρπὸν δικαιοσύνης (v. 11)	τὸν καρπόν (v. 17)
περισσεύῃ (v. 9)	περισσεύω (v. 18; cf. v. 12)
εἰς δόξαν (v. 11)	δόξῃ (v. 19); δόξα (v. 20)

The tense of πεπλήρωμαι indicates that δεξάμενος (nom. sg. masc. of aor. mid. ptc. from δέχομαι) marks antecedent action ("now that I have received" [NIV, NRSV, NJB]). Although formally connected to πεπλήρωμαι, the adv. ptc. loosely modifies the three previous finite vbs. and can be read as causal (Reumann 667).

The acc. pl. neut. art. in τὰ παρ᾽ ὑμῶν is used as a subst. ("the things, i.e., gifts, from you" [BDAG 221b]; "the gifts you sent" [NRSV, NIV, ESV]).

ὀσμὴν εὐωδίας, θυσίαν δεκτήν, εὐάρεστον τῷ θεῷ

The sudden shift from commercial metaphors to the language of worship ("No higher praise could be given" [O'Brien 515]) would not have been abrupt for Paul's audience since temples functioned as banks in the ancient world ("repositories for money and savings accounts" [H-W 272]; Reumann 712 n. 84).

The expressions ὀσμήν, θυσίαν, and εὐάρεστον are all in the acc., in appos. to τὰ παρ᾽ ὑμῶν, and refer to the gifts sent with Epaphroditus (O'Brien 540). Ὀσμήν is acc. sg. fem. from ὀσμή, -ῆς, ἡ, "odor" (BDAG 728d); εὐωδίας is gen. sg. fem. from εὐωδία, -ας, ἡ, "aroma, fragrance," an attributive gen., ὀσμὴν εὐωδίας = "fragrant odor/offering" (BDAG 417c; 728d–729a; most EVV; "a pleasing smell" [NJB]). The imagery "pictures God as literally taking pleasure in the smell of the sacrifices offered by his people" (H-M 272; C. Brown, *NIDNTT* 3.601). The combination ὀσμὴ εὐωδίας occurs frequently in the OT, starting with Noah's offering (Gen 8:21), especially in relation to Israel's cult (Exod 29:18, 25, 41; Lev 1:9, 13) (A. Stumpff, *TDNT* 2.809). Christ "gave himself up for us, a fragrant offering (εἰς ὀσμὴν εὐωδίας) and sacrifice to God" (Eph 5:2; cf. also 2 Cor 2:14, 16). Spiritualization of sacrifices goes back to OT (C. Brown, *NIDNTT* 3.427–28; Amos 5:21–22) and is found at Qumran, as well, where settlers had abandoned animal sacrifices to offer up "a pleasant aroma" through prayer (1 QS VIII, 7–9).

Θυσία (acc. sg. fem., cf. 2:17), associated with all ancient religions, is the common biblical word for animal or grain sacrifices (e.g., Lev 1:9, 13). In the OT the word begins to be spiritualized, so that "a crushed and humbled spirit" (LXX Ps 50:18–19 [EVV 51:16–17]) is acceptable to God, indeed, the kind of sacrifice God actually prefers. Spiritual sacrifices later include prayer and praise (1QS VIII, 7–9; IX, 25; X, 6), doing good deeds, the sharing of possessions (Heb 13:16), and, finally, the worshiper's entire life (Rom 12:1; H-M 272). The adj. δεκτήν is acc. sg. fem. from δεκτός, -ή, -όν ("pleasing, acceptable" [BDAG 217a]; "acceptable sacrifice" [J. Behm, *TDNT* 3.182]; cf. δέχομαι), another term from the LXX sacrificial cult.

The last adj., εὐάρεστον (from εὐάρεστος, -ον, "pleasing, acceptable" [BDAG 403d]; "pleasing" [EVV]), is used only two times in the LXX (Wis 4:10; 9:10), never in relation to the sacrificial system. The ethical meaning of εὐάρεστος is carried over to the NT, where the term is used of conduct that is acceptable to God (Rom 12:1; 14:18; 2 Cor 5:9; Eph 5:10; Col 3:20; Heb 13:21; but cf. Titus 2:9, of slaves ἰδίοις δεσπόταις . . . εὐαρέστους).

The dat. τῷ θεῷ may be taken with just εὐάρεστον (NASB, NIV, HCSB) or with the whole preceding description (NRSV, NJB, ESV), with no appreciable difference in meaning (O'Brien 542).

VERSE 19

ὁ δὲ θεός μου πληρώσει πᾶσαν χρείαν ὑμῶν κατὰ τὸ πλοῦτος αὐτοῦ ἐν δόξῃ ἐν Χριστῷ Ἰησοῦ

Πληρώσει is 3 sg. fut. act. indic. from πληρόω, "to make full" (BDAG 828a). Some commentators are uncomfortable with this comprehensive, apparently unqualified promise. Those who see πᾶσαν χρείαν ὑμῶν as a reference solely (or primarily) to the Philippians' present material needs either (1) project the promise out into the eschatological future (cf. ἐν δόξῃ) (Hansen 326–27), or (2) adopt the aor. opt. var. πληρώσαι (= "a prayer-wish" [H-M 273]). Either option "wards off disappointment or disillusionment when material, physical needs are not met," and "keeps one from having to make excuses for God" (H-M 273). The issues are threefold:

a. A Textual Var.—The aor. opt. πληρῶσαι appears in D* F G Ψ 6 33 81 104 256 263 365 1175 1739 1881, and the entire Latin tradition. H-M claim that the opt. "better reflects the apostle's own reverent attitude. He does not say categorically what God will do for his friends, but he prayerfully asks God to come to their aid" (H-M 258). The fut. indic., however, has the best external support ($\mathfrak{P}^{46}$ ℵ A B D² copsa, bo *Byz* etc.). Ancient scribes, like modern commentators, were likely uncomfortable with the theological implications of the indic. (O'Brien 516; Reumann 671; UBS⁵ = {B} πληρώσει; EVV read fut. indic., e.g., "will/shall supply" [NASB, ESV, HCSB]). The fut. indic. also fits the contextual theme of "the reciprocation of friendship" and is, therefore, "almost surely original" (Fee 449 n. 2; O'Brien 516; Sumney 119).

b. The Meaning of πᾶσαν χρείαν ὑμῶν—O'Brien marshals a persuasive series of arguments for seeing in πᾶσαν χρείαν ("every need of yours" [NRSV, ESV]; "all your needs" [NIV, NJB, HCSB]) more than just the Philippians' material needs, "namely, the fulfilling of their spiritual needs," as well (O'Brien 547; cf. Fee 452 n. 12; Hansen 325; Reumann 671; Silva 208). The addition of the unnecessary πᾶσαν and the expansive doxology (v. 20) both point in this direction (O'Brien 547; 543 n. 203). Material needs, however, remain at the forefront of Paul's mind. The whole discussion of vv. 10–18 has centered around the Philippians' contribution to Paul's material well-being, and the repetition of two key words from the previous context (πληρόω [v. 18] and χρεία [v. 16]) virtually guarantees that the primary referent of πᾶσαν χρείαν ὑμῶν (v. 19) remains "present material needs that can only be met right now by material resources" (H-M 273; Hansen 325).

c. The Sense of ἐν δόξῃ—The prep. phrase has led some to assume that the sweeping promise is eschatological (cf. the eschatological use of δόξα in 1:11; 2:11; 3:21). The meaning of πᾶσαν χρείαν ὑμῶν (primarily = "material needs"), however, excludes an exclusively eschatological interpretation of ἐν δόξῃ, though Paul may have the future partially in view (Fee 452 n. 12; Reumann 724).

Attempts (1) to move the action in πληρώσει out into the eschatological future, or (2) to turn Paul's the promise into a prayer wish by recourse to the var. πληρῶσαι, fail to convince. The apparently unqualifed promise reflected in a straightforward reading of v. 19 can be clarified as follows:

a. Take πᾶσαν χρείαν to include both material and spiritual needs, though the former remains the primary referent. The expansion of πᾶσαν χρείαν to include spiritual needs finds a parallel in Paul's own experience (cf. ὁ θεός μου "my God" [EVV]; "this same God who takes care of me" [NLT]).

God's provision for Paul transcended the physical, for the apostle had found sufficient resources in Christ to be content in a variety of material circumstances, including hunger and lack (vv. 11–13). The Philippians can anticipate the same (v. 19), as they continue to live for Christ.

b. Read the promise as directed to a community, not to each individual member in isolation. Paul assures a church that has contributed generously to the ministry of the gospel that God, in turn, will meet the community's every need (δέ [v. 19] is connective, "and" [EVV]: "by meeting the Philippians' needs God shows in a concrete way his approval of their offering" [O'Brien 545]). With respect to individual needs, it will be the case in Philippi, as in every local church, that some will have more and some will have less. Persons in the church who are particularly blessed in this regard, are expected to share with those in need, according to Paul's ecclesiological convictions elsewhere. In this way the basic material needs of all are addressed.

With the above in view, Paul can confidently assure the Philippians, ὁ δὲ θεός μου πληρώσει πᾶσαν χρείαν ὑμῶν (v. 19).

Τό πλοῦτος is acc. sg. neut., "plentiful supply of someth.," "wealth, abundance" (BDAG 832a; "riches" [EVV]; "blessings" [CEV]). The prep. κατά indicates that God will supply not merely "from" (pace NLT; "out of" [NJB]) his wealth, but "in proportion to" his wealth (BDAG 512c; "according to" [most EVV]).

Δόξη is dat. sg. fem., "in glory" (most EVV; "the condition of being bright or shining," "brightness, splendor, radiance" [BDAG 257b]). Ἐν δόξῃ goes with τὸ πλοῦτος αὐτοῦ, not πληρώσει (in which case it would likely follow the vb. directly), and is intended in a locat. sense. God's riches are ἐν δόξῃ in the sense that they exist "in the sphere of God's glory, where God 'dwells' in infinite splendor and majesty" (Fee 453). An adj. interpretation of ἐν δόξῃ ("glorious/magnificent riches" [NLT, GNB, NAB]) is less convincing grammatically (Fee 454 n. 16) but not far off the mark semantically.

The prep. phrase ἐν Χριστῷ Ἰησοῦ ("in Christ Jesus" [most EVV]; "that come from Christ Jesus" [CEV]) is to be taken with πληρώσει and may be interpreted as sphere ("in Christ" [H-M 274]), or instr. ("through Christ Jesus" [O'Brien 549]). Reumann appropriately wonders whether the Philippians or Paul demanded "exact clarity on the phrase" (Reumann 673).

VERSE 20

τῷ δὲ θεῷ καὶ πατρὶ ἡμῶν ἡ δόξα εἰς τοὺς αἰῶνας τῶν αἰώνων, ἀμήν

Guthrie (Cohesion Shifts, 58) takes v. 20 with vv. 21–23, but it is better to read 4:10–20 as a unit. The dat. τῷ θεῷ may be an indir. obj. or, more likely, a dat. of poss., since some form of εἰμί must be supplied (see below on ἡ δόξα). The art. can be taken with both θεῷ and πατρί "to our God and Father" (NRSV, NIV, HCSB), or with just θεῷ, with καὶ πατρὶ ἡμῶν as epexegetical, "To God our Father" (NJB, NLT, CEV; "to the God, the one supreme God in the universe" [H-M 275]). The first option is more common with an art.-noun-καί-noun cstr. (Wallace 274; O'Brien 549; Reumann 674). Some think Paul has directed τῷ δὲ θεῷ καὶ πατρὶ ἡμῶν against the Roman emperor, who claimed the title "Father of the fatherland" (Witherington 132), a notion more likely for Eph 3:14–15 (τὸν πατέρα, ἐξ οὗ πᾶσα πατριὰ ἐν οὐρανοῖς καὶ ἐπὶ γῆς ὀνομάζεται). The δέ is transitional ("Now" [NLT, NASB, HCSB]; "And so" [NJB]; omit [NRSV, NIV, ESV]), not adversative.

With πατρὶ ἡμῶν (likely emphasizing adoption as God's children [Reumann 674]), Paul shifts from the 1 sg. and 2 pl., which dominated vv. 10–19, to an inclusive 1 pl. (ἡμῶν).

Most EVV supply the opt. εἴη ("be") to the doxology. Commentators, in contrast, prefer the indic. ἐστίν ("the extolling of what is" [G. Kittel, *TDNT* 2.248]; H-M 274; O'Brien 550; Reumann 674; BDF §128[5]; cf. 1 Pet 4:11 [ᾧ ἐστιν ἡ δόξα καὶ τὸ κράτος εἰς τοὺς αἰῶνας τῶν αἰώνων, ἀμήν]; Matt 6:13). The decision rests, in part, on the meaning of δόξα, about which there is no little confusion in the literature. Hansen, for example, (1) defines God's δόξα as "the revelation of God's attributes," (2) claims that God "receives the glory in Paul's worship," yet (3) adds that "Paul is not adding to the glory of God" (Hansen 328). It is hard to see how these three assertions can all be true for a single occurrence of δόξα.

BDAG provides three distinct usages for δόξα: (1) "the condition of being bright or shining," "brightness, splendor, radiance"; (2) "a state of being magnificent," "greatness, splendor"; and (3) "honor as enhancement or recognition of status or performance," "fame, recognition, renown, honor, prestige" (257a–d). On either of the first two options, δόξα is something God already possesses, so we should supply the indic. (ἐστίν). BDAG, instead, prefers the third option for δόξα in v. 20 (BDAG 258a; S. Aalen, *NIDNTT* 2.46), which makes good sense, given Philippi's honor culture. Reading δόξα as "fame, recognition" most naturally requires the opt. (εἴη). The doxology thereby expresses Paul's desire that God would ultimately receive the honor that is his due (cf. 2:9–11). The art. (ἡ) signifies that which properly belongs to God (H-M 274).

The expression εἰς τοὺς αἰῶνας τῶν αἰώνων (acc. and gen. pl. masc. from αἰών, -ῶνος, ὁ, "a long period of time, without ref. to beginning or end" [BDAG 32b]) does not contrast a timeless eternity with chronological time. Εἰς τοὺς αἰῶνας τῶν αἰώνων is an emphatic variation of the common LXX expression εἰς τὸν αἰῶνα τοῦ αἰῶνος (cf. Ps 84:5 [LXX 83:5]) and lit. means "unto the ages of the ages," i.e., time in an unlimited sense ("for evermore" [BDAG 32b]; Fee 455 n. 19; Moule 89). It denotes a succession of cycles, though this should not be pressed philosophically to conclude that the eschatological future is temporal in nature (T. Holtz, *EDNT* 1.45c).

The familiar ἀμήν ("Amen" [EVV]) is a Gk. transliteration of a Heb. term and means "so be it" (Reumann 675; "spontaneous and joyful endorsement of all that has been said" [H-M 275]). The affirmation is not Paul's alone. The liturgical use of the expression suggests that Paul invites "the 'yes' of the worshiping church to God and the acknowledgment and acceptance of the promises he has made in Jesus Christ" (H-M 275; Hansen 328).

FOR FURTHER STUDY

57. Paul and Stoicism (4:11–12)

Engberg-Pedersen, Troels. *Paul and the Stoics*. Louisville: Westminster John Knox, 2000.
Kittel, G. *TDNT* 1.466–67.
Malherbe, Abraham. *Paul and the Popular Philosophers*. Philadelphia: Fortress, 1989.
————. "Paul's Self-Sufficiency (Philippians 4:11)." Pages 125–39 in *Friendship, Flattery, and Frankness of Speech: Studies on Friendship in the New Testament World.* NovTSup 82. Leiden: Brill, 1996.
Rasimus, Tuomas, et al., eds. *Stoicism in Early Christianity*. Grand Rapids: Baker Academic, 2010.
*Sierde, B. *NIDNTT* 3.727–28.

58. The Gift and Paul's Gratitude (4:10–20)

Bassler, Jouette M. *God and Mammon: Asking for Money in the New Testament*. Nashville: Abingdon, 1991.
Elliott, John H. "Patronage and Clientism in Early Christian Society: A Short Reading Guide." *Forum* 3 (1987): 39–48.
Hansen, G. Walter "Transformation of Relationships." Pages 191–204 in *New Testament Greek and Exegesis: Essays in Honor of Gerald F. Hawthorne*. Edited by Amy M. Donaldson and Timothy B. Sailors. Grand Rapids: Eerdmans, 2003.
Marshall, Peter. *Enmity in Corinth: Social Conventions in Paul's Relationship with the Corinthians*. WUNT 2.23. Tübingen: Mohr Siebeck, 1987. See pages 157–64.
SNTSMS 92. Cambridge: Cambridge University Press, 1997.
Peterman, Gerald W. *Paul's Gift from Philippi: Conventions of Gift-Exchange and Christian Giving*.
*————. "'Thankless Thanks': The Epistolary Social Convention in Philippians 4:10–20." *TynBul* 42 (1991): 261–70.
Reumann, John. "Contributions of the Philippian Community to Paul and to Earliest Christianity." *NTS* 39 (1993): 438–57.
Still, Todd D. "More than Friends? The Literary Classification of Philippians Revisited." *Perspectives in Religious Studies* 39 (2012) 53–66.

59. Glory (4:19–20)

Aalen, S. *NIDNTT* 2.44–48.
Hegemann, H. *EDNT* 1.344–49.
Spicq 1.362–79.
Von Rad, G., and G. Kittel. *TDNT* 2.233–55.

HOMILETICAL SUGGESTIONS

Receiving Support with Wisdom (4:10–20)

1. The Need for Positive Affirmation:
   • Paul rejoices over the Philippians's concern for him (v. 10).

- The Philippians have done a good thing by participating in Paul's gospel ministry through their gifts (vv. 14–16).
- Paul has received the gift and is amply supplied (18a).

2. The Need for Tactful Qualification:
   - Paul is not physically dependent on the Philippians. Christ has proven himself sufficient bo.th in times of plenty and in times of want (vv. 11–13).
   - Paul does not seek a gift from the Philippians. He seeks the credit that accrues to their account with God (v. 17).
   - Paul is not obligated to the Philippians. God is the one to whom the Philippians have actually made their offering. He will respond in kind (vv. 18b–19).

3. May God receive the glory forever! (v. 20)

Using Church Finances Wisely (4:10, 14–16, 18)

1. A wise use of church finances meets a genuine need (vv. 10, 14, 18a).
2. A wise use of church finances furthers the spread of the gospel (vv. 15–16).
3. A wise use of church finances pleases God (18b).

A Church that God Blesses (4:10, 15–16, 18b)

God promises to supply every need to a church that . . . (v. 19)

1. Has a missionary mind-set (v. 10).
2. Gives sacrificially to spread the gospel (vv. 15–16).
3. Shares God's priorities (v. 18b).

V. Closing Greeting and Benediction (4:21–23)

21 Ἀσπάσασθε πάντα ἅγιον ἐν Χριστῷ Ἰησοῦ.
    ἀσπάζονται ὑμᾶς οἱ σὺν ἐμοὶ ἀδελφοί.

22 ἀσπάζονται ὑμᾶς πάντες οἱ ἅγιοι,
                      μάλιστα δὲ οἱ ἐκ τῆς Καίσαρος οἰκίας.
23 Ἡ χάρις τοῦ κυρίου Ἰησοῦ Χριστοῦ μετὰ τοῦ πνεύματος ὑμῶν.

Paul's formula for ending his letters typically includes: (1) a closing greeting, using some form of ἀσπάζομαι (cf. vv. 21–22 [3x]) (lacking in Galatians, Ephesians, and 1 Timothy, "each for its own reason" [Fee 456 n. 2]) followed by (2) a concluding benediction (cf. v. 23). This differs markedly from conventional Hellenistic conclusions, which generally consisted of a stark ἔρρωσο/ἔρρωσθε ("farewell"; cf. Acts 15:29) or εὐτύχει ("good luck"), or another such formula. Paul's expansive approach uniquely reveals "the warmth of Christian relations, the marvel of Christian ideas and ideals, and the One who motivates and gives meaning to all" (H-M 279).

VERSE 21

Ἀσπάσασθε πάντα ἅγιον ἐν Χριστῷ Ἰησοῦ

Ἀσπάσασθε is 2 pl. aor. mid. impv. from ἀσπάζομαι ("Greet" [EVV]; "My greeting to" [NJB, cf. NLT, NEB]; in the impv. "greeting to" or "remember me to" [BDAG 144b]). Paul is not asking the Philippians to greet one another, as a narrowly lit. reading of Ἀσπάσασθε πάντα ἅγιον might suggest (for which we would expect ἀσπάσασθε ἀλλήλους [1 Cor 16:20; 2 Cor 13:12] [H-M 280; O'Brien 552 n. 4]). This leaves two remaining options:

1. Paul is addressing not the church as a whole but, rather, individuals within it—likely the "overseers and deacons" of 1:1—who, in turn, are to pass on Paul's greeting to each member of the house church(es) in the colony (H-M 280; Hansen 329 n. 275; O'Brien 552).

*2. More likely, Ἀσπάσασθε simply reflects Paul's greeting to the church as a whole, as indicated by the fact that the letter is so addressed (πᾶσιν τοῖς ἁγίοις . . . ἐν Φιλίπποις [1:1]). "If that is not precise to our thinking, it is surely what Paul intends, and keeps one from the eccentricity of having this singular instance of the second plural imperative addressed to others than those to whom the whole letter is addressed" (Fee 457 n. 6; Fee sees ἀσπάσασθε ἀλλήλους [1 Cor 16:20; 2 Cor 13:12], too, as "Paul's way of greeting the whole community" [456 n. 3]).

See on 1:1 for ἅγιον (acc. sg. masc.); adj. used as subst., "saint" (most EVV; "God's [holy] people" [NIV, NJB, NLT]; "believers, loyal followers, saints," "of Christians as consecrated to God" [BDAG 11c]). The term refers not to the Philippians' moral behavior but, rather, to their position as "people set apart from this world by God's grace," echoing the OT description of Israel (Hansen 329–30).

Some view the sg. adj. πάντα ("every" [NRSV, NJB, HCSB]; "each" [GNB]) as "scarcely different in mng. fr. the pl. 'all'" (BDAG 782b; cf. v. 22). The alternatives for the cstr. with πᾶς, however, are (1) "the whole" or (2) "every" (Moule 94–95), so there is no grammatical justification for the NIV's "all" (Fee 457 n. 7; Hansen 329 n. 276; O'Brien 553). Most commentators, therefore, see in the sg. πάντα (along with the striking absence of personal greetings in so personal a letter) a "deliberate strategy to counter any divisiveness within or between house churches" (Reumann 737; Hansen 329; O'Brien 553; cf. 2:1–4; 4:3). "Paul conveys his love and affection to each individual Christian alike" (H-M 280; Reumann 737).

The prep. phrase ἐν Χριστῷ Ἰησοῦ may be (1) instr. or (2) refer to "where" they are holy, that is, in union with Christ (Reumann 728; "incorporate in Christ Jesus" [NEB]), and can be taken to modify either (a) the vb. Ἀσπάσασθε or (b) πάντα ἅγιον. The alternatives generate four options:

1a. "Greet, by means of Christ Jesus, every saint."

1b. "Greet every one who is a saint by means of Christ Jesus." Perhaps distinguishing them from OT saints.

2a. "Give my greeting, in the fellowship of Christ, to each of God's people" (NEB, cf. NAB; "the greeting is to be 'in Christ Jesus,' who is both the source and focus of their common life together" [Fee 458]).

*2b. "Greet every one who is a saint in Christ Jesus." (cf. "greet each of God's people who belong to Christ Jesus" [GNB]; W. Grundmann, *TDNT* 9.552; H-M 280; Hansen 330).

Reumann maintains that no option should be excluded: "One is a saint 'in (and by) Christ Jesus.' Greetings are extended 'in (and by) Christ'" (Reumann 737). We can be a bit more discriminating. The Gk. word order favors 1b and 2b ("in Christ Jesus" also goes with "saints" in 1:1), with the latter view being the most probable. Any apparent redundancy (i.e., to be "in Christ Jesus" *is* to be a "saint" [Fee 458]) is easily accounted for by Paul's desire to emphasize the inseparable relationship between being a "saint" and being "united with Christ" (H-M 280).

ἀσπάζονται ὑμᾶς οἱ σὺν ἐμοὶ ἀδελφοί

The second (v. 21) and third (v. 22) occurrences of ἀσπάζομαι are both 3 pl. mid. dep. indic. (in the indic., "wish to be remembered, greet, send greetings" [BDAG 144b]). We encounter here the first of three groups greeting the Philippians from Rome. It will help to identify the three in relation to one another:

a. οἱ σὺν ἐμοὶ ἀδελφοί (21b)—Refers to a narrower circle than πάντες οἱ ἅγιοι (v. 22), likely a group of Paul's coworkers ("immediate circle of associates" [Fee 458]), including Timothy (cf. 1:1; 2:19–24) and possibly also Luke (cf. ἡμᾶς [Acts 27:1]) (H-M 281; O'Brien 553–54; Reumann 738). May also include persons sent to Paul from other congregations (Onesimus?) (Reumann 738). Although affectionately labeled ἀδελφοί, the "routine greeting may mask tensions within the circle of apostolic assistants and friends" (Reumann 739; cf. οὐδένα γὰρ ἔχω ἰσόψυχον . . . οἱ πάντες γὰρ τὰ ἑαυτῶν ζητοῦσιν [2:20–21]; cf. 1:15–17).

Gender-inclusive renderings of ἀδελφοί, such as "brothers and sisters" (NIV), are generally helpful ("friends" [NRSV] is "misleading" [Reumann 728]). In this instance, however, Paul's coworkers are in view, and there is some question as to whether women were present in this circle in Rome (Hansen 330 n. 283; Reumann chooses to "leave the possibility open" [738 n. 13]).

b. πάντες οἱ ἅγιοι (22a)—This larger group consists of "all church members in the place of Paul's captivity" (O'Brien 554; Reumann 738).

c. οἱ ἐκ τῆς Καίσαρος οἰκίας (22b)—This subgroup of πάντες οἱ ἅγιοι is made up of representatives (possibly a house church) from "the *familia Caesaris*, slaves and/or those who have gained freedom in the Emperor Nero's lower-level civil-service bureaucracy" (Reumann 739).

VERSE 22

ἀσπάζονται ὑμᾶς πάντες οἱ ἅγιοι

Πάντες οἱ ἅγιοι is now pl. instead of sg. (cf. πάντα ἅγιον [v. 21]).

μάλιστα δὲ οἱ ἐκ τῆς Καίσαρος οἰκίας

Μάλιστα is the superlative form of the adv. μάλα (functioning as an elative, "very" or "exceedingly," like most NT superlative forms [R 670]), "especially" (EVV; "to an unusual degree," "most of all, above all, especially, particularly" [BDAG 613d]).

The phrase οἱ ἐκ τῆς Καίσαρος οἰκίας, along with πραιτωρίῳ ("Praetorian Guard" [1:13]) constitutes the strongest evidence for a Roman origin for Philippians. Both groups are especially "at home" in Rome, while "one must look under all kinds of 'stones' to turn up evidence for their existence in Ephesus or Caesarea" (Fee 459, cf. n. 13; O. Michel, *TDNT* 5.133).

The nom. sg. masc. art., οἱ ("those" [EVV]), functions as a rel. pron.

Καίσαρος (gen. sg. masc., from Καῖσαρ, ὁ) was orig. a proper name, "Caesar" (a cognomen; e.g., Gaius Julius Caesar), then a title, "Emperor," as here (BDAG 498d; BDF §5[3]; J. D. G. Dunn, *NIDNTT* 1.269). Καίσαρος has been placed between the gen. sg. fem. οἰκίας and its art. τῆς. The ἐκ here is equivalent to ἐν, denoting "membership," not source or origin (BDF §437; R 548; Harris 109; cf. τοῖς . . . ἐκ περιτομῆς [Rom 4:12]). Οἰκία can mean either (1) "a structure used as a dwelling," i.e., "house" or (2) the "social unit within a dwelling," i.e., "household, family" (BDAG 695b–c; here either "those in the house" or "those in the household of the Emperor" [BDAG 695c; EVV]). According to prevailing usage, οἱ ἐκ τῆς Καίσαρος οἰκίας denotes not members of the emperor's immediate or extended family (i.e., Roman elites; Fee leaves the possibility open [460 n. 16], but this is not likely), but, rather, those "innumerable slaves and freed persons" who attended to "all sorts of managerial and servile tasks on the Emperor's estates and in government administration" (Reumann 728, 730; BDAG 499a; 695c; O. Michel, *TDNT* 5.133; A. Weiser, *EDNT* 2.236a; O'Brien 554; includes women [Reumann 729]). Common membership in Caesar's οἰκία may have provided a natural foundation for a distinct house church (Reumann 738; less convinced, H. Strathmann, *TDNT* 4.266). It is hard to tell why Paul singles them out. Their background in *familia Caesaris* and government service may have given them a special connection with Philippi, where inscriptions attest to freedmen in the service of the imperial cult (Reumann 740 n. 17). More importantly, "concealed behind this innocuous greeting is a powerful symbol of the day when, even in Rome, the seat of imperial power, 'every knee shall bow' to Christ (2:11)" (Bockmuehl 270; Hansen 331).

VERSE 23

Ἡ χάρις τοῦ κυρίου Ἰησοῦ Χριστοῦ μετὰ τοῦ πνεύματος ὑμῶν

With χάρις, Paul returns (cf. 1:2) to "the self-giving love of Christ demonstrated on the cross" (Hansen 332). Paul desires the Philippians to experience this χάρις in their relationships with one another and in the face of suffering and persecution. We cannot be certain whether benedictions like this were (a) original with Paul (and later used in public gatherings [Reumann 735]), or (b) sourced in early church liturgy (O'Brien 555).

We can supply (1) the indic. (ἐστίν/ ἔσται), (2) the opt. ("be" [NRSV, NIV, ESV, HCSB]; "May . . . be" [NJB, NLT]; cf. opt. πληθυνθείη [1 Pet 1:2; 2 Pet 1:2; Jude 2]), or (3) both: "The grace of the Lord Jesus Christ be—and is—with your spirit" (Reumann 740; "a wish and a statement" [Reumann 740]).

Κυρίου is a title; Ἰησοῦ, a name. Paul likely intends Χριστοῦ as a title ("Messiah"), as well (Reumann 730), though Gentile hearers may have heard it as a name (Κύριος Ἰησοῦς Χριστός according to the analogy of "Imperator Caesar Augustus" [W. Grundmann, *TDNT* 9.542]). An Egyptian papyrus has ἡ χάρις τοῦ κυρίου, referring to Nero (*Pfouad* 21, AD 63, cited by Reumann 730). The switch from "Christ Jesus" (v. 21) to "Jesus Christ" (v. 23) is inconsequential (Reumann 741).

When Paul begins his letters, he generally associates "grace" with both God the Father and the Lord Jesus Christ. In the benedictions, however, he typically writes only of the grace of the Lord Jesus Christ (1 Corinthians; 2 Corinthians; Galatians; Philippians; 1 Thessalonians; 2 Thessalonians). While it is hard to account for this change, it does serve to demonstrate that, for Paul, Christ has the right to perform the divine role of bestowing grace upon the church with full authority (H-M 281).

Τοῦ πνεύματος (gen. sg. neut.) refers not to the Holy Spirit but to either:

1. "a part of the human personality" (BDAG 833c; "that aspect of man through which God most immediately encounters him" [C. Brown, *NIDNTT* 3.693]; H. Strathmann, *TDNT* 4.509; "the mental and spiritual aspects belonging to the personality" [H-M 282]; O'Brien 555, cf. n. 25; Reumann 731); or, perhaps, simply

2. "the whole person" (Hansen 332; "πνεῦμα ὑμῶν means exactly the same as ὑμεῖς" [E. Schweizer, *TDNT* 6.435]). Paul interchanges μετὰ τοῦ πνεύματος ὑμῶν (here; Gal 6:18; Phlm 25; 2 Tim 4:22) with the more usual μεθ' ὑμῶν or μετὰ πάντων ὑμῶν elsewhere in his closing benedictions (Rom 16:20; 1 Cor 16:24; 2 Cor 13:13; Col 4:18; 1 Thessalonians; 2 Thessalonians; μετὰ πάντων ὑμῶν, in fact, appears as a weak var. here [Fee 456; O'Brien 551; Reumann 731]).

C. Brown's interpretation includes elements of both views, above: "man in so far as he belongs to the spiritual realm and interacts with the spiritual realm" (*NIDNTT* 3.693).

Τοῦ πνεύματος is distributive sg., "each of your (human) spirits" (Fee 456 n. 1; cf. πεπωρωμένην ἔχετε τὴν καρδίαν ὑμῶν [Mark 8:17]; BDF §140; "the spirit of each one of you" [Hansen 332]; H-M 282). Some wish to see Paul continuing to stress unity with the sg. πνεύματος (Reumann 732), though the cstr. is hardly unique to Philippians (cf. Gal 6:18; Phlm 25).

FOR FURTHER STUDY

60. Caesar's Household (4:22)

Hall, John F. *ABD* 1.798.

Kyrtatas, Dimitrius J. *The Social Structure of Early Christian Communities*. New York: Verso, 1987. See pages 75–86.

*O'Brien, P. *DPL* 83–84.

Telble, Mikael. *Paul Between Synagogue and State: Christians, Jews, and Civic Authorities in 1 Thessalonians, Romans, and Philippians*. ConBNT 34. Stockholm: Almqvist & Wiksell, 244–45.

Weaver, P. R. C. *Familia Caesaris: A Social Study of the Emperor's Freedmen and Slaves*. Cambridge: Cambridge University Press, 1972.

61. NT Greetings and Benedictions (4:21–23)

Champion, L. G. *Benedictions and Doxologies in the Epistles of Paul*. Oxford: Kemp Hall, 1934.

Cummings, G. J. "Service-Endings in the Epistles." *NTS* 22 (1975–76): 110–13.

Dugmore, C. W. "Jewish and Christian Benedictions." Pages 145–52 in *Mélanges offerts à Marcel Simon*. Paris: de Boccard, 1978.

Jewett, Robert. "The Form and Function of the Homiletic Benediction." *AThR* 51 (1969): 18–34.

Link, H.-G. *NIDNTT* 1.206–15.

*Mullins, T. Y. "Benediction as a NT Form." *Andrews University Seminary Studies* 15 (1977): 59–64.

_____. "Greeting as a New Testament Form." *JBL* 87 (1968): 418–26.

O'Brien, Peter. *DPL* 68–71.

Richards, K. H. *ABD* 1.753–55.

Urbrock, W. J. *ABD* 1.755–61.

Weima, Jeffrey. *Neglected Endings. The Significance of the Pauline Letter Closings*. JSNT, Supplement Series, Vol. 101. Sheffield: Sheffield Academic Press, 1994. See pages 191–201.

Westermann, Claus. *Blessing in the Bible and the Life of the Church*. Philadelphia: Fortress, 1978.

HOMILETICAL SUGGESTIONS

Some Final Greetings (4:21–23)

1. From Paul to the Philippians (v. 21a)
2. From Paul's circle of coworkers to the Philippians (v. 21b)
3. From all the saints in Rome to the Philippians (v. 22a)
4. From believers in Caesar's household to the Philippians (v. 22b)
5. A final benediction (v. 23)

Exegetical Outline

I. Introduction (1:1–11)
  A. Greeting (1:1–2)
    1. Senders and Recipients (1:1)
    2. Greetings (1:2)
  B. Thanksgiving and Prayer for Participation in the Gospel (1:3–11)
    1. Paul Gives Joyous Thanks during His Prayer for the Philippians (1:3-4a)
    2. For Their Participation in the Spread of the Gospel (1:4b–5)
    3. Because It Attests to the Genuineness of God's Work in Their Lives (1:6)
    4. Justification for Paul's Gratitude (1:7)
      a. His Close Affective Ties with the Philippians (1:7b)
      b. Their Partnership in His Ministry and Suffering (1:7c)
    5. Divine Testimony to Paul's Gratitude (1:8)
    6. Paul Prays for the Philippians (1:9–11)
      a. That Their Mission-Oriented Love Might Increase in Knowledge and Discernment (1:9b)
      b. So That They Will Choose the Best from an Array of Options (1:10a)
      c. In Order to Be Blameless on the Day of Christ (10b–11)
II. Paul's Circumstances and the Gospel (1:12–26)
  A. The Gospel Continues to Advance (1:12–18c)
    1. In the Face of Adverse Circumstances (1:12–14)
      a. Non-Christians Hear the Gospel (1:13)
      b. Christians Boldly Proclaim the Gospel (1:14)
    2. In the Midst of Jealousy and Factionalism (1:15–18c)
      a. Some Brothers Proclaim Christ out of Selfish Ambition (1:15a, 17)
      b. Other Brothers Proclaim Christ out of Love (1:15b–16)
      c. Paul Just Rejoices that Christ Is Proclaimed (1:18a–c)
  B. Paul's Future Expectations (1:18d–26)
    1. Paul Will Magnify Christ Whatever the Outcome of His Imprisonment (1:18c–20)
    2. A Personal Soliloquy (1:21–24)

281

3. Expectations for Future Ministry (1:25–26)
III. Body of the Letter (1:27–4:9)
   A. Summary Exhortation to Unity and Steadfastness (1:27–30)
     1. Live as Kingdom Citizens (1:27–28a)
       a. As Evidence of Salvation (1:28b)
       b. Because God Is in Control (1:28c–29)
       c. And Because You Are Not Alone (1:30)
   B. Unity Among Believers (2:1–30)
     1. Plea for Unity through Humility (2:1–4)
       a. God's Blessings in the Lives of the Philippians (2:1)
       b. Responding to God's Blessings by Adopting the Mind-set of Christ (2:2–4)
         i.   The Charge to Unity (2:2)
         ii. The Way of Unity (2:3–4)
     2. Christ Our Example (2:5–11)
       a. Have the Mind-set of Christ (2:5)
       b. Self-Humiliation: A *Cursus Pudorum* (2:6–8)
         i.   Status Level 1 (2:6)
         ii. Status Level 2 (2:7)
         iii. Status Level 3 (2:8)
       c. Divine Vindication: Universal Acclaim (2:9–11)
     3. Humility Lived Out in Community with Others (2:12–18)
       a. Working Out Eschatological Salvation in the Context of Community Relations (2:12–13)
       b. Results in a Shining Testimony and a Proud Apostle (2:14–16)
       c. Who Remains Joyful Even in the Face of Martyrdom (2:17–18)
     4. Paul Commends Timothy as an Example of Humility (2:19–24)
       a. Paul Will Send Timothy to Learn about the Philippians (2:19)
       b. Only Timothy Shares Paul's Other-Centered Passion for the Gospel (2:20–22)
       c. Plan Restated, with Confidence that Paul Will Come Also (2:23–24)
     5. Paul Commends Epaphroditus as an Example of Humility (2:25–30)
       a. Paul Has Sent Epaphroditus to Philippi (2:25a)
       b. Paul Profusely Honors Epaphroditus (2:25b)
       c. Epaphroditus's Illness and God's Merciful Healing (2:26–27)
       d. Sending of Epaphroditus Reiterated (2:28)
       e. The Philippians Must Honor Epaphroditus, As Well (2:29)
       f. Honor Among Christians for Acting like Jesus (2:30)
   C. Steadfastness Toward Opponents (3:1–4:1)
     1. Resisting the Opponents' Fleshly Confidence (3:1–16)
       a. Paul's Relationship with Judaism (3:1–11)
         i.   A Warning that Bears Repeating (3:1–3)
         ii. Paul Plays the Honor Game (3:4–6)

      iii. The Great Exchange: "Everything" for "Christ Jesus My Lord" (3:7–11)
         (a) Everything (3:7–8)
         (b) To Be Found in Him: Justified (3:9)
         (c) To Know Him: Sanctified (3:10)
         (d) To Be Raised with Him: Glorified (3:11)
   b. Pressing Toward the Goal (3:12–16)
     i. Paul's Mind-set in the Midst of the Race (3:12–14)
        (a) Disclaimer 1: Not Perfected but Pressing On (3:12)
        (b) Disclaimer 2: Not Perfected but Pressing On (3:13–14)
     ii. Sharing Paul's Mind-set (3:15–16)
  2. Resisting the Opponents' Fleshly Behavior (3:17–4:1)
   a. Models of Christian Discipleship (3:17–19)
     i. Who to Follow (3:17)
     ii. Who to Avoid (3:18–19)
   b. Why Follow the Right Models (3:20–21)
     i. Because of Our Present Identity (3:20)
     ii. Because of Our Future Hope (3:21)
   c. How to Follow the Right Models (4:1)
D. Final Words of Exhortation (4:2–9)
  1. Restoring a Broken Relationship (4:2–3)
   a. Exhortation to Unity (4:2–3a)
   b. Commendation for Service (4:3b)
  2. The Joy and Peace of Knowing Christ (4:4–7)
   a. General Charge to Rejoice (4:4)
   b. Because the Lord Is Coming Soon, We Can Stop Insisting on What Is Rightly Ours (4:5)
   c. Because the Lord Is Close at Hand, We Can Find His Peace through Prayer (4:6–7)
  3. The Common Good and the Apostle's Example (4:8–9)
   a. Thinking Right (4:8)
   b. Doing Right (4:9a)
   c. Divine Response (4:9b)
IV. Paul's Circumstances and the Philippians' Gift (4:10–20)
  A. First Acknowledgement (4:10)
  B. Qualifier 1: Paul's Christ Sufficiency (4:11–13)
  C. Second Acknowledgement (4:14–16)
  D. Qualifier 2: The Philippians' Reward (4:17)
  E. Third Acknowledgement (4:18)
  F. God's Response (4:19)
  G. Doxology (4:20)
V. Closing Greeting and Benediction (4:21–23)
  A. Greeting (4:21–22)
  B. Benediction (4:23)

Grammar Index

285

Scripture Index

40:10   *110*

Psalms

1:3   *34*
2:11   *130*
8:7   *225*
11:7   *246*
14:2   *136*
17:28   *100*
17:31   *136*
18:8   *136*
22:16   *170*
22:20   *170*
24:1–2   *24*
24:3   *62*
25:5   *179*
33:4   *64*
33:19   *237*
34:26–27   *62, 64*
39:15–17   *62*
49:8   *140*
49:14   *140*
49:23   *140*
50:18–19   *268*
50:19   *140*
51:1   *174*
54:14   *147*
59:6   *170*
59:14   *170*
68:5   *14*
68:29   *233*
84:5   *271*
88:21   *10*
94:4   *174*
96:9   *119*
101:18   *100*
105:31   *179*
111:4   *20*
112:4–6   *100*
118:67   *100*
118:151   *237*
138:18   *69*
139:14   *69*
144:18   *237*

Proverbs

3:9   *34*
5:2   *31*
8:20   *214*
11:30   *34*
14:7   *31*
15:7   *31*
25:14   *174*
27:1   *174*

Isaiah

1:29   *62*
2:11   *100*
6   *120*
6:3   *120*
6:5   *120*
9:7   *179*
12:4   *120*
19:16   *130*
23:16   *20*
26:8   *120*
26:19   *190*
39:4   *103*
40:1   *93*
40:9   *23*
45:15   *223*
45:17   *62*
45:23   *122–23*
48:6   *103*
49:4   *128*
49:23   *62*
51:18a   *93*
52:7   *23*
55:13   *120*
63:12–14   *120*
63:16   *14*
64:8   *14*
65:23   *128*
66:6   *81*

Jeremiah

2:8   *183*
4:4   *172*
4:22   *183*
9:23   *174*
9:23–24   *72, 174*
10:6   *120*
14:7   *120*
18:20   *122*
22:16   *183*
31:33–34   *183*
32:20   *120*

Lamentations

3:12   *204*

Ezekiel

17:24   *100*
18:11   *103*
20:39   *120*
36:20–23   *120*
44:7   *172*

Daniel

4:1   *13*
9:14–15   *120*
12:1   *233*
12:2   *190*
12:3   *127–28, 137–38*

Hosea

4:1   *183*
6:6   *183*
10:12   *34*

Joel

2:2   *25*

Amos

3:2   *183*
5:20   *25*
5:21–22   *268*
6:12   *34*

Jonah

1:2   *49*
3:2   *49*
4:5   *151*

Zephaniah

1:7   *238*
1:14   *238*

Malachi

1:6   *120*

Matthew

1:21   *10*
2:7   *137*
6:13   *271*
6:25   *148*
6:25–33   *149*
6:25–34   *238*
6:26   *32*
6:29   *110*
6:32   *240*
9:13   *140, 250*
9:27   *160*
9:36   *96*
9:37–38   *171*
10:16   *135*
10:20   *60*
11:26   *49, 133*
11:29   *250*
12:7   *140*

16:1   *156*
16:7   *157*
16:17   *214*
16:19   *135*
16:20   *251, 278*
16:21   *9*

1 Corinthians

1:1   *172*
1:2   *11*
1:4   *20–21*
1:7   *223*
1:8   *25*
1:9   *95, 205–6*
1:10   *93*
1:11   *48*
1:18   *46, 217*
1:26   *205*
1:26–30   *72*
1:28–29   *189*
1:30   *69*
1:31   *72, 174*
2:2   *63*
2:3   *130*
2:6   *206*
2:8   *121*
2:10   *208*
2:13   *249*
3:3   *48*
3:9   *152, 171–72*
3:10   *28*
3:10–15   *139*
3:13   *25*
3:22   *58*
4:1–5   *138*
4:4   *200*
4:5   *35, 248*
4:6   *250*
4:7   *72*
4:12   *139*
4:14–17   *150*
4:16   *212, 228*
4:17   *9, 156*
4:19   *146*
5:1   *245*
5:2   *47*
6:2   *207*
6:11   *223*
6:19   *61*
7:5   *189*
7:10   *121*
7:15   *240*
7:17   *227*
7:21   *141, 208*
7:29   *168*

7:30   *216*
7:32–34   *148, 238*
8:4   *62*
8:5   *207*
8:6   *14*
9:3   *28*
9:7   *157*
9:7–8   *245*
9:10   *62*
9:11   *264*
9:13   *245*
9:14   *121*
9:15–18   *24*
9:24   *201, 204, 227*
9:24–26   *139*
9:25   *227*
10:4   *128*
10:10   *134*
10:18   *170*
10:24   *149*
10:31   *36*
10:32   *33*
11   *220*
11:1   *212*
11:2   *250*
11:4–6   *245*
11:17–34   *219*
11:19   *150*
11:23   *124, 250*
11:23–36   *250*
11:28   *227*
11:29   *133*
12:3   *124*
12:4–6   *133*
12:6   *133*
12:13   *79, 95*
12:23   *218–19*
12:25   *148, 238*
12:28   *12*
13:5   *149*
13:12   *32*
13:13   *62*
14:3   *94*
14:6   *208*
14:20   *206*
14:26   *208*
14:30   *208*
14:33   *13, 251*
14:36   *46*
15:1   *250*
15:1–5   *250*
15:3   *250*
15:9   *179*
15:10   *139*
15:11   *227*

15:12–19   *198*
15:20   *192*
15:25–28   *225*
15:28   *124*
15:41   *32*
15:42–47   *224*
15:50–53   *200*
15:58   *128, 139, 163, 198*
16:3   *155*
16:7   *145–46*
16:9   *42, 81*
16:10   *67, 148, 163*
16:13   *79*
16:17   *164, 229, 257*
16:20   *274–75*
16:22–23   *124*
16:24   *278*

2 Corinthians

1   *94*
1:3   *94, 96*
1:3–7   *93*
1:4   *20–21*
1:6   *59*
1:7   *191*
1:11   *60*
1:12   *33*
1:14   *72*
1:21–22   *10, 61*
2:2   *67, 133*
2:4   *52, 216–17*
2:5   *47*
2:12   *23, 42*
2:13   *156*
2:14   *268*
2:16   *268*
2:17   *33, 46*
3:1   *145*
3:1–3   *214*
3:2   *237*
3:6   *12*
3:12   *62*
3:14   *20*
4:1   *159*
4:12   *133*
4:14   *69*
4:15   *36*
4:16   *208*
5:1   *192*
5:4   *202*
5:5   *61*
5:9   *268*
5:10   *138*
5:14   *68*
5:16   *208*